Securities Regulations in Korea

—Problems and Recommendations for Feasible Reforms—

YOUNG MOO SHIN

UNIVERSITY OF WASHINGTON PRESS
Seattle and London
SEOUL NATIONAL UNIVERSITY PRESS
Seoul

Copyright © 1983 by Seoul National University Press
and University of Washington Press
Printed in Seoul, Korea

Library of Congress Cataloging in Publication Data

Shin, Young Moo.
  Securities Regulations in Korea.

  (Asian law series; no. 8)
  Includes bibliographical references.
  1. Securities—Korea(South) 2. Stockexchange—Law and legislation—Korea(South)
I. Title.   II. Series.
Law   346.519'5092 82–4918
ISBN 0–295–95937–1 345.1950.692 AACR2

To My Father & Mother

Acknowledgments

This book is an elaboration of the thesis, "Securities Regulations in Korea," which I wrote for the degree of Doctor of Science of Law from Yale Law School in 1978. While the main text of this book remains essentially unchanged from the original thesis, the Appendix contains substantial additions and updating of developments both in the securities regulations and the securities markets in Korea. In writing the thesis, I was deeply indebted to many people who assisted me in various ways; it is impossible for me to enumerate all those people here, though I am forever grateful for their help and contributions.

My special thanks go to three Professors at the Yale Law School who read and supervised my thesis. Professor Robert Charles Clark, as my supervisor, gave me the benefit of his scholarly criticism from the beginning of my work. He gave me invaluable advice by thoroughly discussing problems of regulation of the Korean securities market, and helped me reshape many of my ideas in better ways. In particular, Professor Clark helped me in formulating a basic policy toward an efficient Korean securities market. Professors Joseph W. Bishop, Jr. and Burke Marshall showed constant interest in the preparation of my dissertation and also gave me invaluable comments on the final draft. Without the intellectual guidance and kind encouragement by these Professors, early completion of this work would have been impossible. Naturally, however, the responsibility for any errors in the thesis remains my own.

My special appreciation is also extended to my former colleagues in the Korean Judiciary, my friends, and members of the Korean

Government for their kind assistance in collecting various materials that made the completion of this study possible. In particular, I owe a permanent debt to Messrs. Choongkeun Cho (CPA), Kuihae Lee (Korea First Bank), Roksang Ryu (Attorney at Law), Byungsung Kim (The Hankook Daily News), and Konghyuk Ahn (Ministry of Finance) who kept me informed of changes in Korean securities laws, the policies behind those changes, and the ways in which new laws were being enforced.

Special appreciation is also extended to Messrs. Richard Yeskoo (J. D. Yale, 1978)and Richard Pile(J. D. Yale, 1978) for their kind editorial assistance; to the Institute of International Education and the Yale Law School for their financial support; to the staffs of the Sterling and the International Law Libraries at Yale for their kind assistance in using library facilities.

This book also marks the first joint-publication by the Seoul National University Press and the University of Washington Press. Therefore, I am sincerely grateful to Professor Dan F. Henderson, Chairman of the University of Washington Press Editorial Committee, Mr. Donald. R. Ellegood, Director of the University of Washington Press and Whan Lee, Director of the Seoul National University Press, and his staff, for their constant and indispensable cooperation in making this publication a reality.

Finally, my appreciation is extended to my wife, Hyunsil, for her patience, sacrifice, and love, shown particularly during our two and a half years at Yale. She gave me the support and encouragement I needed to complete my thesis, and also typed several thousands of pages of manuscripts.

Young Moo Shin
Seoul, Korea
December, 1982

Contents

Acknowledgments vii
List of Tables xiv
List of Abbreviations xvi
Introduction xix

Part One: A Short Survey on the Development Process of the
Securities Market in Korea

Chapter 1: Early Stage of Formation of Securities
Market under Japanese Influences
(Before 1956) 3
Sec. I. *The Origin of the Corporate Structure of Business
and the Securities Market* 3
Sec. II. *The Securities Market under Japanese Occupation
(1910~1945)* 4
Sec. III. *The Securities Market during the Transition
Period (1945~1956)* 7
Chapter 2: Early Stage of Development under
Independently Organized Market System
(1956~1968) 10
Sec. I. *Establishment of the Korea Stock Exchange
and Governing Law* 10
Sec. II. *Early Market Activities and Disasters* 11
Sec. III. *Stock Trading and Some Reforms Established* 15
I. Major Policies Taken and Their Background 15
II. Changes in the Market Activities 17
III. Some Reforms and Supplementary Measures ... 22
IV. Market Activities: A Long Depression 24

Chapter   3:   Securities Markets in a Rapidly Growing
              Economy: Modernization Movement
              (1968~1976) 27
    Sec.   I.   *Issues Raised with Respect to Implementing*
              Economic Development Plans in Korea 27
           I.   Capital Formation and Investment 27
          II.   Some Obstacles Involved in the Financial
              Market 33
         III.   The Excessively Leveraged Corporate
              Capital Structure 44
    Sec. II.   *Policy Measures Taken in a Modernization Movement*
              and Market Activities: Step I (Late 1968~Mid
              1972) 45
           I.   Reforms 45
          II.   Market Activities 54
    Sec. III.   *Further Reforms and Market Activities:*
              Step II (Mid 1972~1976) 60
           I.   Reforms 60
          II.   Market Activities 74
Chapter   4:   Major Reforms of the 1976 Amendments in the
              Securities Laws 92
    Sec.   I.   *Background of the 1976 Amendments* 92
           I.   Role of the Securities Market in the Proposed
              Fourth Five-Year Economic Development
              Plan (1977~81) 92
          II.   Purposes of the Reform 93
    Sec. II.   *1976 Amendments of the Securities Laws* 95
           I.   Reorganization of the Regulatory Structure 95
          II.   Measures Taken to Warrant Continuing Control .100
         III.   Improvement of Disclosure System 102
          IV.   Measures Taken to Ensure Fair Trading 105
           V.   Tax Reform 109

Part Two: Legal Analysis of Securities Laws and
            Problems Raised

Chapter   5:   An Introductory Note: Coverage of
              Securities and Laws Applicable to Securities

		Transaction 115
Sec.	I.	*Coverage of Securities* 115
Sec.	II.	*Sources of Law* 117
	I.	Primary Sources 117
	II.	Secondary Sources 119
Chapter	6:	Regulation of the Distribution of Securities 120
Sec.	I.	*Introduction* 120
	I.	Basic Structure of the Law Governing the Primary Securities Market 120
	II.	Strong Government Involvement in Going Public: Designation Orders and Issuer Registration 121
	III.	Special Problems under the Commercial Code 123
Sec.	II.	*Coverage of Regulation* 125
	I.	Definition of Basic Legal Terms 125
	II.	Exemption from Registration Requirement 131
Sec.	III.	*Securities Analysis for Determination of Offering Prices* 134
	I.	KSDA's Rules 134
	II.	Their Drawbacks 140
Sec.	IV.	*Registration and Distribution of Securities* 143
	I.	Registrant 143
	II.	Restrictions of Transactions in Registration 144
	III.	Processing of the Registration Statement 146
Sec.	V.	*Civil Liability* 154
	I.	Persons Liable under Articles 14 and 197 156
	II.	Materiality 157
	III.	Privity and Reliance 158
	IV.	Defenses 159
	V.	Remedy 159
	VI.	Negative Prescription 160
Sec.	VI.	*Special Problems of Forced Going Public* 161
	I.	A Need for Strict Regulation of Disguising Corporations as Public 161
	II.	A Need for Strict Regulation of Excessive Dividend Payments 164

III. Worsened Capital Structure under Excessive
Public Subscription 167
Chapter 7: Regulation of Trading in Securities (One)......171
Sec. I. *Regulation of Securities Exchange* 171
I. Organization, Regulation and Supervision 171
II. Regulation of Trading in the Exchange
Market 175
Sec. II. *"Manipulation" and "Stabilization"* 211
I. Manipulation 211
II. Stabilization 223
Sec. III. *Regulation of the Over-the-Counter Market and
Securities Companies* 235
I. Regulation of the Over-the-Couner Market 235
II. Regulation of Securities Companies 244
Sec. IV. *Regulation of Securities Credit* 270
I. Types of Credit Extension 270
II. Regulation of Credit Extension by Securities
Companies 273
III. Regulation of the Korea Securities Finance
Corporation (KSFC) 281
Chapter 8: Regulation of Trading in Securities (Two) 286
Sec. I. *Regulation of Takeover Bids* 286
I. Strong Implications to Discourage Potential
Shift in Corporate Control 286
II. Restriction on Increase in Shareholding and
the Owner-ship Reporting Requirement........287
III. Tender Offers 295
Sec. II. *Proxy Solicitations* 318
I. Introduction 318
II. Statutory Proxy Rules 319
III. Enforcement of the Proxy Rules 328
IV. Related Areas: "Going Private" and the "Freeze
Out" 338
Sec. III. *Disclosure and Insider Trading* 358
I. Introduction: Equality of Bargaining 358
II. Disclosure of Information 362
III. Insider Trading: Short-Swing Profits 367
IV. An Urgent Need for Enactment of a New Fraud

Rule 380

Part Three: Recommendations for Feasible Reforms

Chapter 9:   Toward an Efficiently Functioning Securities
              Market 391
    Sec.   I. *Formulation of Basic Policies* 391
            I. Efficient Securities Market 391
            II. Actual Market Features and a Need for
                Government Intervention .396
    Sec.   II. *Specific Recommendations for Reform* 399
            I. Regulation of Distribution of Securities 399
            II. Regulation of Trading in Securities 412
Appendix: Recent Developments 425
Table of Cases 491
Index 493

List of Tables

Table 2.1 Comparison of Trading Volume between
Government Bonds & Stocks during 1957–1961 ...13

2.2 Monthly Trading Volume of KSE Certificates 15

2.3 The Comparison of Monthly Trading during the
Conversion Period 18

2.4 Changes in KSE Stock Price during the 1962 KSE
Stock Crash 21

2.5 Key Statistics for Securities Markets During
1963–1968 25

3.1 Comparison of Investment with GNP 29

3.2 Composition of Savings and Savings Rate 31

3.3 Annual Rate of Return Compared 36

3.4 Changes in the Total Assets of Major Financial
Intermediaries during 1967–1975 39

3.5 Amount of Deposits and Loans at Major
Financial Institutions (1967–1975) 40

3.6 Some Key Statistics Relating to the Financial
Statements of Manufacturing Enterprises
(1966–1974) 44

3.7 Interest Rates on Time Deposits (1965–1972) 54

3.8 Some Key Statistics for Listed Stocks (1968–1972)..57

3.9 Activities of Primary Market (1972–1976) 75

3.10 Capital Increases by Listed Companies
(1967–1976) 76

3.11 Changes in Capital Stock of Listed Companies
(1974–1976) 77

3.12 Key Statistics for Listed Stock (1972–1976) 85

3.13 Distribution of Equity Ownership by Shareholding (1974–1976) 87

3.14 Distribution of Equity Ownership by Owners (1971–1976) 88

3.15 Key Statistics for Listed Bonds (1971–1976) 89

3.16 Maximum Amount of Funds for Margin Trading and Loans Outstanding (1974–1976) 90

3.17 Growth of Securities Investment Trust Funds (1970–1976) 90

4.1 Proposed Investment and GNP Growth (1977–1981) 93

4.2 Proposed Capital Formation for Invesmtnent (1977–1981) 94

4.3 Comparison of Proposed Finance by Sector (1977–1981) 94

Chart 1 Regulatory Structure of the Securities Market 99

List of Abbreviations

AMU	The Association of Managing Underwriters. 139, 140, 142, 169, 402
BOK	The Bank of Korea. 37, 44, 168, 241, 281
CITA	Corporate Income Tax Act (Law No. 1964, Promulgated On Nov. 29, 1967). 47, 48
CMPA	Capital Market Promotion Act (Law No. 2046, Promulgated on Nov. 22, 1968). 45, 46, 53, 67, 118, 164, 394
CPA	Certified Public Accountant. 69, 104, 155, 254, 402
DSITC	Daehan Securities Investment Trust Co., Ltd. 91, 99
EPB	Economic Planning Board. 7, 92
FCIA	Foreign Capital Inducement Act (Law No. 1802, Promulgated on Aug. 3, 1966). 65
GPEA	Going Public Encouragement Act (Law No. 2420, Promulgated on Dec. 30, 1972). 61, 64, 66, 83, 118
KDB	Korea Development Bank. 168
KDFC	Korea Development Finance Corporation. 34, 38, 54
KDI	Korea Development Institute. 79
KIC	Korea Investment Corporation. 42, 49, 54, 80, 99
KIDC	Korea Investment and Development Corporation. 49
KMBC	Korea Merchant Banking Corporation. 41, 91
KSDA	The Korea Securities Dealers Association. 6, 118, 138, 224, 259, 267, 402, 414
KSE	Korea Stock Exchange. 7, 49, 51, 89, 177, 201, 270, 362, 412
KSFC	Korea Securities Finance Corporation. 22, 56, 89, 206, 256, 281, 417

KSIC	Korea Securities Investment Corporation. 71
KSITC	Korea Securities Investment Trust Co., Ltd. 91
KTB	Korea Trust Bank (now, The Bank of Seoul and Trust Company). 38, 51
KUSFC	Korea United Securities Finance Corporation. 11
MBC	Money & Banking Commission. 37
MOF	Ministry of Finance. 8, 65, 96, 182, 242, 400, 412
MS & FC	Mutual Savings and Finance Company. 41
NASD	National Association of Securities Dealers in the United States. 118, 236, 246, 259
NCU	National Credit Union. 41
NYSE	New York Stock Exchange. 193, 201, 327
PCBRA	Public and Corporate Bonds Registration Act (Law No. 2164, Promulgated on Jan. 1, 1970). 118
SAC	Securities Administrative Commission. 95, 182, 223, 250, 330, 366, 400
SDAJ	The Securities Dealers Association of Japan. 119, 239, 240, 268
SEA	Securities & Exchange Act (Law No. 972, Promulgated on Jan. 15, 1962). 16, 51, 69, 93, 104, 115, 223, 250, 341, 399
SEC	U.S. Securities and Exchange Commission. 117, 201, 263, 327, 401
SIPA	Securities Investor Protection Act in the United States. 247
SITA	Securities Investment Trust Act (Law No. 2129, Promulgated on Aug. 4, 1969). 50, 90, 118
SSB	Securities Supervisory Board. 96, 102, 182, 223, 254, 363, 403
STI	Securities Training Institute. 100, 262, 269
STI & FC	Short-Term Investment and Finance Company. 39, 50, 129
TIA	Trust Indenture Act (Law No. 991, Promulgated on Jan. 20, 1962). 118

Introduction

Developing and maintaining a well-functioning securities market which efficiently allocates ownership of the economy's capital stock is vital to the sound development of the national economy in every country. In a developing country like Korea, lacking a capital formation process capable of sustaining the high rate of investment needed for rapid economic growth and depending heavily on foreign capital, promoting the securities market is a vital issue in designing and implementing national economic policies. By introducing a complex system of legal regulation and by effecting a series of law reforms, Korea has struggled to develop securities markets as a strategy to attain efficient capital formation for the past fifteen years.

Securities regulation relates to a wide range of economic activities of market participants and thus raises various legal problems integral to a country's economic system and policies. Securities regulation in Korea is basically structured with the concept of preserving a free and open market by substantially modeling its primary source of law, the Securities and Exchange Act (SEA of 1962), on the federal securities acts in the United States. However, due to unique socio-economic situations in the society, Korea has enacted special laws under which the government becomes extensively involved in the economic activities of the participants, restraining free ownership and economic freedom.

Unlike business corporations in other developing or developed countries, most business corporations in Korea have been traditionally held by a single family or a group of related persons who had never wanted to go public. Although the Korea Stock Exchange

(KSE) was opened in 1956, there were few listed corporations until 1968. Because of this reluctance to go public, most corporations financed their increasing capital needs in a rapidly growing economy through borrowing, leveraging their capital structure further which thereby threatened to become bankrupt. This reluctance to resort to public equity financing also created a serious shortage of commodity supplies in the market; thus, public investors could not commit their savings to enterprises. Indeed, fair competition among the participants has been seriously distorted because of this disequilibrium in the market. Because reasonable production and investment decisions in the management were lacking, the goals of capital formation and economic development plans were significantly frustrated. Since 1968, the government has enacted a series of special laws to encourage and force certain large business corporations to go public.

Through strenuous government efforts, many corporations went public, and the size and functions of the securities markets in Korea grew rapidly until 1976. Along with the rapid growth of the securities markets, the real growth rate of the gross national product (GNP), which had been below 4% in 1957–1961 and 7.8% in 1962–1968, averaged 10.5% in 1967–1971 and 11.5% in 1972–1976. The excessively high share of foreign capital in gross investment, which had been 75% in 1956–1961 and 54% in 1962–1966, decreased to 39.9% in 1967–1971 and 32% in 1972–1976.

Hoping for sustained rapid economic growth and a further reduction of the share of foreign capital, the government placed the heaviest financing burden on the securities market for the implementation of the Fourth Five-Year Economic Development Plan of 1977–1981. In an attempt to achieve the goals of capital formation placed on the securities market, the government also effected a far-reaching reform in securities laws in late 1976. The 1976 Amendments of the securities laws were to strengthen the regulatory structure, to ensure fair and full disclosure, to strengthen anti-fraud regulation, and to spread further equity ownership among the public for an efficient allocation of the real national resources. However, the 1976 Amendments had significant deficiencies, and left many legal problems unresolved.

Achieving the goal of efficient allocation of real resources requires another far-reaching law reform. One purpose of this thesis is to discuss an ideal capital market for Korea and formulate basic policies upon which recommendations for another securities law reform can be based. To understand the needed reforms,the thesis analyzes the present Korean securities laws to identify regulatory loopholes and drawbacks in light of moving toward an ideal market.

This thesis consists of Three Parts and nine Chapters. In Part One, Chapters One through Four, this study closely examines the historical development of the Korean securities markets to clarify the unique social situation in Korea. This study describes how one developing nation Korea, has coped with her capital market promotion problems, especially in a rapidly growing economy. Major emphasis is placed on identifying the barriers to the development of the capital market and appraising the measures taken since 1968, their successes and failures. Finally, Chapter 4 of this study describes the background and contents of the 1976 Amendments of the securities laws, a far-reaching reform completed by early 1977.

In Part Two, this study analyzes the present laws governing the securities markets and identifies regulatory problems. Since Korean securities laws are borrowed substantially from the United States through Japan, the writer compares the Korean laws with those of the United States and Japan. In Chapter 5, he describes the sources of Korean securities laws.

In Chapter 6, the writer analyzes the laws governing the distribution of securities, such as preliminary activities for public offerings and secondary distributions, processing of the registration statement for disclosure of relevant information, and civil liability for misstatements or omissions of a material fact. Because of the strong government involvement in going public, special subjects such as forcing corporations to go public, securities analysis for the determination of offering prices, and problems of forced going public will also be dealt with.

In Chapters 7 and 8, this study discusses the present laws governing trading in securities and other related areas. Chapter 7 discusses the topics of regulations of securities exchanges, manipulating and stabilizing activities, the over-the-counter(OTC) market and securities companies, and securities credit. Chapter 8 discusses the subjects of takeover bids, including ownership increases, proxy solicitation, tender offers, and organic changes and freeze-outs, and disclosure and insider trading. Special emphasis is placed on tracing the regulatory deficiencies revolving around the lack of a proper disclosure standard and a far-reaching anti-fraud rule, a lack which undermines the basic policy goal of a reliable investment climate.

In Part Three, the writer attempts to design recommendations for feasible reforms to move toward the ideal, an efficiently functioning securities market. First, he discusses the concept of an efficient securities market and actual features on the Korean securities markets to formulate a justifiable foundation of which recommendations can be based. The accompanying specific recommendations for reform will be briefly outlined because details have been discussed in the preceding chapters.

Finally, an Appendix is attached, since this thesis was originally written almost five years ago. In the Appendix, the writer describes some of the recent developments in the securities market, the liberalization of the securities market, and the 1982 amendments to the securities laws.

Despite the rapidly increasing importance and growing social demand for studies on Korean securities laws, such studies have been totally neglected thus far. Not even a single article has been written on the securities laws in Korea until the completion of this thesis. Such a lack of previous studies and the resultant scarcity of literature on the Korean securities laws made research on this thesis difficult. In addition, neither the legislature nor the authorities, in enacting or enforcing the securities laws, provided sufficient legislative histories or other materials useful for the clarification of provisions of statutes which are often vague and ambiguous. Another exacerbating condition for the interpretation of the statutes is the lack of court decisions in this field. Therefore, this study had to depend heavily on the inference of the statutes, language by comparing it with those of the United States and Japan on which the former is substantially modeled. It is thus hoped that this study will not only serve as an analysis of the Korean securities laws and a recommendation for legislative actions, but also will provide momentum for more studies in this area.

Part One

A Short Survey on the Development Process of the Securities Market in Korea

In order to plan for the future of the Korean securities market, it is essential to examine its development and identify the present issues. For the sake of convenience, the writer classifies the history of the Korean securities market into four stages: (1) the early stage of formation under Japanese influence (before 1956); (2) the early stage of development under an independently organized system (1956–68); (3) the securities market in a rapidly growing economy (1968–76); and (4) the modern period after a major reform of the securities laws by the 1976 Amendments.

Chapter 1

Early Stage of Formation of Securities Market under Japanese Influences (Before 1956)

Section I. *The Origin of the Corporate Structure of Business and the Securities Market*

"*Sagae Shong-Do Cheeboo-Bub*,"[1] a form of double-entry book-keeping, allegedly originated in the 14th century at the end of the Korea-Dynasty.[2] However, the first business officially recognized as a corporation was probably formed during the late Yi-Dynasty in 1883.[3] Corporate capital at the time was raised through newspaper advertisements.

The king decreed in early 1900 that government-owned businesses be conducted in the form of stock corporation and also encouraged

---

1. This bookkeeping method reportedly developed in the area of Shong-Do, then both the center of commerce and the capital of the Korea-Dynasty. It allegedly preceded Italian double-entry bookkeeping by 200 years. *See* Choong Geuk Kim, *An Analysis of Securities Markets(Cheung-Kwon Seejang Boonseok)* 19–20 (1974) [hereinafter referred to as "Choong Geuk Kim"]; Geun Ho Yoon, *A Study on "Sagae Shong-Do Cheeboo-Bub"(Sagae Shong-Do Cheeboo-Bub Yeonku)* 10–11 (1970). Choong Geuk Kim cites an article by a Japanese scholar, Hirari Shintaro, titled in German, "*Originale Vierfache Buchhaltung in Kaijo*," *Chosen (Korea) Order Chike-Shong Do Chibu*, 6–8 (Z.F.B., 1962).
2. The Korea-Dynasty extended from 918 A.D. to 1392 A.D.
3. *See* Choong Geuk Kim, 13–15. In 1883, six trade companies were incorporated; by 1910, hundreds of corporations existed in the fields of banking, transportation, mining, warehousing, agriculture, publication, and others.

private businessmen to incorporate.[4] The first government bond was issued in 1905 at 7% interest. By law, this government security could be used in lieu of cash.[5] Thereafter, a series of government bonds were issued to meet government financing needs.

Prior to Japanese occupation, the securities market was very rudimentary. There was no organized market in which the public could sell and purchase securities. No evidence can be found to document the existence of underwriting or securities firms prior to 1905. As Japanese influence increased after 1905, a brokerage firm modeled after those in Japan was established in 1909 to meet the emerging spot transaction demands among the public in Seoul.[6] Two significant factors should be noted about public offerings at this time: (1) capital was raised by newspaper advertisements which stated the proposed use of the capital and the reasons for the public offering; and (2) the total shareholdings of promoters were far less than those of the public investors.[7]

Section II. *The Securities Market under Japanese Occupation* (1910~1945)

The first organized securities market was established in April, 1911 by Japanese securities dealers. It was called "The Association of Securities Brokerage Houses on Spot." Members met together at a certain place on every business day and traded securities in accordance with the rules of the Association.[8] The Association, however, was dissolved during the 1910s because of excessive speculation by some members.[9] The Association was reorganized in 1919 and continued to exist until the opening of the "Kyong Sung Stock Market

4. *Id.*, at 18–19.
5. *Decree on the National Treasury Bond* (promulgated in 1905), Art. 11. *See Taehan (Korea) Bubkyu-Ryu Chan* 825; *see* also Choong Geuk Kim, 17.
6. *See* Joo Ryong Kim, *A History of the Securities Market Development in Korea* (*Hankook Cheungkwon Seejang Baldal-Sa*), 8 (1967) [hereinafter referred to as "Joo Ryong Kim"]. Indeed, the number of Japanese coming into Korea after the treaty of 1905 rapidly increased. Their transactions in Japanese stock through a Japanese brokerage firm influenced the Koreans.
7. Choong Geuk Kim, 17.
8. Joo Ryong Kim, 9; Choong Geuk Kim, 21.
9. *Id.*

on Spot" in 1920.[10] The latter was the first organized securities market authorized by the Japanese Government. It was a stock corporation, 60 thousand shares of which were subscribed by Korean and Japanese citizens in proportion to an allotment established by law.[11] The Kyong Sung Market was subsequently followed by the "Chosun Exchange" in 1932,[12] which in turn was succeeded by the "Chosun Stock Exchange" in July, 1943.[13]

The Decree establishing the Chosun Exchange represented the first material law on securities transactions enacted by the Government. Securities transactions had previously been governed by rules adopted by the security traders.[14] The Decree established the Chosun Exchange as the sole securities market in Korea. It consolidated the existing Kyong Sung Stock Exchange on Spot and Inchon Rice and Bean Exchange into the Chosun Exchange. Furthermore, it provided some devices for protecting public investors, such as requiring public notice of fair prices of securities and prohibiting any person from engaging in false transactions.[15] Finally, the Chosun Securities Finance Corporation was established in April, 1932, as the sole securities financing business.[16]

The Japanese promulgated the Decree on Chosun Stock Exchange as a part of a plan to create a centrally controlled national economy in World War II. The organization of the exchange was changed from a private stock corporation to a special government controlled legal entity. The Exchange functioned as a marketplace for the distribution of government bonds to meet the expenses necessary for the continuance of the war economy.[17] In addition, securities

---

10. Joo Ryong Kim, 9; Choong Geuk Kim, 21.
11. For details of the organization of the Kyong Sung Stock Market on Spot, *see* Choong Geuk Kim, 22–23. Kyong Sung was the capital of the country and is now the city of Seoul.
12. *Id.* at 23 and 27. The Chosun Exchange Decree was promulgated by the Japanese Government as Government-General Decree No. 137 in Nov., 1931. Korea was called *"Chosun"* at this time.
13. *Id.* at 31.
14. *Id.* at 27.
15. *Id.*
16. *Id.* at 28. Up until the enforcement of the Decree, the Exchange and securities companies were able to engage in securities financing.
17. *Id.* at 31.

financing was very limited due to the huge amount needed to finance the war. As Japanese military prospects worsened, the prices of Japanese stocks, which made up the bulk of the securities listed, correspondingly declined. When Japan finally lost the war, the market almost completely disintegrated.[18]

It is necessary to understand the Japanese colonial policies to fully understand Japanese policies toward the securities market in Chosun (Korea). Chosun, as a whole, was treated only as a supplier of raw material for Japanese industries and as a market for the consumption of products made in Japan. Thus the securities market in Chosun was used primarily as a market to mobilize the capital needed by industries in Japan. Since it was practically impossible for a Korean to get authorization to engage in major industrial business, the manufacturing industries were dominated by Japanese businessmen. This Japanese control discouraged the process of industrialization and indigenous capital formation in Korea.[19] Furthermore, banking credit privileges and favorable tax treatment were available only to the Japanese.[20]

Of the 284 stocks listed in 1938, 201 stocks were Japanese. Among the manufacturing companies formed by indigenous capital, only Kyong Sung Spinning Corporation was listed on the Exchange.[21] Due to limitations on Korean participation in the securities business, only one of the 15 securities companies was owned by Koreans.[22] Securities transactions on the Exchange were concentrated on a few popular stocks of Japanese companies which had their head offices located in Japan.[23]

Even though the securities market was dominated by the Japanese, some notable developments occurred. During the Japanese

---

18. *Id.; see also* the Korea Securities Dealers Association (KSDA), *The Twenty-Year History of the Korea Securities Dealers Association* (*Cheung Kwon Ub Hyuphoe Isheep-Nyon-Sa*), 43 (1973) [hereinafter referred to as "KSDA, *History*"].
    The matter of remedies for Korean public securities holders who held government bonds or other securities issued by the Japanese Government or private corporations was recently resolved.
19. KSDA, *History*, 43.
20. *Id.*
21. *Id.*
22. *Id.* at 42 and 44.
23. *Id.* at 42.

occupation many Koreans recognized that the adoption of the stock corporation system was important for the modernization of management. Also, some Koreans entered the securities business during the Japanese occupation and later made remarkable contributions to securities administration and market operation during the transition period following independence(August 15, 1945).[24]

Section III. *The Securities Market during the Transition Period* (1945~1956)

The period between the independence of August 15, 1945, and March 3, 1956 was a "transition period" for the securities market in Korea. During that time, there was no organized securities market in Korea. Korea underwent extreme hardship in her political, economical, and social life. The new independence left a power vacuum which lasted for approximately three years. The U.S. Military Government, which temporarily controlled the establishment of a new Korean Government, played a limited role. The Government of the Republic of Korea was established below the 38th Parallel in 1948. But independence was marked by vicious conditions of poverty and social disorder largely due to the Korean War, which broke out in 1950.[25]

In January, 1946, the U.S. Military Government closed the Chosun Stock Exchange.[26] Thus, securities transactions could not be made on an organized market. A few securities, which had been listed on the Chosun Stock Exchange, were traded sporadically by private persons who had experience in the securities businesses during the Japanese occupation.[27] Securities transactions widened as the government issued public bonds. A note for farm-land compensation

---

24. *Id.* at 44.
25. The total amount of property damage incurred during the War was approximately $3 billion, which was equivalent to the GNP of 1965. *See* Economic Planning Board (EPB), *Economic Survey* 14–15 (1963).
26. *See Decree on the Liquidation of the Chosun Stock Exchange* (U.S. Military Government Decree No. 43, released on Jan. 16, 1946).
27. Korea Stock Exchange (KSE), *The Ten-Year History of the KSE* (*Cheung-Kwon Gurae-So Sheep-Nyon-Sa*) 24 (1968) [hereinafter referred to as "KSE, *History*"].

due to agrarian reform[28] was issued in 1949 and a series of government bonds entitled "National Foundation Government Bonds (*Gun-Gook Gook-Chae*)" began to be issued in January, 1950.[29] However, a sustained high rate of inflation caused the holders of 5% government bonds to sell them even at 10% of par value through unauthorized brokers or securities companies located in Busan and Taegu.[30]

In 1947, the leading persons with experience in the field of securities transactions during the Japanese occupation formed an organization called the "Securities Club" with Mr. Dae Soon Song as a central figure.[31] The club was organized to further the establishment of an organized securities market in the near future. In November, 1949, "Dae-Han Securities Company" was incorporated with the authorization of the Ministry of Finance(MOF) through the efforts of the members of the club. The number of securities companies increased to five by 1953.[32] These companies played a significant role in establishing the Korea Securities Dealers Association (KSDA) in late 1953. The KSDA regulated the securities market after the establishment of post-war securities trading until 1956.[33]

---

28. Traditionally Korean landlords owned a large block of land which they leased to many tenant farmers in small sections. In June, 1949, the Government abolished this tenant system and implemented agrarian reform. Under the Agrarian Reform Act, a landlord was limited to a certain amount of land. All excess land was confiscated by the National Government and distributed among the tenant farmers in accordance with statutory priorities. The landlord was issued notes in compensation for the confiscation by the Government.

29. KSE, *History*, 26, 62–64.
     "The National Foundation Government Bond," bearing 5% interest, was first issued in Jan. 12, 1950 to supplement the government deficit. The destruction of the Korean War caused the Government to increase its issues. Government bonds were issued seventeen times in series through Jan. 10, 1963 with a total amount of ₩ 9,150 million. Beginning with the second issue, subscription was compulsory. For details, *see* KSE, *History*, 25–27.

30. *See* KSDA, *History*, 49–51.
     Since there was no securities law after the abrogation of Japanese law, the incorporation of an unauthorized security company might have been legal.

31. *See* id. at 50; *see also* KSE, *History*, 28.

32. *Id.* at 51. Authorized securities companies were Dae-Han, Korea, Ryong-Nam, Tong-Yang, and International (*Kuk-Je*). The latter four were authorized during 1952–53.

33. *See The Rules On Securities Transactions* (authorized by the MOF on March 3,

Its role was ended on February 19, 1956 and was subsequently transferred to the Korea Stock Exchange(KSE).[34]

1955). The members of the KSDA then totaled thirty-one securities companies. For details, *see* KSDA, *History*, 53–55.

34. The Korea Stock Exchange (KSE) was opened on March 3, 1956. For details of the establishment of the KSE, *see* KSE, *History*, 33–37.

Chapter 2

Early Stage of Development under Independently Organized Market System (1956~1968)

Section I. *Establishment of the Korea Stock Exchange and Governing Law*

The first step in the establishment of a stock exchange was the enactment of a securities law. After the establishment of the KSDA, a securities exchange act was submitted to the National Assembly in December, 1953.[1] However, because of legislative dissatisfaction with its incompleteness, the bill died in the second term. Another bill titled the "Securities Exchange Act" was killed in the next session of The National Assembly. The Government was forced to take an alternative route.

Proceeding via an "authorized construction of law,"[2] the government instructed the Establishing Committee to proceed under the "Decree on the Chosun Stock Exchange" enacted in 1943 by the Japanese Government. The Committee completed the start-up procedures by February 11, 1956, and the MOF authorized the opening of the KSE on February 29, 1956.[3]

The general structure of a stock exchange may be classified with

---

1. KSE, *History*, 37–38.
2. The term "authorized construction of law" means an opinion of the competent authority (then the Bureau of Legal Legislation, now the Ministry of Justice) on a question raised when commentators disagree in construing and applying the provisions of a statute.
3. KSE, *History*, 38. For details of the establishment of the KSE, *see id.* at 33-47.

respect to its form, contribution of capital, and operation into three major categories: (1) government operation; (2) stock corporation; and (3) member-firm self-operation. The KSE was incorporated as a special legal entity. Three groups of institutions, viz., banks, insurance companies, and securities companies, each contributed ₩ 10 million of capital.[4] The Government contributed indirectly because it was the controlling shareholder of most of the banking institutions. The KSE as it existed at that time was known as an institutionally operated exchange system (*Yong-Dan-Je*). The government, however, had broad supervisory functions due to the character of the original Japanese Decree. The KSE was, in fact, almost a government controlled structure.[5] There was no change in the structure of the KSE until the Securities and Exchange Act was enacted in 1962.[6]

Section II. *Early Market Activities and Disasters*

In 1956, when the independently organized market opened, there were 49 securities firms of very small size.[7] The Korea United Securities Finance Corporation (KUSFC) did not play a major role in extending securities credit.[8] Only 13 corporations and 3 government bonds were listed.[9] Securities transactions were either spot transactions (*Shil-Mool Gu-Rae*) or deferred clearance transactions (*Chung-San Gu-Rae*).[10] Spot transactions were in turn classified into two forms: the same day clearance transactions (*Dang-il Gyulje Gu-Rae*)

---

4. KSDA, *History,* 57. The total legal capital, ₩ 30 million, was equivalent to $600,000 since the exchange ratio at the time was 50:1. *See* The Bank of Korea, *Economic Statistics Yearbook* 217 (1976).
5. Thus the KSE's Articles of incorporation, the opening of the securities market, membership qualification, listing, and the kinds of authorized securities trading were subject to regulation by the MOF. The election of the directors and officers of the KSE was also controlled by the government. KSE personnel were considered to be government officials.
6. *Securities Exchange Act (SEA)*, Law No. 972, promulgated on Jan. 15, 1962.
7. *See* KSDA, *History,* 58. The amount of capital of the securities company varied from 2 to 3 million Won.
8. *Id.*
9. KSE, *History,* 48. The government bonds were those issued during 1953–55 and known as Ma, Ba, and Sa-Ho, respectively.
10. *Id.* and at 283–84. The latter was tainted with speculative trading which led to a crash (*see* pp. 17–21 and 56–60 *infra*).

and 15 day deferred clearance transactions (*Tukyakil Gyulje Gu-Rae*). Deferred clearance transactions were classified into two types: clearance at the end of the month (*Dang-Han*), or at the end of the next month (*Shun-Han*).

By 1961 the market activities on the Exchange were concentrated in government bonds (*see* Table 2.1). The variety and supply of listed stocks was very limited because large blocks of listed stocks were held by either the government or small numbers of closely-held corporations.[11] Furthermore, public investors avoided stocks due to sustained inflation and an unstable economic situation. The government bonds, however, were very popular after the government announced certain fiscal policies on October 31, 1956.[12] The government exempted from taxation income derived from bond dealings. In addition, the bonds could be legaly used in lieu of cash in mortgage and transactions with governmental institutions. Due to the stability of return, tax advantages, and increasing marketability, the bonds played the dominant role on the Exchange. The average trading ratio of bonds to stock from 1956 to 1961 was 81:19(*see* Table 2.1).

The speculation of securities companies in government bonds led to the first of many tragic experiences, the so-called "January Government Bonds Crash" of 1958.[13] A critical factor which induced excessive speculation was speculation as to whether the eleventh series of government bonds of ₩ 18,000 million would be issued in 1958. There were many discussions in the National Assembly on the matter from mid-September until the final decision was made on December 28, 1957.

During this period of speculation, the purchasing group consisted of 5 securities companies which thought the government would not issue the bonds. They began to corner the ninth and tenth series of government bonds through deferred clearance transactions which permitted them to trade on small margins.[14] Another group of 6

---

11. *Id.* at 51.
12. *Id.* at 49. Until the government released its fiscal policy, there were great fluctuations in the bond's market price due to doubt at to its redeemability.
13. *Id.* at 55-58. KSDA, *History*, 60–61.
14. KSE, *History*, 55–56. In October, the total amount of trading in government bonds was about ₩ 200 million, a 75% increase over that of September. The sharp increase in bond trading continued through early January of the next

Table 2.1 Comparison of Trading Volume between Government Bonds & Stocks during 1957–1961.

Unit: W million[1]

Year	Bonds (A)	Stocks (B)	Ratio % (A:B)[2]
1956	299	394	43:57
1957	2,000	414	83:17
1958	1,481	180	89:11
1959	2,116	763	73:27
1960	1,330	275	83:17
1961	910	440	67:33
TOTAL	10,602	2,466	81:19

Source: Korea Stock Exchange

Notes: 1) The exchange ratio of Korean Won to U.S. $ was 50:1 for the period of 1955–early 1960, 65:1 for the rest of 1960, and 130:1 for 1961. The Bank of Korea, *Economic Statistics Yearbook* 217 (Seoul, 1976).

2) The ratio is calculated by rounding off to the nearest whole number.

securities companies decided to meet the demands of the purchasing group as the price of bonds began to increase. When the MOF declared that the amount of eleventh series bonds might be decreased to W 300 million on November 23, the bond prices rose sharply. In mid-December the Committee of Finance and Economy decided to eliminate the proposal which caused the prices to increase more. The National Assembly, however, passed the proposal on December 28 and the price dropped sharply by 37%. Thereafter, each party tried to manipulate and maintain the price, and the market became a center of frantic speculation. However, when the KSE decided to increase the margin requirement to 50% on January 16, 1958, the purchasing group of 5 securities companies failed to meet the requirement and the manipulation ended with a crash.[15]

The crash was caused both by the excessive manipulation of securities companies without enough funds to meet margin requirements and by the poor market administration of the government. Either the KSE or the MOF should have taken some necessary and appro-

---

year.

15. *Id.* at 57-58. When the contract failed to clear, the MOF arranged special loans immediately. Further, the licenses of the securities companies which had led the purchasing group were cancelled and the licenses of the remaining two were suspended. The whole leadership of the KSE was changed after the crash.

priate actions to discourage the frantic manipulation.[16] Securities businesses as well as the public investors were seriously hurt by the crash. As a result, many public investors were reluctant to participate further in the securities market and thus a long market depression followed.[17]

Another incident occurred on the Exchange in 1959. This incident is known as the "KSE Certificate Accident" (*Dae Cheung-Kwon Sho-Dong*). The crash was caused by excessive manipulations to corner KSE certificates of contribution.[18] The manipulation began in early March, 1959, when the market anticipated a new securities exchange act to reorganize the KSE in the form of a stock corporation or a membership system. Thus, some securities companies started to corner KSE certificates of contribution in the hopes that they would profit by ownership of the institution.

On March 5, 100 million KSE certificates were suddenly traded and cleared on the next day. This news stimulated the price rise sharply. In April, as the likelihood of passage of the new act increased, the speculation intensified and the price went up 66% as compared with the price at the end of February. Even though the KSE, in cooperation with the MOF, increased the margin requirements and required the two-thirds of the KSE certificates held by groups of banks and insurance companies to be traded on the Exchange, the frantic speculation on the market worsened (*see* Table 2.2). No transactions failed to clear in June. But in July, when the securities bill encountered difficulties in the National Assembly, the Kyong-Hee Securities Company, which headed the speculation, defaulted and voluntarily closed its securities businesses.[19] A crash

---

16. A timely increase of margin requirements or the suspension of trading should have been considered.

17. KSE, *History*, 58.

18. *Id.* at 58–69. The total amount of the KSE capital, ₩ 30 million, consisted of 1,200 million certificates of contribution (par value ₩ 0.025 per certificate) which were equally divided among three groups of institutions. Two-thirds of the total outstanding certificates which were held by the two groups of banks and insurance companies had not been traded on the Exchange due to a government policy to freeze them. Thus, only one-third of the total KSE certificates were traded on the market. This small number might easily be manipulated by a few persons.

19. The history of the KSE certificate accident is extracted from the KSE, *History*,

Table 2.2 Monthly Trading Volume of KSE Certificates

Month	Traded (in millions)	Total Price in W mil.	% as Compared to KSE's Total Trading Volume
March	830	43	82
April	1,602	110	93
May	2,088	166	94
June	808	71	58
Total	5,328	391	81.75

Source: Korea Stock Exchange

followed.

These two market crashes which occurred in the early age of the KSE had an adverse impact on the development of the securities markets in Korea by giving the general public an impression that the Exchange was a center of frantic manipulation. They did, however, educate the public about the dangers of a poorly regulated market. The KSE and MOF accordingly tried to improve the system and the regulatory structure of the securities market.

However, the KSE and the Government had not taken any significant measures to reform any regulatory systems by the times of the April Student Revolution which overthrew the government in 1960. Under the subsequent government of Chang Myon, the securities markets in Korea underwent an extreme depression due to social disorder and economic depression. Thirteen months later, General Park led a successful military coup d'etat on May 16, 1961.

Section III. *Stock Trading and Some Reforms Established*

I. Major Policies Taken and Their Background

The government recognized that the securities market was important in mobilizing the domestic capital required for the development of the national economy, and tried to implement some positive policies to promote the market. The policies consisted of enforcement of a new Asset Revaluation Act,[20] improvement of dividend policy, and tax reforms designed to stimulate demand for equity securities. The

58-60 and the KSDA, *History*, 62–63.

20. *See* KSE, *History*, 69–70.

The Asset Revaluation Act was promulgated and enforced in January, 1958. The government replaced it with a new law in May, 1962.

government also promulgated the Securities and Exchange Act (SEA) for the purpose of reforming securities markets with a view to creating a healthy investment climate. It also enacted the Commercial Code, which defined the authorized capital system of stock corporations.

A. Policies Taken for the Stimulation of Stock Demands

The enforcement of the asset revaluation system played a significant role in converting the market activities thus far concentrated on the bonds into stock trading. It stimulated more demand for equity securities by permitting a corporation to revalue its book assets to reflect the appreciation in nominal values of assets due to sustained inflation. By the same token, it encouraged corporations to issue new stock through conversion of the revaluation surplus.[21]

Furthermore, the government forced corporations wholly or partly controlled to declare dividends at an attractive level. In accordance with the policies, commercial banks listed on the Exchange declared their dividends at an 8–12% rate in 1961. Korea Electric Corporation also declared its first dividend at 10% in the same year.[22] In addition, in order to increase the supply of stocks, the government owned companies were ordered to sell stocks through the Exchange.[23]

B. The Securities and Exchange Act (SEA) and the Commercical Code

As noted earlier, the securities markets had been temporarily regulated by the Decree promulgated by the Japanese government in 1943. Thus, the enactment of a new securities law was eagerly awaited to update the laws to Korean needs. The National Assembly passed the new Securities and Exchange Act (SEA) on January 15, 1962.[24] It was modeled after the modern Japanese Securities Exchange Act, which had in turn relied heavily on the Federal securities laws in the United States. Even though the SEA contained many defective provisions,[25] its passage was a pivotal event in the history of the market.

Another piece of legislation which greatly influenced the securities

---

21. *See id.* Table 18 at 70.

   The total amount of revaluation surpluses of listed companies which had been converted into shares totaled ₩ 12,365 million during the period of 1959–64, of which ₩ 10,710 million (87%) was converted in the period of 1963–64.
22. KSE, *History,* **71.**
23. *Id.* at 73–76.
24. Law No. 972, promulgated on Jan. 15, 1962.
25. Some of these problems are discussed at pp. 95–109, *infra.*

market was the enactment of the Commercial Code in early 1962.[26] It replaced the then existing German style system of capital stock incorporation with an authorized capital system similar to that of the United States.[27] It also created other supplementary devices to regulate the structure of a stock corporation. All these devices were geared to enable stock corporations to meet their capital needs more rapidly and more easily.[28]

II. Changes in the Market Activities

A. *Conversion into Stock Trading*

With the help of a series of positive policy measures discussed above, stock trading surpassed bond trading on the Exchange in November, 1961. As the public demand for equity securities began to increase, the supplies were expanded at the same time. Thus, stock trading on the market increased sharply in comparison with bond trading (*see* Table 2.3).

The two major factors which led to the expansion of supplies of stocks during that period were forced trading of government owned stocks and the stock dividends issued from asset revaluation surpluses.[29] Since 12 of the 16 issues listed were owned primarily by the government or government controlled institutions, the simplest way to meet the increasing demands was to have the shares distributed publicly through the Exchange. Among the issues distributed in

---

26. Law No. 100, promulgated on Jan. 20, 1962.
27. *Id.*, Arts. 289(1) (2), 295, 305; *see also* pp.123–125 at Chapter 6, Sec. I, *infra*. The German system was known as "Grundsatz der Vollaufbringung des Kapitals," under which the total capital stock must be stated in the Articles of Incorporation and be paid in full at the time of incorporation. But the new system of authorized capital stock requires that the total number of authorized shares (authorized capital stock) and shares to be issued at the time of incorporation (capital stock in a narrow sense) be stated in the articles of incorporation; and that at least half of the total authorized shares be issued and paid in full at the time of incorporation. Due to these restrictions, the new system is a mixture of the German and Anglo-American systems.
28. The devices included strengthening the power of the board of directors to issue new shares, allowing an issuance of new shares at a price below par in certain circumstances, relaxing the conditions for issuance of corporate bonds or debentures, protecting minority shareholders, and guaranteeing the absolute negotiability of stocks.
29. KSE, *History*, 78–9.

Table 2.3 The Comparison of Monthly Trading during the Conversion Period

Unit: ₩ million

Month		Trading Volume		Ratio (%)
		Stock (A)	Bond (B)	A to B
1961.	7	13.6	65.6	17.2:82.8
	10	24.7	50.2	33.0:67.0
	11	76.7	59.1	56.5:43.5
	12	190.0	66.4	73.7:26.3
1962.	1	609.5	69.0	89.8:10.2
	2	817.7	36.2	95.8: 4.2
	3	3,353.2	89.6	97.5: 2.5
	4	11.768.2	76.6	99.4: 0.6
	5	25,124.7	84.9	99.6: 0.4

Source: Korea Stock Exchange

such a way, those of Korea Electric Corp. and Korea Cereals Warehousing Corp. played remarkable roles;[30] the former increased its number of shares traded on the Exchange by 151.5% and the latter by 1,079%.

Such government distributions were critical, but they were not sufficient to meet the rapidly increasing demands and the distribution prices were set at unreasonably high levels by the government at the expense of investors.[31] However, the total amount of stock dividends from asset revaluation surpluses during 1961–1964 was ₩ 13,216 million.[32] Unfortunately, the sustained boom in stock trading under the shortage of supplies was followed by another big crash in 1962.

B. The So-Called "May Crash"

The so-called "May Crash" began in February of 1962, climaxed in May, and ended in July, resulting in defaults by a large number of stock traders. The crash was caused by excessive speculation by several securities companies who speculated in KSE stock.[33] Clearly, there were some market defects which should be noted as major causes

---

30. *Id.* at 76. The following statistics are based on the number of stocks traded and distributed during Oct., 1961 – May, 1962.
31. *Id.* at 76–7 and 91.
32. *Id.* at 77.
33. *Id.* at 89. The other objects of speculation were the stocks of the Korean Electric and the General Securities Financing Corporations.

of the crash. First, the KSE was reorganized on April 11, 1962 as a profit organization, a pure stock corporation, whose stock remained listed on its own Exchange.[34] Considering the former incident involving KSE certificates, such form of reorganization should have been avoided. The KSE certificates (stock after reorganization) became again a main object of speculation. The system created conflicts of interest and discouraged fair administration by the KSE due to the self-interest of a few controlling shareholders.

Second, the SEA abandoned the deferred clearance method of trading and adopted a "regular way" of trading instead.[35] However, the regular way encouraged speculation because the clearance could be deferred up to two months following the transaction. Thus there was temporarily a large difference in price between the regular and spot transactions.[36] This difference caused many speculators to purchase stocks at the lower price in spot transactions and sell them at higher prices in regular method transactions. This trend in turn brought great pressure on the KSE because it had financing responsibilities for the temporary clearance of securities traded.[37] Indeed,

---

34. The institutionally owned organization of the KSE was appraised during its six year tenure before the SEA was passed. Strong government control under the system was noted as a drawback, and two alternatives——the membership system and the private stock corporation system——were under consideration. However, Korea at this time in its development could not successfully maintain a membership system approach because securities companies could not meet both the capital contribution and self-regulation requirements. Rather, the for-profit stock corporation system was preferred to stimulate stock investment among the public. For details, *see id.* at 81–86; *see also* KSDA, *History*, 72–3.

35. After April 1, 1962, there were four ways to set a clearing date. It could be set on the same day the contract was made, on a specified date within 15 days of the contract, on a date when new shares were expected to be issued, or according to the regular way. Under the regular way the clearance of a contract could be postponed by the parties for up to two months; but the party deferring the clearance must pay all interest charges. The regular way was replaced by the deferred clearance transaction method after two months. For details, *see* KSE, *History*, 86 and 285–6.

36. *Id.* at 86.

37. Since there was no financial institution exclusively established for securities financing, the KSE undertook the role of financing from its establishment. The financing of the money required for the clearance of securities in deferred

the KSE was faced with a shortage of funds for temporary clearance financing unless it could find new sources of capital.

Thus the KSE increased its capital by ₩ 40 million in March, 1962, and a resolution for another capital increase up to ₩ 400 million was approved by the shareholder meeting on April 20.[38] The shareholders approved 900 million shares (12.375% of the total new shares) for public offer. The decisions as to the offering price and the timing were entrusted to the board of directors.[39] The board of directors resolved to adjust the sales premiums on the basis of market prices during the first fifteen days of May. Certain securities companies of the purchasing group which were also large KSE shareholders increased their cornering activities in order to manipulate the market prices.[40] Thus the market became a center of frantic manipulation because there was no rule prohibiting short-sales or insider trading. Furthermore, no measures were taken to deter such manipulation by the authorities.

The price increases of the KSE stock during the manipulation are shown in Table 2.4. This table shows a remarkable increase in price during March and April. The sharp drop on May 1 was due to the closing of the shareholders registry for stock dividends but the price of the stock soon rallied again. The trading volume in May was the highest in history. It almost equaled the total trading volume during

---

clearance or regular way transactions was called "financing for temporary clearance (*Ga-Do Geum-Yung*)."

38. KSE, *History*, 87–9. The total amount of capital contribution was increased to ₩ 500 million.

39. The par value per share was ₩. 05 and the total number of shares issued were 8 billion, of which 7 billion were to be issued *pro rata* to existing shareholders and 10 million were to be issued to employees of the KSE.

40. Under the stock corporation system of the KSE, the controlling shareholders could themselves profit at the expense of the public. The purchasing group, consisting of the Tong-Il, Il-Heung, and Tong-Myong securities companies held a large number of KSE shares. They monopolized securities financing funds and manipulated market prices. The borad decided on May 22 that the new shares would be offered to the public at ₩ 1.45 per share with a 2800% premium (since par value was ₩ .05). Further, the board resolved on June 20 that it would declare stock dividends totaling 20 billion shares (total par value ₩ 1 billion), two shares for each share outstanding, to be accounted for by converting paid-in surplus to capital. *See* KSE, *History*, 87–8.

Table 2.4 Changes in KSE Stock Price during the 1962 KSE Stock Crash

Unit: W (par value per share W .05)

Month and Day		Price (ratio of increase in percent)[1]		
		A[2](%)	B[2](%)	C[2](%)
March	2	.253	.260	.250
	31	.919(263) (on 28th[a])	.855(299)	.990(296)
average	3	.653(158)	.625(140)	.706(182)
April	2	1.987(685)	1.027(295)	1.024(310)
	27	3.450(1,263)	3.390(1,203)	5.100(1,940)
average	3	2.037(705)	1.985(663)	2.402(861)
May	1	*.890(251)	*1.500(477)	*1.500(500)
	31	2.640(943) (on 20th[b])	2.600(900)	4.460(1,684)
average	3	2.001(691)	2.483(855)	2.948(1,079)

Source: Korea Stock Exchange

Notes: 1) The base price for calculations of price increase ratios is that of March 2.
2) A,B and C stand for different types of trading methods:
A stands for "the spot transaction" method during March and "the same day clearance" method thereafter; B stands for "clearance at the end of the month" method during March and April and thereafter for the "regular way"; C stands for "clearance at the end of the next month" method during March and May and the "regular way" during April.
3) The average price is a figure calculated by dividing the total sum of the prices during each month by the number of trading days.
a; There was no available price for March 29–31.
b; The "regular way" was ended on May 28, 1962.
*The drop was due to the closing of the shareholder registry for stock dividends declared from paid-in capital surplus.

the previous six years of the KSE.[41]

Even though the SEA outlawed cornering by the purchasing group as explicit price manipulation,[42] the competent authorities did not take any action to deter such excessive speculation. The KSE had actually relaxed margin requirements,[43] which stimulated the spe-

41. *Id.* at 96. The total trading volume of W 41,062 million for the four months exceeded the W27,400 million traded during the past six years of 1956–61.
42. *See SEA*, Art. 91(2). But there was no provision corresponding to those of American federal securities law which prohibit insider trading (such as Sec. 16(b), Sec. 10(b), and Rule 10(b)–5). *See* p. 105, *infra*.
43. KSE, *History*, 92. The margin requirement was relaxed from 60% on Feb. 7 to 10–30% throughout the crash.

culation. The authority's only limited action was an arrangement of special loans to help finance securities clearances. This financing played a limited role in forestalling the defaults of clearances in June.[44] On June 8, the KSE, under the mandate of the MOF and the consultation with the KSDA, finally acted and cancelled all KSE stock contracts.[45] But the crash had already seriously damaged the securittes market by, *inter alia*, destroying public confidence.[46]

C. Closing of the KSE for 73 Days

Due to the impact of the May Crash, the securities markets entered another long depression. The public mistrusted the brokerage community and tended to regard the KSE as a gambling arena controlled by brokers seeking their own profits. As a result, most securities firms had to sell their stocks to meet their working capital requirements. The forced sales dumped excessive supplies on the market far exceeding the small demand therein and the stock prices accordingly declined. In spite of the government's efforts at reform, speculation again began to center around the stocks of the KSE and Korea Securities Finance Corp. (KSFC).[47] Indeed, the market fluctuated tremendously whenever there were rumors.

With such rampant speculation, the authorities recognized that the way to establish a functioning securities market required a fundamental reform of the system. The MOF closed the Exchange on February 25, 1963, only to be reopened when overall reform work was completed.[48] The resulting closure was the longest suspension of business since the establishment of the KSE.

III. Some Reforms and Supplementary Measures

A. Reorganization of the KSE

Due to the defects involved in the stock corporation system, *i.e.*, conflicts of interest and domination by a few controlling shareholders which, in effect, deterred fair market administration, the SEA was

---

44. *Id.* at 93–5.

45. *Id.* at 95.

46. About ten persons including the Minister of the MOF, officers of the KSE, and officers of the securities companies concerned were indicted. However, they were all found not guilty. *See* KSDA, *History*, 84.

47. The KSFC was organized when the KUSFC was reorganized.

48. *Id.* at 111.

amended to reorganize the KSE.[49] The KSE was reorganized as a special non-profit public entity. Furthermore, the MOF undertook control over personnel decisions regarding KSE officers. Also, the government made a partial capital contribution to the KSE.[50] Though the purpose of the reform was mainly to insure fair administration of the KSE, its certificates were not delisted from its own exchange.

B. Supplementary Measure Taken

1. Unification of Securities Financing System

As noted earlier there had been no institution solely responsible for securities financing. The KSFC would loan upon a pledge of securities as collateral, and the KSE would finance temporary clearance of the deferred clearance method and the regular way transactions. During the May Crash, however, large shareholders of the KSE preempted all other securities firms and concentrated KSE financing on themselves.

Due to such unfair administration, all securities financing was consolidated into the KSFC in December, 1962.[51] This consolidation included a transfer of the clearing business formerly undertaken by the KSE to the KSFC. Unfortunately, the KSFC was controlled by the same group that controlled the KSE, and the same inequities remained.

2. Adoption of a Price Control System

In order to deter excessive speculation or manipulation, a price control technique was provided in The Rules of Business of the KSE.[52] These rules limited the permissible increase or drop in the market price of a stock. Some other provisions of the Rules were also improved.[53]

---

49. *See SEA,* as amended by Law No. 1,334 on April 27, 1963, The reorganization of the KSE was completed on May 3, 1963.

50. *See id.,* Art. 45, and Addenda, Art. 11; *see also SEA,* Addenda, Art. 11, proviso, as amended by Law No. 1,679 on Dec. 31, 1964. The government's capital contribution was made through an exchange of stock with the KSE on Aug. 2, 1965. The government gave the KSE ₩650 million worth of stocks and received 1.3 million certificates of the KSE. The government thus owned 46.3% of the KSE. For details, *see* KSE, *History,* 119–23.

51. *Id.* at 107–9.

52. *The KSE Rules on Business,* Art. 13–2, as amended in Dec., 1964.

53. KSE, *History,* 126–7.

3. Limitation on Short-Sales

To discourage excessive speculation, the KSE was empowered as of August 1, 1965 to enforce a hitherto ignored measure limiting short-sale transactions. A seller who did not hold any securities was forced to pay the whole price in a deferred clearance transaction. The measure, however, was enforced for only two months.[54]

IV. Market Activities: A Long Depression

The KSE reopened on May 9, 1963.[55] The market, however, remained in a long depression through the end of 1968. There were only 24 companies listed on the Exchange by 1967, few of which were considered blue-chip enough to elicit public interest. Since both the KSE certificates and the KSFC issues had not been eliminated from the Exchange listings, they became again objects of manipulation. The high turnover ratio during 1963–1964 shown in Table 2.5 can be attributed to the two issues. Because most business corporations were owned by groups of single families who were reluctant to go public, the primary market for equity securities showed little activity. Some key statistics for the securities market during 1963–1968 are shown in Table 2.5.

The issuance of government bonds was stopped in 1964 due to excessive liquidity and fiscal inflation.[56] During this period, there were not corporate financings through bonds or debentures on the market. Rather, the issuance of corporate bonds or debentures was, in substance, used as an alternative for long-term bank loans.[57] The bonds and debentures were purchased by several financial institutions with annual interest rates in a range of 10–18% and the maturities of 3–6 years. During 1963–1971, 30 issues valued at ₩ 5.68 billion were issued. This private financing resulted from a lack

---

54. The MOF retreat was caused by pressure brought to bear by the KSDA which strongly objected to the short-sale limitation.
55. KSE, *History*, 119. Also on the same day, the par value of KSE certificates of contribution was increased from ₩.05 to ₩ 500.
56. *See* KSDA, *History*, 174.
    Since the annual interest rates of government bonds ranged from 2–5% while those in the private money market exceeded 50%, the BOK had to purchase almost all of them. A negligible part of them was purchased by the public.
57. *Id.* at 170–1.

Table 2.5 Key Statistics for Securities Markets during 1963–1968.

Year	No. of listed Co's.	No. of Sec. Co's.	No. of SH's[a]	Capital Stock listed	Market Value[b]	Trading Volume		Turnover Ratio (%)		Market Values for par value W 5
						No. of Shares[c]	Value	Listed Stocks	Market Value	
1963	17	40	148	17	10	58.00	26	1,071.2	223.2	295
1964	17	36	138	22	17	.30	27	967.9	363.9	284
1965	24	35	148	23	14	.04	9	149.5	64.9	313
1966	24	26	317	32	20	.05	11	125.4	57.2	301
1967	24	25	330	46	38	.07	25	131.7	73.5	407
1968	34	27	399	97	64	.08	20	95.7	48.2	361

Source: KSE, *Securities Statistics Yearbook*, 10–11 (1975).
Units: a; hundred persons
     b; W million
     c; million shares

of public confidence in debt securities caused, for the most part, by low interest rates, since higher yields were available from alternative investments.[58]

---

58. During 1965–71, the official interest rates for one year time deposits ranged from 20.4–26.4%, and rates for two year time deposits were 21.3–30.0%. *See* BOK, *Economic Statistics Yearbook*, 21 (1976).

Chapter 3

Securities Markets in a Rapidly Growing Economy: Modernization Movement
(1968~1976)

Since 1968, the government of Korea has taken a series of measures to promote the Korean securities market. Before reviewing the measures taken and their influence on the securities market, it will be helpful to briefly examine the background of the measures. While implementing its Five-Year Economic Development Plans, the Government realized that the target of rapid economic growth was being frustrated by the deficiencies involving some relevant sectors. The deficiencies were: obstacles to capital formation needed for the planned investment; the dual structure of the financial markets; and the excessively leveraged capital structure of corporations.

Section I. *Issues Raised with Respect to Implementing Economic Development Plans in Korea*

I. Capital Formation and Investment

An important condition for rapid economic development of a less developed country is a capital formation process capable of sustaining a high rate of investment.[1] Unfortunately, the capital formation

---

1. There are various important factors which affect economic development in the long run: capital formation and investment, technology and skilled manpower, entrepreneurial innovation, education and training, a substantial change in the composition of output, and the development of new institutions. *See* A. W. Lewis, *Development Planning* 7–21 (1966); W. Rostow, *The Take Off into Self–Sustaining Growth, Economic Journal* 25–48 (March, 1965); H. W.

process in Korea was not sufficient to meet the needs of the economic development plans implemented after 1962. The economic situation in Korea was a "vicious circle of poverty"[2] Korea was poor because she had little capital, and she could not raise capital because she was poor. The 1950s and early 1960s were marked by an overall economic stagnation. Due to her historical background and political instability, the social environment of Korea had been so fluid from the post-independence period through the early 1960s that no long-term economic development plan could have been implemented.[3] The new government, which overthrew Chang's Cabinet in May, 1961, made economic modernization its first priority. It recognized that economic development was the key to its own political success. In this regard, it began to implement a series of Five-Year Economic Development Plans in 1962.

The long-term economic development plans led to remarkably rapid economic development. As Table 3.1 shows, the average real growth rate of gross national product(GNP), which was below 4% during 1957–1961, increased to 7.8% during the first five-year plan period(1962–1966), 10.5% during the second five-year plan period (1967–1971), and 11.1% during the third five-year plan period (1972–1976). Excluding the first year of the plan, the average annual growth rate of GNP, in real terms, was 13.5% during 1963–1969, and 10.4% during 1970–1976.

The development plans placed top priority on the capital formation required for a sustained high rate of investment in the leading sectors selected throughout the planned periods.[4] Indeed, the increased in-

---

Singer, *International Development,* pts. I & II (1964). Though this thesis deals with regulatory problems involved in a securities market, the issues raised in capital formation and investment, which are central factors in developing countries, will be discussed below.

2. *See* Singer, *supra* at 26; *see also* Nurkse, *Problems of Capital Formation in Under-developed Countries* 4–5 (1961).

3. Two economic development plans, a three-year plan and a five-year plan, were aborted in 1960 and 1961 due to students and military revolutions, respectively. *See* Chan Jin Kim, *On Foreign Capital Inducement (Oe Ja-Doip-Ron)* 39–42 (1976); *see also* I. Adelman, *Practical Approaches to Development Planning: Korea's Second Five-Year Plan* 15–18 (1969); Sung Hee Kim, *Foreign Capital for Economic Development* 159–60 (1970).

4. The strategy of the first five-year plan was based on the theory of unbalanced

vestment stimulated by the plan played a significant role in achieving rapid economic growth in Korea. Subsequent to 1962, investment increased output, and the increased output in turn stimulated added capital formation, which further stimulated expansion of the economy. Gross investment (measured in the current prices) which was only ₩ 14.41 billion in 1956, increased to ₩ 224.48 billion in 1966, to ₩ 805.35 billion in 1971, and to ₩ 3027.2 billion in 1976. Gross investment as a percentage of GNP increased from an average of 12.16% during 1956–1961 to 17.31%, 26.56%, and 26.14% during the first, second, and third plan periods, respectively. *See* Table 3.1.

Table 3.1 Comparison of Investment with GNP

Amount in billion Won

Year	A. GNP (Growth Rate: %)	B. Total Investment	C. Ratio (B to A in percent)
1956	152.44 (0.4)	14.41	9.45
1957	197.78 (7.7)	30.26	15.30
1958	207.19 (5.2)	26.73	12.90
1959	221.00 (3.9)	23.72	10.73
1960	246.34 (1.9)	26.80	10.87
1961	297.08 (4.8)	38.79	13.05
1962	348.98 (3.1)	45.47	13.03
1963	488.54 (8.8)	90.26	18.47
1964	700.20 (8.6)	102.24	14.60
1965	805.32 (6.1)	121.98	15.14

growth, allegedly appropriate for an economy in an early stage of development according to Albert O. Hirschman. In the second plan, the formal planning methodology involved a two-prong approach: a macroeconometric growth model was used to select a growth rate consistent with the supply of foreign and domestic savings and foreign exchange; given the growth rate, a sectoral annual input-output model was employed to assure the balance of demand and supply in each sector and to set minimal levels of investment. In the third plan, a great emphasis was placed on the development of heavy chemical and export-oriented industries as well as the development of agriculture and fisheries. Also, a further increase of domestic savings to 29.5% of GNP to reduce the rate of foreign savings was envisioned. For details of development models and methodologies in Korea, *see* Chan Jin Kim, *supra* at 42–52; *see also* I. Adelman, *supra* at 6, and pt. II; A. O. Hirschman, *The Strategy of Economic Development* (1958).

1966	1,032.45 (12.4)	224.48	21.74
1967	1,269.95 (7.8)	280.97	22.12
1968	1,598.04 (12.6)	427.87	26.77
1969	2,081.52 (15.0)	620.70	29.82
1970	2,589.26 (7.9)	704.66	27.21
1971	3,151.55 (9.2)	805.35	25.55
1972	3,860.00 (7.0)	805.48	20.87
1973	4,928.67 (16.5)	1,292.29	26.22
1974	6,779.11 (8.6)	2,125.88	31.36
1975	9,088.33 (8.3)	2,478.04	27.27
1976	12,108.80 (15.2)	3,027.20	25.00
Averages			
1956–1961	220.31 (3.98)	26.79	12.16
1962–1966	675.08 (7.80)	116.89	17.31
1967–1971	2,138.06 (10.50)	567.91	26.56
1972–1976	(11.10)		26.69

Sources: 1) BOK, *Economic Statistics Yearbook*, 298–301 (1976).
2) EPB, *The Fourth Five-Year Economic Development Plan*, 32–33 and 166 (December, 1976).
3) The Joongang Daily News, February 24, 1977, at 2.

Notes: 1) Figures are calculated at current market prices for 1956–1976
2) The statistical discrepancies between the total investment and total savings during the period of 1960–1972 are shown in Table 3.2.

Gross investment, however, was heavily dependent on foreign savings even though the percentage of foreign savings in gross investment decreased remarkably as the development plans were implemented. The share of foreign savings was 74.48% during 1956–1961 due to large government deficits and a relatively low savings rate in the private sector. *See* Table 3.2. But this share was reduced to 54.16% during 1962–1966, the first five-year plan period. It was further reduced to 39.9% and to around 32.0% during the second and third five-year plan periods, respectively. A further reduction to an average of 7.6% was envisioned during the fourth five-year plan period of 1977–1981.[5] The government hoped eventually to reduce the share of foreign savings to minus 0.26% by 1981. As a consequence, the capital formation needed for the economic development plan would

---

5. The Economic Planning Board (EPB), *The fourth Five-Year Economic Development Plan* 30–32 (Dec., 1976).

depend largely on the capital market.

II. Some Obstacles Involved in the Financial Market

A. *Introduction*

A financial market is simply a place or mechanism for the exchange of financial assets, which unlike goods and services, are not consumed but purchased and sold for money.[6] The market may be classified in a variety of ways such as primary and secondary markets, loan and securities markets, debt and equities markets, exchange and over-the-counter markets, or money and capital markets.[7] The following discussion of some of the obstacles involved in the financial markets in Korea during the late 1960s through the early 1970s will primarily use the distinction between money and capital markets. Money markets are those in which traded instruments have an original maturity of one year or less, while capital markets are those for long-term securities.

B. *Money Market*

1. Dual Structure of Money Market

The money market in Korea can be classified into two sub-markets, an "officially organized" market and an "unorganized" one. The former consists of financial intermediaries which are officially chartered by the Ministry of Finance or a special law, and are subject to government regulation. The latter comprises the private credit or "curb" market, where individual brokers and professional money lenders arrange for or perform creditmaking functions primarily for business borrowers. The activity of this private money market flourished due to the higher interest rates offered in that market. The activity of the private money market was detrimental to the development of both financial intermediaries and a capital market as will be discussed later.

The private money market is hidden, difficult to identify, and usually not subject to any government regulation. The only connection between the market and the government is the tax collected

---

6. *See* C. N. Henning, W. Pigott, and R. H. Scott, *Financial Markets and the Economy* 2 (1975). Further, financial assets are claims that enable their holders, upon disposing of the claims, to obtain consumable goods and services.

7. *Id.* at 5–6.

Table 3.2 Composition of Savings and Savings Rates

Amount in billion Won[1]

Year	Savings (Composition Rate in percent)						Ratio to GNP in percent			
	Total (A + B)	Domestic Savings (A)			Foreign Savings[4](B)	Statistical Discrepancy(c)	A			A + B
		Private[2](a)	Government[3](b)	Subtotal(c)			a	b	c	
1956	14.41(100)	2.35(16.3)	-4.42(-30.7)	-2.07(-14.4)	16.48(114.3)		1.54	-2.89	-1.35	9.45
57	30.26(100)	16.94(56.0)	-6.01(-19.9)	10.93(36.1)	19.33(63.9)		8.56	-3.04	5.52	15.30
58	26.73(100)	16.70(62.5)	-6.43(-24.1)	10.27(38.4)	16.43(61.9)	— —	8.06	-3.10	4.96	12.90
59	23.72(100)	14.60(61.5)	-5.94(-25.0)	8.66(36.5)	15.06(63.5)		6.61	-2.69	3.92	10.73
60	26.80(100)	8.55(31.9)	-5.01(-18.7)	3.54(13.2)	20.99(78.3)	2.27(8.5)	3.47	-2.03	1.44	10.87
61	38.79(100)	16.88(43.6)	-5.30(-13.7)	11.58(29.9)	25.29(65.2)	1.92(4.9)	5.68	-1.78	3.90	13.05
62	45.47/100	10.34(22.7)	-4.86(-10.7)	5.48(12.0)	37.95(83.5)	2.04(4.5)	2.96	-1.39	1.57	13.03
63	90.26(100)	31.81(35.3)	-1.32(-1.5)	30.49(33.8)	52.36(58.0)	7.41(8.2)	6.51	-0.27	6.24	18.47
64	102.24(100)	48.39(47.3)	3.55(3.5)	51.94(50.8)	49.13(48.1)	1.17(1.1)	6.91	0.51	7.42	14.60
65	121.98(100)	46.48(38.1)	14.02(11.5)	60.50(49.6)	57.53(42.2)	9.95(8.3)	5.77	1.74	7.51	15.14
66	224.48(100)	93.37(41.6)	29.08(13.0)	118.45(54.6)	87.63(39.0)	14.40(6.4)	0.04	2.81	11.85	21.74
67	280.97(100)	99.96(35.5)	51.85(18.5)	151.81(54.0)	112.86(40.2)	16.30(5.8)	7.87	4.08	11.95	22.12

68	427.87(100)	117.71(27.5)	100.61(23.5)	218.32(51.0)	184.33(43.1)	25.22(5.9)	7.37	6.30	13.67	26.77
69	620.70(100)	235.63(38.0)	129.55(20.8)	365.18(58.8)	229.02(36.9)	26.50(4.3)	11.32	6.22	17.54	29.82
70	704.66(100)	243.20(34.5)	180.00(25.5)	423.20(60.0)	249.31(35.4)	32.15(4.6)	9.39	6.95	16.34	27.21
71	805.35(100)	268.17(33.3)	190.10(23.6)	458.27(56.9)	354.00(44.0)	−6.92(−0.9)	8.51	6.03	14.54	25.55
72	805.48(100)	427.74(53.1)	149.57(18.6)	577.31(71.7)	215.03(26.7)	13.14(1.6)	11.08	3.87	14.95	20.87
73	1,292.29(100)	864.68(66.9)	225.09(17.4)	1,809.77(84.3)	198.92(15.4)	3.60(0.3)	17.54	4.57	22.11	26.22
74	2,125.88(100)	1,099.90(51.7)	202.98(9.6)	1,302.88(61.3)	917.72(43.2)	−94.72(−4.5)	16.22	2.99	19.21	31.36
75	2,478.4 (100)	1,156.7 (46.7)	479. 2(19.3)	1,635. 9(59.7)	1,023.0 (41.2)	−180.5(−7.2)	12. 7	5. 3	18. 0	27.27
76	2,896.5 (100)	1,608.1 (5.55)	586. 6(20.2)	2,194. 7(75.7)	701.8 (24.2)	—	15. 4	5. 6	21. 0	27.73

Source: BOK, *Economic Statistics Yearbook*, 298–301(1976); EPB, *The Fourth Five-Year Economic Development Plan*, 32–33 and 166 (Dec., 1976); and

The *Joongang Daily News*, February 24, 1977, at 2.

Notes: 1) Figures are calculated at current market prices for 1956–1974 and at 1975 prices for 1975–1976.
2) Includes households, unincorporated enterprises, and private corporations.
3) Includes both general government and government-invested enterprises.
4) Includes both net transfers and net borrowings from the rest of the world.

on the interest received by a lender, which is withheld by the borrower.[8] However, the National Tax Administration Office has encountered difficulties in identifying the moneylender because the borrower is usually reluctant to disclose the identity of the lender. The borrower fears the possible loss of a continued supply of credit or damage to the close personal relationship involved. Furthermore, the private money comes from various sources such as professional moneylenders, private investment clubs "*Kye*"[9], brokers, friends, or relatives.

Because its activities were not regulated by the government, the private money market flourished particularly as the demand for money rapidly increased in response to the tight money market conditions which prevailed during late 1969 through the early 1970s. Interest rates on the private money market were determined by natural market forces, *i.e.*, the demand for and supply of money as well as risk differentials among borrowers, length of the time of the loan, and size of the loan. In 1969 over 80% of the borrowers paid interest ranging from 3.5% to 5% per month.[10] Since 1970 the average monthly rate had been in a range of 4% until the 8.3 Emergency Decree of 1972 was announced.[11] Table 3.3 shows that the private loans were the most profitable investments as compared with other

---

8. Such interest received constitutes taxable income on which a 15.5% tax is imposed. *See Personal Income Tax Act*, Arts. 17(1), 9, 146(1), promulgated by Law. No. 1966 on Nov. 19, 1967.

9. "*Kye*" is a kind of private credit union in which the members share a common bond. The members are usually friends, relatives, employees of the same corporations or institutions, graduates of the same school, or wives whose spouses belong to the same social club. Each member contributes a certain amount of money on a certain day every month during the life of the *Kye* except in the month when he is scheduled to get the total sum contributed by members in that month. The scale of *Kye* money varies with the living standards of its members. Wealthy ladies sometimes operate *Kyes* in which the total sum reaches a couple of hundred million. The member who receives *Kye* money frequently makes loans to the central figure of *Kye* or other businessmen. The interest rates of such loans are far above the official interest rates.

10. *See* KDFC, *Money and Capital Markets in Korea and the Potential for their Improvement* 20, and Table 20 (1970) [hereinafter referred to as "KDFC, *Money and Capital Markets in Korea*"].

11. *See* pp. 61–64. *infra*.

investment alternatives during 1965–1969 at a given curb interest rate of 4% per month, or 60.1% per year.

Such a higher rate of return for private loans stimulated the activities of the private money market even further. Based on the amount of withholding taxes collected, it was reported that the volume of private loans increased from ₩ 49 billion in 1963 to ₩ 438 and ₩ 705 billion in 1967 and 1969, respectively.[12] The total amount of loans made by commercial banks and specialized banks was ₩ 208 billion in 1967 and ₩ 630 billion in 1969, respectively.[13] Considering the fact that such figures are based on the amount of withholding taxes collected, the real figures, including undisclosed private loans, would probably be far above these amounts. The activities of the private money market climaxed in mid-1972 becuase of the downward adjustments of official interest rates on bank deposits and the increased demand for money caused by the Korean government's tight monetary policy during 1969–1972.

In sum, the activities of the private money market thrived as a strong competitor of the organized money market. The more the former thrived, the more the latter suffered. As a consequence, a sustained shortage of funds in the organized sector caused most business corporations to meet their capital needs, especially for short-term working capital, through the more costly private money markets. The corporate capital structure, which had already been highly leveraged, worsened until many companies were on the verge of going bankrupt. In order to achieve an efficient allocation of the national resources, the government sought to absorb the large funds flowing in the private money market through either the organized

---

12. KDFC, *supra* note 10, Table 16 at 84.
    The total volume of loans made through the private money market is hard to assess due to the characteristic secrecy of its operation. One method to estimate the amount of private loans begins with a determination of withholding taxes collected on interest income.

13. *See* BOK, *Economic Statistics Yearbook* 28–29, 36–37 (1976).
    The commercial banks comprise five nationwide commercial banks, local banks, Korea Trust Bank, and foreign banks operating in Korea. The specialized banks comprise Korea Exchange, The Small and Medium Industry, Citizens National, Korea Housing banks, National Agricultural Cooperatives Federation, and Fisheries Cooperatives Federation.

Table 3.3 Annual Rate of Return Compared(1965–1969)

(in percent)

1. Time deposits:[a]	15.0 (low) – 26.4 (high)
2. Government bonds:[b]	32.6
3. Private curb loan:[c]	60.1
4. Common Stock (selected):[d]	
Korea Electric:	39.7
Korea Tungsten Mining:	62.7
Choheung Bank:	33.9
Yuhan Corporation:	41.0
Kyung Sung Spinning:	27.7
5. Real estate:[e]	43.4

Sources: 1) BOK, *Korea Statistics Yearbook*, 21(1976) for item 1.
   2) KDFC, *Money and Capital Market in Korea*, B–13 (1970) for items 2–5.
Notes: Transaction costs were not deducted.
   a; Interest rates of time deposits at commercial banks.
   b; Total yields divided by assumed average purchase prices in January, 1965.
   c; Annual yield compounded at 4% per month.
   d; Cash dividends plus market value of the stock, dividends declared, divided by assumed average purchase.
   e; Selected Seoul areas based on the data compiled by the Korea Bankers' Association.

money market or capital market.[14]

2. Structure, Size, and Intermediary Function of Organized Money Market

The officially organized financial institutions, which function as intermediaries between savers and borrowers, are composed of bank-

---

14. In order to achieve a more efficient allocation of national resources, the functions of both the organized money market and the capital market should be strengthened. In the organized money market, government control over its operation and management, including interest rates and credit extensions, was too strict. Some relaxation of control should have been considered so that the organized money market could flexibly respond to market conditions and compete successfully with the private money market. However, the government approached the problem in a radical way when it took an emergency measure in 1972 which compulsorily froze the activities of the private money market. The measure included a significant constitutional question as to individual property rights. For details, *see the August 3 Emergency Decree*, pp. 61–64. *infra.*

ing and nonbanking financial institutions. The Ministry of Finance regulates them and intervenes in their activities by controlling the interest rates, reserve ratios, and liquidity management under the pertinent banking laws. The Money and Banking Commission (MBC) and the Bank of Korea(BOK), the central bank in Korea, also perform, under the supervision of the MOF, supplementary roles in setting policy and regulating the financial institutions.

The banking system in Korea consists of the BOK, commercial banks, and specialized banks. The BOK's functions as a central bank include currency issuance, receipt of reserve deposits from and extension of credits to other banks, control over foreign exchange operations, and supervision of the operations of other banks. It acts as the government monetary and fiscal agent under the control of the MOF.

Before 1967 there were only six commercial banks with nationwide branch systems.[15] In addition, there were seven specialized banks chartered by special laws to perform specialized functions in compliance with government policies.[16] However, in order to increase capital formation, specialized banks were encouraged to compete with commercial banks in receiving deposits at controlled interest rates

---

15. They were Cho-Heung Bank, Commercial Bank of Korea, Korea First Bank, Han-Il Bank, Seoul Bank and Korea Trust Bank.
16. The functions of specialized banks are as follows: (1) The Korea Development Bank, formerly the Korea Reconstruction Bank, was established in 1954 to perform development financing necessary for industrial projects in key industries through long-term loans at lower interest rates; (2) The Korea Exchange Bank was established in 1967 with a 100% capital contribution from BOK to deal mainly with foreign exchange transactions; (3) The Small and Medium Industry Bank was established in 1961 to provide medium and small enterprises with an efficient financial system; (4) The Citizens National Bank was established in 1962 to serve consumers and small enterprises and especially to function as a savings and loan institution by collecting savings in installment plans and extending loans on a mutual benefit basis; (5) The National Agricultural Cooperatives Federation, which consisted of nationwide members, was established to improve the economic status of farmers; (6) The Fisheries Cooperatives Federation was established to serve as a special credit institution for fishermen and manufacturers of fishing equipment; and (7) The Korea Housing Bank was established in 1967 to finance housing construction.

and thus resemble commercial banks in that context. The government is a large shareholder of the commercial banks and completely owns specialized banks. Thus, the banking system in Korea may be characterized as a government bureau or semi-government agency charged with maintaining organized finance.

In the area of non-bank financial institutions, there were five life and fourteen non-life insurance companies by the end of 1967. Thirteen wrote fire and liability insurance; one wrote educational insurance along with several life insurance companies. There were also postal savings, a savings institution, and the Korea Development Finance Corp.(KDFC), a development institution. The KDFC was established in 1967 as a joint venture among the IFC, foreign banks, and domestic private organizations for the purpose of providing development loans and equity investment in projects with foreign and local currencies. The five commercial banks and the Korea Trust Bank(KTB) also managed trust accounts.[17]

Prior to 1968 there were not any mutual funds or investment companies similar to those in the United States. Private pension plans, unlike government ones, had not entered into the financial markets. In addition, since the organized money market could not absorb the large amount of fractional temporary monies, the holders of such monies placed them in the private money market at higher risk rather than selecting non-interest bearing demand deposits or deposits with lower interests at banks. Furthermore, financial intermediaries could not meet the increasing demand for short-term loans, such as those for less than a 6 month period used mainly for working capital needs of a business borrower, because of the strict government involvement in loan policy. Since the commercial paper market was also underdeveloped, most borrowers chose to depend heavily upon the more liquid private money market and thus were forced to pay higher interests. In sum, structural deficiencies as well as lack of effective policy measures caused the organized money market as a whole not only to fail to meet social demands, but also to misallocate

---

17. However, the trust accounts vary with the objects in trust, such as securities, real estate, and others. Busan Bank, a local bank, opened trust accounts in 1968. On Dec. 4, 1970, the trust accounts of the other banks were transferred to the Korea Trust Bank, which merged into Seoul Bank in mid-1976.

Table 3.4 Changes in the Total Assets of Major Financial Intermediaries during 1967–1975.

In current billion Won

End of	CB[a]	SB[b]	LI[c]	NLI	STI& FC	MS&FC[d]	Total
1967	245.6	331.5	8.3	9.2	—	—	594.6
1968	476.7	577.4	11.3	12.6	—	—	1,077.9
1969	758.6	919.8	19.2	18.1	—	—	1,715.1
1970	1,048.3	1,192.1	24.0	23.7	—	—	2,228.1
1971	1,344.0	1,457.7	32.2	33.4	—	—	2,867.3
1972	1,831.4	1,738.6	40.4	40.9	2.3	—	3,653.6
1973	3,484.6	2,264.1	57.9	59.5	58.7	41.6	4,966.4
1974	3,511.4	2,654.5	80.2	76.3	144.7	55.4	6,522.5
1975	5,302.2	3,199.9	105.3	101.3	220.9	63.7	8,993.2

Source: BOK, *Economic Statistics Year Book*, 30–66, (1976).
Notes: The total assets of each financial institution included both financial assets, real estate, and other assets.
    a; includes five nationwide commercial banks, Korea Trust Bank, ten local banks, and nine foreign banks operating businesses in Seoul.
    b; includes six specialized banks, excluding Korea Development Bank.
    c; includes occupational group insurance, endowment insurance, and educational insurance.
    d; includes only the figures reported to the Cooperatives by memebers.

the national resources. Thus, the size and functions of financial institutions were limited particularly during the period of 1967–1971. *See* Tables 3.4 and 3.5.

Since late 1967, ten new local banks have been chartered and nine foreign banks have begun to operate in Korea, all of which compete with existing commercial banks. Ten Short-Term Investment and Finance Companies (STI&FC) have been chartered since late 1971 to develop short-term credit instruments and to absorb temporary funds. They discount short-term commercial papers and participate in investment banking as well as call money markets for securities dealers. They have achieved remarkably rapid growth during the last few years.[18] *See* Table 3.4. The activities of Mutual Savings and

18. One of the major reasons for the rapid growth of short-term investment and finance companies was attributable to their function as a short-term financial intermediaries. The companies not only offer more favorable interest yields

Table 3.5 Amount of Deposits and Loans at Major Financial Institutions (1967–75)

In current billion Won

the end of—	1967	1968	1969	1970	1971	1972	1973	1974	1975
A. CB (total)	138.7 (109.8)	253.9 (218.4)	419.2 (369.4)	518.2 (451.8)	651.3 (581.9)	912.8 (759.6)	1,202.2 (1,032.1)	1,427.6 (1,627.1)	1,939.2 (2,507.4)
1. NCB[a]	137.7 (108.9)	243.6 (211.7)	393.5 (349.8)	471.3 (415.1)	569.6 (517.8)	765.2 (647.6)	976.6 (826.6)	1,129.2 (1,249.1)	1,523.1 (1,502.0)
2. LB	—	6.7 (4.9)	17.0 (12.0)	32.8 (21.9)	54.8 (37.0)	95.2 (59.3)	146.7 (101.8)	202.1 (195.5)	288.1 (227.6)
3. FB	—	2.0 (1.4)	3.6 (4.5)	5.5 (9.8)	6.5 (18.1)	11.9 (28.9)	17.0 (50.6)	17.5 (70.4)	29.8 (131.1)
4. KTB[b]	—	1.1 (0.3)	5.0 (2.9)	8.4 (4.8)	20.3 (8.7)	40.3 (2.3)	58.8 (47.4)	78.6 (106.3)	98.0 (125.4)
B. SB	69.6 (98.2)	123.6 (167.3)	209.1 (260.7)	285.9 (372.1)	342.8 (494.9)	434.7 (541.1)	578.9 (683.4)	703.4 (995.3)	858.8 (1,211.8)
C. KDB[c]	—	—	20.0 (96.1)	30.5 (128.9)	26.6 (157.4)	19.7 (239.1)	21.5 (318.4) 1	13.8 (384.9)	28.7 (577.8)
D. STI&FC[d]	—	—	—	—	—	1.1 (2.0)	47.6 (53.5)	118.8 (130.2)	180.5 (192.7)
E. MS&FC	—	—	—	—	—		31.3 (35.2)	43.9 (47.9)	43.7 (54.2)
F. TA[e]	—	—	67.1 (47.4)	79.3 (67.6)	124.8 (107.9)	158.4 (115.4)	182.8 (122.6)	190.6 (114.4)	186.4 (112.8)
TOTAL	208.3 (208.0)	—	—	—	1,145.5 (1,234.2)				3,237.3 (4,207.7)

Source: Same as Table 3.4

Notes: Figures in parentheses indicate amount of loans. a; Five nationwide commercial banks. b; Korea Trust Bank.
c; Korea Development Bank. d; Deposits at Short-term Investment and Finance Companies indicate the total amount of bills issued and outstanding at the end of each year. e; Money in trust accounts.

Finance Companies (MS&FC) and the National Credit Union (NCU), which have recently been chartered as a savings institution, are on a negligible scale. In 1975, the Land Bank and the Export-Import Bank of Korea were chartered as development institutions.[19] Since 1976 two Merchant Banking Corporations (MBC) have been organized under the law pertaining to the MBCs.[20] These companies perform a wide range of businesses, *e.g.*, foreign currency finance, loans for projects, discounts of commercial papers, and underwriting of securities, etc.

Table 3.4 shows the growth of major financial intermediaries from the beginning of the second five year economic development plan to 1975. The total amount of assets of major financial intermediaries increased from ₩ 594.6 billion in 1967 to ₩ 2,867.3 billion in 1971, and ₩ 8,993.3 billion in 1975, though the figures are not adjusted for inflation. The STI&FC and commercial banks achieved the most rapid growth. The former grew more than 9600% in 3 years and the latter grew almost 2200% in 8 years.

The intermediary functions of the institutions also increased greatly. As shown in Table 3.5, the amount of savings and loans at both commercial and specialized banks increased almost five-fold in 5 years (1967–71). The total amounts of deposits and loans of major financial institutions increased from ₩ 1,145.5 and 1,234.2 billion in 1971 to ₩ 3,237.3 and 4,207.7 billion in 1975, respectively. Even though some financial intermediaries had grown rapidly, five nationwide commercial banks still played a dominant role, accounting for almost half of the total loans and deposits.

C. Barriers to the Development of the Capital Market

Because of a general reluctance to go public, there were only 24 companies listed on the Exchange at the beginning of 1968. Of these

---

for shorter-term deposits, but also sell their own negotiable commercial papers in the open market, and then buy the short-term commercial papers issued by selected private business corporations (those which have good financial reputations).

19. The former undertakes the efficient operation of lands owned by the government and the latter engages primarily in foreign trade credit finance.

20. *See Merchant Banking Corporation Act,* Arts. 1 and 3, Law. No. 2825, promulgated on Dec. 31, 1975. This banking corporation is allowed to engage in a wide range of businesses, including underwriting.

24 companies, only six were industrial.[21] The survey report of the Korea Investment Corporation (KIC) listed the major reasons for this reluctance to go public as follows:[22]

> First, they thought it would be almost impracticable to declare annual dividends at a level which is equivalent to the interest rates of one year time deposits, *i.e.*, then 22.8%.[23] Second, they were uncertain whether the securities could be successfully distributed through a public offering or secondary distribution; and third, they feared that going public might result in losing control or at least burdensome interventions in management by public shareholders. (Footnote added.)

However, according to the unofficial questionnaire of the Korean Businessmen's Association, the majority of its members deemed the possible result of losing control the primary reason for their reluctance to go public.[24]

Furthermore, there were some institutional deficiencies in the capital market. One of the most critical deficiencies was the absence of an institutionalized investment banking business. While the investment banking or underwriting business is a prerequisite for the promotion of a primary securities market, no financial instution had ever specialized in that business, nor could any securities firm effectively engage in it because of extremely poor financial capacity. By the end of 1968, the total capital of 27 securities companies outstanding had been below ₩ 0.7 billion and the average amount of capital per company had not exceeded ₩ 25 million.[25] Under such circumstances, equities as well as debt securities could not be effectively issued to and distributed among the public. In addition, there was

---

21. *See* KSE, *Securities Statistics Yearbook* 92–96 (1976) [hereinafter referred to as "KSE, *Yearbook*"]. Those six companies traded on the exchange were Korean Shipbuilding Engineering Corp., Kyong Bang Co., Ltd. (then Kyongsung Spinning Corp.), Tong-Il Spinning Co., Ltd., Yuhan Corp., Korea Electric, and Korea Tungsten Mining Corp.
22. *See* KIC, *Survey Report on Going-Public* (1970); *see also* KIC, *Investment (Tooja)*, No. 23 (Oct., 1970) at 15–26. The survey was conducted on May 31, 1970, by the KIC among 654 private corporations whose legel capital was not less than ₩ 50 million.
23. Publicly-held corporations were encouraged to declare dividends at such a level.
24. *See* KSDA, *History*, 93.
25. *See* KSDA, *Yearbook*, 395 (1976).

no call money market available in which brokers and dealers could finance margin trading. The KSFC, the only existing institution for securities finance, played a very limited role because of the shortage of available resources, while institutional investors such as mutual funds or investment companies did not exist prior to 1969.

The rules relating to the securities market did not compel fair trading and timely disclosure of material information so as to deter both manipulation and fraudulent practices. Even after a series of market crashes, few appropriate measures had been enacted. With the self-issued stock trading on the Exchange and the allowance of short-sales, both fair market administration and fair trading could not be attained. Also, a lack of qualified personnel inevitably resulted in the lack of effective policy measures.

The attitude of the public toward the securities market had become extremely negative because of this series of bad experiences, and this attitude could not be changed over the short-term. In addition, the public had more profitable choices for their portfolios: they participated in the boom of real estate investments and provided savings into the profitable private money market as well as into the financial institutions whose sanctioned interest rates were maintained at the highest level.[26]

Under such circumstances, the resources needed for the economic development plan could not be mobilized through the securities market unless appropriate policies were taken to reform the fundamental deficiencies inherent in the overall market. Therefore, the highest priority in economic planning shifted to the promotion of the

---

26. *See* BOK, *Economic Statistics Yearbook* 21 (1976).

The changes in interest rates on time deposits during the period of 1962–1971 were as follows:

Effective Date		3 mos.	6 mos.	1 yr.	Over 2 yrs.
Feb.	1, 1962	9.0	12.0	15.0	——
Sept.	30, 1965	18.0	24.0	26.4	*30.0
Apr.	1. 1968	15.6	20.4	26.4	27.6
Oct.	1, 1968	14.4	19.2	25.2	——
June	1, 1969	12.0	16.8	22.8	——
June	28, 1971	10.2	14.4	20.4	21.3

* Applied to time deposits for 18 months or more.

securities market. Several important policy measures have taken effect since late 1968.

III. The Excessively Leveraged Corporate Capital Structure

As the long-term economic development plans were implemented, most business corporations in Korea encountered difficulties in meeting their rapidly increasing capital demands. Since they were reluctant to resort to direct public financing, the alternatives were borrowing either from financial institutions, private money lenders, or foreign lenders. As a result, the capital structure of most corporations, depending heavily on such borrowing, became excessively leveraged.

As shown in Table 3.6, the average debt/equity ratio of manufacturing enterprises was 1.17 in 1966, the end of the first five-year economic development plan period. It continuously worsened, climaxing in 1971 at 3.45. Consequently, the profit ratio of capital declined during the same period. The 1971 figures are partly attributable to the tight credit controls enforced by the government from

Table 3.6 Some Key Statistics Relating to the Financial Statements of Manufacturing Enterprises (1966–1974)

(In percent)

Year	A. Total Capital Growth Rate	B. Debt/ Equity Ratio	C. Profits Ratio of Total Capital	D. Profits Ratio of Equity Capital[a]	E. Surplus Added to Total Assets
1966	—	54.1/45.9 (1.17)	7.78	16.93	—
1967	—	61.2/39.8 (1.53)	6.77	17.01	7.25
1968	—	66.8/33.2 (2.01)	5.33	16.05	7.80
1969	—	73.0/27.0 (2.70)	3.67	13.57	7.01
1970	—	76.7/23.3 (3.29)	2.49	10.67	5.26
1971	24.10	69.8/20.2 (3.45)	0.99	4.50	4.77
1972	21.66	75.8/24.2 (3.13)	3.77	16.73	6.44
1973	43.44	73.2/26.8 (2.73)	7.90	30.04	7.91
1974	42.31	76.0/24.0 (3.16)	5.66	22.73	6.17

Source: BOK, *Economic Statistics Yearbook*, 170–85 (1976).

Notes: The number of enterprises surveyed was 692, 860, 976, 1026, and 1,272 each year during the period of 1970–1974.

a; Profits indicates net profits.

late 1969 throughout the early 1970s.[27] Regardless of rapidly in-creasing capital demands, most corporations sought large portions of borrowing through the private money markets with the resultant higher expense.

With so highly a leveraged capital structure, most business corpora-tions could not expand their capital budget needed for rapid eco-nomic growth. Rather, many were in danger of going bankrupt. Therefore, the primary concern of the government became to ef-fectively ameliorate the capital structure.

Section II. *Policy Measures Taken in a Modernization Movement and Market Activities: Step I* (Late 1968~Mid 1972)

I. Reforms

The government launched a comprehensive scheme of reform in late 1968, which was designed to promote the securities market. The major reforms were contained in the Capital Market Promotion Act of 1968 (CMPA).[28] Tax reforms followed to provide businesses with incentives for going public. Also, new institutions were established to promote the securities market.

A. Legislation of the CMPA of 1968 and Tax Reforms

The stated purpose of the CMPA was:

> to promote the capital market by creating so sound an investment climate that not only closely-held corporations are encouraged to go public with wide distribution of their securities among the public but also the public investors are elicited to participate in enterprises so as to smooth corporate finance.[29]

To achieve these goals, a series of incentives and measures were in-

---

27. Because of the sustained inflation caused by the implementation of overall economic development plans, the government had pursued a stabilization policy by strengthening control over the fiscal, monetary, and foreign ex-change sectors. The policy was aimed at achieving relatively moderate growth rather than higher growth and worsening inflation due to the resultant rapid expansion of money supplies. *See* KSDA, *History*, 143.

28. Law No. 2046, Promulgated on Nov. 22, 1968. (hereinafter referred to as "*CMPA*").

29. *See CMPA*, Art. 1.

troduced in the CMPA and relevant tax laws.

   1. Decentralization of Equity Ownership and Improvement of
      Investment Conditions

Various measures were enacted to effect wider distribution of
equities among the public as well as improvement of their investment
conditions. First, non-government shareholders of listed corporations were, like holders of non-participating preferred shares, guaranteed to receive annual dividends at a level equal to the interest
rate on one-year time deposits.[30] Second, in order to enhance their
marketability, the securities of listed corporations were allowed to
be used in lieu of cash for the payment of guaranty money or bonding
requirements in transactions with the government or government-
controlled enterprises.[31] Third, the MOF was empowered, despite
Articles 70 and 70–2 of the Budget and Account Act, to sell govern-
ment-held shares without limitation on both volume and price.[32]
This is limited, however, by the requirement that they either be sold
for wide distribution in the public interest or sold to public officials
or employees of government controlled enterprises.

   Further, the CMPA mandated that when a listed or publicly-held
corporation issues new shares, the employees of such corporation have
a right to subscribe up to 10% of such newly issued shares, regardless
of Article 418 of the Commercial Code (preemptive rights of existing
shareholders).[33] This is, in effect, a form of a stock option plan for
employees. Officers and temporary employees of a corporation are
excluded from the coverage of the plan.[34]

   In addition, wide–ranging personal tax exemptions[35] were provided

---

30. *Id.*, Art. 3, and *Presidential Decree* thereunder, Art. 3 (PD No. 3657 promulgated
    on Dec. 9, 1968). The level of annual dividend rates was set at 10% but the level
    was amended later to be the interest rate on a one-year time deposit(as of the
    date when the fiscal year ends). *See Presidential Decree* No. 7219, as amended on
    Aug. 14, 1974.
31. *Id.*, Art. 4.
32. *Id.*, Art. 5.
33. *Id.*, Art. 6. This provision constitutes a special exception to Article 418 of the
    Commercial Code, which gives preemptive rights to existing shareholders. The
    latter should be preempted by the former. *See* pp. 123–25, *infra.*
34. *See Presidential Decree under the CMPA,* Art. 11.
35. *See CMPA,* Art. 7.

to be applicable even to the shareholders of any listed corporation, which does not meet the requirements of a publicly-held corporation.[36] No personal income taxes are to be imposed on the "construction interest,"[37] dividends, or "presumptive dividends"[38] received by shareholders of any listed corporation. Introduction of such exemptions were designed to play a significant role in eliciting public demand for equities of a listed, but non–publicly-held corporation as well as for those of a publicly-held corporation.

2. Incentives for and Relaxation of Obstacles to Going Public

In order to induce closely-held corporations to go public, the CMPA included various measures designed not only to provide incentives for, but also to relax obstacles to, going public. The incentives which fall within the former category were applications of special rates for calculating the amounts of both corporate income taxes due and depreciation for the purpose of tax deduction, in favor of a publicly-held corporation under the Corporate Income Tax Act.[39] Thus, the maximum tax differential between a publicly–held and non-publicly-held corporation can be as great as 20 percent under the corporate income tax table.[40] Also, a 20 percent special depreciation

---

36. The requirements for a publicly-held corporation were stricter in Article 22(3) of the Corporate Income Tax Act and the public corporation had various advantages over non-publicly-held ones. *See* note 43, *infra*.

37. The term "construction interests" is an interest payment to shareholders from working capital in the form of dividends by a corporation whose business has not started yet because the plant is under construction. Construction interests can be paid during the first two years after incorporation. In practice, however, few corporations have paid construction interests because it damages capital stock. *See Commercial Code*, Art. 463.

38. *See Personal Income Tax Act*, Art. 26(2) and (3), Law No. 1966, promulgated on Nov. 29, 1967. "Presumptive dividends" or "dividends on paper *(Jee sang Baedang)*" occur when there are reserves after deducting the amount of corporate income taxes, citizens' taxes, and profit reserves. The shareholders of a corporation, other than a publicly-held or non-profit legal entity, should pay personal income taxes on such presumptive dividends.

39. *CMPA*, Arts. 9 and 10.

40. *Corporate Income Tax Act (CITA)*, Art. 22. The amount of corporate income taxes due should be calculated incrementally in accordance with the following table:

of fixed assets was allowed in addition to the ordinary depreciation.[41]
    The chairman of a shareholders' general meeting, either of a publicly–held or listed corporation, was empowered to stop the speech
of a person acting in bad faith to filibuster the meeting or to disturb
proceedings, and to order hecklers out of the meeting place.[42] Such
provision was designed to eliminate or relax the fears of burdensome
intervention in the management which was noted an obstacle to
going public. Even stronger guaranty for continuing control, however, appears in the requirements for a publicly-held corporation
introduced in Corporate Income Tax Act by the enactment of the
CMPA.[43] It was provided, among vairous requirements, that a share-

Corporate Income Tax Table

(in percent)

Taxable Income (TY)	Non-Public Corps.	Publicly-held Corps.	Difference
TY < ₩1 million	25	15	10
1 ≤ TY < ₩5 million	35	20	15
TY ≤ ₩5 million	45	25	20

41. *See MOF Decree under the CITA*, Art. 26, MOF Decree No. 645, promulgated
    on July 24, 1969. But a "special depreciation" for corporate income tax purposes was provided in favor of listed corporations.
42. *CMPA,* Art. 11–4.
43. *CITA,* Art. 22(3). The term "a publicly-held corporation" was defined as any
    domestic legal entity whose stock is listed on the KSE or whose legal capital
    has been raised publicly either for its incorporation or for a capital increase
    pursuant to the provisions of a Presidential Decree; in addition, it must meet
    the following requirements:
    1) The total number of shares held by one shareholder and other persons who
       have special relations with him (as provided in the Presidential Decree)
       shall not be more than 51% of the total outstanding shares, excluding the
       shares which do not have voting rights;
    2) Total shares held by the minority shareholders (defined as those who hold
       less than 1% of the total shares outstanding) shall be more than 40% of all
       shares excluding any shares held by the government or foreigners (in the
       case of a joint-venture company, the total shares held by domestic persons
       must exceed 51% of the total outstanding shares); and
    3) The number of minority shareholders shall not be less than 300 persons.
    Further conditions were provided in Art. 67 of the Enforcement Decree promulgated under the Corporate Income Tax Act:
    1) If the legal capital of a corporation is to be raised publicly, either for the

holder, with his affiliates, may hold up to 51 percent of the total number of voting shares issued and outstanding.

 B. *Establishment of the Korea Investment Corporation and Other Institutions*
  1. Korea Investment Corporation(KIC)

 The Korea Investment Corporation(KIC), formerly the Korea Investment and Development Corporation (KIDC), was chartered by the CMPA.[44] It was established on December 16, 1968, as a government owned corporation with an authorized capital of ₩ 3 billion. Its purpose was to facilitate the issuance, distribution, and underwriting of securities and to stabilize securities prices.[45] The Investment Deliberation Committee, which consists of nine members, including the Presidents of the KIC and the KSE, was established within the KIC, *inter alia*, to investigate and examine important matters concerning securities and to design a sales plan for government shares.[46]

 The estabilishment of the KIC was a significant event in the history of the securities market. Until its abolition in 1977, it performed a wide range of functions as follows:

  1) underwriting; 2) purchase and sale of any securities as both a broker and

---

    incorporation or for a capital increase, it must be raised through a public offering or a secondary distribution of shares (as provided in the SEA). The total shares publicly offered or secondarily distributed may not be less then 30% of the total outstanding shares, excluding non-voting shares (Paras. 1 and 2);
  2) The stock must be listed on the KSE within six months from the date when the listing requirements are met (the proviso of Para. 1);
  3) The average number of shares traded per month must be not less than 3/1000 of the total outstanding shares, excluding the shares held by the government or foreigners (Para. 3); and
  4) The term "other persons who have special relations with a shareholder" provided in Sub-para. 1 of Article 22(3) of the Law means any person,
     a. Who is an immediate relative as defined in the Family Law;
     b. Who, if the shareholder is a legal person, holds more than 50% of the total outstanding shares of each corporation; or
     c. Who, if the shareholder is an individual, holds more than 50% of the total outstanding shares with his immediate relatives (Para. 8).

44. *CMPA,* Chapter A, Arts. 12–45.
45. *Id.,* Art. 12.
46. *Id.,* Art. 20.

dealer; 3) arrangement for a public offering or secondary distribution of any security; 4) open market operations for the stabilization of securities prices; 5) consignment sales of stocks owned by the government or private corporations; 6) securities analysis and guidance; 7) securities finance on the basis of collateral; 8) securities investment trust; 9) guarantee for the payment of corporate debt securities; 10) securities savings; 11) securities loans; 12) vicarious execution of the issuance of securities; and 13) other business authorized by the MOF.[47]

A series of the KIC Rules were formulated and issued to enhance the performance of such functions.

The CMPA contains many provisions intended to protect the interests of public investors. The members of the Investment Deliberation Committee and the officers and employees of the KIC were prohibited from disclosing or misusing inside information to which they have access in the course of performing their functions.[48] They were also prohibited from trading in securities on the market either in their names or under other names.[49] Any violation of the provision was subject to criminal penalties of up to 5 years imprisonment or W 5 million in fines.[50]

2. Diversification of Financial Institutions

Since late 1971 ten short-term investment and finance companies (STI&FC) have been authorized by the MOF and subsequently established. Through their establishment, the MOF hoped to strengthen the financial capacity of the underwriting community and to develop the short-term money markets, including a market in commercial paper. The STI&FC have grown rapidly due to the strong demand for their services.

Another important event was the establishment of a securuties investment trust. The Securities Investment Trust Act (SITA) was promulgated in 1969 to empower the KIC and other companies to engage in the securities investment trust business.[51] A securities investment trust is a diversified, professionally managed mutual fund. Any

---

47. *Id.*, Arts. 36–38–6.
48. *Id.*, Arts. 28 and 33(2).
49. *Id.*, Arts. 29 and 33(2).
50. *Id.*, Art. 67.
51. Law No. 2129, promulgated on Aug. 4, 1969 (hereinafter referred to as *"SITA"*).

stock corporation whose authorized capital exceeds ₩ 500 million
is eligible for the MOF license permitting it to engage in the business.[52]

C. Institutional Innovations

1. 1968 Amendments of Securities and Exchange Act

The 1968 Amendments of the SEA[53] were designed to strengthen
the financial capacity of the relevant institutions on the one hand,
and to enhance public confidence in the market on the other.

First, the total amount of KSE capital was increased from ₩ 2.6
billion to ₩ 3.0 billion.

Second, the then-existing registration system was replaced by an
authorization system which requires a person to obtain a license from
the MOF to incorporate a securities company. Two kinds of licenses
were created according to the amount of capital a securities company
can have.[54] A company with legal capital between ₩ 30 and ₩ 50
million could transact its business as a dealer and broker; a company
with legal capital above ₩ 50 million could also underwrite securities.
Three big securities companies were incorporated by insurance companies and the Korea Trust Bank(KTB) during early 1969.[55]
Finally, in order to deter another market crash caused by excessive speculation, the 1968 Amendments gave the MOF a power to
cancel contracts made. A minimum working capital requirement was
also adopted to deter excessive speculation and to enhance the public
confidence in the market.

2. Readoption of the "Regular Way" Followed by Another
   Crash

The "regular way" system, which had been abolished in 1962
after only two months of practice, was adopted again in place of the
deferred clearance transaction method in February, 1969. The major

---

52. *SITA*, Art. 12.

53. *SEA*, as amended by Law No. 2066 on Dec. 31, 1968.

54. In January, 1969, the average capital of twenty-seven securities companies was
about ₩ 25 million. Any one company could not underwrite for itself due to
each one's poor financial capacity. With the establishment of new, big companies, the average capital of all securities companies rose to ₩ 85 million in
June, 1969. *See* KSDA, *History*, 138–39.

55. *Id.* They were Hanshin, Hanbo, and Shambo securities companies with legal
capital of ₩ 100, ₩ 120, and ₩ 60 million, respectively.

reason for its adoption was to reduce opportunities for speculation by shortening the time between securities transactions and their clearances. Under the "regular way," clearance was required to be completed by the next day following the transaction.[56] However, clearance could be postponed for up to 30 days by paying additional charges. The thirty-day deferral option made the system similar to the deferred clearance trading system.[57] The opportunity for deferral resulted in speculative transactions which could not be paid for. This deficiency soon resulted in another big crash involving the KSFC stock.[58]

D. Additional Innovations Following the KSFC Stock Crash

After the earlier KSFC stock crash, the MOF designed a comprehensive plan to deter any speculative manipulation existing under the deferral loophole. The plan, known as the "June 3 Decree," was followed by Amendments of the Presidential Decree under the SEA and other Decrees or Rules.[59]

Under the amended Presidential Decree, clearance methods for securities transactions were classified into four types: (1) spot, or immediate clearance; (2) "regular way;" (3) clearance on a specified date within 15 days of the transaction; and (4) clearance on a day designated by the KSE in the case of "when-issued transactions."[60] Under the "regular way," clearance must be completed on the fifth day following the contract. No further clearance beyond such a limit was allowed. In addition, all clearance was required to proceed through the KSE's clearing house. Furthermore, the KSE was empowered at its discretion to increase or decrease the margin requirements up to 100% from time to time as deemed necessary. But the prohibition of short-sales, which was included in the June 3

---

56. *See* KSDA, *History*, 135–36.
57. But the margin accounts must be settled collectively under the deferred clearance system; they are settled individually under the regular way.
58. *See* p. 11, *supra*.
59. Because the operation of the June 3 Decree was enjoined by the Court, the MOF had to effect amendments of the Presidential Decree. For details, *see* pp. 58–60, *infra*.
60. *Presidential Decree under the SEA*, Art. 48, as amended by PD No. 5734 on July 29, 1971. Until this amendment, the kind and method of clearance had been provided only in the KSE Rules on Business.

Decree, did not appear in the Amendments.[61] The refusal to totally disallow short sales probably resulted from the strong objections of the securities companies.

The existing multiple quote system was replaced by a unitary price quote system and the discrete trading session system was replaced by a post system. The result was that securities traded on a continuing basis.[62] Also, with the increase in the number of listed issues, the KSE board was divided into two sections, where the requirements of the first section were similar to those of a publicly-held corporation.[63]

E. *Tight Monetary Policy and Downward Adjustments of Official Interest Rates*

The high official interest rates on bank time deposits were thought to be one of the factors that had an adverse impact on the activities of securities markets. Also, since the interest rate on one-year time deposits was linked under the CMPA with the level of dividend payments by publicly-held corporations, it was desired that the interest rates and the dividends be lowered to a reasonable level. Thus, through a series of six adjustments, the rate on one-year time deposits was lowered from 26.4% to 12% by August 3, 1972, as shown in Table 3.7. The margin of the interest rates over the average dividend rates of listed companies, which was 5.6% in 1969, narrowed and subsequently reversed in 1972. The margin of the latter over the former widened to 4.54%.[64]

---

61. KSDA, *History*, 159–62.
62. There had been four daily market sessions in which securities could be traded: two were in the morning and two in the afternoon. In each session, each trading item was called by the "floor announcer," bidding for and asking for offers. When the number of shares offered matched in number and price those bid for, he struck a wooden bar as a signal of the formation of a transaction. Shares were traded only at the time when each item was called. For details, *see* KSDA, *History*, 162–63; *see also* KDFC, *Money and Capital Market in Korea*, B 3–6
63. *See KSE Rules on Listing*, Art. 12, promulgated on Jan. 1, 1970, as amended on Dec. 1, 1971.
64. The average annual dividend rates of listed companies were 17.12% in 1969 (33 Cos.), 18.29% in 1970 (38 Cos.), 17.0% in 1971 (36 Cos.), and 16.54% in 1972 (35 Cos.). *See* KSDA, *History*, 167. The downward adjustments of interest rates together with tight credit control caused the private money markets to fare better.

Table 3.7 Interest Rates on Time Deposits (1965–1972)

Eff. Date	3 Mon.	6 Mon.	1 Yr.	Over 2 Yrs.
Sep. 30 1965	18.0	24.0	26.4	30.0
Apr. 1 1968	15.6	20.4	26.4	27.6
Oct. 1 1968	14.4	19.2	25.2	—
Jun. 1 1969	12.0	16.8	22.8	—
Jun. 28 1971	10.2	14.4	20.4	21.3
Jan. 17 1972	8.4	11.4	16.8	17.4
Aug. 3 1872	6.0	8.4	12.0	12.6

Source: BOK, *Economic Statistics Yearbook*, 21 (1976).

The government adopted tight credit controls starting in late 1969. It also pursued policies aimed at moderate growth and economic stabilization rather than at sustained rapid growth. These policies were intended to relax the development inflation which had been worsening. The tight monetary policy was also designed to pressure business corporations, which had relied heavily on bank loans, into meeting their capital needs through the securities market.

II. Market Activities
A. Emerging Primary Market
1. Public Offering of Stocks

At first, the business community responded slowly to the various incentives for going public. The public investors also responded slowly to the public offerings. The goal, *i.e.*, promotion of the capital market, could not be achieved over the short term.

Twelve companies made public offerings in 1969. Of these, nine were underwritten by the KIC and three by the KSDA.[65] Eight were underwritten on the basis of best-efforts, two on stand-by, and one on firm commitment. The total value of shares publicly offered was ₩ 2.21 billion, of which 58.4% was placed with public investors. However, subscription rate by the public was relatively low at that time, even though the issues were offered at par.[66]

In 1970, the public attitude toward new issues improved somewhat.

---

65. KSE, *Yearbook*, 371.
66. KSDA, *History*, 140 and 155; *see also* KDFC, *Money and Capital Markets in Korea* 24. But the subscription rate to Seoul Miwon stocks marked 303.5%.

Of the total amount of about ₩ 2.1 billion in new issues, 97.5% was subscribed to by the public. But the primary market activities became depressed thereafter for two years;[67] only four issues, valued at ₩ 0.8 billion, were publicly offered in 1971, and seven issues, valued at ₩ 1 billion, in 1972.

2. Bond Market

There was no public offering of corporate bonds or debentures prior to 1971. The policy measures taken since 1968 were primarily intended to promote the market for equity securities. Thus, as noted earlier, most issuances of corporate debt securities had been used as a means of borrowing from financial institutions.[68] In early 1972, although public offerings of corporate bonds rapidly increased because of higher interest rates, the boom disappeared after the August 3 Emergency Decree was released.[69] In total, thirty-five issues of bonds with an aggregate value of ₩ 9.9 billion were successfully distributed in 1972. The annual interest rate was in a range of 17–28% for a bond maturing in two or two and a half years. These higher interest rates, along with shorter maturities, were due to the sustained inflation at that time.

The government bond market also was active during 1968 through 1972. During this period, ₩ 190.8 billion of government bonds were issued, of which ₩ 74.7 billion were issued in 1972.[70] The purpose of the issuances shifted from financing government deficits to financing development projects such as highways or housing projects. The method of distribution was changed from primary reliance on BOK purchases to public offerings, terms of which were improved in order to elicit more public participation. As the public demand for government bonds increased, their average rate of market yields dropped from around 35% in early 1971 to below 20% in mid-1972, and stabilized thereafter.[71]

---

67. KSE, *Yearbook*, 372–73.
68. *See supra.*
69. When the August 3 Emergency Decree lowered official bank interest rates, public investors were more interested in selecting stocks than less profitable corporate bonds. The coporate need for long-term debt also declined thereafter. *See* KSDA, *History*, 1970.
70. *Id.* at 174–75.
71. *Id.* at 173.

B. Secondary Market with Another Crash

1. In General

The activities of the trading market were enhanced by the positive government policies introduced since 1968. The trading volume increased from ₩ 19.9 billion in 1968 to ₩ 41.9 billion in 1969. *See* Table 3.8. On March 15, 1969, the Busan Stock Exchange, a branch of the KSE, opened in Busan, Korea.[72] From the end of 1971 on, however, market growth slowed and another crash involving the KSFC shares ensued. The crash was caused in large part by speculation enabled by the regular way transaction under which clearance was allowed to be postponed for up to thirty days upon payment of a small fee.

2. The KSFC Stock Crash

As noted earlier, most stock market crashes in Korea were caused by manipulation operated by several groups of securities companies taking advantage of legal loopholes and poor market administration. Such manipulation and excessive speculation often were started by tips of information from senior government officials or other important figures who had access thereto.

The KSFC stock crash of 1970 resulted from extreme market manipulation. The Hanyang Securities Company secretly began to buy the KSFC stock in November, 1969. The market price of the KSFC stock was at that time about ₩ 330, far below its par value of ₩ 500.[73] As far as can be told, Hanyang Securities Company did not have any inside information at the time. It probably intended to profit through manipulation of the KSFC stock price. The KSFC stock with one million outstanding shares was a good target for manipulation. Purchases were facilitated by the ability to make short sales under the existing laws. Under the regular way, as noted earlier, a purchaser or seller could defer his clearance up to one month upon payment of a small fee which depended on the amount sought to be deferred.[74] Furthermore, the purchaser could borrow part of the pur-

---

72. *Id.* at 139–40.

73. *See* Chang Geuk Oh, *Hidden Stories on the Securities Market (Cheung-Kwon Bee-Sa)*, 135 *et seq.* (1977) [hereinafter referred to as "Oh, *Hidden Stories*"].

74. *See* KSDA, *History*, 136; *also see The KSE Rules on Business.* When the amount sought to be deferred by a purchaser exceeded that of a seller, the purchaser paid charges therefor to the seller; if *vice versa*, the seller pays the purchaser.

Table 3.8 Some Key Statistics for Listed Stocks (1968–72)

End of Year	No. of Listed Cos.	No. of Sec. Cos.	No. of SH's (1,000 persons)	Listed Capital		Trading Volume			Market Price Per par Value
				Par Value (W billion)	Market Value (W billion)	No. of shares (million)	Value (W billion)	Composition^a	500 Won
1968	34	27	39.9	96.5	64.3	76	19.9	19:81	361
1969	42	29	54.3	119.9	86.5	98	41.9	27:73	361
1970	48	28	76.2	134.2	97.9	78	42.1	18:82	365
1971	50	28	81.9	141.3	108.7	49	33.7	26:74	385
1972	66	27	103.2	174.3	245.9	82	70.2	17:83	705

Sources: 1) KSE, *Yearbook*, 10–11.
2) KSDA, *History*, 140,158, and 169 for the composition ratio of trading volume,

Note: a; indicates the ratio between the spot transactions and regular way transactions.

chase money from the KSFC and the seller could borrow part of the stock he sold.

Because of Hanyang's cornering of the market, the price of KSFC stock rose sharply to ₩ 540 per share by the end of December, 1969, and to ₩ 764 on January 16, 1970. In response to the rising market, selling and purchasing groups were formed by several other securities companies;[75] also many innocent public investors began to invest in the KSFC stock. The average trading volume, which was ₩ 100–200 million per day prior to November, 1969, increased to almost ₩ 3 billion per day during mid-January, 1970. Starting in early February, 1970, Hanyang ran short of funds, and as it failed to purchase shares, the market price dropped sharply. As many professional speculators left the market, the price continued to decline until early October, 1970. From February to October, most of the public investors were hurt and left the market which had become a center of frantic manipulation. The sale of government-owned KSFC stocks and the open market operations of the KIC in an attempt to stabilize the price were not effective during that period.

In October, 1970, the second round of the market battle commenced with a switch of positions. The former selling group became purchasers and *vice versa*. Due to the secret manipulation of the new purchasing group, the price rose from ₩ 600 in early October to above ₩ 1,000 in December and ₩ 1,239 by February 1, 1971. By the beginning of 1971, the number of the KSFC shares traded in the regular way reached 1,615,800 shares in the aggregate, more than one and one-half times the number of total outstanding shares.[76a] At this time, Hanyang's total short-sales amounted to one-half of the total outstanding shares of the KSFC. The MOF began to consider ways to cool the market and deter manipulation.

On February 16, 1971, the KSE raised the margin requirement for KSFC stock under the KSE Rules in order to dampen the excessive

---

The rate of charges varied with the amount.

75. *See* Oh, *Hidden Stories,* 136–38; *see also* KSDA, *History,* 1961. The selling group was formed by four securities companies, including Choongbo, Shambo, and Dongyang.

76. *See* Oh, *supra* at 138.

76a. *Id.* at 139.

speculation.[76b] The speculation, however, did not stop. Rumors fabricated by the parties caused the price to rise above ₩ 1,500 on March 20.

Following the general elections in May, 1971, the MOF released an order known as the "June 3 Measure or Decree."[77] The order, *inter alia*, prohibited short-sales and required that every transaction based on the regular way be cleared within five days. Lending or other forms of credit making between securities companies were disallowed. Finally, margin transactions for the KSFC stock were abolished.[78]

The Measure shocked the securities companies involved in the speculation. Six securities companies brought suits to enjoin its enforcement on June 15, 1971.[79] On June 23, the Seoul Civil District Court enjoined the enforcement of the June 3 Measure. The Court reasoned:

> ". . . The kind and method of securities trading should be regulated by provisions of Presidential Decree under Article 79(1) of the SEA; because Article 41 of the Presidential Decree provides only the kind of trading and mandates the setting of the method of trading to the KSE, the changes in the methods of trading based on the MOF order was null and void; furthermore, there would be great potential on the part of plaintiffs to incur huge damages due to a resultant sharp drop of the price unless the order was enjoined."[80]

The battle of speculative manipulations reopened following the court decision. The market price again rose sharply in spite of the KSE's measure which had increased margin requirements to 60% of the price. The price rose to ₩ 1,666 on June 25 and ₩ 2,000 on July 15.[81] The major parties finally reached a settlement on July 26 after strenuous efforts by the MOF. The settlement price was ₩ 1,150 per share.[82] The MOF also secured the amendments of the

---

76b. *Id.* at 140; *see also The KSE Rules on Business,* Art. 38. However, the measure was enjoined in a suit brought by the purchasing group. The decision of the court did not present a reasonable statement of the reasons therefor.

77. *See* KSDA, *History* at 159–160.

78. *Id.*

79. *Id.*

80. *Id.*

81. *Id. See also* Oh, *Hidden Stories* at 145.

82. *See* Oh, *supra,* at 147–49.

Presidential Decree on July 29 as noted earlier.[83] The battle finally ended on August 16, 1971, after significant damage to the involved parties and to many innocent public investors.[84]

One of the problems raised by the crash was the failure of government authorities to prevent such blatant manipulation. Clearly, the government should have halted the manipulation by measures, including invoking criminal sanctions pursuant to the SEA.[85] Also, no individual investors brought civil suit under Article 92 of the SEA to recover damages caused by the manipulation. The failure to bring a civil suit was probably attributable to the public's ignorance of relevant law and to the difficulties in proving responsibility.

Section III. *Further Reforms and Market Activities: Step II* (Mid 1972~1976)

I. Reforms

After the KSFC stock crash, the MOF formed an independent bureau in 1972 for the purpose of strengthening its administration and supervision of the securities market. It also began to design a more effective scheme of reform. The economic situation in 1972 presented the government a serious problem. The tight monetary policies adopted in late 1969 forced corporations to excessively leverage their financing. Most corporations, however, did not seek direct public financing, thus hampering the emerging activities of the primary securities market. The corporate community ignored the various incentives provided for going public; rather, they relied heavily on the private money markets. Thus, the activities of the private money market reached its height in mid-1972 and siphoned off resources

---

83. *See The June 3 Decree* pp. 52 and 59, *supra.*

84. It was alleged that the parties incurred damages of more than ₩ 1 billion.

85. *See Old SEA,* Arts, 91, 103, 108, and 129, Law No. 2066, amended on Dec. 31, 1968. Article 91 made it illegal to effect any transaction on the Exchange with the purpose of fixing or manipulating the market price of any security. Any person who violated that provision was subject to civil liability (Article 92), as well as cirminal liability of either imprisonment up to three years or a fine not exceeding ₩ 1 million (item 3 of Article 129). Further, the MOF was empowered, in the public interest or for the protection of public investors, to issue an appropriate order under Article 103, including an order suspending all or a part of the transactions made.

which otherwise would have flown into an organized financial market. As the private money markets flourished, the corporate capital structure and the organized financial market worsened.

The government designed strong measures which limited both the existing private ownership system of corporations and the economic freedom of individuals. The major measures were the so-called "August 3 Emergency Decree"[86] and the "Going Public Encouragement Act (GPEA) of 1972."[87]

A. *The August 3 Emergency Decree*

1. Purpose

The statutory purpose of the August 3 Emergency Decree was to stabilize the household economy and to encourage balanced growth of the national economy.[88] Its specific purpose was to achieve two closely related goals.[89] The first was to eliminate the private money market and direct their resources into the organized financial market. The second was to refinance corporate debt by compulsorily adjusting private indebtedness and by supplying special loans.

2. Measures Taken

To achieve the foregoing purposes, various measures were taken.

a. Compulsory Reports of Private Debt

The Decree provided that all private credit or private debt outstanding as of August 2, 1972, that is credit to or debt of a business enterprise created outside the organized financial markets, to be report to the government by August 9, 1972.[90] The Decree re-

---

86. *See Emergency Decree for Economic Stabilization and Growth,* Presidential Emergency Decree No. 15, released on August 3, 1972 [hereinafter referred to as "**8.3** *Emergency Decree*"]. The Decree was issued on the basis of Article 73 of the Constitution, which empowers the President to take emergency measures in extremely urgent situations such as war, national calamity, or other financial or economic crisis.

87. Law No. 2420, promulgated on Dec. 30, 1972 [hereinafter referred to as *GPEA* of 1972].

88. *See* **8.3** *Emergency Decree* Art. 1.

89. The various measures consisted mainly of compulsory reporting of private debt or credit, compulsory adjustment of debtor-creditor relationships, special adjustment of existing bank loans to improve corporate capabilities for debt service, downward readjustment of interest rates, and stabilization of commodity prices and foreign exchange rates.

90. *See* **8.3** *Emergency Decree,* Arts. 10–12 and 15–17. The private debt required to

gulated repayment of such private debt.[91] Furthermore, any private creditor who failed to report lost his rights as a creditor, including collateral rights.[92]

b. Compulsory Adjustment of Creditor-Debtor Relationships
The private debt duly reported was adjusted as of August 3, 1972.[93] The adjusted principal consisted of the sum of any unpaid interest and the original principal. Interest was fixed by law at 1.35% per month. The adjusted debts were payable in equal semi-annual installments over five years after an initial three year holding period.[94] Small private creidtors were exempted from the act. The adjustments were not applied to private debt of less than ₩ 300,000 and also were less stringent with debt of less than ₩ 3 million. Also, controlling stockholders could convert private loans into their enterprises' capital stock within ninety days of the Decree.[95]

c. Special Measures Regarding Existing Bank Loans
In order to relax the burdens of corporate debt services, existing bank loans to business enterprises were adjusted. The interest rates were lowered and maturities were extended for up to 30% of the total loans outstanding as of June 30, 1972.[96] To raise the required funds,

---

be reported was "any debt of a business enterprise created through non-financial intermediaries (in the private money market) and outstanding as of Aug. 2, 1972." The term business enterprise was in turn defined as "any person who engaged in the business as defined by Article 1 of the Business Tax Act under the license therefor." This definition covers both individual enterprises and legal entities.

91. *Id.,* Art. 13.
92. *Id.,* Art. 18.
93. *Id.,* Art. 19.
94. In the event that a debtor defaults upon his installment payments twice in succession, the Decree denies him an adjusted maturity defense in a suit brought by the creditor. *See id.,* Art. 24.
95. *Id.,* Art. 22. The term "controlling person" was defined as an "oligopolistic shareholder" as defined by Article 15(2) of the National Tax Collection Act. Many controlling persons made private loans to their enterprises to take advantages of favorable tax treatment rather than contributing capital.
96. *Id.,* Art. 32; *see also Presidential Decree* thereunder, Art. 3, PD No. 6309. Existing bank loans with interest rates exceeding 12% per year were converted into new loans. The new loans' interest rates were set at 8% with the exception of loans made from trust funds (12.5%). Their maturities and redemption schedules were set the same as those of adjusted private debt.

₩ 200 billion of special Banking Bonds were issued by financial institutions to the BOK.[97]

d. Other Measures

A Deliberation Committee, consisting of Ministers of Ministries concerned with economic affairs, the Governors of the BOK and the KDB, and two other outstanding scholars recommended by the President, was established to review policies on the "rationalization" of national industries.[98] The Committee was given power to designate certain industries to be eligible for special loans from the Industry Rationalization Funds, special depreciations for favorable tax treatment, and other tax advantages.[99]

Special guarantee funds were created at banking institutions to secure loans to enterprises whose ability to provide collateral appeared to be weak.[100] Also, the existing special guarantee funds for loans to medium size enterprises, fisheries, and agricultural industries were strengthened.[101]

To stimulate private investment in major industries, special tax depreciation rates provided as a privilege for certain categories of corporations were increased from 20–30% to 40–80%.[102] In addition, the official interest rates were again lowered.[103]

3. Accomplishments and Impacts

Creditor and debtors reported ₩ 355.5 billion and ₩ 345 billion of private debt pursuant to the August 3 Emergency Decree, respectively.[104] The average amount of individual credit was ₩ 1.7 million, while the average enterprise debt was ₩ 8.7 million. The discrepancies between the figures given by creditors and debtors is easily attributable to the reluctance to disclose actual figures for fear of possible disadvantages and to conflicts of interest between the

---

97. *Id.*, Art. 33.
98. *Id.*, Arts. 49–51.
99. *Id.*, Arts. 52–64.
100. *Id.*, Arts. 37, 38, and 40–47.
101. *Id.*, Art. 39.
102. *Id.*, Art. 60.
103. The lowering of the official interest rates was noted at note 26, *supra*. The other rates provided in the Act on Limitation of interest Rates were also lowered from 36.5% to 25% per year by a Presidential Decree.
104. KSDA, *History*, 176–77.

parties. Also, the close personal relationships involved and settlements between the parties possibly prevented a considerable amount of private debt from being reported. By the end of 1972, W 264 billion was converted to new debt, W 80.6 billion was converted into capital stock, and the remainder was either released (W 10.6 billion) or disputed.

The August 3 Decree critically affected the activities of the private money markets. As the demand for private credit decreased sharply, the interest rates in the private money market were lowered to around 2.8% per month in the fourth quarter of 1972.[105] The capital structure and profitability of most business corporations improved and public investment in the stock market was stimulated. Corporate bond issues, having been primarily used as a substitute for private debt, decreased sharply.[106]

B. Enactment of the GPEA of 1972 and Relevant Reforms

   1. Purpose and Compulsory Requirements of the GPEA

The purpose of the GPEA was stated as follows:

> "The purpose of this law is to facilitate domestic resource mobilization and improve corporate capital structure by encouraging closely-held corporations to go public and by stimulating public participation in corporate businesses so as to contribute to a sound development of the national economy."[107]

To achieve such goals, major concern was placed on methods to encourage and force corporations to go public. In this regard, the MOF was empowered to issue "designation orders" to "selected corporations" to force them to go public.[108]

The GPEA included several incentives designed to encourage closely–held corporations to voluntarily go public.[109] Furthermore, it provided punitive measures for corporations which remain private in violation of a designation order requiring them to go public.[110] There were two major reasons for providing penalties. First, few corporations had taken advantage of the existing incentives for going

---

105. *Id.*, Art. 178.
106. *Id.*
107. *GPEA,* Art. 1.
108. *Id.*, Art. 4.
109. *See* pp. 65–67, *infra.*
110. *See* p. 66, *infra.*

public in the CMPA and other laws. Hence, stronger measures were needed. Second, the government thought that the corporations in the past, particularly under the August 3 Emergency Decree, had profited at the expense of the public and thus it was legitimate to force them to act in the public interest by going public.[111]

2. Designation Order to Go Public

The Minister of Finance was empowered to issue a designation order requiring a corporation to go public. A designation order contains detailed conditions regulating the process of going public.[112] The process of designation consisted of two steps—the classification of corporations subject to designation and the actual designation of a corporation requiring it to go public. The MOF is required to issue designation orders to corporations finally chosen by the "Committee for Deliberation of Going Public."[113]

a. Standards of Selection and Designation

Two major factors were considered in setting standards for selecting corporations to be forced to go public. The first factor was a consideration of how many financing privileges a corporation had enjoyed. The second factor was a consideration as to the interest of public investors and the securities market as a whole. The specific standards were based on the capital structure, size of loans from domestic institutions and foreign countries, size of adjusted private debt, and earning power and dividend capability of corporations. Thus, the MOF may first select a corporation as a candidate for designation, if:

  a) its total amount of cash loans or capital goods induced pursuant to the Foreign Capital Inducement Act (FCIA) is equivalent to the amount of its legal capital or exceeds ₩ 1 billion;
  b) its total amount of adjusted private debt, including debt converted into capital stock under the August 3 Emergency Decree, exceeds ₩ 100 million;

---

111. *See GPEA,* Art. 5.
112. In this regard, one of the standards set for selecting a corporation to be designated was the size of adjusted private debt. *See* the accompanying text of note 114, *infra.*
113. *See id.,* Art. 4. The Committee was established to deliberate and decide policies relating to going public. The Prime Minister was designated as its chairman.

c) its total amount of loans from financial institutions exceeds
₩ 1 billion; and

d) it was designated by a Presidential Decree as necessary and
appropriate for the development of the national economy to
go public.[114]

In turn, the MOF may, for actual designation, select individual
corporations among the foregoing corporations selected as a candidate
and designate them to go public, if:

a) their legal capital should exceed ₩ 50 (since 1975, ₩ 200)
million;

b) at least two years should have passed since their incorporation;

c) declarations of annual dividends at a rate of not less than 10%
should be deemed possible; and

d) the prices of stock should be expected to be above par on the
exchange.[115]

b. Punitive Measures

A corporation which fails to go public after proper designation is
subject to punitive measures. The punitive measures include unfavorable treatment in calculating corporate and personal income
taxes by eliminating various tax deductions usually available for
corporations.[116] In addition, the MOF may request that financial
institutions restrict loans and other financial support to such corporations.[117] Furthermore, several privileges available for designated
corporations may be refused when they refuse to go public. Such
privileges include exemption from criminal liability for tax evasions
committed prior to the enforcement of the GPEA and revaluation
privileges for non-operating lands.[118]

c. Additional Privileges

In addition to the incentives already provided by law, some additional privileges were provided for publicly-held or designated
corporations. First, publicly-held or designated corporations were
allowed to revalue their non-operating lands.[119] The tax rate on the

---

114. *Id.*
115. *Presidential Decree of the GPEA*, Art. 3, PD No. 6491, promulgated on Feb.
8, 1973.
116. *See GPEA,* Arts. 16 and 17.
117. *Id.*, Art. 18.
118. *Id.*, Arts. 14 and 12; *see also* the accompanying text of notes 119–121, *infra.*

gains from such revaluations was lowered from 40% to 27%.

Second, a 50% exemption from integrated personal income taxes for dividend income was given to shareholders who owned less than 30% of the total outstanding shares of a corporation.[120] This exemption was designed to decentralize equity ownership and to stimulate more equity supplies. As noted above, a further incentive to going public was the exemption from criminal punishment for fraudulent tax evasion committed prior to the enforcement of the law. This privilege is available for designated corporations or other corporations which meet the legal criteria for publicly–held corporations.[121]

3. Other Relevant Reforms

a. Employee Stock Ownership System

Employees of a publicly-held or a listed corporation were already empowered under the CMPA to subscribe for up to 10% of the newly-issued shares of their company regardless of Article 418 of the Commercial Code.[122] The CMPA provision, however, did not provide compulsory preferential rights. To provide employees with privileges and to decentralize equity ownership more efficiently, the GPEA required that employees of designated corporations be allotted in preference to other subscribers up to 10% of new shares to be publicly offered.[123]

b. Incentives Strengthened

Several disincentives to going public were eliminated by amendments to the CMPA in January, 1973. The chairman of a shareholders' general meeting of a publicly-held or listed corporation was empowered to restrict the time and frequency of a shareholder's speech when he deemed it necessary.[124] Despite their guaranteed rights under the Commercial Code, shareholders were also required to show a legitimate reason before inspecting financial records and books of the corporation.[125] Such priviliges for management and

---

119. *Id.*, Art. 12.

120. *Id.*, Art. 13.

121. *Id.*, Art. 14.

122. *See* the accompanying text of note 33, *supra*.

123. *See GPEA,* Art. 8; also *CMPA,* Art. 6(2). These provisions gave such employees preferential rights up to 10% of the new shares.

124. *CMPA,* Art. 11(2) as amended on Jan. 5, 1973.

125. *See id.,* Art. 11–5; *see also Commercial Code,* Art. 466; Hi Chul Chung, *Commen-*

controlling shareholders, however, raise significant problems of fairness for public shareholders. Clearly, such measures could weaken the ability to detect breaches of fiduciary duty by the majority shareholders and management.

Several other provisions were introduced for publicly-held or listed corporations. These provisions simplified the shareholder meeting call notice procedure for notifying shareholders holding less than 1% of the total outstanding voting shares.[126] The provisions also increased the number of new shares which could be issued without shareholder approval.[127] The simplification of call notice procedure, however, may be criticized for the lack of protection of minority shareholders' interest.

C. Fifth and Sixth Amendments of the SEA

The fifth Amendment to the SEA in early 1973 made institutional

---

taries on *Commercial Law*, Vol. 1, (*Sang Bub YoRon, Sang-Kwon*), 437–38 (4th ed. 1972): Ton Kak Suh, *Commentaries on Commercial Laws*, Vol. 1 (*Sang Bub-Kang Euy, Sang-Kwon*), 416–18 (9th rev. ed. 1973) [hereinafter referred to as "Chung, *Commentaries I*," and "Suh, *Commentaries I*," respectively]. The right of inspection of financial books and records was originally aimed at protecting minority shareholders' rights and warranting fairness of management. The right was limited to the restriction of possible abuses so that only a shareholder or shareholders who held more than 5% of the total shares outstanding, and who could show good cause, could request an inspection of books and records. A corporation was not permitted to reject the shareholders' request unless it proved that the request was unfair. If the corporation rejected the request without reasonable cause, the shareholders could bring a suit to force inspection. A temporary injunction was provided to keep financial documents safe.

126. *CMPA*, Art. 11–12. A simplified call notice was also provided which required only that public notices stating the purpose of the meeting be placed more than twice in at least two daily newspapers two weeks prior to the date set for the meeting.

127. *Id.*, Arts. 11–3 and 4.

The total number of new shares which may be issued, without resort to shareholder's approval, is four times the total number of shares outstanding. Article 437 of the Commercial Code, however, restricted the number to twice the total number of outstanding shares. To issue more shares, a special resolution for a capital increase must be passed at a general shareholders' meeting. Also, new non-voting shares may be issued up to half of the shares already issued; Article 370(2) of the Commercial Code restricts this number to one-fourth of the total outstanding shares.

changes designed to increase equity supplies and to strengthen the protection of public interests.[128] First, the category of securities subject to registration requirement was expanded. The Amendment also prohibited sales of securities while in the registration process.[129] Second, to strengthen the financial capability of securities companies, the minimum capital requirements for securities companies were increased from ₩ 30 and ₩ 50 million to ₩ 200 and ₩ 300 million.[130] The Amendment also strengthened auditing standards and introduced civil malpractice liability for certified public accountants (CPAs).[131] Furthermore, some provisions of the Presidential Decree promulgated to enforce the SEA were amended.[132] Most importantly, officers or shareholders directly or indirectly owning more than 10% of the total outstanding shares of listed corporations were prohibited from making short sales of their corporations' shares.

On December 21, 1974, the SEA was amended again in three major areas. First, the 1974 Amendments required that listed corporations register rights offerings and stock dividends with the MOF.[133] This requirement was designed to restrict excessive capital increases which might result in a weakening of corporations' capability to pay dividends.[134]

Second, the 1974 Amendments strengthened the MOF's and the KSE's supervisory functions over the operation of securities com-

---

128. Law No. 2481, as amended on Feb. 26, 1973.

129. *Id.*, Arts. 2(1), 4, 5, and 5–2.

130. *Id.*, Art. 13(3). A securities company whose legal capital was between ₩ 200 and ₩ 300 million could engage in only one business as a dealer, broker, or underwriter.

131. *Id.*, Arts. from 126–2 to 126–9.
   Due to the Amendments, all documents relating to financial matters required to be submitted to the MOF or KSE under the SEA, and must be audited by a CPA in compliance with the new Rules. Also, the CPA auditing report must accompany the public notice of financial statements. In addition, if the corporation concerned so requested, the CPA was required to answer questions raised at a shareholder's general meeting. Such devices along with the adoption of civil liability for malpractice were intended to ensure that auditing be more thorough and accurate.

132. *See Presidential Decree of the SEA*, PD No. 6634, amended on April 20, 1973. Art. 53 prohibited such short sales.

133. *SEA*, Art. 4(1), Law No. 2684, as amended on Dec. 21, 1974.

134. The appropriateness of such a device is discussed below. *See* pp. 143–4, *infra.*

panies.[135] The officers and employees of a securities company were prohibited from disclosing any information concerning customers' businesses without their written consent.[136] Also, a corporation was chartered to perform clearing functions, including receiving securities deposits and stock re-registration.[137]

D. *"May 29 Presidential Special Instructions"*

On May 29, 1974, the President of Korea released special instructions relating to the institutional structure of the securities market as a whole.[138] The Instructions, *inter alia*, encouraged the government institutions to give special support to purblicly-held corporations in the areas of bank loans, foreign capital inducements, and tax incentives. Also, large non-publicly-held corporations and their controlling shareholders were subjected to strengthened supervision of their bank loans and tax payments.

The MOF, pursuant to the May 29 Special Instructions, announced in June, 1974, various policy measures to promote the long term health of capital market.[139] First, "public" corporations were required to have in public circulation at least 30% of their total number of outstanding shares. Controlling shareholders were encouraged to lower their holdings from 51% to 30% of the total number of shares outstanding. Any distribution of securities in the over-the-counter market after the completion of a public offering was prohibited. The MOF measures also contained thorough supervision of controlling persons' shareholdings.[140]

Second, institutional innovations for the underwriting industry were introduced to improve the functioning of the primary market. The "Agreement on Arrangement for Public Offering and Under-

---

135. *SEA,* Art. 34(1) and (2). The KSE could also inspect the operations of the securities companies to deter excessive speculation under the mandate of the MOF.

136. *Id.,* Art. 38–3.

137. *Id.,* Art. 127–2.

138. *See* MOF, *"Policy Measures Taken and Their Major Contents"* (*Chung Chaeck Chochi Mit Jooyo Nae Yong*) 3–6 (unpublished official documents).

139. *See id.,* MOF, Measures taken on June 7, 1974.

140. *Id.,* at 5. Ownership changes in controlling shareholders had already been required to be reported in an annual report (Form 5). *See SEA,* Art. 78, and Presidential and the MOF Decrees thereunder.

writing Business" established an Association of Underwriting Companies.[141] Institutions, eligible for joining the Association, consisted of (1) the KIC, (2) securities companies with legal capital of more than ₩ 300 million, (3) commercial banks, including local banks, the Korea Trust Bank, the Korea Development Bank, and the Korea Exchange Bank, and (4) short-term investment and finance companies.[142] Insurance companies and securities investment trust companies were allowed to join only to the extent of purchasing securities for their own accounts. All other companies were prohibited from underwriting. These innovations institutionalized the securities analysis and underwriting system.[143] In addition, an underwriting fund of ₩ 10 million was established.

Third, in order to stimulate public investment in securities, various securities savings systems were introduced and institutional investors were encouraged to participate in them.[144] In addition, the Korea Securities Investment Corp. (KSIC) was established professionally to operate diversified mutual funds.[145] Also, banking institutions and insurance companies were instructed to give priority to loans secured by listed securities over loans secured by real estate so as to create public demand for securities.

E. Other Institutional Innovations

1. Delisting of Self-Issues, Etc.

Despite the KSE's reorganization which was designed to ensure fair market administration, its certificates of contribution were not eliminated from the KSE's board. The certificate frequently became the object of frantic speculation and manipulation. The conflicts of interest involved between the certificate owners and the KSE prevented fair market administration. The same situation applied to the continued listing of the KSFC stock.

---

141. Promulgated on July 15, 1974 (hereinafter referred to as *"Rules on Underwriting Business"*).
142. *Id.*, Art. 1.
143. The KIC Rules on Securities Analysis (promulgated on March 31, 1973) and the Specific Rules on Securities Analysis (originally promulgated on April 1, 1972) were applied to underwriting companies. *See* pp. 134–38, *infra*.
144. *See* MOF, *"Unpublished Documents," supra* note 138, at 4–5.
145. *Id.*, 5 and 7. The Korea Securities Investment Company (KSIC) was incorporated with ₩ 500 million capital on Sept. 16, 1974.

The MOF finally recognized the urgent need to remove the certificates of interest and delisted the KSE certificates on June 29, 1974.[146] The MOF required securities companies to purchase certain amounts of the KSE certificates. The MOF justified this action by referring to its plan that eventually give the securities companies control over the Exchange. The KSFC stock was delisted on November 15, 1974.[147]

    2. Enactment of Regulation Concerning Accounting Proceedings and Preparation of Financial Statements

To assure uniformity and objectivity of CPA audits of listed companies and certain other corporations, a Presidential Decree and MOF Rules thereunder were promulgated in 1974 and 1975, respectively.[148] The Presidential Decree established standards for fair and proper accounting principles.[149] In order to enforce these principles, the MOF Rules defined the terminology, standard form, method of preparation, and coverage of financial statements.[150]

All persons preparing and auditing the balance sheets, profit and loss statements, statements of surplus application, and other financial statements required by the SEA, were required to comply with the accounting principles, forms, and methods provided in the foregoing laws. However, the MOF did not concern itself with the opportunities for manipulation using accounting procedures. Disciplinary power for malpractice was largely left to self-regulation by the Association of Certified Public Accountants. Although the regulation of the CPA's and their accounting procedures was not sufficient to ensure accuracy, the introduction of uniform rules on accounting standards was an extremely important step in the effort to protect investors and to provide objective standards for regulation.[151]

---

146. *See* Oh, *Hidden Stories,* 159.

147. *Id.* Before delisting, both cash and stock loans for trading in KSFC stock on the Exchange were suspended.

148. *Presidential Decree on Accounting Proceedings for Listed Companies, Etc.,* PD No. 7199, promulgated on July 10, 1974; *MOF Decree on Financial Statements of Listed Companies, Etc.,* MOF Decree No. 1098, promulgated on April 17, 1975 [hereinafter the former is referred to as *"Presidential Decree on Accounting Proceedings,"* the latter as *"MOF Decree on Financial Statement"*].

149. *See SEA,* Art. 126–8; *see also Presidential Decree on Accounting Proceedings,* Arts. 1–3.

150. *See SEA,* Art. 126–9; *see also MOF Decree on Financial Statements,* Arts. 1 and 2.

151. *See August 8 Supplementary Measures to the Policy towards the Enforcement of Going*

3. Supplementary Measures to Enforce the Policies Forcing Corporations to Go Public

The MOF, in 1975, modified its designation procedure to reconcile its policy goal with practical hurdles to issuing a designation order. The new designation procedure consisted of the following three steps:

1) Public Release of the names of corporations selected to go public;
2) Notification to individual corporations requiring them to go public by a prescribed date; and
3) Issuance of a Designation Order in the event that a corporation failed to go public within the designated period.

Such measures were designed to encourage corporations to go public as voluntarily as possible.

Also, new criteria for selection of corporations to be forced to go public were introduced. A corporation had to be selected to go public if it:

1) was the principal corporation among a group of affiliated corporations;
2) was one of the top 100 corporations in terms of sales volume;
3) attracted foreign capital exceeding $5 million;
4) was one of the top 100 corporations in terms of export volume;
5) was chosen by the KIC; or
6) engaged in heavy chemical industries.[152]

Corporations were to be selected for notification in the following order: those meeting more than one of the foregoing criteria were to be selected first; principal corporations among the same groups of affiliated corporations were second; and heavy chemical industries were third.[153]

Designated corporations going public were required to retain either the KIC as their principal managing underwriter or retain the bank with which they had principally dealt as one of their joint managing underwriters.[154] Although designed to deter incorrect

---

Public, released by the MOF on Aug. 8, 1975; *see also* MOF, *"Unpublished Documents,"* 10.

152. MOF, *"Unpublished Documents,"* 9.

153. *Id.*

154. *Id.* at 10.

securities analysis, these requirements also significantly restricted the competition in the underwriting industry. In order to become a managing underwriter, a securities company had to be publicly-held, have legal capital in excess of W 2 billion, have at least three certified public accountants, and have been a managing underwriter at least three times.[155]

Furthermore, even though the existing set of rules[156] for securities analysis and pricing were very conservative, the securities analysis performed by a managing underwriter was subject to reanalysis by the KIC.[157] The KIC review was designed to deter arbitrary securities analysis with resultant overpricing. Also, the managing underwriter could be sanctioned if there was any "remarkable" difference between its analysis and that of the KIC.[158]

II. Market Activities
A. *Primary Market*
1. A Boom of Going Public Accompanied by Hot Issues

The primary market for corporate equities was inactive before 1968. In 1968 it began to develop, but public participation in the market was relatively low until the end of 1972. From the beginning of 1973, however, the activities of the primary market boomed with drastic increases in the number of public offerings and in public subscription rates. This boom was due to the series of policy measures designed to create more supplies of equities and to elicit public demand.

As shown in Table 3.9, the total number of companies which went public increased drastically from only seven in 1972 to forty-five in 1973, and eighty-seven in 1976. Thus the total number of listed companies, which was only sixty-six at the end of 1972, increased to 274 by the end of 1976. As the size of offerings became larger, the amount of total shares distributed through public offerings and secondary

---

155. *Id.* at 10–11.
156. *See* pp. 140–42, *infra.*
157. For details, *see* pp. 78–82, *infra.*
158. *See Rules on Underwriting Business*, Art. 15; *see also* pp. 134, *et seq.*
   When a remarkable difference appears, the Association of underwriting companies may issue a warning or suspend the license for six months to two years.

Table 3.9 Activities of Primary Market (1972–1976)

Amount: in current ₩ 100 million

	1972	1973	1974	1975	1976
A. Public Offerings[a]					
a. number	6	34	13	48	56
b. Amount	10.8	174.0	92.0	280.0	405.6
B. Secondary Distributions[b]					
a. Number	1	11	9	15	31
b. Amount	1.2	33.3	51.0	118.0	334.5
C. Capital Increases[c]	—	—			
a. Number		—	59	67	81
b. Amount	—	—	291.0	815.0	1,019.4
D. Corporate Bonds					
a. Number	35	12	59	68	111
b. Amount	99.2	34.5	278.7	336.0	862.8
Total (A + B + C + D)					
a. Number	—	—	140	198	278
b. Amount	—	—	713.0	1,550.0	2,622.3

Sources: 1) KSE, *Yearbook*, 373–94 (1976), for 1972–75.
      2) KSE, *Stock*, (No. 102, Feb. 1977) at 41–53 for 1976.
Notes: a; Indicates public offerings of new shares by closely-held corporations.
      b; Indicates secondary distributions of shares already issued and outstand-
         ing by closely-held corporations.
      c; Indicates offerings of new shares by listed corporations excluding stock
         dividends.

distributions[159] (A + B in the Table) increased more rapidly than the number of offerings. The total number of shares publicly distributed increased from ₩ 1.2 billion in 1972 to ₩ 73.9 billion in 1976. Corporate bond offerings, which had slowed down after the Emergency Decree, showed dramatic increases from 1974 on both in number and in amount. The total amount of resources mobilized through the capital market, including "capital increases"[160] by listed companies, increased from ₩ 71.3 billion in 1974 to ₩ 155 and ₩ 262.2 billion in 1975 and 1976, respectively. The 1976 total amount was 30% above the proposed target of ₩ 200 billion.

159. Both public offerings and secondary distributions of securities were provided by the SEA as means of going public. For definitions and relevant procedures, *see* pp. 125–26 and 143, *et seq., infra.*
160. *See* note c, Table 3.9, *supra.*

The capital increase by listed corporations, which had slowed down during the tight money period of 1969–72, accelerated again in 1973. The total amount of capital increase by listed corporations, including stock dividends, increased from W 21 billion in 1972 to W 314 billion in 1976. *See* Table 3.10. As a consequence, the number of listed corporations with capital stock of more than W 5 billion increased from thirteen in 1974 to thirty-nine in 1976. *See* Table 3.11.

Despite the rapid increase in the supply of securities on the primary market, almost all the offerings from 1973 through 1976 were oversubscribed. The highest rate of subscription occurred during the first half of 1973 when the issue of Jinro Co., Ltd. (formerly, Jinro Brewery Corp.) was subscribed at a rate of 198.5 offers for each share.[161] The offering of W 15.7 billion shares by the Korea Oil Corporation Subsidiary in June, 1976, constituted the largest public offering of equity securities and netted almost W 120 billion. The boom of public offerings and excessive oversubscription rate resulted from the policies taken by the government, most notably, the broad criteria for selec-

Table 3.10 Capital Increases by Listed Companies (1967–1976)

Amount: Current billion Won

Year	By Offering[a]		In Dividends[b]		Total	
	No.	Amount	No.	Amount	No.	Amount
1967	3	1.3	11	16.2	14	17.5
1968	10	20.3	5	22.6	15	42.9
1969	8	6.1	13	12.0	21	18.1
1970	20	8.0	11	3.8	31	11.9
1971	10	2.8	12	3.1	22	6.0
1972	35	15.6	7	6.3	42	21.9
1973	54	33.8	16	13.3	70	47.2
1974	61	37.0	38	52.3	99	89.2
1975	69	107.0	25	51.2	94	158.2
1976	89	196.1	44	118.7	133	314.8

Source: KSE, *Stock* (No. 102, February, 1977), at 70.

Notes: a; Indicates capital increases actually paid in.

b; Indicates capital increases in the form of stock dividends by converting either reserved surpluses or asset revaluation surpluses into capital stock.

---

161. KSDA, *History*, at 189.

There was 28 public offerings during the first half of 1973, and about half of these were offered at prices with 20–330% premiums.

Table 3.11 Changes in Capital Stock of Listed Companies (1974–1976)

Amount of Capital Stock (in current billion Won)	No. of Listed Cos. at the end of		
	1974	1975	1976
below 0.5	8	9	6
0.5–1	28	40	44
1.0–2	38	51	93
2.0–3	23	37	43
3.0–4	9	22	36
4.0–5	9	4	13
5.0–10	6	16	25
over 10	7	10	14
TOTAL	128	189	274

Source: KSE, *Stock* (No. 102, February, 1977), at 71.

ting corporations to be forced to go public and the government's wide involvement in securities analysis and pricing to protect public investors.[162] However, the rate of subscription for debt securities was very low, which in turn brought great financial pressure on the underwriting companies, as will be discussed later.[163]

The oversubscription of equity securities brought a change in the form of underwriting. In 1974, underwriters switched from the best-efforts or stand-by method to the firm commitment method.[164] In March, 1976, in order to widen the equity ownership among the public, publicly offered shares were required to be allotted on the basis of the "proportional allotment system" rather than the then existing "customer registration system."[165] The customer registration system was faulty. It allotted 45% of the total number of shares offered to certain groups.[166] Many public investors rushed to register

162. *See* pp. 78–82, *infra.*

163. *See* pp. 83–86, *infra.*

164. *See* KSE, *Yearbook,* 337–81 (1976); *see also* KSE, *Stock (Chooshik)* (No. 102, Feb., 1977) at 30–31.
    Along with the adoption of a "proportional allotment system" on March 4, 1976, equity security underwriting was required to be performed on the basis of firm commitments.

165. *See* MOF, *Supplementary Measures to Securities Markets,* released on March 4 and May 12, 1976; *see also* KSE, *Stock* (No. 102, Feb., 1977) at 30–33.

166. *Id., Rules on Underwriting Business,* Art. 6.
    The portions to be preferentially allotted under the customer registration system were as follows:

for the remaining shares before becoming well–informed.[167] The new system abolished part of the preferential allotment and increased the portion available for public investors from 55% to 70–80%.[168] It also limited the allotment of any one person to 1/1,000 of the total shares issued and outstanding or less. However, the problem of too many odd-lot shares could not be resolved under the new system unless supplies of shares were largely expanded. In 1976, the MOF increased the minimum number of shares to be publicly offered to meet going public requirement from 30% to 40% of the total outstanding shares.[169]

2. Problems Raised

a. Conflicts of Interest in Pricing

Many of the difficult regulatory problems considered in going public involve conflicts of interest between the shareholders of a privately–held corporation and the potential public investors. The government placed emphasis on resolving such conflicts, especially in pricing publicly offered securities.

As noted earlier,[170] the MOF attempted to deter overpricing by requiring the KIC to reanalyze every preliminary securities analysis which was performed by a managing underwriter. Such measures bolstered public confidence in the primary market and helped sus-

---

1) 10% to an employee stock ownership union; 2) 10% to a securities investment trust or securities savings plan; 3) 5% to an underwriting syndicate; and 4) 20% to a savings trust for employee asset formation. The savings trusts were introduced in 1970 (Law No. 2, 165, promulgated on Jan. 1, 1970) to increase national savings and to improve the living standards of employees. The 5% allotment to underwriting syndicates were designed to help the managing underwriter perform its duty of stabilizing prices.

167. *See* KSE, *Stock* (No. 102, Feb., 1977) at 31.

168. *Id.* at 33. Under the "proportional allotment system" the securities subcribed to are to be preferentially allotted as follows: 1) 10% to the employee stock ownership union; 2) 10% to a securities investment trust or securities savings plan, one half (5%) of which is to be used for stabilizing purposes; and 3) 10% to savings trusts for employee asset formation.

169. *See MOF Release of May* 12, 1976; *see also* KSE, *Stock* (No. 102, Feb., 1977) at 33. In the case of a joint venture formed with a foreign partner, the minimum requirement was still 30%. It was felt that a lower requirement would hinder the controlling stockholder from maintaining control.

170. *See* the accompanying text of note 156, *supra*.

tain a high rate of public subscription. In fact, according to Dr. Il Sakong,[171] most publicly offered shares were underpriced during 1973–1974.

Dr. Sakong examined the price behavior of thirty-nine new issues during the period from January, 1973 to June, 1974. Dr. Sakong compared their prices on the day of listing, one week, one month, six months, and one year after listing with the KSE composite index. The average margins over the KSE average market price during the respective periods were 6.80, 27.04, 32.42, 22.62, and 16.35%.[172] Only four of the thirty-nine issues performed below the market average during the first two weeks and only three after one month.

Dr. Sakong's study showed that most new issues gave a higher rate of return than other issues already listed, even if sold immediately after listing. Such high returns on short term resale were because of the conservative pricing policy of the government, which purposely kept prices low to assure public participation in the market. The high degree of oversubscription resulted from the public's recognition that investments in new issues were the most profitable course to take. The oversubscriptions were also partly attributable to the fact that government policy disfavored other investment alternatives, such as real estate or bank deposits.[173] The major reason for oversubscription, however, was clearly under-pricing.

The deliberate underpricing raised serious problems. The controlling shareholders of a corporation forced to go public, quite naturally, tried to seek means to offset their losses due to underpricing. They often watered their stocks by converting reserved or asset revaluation surpluses into capital stock immediately before going public.[174] They could realize large profits by either holding such

---

171. *See* Il Sakong, *Some Observations on the Securities Market of Korea* 13–22 (Korea Development Institute (KDI), Working Paper No. 7410, 1974) (hereinafter cited as "Il Sakong, *Working Paper* No. 7410").

172. *Id.* Table 1 at 18. The figures for the six-month and one-year periods were average margins of twenty-six and fifteen issues over the KSE average market prices.

173. The Government enacted high income taxes to deter real estate investment and thus to promote the securities markets. Also, it lowered interest rates on deposits as noted earlier.

174. *See* Maeil Economic Newspaper, Dec. 30, 1976, at p. 3; *see also* Seoul Economic

stocks or selling them after their stocks were listed. Controlling shareholders also attempted to avoid going public by disguising their corporations as public. For the purpose of disguising, they placed a large portion of shares in the names of relatives, employees, friends, or even controlling shareholders of other corporations in reciprocal arrangements.[175]

The MOF has attempted to stop such dishonest practices of controlling shareholders. To deter watering practices, the authority required that the KIC approve any conversion of reserved surpluses into capital stock by a corporation going public.[176] The KIC must deny the application for such a capital increase unless the company, after conversion, retains the capability to declare annual dividends at a level exceeding the official interest rates.

Some controlling shareholders, however, have avoided the KIC examination procedure through the declaration of intermediate dividends, passed at an extraordinary shareholders' general meeting.[177] The Commercial Code requires that a resolution declaring cash or stock dividends be passed at an ordinary shareholder meeting which is held within a certain period after the end of each fiscal year.[178] The Code also places a net asset restriction on the permissible amount of the dividends.[179] However, when a corporation fails to meet such requirements, only creditors of the corporation may

---

Newspaper, Nov. 14, 1976, at p. 4; Joongang Daily News (*Joongang Ilbo*) Dec. 13, 1976, at p. 2. The KIC was empowered to approve the conversion of surpluses into capital stock by a corporation going public. However, some corporations intentionally failed to obtain approval. Kang-won Industries (*"Kangwon Sanup"*) and Shamee Corp. (*"Shamee Sha"*), which had gone public in February and March of 1976, respectively, were reported to have watered their stock by excessive conversions.

175. *See* pp. 105–07, *infra*.
176. *See* pp. 123–25, *infra*.
177. *See* Maeil Economic Newspaper, Dec. 30, 1976, at p. 4.
178. *Commercial Code*, Arts. 447–449 and 365.
179. *Id.*, Arts. 462, 458–60. The legal reserve comprises both earned surplus and capital surplus reserves. Companies were required to set aside at least one-twentieth of net profits every year until the amount of earned surplus reached one-half of legal capital. Capital surplus consists of various paid-in surpluses. Capital reserve may be converted into capital stock in accordance with a special resolution of shareholders. There has been disagreement among com-

bring a suit to recover the corporate funds illegally payed out.[180] Because shareholders usually could not challenge declarations of intermediate dividends, the controlling shareholders could avoid KIC examination and distribute corporate funds to themselves.

Also, the disciplinary power for malpractices which was given to the Association of underwriting companies did not deter fraudulent securities analysis. Sanctions were provided for when there was a "remarkable difference"[181] between the two analyses, *i.e.*, the underwriter's preliminary analysis and the KIC's reanalysis. Becuase of the vagueness of the phrase "remarkable difference," the authority permitted the Association to adopt a set of specific rules governing sanctions in August, 1976.[182] However, the Association did not make the sanctions mandatory and the authority has not exercised any effective oversight in spite of the frequent instances of malpractice.[183] The only enforcement action taken to date for malpractice was a warning issued to the Dongyang Securities Co. on August 28, 1976.[184]

No effective measures have been taken to prevent controlling share-

---

mentators as to the convertibility of the earned surplus reserve, although some companies have frequently converted it. *See* Suh, *Commentaries I,* 408–09 (1973); *see also* Chung, *Commentaries I,* 416 (1972).

180. *Id.,* Art. 462(3).

181. *See* the accompanying text of note 158, *supra.*

182. *See Specific Rules on the Underwriting Business,* Art 11; *see also* Seoul Economic Newspaper, Aug. 25, 1976, at p. 4. The Association may trigger a sanction provided in Art. 16 of the Rules when: 1) the terms of the offering are changed by the KIC reanalysis; 2) the analyses of the profitability values varied more than 50%, or the analyses of asset value varied more than 10%; or 3) the rules were misapplied to the analysis or any fraudulent materials were included.

183. *See* Maeil Economic Newspaper, Dec. 30, 1976, p. 3.
In the second half of 1976, changes were forced in the terms of eight out of twenty-five offerings due to malpractice by managing underwriters.

184. *See* Seoul Economic Newspaper, Aug. 29, 1976, at p. 4.
The Dongyang Securities Co., as a managing underwriter for Keumsung Industrial Corp. (*"Keumsung Shanup"*), had submitted the securities analysis report to the KIC. The KIC found the Dongyang's initial analysis fraudulent because it would mislead the people to think that the company could declare annual dividends at a level exceeding the official interest rate. Thus, the terms of the offerings were changed. A securities company, if warned three times, may have its license suspended for a period of six months to two years,

holders from disguising their corporations as public. The only government action taken to date was a prosecution for tax evasion in the case of the Korea Won-Yang Fisheries Corporation.[185]

b. Problems Relating to Secondary Distribution

Secondary distributions of corporate securities are not a means of corporate finance; nor do they improve the corporate capital structure. Secondary distribution constitute a sale of shares already issued and held by the shareholders of a corporation. A significant number of controlling shareholders of closely-held corporations used secondary distrubtions as a means of going public. Moreover, a large portion of the shares distributed were created by converting reserved or asset revaluation surpluses into stock prior to the distribution.[186]

On August 18, 1976, the MOF announced that it would force corporations, which watered their stock by excessive conversions, to either decrease their capital stock or distribute their securities at prices below par.[187] In addition, specific standards were provided to prohibit certain corporations from going public through secondary distributions. Corporations were prohibited from going public through secondary distributions if their debt equity ratio was above 3:1 or if the total amount of loans exceeded twice their legal capital.[188] Applying these standards for the first time, the KIC stopped the proposed secondary distribution of Daerim Fisheries Corp. stock in August, 1976.[189] However, the standards can be criticized because they are not strict enough to induce corporations to improve capital structure.

c. Other Problems Relating to Enforcement of Government's Public Distribution Policy

The MOF was empowered to issue a designation order to force a

---

185. *See* pp. 161–64, *infra.*
186. *See* Seoul Economic Newspaper, Aug. 19, 1976, at p. 4. Among thirty-seven selected corporations expected to go public in the second half of 1976, nine were suspended due to the excessive conversion of their surplus into capital stock which seriously affected their earning capacity and dividends capability.
187. *See MOF Releases of Aug.* 17, *and* 21, 1976; *see also* Seoul Economic Newspaper, Aug. 18 and 22, 1976, at p. 4.
188. *Id.*
189. *See* Seoul Economic Newspaper, Aug. 19, 1976, at p. 4. The debt/equity ratio was reported to exceed 3:1.

corporation to go public when the corporation failed to go public voluntarily after notification. On October 16, 1975, the MOF selected 105 corporations and notified them that they were required to go public by the first half of 1976.[190] Thirty-seven of these corporations failed to go public by the end of 1976. However, the MOF failed to issue a designation order to any of these corporations. The authority also failed to apply the sanctions of the GPEA to such corporations. Thus, the authority's policy of forcing corporations to go public lacked fairness and consistency.

In addition, public distributions were poorly managed. The public offerings were often closely bunched together in time. Furthermore, the prospectuses were not made available until a few days prior to the deadline for subscription.[191] These procedures should have been improved to enable the public investors to make well-informed investment decisions and thus to promote the securities market.

Finally, there were some cases reported in which corporations did not fulfill the terms of their public offerings. Some corporations which promised in their prospectuses to declare stock dividends subsequent to subscription failed to declare the dividends. However, neither the public nor the authority has sought any legal relief.

d. Corporate Bonds

Unlike that to offerings of equity securities, public response to offerings of corporate debt securities has not been improved. The low rate of subscription has placed great financial pressure on the underwriting companies which have had to hold large portions of unsold bonds on their own accounts.[192] The lack of public participation in the bond market is mainly attributable to three factors—low marketability, fixed interest rates, and lack of variety.[193]

---

190. *See* KSE, *Stock* (No. 102, Feb., 1977) at 33–34; *see also* Seoul Economic Newspaper, Feb. 27, 1977, at p. 4; Maeil Economic Newspaper, Dec. 30, 1976, at p. 3. In July 1, 1976, 101 additional corporations were selected to go public by the first half of 1977. Twenty of them went public in 1976.

191. Many corporations had prepared their prospectus a few days prior to the deadline for subscription because of a lack of regulation.

192. The underwriting had been performed mainly on a stand-by basis through August, 1974, and on only a firm commitment basis thereafter. *See* KSE, *Yearbook*, 385–94 (1976).

193. *See* Maeil Economic Newspaper, Dec. 30, 1976, at p. 3.

The types of corporate debt securities offered to the public have been limited. They are either guaranteed by commercial banks or the KIC or not guaranteed.[194] Convertible bonds are very rare.[195] The annual interest rate of the guaranteed bonds was fixed in 1974 at 18.6%; the rate for the general unguaranteed bonds, 19.5%.[196] The maturities of bonds were fixed between two and three years. Principal was paid in whole at the time of each maturity and interest was primarily paid on a quarterly basis. The Indenture Trustee Act[197] was promulgated in early 1962 to spur bond offerings. However, few corporations have offered under the Act. The reasons why persons did not use the system of indenture trustee are not clear.

Quite naturally, the public normally tries to invest in the most profitable investment opportunities. In 1976, the MOF raised the official interest rate on one year time deposits from 15% to 16.2%.[198] Thereafter, the curb rates of the private money market sharply increased in the first half of 1976, reaching an average of 3.05% per month.[199] The total amount of curb loans was estimated to be ₩ 200 billion in spite of the August 3 Emergency Decree. Due to sustained inflation, the fixed terms of corporate debt securities were not attractive to the public.

To facilitate public participation, the government in early 1976 gave the underwriting companies flexibility to set the interest rates within a limit of 15% to 21% per year.[200] The government has also

---

194. *See* KSE, *supra* note 192.

195. During 1976 only one company issued a convertible bond. At the end of 1976, only three among 180 listed corporate bonds were convertible bonds. *See* KSE, *Stock* (No. 102, Feb., 1977) at 75.

196. *See* KSE, *supra* note 192.

197. Law No. 991, promulgated on Jan. 20, 1962.

198. *See* Seoul Economic Newspaper, Aug. 1, 1976, at p. 1. The adjustment became effective on Aug. 2, 1976.

199. *See* Seoul Economic Newspaper, Oct. 7, 1976, at p. 1; *see also* The Korean Commerce and Industry Association (*Daehan Shankong Hoeuyso*) *"Survey Report on Private Money Finance"* (1976). According to the survey of 626 selected manufacturing industries, the average monthly interest rate in the private money market was as follows: 1.89% and 2.03% in the first and second halves of 1973, respectively; 2.02% and 2.33% in 1974; 3.01% and 2.87 % in 1975; and 3.05% in the first half of 1976.

200. *See* Seoul Economic Newspaper, Aug. 29, 1976, at 3. The notification was sent by the MOF on March 3, 1976.

Table 3.12 Key Statistics for Listed Stock (1972–76)

	End of 1972	1973	1974	1975	1976
A. No. of Listed Cos.	66	104	128	189	274
B. No. of Sec. Cos.	27	30	30	28	28
C. No. of SH's (10,000 persons)	10.3	19.9	19.9	29	56.6
D. No. of Listed Shares (million Shs.)	209	305	487	824	1,583
E. Capital Stock Listed (W billion)	174	251	381	643	1,153
F. Market Value of					
a. Total Listed Stock (W billion)	245	426	532	916	1,436
b. Par value of W 500	705	847	682	718	635
G. Sales					
a. Volume (million Shs.)	83	129	157	310	591
b. Value (W billion)	70	160	178	333	628
H. Turnover of Market Value (%)	38.8	44.5	38.1	48.3	53.7
I. Stock Price Index[a]					
a. Adjusted (W)	1,721	2,364	2,251	2,989	3,148
b. Composite Index	227.0	331.8	293.0	384.3	415.3
J. Average Annual Yield (%)[b]	13.8	7.3	13.2	12.9	13.2
K. PER (times)[c]	—	—	5.5	6.0	6.5

Sources: 1) KSE, *Securities Statistics Yearbook* (1976); BOK, *Economic Statistics Yearbook* (1976) for 1972–75.
2) KSE, *Stock* (No. 102, Feb., 1977) for 1976.

Notes: a; Stock Price Index = (current adjusted stock price average/base adjusted stock price average) ×100:
adjusted stock price average = prices at spot transaction of thirty-five issues with their par value/constant divisor; stock price average of W 758 as of January 4, 1972, was adopted as base; the constant divisor is adjusted in the same way as the Dow-Jones average in case of the ex-right or replacement of any adopted issue, etc.
b; Average Annual Yield = (average annual dividends per share/average stock price) × 100
c; Price Earning Ratio (PER) = stock price/earning per share after corporate income tax.
Figures stand for average PER in December of each year.

been considering devices to improve the marketability of debt securities. The issue is important because the bond market has become increasingly important in the mobilization of private resource due to the limited number of corporations eligible to be forced to go public. Also, most corporations were recently reported to prefer debt financing to equity financing.

B. *Secondary Market*

1. Stock Market

With the boom of the primary market, the activities of the secondary market expanded rapidly as shown in Table 3.12. The toal number of listed shares increased from 209 million shares of sixty-six companies in 1972 to 1,583 million of 274 companies in 1976. The total par value of listed stock increased from ₩ 174 to ₩ 1,153 billion during the same period. The total market value of listed stock increased from ₩ 245 to ₩ 1,436 billion. The trading volume increased from 83 million shares valued at ₩ 70 billion in 1972 to 591 million shares valued at ₩ 628 billion in 1976. Finally, the total number of shareholders of listed companies reached 566,000 persons at the end of 1976. Key statistics for listed stock during 1972–1976 are shown in Table 3.12.

Although the number of shareholders increased drastically during the years preceding 1976, the actual distribution of equity ownership deserves some comment. After the adoption of the proportional allotment system in March, 1976, the total number of shareholders exceeded a record one million at the end of August, 1976.[201] At that time, sixty-seven new companies had completed their public offerings and a larger number of odd-lot shares were available. However, by the end of December, 1976, the number of shareholders decreased to around 566,000. The "penetration ratio" of stock ownership compared to the total population of 35,000,000, is 1.6%. However, because the total number of shareholders was computed on the basis of official shareholders' registries, and many persons would be shareholders of several companies, the actual ratio would be much lower.

In addition, 40% of the total shareholders in 1975 held less than 100 shares. This 40% held only 0.6% of the total listed shares (*see* Table 3.13). On the other hand, 0.3% of the total shareholders held 56.1% of the total shares in 1975. Stock ownership showed increased concentration in 1976; 62.7% of the total shareholders owned 0.8%

---

201. *See* KSE, *Stock* (No. 102, Feb., 1977) at 72. The total number of shareholders at the end of August, 1976, reached 1,074, 811 persons.

Table 3.13 Distribution of Equity Ownership by Shareholding (1974–76)

Shareholding	End of 1974	1975	1976
A. Below 100 shares			
a. 100 persons	1,044.0 (52.5)	1,162.0 (40.0)	3,551.0 (62.7)
b. million shares	3.6 (0.7)	4.6 (0.6)	13.5 (0.8)
B. 100–1,000 shares			
a. 100 persons	669.0 (33.5)	1,253.0 (43.2)	1,351.0 (23.9)
b. million shares	20.0 (4.2)	40.0 (4.8)	43.0 (2.7)
C. 1,000–10,000 shares			
a. 100 persons	230.000 (11.6)	397.0 (13.7)	583.0 (10.3)
b. million shares	69.0 (13.8)	110.0 (13.1)	164.0 (10.2)
D. 10,000–100,000 shares			
a. 100 persons	46.0 (2.3)	83.0 (2.9)	150.0 (2.8)
b. million shares	119.0 (23.9)	216.0 (25.5)	407.0 (25.3)
E. Over 100,000 shares			
a. 100 persons	5.7 (0.3)	8.9 (0.3)	17.0 (0.3)
b. million shares	287.0 (57.4)	475.0 (56.1)	982.0 (60.9)
F. TOTAL			
a. 100 persons	1,996.0 (100.0)	2,906.0 (100.0)	5,663.0 (100.0)
b. million shares	501.0 (100.0)	846.0 (100.0)	1,613.0 (100.0)

Source: KSE, *Stock* (No. 102, February, 1977), at 74.

Notes: 1) Figures in parentheses indicate percentages compared to the total shareholders and shares outstanding.

2) The total number of shares includes non-listed shares.

3) "a" indicates No. of shareholders in 100 persons.

"b" indicates No. of shares in million shares.

of the total shares, and 0.3% of shareholders held over 60% of the total shares. Because these figures were also calculated on the basis of official shareholders' registries, the real degree of concentration would be greater due to hidden beneficial ownership. The changes in the distribution of stock ownership are shown in Tables 3.13 and 3.14.

2. Bond Market

Trading in both government and corporate bonds has been negligible compared with trading in equity securities. No corporate bonds were listed on the Exchange prior to 1972. Until 1968, the percentage of bond trading compared to total securities trading was below 0.1%. The percentage of bond trading increased rapidly after 1968 and peaked in 1972 at 17.4%. The percentage of bond trading thereafter dropped sharply again and returned to 1.7% in 1974. Trading in

Table 3.14 Distribution of Equity Ownership by Owners (1971–76)

End of—	1971	1972	1973	1974	1975	1976
A. Govt. &	62.0	69.0	63.0	76.0	117.0	263.0
Govt. Enterprises	(35.8)	(32.5)	(19.8)	(15.3)	(13.9)	(16.3)
B. Banking Institutions	24.0	20.0	25.0	29.0	68.0	125.0
	(14.0)	(9.5)	(7.9)	(5.8)	(8.1)	(7.8)
C. Securities Cos.	2.0	5.0	11.0	13.0	53.0	179.0
	(1.4)	(2.6)	(3.6)	(2.6)	(6.3)	(11.2)
D. Insurance Cos.	18.0	25.0	41.0	88.0	149.0	240.0
& Other Legal Persons	(10.7)	(12.1)	(13.0)	(17.7)	(17.7)	(15.3)
E. Individuals	65.0	91.0	176.0	289.0	448.0	782.0
	(37.5)	(42.6)	(55.1)	(57.8)	(52.9)	(48.5)
F. Foreigners	1.1	1.4	1.8	3.5	8.7	22.0
	(0.6)	(0.6)	(0.6)	(0.7)	(1.0)	(1.4)
TOTAL	175.0	213.0	320.0	501.0	846.0	1,613.0
	(100.0)	(100.0)	(100.0)	(100.0)	(100.0)	(100.0)

Source: KSE, *Stock* (No. 102, February, 1977), at 72.

Notes: 1) Figures in parentheses indicate percentage compared to the total number of shares, which includes non-listed shares.

2) Unit in million shares.

bonds expanded again during 1975–1976 to 5% of total trading (*see* Table 3.15).

The "turnover ratio," or trading value compared to the total value of bonds listed, was below 10% during 1973–1976. The turnover ratio of bonds was much lower than that of stocks. As noted earlier, such low marketability was caused by the available bonds' fixed rates of return and lack of variety.[202] Corporate bonds were less popular than government bonds. The average yield of government and public bonds on the market was higher than that of corporate bonds during 1975–1976. Some key statistics for listed bonds during 1971–1976 are shown in Table 3.15.

3. Securities Finance for Margin Trading

"Margin" is a credit device which allows a purchaser to trade in securities while paying less than the full purchase price.[203] The device is designed to facilitate securities trading on the Exchange. Investors in Korea may trade on margin by depositing a required margin with

---

202. *See* the accompanying text of note 193, *supra*.

203. For details, *see* pp. 273–78. Ch. 7, Sec. IV, *infra*.

Table 3.15 Key Statistics for Listed Bonds (1971–76)

Unit for sales value and amount outstanding in current ₩ billion

	1971	1972	1973	1974	1975	1976
A. Govt. & Public Bonds						
1. No. of Issues	55	80	128	197	234	254
2. Amount Outstanding	44	64	120	169	167	280
3. Sales Value	7.1	8.2	7.2	2.9	12.7	30.0
4. Average Yields (%)	—	—	17.5	20.9	21.1	21.6
B. Corporate Bonds						
1. No. of Cos.	—	12	14	42	71	105
2. No. of Issues	—	16	18	54	110	180
3. Amount Outstanding	—	4	5	22	52	118
4. Sales Value	—	0.1	0.2	0.2	0.6	6.6
5. Average Yields (%)	—	—	20.8	21.0	20.1	20.4
TOTAL						
1. No. of Issues	55	96	146	251	344	434
2. Amount Outstanding	44	68	125	191	220	398
3. Sales Value	7.1	8.3	7.4	3.1	13.3	36.6
4. Percentage in total Securities Trading (%)	17.4	10.5	4.4	1.7	3.8	5.5

Source: KSE, *Stock* (No. 102, February, 1977) at 72.

their brokers in a margin account. Margin trading is largely financed by the Korea Securities Finance Company (KSFC). Securities companies also extend credit to customers from their own funds.

Because low margin requirements result in destablizing stock prices, excessive speculation, or even market crashes, the MOF and KSE strictly control securities credit. The MOF sets the maximum amount of funds available for extending credit in accordance with market conditions. The KSE regulates the issues eligible for margin trading, permissible collateral loan value, and margin requirements. The lending limits and actual loans outstanding for 1974–1976 are shown in Table 3.16.

The power to control margin requirements and credit extension may be used effectively to stabilize market activities. But authorities in Korea appear to have used these tools too frequently. Twenty-three separate measures were announced for market administration in 1976 alone.[204] Of these measures, eleven changed margin require-

204. KSE, *Stock* (No. 102, Feb., 1977) at 34–37.

ments, eight adjusted the maximum amount of the KSFC's funds for margin trading, and five adjusted the maximum amount of funds of securities companies. It has been alleged that such frequent involvement in market activities probably discouraged or destabilized the prices and performance of the securities market.[205] Investors would not gain confidence in participating in the market due to such instability.

4. Securities Investment Trust

A securities investment trust is a diversified, professionally managed, mutual fund. Under the Securities Investment Trust Act (SITA) of 1969, the KIC began to operate securities investment trusts in May, 1970. This business lagged during the first several years because of the lack of recognition by public investors. To capitalize on the rapid expansion of the securities market, the Korea Securities

Table 3.16 Maximum Amount of Funds for Margin Trading and Loans Outstanding (1974–76)

Amount in current ₩ 100 mil.

End of	KSFC		Sec. Cos.	
	Max. Amount	Loans Outstanding	Max. Amount	Loans Outstanding
1974	100	95.7	20	34.8
1975	168	158.0	60	77.4
1976	200	195.0	110	45.7

Source: KSE, *Stock* (No. 102, February, 1977) at 77.

Table 3.17 Growth of Securities Investment Trust Funds (1970–76)

Amount in ₩ 100 mil.

End of	KIC	KSITC	KMBC	TOTAL
1970	1	—	—	1
1971	2	—	—	2
1972	4	—	—	4
1973	21	—	—	21
1974	21	46	—	67
1975	25	165	—	190
1976	80	399	10	489

Source: KSE, *Stock* (No. 102, February, 1977) at 101–108.

---

205. *See* Maeil Economic Newspaper, Nov. 9, 11, 1977, at p. 3.

Investment Trust Co., Ltd. (KSITC) was established in August, 1974. The securities investment trust industry attained a remarkably rapid growth in the few years following the KSITC's inception.

As shown in Table 3.17, the KIC started its business of securities investment trusts with ₩ 100 million investment. The KSITC launched its trusts with ₩ 4.6 billion in funds in 1974. The KIC's and the KSITC's funds grew rapidly to ₩ 8 and ₩ 39.9 billion, respectively, at the end of 1976. In late 1976, Korea Merchant Banking Corp.(KMBC) entered the business with ₩ 1 billion funds.[206] When the KIC was abolished in 1977, Daehan Securities Investment Trust Co., Ltd. (DSITC) was established to take over the KIC's securities investment trusts.[207]

---

206. *See Stock, supra* note 204, at 108. KMBC started a securities investment trust in November, 1976, with ₩ 0.5 billion in funds. The funds were increased to ₩ 1 billion in the next month.

207. *See id.* at 106–108. The DSITC began operating in mid-February, 1977.

Chapter 4

Major Reforms of the 1976 Amendments in the Securities Laws

Section I. *Background of the 1976 Amendments*

I. Role of the Securities Market in the Proposed Fourth Five-Year Economic Development Plan(1977~81)

During the third five-year economic development plan of 1972–1976, the percentage of total investment compared to GNP averaged 26.6%, and the annual rate of GNP growth averaged 11.1% in real terms. During the fourth five-year plan of 1977–1981, the government has set as its goals maintaining the percentage of total investment at 26.2% and achieving 9.2% annual GNP growth (*see* Table 4.1). The total resources needed for these investment goals are ₩ 18,008 billion in 1975 prices.

Under the proposed plan of capital formation as shown in Table 4.2, the government hopes to get ₩ 16,645 billion (92.4%) from domestic savings and the remainder (7.6%) from foreign savings.[1] To attain ₩ 16,645 billion in domestic savings, the government plans to mobilize ₩ 12,587 billion through private sector savings— ₩ 8,492 billion from corporations and ₩ 4,095 billion from households. The government hopes to reduce the share of foreign savings from 18.2% of total savings to minus 0.3% in 1981. The rate of private savings compared to GNP is projected at an average of 18.3% throughout the plan period.

The government placed the greatest financing burden on the

---

1. *See* EPB, *The Fourth Five-Year Economic Development Plan,* 31–32, 166–167 (December, 1976).

Table 4.1   Proposed Investment and GNP Growth (1977–81)

Amount in billion Won

	year	1977	1978	1979	1980	1981	average or total (1977–81)
A.	GNP[a]	11,486	12,520	13,647	14,875	16,214	—
	(Growth Rate)	(10.0)	(9.0)	(9.0)	(9.0)	(9.0)	(9.2)
B.	GNP per Capital ($)[b]	847	999	1,147	1,317	1,512	—
C.	Total Investment	3,097	3,294	3,540	3,855	4,219	18,008
D.	Shares of Investment (C/A)	27.0	26.3	25.9	25.9	26.0	26.2

Source: The Economic Planning Board (EPB), *The Fourth Five-Year Economic Development Plan*, 156–157 (December, 1976).

Notes: Figures are calculated at 1975 prices.

a; GNP deflator: 1975 = 1000, and 130.0, 142.9, 153.0, 163.7, 175.1 from 1977 to 1981.

b; The GNP per capital figures here are derived by converting the GNP in current prices in thousand won to U.S. dollars at the official exchange rate.

securities market. As shown in Table 4.3, it hopes to mobilize ₩ 5,095.2 billion through the issuance of securities during the fourth plan period. This amount is equivalent to 30.6% of total domestic savings, and 40.5% of total private sector savings, or 93% of the total amount of deposits in bank and non-bank financial institutions. Thus, the ability to raise the capital needed for the fourth five-year economic development plan depends largely on the performance of the securities market.

II. Purposes of the Reform

Due to the strenuous measures taken since late 1968, the securities market in Korea has shown a rapid growth. However, the rapid quantitative expansion produced various regulatory problems that needed reform if the projected performance of the market was to be met. The government began to enact new, far-reaching reforms. These reforms comprise amending the SEA and Decrees thereunder, the KSE Rules, the tax laws, and various other relevant laws. These amendments were completed by early 1977.

Table 4.2   Proposed Capital Formation for Investment (1977–81)

Amount in billion Won

Year	1977	1978	1979	1980	1981	average or total (1977–81)
A. Total Investment	3,097	3,294	3,540	3,855	4,219	18,008
	(27.0)	(26.3)	(25.9)	(26.0)	(26.0)	(26.2)
B. Domestic Savings	2,532	2,874	3,287	3,729	4,231	16,645
	(81.8)	(87.2)	(9.2.6)	(96.7)	(100.3)	(92.4)
1. Private	1,902	2,142	2,476	2,830	3,236	12,587
	(61.4)	(65.0)	(70.0)	(73.4)	(76.7)	(69.9)
2. a. Corporate	1,298	1,474	1,673	1,897	2,149	8,492
	(41.9)	(44.7)	(47.3)	(49.2)	(50.9)	(47.2)
b. Household	604	668	803	933	1,086	4,095
	(19.5)	(20.3)	(22.7)	(24.2)	(25.7)	(22.7)
3. Government	629	732	801	899	994	4,057
	(20.3)	(22.2)	(22.6)	(23.3)	(23.6)	(22.5)
C. Foreign Savings	565	420	261	125	–11	1,363
	(18.2)	(12.8)	(7.3)	(3.2)	(–0.3)	(7.6)

Source: EPB, *The Fourth Five-Year Economic Development Plan*, 166–167 (December, 1976).

Notes: 1) Figures are calculated at 1975 prices.

2) Figures in parentheses of items B and C indicate the share of respective savings in percent as compared to the total savings.

Table 4.3   Comparison of Proposed Finance by Sector (1977–81)

Amount in billion Won at 1975 prices[a]

Year	1977	1978	1979	1980	1981	total (1977–81)
A. Bank Deposit	587.0	642.0	706.9	790.0	872.8	3,598.7
B. Non-bank Deposit	272.1	317.5	379.5	418.7	491.9	1,879.7
1. Insurance & Trust	105.9	115.9	127.6	142.6	157.5	649.5
2. Other Deposit	166.2	201.6	251.9	276.1	334.4	1,230.2
C. Issuance of Securities[b]	727.0	845.4	989.3	1,164.2	1,369.3	5,095.2
D. TOTAL	1,586.1	1,804.9	2,075.7	2,372.9	2,734.0	10,573.6
E. C/D(%)	45.8	46.8	47.6	49.0	50.0	48.18

Source: EPB, *The Fourth Five-Year Economic Development Plan*, 170–171 (December, 1976).

Notes: a; The original figures calculated at current market prices are adjusted and converted into those at 1975 market prices.

b; Includes issuances of equity and debt securities which are non-public offerings.

Six major reforms were made.[2] First, the government reorganized the existing regulatory system to attain more effective supervision. Second, it introduced a device to guarantee continuing control by the incorporators of a corporation with shareholdings of 30% or less. Third, the government strengthened the supervision of the capital structure of listed corporations. Fourth, it improved the disclosure system in order to help public investors make investment decisions with access to relevant information. Fifth, the government designed new systems to ensure a fair trading order in the secondary market. Finally, it effected tax reforms mainly to facilitate decentralization of equity ownership.

Section II. *1976 Amendments of the Securities Laws*

I. Reorganization of the Regulatory Structure

A. Problems of the Existing Regulatory Structure

Prior to the 1976 Amendments, the government agencies which regulated the securities market were the MOF, the KIC, and the KSE. The MOF had supreme power to control and regulate the securities market as a whole. Both the KIC and the KSE performed supplementary roles under the control of the MOF. The KIC helped regulate the primary market; the KSE helped regulate the secondary market.

As the size of the securities market expanded rapidly, the government recognized that the existing regulatory system could not effectively handle the highly complicated work. There were only two Divisions with a total of eight staff members in the MOF's Securities Regulation Bureau.[3] Although the KIC and KSE played supplementary roles, the MOF urgently wanted to establish an institution similar to the SEC in the United States, hoping that the new institution would regulate the securities market more effectively.

---

2. *See* Dong-A Daily Newspaper (*Dong-A Ilbo*), at p. 3. July 29, 1976
3. The Securities and Insurance Bureau of the MOF contains two Securities Divisions. The First Securities Division deals with the primary market. The Second Securities Division regulates the secondary market. Each Division has only 4 staffs.

B. Establishment of the Securities Administrative Commission(SAC) and the Securities Supervisory Board(SSB)

1. Organization

The SAC was established as part of the SSB in February, 1977,[4] and is composed of six commissioners.[5] The outside three commissioners are the Governor of the BOK, the chairman of the KSE, and the Vice-Minister of the MOF. The inside commissioners are appointed by the President of Korea in accordance with the recommendation of the MOF for three years, staggered terms. The chairman of the SAC is appointed by the President from the three inside commissioners.[6]

The SSB was established as a special legal entity without any authorized capital in February, 1977[7]. The budget of the SSB depends on various commissions to be paid by other institutions.[8] In addition, the SSB may be financially supported by the government or the KSE[9]. The SSB has its principal office in Seoul and may be authorized by the MOF to establish regional offices.[10]

The SSB functions as the executive body of the SAC.[11] The SAC's chairman automatically becomes the SSB's Governor.[12] Two Vice-Governors are appointed by the MOF in accordance with the recommendation of the Governor. The Vice-Governors assist the Governor in administrating and controlling nine divisions of the SSB. The SSB has a total of twelve divisions and 206 employees.[13]

---

4. *See SEA*, Art. 119(2), Law No. 2920 as amended on Dec. 22, 1976; *see also* SSB, *Articles of Incorporation*, Art. 7.
5. *SEA*, Arts. 119, 123.
6. *Id.*, Art. 120(1).
7. *Id.*, Art. 131; *see also* SSB, *Articles of Incorporation*, Art. 3.
8. *See SEA*, Art. 143; *see also* SSB, *Articles of Incorporation*, Art. 33; *MOF Decree under the SEA*, Arts. 21 and 22. The commissions are an examination fee and a registration fee. The examination fee is collected from institutions which the SSB examines under the SEA. The registration fee is collected from registered corporations. In addition, the SSB may collect 2/13 of trading commissions from the KSE.
9. *SEA*, Art. 205.
10. *SEA*, Art. 130.
11. *Id.*
12. *Id.*, Art. 133.
13. *See* SSB, *Office Organization of the SSB.*

2. Status and Liability

Unlike the SEC in the United States, the Korean SAC does not constitute an independent, quasi-judicial agency. The SAC must immediately report its decisions to the MOF. The MOF may cancel or suspend part or all of a SAC decision when it deems the decision illegal or inappropriate.[14] Also, the MOF may, in the public interest or for the protection of public investors, request the SAC to take necessary measures.[15] In turn, the SSB is subject to the control and supervision of the SAC.

The commissioners of the SAC and certain employees of the SSB are deemed public officials for the purpose of criminal law.[16] Also, any present or former commissioners of the SAC and all the employees of the SSB are prohibited from disclosing or misusing inside information.[17] Furthermore, they are prohibited from selling or buying securities and from dealing with any securities institutions on their own account.[18] The SAC commissioners are also prohibited from participating in political activities.[19] In addition, they are given full term tenure except for misbehavior or for statutory disqualification.[20]

3. Extent of Powers and Duties

The SAC and the SSB were established to enforce the securities laws, and to ensure the efficient issuance and distribution of securities, fair trading, and supervision of the institutions involved in securities transactions.[21] The SAC's duties are limited to policy making in the area. The SSB enforces the policies of the SAC. The SAC and the SSB, unlike the SEC in the United States, are not independent and are subject to MOF's strong control.

As noted above, the powers of the SAC and SSB extend to the whole securities market. They also enact rules within the power mandated by the SEA and Decree thereunder. Under the SEA, Decrees and

14. *See SEA*, Art. 126(2).
15. *Id.*, Art. 126(3).
16. *Id.*, Arts. 127(1) and 144; *MOF Decree under the SEA*, Art. 23(1). The employees of the SSB here include two Vice-Governors, three Deputy-Governors, twelve division chiefs, and the heads of regional offices.
17. *Id.*, Arts. 127(2), 144 and 83; also *MOF Decree under SEA*, Art. 23(2).
18. *Id.*, and Arts. 83 and 42 of the SEA.
19. *Id.*, Art. 122.
20. *Id.*, Art. 124.
21. *Id.*, Art. 118(1).

their own rules, the SAC and the SSB (under the control of the SAC) administer and deal with matters, *inter alia,* as to (1) registration of the prospective issuers; (2) registration of securities being distributed, including designation of effective dates; (3) detection of illegal activities of the securities companies and other related institutions through inspection power, including discipline for any violations; (4) fair disclosure of information by listed and registered corporations; (5) supervision of over-the-counter (OTC) market trading; (6) registration and supervision of salesmen; and (7) fair disclosure in connection with tender offers and proxy solicitations.[22]

The SAC, unlike the SEC in the United States, was not given a quasi-judicial power. It may only arbitrate disputes arising from securities transactions in the market.[23] The SAC's Arbitral Committee consists of five members with one of the SSB's Vice-Governors always appointed chairman.

C. Reorganization of the KSE

Even though the KSE had been reorganized as a non-profit legal entity, some deficiencies remained. First, the Commercial Code's stock corporation rules were applied to the KSE's certificate of contribution and accounting procedure.[24] These rules, in particular the rule regarding declaration of dividends, in effect made the KSE a profit organization. Second, some KSE certificates remained in individual ownership.[25] The existence of private owners raised burdensome administrative problems such as leakage of confidential information and conflicts of interest.[26]

---

22. *See id.,* Art. 135; *see also* SSB, *Articles of Incorporation,* Art. 28.
23. *See* SAC, *Rules on Administration of the Arbitral Committee* (SAC Rule No. 2, promulgated on April 8, 1977).
24. *See Old SEA,* Art. 48, Law No. 2684, as amended on Dec. 21, 1974.
25. As of Dec. 13, 1976, the distribution of ownership in the KSE was as follows:
    (1) Government: 64.94%;
    (2) Securities Companies: 30.48%;
    (3) Individuals: 1.83%;
    (4) Institutions invested in by government: 1.34%;
    (5) Financial institutions and other corporations: 1.41%.
    Source: KSE.
26. The individual certificate-holders' major concern was naturally profit-oriented. They participated in the certificate-holders' general meeting and pressed the KSE to declare more dividends.

The 1976 SEA amendments deleted the application of the Commercial Code to the KSE.[27] Also, the KSE was empowered to redeem its certificates of contribution held by private persons.[28] On February 23, 1977, the KSE decided to redeem such private stock, thus enhancing its status as a non-profit organization. This redemption also eased the KSE of the burden of converting itself into a membership system in the future when it seemed appropriate in the public interest.

D. Abolishment of the KIC

The KIC was abolished in February, 1977, and its various functions were either transferred or allowed to lapse. The KIC's supervisory function over the primary securities market was transferred to the SAC and the SSB. Its business in securities investment trust was transferred to the Daehan Securities Investment Trust Co., Ltd. (DSITC), a newly chartered company. The Securities Training

Chart 1. Regulatory Structure of the Securities Market

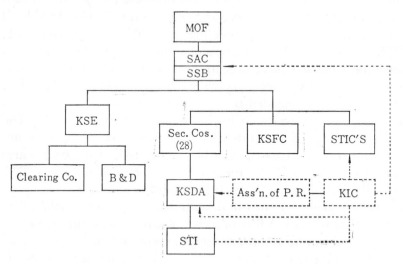

Note: Dotted arrow indicates the transference of the KIC's functions to other institutions.

---

27. *See SEA*, Art. 75. It required that those provisions governing an association incorporated under the Civil Code be *mutatis mutandis* applied to the KSE, unless otherwise specified in the SEA.
28. *Id.*, Addenda, Art. 11.

Institute (STI) attached to the KIC was transferred to the KSDA. Its function of guidance in securities analysis and pricing was also transferred to the KSDA. The remaining assets of the KIC were transferred to the SSB. KIC's other functions, including its underwriting, brokering and dealing, promoting, price stabilizing, consigning of government-owned securities, and guaranteeing of corporate debt securities, were abolished and left to other institutions.

Summary

The new regulatory structure of the securities market is illustrated in Chart 1. The SAC and SSB regulate, supervise, and control the whole securities market under the ultimate control of the MOF. The KSE also shares the regulatory function of the secondary market under the control of the MOF, SAC, and SSB.

II. Measures Taken to Warrant Continuing Control

A. Further Decentralization of Equity Ownership

Despite the strenuous effort of the government, the equity ownership of publicly-held corporations was excessively concentrated in a few controlling persons. Also, the penetration ratio of shareholders as compared to the total population was 1.6% as of December 31, 1976. In order to attain the goals of capital formation and the economic development plan, decentralization of equity ownership was considered urgently necessary to encourage public participation. The government amended the Corporate Income Tax Act to decentralize equity ownership further on November 29, 1976.[29] The amendment applied a tax rate which varied with the degree of equity ownership distribution—33%, when a controlling person's shareholding exceeded 35% of the total shares outstanding, and 27% when the shareholdings were below 35%.

Some obstacles were met in decentralizing equity ownership. The most critical one was a fear of secret takeover. Sometimes a person accumulated the stock through secret purchases in an effort to take control. Because of the lack of antitrust laws regulating monopolistic activities, a takeover is possible for any person who accumulates enough shares to control. To induce more controlling shareholders to lower their ownership to 35% or less, the government introduced measures designed to relax the danger of secret takeovers.

---

29. *See* KSE, *Stock* (No. 102, February, 1977) at 38.

B. *Measures Taken*

1. Restriction on Ownership Increases and Introduction of Tender Offers

The SEA prohibited shareholders from increasing their ownership beyond a certain limit.[30] A person who, at the time of listing, held more than 10% of the total number of voting shares issued and outstanding was prohibited from increasing his ownership. Shareholders holding more than 10% (10% shareholders) were required to report any changes in ownership to the SAC.[31] Shareholders holding less than 10% were prohibited from increasing their ownership over 10%. These maximum limits applied to direct and beneficial ownership of voting shares.

However, some exceptions to maximum ownership limit were provided because the restriction was intended to discourage secret takeovers.[32] First, any person may increase his shareholding beyond the limit through the solicitation of a tender offer.[33] Second, the limitation does not apply to a person purchasing directly from a shareholder who owned more than 10% at the time of listing. Third, the SAC may authorize special exceptions if there appears a reasonable case for ownership increases. Fourth, the limit does not apply to purchases from the government, government-owned corporations, or foreigners.

2. Limitation on Proxy Solicitation and Voting by Proxy

Because stockholders of large, publicly-held corporations do not gather together physically to elect directors or to vote on the matters of mutual concern, a surrogate mechanism was needed to allow all stockholders to be represented at a corporation's annual meetings. The proxy vote process fills that role. Like state corporation law in the United States, the Commercial Code in Korea permits stockholders to designate other persons to act as their agents at the meeting.[34] However, due to a lack of provisions relating to proxy solicita-

---

30. *See SEA*, Art. 200(1).

31. *Id.*, Art. 201.

32. *Id.*, Art. 200(2); *also see **Presidential Decree** under the SEA*, Art. 86, PD. No. 8436, as amended on Feb. 9, 1977.

33. Tender offers are to be regulated according to the SEA and Decrees thereunder. *See SEA*, Arts. 21–27.

34. *See Commercial Code*, Art. 368(3). In this case, a proxy-holder at a sharehold-

tion prior to the 1976 Amendments, shareholders as well as the management were able to solicit proxies without any limitation. They also could use the proxies for a variety of questionable purposes.

The 1976 Amendments regulated proxy solicitations for the first time in order to prevent possible abuses and discourage would-be takeovers. Persons soliciting proxies are required to file a statement with the SSB in compliance with the SAC Rules.[35] Information included in the proxy statement must not be false or misleading. It appears from the legislative history that the proxy rules were designed mainly to make minority takeovers more difficult. To further management control, the rule prohibited brokers and other securities institutions from soliciting proxies from beneficial owners of stock held in the street name.[36]

III. Improvement of the Disclosure System
A. Registration of Prospective Issuers

Prior to the 1976 Amendments, public investors in Korea were not well informed when closely-held corporations went public. Generally, the public did not have access to material information concerning a private corporation. No preliminary prospectus was required when a private corporation effected a public offering or secondary distribution. A final prospectus was usually not available until just a few days prior to a proposed deadline for subscription because the law did not compulsorily require advance delivery of a prospectus.[37] The pre-1976 rules did not compel fair and timely disclosure of information.

The 1976 Amendments required that certain corporations file

---

ers' general meeting must file a written statement establishing his power of representation.

35. *See SEA*, Art. 199; *see also Presidential Decree thereunder*, Art. 85.
36. *See* Draft Committee for 1976 Amendments of Securities Laws, *Basic Outline of Draft Amendments of Securities Laws*, Draft No. 60/200 (1976), at 10; *see also* Hyundai Economic Newspaper, Seoul, July 31, 1976, at p. 1. The category of shares whose voting rights could only be exercised if accompanied by proxies consists of those temporarily held by securities companies, a clearing company, the KSFC, or financial institutions.
37. *See Old SEA*, Arts. 7 and 8, Law No. 2684, as amended on Dec. 21, 1974. The issuer must prepare a prospectus when its registration statement becomes effective. The prospectus must be delivered to a purchaser only if the purchaser so requests.

registration statements with the SAC.[38] Those required to file a registration statement include: (1) corporations intending to list their securities on the Exchange; (2) non-listed corporations intending to make public distributions of any security; (3) non-listed corporations intending to merge or consolidate with listed corporations; and (4) other corporations designated by the SAC in accordance with the provision of the Presidential Decree.[39]

The SAC may require a corporation within any of the foregoing categories to register with it. Regsitration includes filing finanical statements, shareholders' registries, and other information required by Presidential Decree.[40] A corporation which fails to file the required documents with the SAC may be subject to borrowing restrictions by the MOF.[41] Also, any corporation failing to file with the SAC at least one year prior to a proposed public distribution of its securities may not be allowed to distribute the securities.[42]

The SAC may allow public access to the documents filed by a prospective issuer.[43] It also may advise registered corporations to change methods of corporate finance, to improve their capital structure, or to change other matters such as management or public ownership.[44] The adoption of this registration system of prospective issuers was based on two major concerns. The first was to provide potential investors in advance with relevant information. The second was to deter corporations with weak capital structures or earning capabilities from going public.

B. *Adoption of the Semi-Annual Report System*

Prior to the 1976 Amendments, listed corporations were required to file annual reports with the MOF and the concerned Exchange

---

38. *See SEA*, Arts. 3–6.
39. *Id.*, Art. 3.
40. *SEA*, Art. 4; *Presidential Decree thereunder*, Art. 4.
41. *See* MOF, *"Unpublished Documents Prepared for Policy Questions Concerning the Amended SEA,"* at 21–22 (1976).
42. *SEA*, Art. 9(3). For details, *see* p. 151, *infra*.
43. *Id.*, Art. 5.
44. *See id.*, Art. 6; *Presidential Decree thereunder*, Art. 5. Thus, the SAC may affect any capital increase by a registered corporation, including a declaration of stock dividends, and even the issuance of debt securities. However, there is no provision specifying the extent to which the registered corporations would be bound by the SAC's recommendation on the matter.

within the three month period after the expiration of each fiscal year.[45] Since there was no requirement for filing a periodical report, timely and fair disclosure of material information was not ensured. The 1976 Amendments required listed corporations to file with the SAC and the concerned Exchange current and bi-annual reports.[46]

C. Adjustment of Information in a Prospectus

Prior to 1976 the information in a prospectus did not differ from that in a registration statement. The SEA exempted information relating to military secrets or other areas approved by the SAC for exclusion from the prospectus.[47] The exclusion of the former was to protect the national interest due to Korea's peculiar military situation. The purpose behind the latter exclusion, however, is not clear. It is probably to encourage going public by permitting an issuer to keep certain information relating to its business or trade secrets upon showing justifiable reasons.[48]

D. Strengthened Supervision of CPA Auditing

Prior to the 1976 Amendments, all financial documents were required to be audited by qualified, certified public accountants designated by the MOF.[49] The MOF supervised auditing. It was empowered to order the CPA's to submit relevant reports or materials. The MOF, however, was hindered in its supervision by limited manpower and the highly complicated nature of the work involved.

The 1976 Amendments gave the SAC MOF's supervisory function over CPA auditing.[50] The government hoped to ensure the thoroughness of auditing through the strengthened supervision of the SAC. The 1976 Amendments also let corporations choose their own CPA firm from the registered firms. The requirements for the registration of CPA firms are strict, and the MOF may reject or cancel a

---

45. *See Old SEA*, Art. 78, as amended by Law No. 2684 on Dec. 21, 1974.
46. *See SEA*, Arts. 92 and 93.
47. *Id.*, Art. 12; *Presidential Decree thereunder*, Art. 6.
48. Quite naturally, most issuers in Korea are reluctant to disclose material information relating to their business secrets. But the exclusion of material information may raise serious obstacles to investor protection.
49. *See Old SEA*, Art. 126–2, as amended by Law No. 2481 on Feb. 6, 1973.
50. *See SEA*, Art. 182. But the MOF may still issue an order to a CPA with respect to the proper performance of auditing.

registration.[51]

IV. Measures Taken to Ensure Fair Trading

A. Restriction on Insider Trading

Prior to the 1976 Amendments, there was no prohibition against insider trading in the SEA. Even though insider trading is hard to detect, some insider trading has been revealed which hurt public investors. To ensure equality of bargaining power and fair trading, the introduction of provisions like Section 16(b) and Rule 10b-5 of the American securities law appeared essential.[52]

The 1976 Amendments adopted a provision prohibiting short-swing trading by corporate insiders.[53] This provision was modeled substantially after Section 16(b) of the Securties Exchange Act of 1934. Officers, employees, or major shareholders (direct or indirect owners of more than 10%) of listed corporations are prohibited from realizing profits by using inside information, from a purchase and sale or a sale and purchase of an equity security of such corporations within a six month period. A corporation or its shareholders (derivatively) may bring a suit to have profits returned to the corporation. Without clear reason, however, the legislature did not adopt a Rule 10b-5 type of prohibition.

B. Regulation of Trading in the Over-the-Counter (OTC) Market

Prior to the 1976 Amendments, the SEA granted the MOF broad power to regulate the OTC market.[54] The SEA, however, did not

---

51. *See id.*, Art. 182(1) and (2); *Presidential Decree thereunder*, Art. 82; *MOF Decree thereunder*, Arts. 26–28 and 32. The minimum number of CPAs to be qualified for firm registration is five. CPA firms are classified into four categories based on the number of CPAs in their employ: a firm with 5–9 CPAs can audit listed corporations with total assets of W 10 billion or less; a firm with 10–19 CPAs can audit those with total assets of W 30 billion or less; a firm with 20–30 CPAs can audit those with total assets of W 50 billion or less. Only an incorporated firm with more than 30 CPAs can audit corporations of any larger size.

52. *See Securities Exchange Act of 1934*, Secs. 16(b), 10(b), and Rule 10b-5 thereunder, 15 U.S.C.A. §78 p(b), j(b), and 17 C.F.R., §1240, 10b–5.

53. *See SEA*, Art. 188(2) and (3). But a U.S. Rule 10b-5 type of prohibition was not introduced. For details, *see* pp. 380–86, *infra*.

54. *See Presidential Decree under the Old SEA*, Art. 55–2, PD No. 6634, as amended on Apr. 29, 1973; *Old SEA*, Art. 93.

provide the MOF with any specific guidelines for exercising its power so that no detailed regulation followed. Only one provision of the SEA prohibited securities companies from speculating in the OTC market.[55]

The legislature recognized the important role of the OTC market in the performance of the government's fiscal and monetary policies. The MOF hopes to organize the OTC market to perform open market operations that would control the currency in circulation.[56] It also hopes to mobilize a large portion of capital resources needed to implement the economic development plan by distributing public bonds through the OTC market.

The 1976 Amendments gave the SAC broad rule-making power in the OTC market.[57] The SAC was empowered to enact rules concerning the method of trading, clearance, and other matters necessary for the functioning of the OTC market. The SEA also limited market trading to securities issued by listed and registered corporations. Thus, the registration requirement of prospective issuers gained importance in promoting the OTC market although the legislature failed to provide sufficient measures to protect investors.[58]

C. Restriction on Reciprocal Equity-Holding (Shang-Ho-Joo Boyou)

Controlling shareholders of a listed corporation frequently held equity securities of another listed corporation whose controlling shareholders held equity securities of the former in a reciprocal arrangement. This reciprocal equity-holding among listed corporations was used as a means of disguising a corporation as public. For example, a controlling shareholder of corporation A entrusts a large block of his shares to a controlling shareholder of corporation B; under the reciprocal arrangement A's controlling shareholder is entrusted to hold the shares of B's controlling shareholder. Through this reciprocal shareholding, both corporations could meet the formal requirement of a publicly-held corporation that a controlling shareholder hold below 51%. This practice significantly undermined the basic

---

55. *See Old SEA*, Art. 41, Law No. 2066 as amended on Dec. 31, 1968.

56. *See* Seoul Economic Newspaper, Feb. 23, 1977, at p. 1.

57. *SEA*, Art. 194.

58. The need for adequate protection of the public interest will be discussed below. *See* pp. 235–44, Chapt. 7, *infra*.

policy goal of going public. It also resulted in a shortage of trading stocks in the market.

The 1976 Amendments prohibited reciprocal stock ownership arrangements.[59] Only two exceptions to the prohibition of reciprocal-holding were provided in the Presidential Decree.[60] First, a securities company or a financial institution licensed by the MOF to engage in securities business may purchase the equity securities of a listed company for the purpose of selling. Second, a listed corporation may hold equities of another listed corporation in reciprocity, but the percentage of its holding must not exceed 1% of the total outstanding shares.

D. Strengthened Regulation of Securities Companies

As noted earlier, the SAC and SSB succeeded to the MOF's supervisory functions over securities companies. They (mainly the SSB) were empowered to inspect the business and portfolio management of securities companies.[61] Other important amendments followed to broaden regulation of the securities industry.

1. Limitation on Employees' Securities Transaction

Prior to 1976, officers and employees of securities companies were not prohibited from dealing in any securities for their own accounts. They were only prohibited from having credit extended to them by their company in connection with margin trading.[62] However, it was not difficult for them to avoid such prohibition, and profit at the expense of public investors, by using their advantageous positions.

The 1976 Amendments prohibit the officers or employees of securities companies from purchasing or selling any securities for their own accounts with the following exceptions: (1) maintaining a securities saving plan up to a certain percentage of their salary; (2) having transactions in government bonds, municipal bonds, debt securities issued by a special legal entity chartered by a special law, securities investment trust certificates, or a security (including equity interest) issued by a corporation which has not been listed on an Exchange or registered with the SSB; (3) acquiring securities through

---

59. *Id.*, Art. 189.
60. *See Presidential Decree under the SEA*, Art. 84.
61. *See SEA*, Arts. 53 and 54.
62. *See Old SEA*, Art. 26–2, Law No. 2481 of 1973.

an inheritance, gift, or the exercise of a collateral right, and selling such securities; and (4) dealing in securities upon receipt of the SAC's approval therefor.[63]

2. Restriction on Investment Recommendation for Customers

The MOF, prior to 1976, was empowered to issue an order prohibiting a securities company from excessive speculation or from the use of dishonest devices to mislead public investors.[64] However, there was no specific rule concerning undue recommendations or solicitations by the employees of a securities company for customers' investment decisions.

The amended SEA introduced a new provision which sets a standard of unsuitable solicitations or recommendations for the investment decisions of customers.[65] Officers or employees of a securities companies are prohibited from: (1) soliciting business by promising customers to bear all or part of the loss which might be caused by the transaction; (2) will-fully making a false statement of a fact or quotation of a price, or misusing these statements and quotations in connection with any security transaction to get unjustifiable profits; and (3) acting in contravention of the investors' protection or principles of fair trading, or in detriment to public confidence in the securities business in connection with any securities transaction. A violation of these provisions is subject to a criminal sanction. However, the SEA's disciplinary rules do not include revocation or suspension of the license or dismissal of an officer. Nor does the SEA provide an appropriate civil remedy for the injured party.[66]

3. Measures Taken to Enhance Public Confidence

The 1976 Amendements require that a controlling shareholder of a securities company get the SAC's approval when he transfers his

---

63. *SEA*, Art. 42; *Presidential Decree thereunder*, Art. 35.

64. *See Old SEA*, Art. 35; *Presidential Decree thereunder*, Art. 32.

65. *See SEA*, Art. 52. Although the Korean law was modeled after the Japanese Securities and Exchange Act, the regulation of unsuitable solicitation under the two laws varies significantly. *See Japanese Securities and Exchange Act* (hereinafter "*Japanese SEA*"), Art. 50, Law No. 25, as promulgated on Apr. 13, 1948, and as amended by Law No. 5 on Mar. 3, 1971. For details, *see* pp. 258–61, Chapt. 7, *infra*.

66. *See* pp. 235–44, *infra*.

shareholdings.[67] The SAC's power to approve any change in control of a securities company is parallel to the MOF's power to examine statutory qualifications for any entry into securities business. Such administrative control is an indication of a strong concern to restrict any transfer of control to a person who lacks statutory qualifications for the securities business. In order to enhance public confidence in securities companies, the 1976 Amendments also make the controlling shareholder jointly liable for any damages caused by a tortious act of a director or auditor in the course of business.[68] Furthermore, licenses for securities businesses were classified into three categories based on the amount of legal capital.[69] This was to improve the financial capabilities of securities companies by inducing capital increases.

V. Tax Reform
A. Discriminating Corporate Income Tax Rates

Until the 1976 tax reform, the tax code did not favor the highly decentralized ownership distribution of publicly-held corporations. The Corporate Income Tax Act was amended in 1976 to facilitate the decentralization of equity ownership. The amended Act provides discriminating corporate income tax rates in accordance with the degree of ownership decentralization.[70] When a controlling shareholders of a publicly-held corporation holds below 35% of the total voting shares outstanding, the old tax rates are applied; but when his shareholding exceeds 35% of the total voting shares outstanding, an increased tax rate is applied as shown in the following tax table.

B. Personal Income Tax Act Reform

1. Increased Personal Income Tax Rates toward Certain Stock Dividends

---

67. *SEA*, Art. 28(6). A "controlling shareholder" was to be determined by reference to Article 39 of the Basic National Tax Act. *See Presidential Decree*, Art. 19.

68. *SEA*, Art. 58. Under Article 38–2 of the old SEA, the controlling shareholder of a securities company was not liable for such damages.

69. *See id.*, for details, *see* p. 244, *infra*.

70. *See Corporate Income Tax Act*, Art. 22(2), Law No., as amended on Nov. 11, 1976. This amended Act became effective on Jan. 1, 1977. But the operation of the provision concerning the discriminating corporate income tax rates was suspended for two years for existing publicly-held corporations. *See* Addenda, Arts. 1 and 3.

Prior to the 1976 Amendments, the shareholders of publicly-held or listed corporations had personal income taxes imposed on their dividend income at the following rates: 5% for a minority shareholder holding below 3% of the total voting shares issued and outstanding; 10% for shareholders other than the foregoing minority share-holders.[71]

The amended Personal Income Tax Act increased the tax rates on stock dividends converted from any reserved asset revaluation surpluses.[72] Under the amended tax table, minority shareholders pay 10% taxes on such dividend income. Shareholders other than minority shareholders pay 25% taxes on the same income. The main reason for this amendment was to discourage the controlling share-holders of publicly-held or listed corporations from watering their capital stock by excessive conversion of asset revaluation surpluses into capital.[73]

The coverage of the provision, however, contained critical lo-opholes. First, it excluded the controlling shareholders of a registered corporation which is a prospective issuer. These shareholders can avoid higher taxes when they effect stock dividends by converting reserved revaluation surpluses prior to going public. Second, the provision excluded stock dividends financed by converting earned

Table 4.4   Comparison of Old and New Corporate Income Tax Tables

Taxable Income (TY)	Old Table	New Table
A. TY < W 5 million	20%	1. 20%[a]
		2. 25%[b]
B. TY ≥ W 5 million	27%	1. 27%[a]
		2. 33%[b]

Notes: a; Applies to a publicly-held corporation whose controlling shareholder holds below 35% of the total voting shares issued and outstanding.

b: Applies to a publicly-held corporation whose controlling shareholder holds between 35%~51% of the total voting shares.

71. *See Personal Income Tax Act,* Art. 22(2), Law No. 2796, as amended on Dec. 22, 1975. Such taxes, unlike those in the United States or Japan, where capital gains taxes are imposed on dividends recipients, must be withheld by the corporation at the time of dividend payments.
72. *See id.,* as amended on Nov. 29, 1976.
73. *See* KSE, *Stock* (No. 102, Feb., 1977) at 38.

surplus reserves into capital stock. These loopholes create the possible danger of watering stock or impairing capital structure. Such critical loopholes should be seriously reconsidered by the legislature.

2. Relaxation of Tax on Certain Earned Surplus Reserves

Prior to the 1976 Amendment, the shareholders of all the business corporations other than publicly-held corporations were required to pay income taxes on the so-called "paper-dividends."[74] Only shareholders of a publicly-held corporation were exempt from the coverage of such income taxes. The amended act extended the coverage of the exemption to the shareholders of a listed corporation or a corporation in the process of reorganization.[75] It also exempted the amount of earned surplus reserves from the amount of taxable incomes for paper dividend tax purposes. These relaxations were to increase the amount of retained earnings or reserved surpluses for the improvement of corporate capital structure.

---

74. "Paper-dividends" occur when a corporation sets aside profits realized in a fiscal year in excess of the amount legally required. *See* note 38, Ch. 3, *supra*.
75. *See Personal Income Tax Act*, Art. 26(2).

Part Two

Legal Analysis of Securities Laws and Problems Raised

Chapter 5

An Introductory Note: Coverage of Securities and Laws Applicable to Securities Transactions

Section I. *Coverage of Securities*

Article 2(1) of the Securities and Exchange Act (SEA) was amended in 1976 to define the term "securities" as: (1) government bonds; (2) municipal bonds; (3) bonds or notes issued by a legal entity which is chartered by a special law; (4) corporate bonds or debentures; (5) certificates of capital contribution issued by a legal entity which is chartered by a special law; (6) certificates of stock or certificates representing subscription rights for new shares; (7) securities or certificates issued by a foreign country or foreign juridical person which are designated by the MOF; and (8) other securities or certificates as designated by a Presidential Decree.[1] A Presidential Decree designated beneficiary certificates issued under the Securities Investment Trust Act or Trust Business Act as securities within the purpose of the SEA.[2]

The SEA definition of "securities" adopted the limited enumeration approach following the model of Article 2(1) of the Japanese SEA.[3] This limited enumeration approach should be contrasted with

---

1. *SEA*, Art. 2(1).
2. *Presidential Decree under the SEA*, Art. 2.
3. *See Japanese SEA*, Art. 2(1). Securities enumerated in items 1 through 6 of the Japanese Article are almost identical to those in the Korean SEA. Item 7 enumerates the beneficiary certificates of securities investment trust or loan trust. The similar types of beneficiary certificates in Korea are designated by

that of the United States. The Securities Act of 1933 defines the term "security" broadly.[4] The Congress, aware of the states' experience with their blue sky laws, defined the word "in sufficiently broad and general terms so as to include within that definition the many types of instruments that in our commercial world fall within the ordinary concept of a security."[5]

Because of the limited, enumerative definition of the term "securities" in Korea, disputes arise among commentators in determining the coverage of securities regulation. One possible argument for increased regulation is that the securities enumerated in the SEA are merely examples and thus the term "securities" includes other debt or equity instruments not enumerated[6]. This argument is especially cogent when there is a need for the protection of investors. Those opposed to regulation may argue that the term "securities" as defined in the SEA cannot be expanded beyond the types of instruments listed.

The legislative history of the SEA does not provide any relevant indication on the question. The only expansive device provided is

---

a Presidential Decree as securities. Item 8 covers securities issued by a foreign country or foreign juridical person and treats these foreign securities the same as domestic securities. Finally, item 9 covers other securities as designated by a Cabinet Order.

4. *See Securities Act of 1933*, Sec. 2(1), 15 U.S.C.A. §77b(1). As amended in 1934, the term "security" is defined as "any note, stock, treasury stock, bond, debenture, evidence of indebtedness, certificate of interest or participation in any profit-sharing agreement, collateral-trust certificate, preorganization certificate or subscription, transferable share, investment contract, voting-trust certificate, certificate of deposit for a security, fractional undivided interest in oil, gas, or other mineral rights, or in general, any interest or instrument commonly known as a "security" or any certificate of interest or participation in, temporary or interim certificate for, receipt for, guarantee of, or warrant or right to subscribe to or purchase, any of the foregoing."

5. *See* H. R. Rep. No. 85, 63d Cong., 1st Sess. (1933) 11; 1 L. Loss, *Securities Regulation*, 455(2nd ed. 1961). The states' problems were created by various special types of legitimate financing, and by the fringe operators who would treat any definition of "security" in orthodox terms as an invitation to evade the statute by employing other kinds of instruments.

6. Thus the definition of securities may include preorganization certificates or subscriptions, voting trust certificates, certificates of deposit, temporary or interim certificates, receipts for securities, evidence of indebtedness, guarantees, interest in partnerships or non-stock corporations, warrants, and so on.

item 8 of Article 2(1) which provides that a Presidential Decree may "designate" any other securities as necessary or appropriate.

Moreover, it would be difficult, without explicit provision of the SEA or specific designation by a Presidential Decree, to include generally an instrument, investment contract, or other certificate representing indebtedness or right of interest within the statutory definition of the term "securities," and thus to subject these instruments to administrative regulation as well as to civil or criminal liability.[7] Therefore, it is reasonable to see why the legislature took the limited enumeration method in defining the term "securities."

Section II. *Soures of Law*

I. Primary Sources

A. Securities and Exchange Act(SEA) of 1962, Decrees and Rules Thereunder

The major source of Korean securities laws is the SEA of 1962. The 1962 SEA was modeled after the Japanese SEA of 1948, which was in turn modeled after the American securities laws, principally the Securities Act of 1933 and the Securities Exchange Act of 1934.[8] The 1962 SEA regulates both new issues in the primary market and trading of outstanding securities in the secondary market.

The Presidential and the Ministry of Finance(MOF) Decrees, promulgated to enforce the 1962 SEA, also constitute major sources of Korean securities laws. These Decrees, like SEC Rules and Regulations in the United States, amplify the basic securities laws with more detailed regulation. The MOF may also issue orders pursuant to authorization by the 1962 SEA or Decrees thereunder.[9] As the top regulatory body for securities administration, the MOF, is required

---

7. Such construction of the law is also supported by most scholars in Japan. *See* Misao Tatsuta, *Securities Regulation in Japan* 17 (1970) [hereinafter referred to as "Tatsuta"].

8. *Id.*, at 6.

9. These orders differ from "releases," which are announcements by the MOF with respect to the construction of securities laws. The latter does not constitute a direct source of law. It merely reveals guidelines for regulation or construction of law.

to exercise this regulatory power in the public interest and for the investor protection.

The Securities Administrative Commission(SAC), the Securities Supervisory Board (SSB), and the Korea Stock Exchange (KSE) also have various rules and regulations relating to the performance of their duties. These rules and regulations are promulgated with the MOF's approval within the regulatory framework of the SEA. These rules, so long as they do not conflict with the provisions of the SEA, constitute supplementary laws.

B. Other Special Statutes

Various special statutes, resulting from the strenuous governmental effort to promote securities markets in Korea, also regulate the securities markets. These special laws include the Capital Market Promotion Act(CMPA) of 1968, the Going Public Encouragement Act (GPEA) of 1972, the Securities Investment Trust Act(SITA) of 1969, the Trust Indenture Act(TIA) of 1962, and the Public and Corporate Bonds Registration Act (PCBRA) of 1970.[10] Korea has no counterparts to the United States Investment Adviser Act of 1940, the Investment Company Act of 1940, and the Public Utility Holding Company Act of 1935.[11]

C. Self-Regulation

The Korea Securities Dealers Association(KSDA) has its own charter, rules, and regulations to govern its members. The KSDA's members include securities companies (all the twenty-eight existing securities companies are now also KSE trading members) and other financial institutions authorized to do securities business by the MOF. Among other things, the KSDA rules include membership requirements, disciplinary rules, just and fair principles of trade, and rules on underwriting and securities analysis for determining offering prices. These KSDA rules must comply with the SEA's provisions, and the KSDA's rule-making power must be supervised by the SAC.

However, the KSDA, unlike the National Association of Securities Dealers(NASD) in the United States or the Securities Dealers

---

10. For the SITA of 1969 and the TIA of 1962, *see* pp. 83–91, *supra*. The PC-BRA of 1970 was promulgated to simplify the issuance procedure of the bonds and to secure the bondholders' rights. *See* Law No. 2164 as promulgated on Jan. 1, 1970.

11. *See Commercial Code*, Arts. 46 and 47.

Asssociation of Japan(SDAJ), has not yet functioned as a supervisor of trading in an over-the-counter(OTC) market because the authorities in Korea have not yet organized such a market. Recognizing the vital functions of an OTC market, the authorities are now considering how to structure an efficient OTC market.

II. Secondary Sources

A securities transaction constitutes a "commercial matter(*Shangsha*)" under the Commercial Code, and thus is regulated to some extent by the Code, especially by provisions on stock corporations. Therefore, in the absence of an express statutory provision or relevant court decision interpreting the primary securities laws, commercial laws apply to securities transactions. If there are conflicts in the commercial laws, the order of application is first, the Commercial Code; second, the customary commercial law if there is no explicit provision in the Commercial Code; and finally, the civil laws, including the Code of Civil Procedure.[12]

---

12. *Id.*, Art. 1.

Chapter 6

Regulation of the Distribution of Securities

Section I. *Introduction*

I. Basic Structure of the Law Governing the Primary Securities Market

The Securities Act of 1933 in the United States, dealing with the primary securities market, had two basic legislative objectives. One was to compel the disclosure and dissemination of relevant information about securities being distributed to the public. The other was to proscribe the fraudulent interstate sales of securities. To attain these objectives, the Act prohibits offers or sales of a security unless the issuer has complied with these registration and dissemination requirements. Also, it includes several antifraud provisions which greatly expand the common law concept of fraudulent behavior. These provisions also indirectly compel disclosure of information which might not otherwise become available.

The SEA, being substantially borrowed from the United States and Japan, took an approach similar to the American securities laws and governs both primary and secondary markets much like the Japanese SEA. The first three Chapters, which deal mainly with the primary securities market, can be divided into provisions compelling the disclosure and dissemination of relevant information about securities being distributed and provisions barring fraudulent sales of securities.

Another important source of Korean securities laws affecting the primary securities market includes a series of special laws enacted because of some unique circumstances in the society. Through these special laws, the government strongly involves itself in the process of going public.

II. Strong Government Involvement in Going Public: Designation Orders and Issuer Registration

Going public, an efficient means of corporate finance, involves a public offering or secondary distribution of securities. The basic process of effecting the public offering or secondary distribution generally consists of three major steps: preliminary activities, including underwriting; processing of the registration; and distribution of the securities concerned. In these respects Korea is not an exception.

Few corporations in Korea voluntarily went public prior to 1968 because of their fear of losing control or suffering troublesome intervention in management. This traditional reluctance to go public caused excessive leverage of the capital structure of most business corporations, which brought them to the verge of bankruptcy. Because the government has recognized a significant role of the securities market in effectuating economic development plans, it has since 1968 enacted a series of special laws involving it in going public. Responding to the meager response to various incentives provided by the CMPA of 1968, the government in 1972 approached the problem more drastically.[1] The GPEA of 1972 empowered the MOF to issue "designation orders" to force certain corporations to go public, subjecting those remaining private to punitive measures.[2] The 1976 Amendments added a registration system of prospective issuers to the SEA.[3]

As a consequence of these enactments, certain large privately-held corporations in Korea are required to register with the SAC at least one year prior to going public. Through the SAC authority to select such corporations under Article 3(1) of the Presidential

---

1. For various incentives provided in the CMPA of 1968 and responses by the business community thereto, *see* pp. 47–49 and 54 *et seq. supra.*
2. For details of policy measures included in the GPEA of 1972, *see* pp. 64–68 *supra.*
3. For details of registration system, *see* pp. 102–103 *supra.*

Decree, 111 corporations have registered by April 16, 1977.[4] Of
these registered corporations, the SAC selects certain blue-chip
corporations and notifies them to go public within a certain period.[5]
As a last resort, the MOF may force those remaining private to go
public by issuing a designation order. However, few actual designations have been ordered.[6]

The registration requirement for prospective issuers has two major
purposes: enabling public investors to be familiar with the issuers
before the securities issue, and strengthening the SAC's supervisory
function over capital structure, corporate finance, and management
of registered corporations. A corporation subject to this requirement
must submit financial statements, shareholder lists, and other documents prescribed by the Presidential Decree ("registration documents").[7] The public may inspect these documents filed with the

---

4. *See Presidential Decree under the SEA*, Art. 3(1); Seoul Economic Newspaper,
   April 15, 1977, at p.4. Article 3(1) of the Presidential Decree, the SAC may
   select corporations and require them to register with it if any corporation:
   1) whose capital (the sum of legal capital and reserved surpluses) exceed ₩
   200 million; 2) whose sales volume during the last fiscal year (when any
   fiscal year is a six-month period, the late subsequent two fiscal year) exceeds
   ₩ 1 billion; 3) whose total amount of loans from financial institutions exceeds
   ₩ 1 billion; 4) belongs to a group of affiliated corporations whose total
   amount of loans from financial institutions exceeds ₩ 5 billion; 5) whose
   cash loan agreement for capital goods inducement contract, authorized under
   the Foreign Capital Inducement Act, exceeds U.S. $2 million; 6) which is
   designated as a person engaging in a monopolistic or oligopolistic business
   under the Act on Price Stabilization and Fair Trading; and 7) whose usual
   employees are not less than 1,000 persons.
5. The added standards for the selection of blue-chip corporations which are to
   be notified and forced to go public are: 1) the sales volume must exceed ₩
   3 billion per year; 2) the rate of net profits as compared to legal capital must
   exceed 30% for the last fiscal year. But these standards were reported to be
   unreasonably strict because only six among the 111 registered corporations
   met the standards. For details, *see* Seoul Economic Newspaper, April 16,
   1977, at p.4; *also see* p. 66 *supra*, the accompanying text of note 114.
6. The MOF appears to induce and persuade more private corporations to go
   public voluntarily rather than resorting to a compulsory measure. Although
   some selected corporations have failed to go public within a notified period,
   few designations occured.
7. Other documents required to be filed by Article 4 of the Presidential Decree
   include short statements as to the issuer's business operation and facility, and

SAC. However, this registration system differs significantly from that of the United States. The SEA does not impose rules for periodic reports, proxy solicitation, short swing profits, and ownership change reports as the American securities laws do.[8] The Korean statute requires the corporations to report any material changes in the registration documents filed, but does not exact further disclosure.

III. Special Problems under the Commercial Code

The provisions of the Commercial Code affecting corporations, similar to state corporation laws in the United States, create some technical hurdles to going public. The Code's "authorized capital system" requires that corporations' articles of incorporation state the total number of authorized shares ("authorized capital stock") and the total number of shares to be issued at the time of incorporation ("legal capital" or "capital stock" in a narrow sense). It also requires that more than half of the total authorized shares be issued and paid in full at the time of incorporation.[9] The board of directors may increased legal capital by issuing more authorized shares unless prohibited by the Commercial Code or articles of incorporation.[10] The board may issue new shares beyond the total number authorized, however, only by increasing that total through a special shareholders' resolution.[11] New shares may be issued at a price below par only when two years have elapsed after the incorporation, shareholders have passed a special resolution, and a court of competent jurisdiction has

---

CPA's auditing report if the issuer is subject to such auditing.

8. *See Securities Exchange Act of 1934*, Secs. 12(g), 13(a), 14, 16, 15 U.S.C.A. §78 1(g), m(a), n,p. For the insufficiency of the disclosure rule and the lack of other protecting devices for investors in Korea, *see* pp. 242–44 *infra*.

9. *See* Ch. 2, note 27 *supra* and its accompanying text; *also see Commercial Code*, Arts. 289, 415, 317(2).

10. *Commercial Code*, Art. 416.

11. *Id.*, Art. 434. A special resolution must be adopted by more than two-thirds of the votes of shareholders present who hold shares representing more than one-half of the total number of shares issued and outstanding. Further, a substance of any proposal relating to the amendment of the articles of incorporation must be notified in writing to each shareholder at least two weeks prior to the day set for such meeting. In addition, a public notice is required when a corporation has been issued a share certificate to bearer. *See id.*, Arts. 433 and 363.

granted permission.[12]

A public issue of new shares creates a conflict with existing share-holders' preemptive rights. The Commercial Code gives existing shareholders rights to subscribe pro rata to new shares, unless the articles of incorporation specify otherwise[13]. This provision protects the existing shareholders' interest in corporate control and property.[14] Under the Code persons other than existing shareholders could not have subscription rights for new shares unless the articles of incorporations expressly authorize.[15] Because the charters of Korean corporations rarely authorize subscription rights for nonshareholders, amendment of the articles of incorporation is a prerequisite to a public offering.

Some close corporations, however, appear to have gone public by only a resolution of the board of directors, without shareholder amendment of their articles of incorporation. Similarly, some public corporations have publicly distributed their newly issued shares through an underwriting syndicate without these procedures. Although no action has been brought to dispute their validity, these noncomplying offerings raise serious legal questions which should

---

12. *Id.*, Art. 417.
13. *Id.*, Art. 418.
14. *See* Ton K. Suh, *Commentary on Commercial Law, Vol I (Sangbub Kangeuy, Sang Kwon)* 383 (5th rev. ed. 1973) [Hereinafter cited as "Suh, *Commentary I*"].
15. There, however, had been strong disputes among commentators as to whether preemptive rights of existing shareholders can be deprived of by the articles of incorporation. A minority opinion argued negatively on the ground that the preemptive right is a kind of unique right attached to an absolute share-holder's right. In respect to adoption of the authorized capital system and Art. 418 of the Commercial Code, a corporation may give subscription rights to the public in accordance with the special resolution of a shareholders' meeting approving the relevant amendment to the articles of incorporation. This is the present custom of a public offering to mobilize the capital from the public. Another peculiar view is that the subscription rights to new shares of third person should be limited to specified person such as present and former employees, or present and former officers; unless articles of incorporations limit it so, the provision should be null and void. *See* Suh, *Commentary I* at 383; *also see* Hi Chul Chung, *Commentary on Commercial Law, Vol. I (Sangbub Yoron, Sang)* 408 (4th rev. ed. 1972) [Hereinafter cited as "Chung, *Commentary I*"]. But professor Chung exempts the public from the coverage of "third person" here.

be clarified by a court or the legislature.

Section II. *Coverage of Regulation*

I. Definition of Basic Legal Terms

A. Public Offering and Secondary Distribution

The SEA defines a "public offering" of any security as "solicitation toward many and unspecified persons for their offers to acquire any security to be newly issued under uniform terms."[16] The solicitation must be directed toward "many and unspecified persons."[17] The object of the offering must be a new security. And the terms of the offering, including the price and the conditions of acceptance and issuance, must be uniform for every purchaser.

The SEA defines the term "secondary distribution" as "any offer to sell or solicitation for offers to buy an outstanding security to many and unspecified persons under uniform terms."[18] Unlike a public offering, the object of distribution must be limited to a security which has already been issued and outstanding.

B. Issuer

The SEA defines an "issuer" as "any person who has issued or intends to issue any security."[19] Since a natural person cannot issue any security, the phrase "any person" in the definition of the issuer means only a "legal entity" such as a corporation. It does not add any of the other modifications or specifications for certain types of securities which appear in the Securities Act of 1933,[20] since such securities are not common and do not fall within the term "securities" as defined in Article 2(1) of the SEA.

Furthermore, the SEA and Decrees thereunder, unlike the American Act, do not expand the concept of an issuer to include any natural or legal person, directly or indirectly controlling or controlled by the issuer, or any person under direct or indirect common control

---

16. *SEA*, Art. 2(3).
17. The phrase "many and unspecified persons" of Article 2(3) and (4) has been substituted for the word "public" by the 1976 Amendment.
18. *Id.*, Art. 2(4).
19. *Id.*, Art. 2(5).
20. *See Securities Act of 1933*, Secs. 2(1) and (4), 15 U.S.C.A. §77 b(1), (4).

with the issuer.[21] Yet the definition of an issuer is of cardinal importance to the private placement exemption because it determines whether an offer or sale of a security issued by a person falls under that exemption. This definition also is vital to prevention of evasion of registration requirements.

Indeed, a great potential for evading the registration requirement exists in Korea because of such a simple definition of an "issuer" and the filing requirement of the registration statement. It is required under Article 8(1) of the SEA that an issuer file a registration statement with the SAC when the total amount of a public offering or secondary distribution of any security, or an issuance of new shares of a listed corporation exceeds W 50 million.[22] Thus, persons directly or indirectly controlling or controlled by the issuer, or persons under direct or indirect common control with the issuer may distribute a large block of shares to the public through a security firm or any other person without filing a registration statement. Since these entities do not constitute issuers under present law, their transactions are not influenced by criminal sanctions against nonregistration[23] or civil liability for any material representations in the registration statement.[24]

C. Underwriters and Underwriting

Until 1976 the SEA did not explicitly define "underwriting". Article 2(6), amended in 1976, now includes within its definition of "underwriting": (1) acquiring all or a part of a security when issued from the issuer with a view to distributing it; (2) entering into a contract at the time of issue to acquire remaining shares if the security is not fully distributed; or (3) making an arrangement on behalf of an issuer for public offering or secondary distribution of a security, or participating directly or indirectly in a public offering or secon-

---

21. *See Id.*, Sec. 2(11). 15 U.S.C.A. §77 b(11).
22. *See* the accompanying text of note 86 *infra*.
23. *See SEA*, Arts. 208, items 1 and 2, and 213. Any violator of Article 10 must be subject to the imprisonment not exceeding two years or the penalty of a fine not exceeding W 2 million, or both.
24. Under Article 14 of the SEA providing civil liability, an issuer of a security who has made an untrue statement of a material fact in a registration statement or a prospectus must be liable for damages sustained by the person who acquired such security. For details, *see* pp. 154–61 *infra*.

dary distribution, and receiving a commission or remuneration therefor in excess of the usual and customary distributors' or sellers' commission.[25] As in the United States or Japan, the definition of "underwriting" includes the concept that the underwriting commission must be in excess of the usual and customary distributors' or sellers' commissions.[26] The SEA defines "underwriter" as "any person who performs any item of the said underwriting."[27]

The type of underwriting generally varies with the type of underwriter, i.e., whether he acts as a wholesaler, a wholesaler and a retailer, or a retailer. It varies also with whether he acquires securities for his own account, or acts as an agent for the issuer. Under the amended SEA, securities companies[28] are classified in their MOF

---

25. *SEA* Art. 2 (6). The definition of the term "underwriting" has been modeled after the former provision, Art. 2(5) of the Old SEA, which provided the term "underwriter" by eliminating only the phrase "any person who." The term "underwriter" under the old SEA was defined as "any person": 1) who acquires, at the occasion of issuance of any security, all or a part of the security from an issuer with a view to distributing the same; 2) who enters into a contract to acquire the remainder if the security concerned is not fully distributed; or 3) who makes arrangement on behalf of an issuer for a public offering or secondary distribution of any security, or other person who participates directly or indirectly in the public offering or secondary distribution of any security to receive a commission, remuneration, or any other consideration *in excess of the usual and customary distributors' or sellers' commission.* (emphasis supplied.) *See* Art. 2(5) of the old SEA as amended on Dec. 21, 1974.

26. *See Securities Act of 1933*, Sec. 2(11). 15 U.S.C.A. §77b(11); *see also Japanese SEA*, Art. 2(6). This is probably because not only the service of an underwriter is more complicated but also the risk involved is higher than that of a broker or dealer.

   In the first drafted Bill of the 1976 Amendment of the SEA, the phrase "in excess of the usual and customary distributors' or sellers' commission" was deleted. *See* the first drafted Bill for the 1976 Amendment of the SEA, Art. 2(6); *see also* Maeil Economic Newspaper (*Maeil Kyongje Shinmoon*), Oct. 9, 1976, at p.3.

27. *SEA.*, Art. 2(7).

28. The term "securities company" is defined in the SEA as "any stock corporation which is authorized to engage in certain securities businesses under the Law. *See SEA*, Arts. 2(9) and 28(1). In turn, the term "securities business" is defined under Article 2(8) of the SEA as a business of a person who engages in any of the following:

licenses as performing different functions depending upon the total amount of their legal capital.[29] Only companies whose legal capital exceeds ₩ 3 billion can engage in an "underwriting business" as well as brokerage and dealership; a company with legal capital below that amount but above ₩ 2 billion can function as a broker and dealer; but a company whose legal capital is above ₩ 500 million, but below ₩ 2 billion can function only as a dealer. A literal interpretation of this three billion capital requirement for an underwriting business would bar small security companies from participating in an underwriting syndicate. However, the MOF and the SAC have allowed small companies to perform underwriting business other than as a managing underwriter in compliance with the provisions of the KSDA's Agreement on Underwriting Business.[30]

Under the KSDA's Agreement, an underwriting syndicate and a subunderwiring syndicate or selling group perform underwriting and distribution of securities.[31] The underwriting syndicate consists of managing underwriters and members. Because of strict requirements for the eligibility, only nine companies function as managing underwriters (the "big–seven" securities companies, the Korea Short-Term Investment & Finance Corp., and Korea Merchant Banking Corp).[32]

---

1) buying or selling securities;
2) buying or selling securities on consignment;
3) buying or selling securities as a broker or agent on behalf of the person who entrusted;
4) acting as a broker, agent, or proxy with respect to the sale or purchase of any security on the Exchange;
5) underwriting any security;
6) effecting a secondary distribution of any security; or
7) arranging for an offering or secondary distribution of any security.

29. *SEA*, Art. 28(3). For the background behind the policy, *see* p. 109 *supra*.
30. *See* KSDA, *Agreement on Underwriting Business*, Promulgated on March 18, 1977, as amended on April 18, 1977; *see also* Maeil Economic Newpaper, March 16, 19, and 22, 1977, at p.3.
31. *See id.*, esp., Arts. 4 and 5 of the Agreement.
32. *Id.* Under Article 7 of the Agreement on Underwriting Business, a company can function as a managing underwriter, if:
   1) its legal capital exceeds ₩ 3 billion; however, the capital may be more than ₩ 2 billion by January 1, 1980;
   2) it has more than ten professional accountants and security analysts, including at least three certified public accountants;

Of these nine companies, the company who has been entrusted with underwriting responsibilities by the issuer functions as a "principal" managing underwriter; two other companies, upon the designation by the KSDA, function as "co-managers."[33]

The managing underwriters analyze and price the securities, assume any unsold part of securities underwritten, and perform "market formation" activities for a newly listed security if necessary.[34] They can form their underwriting syndicate and selling group with securities companies, banking institutions, trust companies, Short-Term Investment & Finance Corporations (STI&FC), merchant banking corporations, and securities investment trust companies.[35] Institutions other than securities companies, however, must receive MOF authorization for participation. Securities investment trust companies can participate only in underwriting of corporate bonds, and persons other than the "big-nine" companies cannot participate in an underwriting syndicate for equity securities.

Korean law, unlike the securities laws in the United States and Japan, does not segregate banking and securities businesses.[36] Even when the SEA had a provision that apparently assumed seperation in defining "securities business" prior to 1976, the SEA lacked any provision which explicitly prohibited certain financial institutions (including banks and trust companies) from engaging in the securities business as Article 65 of the Japanese law provides.[37] This situation

---

3) it has been audited by an outside CPA firm and the result of the auditing is satisfactory.

33. The purpose of the KSDA's designation appears to deter excessive competition among the managing underwriting community.

34. *See* KSDA, *Agreement on Underwriting Business*, Arts. 4 and 8–10. For the term "market formation," *see* pp. 224–25 *infra*.

35. *Id.*, Arts. 5 and 6.

36. In the United States, for the purpose of protecting the interest of depositors, all the companies engaged in the business of receiving deposits had to stop underwriting, except for government and municipal securities and a few other special types, with the divorcing of commercial and investment banking under the Banking Act of 1933. *See Banking Act of 1933*, Sec. 24(7), 12 U.S. C.A. §24(7). But Japan does not completely segregate the businesses. For the segregation in Japan, *see* note 37 *infra*.

37. In Japan, banks, trust companies, and other financial institutions as designated by a cabinet order cannot engage in "securities business," including

probably reflects the considerable shortage of investment banking funds that has rapidly increased with the boom in public distribution of securities since 1972. Indeed, commercial banks and other financial institutions have played a significant role in the investment banking business in Korea.

The 1976 Amendments eliminated the phrase implying the segregation of banking and securities businesses, and added a new provision to the SEA. Banks, trust companies, STI&FC's, and other financial institutions permitted by a Presidential Decree may engage in securities business upon the MOF's authorization.[38] The MOF authorized the STI&FC's to participate in underwriting beginning on

---

underwriting except for government and few other special types of securities, since Congress adopted Article 65. Article 65 was borrowed from the American Banking Act of 1933, but does not restrict acquisition of securities for an investment purpose. The provision of Article 65 provides that a bank may engage in sales of a security upon a written order of its customer, and that a bank, trust company, or other financial institutions designated by a cabinet order may buy and sell securities for the purpose of investment or in the account of a person who makes *cestui que* trust pursuant to a trust agreement. Thus, the goal of Article 65 might lie in improving the business conditions of securities companies by enlarging their range of transactions rather than in protecting bank depositors as sought by the United States Act. *See Japanese SEA*, Art. 65; *also see* Tatsuta, 39–40.

However, the legislature in Korea has never adopted a provision like Article 65 of the Japanese SEA, and in practice banking institutions have largely engaged in the underwriting business. Article 2(6) of the old SEA, as amended on Feb. 6, 1973, provided: "securities business in this law shall mean a business of a person *other than a bank, trust company or other financial institutions* as may be designated by a Presidential Decree who engages in any item enumerated in the following: 1) to buy or sell any security; 2) to buy or sell any security on a consignment of other person for his account; 3) to act as a broker, agent, or proxy with respect to buying or selling transactions of any security; 4) to underwrite any security; 5) to arrange for a public offering or secondary distribution of any security; and 6) to act as a broker, agent, or proxy with respect to entrusting of buying or selling transactions of any security on a security market. (Emphasis mine.) Legislative intention is far from clear since no material on the matter is available. It seems to be modeled after Art. 2 (8) of the Japanese SEA. Also, no financial institution had been designated by a Presidential Decree in accordance with Art. 2(6) of the old SEA.

38. *SEA*, Art. 29(1).

March 28, 1977.[39] This arrangement creates a significant problem for the wider applicability of the SEA, because Article 29(2) expressly states that only the securities business chapter of the act (Chapter 5) applies to the authorized business of such financial institutions.[40]

The SEA also produces the possible problem of disclosure rule evasion by companies enjoying the private placement exemption because of the narrow definition of the term "issuer."[41] An actual underwriter may evade the prospectus delivery requirement and any risk of civil liability for misrepresentation by purporting to facilitate a private placement.[42]

II. Exemption From Registration Requirement
A. Exempted Securities

Provisions for filing a registration statement and providing a prospectus are not applicable to some securities. These securities include government bonds, municipal government bonds, bonds or notes issued by the government or any legal person in accordance with a special law, investment trust certificates or notes issued by a legal person established under a special law, and other securities designated by Presidential Decree.[43] The reasons for this exemption are that these securities are safe by nature and sufficient information already is disclosed.

The trust certificates of securities investment trust companies were designated as a category of securities by Presidential Decree in 1977, and they were included as a category of exempted securities from registration under the SEA.[44] However, full disclosure of a trust fund's portfolio and management is important for the investment decisions by public investors. Hence the exemption should be reap-

---

39. *See* Maeil Economic Newspaper, March 28, 1977, at p.3.
40. *SEA*, Art. 29(2).
41. *See* the accompanying text of note 21 *supra*.
42. Civil liability of an underwriter under the SEA is limited to the misrepresentation by way of using prospectus. *See SEA*, Art. 14. For details, *see* pp. 154–61 *infra*.
43. *SEA*, Art. 7.
44. *Presidential Decree under the SEA*, Art. 2, as amended on Feb. 9, 1977, by PD No. 8436.

praised in the interest of protecting investors.

Several questions remained unresolved. Perhaps, public corporations meeting continuing disclosure requirements under the SEA should not be subject to registration requirements for new issuances of their securities, because this registration requirement generates complexities, excessive costs and double registration.[45] Simplification of registration or else a temporary exemption should be considered to avoid unnecessary complexities of administration when continuing disclosure has been met or when preferred payments of debt securities of corporations are highly guaranteed or warranted.[46]

B. Exempted Transactions

1. Private Placements

The SEA does not refer to "private placements" or "private offerings." However, it provides an exemption for private placements by construction of such sentences as "any public offering or secondary distribution . . . shall not be effected unless the issuer files the registration statement"[47] or "the issuer whose registration statement has become effective shall prepare a prospectus prior to the public offering or secondary distribution."[48] Because the SEA defines public offerings or secondary distributions as distribution to "many and unspecified persons," the legislature apparently intended an exemption for private placements.[49]

Unlike the situation in the United States, however, no specific rule or standard has been adopted for determining when an offering is private.[50] The only statutory criterion is the "many and unspecified persons" rule pertaining to a public offering or secondary distribution. An offer or solicitation to buy or sell a security is a private placement if it is presumably made toward a "small number of specified

---

45. In the United States, the registration statement is largely simplified in this case.
46. In Japan, the temporary exemption for secured corporate debentures and corporate debentures having statutory guaranty with respect to their preferred payment was introduced in 1953, except convertible debentures. Since the provision exempted most corporate debentures from registration, Prof. Tatsuta argued critically for its elimination. *See* Tatsuta, 20 and n. 15 therein.
47. *SEA*, Art. 8(1).
48. *Id.*, Art. 12.
49. *See* the accompanying text of notes 16 and 18 *supra*.

persons." In practice, however, it is difficult to decide whether offerees in a complicated transaction are "small" or "specified." For example, it is hard to determine whether an offer or solicitation toward existing shareholders, employees, or customers is a private placement, without more specific and precise standards.[51]

The question is important because of the great potential for evasion of registration requirements and civil liability created by the narrow definitions of the terms "issuer" and "underwriter". Indeed, under the present structure of regulation, it is not difficult for any controlling person to evade the registration requirement and civil liability under the pretext of a private placement. The only feasible resolution is new legislation providing specific standards.

2. Small Issues

A public offering or secondary distribution of any security, or an issuance of any new shares by a listed corporation, requires the filing of a registration statement with the SAC. An issuer whose total offering or secondary distribution is less than ₩ 50 million, however, may file a notification statement in lieu of a registration statement.[52] To prevent evasion of the registration requirement by splitting offerings to get the amount below ₩ 50 million, the provision of notification statement must not apply to an issuer whose total public offerings of the same class of a security during one year, including the amount of the offering concerned, exceeds that amount. However, it is difficult to understand why no analogous provision exists to guard against the same evasion in secondary distributions.[53]

---

50. *See Securities Act of 1933*, Sec. 4(2) 15 U.S.C.A. §77 d(2), and SEC Rule 146 thereunder.
51. *See S.E.C. v. Ralston Purina Co.*, 346 U.S. 119 (1953). There the court noted that the exemption must be interpreted in the light of the statutory purpose to "protect investors by promoting full disclosure of information thought necessary to informed investment decisions" and held that the applicability of the exemption should turn on whether the particular class of persons affected needed the protection of the Act. The exemption does not deprive corporate employees, as a class, of the safeguards of the Act, though some employee offerings may come within the exemption (e.g., one made to executive personnel).
52. *SEA*, Art. 8(1), proviso and *MOF Decree* thereunder, Art. 2, MOF Decree No. 267 promulgated on May 30, 1962, as amended by MOF Decree No. 1232 on February 15, 1977.
53. *See MOF Decree, supra*, Art. 2(1) and (2).

When a notification statement is filed by an issuer, the notification statement becomes effective on the date of its receipt by the SAC.[54] In addition, such an issuer is not required to prepare a prospectus.[55] Although there might be some defects in the form required or omissions of material facts, the law does not require the issuer to submit any amendments to the notification statement filed and does not impose civil liability for any damages from misrepresentation or omission of a material fact in the notification statement. These defects in the rule should be seriously reappraised for better protection of public investors.

3. Other Exempted Transactions

The registration and prospectus requirements should not apply to certain transactions despite the absence of a provision in the SEA for exempted transactions. These exempted transactions include: 1) transactions by any person other than an issuer, underwriter, or dealer; 2) dealers' transactions or any transactions by a securities company, except through direct or indirect participation in a public offering or secondary distribution of any security which it has underwritten; and 3) brokers' transactions executed upon customers' orders on any exchange or in the over-the-counter market, except the solicitation of such orders.

The SEA, however, should have explicitly provided these exemptions as American law does.[56] Unless these exemptions are clearly specified, risk of evasion and disputes will likely arise, especially in the case of an exempted transaction of a dealer, or former underwriter.

Section III. *Securities Analysis for Determination of Offering Prices*

I. KSDA's Rules

A. Pricing Formula and Application

Analysis of the value of any security to be distributed among the public and determination of its offering price are critically important

---

54. *SEA*, Art. 9(1).
55. *Id.*, Art. 12. It provides that only the issuer whose registration statement has become effective must prepare a prospectus.
56. *Securities Act of 1933*, Sec. 4. 15 U.S.C.A. §77d.

issues for the protection of public investors and for the promotion of the securities market. Overpricing hurts public investors and the securities market; underpricing, on the other hand, hurts the interest of existing shareholders and discourages corporations from going public. Reconciling these conflicting interests is essential in a securities analysis to determine offering prices. Pricing of an equity security is more important and complicated and thus deserves detailed discussion.

When an effectively functioning securities market exists, offering a comparable price, it would be reasonable to refer to the market price in valuing and pricing securities. In Korea, however, where the securities market has not been extremely thin but its functioning has been imperfect, application of such a method is impossible or meaningless. Therefore, pricing prior to the 1976 Amendments was based mainly on the intrinsic value of the stock concerned, and was determined by both the quantitative and qualitative analyses of the business. The intrinsic value was primarily based on the earnings evaluation of the stock concerned and secondarily on asset value.[57] The comparative value could be reflected only when more than two similar issues engaged in the same field of business were listed on the KSE. Since no detailed rule followed on the determination of the comparative value, the offering prices were wholly based on the intrinsic and asset values.

Through the KIC the government strictly controlled the securities analysis and pricing. The KIC reanalyzed every preliminary price analysis made by the managing underwriter to prevent possible overpricing.[58] As a consequence of this conservative evaluation policy and supervision, public participation in the market has been greatly expanded. However, some practices detrimental to the interest of public investors and the promotion of the securities market have occurred, such as the frequent practices of watering stock and

---

57. KIC, *Rules on Securities Analysis*, Arts. 3, 7–11 and 11–2 (promulgated on March 31, 1973, as amended on Sep. 19, 1975). It was required under Article 5(5) of the then Agreement on Underwriting Business that any underwriter (managing) follow the KIC Rules on Securities Analysis in evaluating and pricing a security.

58. *See* pp. 78 *et seq. supra.*

disguising corporations as public.[59]

Following the 1976 Amendments, the government in 1977 amended the rules concerning securities analysis in an effort to eliminate shortcomings and to discourage the frequent cases of evasion.[60] First, the securities analysis and pricing are subjected to self-regulation by the KSDA. Second, comparative value may be more clearly reflected in the offering price than permitted under the KIC's Rules. Third, the analysis and pricing must be performed by three managing underwriters, including one principal manager; the KIC reanalysis has been abolished.

Under the KSDA's Rule on Securities Analysis, the pricing is still based largely on the intrinsic value of the stock concerned, which is determined by the same formula provided by the KIC's Rules. The asset and comparative market values are partly considered. The intrinsic value of a stock is generally defined to mean the present value of expected returns which in turn depends on the degree of risk deciding a capitalization rate. Also, the growth rate of the corporation is an important factor considered in evaluating the expected returns. Basically, the KSDA's Rule follows this concept in evaluating an intrinsic value, but asset value must be partly reflected.[61]

The profitability value, asset value, and comparative market value of common stock under the KSDA's Rules are evaluated in compliance with the following formulas:[62]

1. Profitability Value (expected earnings) per share $= \dfrac{\text{expected average dividends per share (E)}}{\text{capitalization rate (\%)}}$

   $= E \times K(\text{multiplier})$

2. Asset Value per share $= \dfrac{\text{net asset value} + \text{amount of capital raised through the proposed public offering or secondary distribution}}{\text{total number of shares outstanding} + \text{number of shares proposed to be issued}}$

---

59. *See id.*
60. *See* KSDA, *Agreement on Underwriting Business; Rules on Securities Analysis* (promulgated on March 27, 1977).
61. KSDA, *Rules on Securities Analysis*, Art. 9(1)(2).
62. *Id.*, Arts. 10–12.

$$
\begin{array}{l}
\text{3. Comparative Market} \\
\text{Value per share}
\end{array}
=
\left\{
\begin{array}{c}
\dfrac{\text{market price of the comparative issue}}{} \times \left(\dfrac{\text{earnings per share of the issuer}}{\text{earning per share of the comparative issuer}} \right. \\[2em]
+ \left. \dfrac{\text{net asset per share of the issuer}}{\text{net asset per share of the comparative issuer}} \right)
\end{array}
\right\} 1/2
$$

In turn, Earnings, "E", is defined as the weighted arithmetic mean calculated from the probable dividends as estimated in the prospective financial statements of the first and second subsequent years at a weighting ratio of 3 to 2 in the following formula:[63]

$$ En = \frac{(Y - T - L - B - A)}{N} $$

where: En = total amount of expected dividends of each year;
      Y = expected net profit at the end of each fiscal year;
      T = corporate taxes due;
      L = losses being carried over;
      B = bonuses or other extra compensations other than regular wages for the officers and directors; and
      A = "profitability adjustment factor" reflecting probable risks respectively.

"A" in turn is calculated as follows:

$$ A = (Y - T - L - D - t - B) \times 1/4, $$

where: D = amount of special depreciation provided as a privilege;
      t   = amount of exempted taxes.
      Finally, the interest rate on one-year time deposits is to be used for the capitalization purpose.[64]

The net asset value used for asset value analysis is to be calculated on the basis of the latest financial statements in the following formula:[65]

Net asset value= Total Value of Assets — (the value of absolute intangible assets + some deferred accounts + total liabilities +

---

63. KSDA, *Specific Standards under the Rules on Securities Analysis* (promulgated in 1977) Art. 7.
64. *Id.*, Art. 8.
65. *Id.*, Art. 11.

> taxes due + bonuses and other extra compensations +
> dividends expected to be declared for the period) ± (the
> amount of surplus decreased or increased for the period +
> special profits or losses + reserved surplus)

The market price of the comparative issue selected is to be the average closing price during the latest six months.[66] Earnings per share is to be calculated on the basis of the financial statements for the past two calendar years.

The profitability, asset, and comparative market values per share thus calculated are to be used for the pricing according to the following standards:[67]

a) if asset value ≥ profitability value, the profitability value must be used;
b) if asset value < profitability value, an arithmetic mean must be used;
*c) if comparative market value ≥ profitability value, an arithmetic mean must be used; and
*d) if comparative market value < profitability value, the comparative market value must be used.

* Items (c) and (d) above were added by the KSDA in its 1977 Amendments to reflect the market prices of the comparative issues.

A syndicate of managing underwriters must appropriately determine the offering price in consultation with the issuer within the limit of the foregoing standards;the offering price thus determined must not exceed double the asset value.[68] When a dispute over the offering price arises among the managing underwriters as to the determination of the offering price because of different results from their independent analysis, the KSDA must arbitrate.[69]

B. Enforcement Procedures

If a significant overestimation of expected earnings or other malpractice should lead to an overpricing, the SAC under the SEA may not designate the effective date of the registration statement filed therewith or may withhold the proposed public distribution. The determination of such significant overestimation is left to the SAC's discretion. By May 15, 1977, three of eleven proposed distributions were not allowed by the SAC due to overestimation. In addition, the underwriters who delivered the defective prospectus may

---

66. *Id.*, Arts. 9–10.
67. KSDA, *Rules on Securities Analysis*, Art. 17.
68. KSDA, *Agreement on Underwriting Business*, Art 9; *Rules on Securities Analysis*, Art. 18. Any offering with premiums must be determined as 30%, 50%, 70%, or 100%, etc. over par value of the stock.

under the SEA be liable for damages sustained by purchasers due to any material misstatement or omisson of a fact.[70] The enforcement of rules governing underwriting business, however, is largely left to the KSDA and the Association of Managing Underwriters (AMU) themselves.

The KSDA's Agreement on Underwriting Business (hereinafter "Agreement") became effective as a self-regulatory rule by virtue of agreement among the nine managing underwriters and the KSDA.[71] The foregoing underwriters and the KSDA constitute the AMU; but AMU is subjected to the KSDA's control.[72] The KSDA may enact specific rules to enforce the Agreement and must report the rules to the SSB.[73] Also, the KSDA has a broad power to investigate any violation of the Agreement and must immediately report the results of investigations to the SSB.[74] However, the Agreement gives disciplinary power only to the AMU and includes no provision for KSDA disciplinary power.[75] Although uncertainty remains as to the relationship between the disciplinary powers given to the two self-regulatory bodies, the KSDA is empowered with strong disciplinary powers under Article 48 of its Articles of Association to expel its members, suspend memberships, or issue warnings.[76]

The KSDA's Agreement prohibits members from promising to underwrite any security offered with unreasonable premiums or discounts of commissions, and from unreasonably soliciting business.[77] The Agreement also prohibits a member who has "a special relationship" with any issuer from acting as a managing underwriter for such issuer.[78] These prohibitions discourage excessive competition among the underwriting companies and prevent possible conflicts of interest. The term "a special relationship" is not defined,

---

69. *Agreement on Underwriting Business, supra*, Art. 10.
70. Civil liability of an underwriter is, under the SEA, limited to the misrepresentation by way of using a prospectus. For details, *see* pp. 154 *et seq. infra.*
71. KSDA, *Agreement on Underwriting Business*, Art. 1 and Addenda, Art. 1.
72. *Id.*, Art. 2.
73. *Id.*, Art. 26.
74. *Id.*, Art. 17.
75. *Id.*, Arts. 22 through 24.
76. For details, *see* pp. 265–70 *infra.*
77. KSDA, *Agreement on Underwriting Business*, Art. 21, items 4 and 5.
78. *Id.*, Art. 4(2).

however, and its application is not specified. The KSDA and the SAC allowed the Dongyang Securities Company in 1977 to function as the principal manager for a corporation controlled by the same person controlling Dongyang without taking proper actions.[79]

The disciplinary powers given to the AMU include the imposition of fines or the suspension of membership.[80] The AMU may impose a fine not exceeding half the amount of commissions that the member has received; the fine paid becomes part of KSDA's funds. The AMU may also suspend a member for a period of fifteen days to one year. When any "significant" difference has occurred between the expected earnings or losses estimated by a managing underwriter and the actual results, such underwriter is subject to a penalty within the amount of commissions received. The penalty is based on the following formula:[81]

$$\text{Amount of the penalty imposed for the misestimation of the earnings for the 1st or 2nd prospective year} = \text{the amount of commission received (W)} \times \left(1 - \frac{\text{earnings realized} \times 1.5^*}{\text{earnings estimated}}\right)$$

* or 2.0 for the second year

Thus, the penalty cannot be imposed unless the difference of the estimation exceeds 50% for the first prospective year or 100% for the second prospective year.

II. Their Drawbacks

The 1977 Amendments moved one step further toward a pricing method based on the market prices. The Amendment has two purposes—protecting the interests of existing shareholders from a con-

79. *See* Maeil Economic Newspaper, May 26, 1977, at p.3. The Dongyang Securities Company is controlled by the Daewoo Industrial Co., Ltd., and individuals who have incorporated the latter, the Daewoo Industrial Company. However, Dongyang functioned as a principal managing underwriter for the Daewoo Development Co., Ltd. (*"Daewoo Gaebal"*) which is controlled by the same group of persons controlling Dongyang. Curiously enough, no criticism has been raised about such an illegal practice.

80. KSDA, *Agreement on Underwriting Business*, Arts. 23 and 24.

81. *Id.*, Arts. 23(1), 25, 8(4). Managing underwriters must report the difference to the KSDA within seven days after they received financial statements from the issuer.

servative evaluation policy and resultant underpricing; and eliminating reported abuses by controlling shareholders to offset the losses from such underpricing. However, the essential features of the pricing formula include some drawbacks as they did under the KIC's Rules.[82] The basic formula calculating the intrinsic value of a stock is based on both earning capacity and asset value. The expected earnings per share is evaluated on the basis of estimated financial statements prepared by the issuer for the immediate two prospective years only. This formula presents great dangers of overestimation. First, the rule does not formally require the managing underwriters to estimate expected returns by analyzing past performance and weighing future risk factors. As of May 16, 1977, the SAC did not allow three proposed public distributions out of eleven due to overestimation of earnings or sales volume.[83] Second, the automatic application of the interest rate on one-year time deposits for capitalization purposes appears to be unfair and unreasonable. The capitalization rates should be tailored to the individual issuer by weighing past performance against future risks or by comparing a stock's price-earning ratio to that of comparable issues on the market. Third, an automatic 25% reduction of expected earnings for risk adjustments should be reappraised to formulate a fairer standard.

Also, the KSDA's Rules require the managing underwriters to reflect partly a comparative market price regardless of whether a security of the same class is listed on the exchange. However, in the case of a public offering of the same class of a security by a corporation already listed, a situation which is rapidly increasing in Korea, application of the market price of the same issue appears to be advisable unless the price is manipulated or is formed by an unusual market force. No other reasonable method of pricing for securities whose price is formed by natural market price seems to exist. Also, the regulation of controlling shareholders' abuses to offset the losses from underpricing can be justified when an offering at market price is allowed. When an offering price is determined with reference to the market prices, the potential for manipulation of securities prices by the

---

82. *See* Il Sakong, *Some Observation on the Securities Market of Korea*, 13–22 (KDI, Working Paper No. 7410, 1974). He critically noted some drawbacks included in the KIC's Rules on Securities Analysis.
83. Maeil Economic Newspaper, May 16, 1977, at p.3.

persons interested in the distribution would be even greater. Hence, a prohibition of purchases by such persons is a prerequisite to utilization of a market price standard. However, the authorities have failed to concern themselves about this problem in amending the pricing formula. Article 105 of the SEA, which prohibits manipulation of listed securities, is not applicable because of its limited scope.[84] In order to deter effectively purchases by the interested persons, the concept of manipulation should be broadly expanded as it is in the United States.[85] The concept of manipulation should also include trading in similar issues whose market prices are being used for the determination of offering prices.

Another drawback is included in regulating co-managing underwriters in connection with securities analysis for pricing. Requiring two co-managers to analyze and price the security along with the principal manager and subjecting them to liability for malpractice, the authorities have failed to require them to submit or disclose the result of securities analysis. Thus, co-managers are actually freed from legal restraints and thus tend to remain indifferent to pursuing fair analysis. To make them eagerly participate in securities analysis, it seems advisable to require the result of co-mangers' analysis to be disclosed in the registration statement as a special note. This short remark would also help public investors to make investment decisions and help the authorities to determine whether co-managers have exercised due diligence in investigation.

One more critical problem involves the deficiencies in the regulatory framework and the enforcement techniques. First of all, the current regulation of the underwriting business is largely left to self-regulation by the KSDA and the AMU. Particularly, the AMU is given almost exclusive power to discipline for malpractice. The KSDA must report to the SSB any violation of the Agreement by its members, but both the KSDA and the AMU are not obligated to report to any regulatory agency the disciplinary action under consideration or finally taken. Also, the authorities have failed to provide

---

84. *SEA*, Art. 105. For details, *see* pp. 211 *et seq. infra.*
85. As in the United States, a set of rules should have been introduced to prevent trading in securities by any person interested in the distribution. For details, see pp. 232–35 *infra.*

the regulatory agency with superior power to review and amend any sanction taken by the self-regulatory bodies or power to independently impose sanctions on underwriters. Since empirical evidence strongly indicates that a self-regulatory body cannot properly function in regulating its fellow members, the authorities should reallocate the enforcement power in a way that the regulatory agency can ensure an impartial exercise of the AMU's and the KSDA's disciplinary power, and that it supplement their failure to act.

Also, the sanctions currently available for violations of the Agreement are too mild to deter effectively malpractice. Penalties may only be imposed within certain limits of the commissions received. Stricter sanctions such as expulsion from the AMU should have been included. In addition, effective sanctions for malpractice should have been extended to CPA's and securities analysts because accounting reliability is of cardinal importance for accurate pricing.

Section IV. *Registration and Distribution of Securities*

I. Registrant

The issuer must file a registration statement with the SAC when the total amount of a public offering or secondary distribution of any security by a close corporation or when the amount of an issuance of new shares by a listed corporation exceeds ₩ 50 million.[86] The filing requirement of the public offering or secondary distribution is to ensure disclosure of relevant information about the securities being distributed to protect public investors. The general filing requirement for an issuance of new shares by listed corporations, however, deserves some comments.

This category was provided by the 1974 amendment of the SEA requiring even stock dividends by listed corporations to be subject to a filing requirement.[87] It was designed to strengthen supervision

---

86. *See SEA*, Art. 8(1); *MOF Decree thereunder*, Art. 2.
87. *See* MOF, *"Policies Taken and Their Main Contents" (Chungchaek Jochi Mit Chooyo Naeyong)*; *see also Old SEA*, Art. 4(1), as amended on Dec. 21, 1974, by Law No. 2684. Article 4 (1) provided: "A public offering or secondary distribution of any security, and an issuance of new shares by a listed corporation to the subscriber thereto shall not be effected unless the issuer has filed a registration statement as to such security with the Ministry of Finance."

over excessive capital increases by listed corporations, which might result in weakened dividend capacity or in depression of market prices below par value. A capital increase through excessive conversion of revaluation, capital, or earned-surplus reserves into capital stock might hurt dividend capacity or result in watered stock since it constitutes a distribution of corporate assets. Therefore, the Commercial Code requires that such capital increase be subject to shareholders' approval and that such new shares be issued to existing shareholders in proportion to their current shareholdings.[88] However, the authorities wanted to provide a safeguard against an excessive capital increase probable under a controlling group's domain.

Newly-issued shares not involving a stock dividend must be subscribed by and issued to existing shareholders upon their approval unless otherwise provided in the articles of incorporation.[89] Since such offering is acquired by existing shareholders directly from the issuer without participation by an underwriter, it seems unnecessary to require the issuer to file the same registration statement; rather, the requirement to file a full registration statement creates the complexity, cost, and time both in the preparation and in administrative review. If the statement is required to supervise possible excessive capital increase, it would be more reasonable to require the issuer to file a statement including only the information needed to meet the supervisory purpose. Thus, only when a listed corporation intends to offer its new shares toward the public in a way that would deprive its shareholders of their preemptive rights upon shareholders' approval, should it be required to file a full-scale registration statement.

II.   Restrictions of Transactions in Registration

Before the 1976 amendments, Article 4(1) of the old SEA made it unlawful for any person to offer to sell or to solicit an offer to buy a security unless a registration statement had been filed with the Ministry of Finance. Further, Article 5-2 made it unlawful for a person offering to buy or acquire a security to buy or acquire it until the registration statement had become effective.[90] During the pre-filing

---

88. *Commercial Code*, Art. 461.
89. *See* the accompanying text of note 13 *supra et seq.*
90. *Old SEA*, Arts. 4(1) and 5-2, as amended on Feb. 6, 1973, by Law No. 2481.

period, only preliminary activities, including underwriting, were allowed. During the waiting (the post-filing but pre-effective) period, it was implicit from Article 5–2 that a security could be offered legally. An offer to sell or solicitation of an offer to buy was legal whether it was oral or written since no requirement existed to use preliminary prospectus or other written material required under the relevant law.[91] The purchase or sale could still not be made legally until the registration statement became effective.

Under the new SEA, however, more complicated restrictions on transactions are provided because of the adoption of an additional waiting period after the effective date of the registration statement. Article 8(1) makes it unlawful to sell a security unless a seven-day additional waiting period has passed after the registration statement has become effective.[91a] On the other hand, Article 10 makes it unlawful to accept an offer to buy or acquire a security unless its registration statement has become effective.[92] The legislative intention is unclear, but it probably was to provide a cooling period for the issuer, underwriter, and dealer as well as for the public investors. These two provisions, however, conflict with each other.

It is clearly illegal under the SEA for any person to offer a security prior to the filing of a registration statement. After an additional cooling period, it is clearly allowed to consummate sale and purchase transactions. Article 10 seems to postulate that it is legal to make an offer to sell or solicit an offer to buy a security even during the waiting period, while article 8(1) makes it illegal to do so until the additional

---

91. It was the same under the old SEA that the prospectus should be prepared by an issuer after the registration statement became effective, and the delivery of the prospectus was required only when asked for. *See Old SEA*, Art. 8(1), as promulgated on Jan. 15, 1962 by Law No. 972.

91a. *SEA*, Article 8(1) and *the MOF Decree thereunder*, Art. 1. Article 8(1) provides: "A public offering or secondary distribution of any security and an issuance of new shares by a listed corporation shall not be effected *unless a registration statement as to such security filed by the issuer with the SAC has become effective and a period thereafter prescribed by the Ministry of Finance Decree has passed.*" (Emphasis added.)

92. *Id.*, Art. 10. It provides: "*Any issuer, seller or its agent shall not accept an offer made to buy or acquire a security unless* the registration or notification statement as to such security has become effective in accordance with Article 9." (Emphasis added.)

cooling period has expired. Unless the conflicts are clarified by a MOF's Release or otherwise, there will be great confusion and questionable practices.

In addition, the SEA failed to give explicit definitions of some basic terms such as "sale", "sell", "offer to sell", "offer for sale", and "prospectus". This failure provides a loophole in identifying the types of transactions restricted during registration. It would be extremely difficult for the regulatory agencies to identify whether a specific case constitutes an offer to sell, or a solicitation for an offer to buy a security.

The SEA also requires a prospectus to be prepared after the registration statement has become effective and to be delivered only when it is asked for,[93] but no other provision regulates a preliminary prospectus. Therefore, any freely written materials can be used for an offer to sell, or solicitation of an offer to buy. Even though few serious problems have been raised because of such loopholes,[94] a great potential for misuse exists in the structure. If the purpose of the restriction is to enable public investors to make well-informed investment decisions, the present rule cannot properly perform its function.

Another drawback is an ambiguity in Article 10, which provides that "any issuer, seller, or its agents shall not accept an offer made to buy . . ." The meaning of the term "seller" is not clear. No supplementary rule or legislative history is available on the matter. Although the term "seller" usually means any person who sells a security, viz., a dealer, it is not clear if it also includes an underwriter. To achieve the purpose of the restrictions, underwriters should be included. When an underwriter purchases an entire issue from the issuer for its own account or enters into a stand-by commitment, it is not an agent of the issuer. Thus, the provision should be revised to include an underwriter explicitly.

III.   Processing of the Registration Statement
A. Information and Attached Documents
The registration or notification statement must contain a wide

---

93. *Id.*, Art. 12.
94. Since there have been excessive subscriptions for the securities publicly offered in the field of equity securities, the sales efforts on the part of issuers, underwriters or dealers felt little need to take advantage of these loopholes in order

range of relevant information for the offered security: the purposes of business, trade name, matters pertaining to the business operations and the financial affairs of the company, and other information prescribed by MOF Decree.[95] The registration or notification statement must also be accompanied by the documents specified by the MOF Decree.[96]

Information specified in Article 3(1) of the MOF Decree and the attached Form-1 is summarized as follows:[97]

item 1. Brief Description of the Corporation, including the purpose, history, changes in capital, kind and class, number and par value of the shares issued and outstanding, and matters on the declaration of dividends during the past three financial years of the issuer;

item 2. Description of Business, including the principal products in the respective field, its productive capacity and actual production, sales volumes, and material contracts involving business operation;

item 3. Statement of Financial Affairs, including balance sheets, profit and loss statements with production cost statement and surplus or loss calculation statement, surplus application or loss disposition statement, a table showing the changes in liability and capital before and after the offering, and a table showing material changes in profit or loss;

item 4. Plan of Offering or Distribution, including the description of classes of securities, underwriting, distributions of securities to specified subscribers, and terms or conditions of offering;

item 5. Use of Proceeds to Registrant, including the calculation of net proceeds;

item 6. Other matters, including but not limited to special profits received by promoters, contribution in kind, property promised to be transferred to the registrant after incorporation, and other matters specially intended to state;

item 7. Brief Opinion of CPA's on the result of auditing, including some notes on accounting principles applied, propriety of the financial statements, major corrections made, and other supplementary matters if necessary; and

item 8. Opinion of Underwriters on the security concerned, including dispersion of shares among shareholders, directors and officers, wages and compensation for employees, facilities, and other documents attached to financial statments.

---

to make full distribution.

95. *SEA*, Art. 8(2).

96. *Id.*, Art. 8(3).

97. *See MOF Decree*, Art. 3(1) and Form-1, as amended by MOF Decree No. 1232 on February 15, 1977. The information required to be stated is common for the purpose of the registration and notification statements.

The documents required to be attached to the registration or notification statement are:[98] (1) the articles of incorporation; (2) a certified copy of corporate registry; (3) a copy of the resolution of the promoters, shareholders or board of directors which has approved the pending offering or distribution; (4) a copy of an authorization of competent authority if authorization is required for the issuance of the security concerned; (5) a copy of the underwriting agreement; and (6) an audit report made by a CPA firm.

Even though the information required in the registration or notification statement seems to cover all the necessary information for public investors, a critical loophole exists because of the lack of precise and specific disclosure standards. A standard of disclosure, "materiality" of information, is provided indirectly in a provision on civil liability, which makes a registrant, directors or promoters, or a person who prepared or delivered a prospectus liable for the damages incurred by an acquirer due to false or withheld information.[99] No rule has, however, clarified the standard of materiality.[100] Moreover, no relevant case has been brought to court for a decision. In this circumstance and with restricted administrative review a registrant may easily omit material information. Since the factual setting of a specific case is often too intricate to resolve, civil liability provisions or even stricter criminal sanctions will not work effectively unless more specific disclosure standards are provided.

Except for the registrant (actually a representative director or promoter) no one is required to sign the registration statement though directors or promoters at the time of filing the registration statement are subject to civil liability. Expansion of the signers should be considered to promote fair disclosure of information. In addition, the registration statement thus far has not been prepared or reviewed by an attorney, and thus a question arises as to the propriety of pre-

---

98. *Id.*, Art. 3(2).
99. *SEA*, Art. 14.
100. Item 6 of the Guidelines for Description included in the attached Form-1 of MOF Decree, requires the issuer to specifically state: Such matters occurred during the period between the preparation of financial statements and filing the registration statement and as affected materially or deemed assuredly to affect materially the financial statements. But this guideline cannot be qualified as a standard for materiality in its nature and coverage.

paration of complicated documents without even review by a lawyer.

B. *Administrative Review, Examination, and Sanction*

The SAC (in fact, the SSB) under the SEA must review the registration statement and accompanying documents. When defects in terms of the required form or omissions of pertinent facts appear, the SAC orders the registrant to submit an amendment to the registration statement.[101] Also, the registrant may voluntarily file an amendment until the registration statement has become effective.[102] When an amendment order has been issued by the SAC, the registration statement filed must be deemed not to have been received by the SAC from the date of the issuance of such order.[103] When a registration statement has been amended either in accordance with an amendment order or voluntarily under Article 11(3), it must be deemed to have been received from the date of the receipt of such amendment.[104]

Further, the SAC may order the registrant, issuer, underwriter, or other related persons to submit any report, materials and documents for review, or may order its staff to examine the books and records, documents, or other materials kept by such persons, whenever it deems doing so to be necessary and appropriate for the public interest or for the protection of public investors.[105] When the registration statement, prospectus, or report of actual distribution submitted under Article 17 appears to include any misstatements or omissions of material facts, the SAC may, after accounting for the reasons therefor and giving public notice, order the issuer of such security to correct the defects, or may issue a stop order suspending the issuance, public offering, secondary distribution, or other transactions of such security.[106] The SAC may exercise its inspection power in any case in order to determine whether a stop order is to be issued. When the stop order is issued, the effectiveness of the registration statement of the security may, temporarily or permanently, be suspended. Any person aggrieved by a SAC order may obtain review of such order

---

101. *See SEA*, Art. 11(1).
102. *Id.*, Art. 11(3).
103. *Id.*, Art. 11(2).
104. *Id.*, Art. 11(4).
105. *Id.*, Art. 19(1).
106. *Id.*, Art. 20.

in the MOF with appeal to the High Court.[107]

Because the MOF had not been equipped with a sufficient number of personnel, the function of the administrative review was transferred to the SAC and the SSB by the 1976 Amendments. The problem still remains, however, of securing enough personnel qualified to undertake such highly technical work. The SAC and the SSB have few CPA's and no lawyers. In addition, the SEA has failed to provide a statutory procedural device to ensure accuracy in issuing an amendment or a stop order. As in the United States, the SEA should have provided a hearing procedure which gives issuers an opportunity to defend themselves against any charges.[108]

The registration statement becomes effective on the date designated by the SAC; however, the notification statement required for a small issue becomes effective immediately.[109] If the SAC does not designate an effective date within thirty days after receipt, it must notify the registrant of the reasons therefor.[110] When an amendment to the registration statement has, either voluntarily or by order, been filed, the thirty-day period commences from the date such amendment is received. It is not clear if SAC's default to designate an effective date within thirty days without providing reasons therefor would entitle the registration statement to take effect automatically. A default should not lead to automatic registration because the thirty-day limitation should be construed as a "disciplinary provision" to facilitate the SAC's administrative review.[111]

The SAC may not designate the effective date if a registrant failed

---

107. *Id.*, Art. 206.

108. *Securities Act of 1933*, Sec. 8(d), 15 U.S.C.A. §77 h(d).

109. *SEA*, Art. 9(1).

110. *Id.*, Art. 9(2).

111. When obedience to a certain provision is required for the protection of public interests, it is a mandatory provision; if vice versa, a disciplinary one. The SAC might fail to complete its work within the thirty day period under certain circumstances. If it should be construed as a mandatory provision, a serious question occurs as to the effect of a SAC's failure. Furthermore, it is more important for the protection of public interests to achieve accuracy in the work than to make the reviewer finish his work within a limited period with the possible risk of mistakes. Weighing the public interests involved in the case of a default, the provision should not be construed as a mandatory one.

to register itself in accordance with Article 3 one year prior to the pending registration. In addtion, the SAC may refuse to designate the date if it deems refusal necessary for the stabilization of the security's fair market price or for the protection of public investors.[112] This provision expresses the government's strong intent to maintain a fair market price for listed stocks. The success of this kind of supervisory function will largely depend on the administrative agencies techniques and impartial performance of their duties.

The designation of an effective date does not mean that the information stated in the registration statement is true or correct, or that the government or the SAC guarantees or approves the value of such security.[113] A warning to this effect must appear in red letters on the bottom of the front cover of the prospectus.

C. Prospectus Requirement in Distributing Securities

The Commercial Code requires that persons wishing to subscribe to stock, bonds and debentures to describe the kind and number of securities subscribed for on a form provided by promoters or directors.[114] The SEA, however, adds a prospectus requirement because the statements in a subscription form do not give sufficient information to public investors and because the subscription form requirement is not applicable to a secondary distribution of securities.[115]

Under the SEA, any issuer whose registration statement has become effective must prepare a prospectus for the security concerned.[116] As noted earlier, however, a prospectus may only be delivered when asked for by a person intending to acquire such security.[117] It is implicit from those provisions that a prospectus is not required in the

---

112. *SEA*, Art. 9(3). It is also required to notify a registrant of the reasons therefor when the SAC decides not to designate an effective date.

113. *Id.*, Art. 3(4).

114. *See Commercial Code*, Arts. 302, 420 and 474.

115. *See SEA*, Arts. 12 and 13. Since the SEA is modeled after American securities laws through Japan with some modifications, the legislative intent of provisions is basically the same as that of Japan. *See also* Tatsuta, at 50.

116. *Id.*, Art. 12(1).

117. *Id.*, Art. 13(1). It provides: "With respect to any security of which the registration statement has taken effect, any person shall not cause the security to be sold or acquired *unless he delivers a prospectus* prepared in conformance with the provision of Article 12 *upon request by a person intending to acquire such security.*" (Emphasis added.)

following transactions:

1) where a securities company sells the security to another security company;
2) where a transaction is made by any person other than by an issuer, one who makes a secondary distribution, underwriter, or dealer;
3) where an issuer or one who makes a secondary distribution sells the security other than through a public offering[118] or secondary distribution;
4) where a transaction is made by a dealer or one who acted as an underwriter with respect to the security concerned after the expiration of the underwriter's function;
5) brokers' transactions executed upon the customers' orders so long as the orders are not obtained through the former's solicitations; and
6) any other transactions by an issuer, underwriter, or dealer which involve a public offering or secondary distribution of a security but where an acquirer does not request the delivery of a prospectus.

These exemptions are proper, considering the nature of the respective transactions and the legislative intention behind the prospectus requirement. The exemption in the case of item 6, however, raises a critical question on the basic policy of disclosure of information. Clearly, many investors will make their investment decisions without having access to the prospectus. The delivery of a prospectus should have been made compulsory by the statute.

Furthermore, the use of free written materials is not prohibited. Under Article 13(1), it is required only that a prospectus prepared in accordance with Article 12 be delivered to purchasers upon their request. In turn, it is provided that any prospectus prepared in contravention of the requirements of Article 12(2) and (3) should not be used for any transaction involving a public offering or secondary distribution of any security.[119] Since there is no definition of the term "prospectus" in the SEA,[120] any free written material, unless named as a prospectus, may be used. Further, newspaper, radio or television

---

118. Public offering here includes any issuance of new shares required to file a registration statement under the SEA.
119. *SEA*, Art. 13(2).
120. The Japanese SEA, by which Korean legislators have been greatly influenced, defines the term prospectus as follows: "The term prospectus in this law shall mean a document purported for public dissemination, containing an explanatory statement concerning the business activities of an issuer of any security for public offering or secondary distribution." *See Japaneses SEA*, Art. 2(10).

advertisements, are not prohibited under the SEA.

Civil liability under the SEA is limited to cases of the misrepresentation of a fact or the omission of a material fact in a registration statement or prospectus. Therefore, (1) any person may use any free written materials to solicit an offer to buy from or an offer to sell a security to the public in person, by mail or through an advertisement in any newspaper, or on radio or television without accompanying it with or following it by a statutory prospectus; (2) a prospectus need be delivered to investors only when requested; and (3) any person who uses free written material is not subject to any civil liability, at least under the SEA,[121] for damages sustained by purchasers of a security due to any misrepresentation or omission of a material fact unless such material qualifies as a statutory prospectus. In view of the goal of investor protection in this area, the following are needed: (1) a coordinated set of reforms; (2) an explicit statutory definition of the term "prospectus"; (3) a compulsory delivery requirement of a prospectus prepared legally; (4) an appropriate prohibition against the use of free written materials; (5) introduction of a preliminary prospectus concept; and (6) the reorganization of the civil liability system.

The information which must be stated in a prospectus, as a rule, is the same as that contained in the registration statement. A prospectus must not contain any information differing from that in an effective registration statement and must not omit any information included in the registration statement.[122] Therefore, the propriety of disclosure in the prospectus should be attacked on the same basis as the propriety of disclosure in the registration statement. The 1976 Amendments provided that certain information such as military or business secrets may be exempted upon the SAC's approval.[123] On the other hand, an issuer must state such additional information as prescribed by a MOF Decree.[124]

---

121. A victim may bring a suit to recover damages in tort under civil law; but it would be almost impossible to prove the requirements of a case, like intent to defraud (*scienter*), material misrepresentation of a fact, reliance thereon, causation and damages. For details, *see* pp. 217 *et seq. infra.*
122. *SEA*, Art. 12(2).
123. For the information exempted, *see* pp. 103–4 *supra.*
124. *See MOF Decrees*, Art. 4. The required information includes: (1) the fact that a registration statement has been filed and become effecive; (2) a place

Finally, no provision exists stating the length of time during which a prospectus may be validly used. Since the information contained therein does not reflect all the material information on the current situation of an issuer, a prospectus prepared more than a certain period prior to its use should be invalid. No serious problem has yet occurred due to oversubscription in the market. Sometime in the near future when the market conditions change, however, this problem may arise in transactions involving parts of securities offerings remaining unsold.

D. *Report of Actual Distribution*

The SEA requires any issuer whose registration statement has become effective to file a report with the SAC of the actual distribution of the security immediately following the completion of the public distribution; any violation of the provision is subject to a fine.[125] The SAC must keep this report together with the registration statement for two years for public inspection. This reporting requirement appears to perform two functions. First, it provides the SAC with information on the actual distribution of issued securities, including the rate of subscription and the method of allotment so that the SAC can effectively perform its supervisory functions. Second, it discourages any issuer from evading the requirements for a publicly-held corporation.

Section V. *Civil Liability*

The Securities Act of 1933 in the United States included several separate sections creating civil liabilities in connection with distribution of securities.[126] Section 11 subjects the issuer of registered securities and numerous other classes of persons to liability (damages) for

---

where a copy of the registration statement may be examined by public investors; (3) the price of the public offering or secondary distribution of the security involved; and (4) the fact that the information stated in the registration statement shall not be taken to be approved by the government as true or correct or that the value of the security is not guaranteed or approved by the government.

125. *SEA*, Arts. 17, 213 item 1; *Presidential Decree thereunder*, Art. 7.
126. *See Securities Act of 1933*, Secs. 11, 12, 15 and 17, 15 U.S.C.A. §77 k, l, o, and q.

a material misstatement or an omission in the registration statement. Section 12(1) imposes liability (rescission or damages) on anyone who offers or sells securities in violation of Section 5 which requires the registration and delivery of a statutory prospectus. Section 12(2), which is not directly related to the registration requirement, creates broad civil liability (rescission or damages) for a false or misleading statement in a prospectus or any other written or oral communications. In addition, Section 15 imposes liability on any person who controls a person liable under Section 11 or 12, subject to a special defense of innocence. Finally, Section 17(a), like Section 10(b) of the Exchange Act and Rule 10b–5, broadly prohibits any person offering or selling securities from employing or engaging in any fraudulent or deceptive acts, practices or devices. Civil liability may also be available to an injured buyer under this section.

These civil liability provisions have exerted indirect pressure on companies to disclose relevant information through the expansion of their reach far beyond the common law concept of fraud or deceit.[127] Plaintiffs are not required to prove reliance upon a false or misleading statement under Section 12(2) nor normally under Section 11, though they must prove their lack of knowledge under Section 12(2). Lack of knowledge after due diligence is not available under Section 12(2), while it may be a defense under Section 11, except for the issuer itself. Privity is not required under Section 11, but it is necessary under Section 12(2).

The SEA includes two provisions, Articles 14 and 197, creating civil liabilities in connection with distribution of securities. Article 14 provides civil liability for false or misleading statements in a registration statement or prospectus.[128] Article 197 creates civil liability for independent certified public accountants (CPA's) who falsely certify financial statements which are to be included in the registration statement, prospectus or other required reports.[129] Article 14 provides;

---

127. *See id*; *also see* R. W. Jennings & H. Marsh, Jr., *Securities Regulation* 777–843 (4th ed. 1977); 3 Loss, *Securities Regulation* 1682 *et seq.* (2d ed. 1961).
128. *SEA*, Art. 14.
129. *Id.*, Art. 197. Article 197(1) provides: "A certified public accountant who certifies financial statements required to be filed under this law shall be liable for any damages sustained by an innocent investor due to the CPA's statement that such financial statements have not included any material missta-

"In case any person, who has acquired or purchased a security, incurs damages due to any false or untrue statement of a fact contained in the registration statement or prospectus, made by an issuer under Article 8 or Articles 12(1) and 13(1), or omission of a material fact required to be stated therein, the registrant of such security and its directors at the time of filing the registration statement (or its promoters in case such registration statement has been filed prior to the incorporation of the company), or any person who has prepared or delivered the prospectus shall be liable for the compensation of such damages; provided, however, that this shall not apply, if any person, who is liable to compensate, proves that he could not have known, in the exercise of reasonable care, such untruth or omission, of if the acquirer or purchaser knew such untruth or omission when he made an offer to acquire or purchase."

Unlike the civil liability provisions of the Securities Act of 1933, these provisions do not appear to cover broadly fraudulent and deceptive acts or practices in connection with distribution of securities. Despite vagueness and ambiguity, no judicial interpretation on the coverage of these provisions is available. Thus, the following discussion on the elements of liability will be based mainly on the inferences drawn from the statutory provisions.

I. Persons Liable under Articles 14 and 197

The foregoing SEA Articles specifically set forth persons who may be liable:

(1) the registrant, *i.e.*, the issuing corporation which has filed a registration statement and prepared a prospectus;
(2) all directors or promoters of the issuer, at the time of filing the registration, but excluding all other persons later named as directors;
(3) an underwriter or dealer who has actually delivered the prospectus; and
(4) an independent certified public accountant who has certified the financial statements.

The SEA does not include any indication that the courts may go beyond any of these categories to include any other person (*e.g.*, an aider and abettor of fraud). Thus the statute does not include within its coverage any inside auditor, or other similarly important figures

---

tement or omission of a fact."
Article 197(2) requires that Articles 15 and 16 *mutatis mutandis* apply to the CPA's civil liability.

such as officers or senior staff members of the executive (or general affairs), the financial, and the accounting divisions who are in charge of preparing the registration statement. Unlike American securities laws, the SEA does not extend civil liability to any person who has signed the registration statement, or who has been named as having prepared or certified any report or valuation used in connection with the registration statement and prospectus.[130] Thus, the civil liability provision does not reach experts who occasionally provide information for the registration statement, such as geologists who give opinions on mineral reserves, lawyers who give title opinions on real property, or appraisers who give authoritative evaluation reports on certain property.

Some more critical drawbacks in the coverage of civil liability under the SEA can be found in connection with any person who offers or sells a security, whether exempted or not. Because of a lack of provisions like Section 12(1) and (2) of the Securities Act of 1933, civil liability cannot reach persons who effect the distribution of securities by means of a false and misleading statement, through either oral or written communications. In addition, any underwriter or dealer who sells or solicits offers to buy through other than a statutory prospectus is not subject to civil liability under the SEA because the civil liability provision reaches only the person who delivers a statutory prospectus prepared by the issuer.

Finally, the SEA includes no provision for joint and several liability for a person who controls any person liable under Articles 14 and 197. Introduction of a provision like Section 15 of the Securities Act of 1933 is important to meet the purposes of fair disclosure and broader remedies.

II. Materiality

The foundation of an action under Article 14 is an "untrue or false statement of a fact" or "an omission of a material fact" either required to be stated or necessary for clarity. Although the statute does not indicate so explicitly, the first half of the provision should also be read as referring to an "untrue or false statement of a material fact" as indicated in Article 197.[131] Therefore, whether misstatements or

---

130. *See Securities Act, supra* note 126, Sec. 11(a).
131. *See* note 128 *supra.*

omissions of fact in a registration statement or prospectus are actionable depends on their materiality.

The term "materiality" is not defined in the SEA, nor can one find a court decision interpreting it. An alternative definition of materiality could be that established in the field of civil law fraud; a material fact is "one of such a character that it might have been considered important by a reasonable person in the process of deciding how to act under the circumstances."[132]

III. Privity and Reliance

Since the SEA includes no explicit indication as to whether any privity of contract is required for plaintiffs in an action under Articles 14 and 197, a dispute would be raised among commentators. Since these provisions create civil liability for misstatements or omissions in the registration statement, requiring privity would make the provisions almost unenforceable. A reasonable interpretation, meeting the legislative purposes, is that privity is not required under Articles 14 and 197 as under Section 11 of the Securities Act.

Because the statute is not specific, another crucial question arises as to whether the civil liability provision requires a showing of reliance upon the false statement or omission. If such a requirement is made, the questions of who has the burden of proving reliance, and to what extent the reliance must be proved remain. No legislative history is available on the matter. One could argue that the burden of proof is on the plaintiff to show reliance because it is an essential element of liability in tort law, and the provision failed to include any statements allowing for relaxation. Conversely, one could argue that it is enough for a plaintiff to show a material misrepresentation and damages because providing specific proof of reliance would be very difficult.

In order to make the provision enforceable for remedial purposes, the legislature should have included a phrase on burden of proof, as in the United States.[133] Otherwise, the introduction of the civil

---

132. Such a definition is firmly established in the civil and criminal fraud actions in Korea.

133. *See* Section 11(a), the second Paragraph of *Securities Act, supra* note 126. It requires proof of reliance if a plaintiff has acquired the security after the issuer made an earnings statement covering a twelve-month period after the

liability provision of the SEA would almost reiterate an established civil law tort concept.

IV. Defenses

While Article 197 is silent as to any defense available for CPA's, the proviso of Article 14 stipulates two exceptions from liability.[134] First, defendants are not liable under Article 14 if they prove that they could not have known the defect in question upon the exercise of reasonable care. Second, they are not liable if the acquirer or purchaser had knowledge of the misstatement or omission at the time he made an offer to acquire. However, the second exception is ambiguous about the burden of proof, because the latter part of the proviso, unlike the first part, ignores the question. One may argue that the plaintiff must show his lack of knowledge to maintain a case. To meet broader remedies, it would be a more reasonable interpretation to require the defendant to show plaintiff's knowledge.

The "reasonable care defense" is explicitly provided for all defendants under Article 14, including the issuer. Thus if a representative director proves that he could not have known the untruth or omission with the exercise of reasonable care, neither he nor the issuer would be liable. In order to give the provision broader remedial power, however, the issuer should not have been given the due diligence defense, as in the United States. A critical question also arises as to the standard of diligence. Unlike the Securities Act of 1933, the SEA does not include any clear standard of how much care is due for the defense. Nor does the SEA classify the degree of care according to the portion of the registration statement (*e.g.*, expert or non-expert) or with respect to the status of person (*e.g.*, inside versus outside directors).

V. Remedy

A. Damages Recoverable

In an action under Article 14 or 197, the plaintiff may recover the difference between the price he paid and the value of the security.[135]

---

effective date.

134. For the respective text, *see* p.155 and note 129 *supra*.

135. *See* Section 11(b)(c) of *Exchange Act supra* n. 126; *see also* Folk, *Civil Liabilities under the Federal Securities Laws: The Barchris Case*, 55 VA L. REV. 1 (1969)

The value of the security is determined by the market price at the time of closing the fact-finding procedure at the court where the action is pending (or the price at which the security is assumed to be sold when there is no active market for the security) if the plaintiff holds the security; or it must be the price at which he previously sold it.[136]

It appears from the foregoing method of calculating the damages recoverable that the SEA does not require the plaintiff to show any causal connection between the decline in the price and a defective statement so long as materiality is established. The plaintiff is required only to prove the damages sustained. Further, the SEA does not indicate whether the defendant can escape his liability by proving that all or any portion of the damages represent something other than depreciation in the security's value resulting from a defective statement. Nor does the SEA indicate whether interest on the damages to the date fully recovered should be added or not. These questions, however, may be affirmatively resolved under the civil law principles.[137]

B. Rescission of Contract

In a civil law fraud action, rescission of a contract is available for a purchaser upon the tendering of such goods to recover the amount paid with the interest thereon. The SEA, however, explicitly provides for a monetary remedy in Articles 14 and 197. Disputes may arise as to the availability of rescission. In order to stabilize the social interests involved, it would be more reasonable not to allow an action for rescission as far as Articles 14 and 197 are concerned.

VI. Negative Prescription

Articles 14 and 197 provide that no action to enforce liability shall be taken unless the purchaser claims fraud within one year after the discovery of an untrue statement or within three years from the the date when the registration statement become effective under Ar-

---

136. *SEA*, Arts. 15, 197(2).
137. Since the matters otherwise specified in the SEA may be governed by other laws such as the Commercial Code or Civil Code, defendants may escape liability by proving the non-existence of causal connection between the damages and decline in the price; also plaintiffs may recover interest under civil law doctrine.

ticle 8.[138] This short statute of limitations encourages the purchaser of a security to exercise his right as soon as possible after he discovers fraud to resolve disputes with evidence which might otherwise be destroyed or unavailable.

There is no explicit indication as to whether the persons subject to civil liability under Article 14 or 197 will be jointly and severally liable or not. As far as they constitute joint tort-feasers, however, it would be reasonable to interpret that they may be liable jointly and severally as in a civil tort action.

Section VI. *Special Problems of Forced Going Public*

Due to the unique social and economic background surrounding the business community in Korea, the government has been strongly involved, under various special laws, encouraging and forcing certain corporations to go public. The strong government involvement has been extended to a wide range of corporate activities, including the analysis of securities to determine offering prices and dividend declarations as well as the disclosure of relevant information. This government policy toward going public has contributed to the rapid growth of the securities market in Korea, at least in terms of quantitative expansion, and has enhanced public participation in the primary securities market.

However, some serious problems appear to be by-products either of the strong government involvement or of a lack of effective regulation. The problems include the frequent disguising of corporations as public and the declaration of high rates or dividends impairing the corporate capital structure. In addition, the highly leveraged corporate capital structure has worsened despite the government's policy. Since these problems are important both for the soundness of the national economy and for the protection of public investors, they require special consideration for possible reforms.

I. A Need for Strict Regulation of Disguising Corporations as Public

The concept of a "publicly-held corporation" was introduced in the Corporate Income Tax Act in 1967 to provide public corpora-

---

138. *SEA*, Arts. 16, 197(2).

tions with various privileges over non-publicly-held corporations as an incentive for going public.[139] Regardless of these various privileges, however, controlling shareholders forced, though not legally, to go public were reported to have frequently disguised their corporations as public by placing a large portion of shares in the names of trusted persons to reduce their holding below 51%, thus meeting the requirements of a publicly-held corporation. Such a practice of disguising may be partly attributed to the traditional reluctance to go public. But it was reported that the strong government involvement in securities analysis and the resultant underpricing tended to have strongly induced the controlling shareholders to develop such practices. Indeed, disguising corporations as public is facilitated by the peculiar Korean custom which permits controlling shareholders to list their shares under the names of close friends, relatives, employees, and occasionally, controlling shareholders of other corporations in a reciprocal arrangement.

However, it is difficult for the authorities to identify specific cases of disguised-as-public corporations due to close human relationships between the persons involved. Furthermore, the authorities appear to have been inactive in investigating and regulating such practices for fear of discouraging corporations from going public.

Only in late 1976 did a case of a disguised-as-public corporation occur which led to prosecution. Haksoo Lee, the representative director and controlling shareholder of the Korea Wonyang Fisheries Co., Ltd. (*Korea Wonyang*), was prosecuted and convicted on the grounds that he had evaded approximately ₩ 247 million of taxes for the years 1973 and 1974 by having disguised Korea Wonyang as a publicly-held corporation.[140] He had represented himself to hold 50.9% of the total outstanding shares of Korea Wonyang, while he actually held approximately 91% of the shares. He had listed the difference (40.1%) under the names of other persons, including some controlling shareholders of other public corporations, officers, and employees of the corporations concerned.

The Korea Wonyang case greatly shocked the society. Considering

---

139. For the requirements of a "publicly-held corporation" and various incentives therefor, *see* note 43 at p. 48 and pp. 45 *et seq. supra*.

140. *See* Joong-Ang Daily News (*Joong-Ang Ilbo*), Dec. 7, 1976, at p. 7.

the fact that it is only one case detected among numerous similar cases, however, the basic policy of forcing corporations to go public was significantly challenged. Under the pretext of a publicly-held corporation, a large number of disguised-as-public corporations have enjoyed only various privileges and evaded a large amount of taxes. In addition, such disguises largely resulted in a highly concentrated equity ownership which seriously undermines the basic policy goal of going public. Due to such monopolistic domain in equity-ownership (wealth) by a few business elites (controlling shareholders), the actual penetration ratio would be far smaller than the reported 1.6% in 1976. Indeed, the major goal for the promotion of the securities market——capital formation through direct public financing to achieve a sound development of the national economy——will not be attained as long as such disguises remain in the society.

Several approaches are available to resolve this question. First, finding major reasons for such disguises, the authorites should seek to eliminate or relax them. Fear of losing control, one of the reported reasons, has been largely eliminated by the 1976 Amendments because of devices such as the restriction on secret ownership increases, proxy rules, and rules of takeover bids. Another major reason, conservative evaluation or underpricing, has also been largely improved though the pricing formula is still far from a market pricing or offering. A further improvement of the pricing rule should seriously be considered to reconcile the conflicting interests.

Second, the authorities should have fully exercised their enforcement techniques to detect and prevent such disguised ownership even though detection is extremely difficult in practice. The SAC and the SSB are given broad power to inspect securities institutions as well as listed corporations. To facilitate detection of disguised ownership, some improvement of the present rule is essential, especially in the area of identifying beneficial ownership and trading under such ownership as will be noted in the next Chapter.[141] Once detected, an appropriate sanction should be imposed on any violator. In addition to penalties for tax evasion, a criminal penalty should be available for a false entry or fruad in the ownership report. But, an administrative sanction of delisting may hurt public investors due to

---

141. *See* pp. 205–53 *infra*.

destruction of the public market. An appropriate remedy should be designed for those injured by delisting.

II. A Need for Strict Regulation of Excessive Dividend Payments

The Commercial Code requires that stock corporations declare dividends within the limit of net assets stated on the balance sheet after deducting the total amount of legal capital, statutory capital reserve and earned surplus reserve already retained, and earned surplus reserve to be set aside for the fiscal year.[142] Any dividend declaration made in violation of this provision may be voided by a shareholder's suit, and any creditor of the company may bring a suit to have the dividends paid returned to the company.[143] Directors concerned may be jointly and severally liable for damages sustained by the company and also may be subject to criminal penalty of an imprisonment or fine.[144] These provisions are designed to prevent dilution of equity and impairment of the corporate capital structure by maintaining the strict net asset limit in declaring dividends.

A special provision, however, was introduced in the Capital Market Promotion Act (CMPA) of 1968 to warrant non-government shareholders of a listed corporation to be paid dividends at the minimum level of interest rates on one-year time deposits.[145] It requires that listed corporations declare and pay dividends to non-government shareholders at such an interest rate level per year in preference to any government shareholders. Regarding the question of whether listed corporations may declare dividends beyond the Commercial Code's net asset limit, the Ministry of Justice has responded that the net asset limit still binds; thus, the CMPA's provision only warrants non-government shareholders a preferred right to dividends within the limit over government shareholders in order to stimulate public demand for listed stocks.[146] Thus, non-government shareholders of listed corporations in Korea are treated like non-participant preferred shareholders as far as the right to dividends is concerned.

---

142. *Commercial Code*, Art. 462(1).
143. *Id.*, Arts. 462(2), 380; *also see* Suh, *Commentary* I, 424–14.
144. *Id.*, Arts. 399, 625 item 3.
145. *See* note 30 and its accompanying text *supra* Ch. 3.
146. *See* Taero Lee, *Corporations* 554–55 (1975), citing the Justice Ministry's authoritarian interpretation on the question, *MOJ* 810–8078 (July 24, 1969).

In response to the government's encouragement, it has been a general trend in Korea that listed corporations declare dividends at an unusually high level, usually 20–30% per year, frequently impairing their capital. According to a recent report, fourty-two of the 200 listed corporations whose fiscal year ended on December 31, 1976, declared and paid out dividends in excess of the net earnings after audit by a CPA firm.[147] They were reported to have inflated the amount of earnings in various ways, for example,by alloting a smaller amount than the required depreciation, or overvaluing the assets carried over. More significantly, twelve of these fourty-two corporations declared dividends in excess of the net earnings shown on the balance sheet even prior to correction by a CPA's auditing.

In addition to the government's encouragement, such excessive dividend payments were largely attributable to the corporations' desire to maintain or induce a good market reputation concerning the price behavior of their issues. Also, some critical loopholes or drawbacks in the pertinent laws enabled the corporations to manipulate and apply net earnings to declaration of dividends. First, the present rules do not necessarily require listed corporations to reflect the result of the CPA's auditing in their financial statements and to declare dividends on the basis of corrected net earnings.[148] The rules only require such corporations to have their financial statements au-

---

147. *See* Maeil Economic Newspaper, May 20, 1977, at p .3. Joong-Ang Daily News, May 23, 1977, at p.2.

148. *See SEA*, Arts. 182–185; *Commercial Code*, Arts. 447–449. Listed corporations in Korea are required to have their financial statements audited by a qualified, independent CPA firm when they file the financial statements with the SAC and the KSE under the SEA. Also, they are required to have their financial statements sent to such CPA firms four weeks prior to the day set for an ordinary shareholders' general meeting; the auditing report of the CPA firm together with the original financial statements must be kept at the principal office of the company for public inspection one week prior to the day set for the shareholders' meeting; when the shareholders approved the financial statements and a proposal for dividends at the meeting, the corporation must give a public notice of the financial statements with the CPA's auditing opinion. Thus, the present rule neither requires listed corporations to correct their financial statements in accordance with the CPA's auditing results; nor does it require them to declare dividends on the basis of the CPA's auditing result.

dited by a qualified CPA firm and to keep the financial statements with the CPA's auditing report for public inspection prior to a shareholders' general meeting where dividends will be declared. Taking advantage of this loophole, corporate insiders can declare dividends on the basis of the net earnings manipulated for dividend purposes.

Another drawback is found in the area of enforcing the net asset limit rule. Although excessive dividend payments impair the capital and violate the net asset rule, enforcement is largely left to private actions, which have not been instituted thus far. General creditors and the company itself may bring suit against the shareholders to return excessive dividends to the company. Also, the company and its shareholders (in a derivative capacity) may institute an action against the directors concerned to recover damages sustained by the company through illegal dividend payments. Enforcement by the government is only through criminal prosecution by a prosecuting attorney. But, the authority has never instituted a prosecution for violation of the rules without clear reason.

The present enforcement techniques do not appear to be effective from the empirical evidence. It would be impractical to expect the company to bring an action against its shareholders or directors and inside auditors. General creditors do not feel any strong interest in instituting an action against scattered shareholders at a large cost for a small benefit which would not be immediate or direct. Public shareholders in general are reluctant to attack, in a derivative capacity, directors' misconduct which brought them higher yields at least in the short run, and in which they also have partly participated by approving the proposal. Though objected at the meeting, the minority shareholders have a 5% hurdle to standing to sue under Article 403 of the Commercial Code,[149] and the recovery belongs to the company in which they have only pro rata interests. Thus, the present rule of enforcement, largely left to private remedies almost unavailable, should be strengthened.

Under the SEA, the SAC is given broad powers to enact rules regulating the financial affairs of listed corporations, including the power to require special reserves in addition to the Commercial

---

149. *See* pp. 355–56 *infra.*

Code's reserve requirements.[150] The SAC, however, has not exercised its power. Under this power, the SAC should include provisions designed to prevent or discourage an excessive dividend payment, and provisions designed to strengthen enforcement techniques. First, it is urgently necessary to require listed corporations to have their financial statements corrected in accordance with the CPA's auditing report prior to any disposition of earnings. Second, it would be effective as an enforcement technique to require listed corporations to file with the SAC their financial statements, CPA's auditing report, and proposed dividends made on the basis of the corrected financial statements at least one week prior to the date set for a shareholders' meeting. Third, the SAC should be given appropriate disciplinary power for any violation of its rule, though the SEA has not explicitly given the SAC power in this area.

It is equally necessary to strengthen the regulation of financial affairs of the registered corporations which are prospective issuers. The SEA, however, granted the SAC power to advise these corporations in the area of corporate finance, going public, and other financial affairs for the purpose of improving capital structure.[151] The SAC's recommendation is not legally binding and thus would not be so effective as to prevent practices of impairing capital or diluting stock which have been prevalent prior to going public. In order to prevent effectively the registered corporations from impairing their capital, the SEA should include these corporations in the coverage of the SAC's rule on financial matters. The financial affairs of registered corporations should not be treated differently from those of listed corporations.

III. Worsened Capital Structure under Excessive Public Subscription

One of the major purposes behind the government's policy forcing corporations to go public was to ameliorate problems of the corporate capital structure by shifting the traditional method of private debt financing to public equity financing. As a consequence of this policy, the average debt/equity ratio somewhat improve from the record 3.95 in 1971 to 2.73 in 1973. However, since 1974 corporations

---

150. *SEA*, Art. 192; *Commercial Code*, Art. 458.
151. *See* p. 103 *supra*.

have leveraged their capital structure even further. The debt/ equity ratio of manufacturing industries averaged 3.12 in 1975 and 3.65 in 1976.[152] The highest debt/equity ratio for a single corporation was 58.[153]

The reason for such leveraging has not been closely examined yet. It is understood, however, that in rapidly expanding economies most corporations met their increasing capital demands with borrowed capital rather than with equity financing. In fact, the government restricted equity financing by corporations whose rate of dividend payment falls below the level of the interest rate on one-year time deposits.

On the other hand, public subscription rates for newly offered shares have been excessively high throughout the first half of 1977. Because of such oversubscription, most public subscribers were allotted only odd-lot shares, and small subscribers received no allotment. For example, the aggregate amount of subscription for three public distributions offered in June, 1977, reached ₩ 100 billion, more than 5% of the total currency in circulation.[154] Of these three offerings, *"Chinheung"* shares were allotted as follows: none for those subscribed for less than 300 shares; five shares for those between 350–900; ten shares for those between 950–1550: fifteen shares for those from 1600 to the maximum limit of subscription (2,000 shares). Most subscribers for the other two offerings were similarly allotted only odd-lot shares due to excessive oversubscriptions.

Such excessive oversubscriptions are attributable to the under-pricing trend and short-term speculation by public investors. However it is equally true that the public has never had enough access to equity ownership of the large corporations in Korea. Whatever the reasons for such oversubscription, the government could have taken advantage of the strong public demand for cor-

---

152. For 1974 figure, *see* Table 3.6 at p. 44 *supra*. For 1975–1976, *see* Joong-Ang Daily News, July 5, 1977, at p. 2, citing the two different statistics made by the BOK and the KDB. The figures in the text are adopted from the BOK's result to maintain the consistency with the 1974 figure of the BOK.

153. *See* Joong-Ang Daily News, June 6, 1977, at p.2. It was the Hyundai Shipbuilding Co., Ltd., with the total capital of ₩ 4 billion, the largest shipbuilding company in Korea. But Hyundai has not yet gone public.

154. *See* Seoul Economic Newspaper, June 8, 1977, at p. 4.

porate equity securities to ameliorate the highly leveraged capital structure which has been on the verge of going bankrupt. Using this opportunity, the government could also have attained the ideal of decentralizing equity ownership which in turn would have contributed to an efficient allocation of the national real resourses. Unfortunately, the opportunities were not taken.

SUMMARY

The preceding analysis of the present rules governing the distribution of securities reveals numerous shortcomings. These shortcomings should be eliminated by another major reform to ensure that the primary securities market effectively performs its function of direct financing for enterprises and to attain the goals of the economic development plan. The problems may be classified into four major categories; problems involving primary activities, the distribution process, civil liability, and enforcement of the basic policy of going public, including the supervision of financial affairs of registered and listed corporations. Many of these regulatory problems are interrelated and thus cannot be considered separately.

First, a critical question in the area of regulating preliminary activity is the problem of formulating an ideal pricing formula. From the empirical evidence, conservative underpricing, mainly determined by intrinsic value, stimulated an artificial public demand which resulted in excessive oversubscription. Controlling shareholders have developed various devices to avoid losses caused by such underpricing. The new pricing formula, however, still includes several factors which may lead to an unreasonable offering price in one way or another. To reconcile the conflicting interests between public investors and controlling shareholders, such unreasonable factors in pricing should be refined.

Another drawback is the lack of effective enforcement techniques to ensure fairness and impartiality in evaluating and pricing procedures. A critical drawback involves the self-regulation of the industry by the Association of Managing Underwriters (AMU) and the KSDA. In addition to the lack of effective disciplinary power given to these self-regulatory bodies, there are no devices designed to ensure impartiality.

Second, another critical drawback involves inadequacies in the disclosure system. Because the SEA does not define the term "prospectus," free-written sales materials are exempted from legal regulation. The SEA does not provide a precise disclosure standard for the preparation of registration statements and statutory prospectuses. The concept of a preliminary prospectus has not been introduced, and delivery of the statutory prospectus is not compulsory. The inadequacy is extended to the regulation of sales activities while in registration. In addition, due to a limited definition of the terms "issuer" and "underwriter" and the lack of specific standards regarding exempted "private placements," a great potential of evading registration rules exists. Finally, special concern is needed in connection with improving the efficiency and accuracy of reviewing the registration statement and issuing a correction or stop order.

Third, civil liability rules are almost unenforceable because of some critical deficiences and loopholes. Unlike the United States, the elements of liability are not relaxed to ensure a broad remedial function. Coverage of persons subject to the rules is very limited. In order to make the liability rules effective to prevent fraud and thus to compel full disclosure of relevant information, the legislature should expand the concept of fraud in the SEA.

Finally, strong government involvement is needed to enforce the basic policy goal of going public. Regardless of the various privileges given for going public, frequent practices of disguising corporations as public seriously undermines the basic policy goal. As long as a few business elites try to monopolize the national real resources by employing various dishonest practices, the public in general will be given only limited opportunities to share in the resources. Indeed, most business corporations are in danger of bankruptcy due to the highly leveraged capital structure and a reluctance to resort to direct equity financing; however, public investors do not have opportunities to invest in equity because of significant shortages of supplies in the primary securities market. Also, some practices which impair the capital structure of both registered and listed corporations are critically detrimental to the national economy and public investors. A sound development of the national economy will not be achieved until these evils are effectively regulated.

Chapter 7

Regulation of Trading in Securities (One)

Section I. *Regulation of Securities Exchange*

I. Organization, Regulation, and Supervision

Both the United States and Japan have organized their securities exchanges as self-regulating organizations formed by member broker-dealers. The United States Securities Exchange Act of 1934 requires that national exchanges file an application for registration with the SEC and that the exchanges to be registered meet legal requirements designed to protect broader public interest.[1] The Japanese SEA also requires exchanges to apply for licenses from the Ministry of Finance and requires the Ministry to deny licenses when the applications fail to meet the statutory criteria.[2] An exchange exists in per-

---

1. *See Securities Exchange Act of 1934*, Secs. 6 and 19, 15 U.S.C.A. §78 f and s. Within 90 days of the date of publication of notice of filing, the Commission may by order grant the registration or institute proceedings to determine whether the registration should be denied. The Commission must grant the registration if it finds that the requirements of the Act and the rules and regulations thereunder with respect to the applicant are satisfied. To meet the requirements, an exchange, *inter alia*, must be so organized and must have the capacity to be able to carry out the purposes of the Act and to comply, and to enforce compliance by its members and persons associated with its members, with the provisions of the Act, the rules and regulations thereunder, and the rules of the exchange.

2. *See Japanese SEA*, Arts. 80–84. Articles 80 and 81 require that an exchange be a juridical person, which is incorporated by its members, securities companies. Article 82 concerns the application procedure for a license. Article 83 enumerates the requirements for license, which are basically the same as those in the United States. The MOF of Japan must examine thoroughly whether

petuity after being licensed unless its license is cancelled by the regulatory agency or is withdrawn by itself.[3] The exchanges' new or amended rules are subject to the approval of the regulatory agencies. The regulatory agencies are also empowered to order the exchanges to amend their rules.[4]

Unlike the United States or Japan, the Korea Stock Exchange (KSE) was chartered by the SEA and incorporated under the MOF's authorization as a special non-profit legal entity.[5] The KSE's principal office must be located in Seoul and a regional branch may be established pursuant to the MOF's authorization when it appears necessary.[6] At one time, one regional branch was established in Busan, the second largest city in Korea.[6a]

The KSE's organs consist of the certificate holders' meeting, the chairman, managing director, directors, and auditors.[7] The certificate holders' meeting is empowered to resolve such matters as prescribed by the SEA or articles of incorporation.[8] Its resolutions must be approved by the MOF to become effective.

---

an application complies with the respective requirements. Article 84 provides the procedure for denial of license. The Japanese MOF must hold a hearing for further examination and notify the applicant in writing of the reasons thereof when the application is denied.

3. *See Securities Exchange Act of 1934*, Sec. 19(a) (3), 15 U.S.C.A. §78 s(a) (3); *also see Japanese SEA*, Art. 85.

4. *See Securities Exchange Act of 1934*, Sec. 19(c), 15 U.S.C.A. §78 s(c); *also see Japanese SEA*, Arts. 85–2 and 156. The term "amend" here means to abrogate, add to, or delete from the rules of self-regulatory organization.

5. *See SEA*, Arts. 71 and 75. Prior to the 1976 Amendments, however, the KSE did not constitute a pure non-profit organization due to dividend payments and the application of the Commercial Codes' provisions on stock corporations. *See* pp. 98–99 *supra*.

6. *SEA*, Art. 71(3)

6a. The KSE Busan Branch which was established on March 5, 1969, was closed on March 15, 1979, for the reason, among other things, that the KSE located in Seoul performed the role as a national exchange along with rapid developments in both transportation and communication systems.

7. *Id.*, Arts. 77–8 and 75; *also see Civil Code*, Arts. 57–76. The Board of director does not constitute an organ under these articles. There must be one chairman and one managing director, not more than four directors, and not more than two auditors.

8. *Id.*, Art. 77.

The chairman of the KSE is appointed by the President of Korea in accordance with the MOF's recommendation. The Chairman represents the KSE and fully administers the KSE's business. The managing director helps the chairman and takes his place when the latter is unable to perform his duties. The directors help the chairman and managing director by sharing administrative duties. The MOF appoints both the managing director and the directors. The MOF also appoints two auditors, one of whom is required to be an insider. The chairman's, managing director's, and directors' terms of office are three years while the auditors' terms are two.

The KSE's capital was originally contributed in equal amounts by the three associations of securities businesses, banking institutions, and insurance companies.[9] In order to strengthen governmental involvement in market administration, however, the government amended the SEA in 1963 and made a direct capital contribution.[10] Because the KSE's certificates of contribution were listed on the exchange until 1974, they are now held by the securities companies, government, individuals, financial institutions, and other legal entities. To ensure fair market administration, the MOF was empowered to restrict the certificate holders' voting power.[11] Nongovernment certificate holders are restricted to 1/10 of the total votes eligible to be cast in a certificate holders' general meeting. In addition, the amended SEA of 1976 empowered the KSE to redeem certificates held by persons other than the government or securities companies. This compulsory redemption procedure was designed to ensure a fair market administration and to go one step further toward a true membership system. Elimination of divided payments and the application of the Commercial Code's stock corporation provisions were a significant move toward a true non-profit status.[12]

The KSE is empowered to make various rules and regulations concerning its business, listings, trading members, and their activities. The whole rulemaking process is subject to review by the SAC and

---

9. *See* pp. 10–11 *supra*.
10. *See* p. 19 *supra*.
11. *SEA*, Art. 82 and Presidential Decree thereunder, 44(2). The KSE also could not exercise the voting power of its treasury certificates.
12. *See* pp. 98–99 *supra*.

approval by the MOF.[13] The MOF may also order the KSE to amend its articles of incorporation, rules, and regulations when amendments appear to be necessary and appropriate in the public interest and to protect investors.[14]

The government thoroughly reviews the KSE's budgeting, accounting, and auditing. Its budget and financial statements are approved by the MOF every year.[15] The disposition of surpluses must be approved by the MOF. Furthermore, to ensure fair administration of the KSE, the MOF may order the KSE to submit a report or other materials on its business and assets or have the KSE's business, assets, books and records, instruments, and other materials inspected.[16]

The KSE's officers must meet certain qualification requirements provided in the SEA.[17] To avoid conflicts of interest, any person affiliated with a securities company as a shareholder, officer, or employee cannot be appointed as an officer of the KSE.[18] A KSE officer who violates the pertinent laws or KSE's rules can be removed from office.[19]

Strict restrictions are placed on the KSE's officers and employees to ensure fair market administration.[20] First, present or former officers and employees are prohibited from tipping or misusing any non-public information obtained in the course of their business performance. Second, officers and employees are prohibited from transacting in securities, either in their own names or other persons' names, for their own accounts. Only certain securities savings are permitted. Third, officers and employees are prohibited from supplying money to, making profit sharing agreements with, or having any other business relations with any securities institution.

---

13. *SEA*, Art. 115. As far as the articles of incorporation is concerned, the SAC's deliberation is not required.
14. *Id.*, Art. 116.
15. *Id.*, Arts. 113 and 114.
16. *Id.*, Arts. 112 and 53(3). The inspecting officials must prove the evidence of power prior to their inspection.
17. *Id.*, Art. 80.
18. *Id.*, Art. 78(6).
19. *Id.*, Art. 81. The President or MOF, which appoints such persons, also has the power to remove them.
20. *Id.*, Arts. 83 and 42.

II. Regulation of Trading in the Exchange Market
A. *Trading Members and Discipline*
1. Trading Members

Although the amended SEA of 1976 allows securities companies to trade in certain securities in the over-the-counter market, the exchange market still dominates securities trading in Korea.[21] Only the KSE's "trading members" may trade in the exchange market.[22] Other persons are prohibited from having direct access to the exchange market. Non-trading-member securities companies or public investors can effect a securities transaction in the exchange market by placing their orders through trading members.

The KSE, unlike the United States' national stock exchanges, does not have "specialists" who function on the floor as a broker's broker and as a dealer in a particular stock or group of stocks.[23] In 1976,

---

21. Art. 2(10) of the SEA defines the term "securities market" to mean "the market opened by the Korea Stock Exchange." This definition is not correct because another securities market exists off the Exchange. Therefore, the writer refers to "the securities market opened by the KSE" as "the exchange market" and "securities trading in this market" collectively as "floor trading." *See SEA*, Arts. 2(1) and 194; *also see* pp. 185–97 *infra*.

22. *Id.*, Art. 85. The term "a trading member" is defined as "a person who can ordinarily engage in the business of securities transactions on the exchange market." *See id.*, Art. 2(11).

23. As a broker's broker, the specialist holds and executes orders, which are generally "limited price" orders entrusted to him by other brokers. The "limited price" orders cannot ordinarily be immediately executed since they specify prices "away" from the market, that is, orders to buy if and when the price declines to a particular point, or orders to sell if and when it rises to a specified figure. Thus, these orders are left with the specialist, who acts as a central repository for them. The second function of the specialist is to purchase and sell securities for his own account in order to assist in maintaining a fair and orderly market in each security in which he is registered. Section 11 of the Securities Exchange Act of 1934 permits the specialist to act as a dealer but his functions must be restricted "so far as those reasonably necessary to permit him to maintain a fair and orderly market." In general, the specialists contribute to a fair and orderly market by using their own capital to minimize temporary disparities between supply and demand and, thus, to contribute to price continuity. There have been great objections to the specialist system and discussions on the regulation framework of the specialist. For the detailed description of the specialist system and its regulation

the amended SEA adopted the system of a "broker's broker" or "sub-broker" similar to the Japanese "*saitori*" member, who performs half the function of the United States "specialist"; to act as a "broker's broker" in the exchange market, a person must be incorporated as a stock corporation subject to the MOF's license.[24] However, no person has yet been chartered to act as a broker's broker. Thus, the KSE's trading members all share in the securities transactions in the exchange auction market, the operation of which will be discussed in the section on floor trading (*see* pp. 189–94, *infra*).

2. Membership and Discipline

a. Membership Regulation

The status of the KSE's members is quite different from that of

---

in the United States, *see* SEC, *Report on the Feasibility and Advisability of the Complete Segregation of the Functions of Dealer and Broker* 25–42 (1936); Jennings & Marsh, Jr., *Securities Regulation* 612–14 (4th ed., 1977). [Hereinafter cited as "Jennings & Marsh"].

24. *SEA*, Art. 179. A person who functions as a brokers' broker in the exchange market must be a stock corporation which is chartered by authorization of the MOF through the KSE. The KSE should investigate and examine the business operation and asset management of this corporation. This corporation may not effect securities transactions for its own account. This brokers' broker system is modeled after the Japanese "*saitori*" member system of the Tokyo Stock Exchange. Membership in stock exchanges in Japan is limited to securities companies and is classified, according to the nature of operation, into three categories—regular members, "*saitori*" (called "*nakadachi*" in Osaka) members, and special members. Regular members transact securities on the exchange either for their own accounts or for the accounts of customers. Non-member securities companies can participate in securities transactions on the exchange indirectly by placing their orders through regular members. Saitori members specialize in acting as intermediary for securities transactions among regular members in the exchange market. They are prohibited from receiving orders from public investors and from trading for their own accounts. There are twelve saitori members on the Tokyo Exchange, five on Osaka, three on Nagoya, and none on other exchanges. Special members are securities companies specializing in handling sales and purchases in the exchange markets of Tokyo and Osaka for orders which could not be consummated on regional exchanges. In addition, there is one member on each of the Tokyo and Osaka stock exchanges which performs the special function of receiving orders only from non-member securities companies which are its shareholders. For the detailed description of membership system of Japanese stock exchanges, see Japan Securities Research Institute, *Securities Market in Japan* 75–76 (1975).

the exchange members in the United States or Japanese membership system because the KSE was organized as a semi-government agency rather than as a membership system. While the regulatory structures of the three countries differ, however, the basic membership regulation and disciplinary rules are very similar.[25]

In the United States, a national securities exchange may give membership to any person or entity if it finds the person or entity meets the qualifications prescribed in the Securities Exchange Act of 1934 and the rules of the exchange.[26] The SEC may, in the public interest or for the protection of investors, direct the exchange to deny membership to any person or to bar any person from becoming associated with a member. The exchange must scrutinize (1) whether potential members or associates meet such standards of financial responsibility, operational capability, training, experience, and competence as are prescribed by its rules, and (2) whether they have engaged in and there is a reasonable likelihood that they may again engage in acts or practices inconsistent with just and equitable principles of trade.[27]

In Japan, membership in a securities exchange is confined to securities companies which are incorporated under the Finance Ministry's authorization. The exclusion of foreign controlled securities com-

---

25. It is because the basic goals of such regulation are the same, i.e., to enhance the public interest and to protect public investors.

26. *Securities Exchange Act of 1934*, Sec. 6(c), 15 U.S.C.A. §78 f(c).

27. *Id.*, In the case of permitting a natural person to become associated with a member, there are two additional statutory requirements: (1) the person must agree to supply the exchange with such information with respect to its relationship and dealings with the member as may be specified in the rules of the exchange; (2) the person must agree to permit the examination of its books and records to verify the accuracy of any information so supplied. These additional requirements are unnecessary in the case of a registered broker or dealer because Section 17 of the Exchange Act empowers national securities exchanges to make, keep, or examine the accounts and records or reports of members, brokers, or dealer. The exchange must file notice with the Commission not less than 30 days prior to admitting any person to membership or permitting any person to become associated with member, if the exchange knew, or in the exercise of reasonable care should have known, that such person was subject to a statutory disqualification. Also, the exchange may limit the number of its members.

panies was eliminated in 1971.[28] Membership applications are subject to approval by the exchanges' board of directors.[29] Strict examination of applicants is not required; however, approval is very rare
due to the maximum limits on exchange memberships.[30] The exchanges' relaxed examination is also accounted for by the strict
governmental regulation of securities companies which requires
minimum capital for brokers, dealers, and underwriters and imposes
strict qualifications on securities companies' directors and auditors.[31]
The regulation of exchange members also places strong emphasis on
discipline as in the United States. In its Articles of Association, the
exchange must include provisions concerning expulsion or suspension
of members, impositions of fines upon members for illegal acts and
practices, or acts or practices inconsistent with just and equitable
principles of trade.[32]

---

28. *Japanese SEA* (Law No. 5 as amended on Mar. 3, 1971), Arts. 90 and 28;
    Cabinet Order thereunder, Art. 18–2, CO. No. 32, Sept. 30, 1965 as amended by
    CO. No. 267. Aug. 13, 1971); *Law Concerning Foreign Securities Dealers*. Art. 3
    (Law No. 5, Mar. 3, 1971). Only securities companies or foreign securities
    companies, as prescribed by Cabinet Order, may be members of a securities
    exchange. The Cabinet Order of 1971 sets no restrictions on the membership
    of a securities company which is controlled by an alien or a foreign corpora-
    tion. Prior to the 1971 amendment, however, the Articles of Association
    of the exchanges stipulated that a member should not be under the control
    of an alien or foreign corporation and that the board of directors of the
    exchanges must set up criteria under which control by an alien would be
    determined. *See* the old *Articles of Associations of the Tokyo and the Osaka Securi-
    ties Exchanges*, Arts. 8.
29. *Japanese SEA*, Art. 88. item 5; *Articles of Association of the Tokyo Securities Ex-
    change*, Arts. 38, 39(1). A securities company may make an application for
    membership to the exchange with introductory statements by more than two
    members in the same kind of membership.
30. The maximum number of the exchange regular members is limited to not
    more than 83 securities companies in Tokyo and 58 in Osaka, due to the
    limited exchange facilities and the fear of possible unfair competition. *See*
    the Committee of Studies on the Finance and Banking Law, ed., *Commentary
    of Law on Securities and Corporate Finance*, Vol. I. 514–25 (1970).
31. *Japanese SEA*, Art. 32.
32. *Id.*, Art. 98. Cf. *Securities Exchange Act of 1934*, Sec. 6(b) (6), 15 U.S.C.A. §78f
    (b) (6). On the other hand, the Minister of Finance is empowered to revoke
    the license or order the suspension of all or part of the business of a member
    who violates a law, order, or administrative decree or who commits a certain
    misconduct resulting in insolvency. *See id.*, Art. 35.

The KSE's regulation of its trading members is similar to the Japanese regulation. Natural persons cannot be trading members or associate with trading members. Only securities companies which were incorporated under the MOF's authorization are eligible for a KSE trading membership.[33] To act as a trading member, such securities companies must register with the KSE in accordance with the KSE Rules on Trading Members. These KSE Rules must, *inter alia,* cover the maximum number, registration, denial, and revocation of trading memberships; and supervision of the trading members.[34]

As in Japan, entry into the securities business in Korea is subject to the MOF's license. Before issuing a license, the MOF scrutinizes such things as the financial capability and prospective profitability of the applicant and the applicant's incorporators and officers for any statutory disqualifications.[35] Because of the MOF's strict entry and post-entry regulation of securities companies, the regulation of the trading membership is relatively relaxed. No non-member securities company has existed thus far; thus, in Korea, no regulatory problems have been raised between member and non-member firms as in the United States.[36]

b. Discipline of Exchange Trading Members

In both the United States and Japan, where exchanges are organized by members as self-regulatory bodies, the discipline of exchange members is largely the responsibility of the respective exchanges. The regulatory agencies—the SEC in the United States and the Ministry of Finance in Japan—primarily supervise the exchanges' regulation with limited direct involvement in their rule-

---

33. *SEA.,* Art. 84 (1).
34. *Id.,* Art. 84(3).
35. *Id.,* Arts. 32–3; *also see* pp. 244–47 *infra.*
36. Many regulatory problems were raised in the United States because of the existence of many non-member broker-dealers, dual-trading, and so on. These were, *inter alia,* anti-trust questions about the monopolization of the exchange by members and problems about the commission rates. *See Silver v. New York Stock Exchange,* 373 U.S. 341, 83 S. Ct. 1246 (1963); *Kaplan v. Lehman Brothers,* 250 F. Supp. 562 (N.D. III. 1966), *aff'd,* 371 F. 2d 409 (7th Cir.), *cert. denied,* 389 U.S. 954(1967); *Thill Securities Corp. v. New York Stock Exchange,* 433 F. 2d. 264 (1970), *cert. denied,* 401 U.S. 994 (1971).

making and disciplining of members.[37] The discipline of exchange trading members in Korea is threefold; by the KSE, by the MOF, and by the SAC.

---

37. *See Securities Exchange Act of 1934,* Secs. 6(b), 17(d), and 19(a), (g), (h), 15 U.S.C.A. §78 f(b), q(d), and s(a), (g), (h); *Japanese SEA,* Arts. 98, 155 item (1), and 35. The exchange in the United States, as a selfregulatory agency and within the mandate of the Exchange Act of 1934, must provide in its rules that its members and persons associated with its members should be appropriately disciplined for violations of the provisions of the Exchange Act of 1934, the rules or regulations thereunder, or the rules of the exchange. The disciplinary sanctions to be provided should include: explusion; suspension; limitation of activities, functions, and operations; fines; censure; or any other fitting sanction. The SEC has the supervisory power to approve and amend, by order, the rules of the exchange. It also may, if in its opinion such action is necessary or appropriate in the public interest, for the protection of investors, or otherwise in furtherence of the Exchange Act, order the suspension of or expel any member of the exchange or participant therein for violations of federal securities laws. In addition, the exchange must promptly file notice with the SEC when it imposes any final disciplinary sanction on any person associated with its member. The SEC will review the sanction reported by the exchange, on its own motion or upon application by an aggrieved person, and will affirm, modify, or remand the sanction, may cancel, reduce or require the remission of the sanction, or may dismiss the proceeding by order.

In Japan too, an exchange, under the mandate of the Japanese SEA, must include in its Articles of Association provisions concerning expulsion, suspension, or fines for the violation of law, administrative orders, or rules of the exchange or for acts or practices inconsistent with just and equitable principles of trade. The exchange may suspend all or part of the privileges of a member to deal in securities on the exchange. The Ministry of Finance in Japan supervises the performance of the exchange with respect to the discipline of members. In the case of a member who commits any violation of a law, order, or rules and regulations and the exchange fails to impose its disciplinary sanction on that member, or neglects to take other necessary measures to cause the member to comply with the law, the Minister of Finance may: (a) cancel the license of the exchange's incorporation; or (b) order the exchange (1) to suspend all or part of the guilty member's business for a period not exceeding one year, (2) to prohibit a part of the member's business, (3) to dismiss the member's officers, or (4) to take necessary measures as stipulated in its Articles of Association. On the other hand, the Finance Minister may revoke the license of a securities company which is a member of an exchange, and a member which is deprived of its license as a securities company necessarily loses its membership.

(1) *Discipline by the KSE*

Like securities laws in the United States and Japan giving the exchanges broad rulemaking powers, the SEA authorizes the KSE to prescribe in its Rules on Trading Members disciplinary rules for its trading members and their registered representatives.[38] The KSE has not enacted the rules on trading members, but it included a disciplinary provision in its Rules on Business.[39] In order to enforce it, the KSE enacted a separate rule prescribing sanctions for specific acts.[40] The disciplinary measures provided are revocation of registration, suspension of the transaction, and issuance of a warning.

Under the Specific Rules on Disciplinary Standards, the statutory bases for the suspension of a transaction are:[41] (a) violation of any rule relating to the minimum capital requirement, maximum debt-capital ratio, or the reserve requirement for securities transactions; (b) failure to pay the additional guaranty amount; (c) "swallowing";[42] (d) failure to supplement a bonding requirement shortage or default in delivery and settlement; (e) violation of margin requirements; (f) failure to comply with customer's order or other unfair activity which impairs customer's confidence; and (g) other activities which obstruct or impede the business of others, or cause disorder among trading members. The period of suspension varies with the

---

38. *SEA*, Art. 84(3). The registered representative of a trading member handles securities transactions on the exchange, for the trading member. The KSE Rules on Trading Members should include, among other things, provisions concerning the number of trading members; registration and its denial or revocation; disciplinary rules for the supervision of trading members; and the qualification, suspension, registration, and revocation of registration of the registered representative of trading members.

39. *See the KSE Rules on Business* (as amended on Jan. 20, 1976) Art. 60. The KSE may suspend the transaction of a trading member who violates the provisions of the SEA on minimum working capital requirement, maximum debt ratio as compared to net assets, or the required reserve for securities transactions.

40. *See* KSE, *Specific Rules on Disciplinary Standards* (promulgated on july 4, 1973).

41. *Id.*, Arts. 2 through 10.

42. The term "swallowing" commonly means a practice that brokers, who have been entrusted with a customers' order to buy or sell securities on the exchange market, effect the transaction by acting as a dealer without executing the order on the exchange. This practice is illegal as in Japan and constitutes a statutory cause for criminal sanction. *See SEA*, Arts. 101, 210; *Japanese SEA*, Art. 129.

respective act, but does not exceed three days if the violation is corrected.[43]

The statutory bases for revocation of registration are restricted to
failure to correct a violation of (b), (c), or (d) above within one month
of suspension, and more than three suspensions in a year for violation
of (b), (c), or (d) above.[44] Violations of any other rules not specified
above may be cause for issuing a warning. The issuance of more than
three warnings in a year can be cause for the suspension of a transaction.[45]

The foregoing sanctions, including the suspension period for discipline, are too mild to enforce effectively the purposes of the SEA in
the public interest and for the protection of investors. The grounds for
the expulsion of a member are too limited to compel members to
comply with the rules and principles of fair trade. Also, they are not
consistent with other disciplinary provisions of the SEA. For instance,
violations enumerated in (d) above are disciplined by suspension of a
transaction; under the SEA the same violations are disciplined by the
revocation of broker-dealers' licenses by the MOF.[46] The disciplinary
rules should, therefore, be strengthened and integrated.

(2) *Discipline by the MOF and by the SEA*

Unlike the securities laws in the United States and Japan, the SEA
does not empower the Korean regulatory agencies (the MOF, the
SAC, and the SSB) to expel or directly suspend KSE trading members
who violate provisions of the SEA, Decrees thereunder, or the KSE's
rules and regulations.[47] Nor does the SEA require the KSE to notify
the regulatory agency of a charge under consideration or a disciplinary sanction finally taken by the KSE. Rather, the SEA took the
approach that the regulatory agency may indirectly supervise or
discipline the KSE trading members by imposing a sanction on
securities companies which are at the same time KSE trading members.[48]

---

43. *Id.* Only in the case of "swallowing," may the maximum period to suspend
transaction be more than four days, and only if the amount "swallowed"
exceeds ₩ 10 million(Art. 6).

44. *Id.*, Art. 12.

45. *Id.*, Art. 11.

46. *SEA.* Art. 55 item 4.

47. *See* note 37 *supra.*

48. *SEA*, Arts. 55 and. 57

The disciplinary sanctions to be imposed on securities companies by the regulatory agency under the SEA include: (1) the revocation of a license for a securities business; (2) the suspension of all or a part of the securities businesses; and (3) issuance of an order to remove officers. The MOF may, after specifying the underlying reasons, revoke the license of a securities company which falls within any statutory cause provided in Article 55 of the SEA.[49] The SAC, on the other hand, may suspend all or a part of the securities businesses of a company or order a company to dismiss its officers for violation of certain provisions of the SEA.[50]

When a sanction (revocation or suspension) is imposed on a securities company by the MOF or the SAC, the company must be expelled from the exchange or its KSE trading membership must be suspended.[51] The regulatory agency's discipline does not differ greatly in its effect from that imposed in the United States or Japan. However, Korean disciplinary rules for securities companies include too many significant loopholes and deficiencies to attain the regulatory purpose of the SEA which will be discussed in detail later(*See* pp. 264–67 at Section III, II, B, *infra*).

A significant question arises about the regulatory framework; would it be more effective to allow a regulatory agency to be directly involved in disciplining the KSE trading members? It is hard for a self-regulatory agency to discipline its fellow members; the empirical evidence in Korea strongly supports this idea. The KSE has no legal obligation to notify a regulatory agency of the disciplinary sanction finally taken or under consideration, and enjoys broad discretion in imposing disciplinary sanctions. Unlike regulatory agencies in the United States and Japan, however, the MOF may, under the SEA, remove any KSE officer from his office when he has violated laws or decrees, administrative dispositions, or KSE's articles of incorporation and other rules.[52] Because of this power of removal, it could be argued that direct government involvement in the disci-

---

49. For details of the MOF's disciplinary power, *see* pp. 264–67 *infra*.
50. For details of the SAC's disciplinary power, *see* pp. 264–67 *infra*.
51. This is so because, as noted earlier, licensing of a securities company by the MOF is a prerequisite under the SEA for registration as a KSE trading member.
52. *SEA*, Art. 81

plining of the KSE trading members is unnecessary. However, the administration of the disciplinary rules is left to the full discretion of KSE's board of directors: thus, it cannot be construed as a violation of the law when the board has failed to take disciplinary action against a violation of a KSE trading member. Hence, the MOF may not remove KSE's directors because of their failure to impose a sanction on any guilty trading member. Therefore, the MOF's power to remove any KSE officer cannot be an effective device to compel the KSE's board to administer fairly the disciplinary rules.

To accomplish the regulatory purpose of the disciplinary rules, it is necessary to reorganize the present framework. One possible approach would be to introduce a device disigned to oversee the KSE's self-administration and ensure impartial exercise of its broad discretionary power. Another approach would be to give the MOF or the SAC superior powers to be involved directly in disciplinary decisions under certain circumstances. These approaches are interrelated and would supplement each other. To meet such purposes, the KSE should be required to file a report with the SAC of any charge under consideration and finally determined; the SAC or the MOF should be empowered to amend the sanction imposed or directly impose any sanction, including expulsion, suspension, or other administrative dispositions.

Another drawback is the lack of a statutory proceeding designed to ensure fairness in disciplinary decision-making and to provide the aggrieved party with sufficient opportunities to appeal for review of the sanction imposed. The SEA does not include any proceeding which gives a person charged with a violation an opportunity to defend himself against it prior to a final decision. When a sanction is imposed by the MOF or the SAC, the aggrieved party may bring an appeal or a suit against the MOF only if the sanction is illegal or significantly unfair.[53] As to the sanctions imposed by the SSB and the KSE, the SEA strictly restricts the bases for bringing an appeal to

---

53. *Id.*, Art. 206; *Presidential Decree thereunder*, Art. 90. When the license of a securities business is cancelled by the MOF, the aggrieved party may bring an appeal and administrative action under the pertinent laws, only if the revocation is illegal or significantly unfair. *See the Appeals Act of 1951* (Law No. 221. promulgated on Aug. 3, 1951) and *the Administrative Procedure Act of 1951* (Law No. 213, promulgated on Aug. 24, 1951).

only the discipline of officers by the SSB and revocation of the trading membership registration by the KSE. The legislature should seriously reappraise these deficiencies to ensure fair administration of the disciplinary rules.

Finally, the legislature also failed to include in the SEA or other pertinent laws a provision preventing a former KSE officer who has been removed or has resigned by reason of any misconduct from being employed by a securities company or other securities institution. Though the actual cases of such employment have been rare in Korea, a great potential for such practice exists because of the lack of regulation. Considering the possible conflicting interests and a strong need to establish a higher ethical standard in the securities industry, introduction of a provision preventing such an employment is necessary and appropriate. The same prohibition should be applicable to the officers and employees of other regulatory agencies who have resigned or who have been removed for the same reason.

B. Regulation of Securities Transactions on the Exchange Floor

   1. Basic Structure of Regulation

      a. Listing, Delisting, and Supervision over Listed Corporations

Securities transactions to be effected on the exchange floor are limited to securities listed on the exchange.[54] The listing of securities means to designate securities as objects of trading on the exchange. The listing of a security may, under the SEA, be effected in two ways: by an application of issuers and by a MOF order. When issuers file an application accompanied by the required documents with the KSE, the KSE must examine the application and get the SAC's approval for the listing.[55]

Modeled substantially after the Japanese exchange rule, the KSE has enacted specific standards for listing requirements which concern the size and business condition of the issuer, liquidity of the securities, and other pertinent factors to ensure fair price formation and mar-

---

54. There, however, appears no explicit provision in the SEA or Decrees and rules thereunder which makes it unlawful for any trading member to effect a transaction on the exchange in any non-listed securities.

55. *SEA*, Art. 88; *Presidential Decree thereunder*, Arts. 45–6. Listing of a certain exempted security need not be subject to the SAC's approval.

ketability.[56] The listing standard for equity security is substantially the same as the requirements for a publicly-held corporation. To deter any forgery, all the share certificates of listed stocks must be issued in compliance with a standard form prescribed by the SSB. The MOF may order the KSE to list certain securities if it deems such listing necessary and appropriate in the public interest and for the investors' protection.[57]

The KSE has two Sections on its floor board for listed securities. All stocks newly listed and debt securities are in Section II.[58] Strict qualifications must be met for any stock to be designated as a stock of Section I.[59] If a stock fails to meet such qualifications, the KSE changes its Section. Issues listed on the first Section are usually eligible for margin trading.

With the SAC's approval, the KSE may delist any security which comes under the delisting standards.[60] Any issuer of a security may

---

56. *KSE Rules on Listing*, Arts. 2 & 11 (promulgated on July 1, 1971, as amended on Jan. 20, 1976); *KSE Standards for the Examination of Listing*, Arts. 3 & 4 (promulgated on July 1, 1971, as amended on Jan. 20, 1976). For the listing standards in Japan, *see* as an example Tokyo Stock Exchange, *Rules on Listing Securities; Screening Standards for Listing;* Japan Securities Research Institute, *supra* note 24, at 97–99.

57. *SEA*, Art. 90.

58. *KSE Rules on Listing*, Art. 17 (as amended on July 1, 1974).

59. *KSE Standards for the Section Designation and Its Changes*, Arts. 2–4 (promulgated on July 1, 1974, as amended on May 1, 1975). When any corporation has been listed on Section I, its new shares belong to the same Section. To be designated as a listed stock of Section I, a corporation must meet the following requirements: (1) its paid-in capital should exceed ₩ 1 billion; (2) its dividend payments to non-government shareholders should exceed 10% per year; (3) the average trading volume of the stock concerned for the last six months should exceed 1% of the total liquid stock; (4) the stock concerned should have been traded on the exchange for more than half of each business day during the last six months; and (5) at least six months should have passed since the listing of the stock concerned.

60. *SEA*, Art. 89(1); *KSE Rules on Listing*, Art. 20; *KSE Delisting Standards*, Arts. 2 and 3 (promulgated on July 1, 1974, as amended on Mar. 1, 1975). Any listed stock may be delisted when it or its issuer falls within any of the following categories: (1) the paid-in capital is reduced to below ₩ 200 million; (2) the number of minority shareholders is reduced to below 50; (3) the total holdings of the minority shareholders is reduced to below 5/100 of the liquid stock; (4) the total holdings of a controlling person or persons exceeds 51% of the total

file an application for delisting with the KSE.[61] The KSE is also empowered to suspend the listing of any security if it appears to be necessary.[62] Under the SEA, listed corporations are required to file annual and semi-annual reports, following prescribed forms, with both the SAC and the KSE.[63] In addition, they must meet the provisions of the KSE rules and resolutions of the KSE board, by virtue of their agreement in the listing contracts. The KSE rules, *inter alia*, require listed corporations to make timely disclosures in writing to the KSE when a certain material fact has occurred.[64] Further, the KSE may, in writing or by phone, ask any listed corporation about any rumor or non-public information in order to confirm it. The corporation should immediately respond to this request through its personnel (the three selected disclosure officers) who are in charge of making

---

number of shares issued and outstanding; (5) no trade in the stock has been executed on the exchange for the last six months; (6) a readjustment or reorganization proceeding under the pertinent law is deemed to be necessary for the issuer; (7) the issuer violates a material provision of the KSE Rules on Listing or the listing agreement; (8) the issuer is legally confirmed as dissolved or merged into or consolidated with other corporation; (9) material misrepresentation is stated in a document filed by the issuer with the KSE; or (10) it appears necessary or appropriate in the public interest or for the protection of investors that the KSE delist any listed stock.

61. *KSE Rules on Listing,* Art. 19. It is required that a copy of the resolution, passed at a shareholders' meeting, to delist any security be submitted to the KSE.

62. *SEA,* Art. 89 (2); *KSE Rules on Listing,* Arts. 80 (2) and 22. The KSE may suspend any listed security, if: (1) such security appears to be traded excessively or there is a likelihood of manipulation in the trading in that security; (2) the issuer of such security fails to meet a duty to make any required report, notice, or answer to an inquiry and that results in an adverse impact on the protection of investors; (3) any documents filed by the issuer include a false statement of a fact; or (4) it appears to be necessary or appropriate in the public interest and for the protection of investors that the KSE suspend the listing of such security.
When the KSE suspends the listing or cancels the suspension, it must report this to the SAC without delay.

63. *SEA,* Arts. 92 and 93 and 186; *Presidential Decree thereunder;* Art. 47; and *MOF Decree thereunder,* Arts. 15 and 16. For the SEA's reporting requirement of current information, *see* pp. 244–49 *infra*.

64. *KSE Standards for the Administration of Listed Securities,* Art. 2 (promulgated on July 1, 1974, as amended on Jan. 20, 1976). The Article lists nine categories of material facts which fall under the current reporting rule.

timely disclosures of material information.[65]

Such requirements for filing periodic reports and for disclosing material inside information could play a significant role for the protection of investors. The rules will not effectively work to enforce a timely and fair disclosure and to maintain a fair and orderly market unless a complete and properly functioning regulatory or supervisory structure exists. Unfortunately, the supervisory structure of listed corporations has several drawbacks.

First, the supervisory power to delist or suspend any listed securities rests mainly in the KSE. The SAC is empowered only to approve the delisting by the KSE. In the case of a suspension, the SAC must be notified by the KSE immediately following the suspension order. When the KSE fails in the timely exercise of its supervisory powers, no back-up measures in the SEA oversee or supersede the KSE's functioning. Thus, reallocation of the supervisory power is necessary to carry out the fair, timely supervision of listed corporations.[66]

Second, a disciplinary device is more efficient than delisting or suspension is. Delisting or suspension sometimes only costs minority shareholders at the loss of a trading market. Under such circumstances, the imposition of a considerable fine or other criminal sanction on a person violating a rule would be a more effective deterrent.[67]

Third, the present procedure for delisting or suspension is far from meeting the Constitution's basic philosophy on due process of law. Providing an issuer with an appropriate notice and an opportunity to defend himself prior to a final decision is essential to the fair administration of the rules.[68]

---

65. *Id.*, Art. 3.
66. In Japan, the Ministry of Finance is empowered to order an exchange to delist or suspend certain listed securities even though the exchange has the supervisory power to delist or suspend. *See Japanese SEA*, Arts. 112, 117, and 119.
67. The SEA has a provision imposing a fine of not more than ₩ 5 million on any issuer who fails to file periodic reports. It is hard to construe this provision to cover the misrepresentation of material fact made in the report because no explicit phrase on the matter appears in the context of the provision. No other supplementary provision appears in the Decrees thereunder or the KSE rules. *See SEA*, Arts. 211, item 1, 92 and 93.
68. Article 119 of the Japanese SEA also requires that the regulatory agency give the issuer an appropriate notice and opportunity for a hearing.

b. Regulation of Floor Trading
(1) *Kinds and Methods of Securities Transactions*

As in Japan, the kinds and methods of securities transactions in Korea are prescribed in the KSE Rules on Business by the mandate of the SEA.[69] Four types of transactions are allowed on the KSE floor:[70] a) spot transactions; b) regular-way transactions; c) specified-date transactions; and d) when-issued transactions. Among these, the regular way is the most popular one as in Japan and the United States. All these transactions must be cleared through the KSE's clearing house.[71]

In every trading session the KSE provides a two-way auction at which its trading members buy or sell securities for their own accounts or for their customers' accounts.[72] All bids (offers to purchase) or offers (offers to sell) at this auction are made publicly by the KSE floor officer and are written down in the form prescribed by the KSE.[73] Each broker must attempt to get the best price possible for its customers.[74] At the auction the KSE rule provides priorities among the bids and offers made according to their price, time, or size. A broker must report to its customer without delay about the execution of an order in a form prescribed by the SAC.[75]

---

69. *SEA*, Art. 94; *KSE Rules on Business*, Art. 4–3. Cf. *Japanese SEA*, Art. 108.
70. *See KSE Rules on Business*, Arts. 4–3 and 31; *see also* note 42 *supra*. Settlement and clearance in the regular way in Korea must be completed on the third business day after the transaction. In the specified-date transaction, the clearance should be completed on a specified date as may be agreed upon by the parties concerned within 15 days after the transaction. The when-issued transaction is available only for shares to be newly issued by a corporation already in existence. The date for the clearance under this method should be designated by the KSE as one of the days after the completion of capital contribution(or a proposed date for the distribution of new shares in the case of stock dividends).
71. *Id.*, Art. 28.
72. *Id.*, Arts. 5–7.
73. *Id.*, Arts. 9–10.
74. *See* KSE, *Specific Rules on the Execution of Contract Under the Rules on Business*, #1. The highest bid and lowest offer must be granted precedence in all cases. In the case of the same price, the priority must be given to the earliest in time. If the price and time are same, the priority must be given to a larger one over a smaller one.
75. *SEA*, Art. 46.

The so-called "swallowing" practice is prohibited in Korea as in the United States or Japan.[76] When a broker has been entrusted with a purchase or sales order from its customers on the exchange market and sells stock owned by itself, it must execute such orders through the exchange floor. Although the prohibition of "swallowing" was mainly to concentrate tradings in the exchange market, this prohibition could also eliminate possible conflicting interests inherent in such a transaction. In order to guarantee the customer concerned the best possible price in such a transaction, the KSE Rules require the broker to go through the auction procedure first before it deals for an account in which it, either directly or indrectly, has an interest.[77]

(2) *Trading Units and Block Transactions*

A trading unit consists of 100 shares of stock or debt securities with a par value of ₩ 50,000.[78] But, "odd-lot" shares, those below the trading unit, may be traded on the exchange floor if the KSE deems it necessary. A special auction procedure is provided for a large block of shares which is 1,000 trading units or more on floor Section I, or 500 trading units or more on floor Section II.[79]

In the United States and Japan, a block transaction in a listed security exceeding a certain number of trading units may be executed off the exchange floor. This is an alternative device designed to handle a large volume of transactions with which the classic auction market mechanism cannot cope.[80] The KSE rules, however, do not have

---

76. *Id.*, Arts. 101, 44; *Japanese SEA*, Art. 129; *NYSE Rule 76*. For the term "swallowing," *see* note 42 *supra*.

77. *KSE Rules on Business*, Arts. 46–7.

78. *Id.*, Art. 12. Usually, the "odd-lot" shares are traded in the OTC market.

79. *Id.*, Art. 7–2; *KSE Specific Rules on Execution of Contract*, #3.

80. *See* Jennings & Marsh 608–12 (4th ed. 1977); Tatsuta, 92–95.

In the United States

The economic mode upon which the rules of the New York Stock Exchange have been based contemplates a continuous central auction market where all buyers and sellers will congregate and effect transactions in securities through the free competition of bids and offers. The specialist system developed as an essential lubricant to the maintenance of the continuity of the market and a fair and orderly market.

Since 1960, however, institutional trading (by mutual funds, pension and profit-sharing funds, and other fiduciaries) increased rapidly, and as a consequence, the specialist was unable to play its role due to the lack of sufficient capital to assume large positions. Even though the required minimum capital

any provision allowing an off-floor transaction in a large block of

was increased several times, the capitalization of the specialist firms was inadequate to meet the demand. Block transactions were impossible to execute immediately in the auction market, since it was unlikely that there would be buyers already in the crowd bidding for 15,000 or 25,000 shares of a particular stock.

The Exchange developed new devices: Special Offer or Special Bid which had to remain open for a minimum period of 15 minutes, and the seller or buyer may offer an extra commission; and a so called Exchange Distribution or Exchange Acquisition, which was somewhat similar to an underwritten public offering, although the transactions were effected on the Exchange floor rather than in the over the counter market by a syndicate of members. These techniques, however, were insufficient to solve the problem, and as a result off-floor block transactions (the third market) were in fact conducted.

The off-floor transactions were conducted as negotiated sales or purchases, which were merely recorded on the floor of the Exchange, but were not in fact a part of the auction market process. The other side of the market typically was found from one or more of four types of investors—specialist, other member firms of the NYSE ("positioners"), other institutional investor, and a so-called "market maker" who was not a member of the NYSE but who engaged in trading as a principal in listed securities on the NYSE. On Nov. 7, 1966, the NYSE amended its Rule 394 so that a member could, under certain broadened circumstances, effect a transaction with an off-floor market maker in any listed stock. The member had to first make a diligent effort to explore the feasibility of obtaining a satisfactory execution of the order on the floor and then report the facts concerning the proposed transaction to a Floor Governor. Also the member had to ask other members in the crowd whether they had orders to execute at the same price and on the same side of the market. These provisions were criticized as inadequate at the time they were issued by persons active in the third market, and apparently were not used very extensively. Finally, along with the 1975 Amendments of the Securities Exchange Act, the SEC released its intent to repeal Rule 394 as to principal transactions and agency transactions.

In Japan

Securities exchange in Japan prohibit generally their members from effecting a transaction off the floor of exchanges in listed securities. To meet increasing demands for bulk sales, a so-called *"baikai"* was developed and prevailed until its abolishment in 1967. The *"baikai,"* a special term used only in securities and commodity industries, was a way of effecting a transaction by matching a sell order with a buy order for the same security in the hands of a single exchange member, (*"tsukeawase baikai"*), or by matching a customer's order with the member's own bid or offer (*"shikiri baikai"*), at a price at which the last sale of the security concerned was executed on listed securities. Rather, the KSE rule provides a procedure of "Spe-

---

the exchange floor. Heated arguments arose on the legality of this practice, since a single member assumed both roles in the contract and "swallowing" was prohibited. But commentators were in agreement in their conclusion, though their grounds varied, that the *"baikai"* was legal and valid and a court also supported this conclusion.

The *"baikai,"* however was completely abolished in October, 1967, due to abuses and its drawbacks. Its drawbacks were: (1) since a single member matches a selling order with a buying order for the same security, *"baikai"* prevents concentration of trading on the floor and hinders determination of the fair market price of the security; (2) *"baikai"* is an exception to the principle of time priority ("first come, first served") and deprives other members of an opportunity for favorable trading; (3) the customer's interest conflicts with that of the member who executed the order according to the *"shikiri baikai"* method. Along with the abolishment, exchanges adopted two new techniques for off-floor trading in listed securities.

One is an off-floor distribution of listed securities, which was modeled after "Special Offer" provided in Rule 391 of the New York Stock Exchange. But the procedure differs from that of a "Special Offer." When a member has a customer's selling order for a block of securities which exceeds the volume prescribed by the exchange and which is difficult to execute on the floor in a reasonable time and at a reasonable price, he may, with the prior approval of the customer as to a special fee in addition to the usual commission, execute the order off the floor. The member must obtain the prior approval of the exchange during the trading hours and the transaction should be executed within the next business day. The exchange must announce the terms of such a transaction after the closing of floor trading on the day when it gave approval. The off-floor distribution must be executed: (1) by matching buying orders with the offering at a price fixed by the customer ranging between the closing price of the day when the exchange gave the approval and 95% of that price; or (2) by resorting to an auction in which bid should exceed 95% of such closing price.

Another technique adopted in 1967 is the procedure of "Block Sales" or "Block Purchases," which was modeled after the "Exchange Distribution" or "Exchange Acquisition" provided in Rule 392 of the New York Stock Exchange. When a member has a customer's order of a block of securities which exceeds the volume prescribed by the exchange, and which is difficult to execute in a reasonable time and at a reasonable price, the member may solicit others off the floor for an offer to sell or to buy and may execute the order through auction on the floor. With the prior approval of the customer, the member may charge a special fee in addition to the entrustment commission at a special rate. The member also must obtain the prior approval of the exchange and file a report with the exchange after the completion of

cial Offer" or "Special Bid," which is similar to that of Rule 391 of the New York Stock Exchange.[81] This procedure requires that any order for block trading be marked on a call sheet for bid or offer, "block (dai)," and that such Special Bid or Special Offer remain open for five minutes during which time the auction procedure for other bids or offers is suspended. Then, the offers or bids received during the period must be executed in accordance with the prescribed priority.[82] No extra commission is required from the customer.

Indeed, there was no urgent need for a new technique for off-floor block transaction in Korea since institutional trading by organizations was not so large that the existing auction market mechanism could not cope. Even though no special study on the volume of institutional trading and block transactions has been made thus far, the demand for block transactions has been rapidly increasing along with the rapid expansion of mutual funds and financial intermediaries.[83] Thus, in the near future the KSE will face difficulties because of the increasing market demand for block transaction and new techniques should be designed to cope with these problems.

(3) *Daily Report of Floor Trading*

The KSE is required under the SEA to file a report of daily trading on its floor with the MOF and the SAC by the next day.[84] The report must include the kinds of transactions executed, their volume per each listed security, and the prices. The price must be classified into

---

such a transaction.

Also available is "crossing" of customers' orders or "crossing" for the account of the member firm. Unlike the *"baikai,"* a member, prior to its crossing, must try for an asked price on the floor which is higher than his bid price by the maximum fluctuation. A cross is effected in an open way and constitutes a part of floor trading.

81. *KSE Rules on Business*, Art. 7–2; KSE, *Specific Rules for the Execution of Contract*, #3. Cf. 2 *CCH NYSE Guide* 2391 (Rule 391).

82. *Id.* The price in a Special Bid or Special Offer for a block transaction must have priority over other bids or offers already made. When a customer's order for block trading is not completely executed through this special auction procedure, the remaining volume must be executed by matching offers or bids made prior to the five minute suspension in accordance with their priority.

83. Unfortunately, no material is available on the volume or share of institutional trading in listed securities on the floor of the KSE.

84. *SEA*, Art. 102; *Presidential Decree Thereunder*, Art. 57. In addition, the MOF may request the KSE to report when necessary or appropriate.

the opening, closing, highest, and lowest prices of the day. In addition, the KSE must release every day the trading volume and prices to the public as well as quote them on the floor board. Considering the importance of rapid report and quoting systems both for the regulatory agencies and for public investors, the computerization of the system with automatic quotations like those in the United States is essential.

(4) *Entrustment of Orders and the Commission Rate Structure*

(a) Entrustment of Order

It is illegal under the SEA for any member to entrust itself with a customer's order for a securities transaction which is to be executed on the exchange at any place other than its head office, branch, or other business offices.[85] Under the mandate of the SEA, the KSE enacted Rules, which specify (i) the terms of conditions of being entrusted with a customer's order; (ii) delivery and method of settlement; (iii) rate of commission and method of its collection; and (iv) other matters necessary for the entrustment of a customer's order.[86]

The KSE Rules require that every member, prior to being entrusted with an order, receive the customer's written consent stating that he shall abide by the KSE Rules.[87] Every customer's order (even by phone or telegram) must be in compliance with the form prescribed in the KSE Rules.[88] The matters required in the form are the kind of trading, name of a security, volume, designation of price, time or period to execute the order, and the trading classification such as cash or margin. In the case of margin trading, credit extension by a member to his customer must be made on a "first come, first served" basis.

No person may entrust an order to buy or sell a security on the market under the condition that the security will be purchased or sold if and when the quotation of the security rises over or drops from his specified price.[89] The prohibition of entrusting such a "stop-loss" order was modeled after a similar prohibition in the Japanese SEA, which in turn was borrowed from the United States; however, this

---

85. *SEA*, Art. 109.
86. *Id.*, Art. 110.
87. *KSE Rules on Entrustment of Order*, Arts. 2 and 3.
88. *Id.*, Art. 4.
89. *SEA*, Art. 111.

prohibition in Korea is not effective.[90]

The purpose of such a "stop-loss" order, as Professor Loss has pointed out,[91] may be to limit the loss on an open commitment; to safeguard a profit on an open commitment; or to insure the making of a new commitment when a specific price level is reached. Such purposes belong to a category of natural instincts inherent in every human being; therefore, an absolute prohibition against these natural instincts of investors would be almost impossible to enforce. In addition, insofar as an order is allowed at a member's complete discretion, such prohibition would be meaningless.[92]

Except for the prohibition of a "stop-loss" order, no other prohibition of or restriction on entrustment appeared either in the SEA or in the KSE Rules. Therefore, a market order, a limited price order, or even an order at a member's complete discretion (discretionary order) is available for investors.[93] Since the discretionary order could result in abuses inconsistent with the member's fiduciary duty as an agent and could raise disputes between the parties involved, the SEA requires that each member file a report on the execution of such an

---

90. For the rule in Japan, *see Japanese SEA*, Art. 133 item (2); Tatsuta 90–91; also for the rule in the U.S., *see Securities Exchange Act of 1934*, Sec. 10 (a), 15 U.S.C.A. §78 j(a); Jennings & Marsh, 558 at n. 10 and its accompanying text. Article 133 of Japanese SEA authorizes the prohibition of a "stop-loss" order in a Cabinet Order. But, no Cabinet Order has been enacted to effect such a prohibition. In the United States, the Exchange Act authorized the SEC to prohibit stop-loss orders in its rules, but no rule has yet followed. Thus, "stop-loss' orders can be used in these countries.

In Korea, however, the text of Article 111 of the SEA includes no such mandate to others. Thus, the prohibition provided in Article 111 is effective itself as a matter of law.

91. 2 Loss, *Securities Regulation* 1202 (2d ed. 1961).

92. *See infra*, note 93 and its accompanying text.

93. A market order is an order to buy or sell a stated amount of a security at the most advantageous price obtainable as promptly as is reasonably practicable. The limited price order is an order to buy or sell a stated amount of a security at a stated price or at a better price if obtainable. The bulk of the trading member's brokerage business consists of executing limited price orders. A discretionary order is an order to sell or buy a security at the member's sole discretion, that is, without any restrictions on the kind and method of trading, or the amount and price of a security.

order with the KSE by the fifth day of the next month.[94] Also, the member must refrain from effecting, for the discretionary account, securities transactions which are excessive when compared to the customer's intention and the amount entrusted in the account. Because of the experiences of developed countries like the United States and Japan, a more sophisticated rule for discretionary accounts should be designed so that possible abuses, detrimental both to the customers' interest and to the maintenance of a fair and orderly market, could effectively be deterred.[95]

A customer must, at the time of his entrustment of an order, deposit a certain amount of money, or securities equivalent thereto, with the trading member.[96] The amount of security money required is determined by the KSE from time to time in accordance with trading conditions. However, the KSE rules provide an exception to this deposit requirement for cash transactions for an institutional investor who submits a certificate of the "registered seal-impression" of its representative prior to the entrustment.[97] Such an exception deserves some

---

94. *SEA*, Art. 107.
95. *Japanese SEA*, Art. 127; Tatsuta, 90. The restriction provided in the Korean SEA on the discretionary accounts is modeled after that of the Japanese SEA. The Japanese restriction, however, is stricter and more sophisticated due to frequent disputes which resulted from the discretionary accounts and adverse impact on the maintenance of an orderly market. In addition to the restraint on excessive trading and the report filing requirement in the SEA, the authority (MOF), in a release, requested securities companies not to engage in discretionary account transactions except in accordance with strong demands on the part of their customer. Each association of securities companies responded to this release by providing in its rules that each member must prohibit its registered representatives from accepting discretionary orders from customers. The authority recommended as a matter of regulation that securities companies have the customer execute a written contract form with a clause to the effect that all profits and losses belong to him. Unlike Korea, Japan requires that a more important item be stated in a monthly report on discretionary accounts—the number of accounts which have gained profits and the number of those which have suffered loss.
96. *KSE Rules on Entrustment of Order*, Arts. 7, 17, 17–2. The money or security under this requirement is called as *"Wetag-Cheunggoekeum"* in cash transaction or *"Bocheungkeum* (margin)" in margin transaction. The minimum amount must be 30% in the former and 40% in the latter.
97. *Id.*, Art. 7, proviso (as amended on Jan. 20, 1976). The "registered-seal" of a

comment since it represents a great advantage for institutional investors over individual investors.

Institutional investors usually have stronger financial capacity than most individual investors have. Although a certificate of the representative's "registered seal-impression" ensures to some extent the specific performance of the transaction, the purpose behind requiring the deposit of security money is not only to facilitate full payment of the consideration, but also to deter excessive trading and speculation beyond the customers' financial capability. Therefore, such an exception for institutional investors is unfair for individual investors, and allows the institutional investors an opportunity for excessive trading and speculation.

(b) Commission Rate Structures

Like the Japanese exchange, the KSE adopted a fixed minimum commission structure, the rate of which is classified into three categories depending upon the trading volume to reflect quantity discounts; every KSE trading member must charge minimum commissions at the same rate if the volume of trading belongs to the same category.[98] The KSE rule denies members the freedom to bargain over commissions. Any violation of this fixed commission rule may be subject to the issuance of a warning or the suspension of a transaction, but the KSE has not exercised this disciplinary power to date.[99]

Because Korea adopted a single, central exchange market system

---

person is a peculiar device in Korea designed to prevent any forgery of a legal document to lighten the burden of proving the effectiveness of a contract or agreement entered into. Usually, the parties making a contract are required to press the "registered-seal" at the bottom of the signature.

98. *KSE Rules on Entrustment of Order*, Art. 23. The commission rate schedule is as follows:
    a. Stock (as amended on Jan. 20, 1976)
        (1) "round-lot" trading:

Trading Volume	Rate
a) below W 1 million:	1.0%
b) between W 1 and W 5 million:	0.9%
c) over W 5 million:	0.8%

        (2) "odd-lot" trading: 1% of trading volume.
    b. Debt Securities (as amended on Mar. 10, 1976): 0.2% of the trading volume.
99. KSE, *Specific Rules on Disciplinary Standards*, Art. 13; *KSE Rules on Business*, Art. 60.

where all securities companies have been registered as KSE trading members, the commission rate structure is relatively simple, and few serious regulatory problems have arisen. However, as the volume of institutional trading has increased recently, the fixed commission rate rule is frequently violated by members who offer favorable rebates or discounts to induce or maintain large institutional customers. This practice raises a basic question as to whether the fixed commission rates should be maintained or replaced by an alternative such as the competitive commission rates adopted in the United States in 1975.

The lengthy history of the United States' fixed commission rates originated in the enactment of the Securities Exchange Act of 1934, which gave a clear authority to supervise exchange self-regulation with respect to the "fixing of reasonable rates of commission."[100] This system of fixed rates for brokerage commission raised a significant antitrust question because it constituted price-fixing and no explicit antitrust exemption for exchanges was included in the statute.

The applicability of the antitrust law to stock market regulation in the United States has not been clearly resolved by either a court or statute.[101] Nothing that the Securities Exchange Act of 1934 contains no explicit antitrust exemption for exchanges, the Court in *Silver* laid down a substantive test for reconciling antitrust laws with securities regulation: "Repeal of the antitrust laws is to be regarded as implied only if necessary to make the Securities Exchange Act work, and even then only to the minimum extent necessary."[102]

---

100. *See Securities Exchange Act of 1934*, Sec. 19(b) (9), 15 U.S.C.A. §78s(b) (9) (1970).

101. *See* generally Pozen, *Competition and Regulation in the Stock Markets*, 73 MICH, L. REV, 317, 323 *et seq.* (1974). In resolving conflicts between competition and regulation in the stock markets, the courts and Congress in the United States have used the anti-trust laws and the 1934 Securities Exchange Act as proxies for opposing policies. Such conflicts have been approached as jurisdictional disputes involving procedural and substantive questions. However, these questions have been answered inconsistently.

102. *Silver v. New York Stock Exchange*, 373 U.S. 341, 357 (1963). There, a non-member broker brought an action against the NYSE under the Sherman Act after it ordered the discontinuance of his wire connections with the offices of NYSE members without notice, explanation, or a hearing. The Court held that the anti-trust court should adjudicate Silver's claim without

However, the antitrust question has been answered differently in the area of fixed commission rates in subsequent cases.

In *Kaplan v. Lehman Brothers*, where shareholders of certain mutual funds alleged the NYSE's fixed commissions to constitute *per se* a violation of the antitrust laws, the district court distinguished *Silver* on the ground that agency review was available in *Kaplan*, because "the SEC exercises a general and continuing power to change, alter, or supplement the Exchange fixing the rates of commission."[103] Although the court in *Thill Securities Corp. v. NYSE*[104] deviated to some extent from *Kaplan*, the Supreme Court in *Gordon v. NYSE* confirmed *Kaplan* by holding that "the system of fixed commission rates, which is under the active supervision of the SEC, is beyond the reach of the antitrust laws."[105]

During over forty years in practice, the fixed rates raised serious regulatory problems because of the frequent circumvention and erosion of the rule caused by fragmentation of the market and multiple trading.[106] Such frequent circumvention or evasion was also largely

---

prior consideration by the SEC, on the grounds that the SEC lacked jurisdiction.

103. 250 F. Supp. 562 (N.D. Ill. 1966), *aff'd*, 371 F. 2d 409 (7th Cir.), *cert. denied*, 389 U.S. 954 (1967).

104. 433 F. 2d 264 (7th Circ. 1970), *cert. denied*, 401 U.S. 994 (1971). Although the court did not overrule *Kaplan*, it attempted to distinguish Kaplan on the grounds that the plaintiffs in *Thill* did not allege a per se violation of the anti-trust laws, that the anti-rebate rule, unlike the fixed commission rule, could be used to injure particular competitors, and that there was no evidence that the SEC was currently exercising its jurisdiction over anti-rebate rules. 433 F. 2d at 270–71.

105. *See* CCH Fed. Sec. L. Rep. 95215 (U. S. 1975).
Three factors influencing such holding were noted: (1) statutory authorization for regulation by the SEC under Section 19 (9) of the Exchange Act; (2) the long history of SEC's oversight, which culminated in the adoption of a rule requiring a transaction to competitive rates; and (3) continued Congressional approval of the SEC's authority over the commission rate system.
For the lower court decision, *see* 498 F. 2d 1303 (2d Cir. 1974).

106. Significant regulatory problems, in connection with the implementation of the fixed commission rates, were created largely by the existence of many regional exchanges, non-member brokers and dealers, and multiple-trading. Until the abolition of the fixed commission rates in 1975, there were various

attributable to institutional investors who held larger portfolios than individuals, sought short term capital appreciation more actively, turned over portfolios much faster, and traded larger quantities of stock. They undermined the backbone of the exchanges' auction market, refused to pay the fixed minimum rates, and found members offering more favorable terms by means of rebates, "give-ups," or better services.[107]

Regulations to maintain the fixed minimum commission rates are noted to impose both large efficiency losses and administrative expenses.[108] A fixed rate would never be efficient in fully competitive markets. Also, administrative bodies must guard against black markets and kickback schemes to ensure that investors and brokers do not circumvent a fixed rate. Professor Pozen argues that trading restrictions on marketplaces tend to impose relatively high efficiency losses and relatively low administrative expenses because of the existence of so few marketplaces; and that restrictions on brokerage activity tend to have the opposite effects, because of the existence of so many brokers.[109] He further asserts that both efficiency losses and administrative expenses imposed by a regulatory restriction would generally be passed on to investors in the form of higher prices for transactional serivces. Thus, he concludes that regulatory restrictions designed to promote the purpose of the 1934 Act should be judged according to a revised *Silver* test: "a regulatory restriction should be

---

types of erosion and circumvention of the exchanges' minimum commission structure, including customer directed "give-ups," reciprocity, end run, and incorporated give-up pocket. For a detailed discussion of the fragmentation of the securities markets and the erosion of the fixed commission rates, *see* Werner, *Adventure in Social Control of Finance: The National Market System,* 75 COLUM. L. REV. 1233 (1975).

107. *Id.,* 1256 *et seq.* Institutional investors, using the existing relationships between single and dual members on the regional exchanges, placed their orders with a dual member. After this "lead broker" had assembled matching sides, the institution would direct it to place the transaction on a regional exchange and to give up part of its commission to sole members and sometimes even to broker-dealers, non-members of the exchange. Give-up deals often became highly complex. Some were structured to return the institutional customer a benefit of 90% of the commission nominally paid.

108. *See* Pozen *supra* n. 97 at 351–54, citing *The SEC's Institutional Investor Study Report.* H.R. Doc. No. 64, 92d Cong., 1st Sess. 2182–89 (1971).

109. *Id.,* 352

violated only if its regulatory benefits outweigh the efficiency losses and administrative expenses imposed by the restriction."[110]

After the completion of a comprehensive study on the impact of block trading by institutional investors and the structural change of the securities markets, the United States' Congress finally eliminated the fixed commission rates and effectuated competitive commission rates as of May 1, 1975.[111] Along with adoption of a central market system, this replacement of the commission rates was a move toward an efficient securities market by eliminating restraints on competition and market fragmentation and by providing the best execution both for investors and brokerage firms.

Although it is too early to make a decisive conclusion as to the impact of competitive commissions on the securities industry, the SEC's report thereon is revealing. The commission, for the period of twenty months from May 1, 1975, through December 31, 1976, found: (1) New York Stock Exchange member firms' revenue foregone as the result of competitive commission rates is estimated to be $682 million or about 6.3% of their total revenue; (2) that because trading activity has been very high compared to preceding periods, the financial condition of broker-dealers in the aggregate has actually improved substantially in spite of the lost commission revenue; (3) institutional investors and individuals who transact larger orders (between 1,000 and 10,000 shares) appear to have benefited from substantially reduced commission rates, but rates on 90 of individual orders (those for less than 1,000 shares) have edged slightly upward in current dollars.[112]

---

110. *Id.*, 353

111. *Institutional Investor Study Report supra* n. 104; *Statement on the Structure of the Securities Markets*, 37 Fed. Reg. 5286 (1962); *Policy Statement on the Structure of a Central Market System* (March 29, 1973), SRLR No. 196, at D–1 (1973); *also see Securities Exchange Act of 1934* Secs. 6(e), 11A (a) (1) (c), as added by the 1975 Amendments, 89 Stat. 97 §7; SEC, *Sec. Exch. Act Rel. No. 11073* (Oct. 24, 1974), CCH Fed. Sec. L. Rep. 79, 991 (proposed rule 19b–3, which requires all exchanges to eliminate fixed commissions by May 1, 1975): SEC, *Sec. Exch. Act Rel. No. 11203* (Jan. 23, 1975), CCH Fed. Sec. L. Rep 80,067. For a detailed discussion of policy behind the 1975 Amendments, *see* Werner *supra* note 106, at 1266 *et seq.*

112. *See* SEC, *Fifth Report to Congress on the Effect of the Absence of Fixed Rates of Commission* i.v. and 3–60 (May 26, 1977). The Commission, however, noted

Such an argument for the competitive commission rates and the SEC's findings are useful to determine the question of whether Korea also should abolish the current fixed commission rates in order to move toward competitively determined rates. Since Korea to date has not enacted modern antitrust laws similar to those in the United States, fixed rates of commission will not raise any antitrust question until an enactment of such laws. Fragmentation of the market does not appear to be serious because of the single national exchange system in which all the existing securities companies are registered as members. Practices circumventing the fixed commission rule have raised few significant regulatory problems although trading by institutional investors is increasing. In addition, since the current rule allows quantity discounts for customers of large orders, it tends to reduce the disadvantages of the fixed commission rates. If competitive commission rates are put into effect, the benefits would be available only for the institutional investors or individuals of large orders as experienced in the United States. The large number of small public investors would not be better off either in terms of costs or quality of services.

On the other hand, economic arguments[113] against moving toward the competitive commission rates may have strong ground, because the Korean securities industry is now in a developing stage. To eliminate fixed rates would create serious temporary disruptions during the transition period. Most inefficient firms will be hurt; some of them would be expected to leave the brokerage business, while others might improve efficiency or merge with more efficient firms. A reduc-

---

that the impact of competitive commission rates on the securities industry had been assessed during very favorable market conditions; thus, the impact which competitive rates might have during a down-cycle remains unknown.

113.   The two economic arguments against moving toward competitive commission rates generally take one of two forms. First, the transitional disruptions of moving from fixed to competitive rates are so severe that they outweigh any potential permanent advantages of such a move.; Second, even after the adjustement to competitive commissions, the overall characteristics of the brokerage industry would be inferior to the industry as it is currently structured, *See* generally Friend & Blume, *Competitive Commissions on the New York Stock Exchange*, 28. J. FIN. 795, 798–802 (Sep., 1973); *also see* NYSE, *Economic Effects of Negotiated Commission Rates on the Brokerage Industry, the Market for Corporate Securities, and the Investing Public* (1968).

tion in the number of brokerage firms could have an adverse impact on competition resulting in services of lower quality and reduction of public participation in the market. More critically, because of the lack of antitrust laws, the remaining smaller number of brokerage firms might move to fix commission rates at a higher level than they are now.

Therefore, adoption of competitive commission rates would not be desirable now for either the protection of investors or the promotion of the securities market. Competitive rates should be seriously considered only in the future when the securities industry is strengthened and when market conditions show serious inefficiency, cost, and regulatory problems.

2. A Need for Restriction on Floor Trading

"Floor trading" is trading by members of the securities exchange for their accounts while personally present on the trading floor of an exchange. Floor trading by members may contribute to the maintenance of continuous and liquid markets. On the other hand, it raises some regulatory issues because of the special advantages enjoyed by floor traders due to their presence on the floor, their tendency to trade with the trend, and the conflicts of interest involved in acting as both a floor trader and a commission broker. Section 11 of the Securities Exchange Act of 1934 in the United States limits and restricts floor trading and specialists' dealer activity to protect the public against excessive speculation, conflicts of interest, and the unfair advantages of market insiders.[114]

As noted earlier, the SEA allows all the KSE trading members to

---

114. Secs. 11(a) and (b). 15 U.S.C. § 78 k(a) & (b); NYSE, *Rules of Board of Governors*, Rules 108–12. Section 11(a) of the Exchange Act restricts floor trading by a member of a national securities exchange for any account in which he has an interest or in which he is vested with more than the usual broker's discretion by prohibiting such trading unless it comes under specified exemptions or conditions. Exempted transactions include: (1) transactions by dealers acting in the capacity of market maker; (2) transactions by specialists or odd-lot dealers in the performance of their respective functions; (3) bona fide arbitrage transactions or stabilizing transactions effected in compliance with the rules thereon; (4) any transactions to offset a transaction made in error; and (5) certain other transactions designated by the SEC consistent with the purpose of the exemption, the protection of investors, and the maintenance of fair and orderly markets.

effect floor trading; those with legal capital of more than ₩ 2 billion may also act as brokers. However, the SEA does not include a provision which restricts or limits floor trading in the public interest and for the maintenance of a fair and orderly market.[115] Most stock market crashes in Korea were caused primarily by the excessive floor trading of the KSE members—manipulations, excessive speculations, and sudden and unreasonable fluctuations in the prices of securities. Such evils impaired the maintenance of a fair and orderly market as well as public confidence in the mechanisms of the market. Therefore, a device to restrict floor trading should be carefully examined by weighing the potential harms and against advantages of unrestricted floor trading.

First, floor trading is usually defended on the grounds that added market liquidity and continuity have been a beneficial by-product of the presence of professionals on the floor. In Korea, where the KSE has no specialist who is functioning to insure the maintenance of a fair and orderly market, this defense is strong. In addition, because of the prohibition of off-floor block transactions, floor trading in Korea may play a significant role by providing capital on the floor to aid in the orderly assimilation and liquidation of large blocks of securities without disruption of the auction market. The experiences of stock market crashes, however, raise doubts as to whether such advantages to the continuity and liquidity of the market outweigh the potential evils inherent in floor trading. Furthermore, floor trading actually tends to have a destabilizing influence on prices because floor traders are generally buyers in rising markets and sellers in declining markets.[116] Their trading, as a result, appears to be inimical to the orderly functioning of the market, tending to accentuate price movements. Also, floor trading is usually heavily concentrated in the active securities, where additional liquidity is least needed. More fundamentally, the maintenance of a fair and orderly market and its con-

---

115. This is probably because the legislature overlooked this matter when modeling the framework of the SEA after the Japanese SEA which had no provision restricting floor trading.

116. In order to make more profits or reduce possible loss, trading with trend is quite natural for floor traders. This tendency was the same in the United States, *See* Jennings & Marsh 615–17 (4th ed. 1977) and 771–75 (3 ed. 1972). citing SEC, *Sec. Ex. Act Rel. No. 7290* (Apr. 9, 1964).

tinuity is the responsibility of the authorities, including the KSE itself, and floor traders are not explicitly obligated to share such responsibility.

Second, defenders of unrestricted floor trading may argue that the potential evils inherent in floor trading could be controlled and avoided by several regulatory provisions in the SEA and Decrees or Rules thereunder. Under the SEA, the SAC is empowered to issue an order concerning the trading members' portfolio management, and to prohibit excessive trading as well as deceptive and fraudulent practices on the floor.[117] The SEA prohibits manipulation and restricts stabilization.[118] In addition, any daily change in the price of a security must not exceed an upper or lower limit as specified in the KSE rules. On the other hand, to avoid conflicting interest, the KSE rules require that a floor trader should not, prior to the execution of a customer's order, effect a transaction for an account in which the trader has any direct or indirect interest.[119]

Enforcement of these rules over the past decade, however, demonstrates that these rules were not effective in restraining floor trading. The regulatory agency's power to issue an order, in effect, has not been preventive but curative. Limits on daily price changes have been ineffective in restraining floor trading since floor traders could accentuate price movements continuously within the limits. Such a set of rules fails to restrict effectively floor trading of members who enjoy various advantages over the public. Even in the United States, whose exchanges enforce more sophisticated rules to restrict floor trading, a special study concluded that "the existing regulation of floor trading has not been generally effective but in a most important respect it has been misdirected" and that "despite the great variety and complexity of exchange rules experimented with to date . . . floor traders still retain their significant private trading advantages in a public market, continue to concentrate their activities in the more active stocks, and continue to accentuate price movements."[120]

---

117. *SEA*, Arts. 54, 64, 108, 209 (item 7), and 210 (item 4); *Presidential Decree thereunder*, Arts. 37 (item 1), 66.
118. *SEA*, Art. 105. For details *see* pp. 211 *et seq. infra.*
119. *KSE Rules on Business*, Art. 46.
120. The original 1934 bills carried an outright prohibition of floor trading. The Exchange Act as passed, however, incorporated a more deliberate approach

3. A Need for Restriction on Short Selling

Short selling is usually a device whereby the speculator sells a security which he does not own, anticipating that the price will decline and that he will thereby be enabled to cover, or make delivery of the stock sold, by purchasing it at the lesser price or by borrowing it from others. If the decline materializes, the short seller realizes as a profit the difference between the sales price and the lower purchase or covering price. When an order is given to a KSE trading member to sell the stock short, the order is executed on the floor of the exchange and recorded in precisely the same manner as any other order to sell.[121] The purchaser is unaware whether he is buying from a short seller or an actual owner of stocks. The seller is required to make delivery of stocks he has sold within the period prescribed by the KSE Rules on business. Since he has no shares to deliver, he must obtain them somewhere. Usually, the trading member executing the sale either borrows the stock from the KSFC on its customer's behalf or makes loans in stock to the customer from the stock held in its own account.[122] When the short seller covers and returns the stock, the

---

and directed the SEC to prescribe such rules as it deems necessary or appropriate. In pursuance of the Congressional mandate the SEC had studied floor trading on at least 15 occasions between 1934 and 1963 (The most comprehensive were those conducted in 1936, 1945, and in 1962–63). The SEC determined tentatively to abolish floor trading in August 1945, but after considering the matter and holding conferences with the exchange, it determined not to abolish floor trading in light of repeated assurances that the exchanges would develop effective self-regulation of this activity. Subsequent to this, the New York Stock Exchange (NYSE) adopted rules designed to meet the problem. Two of these rules, Rule 108 dealing with priority or precedence and Rule 109 prohibiting "stopping" of stock for floor traders, have continued in effect substantially unchanged. The more important rule, now Rule 110, has undergone a steady process of amendment and erosion. For details, *see SEC, Sec. Ex. Act Rel. No. 7290,* cited in Jennings & Marsh 774–77 (3rd ed. 1972).

However, under the Securities Acts Amendments of 1975 floor trading is completely prohibited after May 1, 1978, except as may be otherwise expressly permitted by rule of the Commission. *See* Jennings & Marsh 616 (4th ed. 1977).

121. Also, a KSE trading member may sell the stock short for its own account. This transaction is executed and reordered in the same manner as any other transaction.

122. *See SEA,* Art. 49 and *MOF Decree thereunder,* Art. 12; KSFC, *Rules on Finance*

lender repays the sum which is on deposit with it, and the transaction is closed.

There were two extreme views of the impact of short selling practices on the securities market as a whole in the United States. Prior to the enactment of the Exchange Act of 1934 in the United States, the Banking and Currency Committee found in its 1934 report:

Few subjects relating to exchange practices have been characterized by greater differences of opinion than that of short selling. The proponents of short selling contend that *it is a necessary feature of an open market for securities*; that in a crisis short sellers are useful in maintaining an orderly market; and that their activities serve as a cushion to break the force of a decline in the price of stocks. Its opponents assert that *short selling unsettles the market, forces liquidation, depresses prices, accelerates declines, and has no economic value or justification.*[123] (Emphasis supplied.)

The grounds on which short selling is justified are that it does not operate as a depressive influence on the market as a whole, that it has little permanent influence on the long-term price of a stock, and that it sometimes performs useful functions in the securities market. However, opponents argue that short selling performs no useful services in the market; rather, it has harmful effects, as Mr. Flynn stated:

". . . that it (short selling) is purely an instrument in the hands of the pool operator, the floor trader, and the speculating specialist; that it can be used to hammer down the price of individual stocks and is used for that purpose; that it could perform a useful purpose in checking inflationary price rises if it were not for the fact that in practice the technique of trading has taught the broker that the time to apply short selling to the market is after the stock has begun

---

for Securities Trading (promulgated on Mar. 2, 1974, as amended on Mar. 3, 1975), Arts. 1, 4, 8–2, 10–17. There must be deposited with the lender of the stock the market value of the stock loaned, and the amount of this deposit varies with changes in the price of the security. If the market price rises, the deposit must be increased; and if the market price drops, the lender should return the difference between the amount deposited and the then market value of the security. The lender, during the life of the loan, may exercise the rights of the security deposited. Reasonable restrictions on the lender's right should be provided for the protection of borrowers.

123. *Stock Exchange Practices,* Report of Com. on Banking & Currency, S. Rep. No. 1455, 73d Cong., 2d Sess. (1934) at 50. For the details of pre–SEC selling, *see* Loss, *supra* note 91 at 1224–28.

to decline as a result of other forces."[124]

Apparently finding it impossible to discover where the truth lay between the extreme views expressed, Congress adopted Section 10(a) in the Exchange Act.[125] Section 10(a) mandated the SEC to frame a set of rules regulating short sales as the SEC deemed necessary or appropriate in the public interest and for the protection of investors.

Studying the effects of short selling in a rapidly declining market in the fall of 1937, the SEC concluded "that members trade predominantly with the price trend on balance" and "that in a declining market certain types of short sales are seriously destructive of stability."[126] It adopted rules on short sales in 1938 which were designed merely to curb certain harmful uses of the short sale and not to affect the underlying economic causes of market movement.[127] These short selling rules were amended several times to, *inter alia*, define the coverage of "short sale," set price restrictions, require marking of orders, and provide the requirements for covering purchases.[128]

---

124. *See* Flynn, *Security Speculation,* 227 (1934), cited in 2 Loss, *supra* at 1227.

125. *The Securities Exchange Act of 1934,* Sec. 10(a), 15 U.S.C.A. §78 j(a); S. Rep. No. 792, 73d Cong., 2d Sess. (1934) at 9. The text of Section 10(a), in part, reads: "It shall be unlawful for any person, directly or indirectly,. . . (a) To effect a short sale, or to use or employ a stop loss order in connection with the purchase or sale, of any security registered on a national securities exchange, in contravention of such rules and regulations as the Commission may prescribe as necessary or appropriate in the public interest of for the protection of investors." Under this mandate, the SEC enacted the Rules on short sales in 1938 but never adopted any rules on stop-loss orders. For the SEC Rules on short sales, *see* note 128 *infra*.

126. *See* SEC, *Sec. Ex. Act Rel. No. 1548* 5, 8 (1938); Loss, supra note 91, at 1229.

127. SEC, *Sec. Ex. Act Rel. No. 1548* 1-2 (1938). The then existing rules of the New York Stock Exchange (NYSE) prohibited short sales at a price below the last sale price. But the SEC found that these rules had not proven effective. *See* NYSE, *Rules of the Board of Governors,* Rule 435(1); Loss, *supra* note 91, at 1229, 1211.

128. *Rules under the Exchange Act,* Rules 3b-3, 10a-1, and 10a-2. Rule 3b-3 defined the term "short sale" to mean "any sale of a security which the seller does not own or any sale which is consummated by the delivery of a security borrowed by, or for the account of, the seller," It also defines the situations in which a person should be deemed to own a security; a person must be deemed to own securities only to the extent that he has a net long position.

Japanese short selling rules were copied after the American model. Article 133 of the Japanese SEA made it illegal for any person to effect a short sale in contravention of the provisions prescribed by Cabinet Order.[129] But, a special Rule of 1948 on Short Sale is still effective by virtue of a Cabinet Order.[130] The Rule requires that every order to sell be marked either "short" or "long."[131] It, however, prohibits short sales effected by a member only at a price below the last sale price on the floor, regardless of the next preceding different price.[132]

Rule 19a–1 sets a price restriction, which makes it illegal for any person to effect a short sale on the national exchanges at below the last "regular way" sale price or at such price if the price was itself higher than the last different regular way price which preceded it. Thus, after sales $49 7/8 and 50 an indefinite number of short sales may be effected at 50; but, after sales at 49 7/8 and 49 3/4, the minimum price at which a short sale may be effected is still 49 7/8. In determining the price at which a short sale may be effected after a security goes ex-dividend, ex-right, or ex-any other distribution, all sale prices prior to the "ex" date may be reduced by the value of such distribution. In addition, the rule requires that every sell order be marked either "long" or "short." The reason for marking this type of customer order "long" is that the sale is more apt to turn out to be long than short. Rules 10a–2 requires a broker or dealer to cover the open position for the delivery of securities sold pursuant to an order marked "long." However, these rules contain a number of exemptions, most of which have been added since 1939 as experience demonstrated the propriety of relaxing the restrictions. For details, *see* Loss, *supra* note 91, at 1229–35.

129. *Japanese SEA*, Art. 133 item (1). Law No. 270 as amended on July 31, 1952.
130. *Cabinet Order on the Enforcement of the SEA*, Art. 28; *Rules on Short Sale of Securities*, Japanese SEC Rule No. 16, as promulgated on July 24, 1948. Article 28 of the Cabinet Order provided that "the Cabinet Order under Article 133 (Short Selling Rule) and Article 194 (Proxy Rule) of the SEA must be as specially prescribed." Therefore, the Japanese SEC Rule on Short Sale and the Rule on Proxy Solicitation (Japanese SEC Rule No. 13, as promulgated on July 10, 1948) are still effective and, in fact, they constitute a part of the Cabinet Order.
131. *Rule on Short Sale of Securities*, Art. 1. But in actual practice a sell order is not marked since marking is no longer as necessary as it was in pre-war days when future transactions prevailed. *See* Tatsuta, 92.
132. *Id.*, Art. 2. Regulations of the securities exchanges provide the same rule. *See* e.g., Tokyo Securities Exchange, *Business Regulations*, Art. 85; Osaka Securities Exchange, *Business Regulations*, Art. 113. Like those in the United States, the rules also require that all sale prices prior to the "ex" date be

In Korea, only short sales in connection with insider short-swing trading are prohibited. This rule was modeled after Section 16(c) of the Exchange Act of 1934.[133] There are no other restrictions on short sales by the KSE trading members. Speculators and manipulators in every stock market crash employed short sales which accentuated price declines. The authority's efforts to prohibit short sales were in vain because of the strong objections from the securities business community and the fear that the activities of the secondary market might be significantly depressed if short selling were completely prohibited.[134]

The short selling practices in Korea have frequently been reported as still being prevalent with a serious destructive effect on the stability of a declining market. The Seoul Economic Newspaper reported that as of April 29, 1977, the volume of stock made loans for short sales increased four times as compared to the volume at the end of 1976; such an increase in short sales in the declining market tended to accentuate the price decline further, and many speculators, with support from securities companies, were interested in making short-term margins at the expense of some public investors.[135] Under the

---

reduced by the value of ex-dividend or ex-right.
In addition, both odd-lot and arbitrage transactions are exempted from the pricing restrictions.

133. *SEA*, Art. 188(1), Certain categories of insiders——officers, employees, and more than ten percent shareholders——of a listed corporation are prohibited from effecting a short sale of any security issued by their corporation, Originally, this prohibition was adopted in 1973 in a Presidential Decree, *See Presidential Decree under the SEA*, Art. 53 (PD No. 6634, as amended on Apr. 20, 1973). Cf. *The Securities Exchange Act of 1934*, Sec. 16(c), 15 U.S.C.A. §78 p (c); *The Investment Company Act of 1940*, Sec. 30(f).

134. *See* p.52 *supra*.

135. Seoul Economic Newpaper, Apr. 21, 1977, at p.4 and Apr. 22, 1977, at p.4. The KSFC and securities companies make loans in stock for short sellers. The former does so indirectly through the securities companies, while the latter does so directly with the portfolios which it held in its own account. *See* the accompanying text of note 122 *supra*. As of April 20, 1977, the percentage of loans made directly by securities companies for their customers reached 30% of the total volume of stock loans. Since the authority strictly controls only the extension of credit in cash, the securities companies were able to use their stocks held in their own accounts to make loans to support sellers. When they loaned stock, the securities companies receive interests as well as commissions from the customers.

present regulatory system, which allows broad freedom in short selling, such evils are almost inevitable. Indeed, the introduction of a set of rules designed to restrict the destabilizing effect of such short selling is urgently needed in Korea to ensure a fair and orderly market and to avoid a probable market crash like those in the 1960s and early 1970s.

Section II. *"Manipulation"* and *"Stabilization"*

I. Manipulation
A. *Legal Doctrine*

To maintain a free and open market, the SEA adopted Article 105 (formerly, Article 91) which prohibits manipulative and deceptive devices.[136] This Article prohibits certain activities raising or depressing the market prices of any listed security if such activities are effected for any statutory illegal purpose. It enumerates the activities that constitute objective requirements for manipulation as follows:

(1) to execute "matched orders;"[137] (2) to effect "wash-sales;"[138] (3) to entrust or to be entrusted with any order to effect (1) and (2) above;[139] (4) to operate "pool manipulations,"[140] manipulation in a narrow sense, or to entrust or to be

---

136. *SEA,* Art. 105. This provision was originally adopted as Article 91 in 1962 when the SEA was enacted.

137. *Id.,* Art. 105(1) items, 1 and 2. The term "matched orders" means the entry of an order or orders for the purchase (or sale) of any security with the knowledge that an order or orders of substantially the same size and at the substantially the same time and price for the sale (or purchase) of such security has been or will be entered by or for the same or different parties.

138. *Id.,* Art. 105(1), item 3. The term "wash sale" means any transaction in a security which involves no change in the beneficial ownership thereof. The operator of a "wash sale" is both buyer and seller of the same security.

139. *Id.,* Art. 105(1), item 4.

140. *Id.,* Art. 105(2), item 1. The concept of ''pool manipultion'' signifies a joint undertaking by a group of speculators to alter the price of a security artificially and to profit by price movement so engineered. For details of the control on pool manipulation in the United States, see Notes, *Manipulation of the Stock Market Under the Securities Laws,* 99 U. PA. L. REV. 651, 659 *et seq.* (1951); *Regulation of Stock Market Manipulation,* 56 YALE L.J. 509, 519 *et seq.* (1947). The text of this item reads: ''to effect, alone or with one or more other persons *in conspiracy, any transaction* in the security creating actual or apparent

entrusted with an order thereof; (5) to circulate or disseminate information to the effect that the price will or is likely to rise or fall because of manipulation;[141] and (6) to make a willful misrepresentation of a material fact which is false or misleading.[142]

These activities are not made illegal of themselves but are made illegal if they are effected for the statutory illegal purposes provided in the Article. The activities of items (1) through (3) above are prohibited only if they are effected "for the purpose of creating a false or misleading appearance of active trading in any listed security— or a false or misleading appearance with respect to the market for such a security."[143] The activities of items (4) through (6) above are prohibited only when they are effected "for the purpose of inducing the purchase or sale of such security by others."[144] Any person who violates any of these items is subject to criminal liability as well as civil liability.[145]

The Article on market manipulation was copied from the Japanese rule which in turn had been modeled on the Federal securities laws in the United States.[146] The text of the Article shows differences only in the "pool manipulation" provided in Paragraph 2, item 1. Unlike Japan or the United States, the text does not include the phrase "a series of" transactions but indicates "any" transaction.[147] In effect, however, the text would not make a big difference in determining pool manipulation because "any" transaction is required to be a transaction which is "creating actual or apparent active trading in any security or raising or depressing the price of such security;" and because the trading in such security will not appear actually or ap-

---

trading in such security or raising or depressing the price of such security, or to entrust or to be entrusted with such order." (emphasis added.) The phrases italicized show the differences in the text from those of the Japanese and American rules on pool manipulation. *See* the accompany texts of notes 147 and 148 *infra*.

141. *Id.*, Art. 105(2), item 2.
142. *Id.*, Art. 105(2), item 3.
143. *Id.*, Art. 105(1).
144. *Id.*, Art. 105(2).
145. *Id.*, Arts. 106, 208, 210.
146. *See Japanese SEA*, Art. 125; *also see The Securities Exchange Act of 1934*, Sec. 9(a) 15 U.S.C.A. 78i(a).
147. For the text of the item, *see* the italicized part of note 140 *supra*.

parently active or the price of such security will not rise or fall unless there are a series of transactions. However, the phrase "in conspiracy" in the same text, which is a counterpart of "with" or "in concert (or in conjunction with)" in the United States or Japan, would raise some difficulties and disputes in determining the coverage of the illegal activities of persons involved in any pool manipulation.[148]

B. Coverage of the Legal Doctrine

In the United States, the legal approach toward the problem of market manipulation was primarily developed through the concept of fraud in common law.[149] Because the reach of the strict fraud doctrine was inadequate, no case prior to 1934 had established the illegality of manipulation by actual purchases and sales.[150] Although the inadequacies of common law fraud doctrine were bolstered to some extent by statutory expressions of a broader concept of fraud,

---

148. For the text of the item, *see* the italicized part of note 140 *supra*. Due to the phrase "in conspiracy," the coverage of persons who are jointly liable for manipulative and deceptive devices would be limited. In practice, it is very hard to prove conspiracy to defraud or manipulate since it must be established that the persons involved acted in concert and with a prior understanding of the purpose of the activity.

149. *See* Note, *Regulation of Stock Market Manipulation*, 56 YALE L.J. 509, 516–18 (1947). Prior to 1934, legal remedies were usually called into play only when invoked by an individual who thought he had been cheated, or when the manipulators had a "falling out" and went to court to settle their differences. Wash sales and matched orders came early to be regarded as "fictitious" transactions, since they were used to misrepresent the actual state of the market. False rumors designed to unsettle security prices were condemned, largely because of their use to defraud the public.

150. *Id.*, at 517–18. The damage to a person who bought a worthless stock in reliance on the apparent activity created by wash sales might be regarded as too remote a consequence of the manipulative activity or the wash sale might not be regarded as a representation on which anyone had a right to rely [*McGlynn v. Seymour*, 14 Daly 420 (N.Y. 1888)]. The fraud concept largely failed to reach manipulation by actual purchases and sales [*Scott v. Brown*, 2 Q.B.D. 724 (1892)]. In *Scott*, the court in England refused, on the ground of public policy, to aid a party to a contract having as its object the purchase on the market of the shares of a new corporation in order to raise the market price and induce the public to subscribe. By way of dictum, the court declared that this would be ground for a civil action for damages and a criminal indictment for conspiracy to defraud.

the scope was still too limited.[151] After the market crash of 1929, caused, *inter alia*, by fraud, manipulation, and excessive speculation, Congress passed the Bills of Federal Securities Acts—the Securities Act of 1933 and the Securities Exchange Act of 1934.

The legal doctrines on manipulation expressed in the Federal Securities Acts are varied in order to cover the many techniques of manipulation. Manipulation on the exchanges is broadly prohibited by Sections 9 and 10(b) of the Exchange Act and Rules thereunder.[152] Manipulation in the over-the-counter market is also broadly prohibited by three overlapping sections—Sections 15(c)(1) and 10(b) of the Exchange Act, and Section 17(a) of the Securities Act.[153]

---

151. *Id.*, at 518. New York passed laws against wash sales, matched orders and the use of rumors designed to unsettle security prices (The Martin Act, New York Business Law, Art. 23–A).

152. *The Securities Exchange Act of 1934*, Secs. 9, 10(b). 15 U.S.C.A. §78 i, j(a); Rule 10b–5 and 6 thereunder. Section 9 prohibits fraudulent or manipulative practices on the exchanges, while Section 10(b) prohibits such practices both on the exchanges and in the over-the-counter market with respect to the purchase or sale of securities in interstate commerce.

Under the mandate of Section 10(b), the SEC enacted a broad range of rules to control manipulative and deceptive devices and contrivances. Rule 10b–5, *inter alia*, broadly prohibits use of such practices in connection with the purchase or sale of any security in interstate commerce, and Rule 10b–6 prohibits trading by persons interested in a distribution. Rule 10b–5, in part, reads: "It shall be unlawful for any person: (1) to employ any device, scheme, or artifice to defraud; (2) to make any untrue statement of a material fact or to omit to state a material fact necessary in order to make the statements made, in the light of the circumstances under which they were made, not misleading; or (3) to engage in any act, practice, or course of business which operates or would operate as a fraud or deceit upon any person, in connection with the purchase or sale of any security."

153. *See The Securities Exchange Act of 1934*, Sec. 15(c) (1), 15 U.S.C.A. §78 o(c) (1); *Also see The Securities Act of 1933*, Sec. 17(a) 15 U.S.C.A. §77 q(a). Section 15(c) (1) of the Exchange Act specifically prohibits the use of fraudulent or manipulative acts or practices by brokers and dealers in the over-the-counter market, while Section 10(b) of the Exchange Act and Section 17(c) of the Securities Act broadly prohibit the use of such practices in the offer or sale of all securities in interstate commerce. For details of regulation of broker-dealer manipulation in the over-the-counter market, *see* R.B. Martin, Jr., *Broker-Dealer Manipulation of the Over-The-Counter Market Toward a Reasonable Base for Quotations*, 25 BUS. L. 1463 (1970); H.S Bloomenthal, *Market*

The origin of these Sections was largely based on the concept of common law fraud. The Sections expanded the concept of fraud, however, to take within their scope all fraudulent or manipulative devices.[154] Although most private parties would have difficulty establishing a civil case under Section 9(e) of the Exchange Act, they could successfully bring a suit under other overlapping provisions such as Section 10(b) of the Exchange Act and Rule 10b-5. Indeed, because the so-called "five-finger fraud concept"[155] in common law tort was largely relaxed by the courts, the Federal Securities Acts in the United States established a new concept of fraud to control manipulative and deceptive devices in securities transaction. (For the detailed elements of liability under Rule 10b-5 and recent developments therein toward curtailments, *see* pp. 380–86, *infra*.)

The legal doctrine of manipulation in Korea, as in Japan, does not take within its scope such a broad fraudulent or manipulative practices as expressed in the Federal Securities Acts in the United States. Modeled after the Japanese SEA, the SEA has never adopted any other provision except Article 105.[156] The SEA has no counterparts to

---

Makers, Manipulators and Shell Games, 45 ST. JOHN'S L. REV. 597 (1971); Notes, *Manipulation of the Stock Markets Under the Securities Laws,* 99 U. PA. L. REV. 651–665 (1951); SEC, *Opinion of the Director of the Trading and Exchange Division,* Exch. Act. Rels. Nos. 3505, 3506 (Nov. 16, 1943).

154. For the early expansion of the fraud concept under Section 9 of the Exchange Act, *see Regulation of Market Manipulation,* 56 YALE L.J. 509, 519–21 (1947). For the expansion of the fraud concept under other overlapping Sections, *see* pp. 349, 380–86 *infra*.

155. *See* generally W.L. Prosser, *The Law of Torts* 683–736 (4th ed. 1971). To establish the tort cause of action in deceit, a plaintiff should establish the following five elements: (1) a false representation of a fact; (2) *scienter*; (3) an intention to induce the plaintiff to act or to refrain from action in reliance upon the misrepresentation; (4) justifiable reliance; and (5) damages resulting from such reliance.

156. Japan and Korea, unlike the United States, prohibit only such manipulative or deceptive devices as expressed in Section 9(a) of the Exchange Act of 1934. But Article 105 of the SEA and Article 125 of the Japanese SEA do not include a provision like Section 9(a) (5) of the Exchange Act, prohibiting the dissemination of information as to the likelihood of a rise or fall in the price of a security due to manipulation by any person receiving a consideration for the dissemination from any prospective seller or purchaser. Both do, however, have a provision prohibiting the dissemination of such infor-

Section 10(b) of the **Exchange Act and Rule** 10b-5 thereunder which prohibit broadly the use of fraudulent or manipulative practices in connection with the purchase or sale of a security both on the exchange and in the over-the-counter market. It also lacks a counterpart to either Section 17(a) of the Securities Act or 15(c) of the Exchange Act which controls such practices in the over-the-counter market.

On the other hand, just as Section 9(a) of the Exchange Act does not outlaw speculation, neither does Article 105. There is no explicit text on the matter in the SEA nor in the Decrees thereunder, but it is clear from the legislative intent and purpose of Article 105 that speculation is not outlawed. Only when speculation appears to be "excessive," may the SAC under the SEA issue an order necessary to prevent it, in the public interest and for the protection of investors.[157]

Classical economists accepted specialized risk-bearing as a useful and necessary function, and speculation was regarded as a productive force which shifted funds from less to more profitable areas and tended to reconcile money rates. Generally, it has been said that the functions of speculation is to maintain market price at a reasonable equivalent to investment value or intrinsic value. Alternatively it is also said that maintenance of the stability of market price is a function of speculation.[158] Recognizing legitimate functions of speculation, the United States' Congress in 1934 reported:

> "There is plenty of room for legitimate speculation in the balancing of investment demand and supply, in the shrewd prognostication of future trends and economic directions; but the accentuation of temporary fluctuations and the deliberate introduction of a mob psychology into the speculative markets by the fanfare of organized manipulation menace the true functioning of the exchanges,

---

mation by any person without raising the issue of any consideration for the act.

157. *See SEA,* Art. 54; *Presidential Decree thereunder,* Art. 37.
158. These, however, are not necessarily parallel functions; they may conflict. For the theories of speculation and the classical economic doctrines of the free market, *see* generally Hardy, *Recent Development in the Theory of Speculation,* 27 AM. ECON. REV. 263 (Supp. 1937); Ross, *Speculation, Stock Prices and Industrial Fluctuations* (1939) ch. 11; Lerner, *The Economics of Control* (1944) ch. 8.

upon which the economic well-being of the whole country depends."[159]

In this context, it is reasonable that Article 105 does not outlaw speculation but generally prohibits manipulating the prices of securities up or down for statutory illegal purposes. Also, the rule of manipulation applies to trading in a listed security on the exchange only.

The methods of manipulation prohibited by Article 105 are, in their substance, closely related to the fraud concept of both civil and criminal laws in Korea as they are in the United States. Unlike the United States, however, Article 105 in effect does not expand the fraud concept of civil and criminal laws. To constitute a fraud case under civil or criminal law, the following requirements must be established: (1) a misrepresentation of a material fact or a failure to state it, or an employment of any fraudulent or deceptive acts, devices, and contrivances; (2) *scienter* or willfulness; (3) an intention to induce the plaintiff to act or to refrain from action in reliance upon the misrepresentation; (4) justifiable reliance upon the misrepresentation on the part of the plaintiff, in taking action or refraining from it; and (5) damage resulting from such reliance.[160] The execution of "wash sales" and "matched orders" or any entrustment therewith prohibited by Article 105(1) may constitute the employment of a fraudulent or deceptive device or contrivance within the fraud concept of civil and criminal laws if it was effected "for the purpose of creating a false or misleading appearance of active trading in any security or a false or misleading appearance with respect to the mar-

---

159. *See* H.R. Rep. No. 1383, 73d Cong., 2d Sess. (1934) 11.
160. *See The Civil Code,* Arts. 750, 760 (Law No. 471, promulgated on Feb. 22, 1958); *The Criminal Code,* Arts. 347–8, 352 (Law No. 239, promulgated on Sept. 18, 1953). It is unlawful for any person, alone or with one or more other pesons in conspiracy, to make a willful misrepresentation or willfully omit to state a material fact under the circumstances and thereby obtain any pecuniary interest or advantage from the person who acts in reliance on such misrepresentation. The person or persons who defrauded another person would be subject to an imprisonment for not more than 10 years or a fine not exceeding ₩ 200,000 as well as civil liability. It is the same when a person employs fraudulent or deceptive devices and contrivances to defraud another person for such purpose. The criminal penalty can be invoked when a person attempted to commit fraud, while the civil remedy presupposes the actual damages caused by the fraudulent act.

ket for any security." Also, operation of "pool manipulation" prohibited in Article 105(2), item 1, or any entrustment therewith
creating actual or apparent active trading in any security or raising
or depressing the price of such security may constitute the employment of a fraudulent or deceptive device or contrivance within the
same fraud concept if such actions were effected "for the purpose of
inducing the purchase or sale of such security by others." Dissemination of impending manipulated price changes and willful misrepresentation of a material fact prohibited by Article 105(2), items 2 and
3, may constitute a basic illegal activity within the same fraud concept if these activities were effected "for the purpose of inducing the
purchase or sale of any security by others." Therefore, the Article is
important only to the extent that criminal sanctions can be imposed
thereunder with no need of proving damages.[161] In practice, however, enforcing such prohibition would be almost impossible because
the eivdence necessary to prove a manipulation case is usually unavailable.

A series of stock market crashes, occurring in the early 1960s and
1970s in Korea, were caused by habitual manipulations, excessive
speculations, and fraudulent practices. Disseminations of false information of material facts, pool operations, and short selling practices
were frequently employed by brokers and dealers to manipulate the
prices of a security up and down. Interestingly enough, however,
Article 105 (then Article 91) was never invoked by either the authorities or the injured parties for the purpose of criminal penalty and civil
remedy. Among the difficulties in establishing a case, proof of an
illegal statutory purpose was probably impossible under circumstances existing in Korea where even the authority lacked effective
enforcement techniques to detect manipulative devices and operations. Another reason which probably deterred the authorities from
taking any impartial action were the peculiar non-legal factors involving Korean society, such as outside pressures by influential figures on
governmental officials and close human relationships between government officials and management of the securities industry.

---

161. Such a prohibition has a little importance because the criminal penalty
under the Criminal Code can be invoked in a case of attempted fraud where
no damages resulted. *See* note 160 *supra*.

From the foregoing analysis of the legal doctrine of manipulation and its application, it is a clear loophole that Article 105 did not expand its coverage beyond the concept of fraud in civil and criminal laws. Indeed, the doctrine expressed in Article 105 is no more than a detailed reiteration of the fraud concept which had already been established in the areas of civil and criminal laws, and could not meet the purpose of maintaining a free market. Therefore, a new legislation is urgently needed in Korea so that the rule of manipulation can cover all fraudulent and manipulative practices.[162]

C. Enforcement Techniques

The legal doctrine of manipulation requires the proof of an illegal purpose to establish a case. Moreover, in actual practice the types and operational techniques of manipulations are so varied and sophisticated that it is hard to detect them. Therefore, a big gap exists between the legal doctrine and actual practice.

In the United States, the Exchange Act bridged this gap by providing the SEC with broad investigative powers to detect manipulation and a wide variety of remedies with which to proceed.[163] In utilizing these powers, the professed purpose of the SEC has been to detect manipulation at its inception and to prevent it, rather than to

---

162. The question of what form the new fraud rule should take will be considered in the Section on insider trading. *See* pp. 380–83 *infra*.

163. *The Securities Exchange Act of 1934*, Sec. 21.15 U.S.C.A. §78 u. The SEC was empowered under this Section to make, at its discretion, such investigation as it deems necessary to determine whether any person has violated, is violating, or is about to violate any provision of the Exchange Act. Also, a wide choice of remedies is offered. Under Section 2 a(d) (e), the SEC may bring an action in the federal courts for a temporary or permanent injunction "whenever it shall appear to the Commission that any person is engaged or is about to engage" in any illegal activity. Under Sections 19(a) (3), 15(b), and 15 A(1) (2), proceedings may be instituted for administrative remedies. These remedies have been most important ones. Expulsion, revocation, or suspension of membership is a serious penalty due to the loss of membership or damage to reputation. In Section 32, criminal prosecution is provided for any willful violation of the Act. Although criminal prosecutions are in form brought by the Attorney General, the evidence on which a prosecution is based is furnished by the SEC alone with its recommendation for prosecution under Section 21(e). Finally, a theoretical means of enforcement is civil liability for manipulative activity based on Section 9(e).

apply the statutory remedies after the damage has been done.[164] In Japan, the Ministry of Finance has resorted to the "Soundness Rule"[165] to avoid the need for proof of purpose. This rule includes a provision making it unlawful to effect a series of securities transactions if such transactions are likely to create an artificial market price deviating from the actual market, and thus proving a statutory illegal purpose is not required.

Under the SEA, the SAC was empowered to make such investigation as it deems necessary to determine whether a person has violated any provisions of the SEA, Decrees thereunder, or Rules and regulations of the SAC.[166] For this investigation, the SAC may require the person concerned to submit statements, books, records, and other relevant materials, and may demand the attendance of any witness. To perform its duty, the SAC may also order officers of the SSB to investigate such person, and may "invoke the aid of any administrative office or other institutions concerned."[167] Unlike the United States, the text of the provision does not clearly state whether the

---

164. *Regulation of Stock Market Manipulation,* 56 YALE L.J. 483, 521 (1947). Thus, much of the enforcement activity consisted of informal investigations, personal consultations, and the answering of detailed questions posed to the Commission concerning its interpretation of the law. *See Id.,* citing Purcell, *The Structure and Functions of the Securities and Exchange Commission,* 6 FED. BAR, ASS'N. J. 241. 252 (1945).

165. *See Japanese SEA,* Art. 50 item 3; *MOF Rules on the Soundness of Securities Companies.* Art. 1, item 3 (MOF Order No. 60 Promulgated on Nov. 5, 1965, as amended by MOF Order No.2 in 1973). The item prohibits "a series of sales or purchases or entrustment thereof which is likely to create an artificial market price deviating from the actual market, or the act of being entrusted with a series of sales or purchases with the knowledge that an artificial market price deviating from the actual market is likely to be created." However, the Japanese MOF can issue only an administrative order based on this soundness rule, whereas the violator of the anti-manipulation provision is subject to civil liabilities as well as criminal sanctions. *See* Tatsuta, 87–88; *also see* Takeo Suzuki & Ichiro Kawamoto, *Securities Exchange Law* (53 Horitsu-Gaku) 240 (1968) [Hereinafter cited as "Suzuki & Kawamoto"].

166. *SEA,* Art. 128. The SAC, under this Article, was empowered to exercise its investigation power when it deems the exercise to be necessary in the public interest and for the protection of investors. Thus, the SAC may investigate to determine whether any person is engaging in or is about to engage in any illegal activities.

167. *Id.,* Arts. 130, 135–36, and 129.

SAC may invoke the aid of any courts.[168] However, since the SAC was empowered to demand the attendance of witnesses and since the phrase "other institutes concerned" may include any courts, it can be assumed that the SAC may invoke the aid of a court for investigative purposes.

The statutory remedies or enforcement techniques are various. First, the MOF and the SAC were empowered to issue any necessary order to stop manipulation or excessive speculation when they deem it necessary and appropriate in the public interest or for the protection of investors.[169] Second, the MOF may revoke the license of a security company which fails to obey this stop order.[170] The SAC may suspend the buisness of a securities company which violates its order to stop manipulation and excessive speculation.[171] Third, a provision on criminal penalties may be invoked for the violation of the manipulation rule.[172] Although prosecution belongs to the power of a prosecuting attorney, the SAC may, at its discretion, recommend prosecution by furnishing the evidence. Finally, the SEA includes a provision on civil liability for manipulative or deceptive devices.[173]

As noted earlier, however, none of these enforcement techniques were effectively employed during the last decades. Rather, some securities companies which operated manipulations and excessive speculations voluntarily withdrew their businesses after the market crashes.[174] The provision on criminal penalty was never invoked against the manipulations. Neither did any injured person bring a

---

168. There is no explicit provision in the SEA on whether the SAC may invoke the aid of the courts in requiring the attendance and testimony of witnesses and the production of books, records, and other related materials. Cf. *The Securities Exchange Act of 1934*, Sec. 21(c). 15 U.S.C.A. §78 u(c).

169. *Id.*, Arts. 117, 54. What the phrase "any necessary order" means is not clear. To stop manipulation or excessive speculation, however, an order suspending the transaction would be usual.

170. *Id.*, Art. 55, items 7,8.

171. *Id.*, Arts. 57(1) and 54. The SAC may suspend all or a part of the business of such a securities company.

172. *Id.*, Arts. 208, item 3 and 214. Any person who violates Article 105 is subject to a sentence of criminal servitude not exceeding 3 years or a fine not exceeding W 5 million, or both.

173. *Id.*, Art. 106.

174. *See* p. 14 *supra*.

suit to recover damages, probably because the evidence necessary for proof of a manipulation case is not available to most private parties. The crucial question in establishing either a criminal or a civil case is how to prove the statutory illegal purpose for which transactions are effected. Although proving the statutory illegal purpose was not a precondition of issuing a stop order, the MOF seldom exercised its power without clear reason.

Only recently, the authority indicted the accountant department's chief of Wonpoong Industrial Corp.(*Wonpoong Shanup*) who was convicted that he manipulated the market prices of *"Wonpoong"* stock by disseminating an information of a material fact which was false and misleading.[175] On March 22, 1977, the department chief of the company falsely disseminated the information that the company had decided to participate in a construction business in Saudi Arabia by incorporating a subsidiary there which is to be jointly ventured with a Saudi Arabian company. In response to this information, *"Wonpoong"* stock, which operated at ₩ 518, closed at ₩ 568 on the same day, and showed a sharp rising trend thereafter. Between March 28 and 30, the controlling shareholder of the company sold out 92,300 shares on the exchange, gaining profits of about ₩ 100 million. Immediately after these sales, the company announced that it had no plan to participate in a Saudi Arabian construction business and that the information concerned had had no reasonable base.

The detection of the case was possible because the controlling shareholder filed a report of his ownership changes with the SSB so that the company would be treated favorably for corporate income taxes.[176] Receiving this report, the SSB investigated the company to determine where there had been any violation of the manipula-

---

175. Joong-Ang Daily News, May 18, 1977, at p.4; May 19, 1977, at p.7; Seoul Economic Newspaper, April 20, 1977, at p.4; Maeil Economic Newspaper, April 14, 1977, and April 16, 1977, at p.3.

176. Maeil Economic Newspaper, April 14, 1977, at p.3; April 16, 1977, at p.3. According to the ownership change report, the controlling shareholder of *"Wonpoong"* reduced his shareholding from 36.62% to 25.08%. If the controlling shareholder of a company owns below 35% of the total number of shares issued and outstanding, the company is eligible for the most favorable corporate income tax rate of 27%.

tion rule. However, the SSB failed to detect a case of manipulation, and issued only a warning to the company on the ground that the company had failed to meet disclosure requirements.[177] Also, the prosecuting attorney concerned failed to detect illegality in the controlling shareholder's activity, even though he could have assumed the activity to be closely connected to the dissemination of the false information by the department chief. The attorney prosecuted only the department chief, who received imprisonment, and the company, which received a fine of ₩ 5 million. It is unclear why the controlling shareholder, who made a great profit at the expense of public investors, was free from any conviction under the relevant law. Unless a criminal case is established against the controlling shareholder, individual parties concerned are unable to prove the case for recovery. Therefore, reappraisal of the existing enforcement techniques, together with an enactment of sophisticated rules, is of cardinal importance.

A crucial drawback of the enforcement machinery in Korea is the lack of a market watching system. The system of market watching is the most significant base upon which all the enforcement activity rests. Without installing the watching system in the SAC, detecting manipulation at its inception would be impossible; thus, no enforcement devices could work until after the damage had been done. In addition, the SAC should have power to compel the attendance of any witness who refuses to obey a demand. Otherwise, the SAC's investigation power given by the SEA could not meet the legislative purpose. On the other hand, the SAC should be empowered to bring a temporary or permanent injunction to the court in order to prevent any manipulative and deceptive devices in advance. To strengthen its enforcement activity, the SAC should also have the mandatory duty to recommend prosecution when it has detected a manipulation case.

II. Stabilization

A. Exemption from the Rule of Manipulation

Although Article 105 of the SEA generally prohibits manipulating security prices up and down, it does not prohibit certain other kinds

---

177. Seoul Economic Newpaper, April 20, 1977, at p.4.

of manipulation. Like Section 9(a)(6) of the Exchange Act and Article 105(3) of the Japanese SEA, Article 105(3) of the SEA provides:[178]

> "It shall be unlawful for any person to effect either alone or with one or more other persons any transaction, or to entrust or to be entrusted with an order thereof for the purchase and/or sale of any security on the exchange for the purpose of *pegging, fixing, or stabilizing the price of such security in contravention of such rules as a Presidential Decree may prescribe.*" (Emphasis supplied.)

Within its authorized rulemaking power, the Presidential Decree, unlike the United States or Japan, permits two kinds of stabilizing activities.[179] In addition to the "pegging, fixing or stabilizing" (hereinafter all these referred to as "stabilizing" or "stabilization" only) to facilitate a distribution of a security, it allows "market formation (*Seejang Chosung*)" to facilitate supplies of and demands for a newly listed security.

The term "stabilization" under the Presidential Decree may be defined as "purchasing a security by the syndicate manager of such security being distributed for the limited purpose of preventing or retarding a decline in its market price in order to facilitate its distribution to the public."[180] The term "market formation" may be defined as "purchasing or selling a security by a syndicate manager for a limited purpose of maintaining its market price in order to facilitate trading in such security.[181] Stabilization and market formation are thus forms of manipulation which fall within the coverage of prohibition prescribed in Article 105(2), item 1.[182]

---

178. *SEA*, Art. 105(3) Cf. Japanese Art. 125(3) and Section 9(a) 6 of the Securities Exchange Act of 1934 in the United States. The exemptions of certain kinds of stabilizations from the prohibition of manipulation area, in their principles, the same among the three countries. The prescriptions as to the coverage of such exemptions are fraud in the SEC Rules and Regulations in the United States and in the Cabinet Order in Japan, while such prescriptions are set out in the Presidential Decree in Korea.

179. *See Presidential Decree*, Art. 59(1). Cf. *Cabinet Order under the Japanese SEA*, Art. 20(1); SEC, Rule 10b–7 under the Securities Exchange Act of 1934.

180. *Id.*

181. *See id.; also see* KSDA, *Agreement on Underwriting Business*, Art. 9(9).

182. Stabilization is a negative form of manipulation since a syndicate manager purchases a security to prevent or retard a decline. Market formation is also a form of manipulation which can be either negative or postive, since a syn-

The permission for these stabilizations and market formations, therefore, is an exemption from the rule of manipulation. When an underwriting syndicate distributes a large number of a security at a fixed price, it is possible for the market price of such security to drop below the offering price because of a temporary oversupply in the market. In part, this oversupply comes from the so-called "free-riders" or speculators who purchase with the hope of quickly selling out and taking a profit from an early rise. If this oversupply is not absorbed by and balanced with the market demand, its pressure will tend to force the market price below the offering price and could impede the success of distribution by the syndicate. Thus, the policy behind the permission for stabilization is to facilitate the distribution of a security by the syndicate manager.[183] In practice until the 1976 amendments, stabilization was not needed in Korea where a security

---

dicate manager can both purchase and sell a security to maintain the security's price and to artificially form a market for that security. Market formation is different from the resale price maintenance practice in the United States. The latter is a practice in which the typical underwriting agreement and selling group agreement require all underwirters and selling group members to adhere to the public offering price as stated in the prospectus to prohibit a price-cut. This raises an anti-trust question. In *Morgan,* the Court held that resale price maintenance in securities distributions was not *per se* illegal under the Sherman Act. *See United States v. Morgan,* 118 F. Supp. 621, 699 (S.D. N.Y. 1953).

183. In Korea, no material on the policy behind the permission of stabilizing activity appears. In the United States, the questions of policy involved in any regulation of stabilization were of such fundamental significance as to require a discussion of the considerations which led to the SEC's conclusion to attempt to embark upon a broad program of regulation. Faced with the three choices—a complete permission, complete prohibition, and partial permission of stabilization—the SEC adopted piecemeal regulations reconciled and designed to eliminate particular abuses which, in the absence of regulation, were being employed. Recognizing that stabilization must be an integral part of the American system of fixed security distribution, especially under firm commitment underwriting contracts, the SEC allowed stabilization by the syndicate manager (originator) to facilitate its distribution while regulating possible abuses. Such an approach was to reconcile the conflicting interests between industry and purchasing investors; to guard the welfare of the multitude of direct individual investors against injury from stabilizing; impeding the flow of individual savings into industrial expansion. For details, *see* SEC, *Sec. Ex. Act. Rel.* No. 2446 (March 18, 1940).

was offered at a fixed price under a firm commitment contract because of the sustained bull market and underpricing trend based on intrinsic value. However, if any security is offered at a fixed price largely reflecting market price under the new pricing system, a practical need for stabilization of the market price would arise, as in Japan.[184]

Market formation for a newly listed security was adopted because of a unique situation in Korea. Although the existence of a continuing trading market for a security is a prerequisite to the distribution of such a security, privately-held corporations have never had a continuous trading market for their securities. Also, since Korea has no specialist system to maintain a fair and orderly market for a listed security, it is uncertain that a continuing trading market could be formed for a newly listed security, especially immediately following the listing of such security. The permission of market formation is thus probably designed to create a trading market for only a newly listed security at a certain price level.[185] The Agreement on Underwriting Business includes a provision imposing on an underwriting syndicate a duty to perform market formation for two months after the listing of any security.[186] Also transactions by a syndicate manager for market formation mainly consists of purchasing activity to prevent or retard a decline in the market price since the 5% preferential allotment of new shares to an underwriting syndicate over the public subscribers was abolished in 1976.[187]

B. The Rule of Stabilization

1. Permissible Purpose of Stabilization

Under the Presidential Decree, the permissible purpose of stabiliza-

---

184. In Japan, there had been 278 cases of stabilization notified to the authority from July 1, 1971, to the end of 1974. Japan revised the rule of stabilization on July 1, 1971, by amending the Cabinet Order for Enforcement of the SEA (Arts. 20–26). For details, *see* Japan Securities Research Institute, *supra* note 24, at 93–95.

185. There is no written material on the policy behind the adoption of market formation system.

186. KSDA, *Agreement on Underwriting Business*, Art. 9(9).

187. *See* pp.77–78 *supra*. This 5% of new shares were allotted for the underwriting syndicate concerned to perform the function of market formation by selling them out to retard a rise in price over a certain level.

tion is limited to facilitating the distribution (both a public offering and secondary distribution) of a security and to forming a trading market for a newly listed security. Thus, stabilizing otherwise than to facilitate a distribution or to form a market is completely prohibited even though such activity does not amount *prima facie* to "manipulation." In this respect, the regulation of stabilization in Korea shows a difference from that in the United States where stabilization is prohibited only to the extent that the SEC has adopted rules under Section 9(a)(6) of the Exchange Act; the SEC's stabilizing rules specifically apply only to the regulation of stabilizing in connection with the distribution of securities.[188]

Since stabilizing activities actually maintain an artificial market price not based on the natural power of supply and demand, and since such activities are not in the interest of public investors, complete prohibition of stabilization except to facilitate a particular distribution appears to be proper. In Korea, where the ethical conduct of professionals is relatively low and where manipulative practice is hard to detect, such a prohibition is even more necessary. However, ensuring a fair and orderly market which is unaffected by unnatural restraints and stimulation would largely depend on impartial enforcement rather than on the strictness of the rule.

2. Persons Eligible to Operate Stabilization

The persons who can effect stabilizing transactions, including "market formation" for their own accounts or for the accounts of other persons, are limited to "as securities company stated in the registration (or notification) statement as an underwriter who entered into a contract with an issuer or owner of the security."[189] The per-

---

188. *See SEC Rules under the Securities Exchange Act of 1934,*10b–6,10b–7 and 10b–8; *also see* Jennings & Marsh, *Securities Regulation,* 640 (4th ed. 1977); 3 Loss, *Securities Regulation*1583–85(2d ed. 1961). Since the SEC adopted piecemeal regulation of stabilizing in connection with a distribution of securities, activities undertaken to maintain the collateral value of a security or to maintain the prestige of distributors or the good will of purchasers after the completion of a distribution, or for some purpose other than to facilitate a distribution are not *per se* illegal without any public notice or reports to the SEC. In 1959, the SEC proposed an amendment to Rule 10b–7 which would have prohibited all stabilizing except to facilitate a particular distribution, but for some reason the amendment was never adopted. *See* SEC, *Rx. Act Rel. No. 6127* (1959).

sons who can entrust stabilization to such a managing underwriter who is a securities company are: (1) officers of an issuer; (2) owners of outstanding securities; (3) a company which has a special relationship (more than 35% holder or more than 10% holder with participation in management) with the issuer, or officers thereof; and (4) the persons having been previously notified by an issuer to the exchange as a person who can entrust stabilization.[190] Thus stabilizing activities in Korea cannot be directly effected by the issuer itself, while stabilization in the United States can be effected by an issuer as well as by an underwriter.[191]

3. Disclosure and Reporting Requirements

No stabilization or market formation can be effected unless the prospectus concerned includes a statement that such transaction is to be made on a certain exchange.[192] Also, the rule of stabilization requires that a stabilizer file a notification of its initial operation with the SAC and the KSE immediately after completing the initial stabilizing operation; the rule of market formation, however, requires an underwriter willing to effect such transaction to file a notification thereon with the SAC and the KSE prior to effecting it.[193] In addition, an underwirter is required to file a report with the SAC and the KSE after completing the operation of stabilization or market formation.[194] This report must be made to the authorities by the first business day following the completion of the operation, and must comply with the form prescribed by the MOF Decree. All these notifications and reports must be made available for public inspection.[195]

---

189. *Presidential Decree Under the SEA*, Art. 59(2). In Japan, a securities company entering into a principal underwriting contract can effect stabilizing transactions for its own account only. *See Cabinet Order under the Japanese SEA,* Art. 20(2).

190. *Id.*, Art. 59(3); *MOF Decree thereunder*, Art. 17. These are the same as Art. 20(3) of Japanese Cabinet Order and Art. 1 of the MOF order on Stabilization under the SEA.

191. Loss, *supra* note 188, at 1593–94; SEC, *Sec. Ex. Act. Rel. No.* 1463(1948)

192. *Presidential Decree Under the SEA*, Art. 60.

193. *Id.*, Art. 62(1) and (2). The report must comply with the form prescribed by the MOF Decree (Arts. 18 and 19) thereunder.

194. *Id.*, Art. 64 and *MOF Decree thereunder*, Art. 20.

195. *Presidential Decree under the SEA*, Art. 65.

However, the Korean stabilization rule, copied after the Japanese rule, does not have any provision like Rule 10b-7(k) in the United States, which requires that any stabilizer give or send to the purchaser, at or before the completion of the transaction, a notice to the effect that stabilizing purchases may be or have been effected.[196] Such a requirement, which supplements the rule requiring the disclosure of stabilization in the prospectus, is of cardinal importance to protect investors in Korea. This is because the prospectus under the SEA is not required to be compulsorily delivered to the buyers at or prior to the completion of transaction.

Furthermore, the non-compulsory requirement of prospectus delivery reduces the importance requiring the description of planned stabilization in the prospectus. Also, the public could not have access to the initial operation of stabilization since the notification of stabilization must be made to the authorities only after its completion. Another critical drawback of the disclosure rule on stabilization is that the rule does not require the authorities to make public notice of all the notification and reports filed by stabilizers but only requires them to be available for public inspection. In these respects, the disclosure rule should be reappraised for the protection of investors.

4. Stabilizing Place, Period, and Level

The place to effect any stabilization or market formation is limited to an exchange stated in the prospectus.[197] The period to effect any stabilization is for twenty days from the last date for subscription,

---

196. SEC Rule 10b–7(k) under the Securities Exchange Act of 1934. The Japanese stabilization rule does not include such a disclosure requirement either, which is important for the protection of investors. Apart from the reporting requirements of Rule 17a–2, which Rule 10b–7 incorporates, the latter rule supplements the Securities Act rule requiring disclosure of stabilization in the prospectus by requiring any stabilizer who is a seller or a buyer's broker to give or send a written notice to the buyer that stabilizing purchases may be or have been effected. The notice must be given "at or before the completion of each transaction entered into while the distribution is in progress." This requirement is excused if, at or before the completion of transaction, the buyer receives a prospectus, offering circular, confirmation or other writing containing a statement similar to the legend required by Rule 426 under the Securities Act of 1933.

197. *Presidential Decree under the SEA,* Art. 61(1).

while the period to effect market formation runs for six months from the date of listing of any security.[198] The rule also provides that if a security goes ex-dividend or ex-rights during the six-month period for market formation, the period must be reduced to the date just prior to the ex-distribution day.[199]

Even though an offering at the market is not allowed under the Korean securities laws, a question is raised about the period for stabilization. To protect the interest of investors, stabilization must not be effected before an offering price is set. If the total amount of securities to be offered or secondarily distributed exceeds ₩ 50 million, stabilization cannot practically be effected before the offering price is set because the registration statement in which an offering price is stated becomes effective by SAC designation within thirty days. If the amount is below ₩ 50 million, however, the notification statement becomes effective on the day of its receipt by the MOF. Therefore, if the last date for subscription is set for a few days after the filing of the notification statement, stabilization can be effected even before the offering price is set. The legislature clearly overlooked this problem.[200]

The level to effect stabilization is classified differently between the price at which the first stabilization is initiated, and the price

---

198. *Id.*, Article 9(9) of the Agreement on Underwriting Business, however, requires a syndicate member to operate market formation for a two-month period following the listing; it also provides that if the security goes ex-dividend or ex-rights during the period, the price to effect market formation must be reduced to a theoretical price which is reduced by an amount equal to the value of the dividend or right. This provision conflicts with Article 61(2) item 2 of the Presidential Decree under the SEA and raises a question on its legality. The only solution is new legislation.

On the other hand, the rule is silent on a case in which a security goes ex-dividend or ex-rights during the twenty-day period for stabilization. It would be reasonable to construe that stabilization can still be effected at a theoretical price which is reduced by an amount equal to the value of the dividend or right.

199. *Id.*, Art. 61(2).

200. In Japan, the rule provides that no stabilization can be effected until the offering price is decided and the issuer informs the securities exchange concerned of such price. *See Japanese Cabinet Order for the Enforcement of the SEA*, Art. 22(3).

thereafter.[201] A person is prohibited from initiating stabilization of a security at a price higher than the closing price of the preceding business day on the principal exchange (if no transaction for the security was effected on that day, the latest sale price) or at the lower of the latest prices of the preceding business day. When initial stabilization is effected, a person must not effect stabilization on that day at a price higher than the initial stabilizing price. After the initial stabilizing day, a person is prohibited from effecting stabilizing at a price higher than the initial stabilizing price (or, when more than two securities companies effected the initial stabilizing on the same day, the lowest initial stabilizing price) or at the lower of the latest stabilizing prices. This rule may also apply to stabilization effected after stabilization has been discontinued. A securities company effecting market formation for a newly listed security is prohibited from purchasing or selling the security at a price in excess of the price at which the security has been offered or secondarily distributed.

This rule on stabilizing levels is not so sophisticated as that in the United States, and includes some drawbacks for investors.[202] First, the rule does not include any explicit provision prohibiting a person from initiating stabilization or stabilizing at a price above the price at which a security is being offered or distributed.[203] Thus, it may be possible for a stabilizer to begin stabilization at a price above the offering price because, even though the concept of stabilization may be extended to prohibit such transaction, the stabilizer is only required to file a notification of the stabilization with the authorities just after its completion. Second, the rule includes no provision on the stabilizing level of a security when such security goes ex-dividend or ex-rights during the period stabilizing is being done.[204] Third, the rule does not include any lawful price for a security which is also traded in the over-the-counter market.[205]

---

201. *Presidential Decree under the SEA*, Art. 63. This provision is fully copied after Art. 24 of the Japanese Cabinet Order for the Enforcement of the SEA.
202. *See* SEC, Rule 10b–7(j), 17C.F.R. §240, 10b–7(j).
203. In the United States the rule includes a special provision that prohibits stabilizing a security at a price above the current distribution price. *See id,* Rule 10b–7(j) (5).
204. Cf. *Id.*, Rule 10b–7(j) (6).
205. Cf. *Id.*, Rule 10b–7(j) (1). In Korea, the SAC has not yet enacted any rule

C. Related Problems

1. Trading by Persons Interested in a Distribution

Both the rule of manipulation and the rule of stabilization prohibit manipulative and fraudulent activities if the purpose of the fraud or manipulation is found to fall within the statutory illegal standards. Proving such a purpose, however, is extremely hard in practice. Therefore, it would not be difficult for any person interested in the distribution of a security to avoid such rules. Persons such as underwriters, prospective underwriters, or other participants in a distribution, or any person on whose behalf such a distribution is being made, can directly or indirectly purchase a security being distributed or attempt to induce anyone else to purchase such security prior to or during a distribution. Such activity could be effected with or without a statutory illegal purpose which would determine legality of the activity. Even if an illegal purpose existed, the manipulation or stabilization rule would not be enforced in many cases due to difficulties in detecting such purpose.

Some persons interested in the distribution of a security would feel even greater practical desire for trading in such security to influence pricing since the pricing method has been changed along with the 1976 amendments of the SEA so that the market price of a security (or a security similar to it) could be substantially reflected in an offering price. Also, persons interested in the distribution would be more tempted to trade in such a security as offered at a market price or a price closer to a market price during the distribution thus maintaining the market price at a more favorable level. This would be the same when a security is not fully sold out and a large portion of it still remains in the hands of a syndicate manager or other persons. Furthermore, stabilizing or manipulating activities which occur off the exchange floor are beyond the reach of the prohibition.

In the United States, a set of rules is enacted to prohibit any person interested in a distribution from using the mails or interstate or exchange facilities, either alone or with others, to bid for, or to purchase, directly or indirectly, any security which is the subject of distribution, or any security of the same class and series, or even any

---

on trading in securities in the OTC market, even though any security of a registered or listed corporation can be traded there.

right to purchase such security.[206] Japan also enacted a rule which, if not so sophisticated as the rule in the United States, prohibits certain kinds of trading by a managing underwriter such as: (1) purchasing the security concerned during the period of stabilization for its own account unless such purchase is effected for stabilization; (2) being entrusted with any order to buy or sell the security concerned during the same period unless such indication is made as stabilization is being done.[207]

In Korea, however, no provision prohibits any person interested in a distribution from purchasing a security which is the subject of distribution prior to or during distribution. The lack of such a fundamental prohibition clearly constitutes a critical loophole in rules of manipulation and stabilization for which practical enforcement is difficult. New legislation is an urgent need in Korea since the method of determining an offering price has been amended to reflect substantially a market price as noted earlier.

2. Regulation of Trading in Connection with Rights Offerings

A need to prohibit manipulative or deceptive devices or contrivances in order to maintain a free market is the same in the case of a rights offering, a distribution of a security being offered through

---

206. *Id.*, Rule 10b–6. This rule prohibits trading only in the sense of buying, not selling. This rule also includes a series of exemptions, two of which are for transactions permitted by Rule 10b–7 (Stabilizing to Facilitate a Distribution) and Rule 10b–8 (Distribution Through Rights). When these rules are viewed together, Rule 10b–6 is the central rule. Even though they contain their own prohibitions with their own exemptions, a transaction which is not permitted by Rule 10b–7 or Rule 10b–8 violates one or the other of the rules and also, as a result of the distribution of the exemptions from Rule 10b–6, the latter rule as well. The prohibition against bidding and buying is subject to different commencement and terminal dates in the case of (1) underwriters, (2) brokers, dealers or other participants in the distribution, and (3) issuers or security holders making a secondary distribution. For the details of the prohibitions and exemption by Rule 10b–6, *see* Loss, *supra* note 188 at 1595–1604; J.M. Whitney II, *Rule 10b–6; The Special Study's Rediscovered Rule*, 62 MICH. L. REV. 567 (1964); *The SEC's Rule 10b–6; Preserving a Competitive Market during Distributions*, 1967 DUKE L.J. 809; W.W. Foshay, *Market Activities of Participants in Securities Distributions*, 45 VA L. REV. 907 (1959).

207. *The Japanese MOF Order on Standards, etc. for Soundness of Securities Companies*, Art. 1, items 6 and 7. However, this rule does not include a wide range of

rights issued on a pro-rata basis to security holders. In addition to Rule 10b-6 and Rule 10b-7, which also apply to bids for or purchases of the "underlying security," the SEC in the United States enacted Rule 10b-8, which was designed to prevent fraud and manipulation in rights offering by controlling the price of sales of the "underlying security" as well as the prices and conditions of purchases of rights, by any person participating in a distribution of a security being offered through rights.[208] With respect to rights offerings, Japanese rules of stabilization and manipulation include a special treatment only in the light of the period to effect stabilization;[209] stabilization in the case of rights offerings is allowed for twenty-four days, while other cases of stabilization are allowed for either twenty-one days or ten days. Except for this, the Japanese rules of manipulation and stabilization fully apply to any illegal practices in rights offerings.

The Korean rules of manipulation and stabilization include neither a special provision with respect to rights offerings, nor general application to any fraudulent or deceptive practices employed in a distribution through rights. Since going public has been only a recent trend in Korea, few significant problems in connection with rights offerings have occurred. As the number of publicly-held corporations

---

prohibition against trading by any person interested in a distribution.

208. *See supra*, note 206; *also see* Loss, *supra* note 188, at 1604–14. The regulation on rights offerings was established in the United States due to the development of complicated devices by the stand-by underwriters to reduce risk in such offerings. When a security is offered to existing security holders by means of rights or warrants at a price below the current market, and an underwriter agrees to stand-by and take up any amount of the issue not purchased by the security holders with a view to offering it to the public at or about the current market price after the expiration of offerings, Rules 10b–6 and 10b–7 fully apply to bids for or purchases of such underlying securities. Even though Rule 10b–8 is silent with respect to the filing of reports, reports must be filed if the syndicate manager does any purchasing of the underlying security since such purchasing may be effected only by way of lawful stabilizing transactions. Also, a stabilizing legend must appear on the prospectus.

209. *See Japanese Cabinet Order for the Enforcement of the SEA*, Art. 22(2). Stabilization in the case of rights offerings is allowed for two weeks from the closing date of subscription and an additional 10 days thereafter by the date of payment due. In other cases of stabilization, the period expires either on the closing date of subscription for new shares or on the final date for sales of outstanding securities.

rapidly increases, however, the regulation of manipulative and deceptive devices in connection with rights offerings will gain importance for the protection of public investors. An adoption of the Rule 10b-8 type of prohibition of the United States is necessary and appropriate.

Section III. *Regulation of the Over-the-Counter Market and Securities Companies*

1. Regulation of the Over-the-Counter (OTC) Market
A. Lack of Organization

The OTC market, in general, refers to a marketplace, other than an organized securities exchange, where transactions in securities take place.[210] Organized securities exchanges furnish auction markets for exchange members who normally act as brokers for a disclosed commission; the OTC market is a negotiated market in which, for the most part, dealers who act as principals buy from and sell to investors or other dealers for an undisclosed profit.[211] These fundamental differences between the two markets are reflected in the manner of publishing transactions or quotations, and therein lies much of the regulatory problem.

In the United States, the OTC market is much bigger than all the exchanges combined, and performs vital economic functions which can not be performed by the exchanges.[212] Because of the OTC's

---

210. The Securities Exchange Act of 1934 nowhere uses the term "over-the-counter market," but refers simply to transactions effected "otherwise than on a national securities exchange." Under the Securities Exchange Act of 1934, the OTC markets are deemed to include all transactions in securities which take place otherwise than upon a national securities exchange. *See* S. Rep. No. 1455 and H.R. Report No. 2307, 75th Cong., 3rd Sess. 2(1938).

211. In the OTC market, there is a substantial amount of trading for customers on a brokerage basis. For details of OTC trading in the United States, *see* Loss, *supra* note 91, at 1277–1417; Jennings & Marsh 667–714 (4th ed. 1977), and references cited therein.

212. The size of the OTC market is undoubtedly much bigger than all of the exchanges combined, although the number of issues traded over-the-counter can only be estimated, and the proportion as compared to exchange trading varies considerably in accordance with the kinds of securities. Most common stock of banks and insurance companies as well as corporate and government bonds are traded over-the-counter. A substantial portion of the OTC trading

large trading volume, its vital economic function, and the increasing need for adequate protection of the public interest involved therein, the Securities Exchange Act was amended several times. By the 1936 amendments, all the brokers and dealers in the OTC market were required to register with the SEC and to comply with the rules of bookkeeping, periodic reports, and SEC inspection.[213] In 1938, the National Association of Securities Dealers (NASD) was established by the Maloney Act to supplement direct government regulation as a "cooperative" regulatory agency.[214] Since investors in the

---

is in issues which are listed or admitted to unlisted trading privileges on exchanges. In addition, both rights offering (of listed issues) and the whole field of underwriting and distribution of securities are part of the OTC market.

The OTC market performs vital economic functions which could not be performed by the exchanges as they are constituted. This is especially true with respect to distributing securities, creating a market for local issues or those which are not distributed widely enough for auction trading, and buying and selling of large blocks of securities which are too large to be readily digested by the exchange markets. It is also true with respect to the performance of monetary and fiscal policies by distributing Federal and municipal bonds. For the details of size and economic functions of the OTC market, *see* Loss, *supra* note 91, at 1284–87 and references cited therein.

213. The original Section 15 of the Exchange Act made it unlawful, in contravention of the SEC's rules, for any broker or dealer to trade in securities otherwise than on a national securities exchange. Under the Exchange Act as amended in 1936, the regulation of the OTC market consisted of the registration and inspection system together with several anti-fraud provisions. Section 15(a) required all brokers and dealers, for OTC trading, to register with the SEC with some exceptions, and Section 15(b) gives the SEC a broad power to grant, deny, revoke, cancel, postpone, or suspend the registration for statutory causes. Under Section 17(a), all brokers and dealers were required to make, keep, and preserve various kinds of books and records, make such periodic reports as the SEC may prescribe, and be subject at any time to periodic, special, or other inspections by the SEC. For details of the registration requirement and the SEC's inspection power, *see* Loss, *supra* note 91, at 1288–1358.

214. In 1938, the Maloney Act added Section 15A to the Exchange Act to supplement then existing direct regulation of a complex business through the machinery of government by establishing a cooperative regulatory body, the NASD. *See Securities Exchange Act of 1934*, See. 15A, as added, 52 Stat. 1070 (1938), 15 U.S.C.A. §78 0–3(1958). At the same time, the 1938 amendment expanded the SEC's direct authority over the OTC market by au-

OTC market still lacked adequate information to assess their investment worth in relatively unknown securities, the Exchange Act was
amended again in 1964 to extend the same protection afforded those
in listed securities to investors in certain OTC securities.[215] An issuer
meeting the statutory tests must file a registration statement with the
SEC; rules of periodic reporting, proxy solicitation, and insider
trading were extended to apply to such registered corporations.[216]
Also, the 1964 amendment strengthened the regulation of OTC
broker-dealers, including strict qualification standards and disciplinary controls.[217]

---

thorizing it in Section 15(c) (2) and (3) to adopt rules to prevent fraud as
well as to define it and to protect financial responsibility. Under these provisions, the SEC adopted its rules on hypothecation of customers' securities and
debt-capital ratio. For the details of the cooperative regulation by the NASD,
see Loss, *supra* note 91, at 1359–91; R.W. Jennings, *Self Regulation in the Securities Industry: The Role of the Securities and Exchange Commission,* 29 LAW &
CONTEMP. PROB. 663 (1964); Cary, *Self-Regulation in the Securities Industry,*
49 A.B.A.J. 244 (1963); Note, *The NASD-An Unique Experiment in Cooperative
Regulation,* 46 VA. L. REV. 1586 (1960).

215. *See 1964 U.S. Code Cong. & Adm. News* 3013 *et seq.;* Public Law No. 88–467,
Approved Aug. 20, 1964 (78 Stat. 565). Although some anti-fraud provisions
[Section 10(b) and Rules thereunder] were applicable to trading in securities in the OTC market, the need for full disclosure and extension of other
investor protections provided in listed securities appeared to be urgent.

216. *Securities Exchange Act of 1934,* Secs. 12 (g) (1), 13, 14, 16, 15 U.S.C.A. §78
(g) (1), m, n, p. The amendments extended the same requirements that
apply to issuers of securities listed on an exchange to any issuers of securities
traded in the OTC market, if the issuers have over $1 million in total assets
and 750 stockholders of record (reduced to 500 after 2 years); namely: (1)
registration requiring disclosure of certain information about the issuer including financial statements (sec. 12); (2) periodic reporting (sec. 13); (3)
information, including financial statements to accompany proxy solicitation;
or if no solicitation, equivalent information to be supplied (sec. 14); (4)
reporting of changes in stockholdings in an issuer by officers, directors, or
ten-percent stockholders of the issuer, and making any short-term profits
resulting from transactions in the stock subject for a period of two years to
recapture by the issuer (sec. 16).
Certain classes of securities are specifically exempted from these requirements: those of an investment company: of building and loan associoctions;
and of charitable, educational, religious, and other institutions. Securities
of a foreign issuer may be exempted by the SEC upon the determination that
such action is in the public interest.

217. *See 1964 U.S. Code Cong. & Adm. News* 3013 *et seq.* The amendment (Bill,

In Japan the term OTC market or OTC trading does not appear in the SEA either except for the phrase "other than on a securities exchange," which is included in Article 27–2 concerning tender offers, although a large portion of bonds and some equity securities are traded in the OTC market.[218] However, in extending disclosure requirements to those issuers who issued a category of unlisted securities but whose "marketability" or "trading" is similar to the listed securities, Articles 6 and 24 of the Japanese SEA mandated Cabinet Order to prescribe such securities.[219] Under the power mandated, Article 3 of the Cabinet Order provided that such securities must be "OTC trading securities" which are registered with the Securities Dealers

H.R. 6793) strengthened the regulation by: (1) requiring the NASD to establish standards of training, experience, and competence for members and employees, and capital requirements for members; (2) permitting the SEC, and the NASD, in a disciplinary action to proceed directly against an employee of a broker-dealer. Instead of against the firm, and permitting the SEC to employ sanctions, such as suspension, short of revoking registration; (3) requiring that the NASD have rules designed to produce fair and informative retail quotations for unlisted securities; (4) broadening the SEC's power to alter or supplement the NASD's rules relating to organization, discipline, and eligibility for membership; (5) granting the SEC power to brokers and dealers who chose not to become members of a registered securities association, in order to insure that all the brokers and dealers be subject to the expanded regulation provided by the Exchange Act either through a registered association which they voluntarily join or alternatively by the SEC itself.

218. *See Japanese SEA*, Art. 27–2. The Article makes it unlawful for any person to make a tender offer toward many and unspecified person to purchase certain securities "other than on a securities exchange" unless a notification statement filed with the MOF has become effective. On the other hand, trading in bonds in Japan, unlike trading in stock, is effected mainly in the OTC market. This is because of the technical difficulties involved in large volume of trading and simplicity in character and price. But, OTC quotations and publications are strictly controlled because of their significance. *See* Japanese Securities Research Institute, *Supra* note 24, at 69–71.

219. *See Japanese SEA*, Arts. 6, item 2 and 24 (1), item 2. Article 6 requires issuers of such securities to submit a copy of the same registration statement to the securities business association immediately after the issuer has filed the registration statement with the MOF in connection with a public offering or secondary distribution, whereas Article 24 requires such issuers to file periodic reports with the MOF in triplicate in compliance with the provisions of the MOF Order thereon.

Association.

The Securities Dealers Association of Japan (SDAJ), which had been given a broad rule-making power by Article 71 of the SEA, promulgated a wide range of rules relating to maintaining a fair and orderly market and protecting investors in the OTC market.[220] The SDAJ requires certain securities upon various tests[221] to register with it in compliance with the rules; such registered securities are then qualified for OTC trading. Any purchase or sale of the registered securities effected between the SDAJ members must be publicly released each day through the quotation system, and published in the Japanese Economic Newspaper specifying the highest and lowest prices of the day.[222] On the other hand, another type of OTC trading is effected by exchange members within the regulation of the exchange.[223] Thus, the regulatory framework of OTC trading in Japan

---

220. *See*, e.g., SDAJ: *Articles of Association; Fair Customary Rules; Uniform Customary Rules; Fair Customary Rules and Uniform Customary Rules of the Old Securities Dealers Association.*

221. SDAJ, *Rules on Quotations and Public Release of Trading in Registered Securities* (Uniform Customary Rule No 7, promulgated on Dec. 18, 1962, as amended on July 29, 1971) Arts. 3–11. To be registered with the SDAJ, any security in principle must meet eight requirements: among other things, the legal capital must exceed ¥100 million; at least two years must have passed after the incorporations; annual dividend rate must have exceed 8% in previous years and such rate must be expected to continue in the future; and the CPA's opinion must be concluded to be "proper" after the completion of a fullscale auditing of the financial structure of the issuer of such security.

222. *Id.*, Art. 2.

223. While exchange members must in principle carry out their trading in listed securities on the floor of the exchange through the auction system, they are also permitted to effect OTC trading as prescribed by the exchange's Articles of Association and Rules on Business (The Exchange's rule making power was given by Article 108 of the Japanese SEA to prescribe kinds and methods of trading in securities). Such exceptional cases are when a member company: (1) participates in competitive bidding held outside an exchange by the government or by a securities finance company; (2) effects odd-lot transactions; (3) effects trading in certificates of rights to be issued a new share; (4) which is also a member of another exchange, effects transactions on another exchange; (5) upon the exchange's approval, makes a secondary distribution among the public or participates in such distributing; (6) effects trading in bonds; and (7) buys as an agent of a tender offeror or sells securities in response to such tender offer. *See Japanese SEA* Art. 108; Tokyo Secu-

consists largely of self-regulation by the SDAJ and securities exchanges. The Japanese MOF indirectly involves itself in the OTC market by controlling and supervising these self-regulatory bodies.[224]

Regulation of OTC trading in Korea has recently been framed by the 1976 Amendments because of the recognition that OTC trading performs significant economic functions not performed by the exchange market.[225] The MOF hopes to develop an OTC market in which it could effectively apply its monetary and fiscal policies. Also, the MOF hopes to promote an OTC market in which registered securities (also listed securities in exceptional cases) could be widely distributed. In this respect, the SEA gave the SAC broad rulemaking power to design detailed regulation of the OTC market, but as yet the SAC has not exercised this power.

No survey has been conducted to estimate and appraise OTC

---

rities Exchange, *Rules on Business,* Arts. 93–96; Japan Securities Research Institute, *supra* note 24, at 92.

In addition, there are two kinds of inside-exchange but off-floor transactions for cases in which it is difficult to effect transactions on the floor. These are (1) transactions effected off the floor between a member and its customer within exchange's approval when there is unavoidable error or a breakdown of communication facilities on the floor and (2) off-floor block distributions, after trading hours. In a strict sense, however, these do not constitute OTC trading since they are required to be effected inside the exchange.

Finally, there is a third market, where a securities company functions as an intermediary to conclude transactions between non-members such as institutional investors, without acting as their agent. The securities company is only required to report details of transactions, to the exchange. *See* Japan Securities Research Institute, *supra* note 24, at 92.

224. *Japanese SEA*, Arts. 67–78 (for SDAJ) and 81–89 (for exchanges). Any securities dealers association is required to register with the MOF, which scrutinizes qualifications, rules and regulation for a denial or approval of application. Also, the MOF may, in the public interest and for the protection of investors, require the applicant to amend, delete, or add its rules and regulations, and any charges therein by the association must be reported. In addition, the MOF was empowered to inspect the association and to discipline the association. The MOF may issue an order to suspend or revoke the registration of any association, or an order to the association to expel a member or to dismiss an officer.

For regulation of the Japanese securities exchange by the MOF, *see* pp. 171 *et. seq. supra.*

225. *See* p. 105 *supra.*

trading in Korea.[226] Quotations are not made for OTC trading nor is any reporting on trading required. It can be assumed, however, the size of OTC trading as a whole in Korea is not insubstantial though it varies with the kinds of securities. First, large amounts of bonds either public or corporate, and listed and non-listed securities are traded in the OTC market. The Bank of Korea and the National Government sometimes hold competitive bidding for public bonds; institutional investors, including financial institutions, securities companies, and securities investment trust companies participate in such bidding.[227] Second, it is not unusual for speculators to trade in certificates of rights for new shares in the OTC market prior to the completion of distribution or the listing of such security in order to realize short-term profits.[228] Third, substantial amounts of odd-lot shares, from excessive oversubscription and pro-rata allotment with a maximum limit, come out and are traded off the exchange. Fourth, various types of private placements are effected by controlling shareholders of close corporations because they are deeply concerned about offsetting loss caused by possible underpricing and maintaining their control after their corporations go public. Finally, some investors can trade in securities in the OTC market even without the help of securities companies thus reducing transaction costs.

---

226. Although both public offering of new shares and secondary distribution of outstanding shares under the SEA belong to coverage of OTC trading in a broader sense, the writer excludes these two types of distribution from the coverage of discussion on OTC trading here.

227. *See* Seoul Economic News Paper, May 22, 1977, at p. 1. The Bank of Korea held competitive bidding for ₩ 5 billion of "currency stabilization bonds" in May, 1977. This was an open market operation launched in Korea to control money supplies rapidly expanding, especially by unexpected surpluses of balance of payment which reached a record of $3.45 billion in May 1977, from $1.5 billion at the end 1975. *See* Joongang Daily News, June 2, 1977 at p.1.

228. *See id.*, May 4, 1977, at p.4; May 7, 1977, at p.4; May 14, 1977, at p.4. The reason that such OTC trading is popular in Korea is attributable to the gap between an offering price and market prices after the listing. Many speculators make double subscriptions in a illegal way by avoiding the maximum limit imposed on subscribers in order to get short-term profits. The more such speculators are allotted new glamour shares, the more they can realize profits prior to the listing by selling such shares in the OTC market at a price far above the offering price.

How to organize an efficiently functioning OTC market has become an urgent issue in Korea because of a variety of reasons. Needs for the adequate protection of the interest of investors is growing as the size of OTC trading increases rapidly. The exchange market cannot cope with the increasing number of large orders from institutional investors. Public shareholders who are deprived of the trading market due to delisting or who hold below the unit of trading should have an alternative public market offering an opportunity for fair trading. Furthermore, absent an organized OTC market, the government could not apply its open market operation to control money supplies effectively, nor could it mobilize capital resources efficiently from the public for its application of fiscal policy. Clearly, the government should urgently organize and develop the OTC market to protect the interest of investors and to let that market perform vital economic functions which cannot be performed by the KSE.

B. Drawbacks in Law and the Institutional System

In designing the 1976 Amendments of the SEA, the legislature overlooked some critical points about the OTC market. First, Article 194(2) of the SEA limited the coverage of securities eligible for OTC trading to only two categories, the securities issued by listed corporations or those issued by registered corporations. This provision explicitly undermines a fundamental principle of commercial law, the "free transferability" of securities which are issued by non-listed or non-registered corporations.[229] Although enforcement of the provision is practically impossible, the provision must be amended to cover all the securities within the protections of the SEA as in the United States.

Second, another drawback is in the registration system for certain

---

229. The "free transferability" of securities is a fundamental principle under the Commercial Code in order to enhance marketability. As to the equity securities, the Commercial Code made it illegal to limit the negotiability of stock, *See Commercial Code,* Art. 335 (1). Also, any bearer form stock is transferred by an agreement to sell and buy and delivery of the certificate of stock. Any stock of register form is transferred by either endorsement and delivery or delivery with a certificate of transfer. But the transferee of register form stock should not claim against the corporation that he is entitled to the rights of a shareholder until his name and address are recorded in the shareholder registry. *See Commercial Code,* Arts. 336, 337.

issuers. The registration system was adopted to strengthen the disclosure system by requiring prospective issuers and some related corporations to file registration documents with the SAC. As of May 7, 1977, 108 designated corporations filed their registration documents with the SAC.[230] These required documents include financial statements, shareholder registry, statements of the business, marketing and production facilities of the company, and any material changes therein.[231] However, the SEA did not extend further disclosure rules and protections, such as periodic reporting, proxy solicitation, report of ownership changes, and prohibition of insider trading, to registered corporations.[232] The legislature might not perceive any need for the extension of such rules to registered corporations because traditionally they were all held by a small group of persons or by families. However, the need for extending the same rules of full disclosure and adequate protections provided for listed securities is essential as a safeguard for investors, as long as any securities of registered corporations are traded in the OTC market.

Finally, the existing regulatory system of the OTC market should be reappraised in terms of efficient allocation of power. Presently, the OTC market is regulated directly by the MOF and the SAC, which is an arm of the government. Experiences in the United States and Japan, however, indicate that direct regulation of a complex business through the machinery of government is insufficient and must be supplemented by a substantial degree of self-regulation.[233] In this respect, the government should, in organizing regulation of the OTC market, give the KSDA a substantial degree of self-regulation in the areas of denial of membership for a market-maker, registration of OTC securities, quotations and trading report, fair and equitable principles of trade, disciplining members, and relevant rule-making. However, these self-regulations should be properly su-

---

230. Seoul Economic Newspaper, May 8, 1977, at p.4. The 108 registered corporations were those which had been selected by the MOF in 1975 to go public, but failed to do so. Among these, forty-eight corporations were selected by the SAC to go public in 1977.

231. *SEA*, Art. 4; *Presidential Decree thereunder*, Art. 4.

232. *SEA*, Arts. 91, 92, 188, and 199.

233. *See* Loss, *supra* note 91, at 1361; S. Rep. No. 1455 at 3 and H. R. Report No. 2307 at 4, 75th Cong., 3d Sess. (1938).

pervised by the regulatory agency to avoid possible inefficiency of self-regulation. Through this cooperative regulation, the securities industry will build up its ethical standards and enhance the confidence of public investors.

II. Regulation of Securities Companies
A. *Regulation of Entry*
1. Corporate and License Requirement

Like Japan, entry into the securities business as a broker or dealer in Korea is limited to stock corporations chartered by a MOF license.[234] No individual, partnership, or legal entity other than a stock corporation can apply for a license for an independent business or for approval to be associated with any broker or dealer. The purpose behind this restraint is not clear, but it is probably to strengthen the financial capability of broker-dealers and to eliminate possible regulatory burdens inherent in allowing individual broker-dealers. Prior to 1976, the SEA kept silent on whether any foreign national could enter into the securities business. The amended SEA, however, liberalized its policy toward an internationalization of the securities market by allowing foreigners to participate in the securities industry with a requirement that such a securities company be controlled by domestic persons.[235]

Modeled after Japan, licenses for the securities business are classified into three categories based on the amount of legal capital.[236] If an applicant has legal capital of more than ₩ 3 billion, it is eligible

---

234. *SEA*, Art. 28(1), Cf. *Japanese SEA*, Art. 28.
235. *Id.*, Art. 28(4). It is required that more than 50% of legal capital or voting shares of a securities company be held by a Korean national or a legal person incorporated under the Korean law. But, the latter phrase would raise a problem among commentators because any alien may control a securities company by acquiring controlling stock through a corporation incorporated under the local law.
236. *Id.*, Art. 28(2), (3); *Japanese SEA*, Arts. 28(2), 32, item 1. But, Japan has four types of securities business license. The fourth type is a license for the business of handling public offerings or secondary distributions. Unlike underwriting, this business does not assume any risks. A security company performing this business receives commissions from issuers, shareowners, or underwriters for whom it rendered services. For details, *see* Japanese Securities Research Institute, *supra* note 24, at 109.

for the three kinds of businesses as a dealer, broker, and underwriter; if its capital is between W 2 and W 3 billion as a dealer and as a broker; if its capital is below W 2, but over 0.5 billion, as a dealer only. Thus, the businesses of broker, dealer, and underwriter are not segregated by law. Although some segregation can be attained by the provision subjecting separate licenses for more than one kind of business to minimum amounts of legal capital, the real legislative intent of such requirement was to induce capital increases in securities companies.

2. Qualifications for License

When application for a license is made, the MOF must examine the financial status and profitability of the applicant, promoters, and other management personnel, and securities transactions and other economic circumstances in the projected area of business.[237] In addition, the statute disqualifies certain individuals as officers, including the legally handicapped or persons who have been officers of a revoked securities company at the time of the revocation of its license, a disqualification which applies for a period of two years after the revocation.[238] When a securities company intends to either merge with another securities company or take over all or part of business from or transfer of its business to another company, it must obtain MOF approval; prior to issuing authorization, the MOF scrutinizes the same qualifications and other factors as required for the issuance of license.[239]

These qualifications, which the MOF must examine before granting or denying a license, are too abstract and ambiguous to indicate definite guidelines. In the United States and Japan, the statutes provide more specific grounds under which an application must be denied or approved.[240] Since specific criteria for granting or denying

---

237. *Id.*, Art. 32; *see also Presidential Decree under the SEA,* Art. 17.
238. *SEA,* The legally handicapped include any person who has not become an adult by law, who has been sentenced to be a permenant or temporary incompetent, or bankrupt by a court, or who had been imprisoned less than two years before. The provision also includes any person who had been sentenced a fine for the violation of the SEA less than two years before.
239. *Id.*, Art. 35.
240. *See Securities Exchange Act of 1934,* Secs. 15(b), 15A(f), 15 U.S.C.A. §78 o(b), o-3(f); Loss, *supra* note 91, at 1301–44; *Japanese SEA,* Arts. 31, 32. Section

a license in Korea are lacking, the MOF might exercise excessive discretion in a licensing procedure in contravention of the public interest. Furthermore, the SEA, unlike the counterparts in the United States or Japan, does not provide applicants with any statutory proceeding such as notice of the grounds for denial under consideration or opportunity for a hearing, to insure fairness in the denial of a license.[241] Appropriate amendments to the law could cure these deficiencies.

15(b) of the Exchange Act specifically provides a wide range of statutory causes for denial, including misstatement in application, conviction, injunction, willful violation of Federal statutes concerning securities industry and rules or regulations thereunder, willful aiding, abetting, counseling, or inducing any such violation, and far from or suspension of any functions or activities by an SEC order. In addition, as Section 6(c) empowered the exchange, with respect to the approval or denial of membership, Section 15A (g) empowered the NASD to examine statutory qualifications of its members, and to deny membership to any person, who is subject to a statutory disqualification. The NASD may deny membership to, or condition the membership of, a registered broker or dealer if:(1) such broker or dealer does not meet such standards of "financial responsibility", "operational capability", or "training, experience, and competence" as are prescribed by the NASD's rule; (2) there is a reasonable likelihood such broker, dealer, or any associated person therewith will again engage in acts or practices inconsistent with just and equitable principles of trade.

Article 31 of the Japanese SEA, which enumerates the matters to be examined by the MOF as Article 32 of the Korean SEA does, provides more specific terms. In addition, the Japanese SEA has some specific standards for denial of an application. Under Article 32, the MOF must deny a license if: (1) an applicant is not a joint stock company with its legal capital more than a certain amount prescribed by a cabinet order; (2)an applicant is a company which had been fined under the SEA, and five years have not yet passed after the completion of the execution of such penalty or from the date on which the execution was withheld; (3) an applicant is a company whose license had been cancelled, and five years have not yet passed from such cancellation; or (4) any officer of an applicant comes under a statutory disqualification.

241. *See Securities Exchange Act of 1934*, Sec. 15(b) (1), 15(b), 15 U.S.C.A. §78 o (b) (1); *Japanese SEA*, Art. 36. These provisions require that the authorities in both countries institute proceedings to determine whether an application should be denied. The proceedings must include notice of the grounds for denial under consideration and opportunity for hearing within a reasonable period of time.

3. Bonding Requirements

The SEA requires a securities company to post surety bonds when it is granted a license to engage in securities business or an authorization to establish a branch office.[242] The amount of required bond is ₩ 1 million for every business office, main office or a branch; the SAC may increase this amount to ₩ 10 million if the increase is necessary or appropriate in the public interest or for the protection of investors. Any appropriate deposit of listed securities may be accepted in lieu of cash. The bonds deposited must not be withdrawn except for statutory causes, such as the liquidation of business, so that any person who has a credit with the securities companies due to securities transactions has a right for repayment from such bonds in preference to other general creditors.[243] Unlike the blue-sky laws[244] or the Securities Investor Protection Act (SIPA) of 1970[245] in the United States, the bonding requirements in Korea were provided as mandatory provisions for entry into the securities business, thereby protecting the interest of public investors.

4. Problems of Public Policy toward Entry Regulation

As Section Three has indicated, entry into the securities businesses in Korea as a broker, dealer, or underwriter is limited to a stock corporation chartered by a MOF license and meeting certain bonding requirements. The MOF since 1973, however, stopped granting new entry under the pretext of avoiding excessive competition within the securities business community.[246] Such a public policy toward entry restrictions raised some interesting issues in the securities industry.

First, twenty-one among the twenty-eight existing securities com-

---

242. *SEA,* Art. 34; *Presidential Decree thereunder,* Arts. 19–23.
243. *SEA,* Art. 34(2).
244. *See* Loss, *supra* note 91, at 1350 and Loss, *supra* note 188, at 1654 *et seq.* Unlike the federal securities Acts, many of the blue-sky laws in the United States impose bonding requirements upon brokers and dealers. Though the legislative types of bonding requirements vary with states, they are not inserted to regulate the entry into securities business but to protect injured persons due to securities transactions.
245. 15 U.S.C.A. §78, 78aaa–78lll (1970). Basically the Act insures against loss or theft of securities purchased by customers but kept with their broker-dealers. For a discussion of the Act, *see* R.C. Clark, *The Soundness of Financial Intermediaries,* 86 YALE L.J. 1, 88 at note 254 (1976).
246. Seoul Economic Newspaper, April 19, 1977, at p.3.

panies are under the control of large business groups as of April 19, 1977.[247] The motivation of large business groups to participate in the securities business is to maintain continuing control after their corporations go public and to stabilize the market prices of their listed securities. Also, securities businesses appeared to be an attractive form of financing industries because of the government's positive policy in promoting securities markets. Since the MOF stopped granting new licenses, most large business groups could easily take over existing securities companies. The MOF appeared to welcome such takeovers with the expectation that new owners could improve the financial capability of the companies. However, few business groups have actually increased the capital stock of the companies taken over; rather, such companies have been misused as tools to simply serve the purposes of the respective business group.

Although a large volume of listed securities are issues of business groups directly or indirectly controlling a securities company, authorities are not seriously concerned about conflicting interests and potential unfair practices by such securities companies, and a law that prohibits a securities company having "special relations" with an issuer from becoming a managing underwriter for such issuer is the only law regulating conflicting interests or unfair practices.[248] To protect the public interest and maintain a fair and orderly market, the authorities should design a set of rules regulating or eliminating these conflicting interests and possible unfair practices.

Second, the existing securities business community is smaller in number and weaker in financial capability than the government intended for the smooth functioning of the securities market in the national economy. As noted earlier, Korea does not have even a single non-member securities company which exclusively engages in the OTC market. The total capital stock of twenty-eight securities

---

247. *Id.* The type of control varies with securities companies. Some securities companies exist as an affiliated corporation with a large business group, while some others are controlled by controlling shareholders or corporations of such large business group. Recently, the price of an existing license only is traded at about ₩ 150 million.

248. KSDA, *Agreement on Underwriting Business,* Art. 4(3). The term "special relations" should have been defined there. For details, *see* pp. 139–140 *supra.*

companies was about ₩ 32 billion as of December, 1976.[249] To help the securities markets in Korea, including the OTC market, to perform their economic functions effectively, the securities business community as a whole should be expanded by allowing more entries and by inducing capital increases in existing securities companies. The existing restraints on entry should be amended so that individuals or partnerships could participate in securities business under a reasonable capital requirement and qualification standard. Qualification standards should include personal factors such as professional career, experience, training, and ethical standards to insure protection of the public interest. These amendments should be designed so that the OTC market could effectively be developed as well.

B. *Post-Entry Regulation*

1. Portfolio Regulation

To regulate excessive transactions by securities companies compared to their financial condition and to protect customers against the risk of a broker's insolvency, the SEA restrains asset management by securities companies through a series of rules. These rules are working capital requirements, maximum debt-asset ratios, and reserve requirements. The SAC was empowered to inspect any securities company which appears to effect securities transactions, make loans, or to hold assets in contravention of these rules; it also was empowered to issue an order or take other necessary actions to prohibit such violations.[250]

a. Working Capital Requirement

In the ordinary course of business, every securities company is required to maintain a certain amount of working capital, which varies with the respective license for business.[251] If a securities company engages only as a dealer, working capital is to equal 30% of its capital stock; if both as a broker and a dealer, 25%; if as a broker, dealer, and an underwriter, 20%.

However, the current working capital requirement based on the

---

249. *See* KSE, *Securities Statistics Yearbook for 1976.* 368 (May, 1977).

250. *SEA,* Art. 64.

251. *Id.,* Art. 38, *Presidential Decree thereunder,* Art. 32; and *MOF Decree thereunder;* Art. 11. Under the MOF Decree, the amount of required working capital must be calculated by deducting the sum of the total amount of outstanding debts and fixed assets from the total amount of assets.

amount of capital stock does not seem to be rational. To make it rational, this requirement should be related to volume of business of each company.

b. Maximum Debt-Asset Ratio

The SEA makes it unlawful for any securities company to have aggregate indebtedness exceeding ten times the amount of net assets.[252] The amount of net assets must be the amount of existing total indebtedness deducted from that of existing total assets. The SAC was empowered to prescribe specific rules on the coverage of total indebtedness and assets. However, since the SAC has not yet enacted any specific rule on the matter, the rule preventing every securities company from borrowing ten times its net assets is hard to enforce in practice.

c. Reserve Requirement

Since a securities company is required to be a stock corporation under the Commercial Code, it must set aside at least one-twentieth of its earned surplus at the end of each fiscal year until such surplus reserves reach half the capital stock.[253] The SEA requires that every securities company set aside a certain portion of revenues as a loss reserve for securities transactions.[254] The portions to be set aside are determined by the size of trading volume and profits. The securities companies must not use these reserves for purposes other than writing off deficits caused by securities transactions.[255] This requirement thus concerns dealer's activities of securities companies. But the SEA, unlike Japanese law, requires no liability reserves to be used for compensating civil liabilities caused by securities transactions, especially a broker's.[256]

---

252. *SEA*, Art. 39 and *Presidential Decree thereunder*, Art. 33. In the United States the maximum debt ratio for brokers and dealers is fifteen times their net capital, while in Japan it is ten times the net capital as in Korea. But, the Japanese MOF may at its discretion issue any correction order, if the amount of the total net assets falls below that of capital stock. *See*. SEC Rule 15c 3–1. 17 C.F.C. §240. 15c 3–1; *Japanese SEA*, Art. 54; *MOF Order on Securities Companies*, Art. 3.

253. *See Commercial Code*, Art. 459; *also see* notes 142–144 and their accompanying texts *supra* Ch. 6.

254. *SEA*, Art. 40(1) and *Presidential Decree thereunder*, Art. 34.

255. *SEA*, Art. 40(2); It can be used for other purposes when the SAC approves.

256. *See Japanese SEA*, Arts. 56, 57, 57–2 and *MOF Order on Securities Companies*,

2. Bookkeeping Rules

Since all the securities companies in Korea are required to be incorporated as stock corporations, they are subject to the bookkeeping and accounting rules of the Commercial Code.[257] But these rules of the Commercial Code were designed mainly to protect the interest of shareholders and general creditors, and thus are insufficient to meet the purpose of the SEA—*inter alia,* for the protection of customers and investors and for the maintenance of a fair and orderly market by supervising the activities of securities companies. Enforcement of separate bookkeeping rules designed to meet these special concerns of the SEA is needed to compel securities companies to comply with the rules imposed upon them. In this respect, the bookkeeping rules of the United States and Japan require all brokers and dealers to make, keep, and preserve all such books and records as necessary or appropriate in the public interest or for the protection of investors.[258]

Arts. 7–2, 8.

257. *Commercial Code,* Arts. 447 *et seq.*

258. For the bookkeeping rules of the United States, *see Securities Exchange Act,* Sec. 17(a), 15 U.S.C.A. §78 q(a) and *SEC Rule* 17a–3, 17 C.F.R. §240. 17a–3; for those of Japan, *see Japanese SEA,* Arts. 53, 54; *Cabinet Order thereunder,* Art. 16; *MOF Order on Securities Companies,* Arts. 5, 5–2;7 and *MOF Releases on Bookkeeping, Accounting, Auditing Standards and Making Periodic and Business Reports,* MOF. Sec. Rels. No. 1740 (July 1, 1971, as amended by No. 1108, 2613, 3147 in 1973), No. 2018 (Aug. 14, 1972, as amended by No. 132 in 1975).

In the United States, books and records required to be made and kept by exchange members, brokers and dealers are:

1) blotters containing an itemized daily record of all purchases and sales of securities, all receipts and deliveries of securities, all receipts and disbursements of cash and other debts and credits;

2) ledgers reflecting all assets and liabilities, income and capital accounts;

3) ledger accounts itemizing separately each account of every customer and other related persons;

4) ledgers reflecting securities in transfer, dividends, and interest received, securities borrowed and loaned, monies borrowed and loaned, securities not received or failed to be delivered, and all long or short stock record differences.

5) a record or ledger reflecting separately for each security all "long" or "short" positions carried as of the clearance dates;

6) a memorandum of each brokerage order;

7) a memorandum of each purchase and sale for each, showing the price

Under the amended SEA, every securities company is required to make and keep books and records relating to its business in compliance with such bookkeeping rules as the SAC may prescribe.[259] Within the mandate, in 1978,[260] the SAC enacted a set of rules on Bookkeeping of Securities Companies. As in Japan, the securities companies must calculate the amount of their assets, debts, and net assets in accordance with the Bookkeeping Rules of Securities Companies. In conducting bookkeeping, securities companies must segregate their own assets from those entrusted by their customers.[261] All the statutory books, ledgers, and records (collectively referred to as "statutory ledgers") required to be kept must also comply with special forms and methods provided in the Bookkeeping Rules.[262] The financial statements to be made after the expiration of a fiscal year must follow a specified form.[263]

The statutory ledgers are classified into the principal ledgers and the supplementary ledgers. Principal ledgers include journals con-

---

and, "to the extent feasible," the time of execution;
8) copies of confirmation;
9) the name and address of the beneficial owner of each account, including the owner's signature in the case of margin account;
10) a record of puts, calls, and other options in which the member, broker, or dealer has any direct or indirect interest; and
11) a record of the proof of money balances of all ledger accounts in the form of trial balances, prepared currently at least once a month.

Japanese bookkeeping rules appear to have been modeled substantially after the American rules. Although the bookkeeping rules designed in the Japanese SEA and Cabinet and MOF Orders thereunder concern only coverages of assets and debts and methods of calculating the amount of net assets to be stated in financial statements, the MOF releases require that all the statutory ledgers, books and records be made and kept in compliance with the rules prescribed therein.

259. *SEA*, Art. 47.
260. The Bookkeeping Rules of Securities Companies (Promulgated as SAC Rule No. 11 on January 1, 1978, as last amended on May 28, 1979). With respect to the matters not specified in the Rules securities companies must comply with the provisions of the Bookkeeping Rules of listed corporations (P.D. No. 7199 of July 18, 1974, as last amended by P.D. No. 10061 of November 11, 1980). *See* Art. 2 of the Rules.
261. *Id.*, Art. 3.
262. *Id.*, Arts. 6 through 9.
263. *Id.*, Arts. 5 and 10.

taining an itemized daily record of all purchases and sales of securities, all receipts and deliveries of securities, all receipts and disbursements of cash and other debits and credits, and ledgers reflecting all assets, liabilities, and capital accounts. Supplementary ledgers include a wide range of ledger accounts itemizing separately each account which appeared in the principal ledger.[264]

By failing to include some important ledgers, the coverage of such statutory ledgers, unlike the coverage in the United States, is not adequate to meet the purposes of efficient supervision and protection of investors. First, the bookkeeping rules failed to include a ledger reflecting separately for each security all "long" or "short" positions carried as of the clearance dates. The rules also failed to include ledgers reflecting dividends and interests received, and securities, not received and delivered. In addition, although the identification of the beneficial owner of each account is of critical importance for supervisory purposes, the bookkeeping rules failed to require securities companies to record names and addresses of all the beneficial owners.

3. Reporting Requirements
a. Reporting Requirements

The SEA requires securities companies to file three kinds of reports with the SAC: (1) a business report reflecting business operations and financial status;[265] (2) a report on any changes in registered salesmen;[266] and (3) other reports on such material matters prescribed by the SEA and the Presidential Decree thereunder.[267] Reports of

---

264. *See id.*, Art. 8 and attached forms specified respectively.
265. *See SEA*, Art. 47. This reporting requirement is, in a sense, a ramification of the bookkeeping rules.
266. *Id.*, Art. 68. The matters required to be reported on registered salesmen include: (1) any changes in the matter registered with the SAC; (2) any causes making a salesmen legally handicapped; and (3) retirement or other cause dismissing a salesman from his business.
267. *Id.*, Art. 36 and *Presidential Decree thereunder*, Art. 31. The matters required to be reported by these provisions include a wide range of information on material facts, such as changes in management, criminal sanctions for violations of the SEA, bankruptcy, changes in shareholdings of controlling shareholders, and so on.
To protect the interest of public investors, the public must be informed of termination of security business by inserting public notices at least three

items (2) and (3) must be filed immediately when any statutory cause has occurred, while the business report of item (1) must be filed in compliance with provisions of the SAC's Bookkeeping Rules.[268]

Under the SAC's Bookkeeping Rules of Securities Companies, securities companies must file with the SAC, among other things, profit and loss statements, balance sheets, and business reports, all on a monthly basis, by stating current financial status, profits and losses, and monthly status of securities transactions, margin trading, and monies loaned and borrowed.[269] The financial statements and other reports are required to be made in compliance with specified forms respectively.[270]

Along with the inspection power conferred upon the SSB (in effect, the SAC),[271] the purposes of reporting requirements were to detect and prevent any violation of law by securities companies. To meet purposes, the accuracy of a report is of cardinal importance. However, unlike the United States, Korea's reporting rules do not require the financial statements to be audited by an independent CPA firm.[272]

b. Other Administrative Restrictions

Administrative control affects other important activities of securities companies. A statutory merger, consolidation, transfer or acquisition of all or part of any securities business cannot, as in the case of a new entry into the securities business, become effective without a prior authorization by the MOF.[273] On the other hand, a securities company must get SAC authorization when it: (1) changes its name

---

times in more than two daily newspapers, and thirty days prior to the proposed termination. *See id.*, Art. 37.

268. *See* note 260 *supra* Until the Bookkeeping Rules was enacted, the old MOF Bookkeeping Rules were made applicable by virtue of addenda, Art. 4 of the SEA.

269. *The Bookkeeping Rules of Securities Companies*, Art 12. The monthly report must be filed by 20th of the next month except the month when a fiscal year ends.

270. *Id.*

271. *See* pp. 380–82 *infra*. Since the SSB is under the control of the SAC, the SSB's inspection power, in effect, belongs to the SAC.

272. SEC Rule 17a–5, 17 C.F.R. §240. 17a–5. The financial report must be made on a monthly, quarterly, and annual basis.

273. *SEA*, Art. 35(1), Cf. *Japanese SEA*, Art. 35.

or the amount of stated capital; (2) sets up a branch or other office, or changes the location of its principal or other office; (3) suspends, reopens, or discontinues its business; or (4) does any other matters as prescribed by the Presidential Decree, such as disposition of any capital or surplus reserves.[274]

In order to prevent any person from avoiding the license requirement, the SEA made it illegal for any securities company to lend the license to another person.[275] In addition, the amended SEA adopted a provision requiring any controlling shareholder to get SAC approval prior to the transfer of his shareholdings.[276] Furthermore, a securities company is prohibited from engaging in a business other than the securities business or a business authorized by the MOF.[277] Inside directors and full-time officers are also forbidden to engage in a daily business for other companies or their own business without prior SAC approval.[278]

4. Protection of Customers
    a. General Protection

Like the Japanese SEA, the SEA in Korea includes provisions to protect customers' interest from their brokers. When a securities company receives an order from its customer, the company must inform him in advance whether it acts for its own account or executes the order for his account; the company is prohibited from acting as both dealer and broker in the same securities transaction.[279] In addition, a securities company is required to send a report to its customer immediately after the execution of an order.[280] It also is generally prohibited from lending or hypothecating customers' securities.[281]

In addition, customers who have entrusted securities companies with an order to sell or buy a security have a definite right to the protection of their privacy on securities transactions, monies and securities in deposit, and any other transactions. Officers and other

---

274. *Id.*, Art. 35(2) and *Presidential Decree thereunder*, Arts. 27–30.
275. *SEA*, Art. 63.
276. *See* p.109 *supra*.
277. *SEA*, Art. 51.
278. *Id.*, Art. 48.
279. *Id.*, Arts. 43–44. Cf. *Japanese SEA*, Arts. 46, 47, 129.
280. *Id.*, Art. 46. Cf. *Japanese SEA*, Art. 48.
281. *Id.*, Art. 45. Cf. *Japanese SEA*, Art. 51.

employees of a security company are prohibited from disclosing any information about customers' accounts and securities transactions to others without prior written consent of such customers.[282] This privacy rule on securities transactions, the same as that on bank deposits, is to induce more participation by public investors in Korea. The exceptions provided to this privacy rule are restricted to cases accompanied by a written instrument or warrant issued by a court of competent jurisdiction, prosecuting attorney, the SSB, the KSE, the KSFC, or a national tax administrative office of a competent jurisdiction.[283]

b. Civil Liability

The SEA, unlike the Japanese SEA, includes two provisions concerning civil liabilities of a securities company or its officers and controlling shareholders.[284] One is Article 41, which makes any securities company liable for "damages done to others by its branch or other business offices in purchasing or selling a security, or performing other transactions." The other is Article 58, which makes directors, auditors, and controlling shareholders "jointly and severally" liable for "damages done to a third person by any willful or negligent act of officers or directors in performing their business; provided, however, that a controlling shareholder shall not jointly be liable, if he proves that such activities of directors or auditors were not made by his request or approval;[285] and the securities company concerned shall not be exempted from its civil liability in any of the foregoing cases." However, introduction of these civil liability provisions makes little difference in the public interest or for the protection of investors because these provisions have incorporated into the SEA the substance of existing legal doctrine in civil and commercial

---

282. *Id.*, Arts. 59, 60. Any violation of this prohibition is subject to criminal sanctions of an imprisonment or a fine. *See id.*, Arts 280, 214, 215.

283. *Id.* and *Presidential Decree thereunder*, Art. 38. In the Japanese SEA and other Rules thereunder, this privacy rule does not appear.

284. *Id.*, Arts. 41, 58. But the Japanese SEA does not have any special provision of civil liability of securities companies. *See Japanese SEA*, Ch. 3 (Securities Companies).

285. *Id.*, Art. 58(1). Also, any officer can avoid his liability if he proves that he dissented from the passage of a resolution. *See id.*, Art. 58(3) and *Commercial Code*, Art. 399(2), (3).

laws with only minor, insignificant variations. As a matter of corporate law, securities companies, being corporate entities, must be liable for damages done to others by their branches or other business offices. As corporate entities, securities companies are also subject to vicarious liability in a civil law tort.[286] Furthermore, directors, auditors, and controlling shareholders, if controlling shareholders are joint tort-feasors, must be jointly and severally liable for damages done to a third person, and the corporation concerned must not avoid its liability by pointing to such officers' liability.[287] Article 58 only expanded existing protection by extending officers' liability to all negligent acts; under the commercial code liability is limited to "gross or material" negligence.

Introduction of Article 41, however, raises significant disputes among commentators due to the vagueness of the text. Requiring that a securities company be liable for damages done by its branch or other business office, the text of Article 41 includes no indication about the coverage of liability. The text appears to impose a "strict" liability on securities companies because it, unlike Article 58, does not include a phrase "willful or negligent," explicitly limiting the coverage of liability. No legislative history on this matter is available. A securities business is not an insurance business, and a securities company does not insure or undertake all the risks of securities transactions which belong to other parties. In this respect, Article 41 should be amended to clarify the extent of liability.

In the United States, general fraud sections as applied to broker-dealers comprise Section 17(a) of the Securities Act of 1933, Sections 10(b) and 15(c) of the Securities Exchange Act of 1934, and Rules 10b-5 and 15c 1–2 thereunder, all of which have appropriately modified common law tort theory in order to meet the purpose of the securities law.[288] Unlike the United States, the SEA included the fore-

---

286. *See Civil Code,* Art. 756.
287. *Commercial Code,* Arts. 389 (3), 210, 401, 414. Officers' liability to a third person is limited, under the Commercial Code, to a willful, or "materially" negligent act. Controlling shareholders of a company also may be joint tort-feasors if involved in any tortious act by officers of the company, even though there is no explicit provision in the statutes.
288. These sections all prohibit manipulative, deceptive, or fraudulent acts in the securities markets. Section 17(a) outlaws: (1) any device, scheme, or artifice

going two Articles which incorporated the substance of the existing tort doctrine without appropriate modifications to relax the difficulties in establishing a case. Although no case on the matter has been brought to and decided by a court thus far, establishment of a case is almost impossible by any injured party under the existing rules unless appropriate modifications are provided by the legislature.

c. Prohibition of Unsuitable Recommendations

As noted in the historical analysis,[289] the amended SEA introduced Article 52 prohibiting unsuitable solicitations, recommendations, or other fraudulent practices by officers and employees of a securities company. Introduction of this Article is of critical importance in terms of maintaining a fair and honest market and enhancing public

---

to defraud; (2) any untrue statement of a material fact or any omission to state a material fact necessary to make the statements made not misleading; and (3) any transaction, practice, or course of business which operates or would operate as a fraud or deceit. Section 10(b) itself only refers to "any manipulative or deceptive device or contrivance," but Rule 10b–5 has copied the language of the three subdivisions of Section 17(a). Section 15(c) (1) refers to "any manipulative, deceptive, or other fraudulent device or contrivance." But again Rule 15c 1–2 has incorporated the substance of the three subdivisions of Section 17(a) into this section.

The major difference between these three sections and the rules implementing them are that Section 17(a) applies only to sales, whereas Section 15(c) (1) applies to both purchases and sales, and that Section 15(c) (1) applies only to a "broker or dealer," whereas Sections 17(a) and 10(b) apply to "any person."

There are some related rules evolved and established both by the SEC and courts. Above all, the "shingle theory" referred to by Judge Clark in *Kahn v. SEC*, 297 F. 2d 112 (2d Cir. 1961) was evolved by the Commission as a basis for finding statutory fraud under these sections in a case where no intentional misstatement or omission on the part of the broker-dealer could be established. In brief, the theory is that when a broker-dealer goes into business (hangs out his "shingle"), he implies that he will deal fairly and competently with his customers and that he will have an adequate basis for any statements or recommendations which he makes concerning securities. Since Congress has given the Commission a broad, though not limitless, grant of authority to interpret and apply the statutes under which it operates, the Commission's interpretations of the statutes as expressed in a Release indicate a guideline for courts to apply rules to specific circumstances. For details, *see* Jennings & Marsh 676–81 (4th ed. 1977).

289. *See* pp.108–109 *supra*.

confidence in the securities industry. The coverage of this Article, however, is insufficient to prevent professionals in the securities industry from effecting securities transactions by means of manipulative, deceptive, or other fraudulent acts, devices or contrivances, or from making any unsuitable recommendations without having reasonable grounds.

First, since item 2 of Article 52 prohibits false statement of a fact or false quotation of a security price that is "willfully" made in order to get unjustifiable profits, the actual coverage of prohibition would be limited to outright fraudulent practices. Providing proof of such willfulness and illegal purpose in complicated securities transaction is generally beyond the competence of authorities or individual parties.

Second, the phrases "in contravention of investor protection or fair and equitable principles of trade or in detriment to public confidence in the securities business" as expressed in item 3 of Article 52 appear too vague and abstract to determine guidelines for prohibited practices or acts. Modeling the phrases after the Japanese rule,[290] the legislature failed to specify certain categories of illegal activities in an enforcement decree. Unlike the NASD in the United States, the KSDA in Korea failed to exercise appropriately its rulemaking power provided by the SEA concerning the matters of investor protection or fair and equitable principles of trade.[291] The ambiguity of the rule

---

290. *See Japanese SEA,* Art. 50, *MOF Decree on Securities Companies,* Art. 15, and *MOF Decree on Soundness, Etc. of Securities Companies,* Art. 1. Article 50 of the Japanese SEA, like its Korean counterpart, has three items: item 1 made it illegal for any officers or employees of a securities company, in recommending the purchase or sale of a security, to provide their customers with a dogmatic conclusion or belief that the market price of such security would rise or fall; items 2 and 3 correspond to items 1 and 3 or the Korean SEA's Article 52 respectively, but Japanese item 3 mandated to the MOF Order to prescribe specific coverage of illegal activities or practices which are in contravention of investor protection or fair and equitable principles of trade, or in detriment to public confidence in the securities industry. The MOF Order within this mandate enumerates 7 categories of such illegal activities of practices in more specific terms.

291. *SEA,* Art. 163, *Presidential Decree thereunder,* Art. 78 item 11, and KSDA, *Articles of Association,* Arts. 8, 9, and 48, items 1 and 2. The NASD in the United States enacted the Rules of Fair Practice which incorporate basic

would result either in abuses of administrative power broadly left at authority's discretion or in incompetence in exercising the power.

Third, the foregoing Article presents enforcement problems because adequate remedies for rule violations are lacking. The SEA provides a criminal sanction of only a fine or imprisonment.[292] The SEA has not empowered the MOF or the SAC to impose an appropriate disciplinary sanction on any natural person violating the rule or on an involved securities company.[293] Nor has the SEA provided any injured party with adequate means of civil remedy since, as noted earlier, establishing a case under the two civil liability provisions is still difficult for the injured party because elements of liability under the provisions are no more relaxed than those already established in civil and commercial laws.[294] Both the lack of disciplinary sanctions

---

requirement that a member in the conduct of his business "shall observe high standards of commercial honor and just and equitable principles of trade." This is followed by a number of particularized requirements. Some of these are patterned after the SEC's fraud and disclosure rules. Others are more specific. For example, a member recommending that its customer purchase or sell a security must have reasonable grounds for believing that the recommendation is suitable for such customer upon the basis of facts, if any, disclosed by such customer as to his other security holding and as to his financial situation and needs. *See NASD Rules of Fair Practice*, Art. III, Sec. 1, 2, CCH NASD Manual ¶ 2152.

Also, if a salesman makes statements knowing they have no "adequate basis," or if he is "grossly careless or indifferent to the existence of an adequate basis" for his statements, then he has violated the anti-fraud provisions of the securities laws. This rule has been evolved by the so-called "shingle" theory— one who hangs out his shingle implicitly warrants the soundness of statements of stock value, estimates of earnings potential, and the like. *See* note 288 *supra*.

292. *SEA*, Arts. 209 item 6, 214, 215. Any person who violates Article 52 must be subject to an imprisonment of not more than two years or a fine not exceeding W 2 million. At the same time, the securities company employing such person is subject to a fine not exceeding W 2 million.

293. *Id.*, Arts. 55, 57. These Articles do not make any violation of Article 52 a statutory cause for revocation or suspension of a license for securities business. Nor does Article 57(3) empower the SAC to order securities companies to dismiss an officer concerned.

294. *See* the accompanying text of note 160 *supra*. An injured party may have a cause of action under both Civil Law and the SEA to recover damages done by unsuitable recommendations or other fraudulent and deceptive devices

and the lack of enforceable civil remedies are critical drawbacks; the legislature should act quickly to cure them in order to protect investors and promote the securities market by enhancing public confidence.

5. Insider and Salesman Regulation

a. Insider Regulation

In its 1976 Amendments the SEA adopted a provision prohibiting trading in securities by officers and other employees of a securities company for the accounts in which they, directly or indirectly, have an interest.[295] This prohibition was to control unfair trading by insiders of the securities industry at the expense of public investors due to insiders' advantageous positions. A violation of this prohibition constitutes a statutory cause for the SAC's suspension order of a license, and a cause for imprisonment of not more than one year or a fine not exceeding ₩ 1 million.[296] The SEA, however, does not make this violation a direct cause for the MOF's revocation order or the SAC's order to securities companies to dismiss the officers concerned.[297] To discipline securities companies and strengthen administrative control over them, the SEA should have diversified the statutory sanctions for this violation.

On the other hand, the insider trading rule includes a loophole by not extending its prohibition to cases in which any insider or tippee discloses or tips inside information of a material fact on securi-

---

made by employees of a securities company. He may bring a suit against such employees or the company itself. But unlike the United States, neither the statutory requirements for proving a case were relaxed for the protection of investors, nor did any authorities or a court interpret statutes and evolve or establish specific rules to relax the existing fraud doctrine so that individual investors could successfully bring a suit.

295. *See* pp. 98–107 *supra*. They can trade in registered or listed securities upon receiving SAC approval in compliance with the rules thereon (*SAC Rules on Trading in Securities by Officers and Employees of Securities Companies*, SAC Rule No. 5, as promulgated on Mar. 30, 1977).

296. *SEA*, Arts. 57(1), 210, item 2, 214, 215, and 42.

297. *Id.*, Arts. 55, 57(3). Under Article 55 item 4, any securities company whose license has been suspended and which has failed to meet conditions attached to the suspension order within a month may have a statutory cause for revocation. But from the viewpoint of an efficient administrative control, the authorities should order the securities companies to dismiss their officers concerned or issue a revocation order under the circumstances.

ties to close friends or other persons so that they can effect transactions in such securities for accounts in which the insider has no direct or indirect interest. This practice also falls within the category of fraudulent practices which the SEA should have included within its coverage.[298] Even though no case has been brought to court, such practice appears to have frequently occurred in Korea at the expense of public investors; therefore, the legislature needs to expand the fraud concept to prevent such fraudulent transactions.

b. Salesman Regulation

Salesmen of securities companies are required to register with the SAC in accordance with provisions of the SEA, the Presidential Decree thereunder, and the SAC's Rule on Salesman Registration.[299] Statutory qualifications for the salesman registration, *inter alia*, include the completion of a training course at the Institute of Securities Training, a certificate for passing the examination for salesman, and professional experience of not less than one year at a securities company, after having passed the examination. The SAC, upon the receipt of an application, must examine whether the application meets statutory qualifications, and must deny the application if it fails to meet the qualifications or includes a false statement or any statutory disqualifications.[300]

When a salesman registered with the SAC has violated any provisions of the SEA or Decrees and Rules thereunder, the SAC may

---

298. *See* the accompanying texts of notes 289–291 *supra*. Such practice clearly constitutes an act which is in contravention of "investor protection" or "fair and equitable principles of trade" or in detriment to "public confidence in the securities industry" as provided in Article 52 item 3. However, due to the lack of relaxed and expanded fraud doctrine and specific rules on fair and equitable principles of trade in Korea, establishing a civil case for such an act is almost impossible for an injured party, especially against tippees who have special access to inside information from insiders of a securities company.

299. *SEA*, Arts. 65–66; *Presidential Decree thereunder*, Arts. 40–41; *SAC Rule on Salesman Registration* (SAC Rule No. 6, as promulgated on April 22, 1977).

300. *SEA*, Art. 66; *SAC Rule on Salesman Registration*, Arts. 4–6. The application for registration also must be denied if the applicant: (1) has had his registration revoked and two years have not yet passed after the revocation; (2) has already been registered as a salesman of another securities company; or (3) has made the application by means of fraudulent or unlawful acts or devices.

revoke or suspend his registration. In addition, the SAC must eliminate a salesmen's registration if any statutory disqualification or other statutory cause has been discovered.[301] In order to facilitate the SAC's supervisory functions, securities companies must immediately file a report when any material changes occur in the status of their salesmen[302].

6. Inspection Power

Like the SEC in the United States, the SSB (in effect, the SAC) was granted broad inspection powers over the financial situation and business operation of securities companies.[303] This inspection power was intended to play a significant role in detecting any violations of laws and in discouraging or preventing securities companies from engaging in any illegal practices. Also, through inspections, brokers, dealers, and all the professionals in the securities industry could be educated in the legal requirements. Prior to the 1976 Amendments, the MOF had been granted the same inspection power, but the MOF could not exercise this power because of insufficient personnel to perform this duty.

The SSB may inspect securities companies periodically, on a surprise basis at any time that appears necessary, under the direction of the MOF and the SAC or upon the consignment of other governmental agencies.[304] The inspection sometimes may be limited to particular matters of a company's operation, but it generally involves a full scale examination. After their establishment, the SAC and the SSB made full scale examinations both periodically and on a surprise basis. Prior to conducting an examination, personnel of the SSB must show a certificate representing the right of inspection power to persons of the securities companies concerned. If necessary,

---

301. *SEA*, Art. 69.
302. *See Id.*, Arts. 68, 213. Any violation for this reporting requirement is subject to criminal sanctions.
303. *Id.*, Arts. 53, 135. Since the SSB was established as an enforcement or executive division of the SAC and must be subject to the control of the SAC, the inspection power in effect is exercised by the SAC. For the SAC inspection power in the United States, *see Securities Exchange Act of 1934*, Sec. 17(b) 15 U.S.C.A. §78q(b); *also* Loss, *supra* note 188, at 1356–58.
304. *SAC Rules on Inspection* (SAC Rule No. 1, as promulgated on March 14, 1977), Arts. 2, 3, and *SEA*, Arts. 135, items 3 & 7, 112 (3).

the SSB may require the securities companies to file a report on business or asset management, to submit books, records, or other related materials, to compel the attendance of a witness, or to have persons involved make a statement.[305] Also, the SAC can invoke the aid of any other concerned institutions to facilitate the inspection.[306]

Upon completion of the inspection, the SSB must make a report thereon to the SAC with an opinion on any appropriate measure or disposition to be taken for violations made.[307] If a violation constitutes a statutory cause for revocation of a license, the SAC recommends that the MOF revoke the license;[308] if the violation constitutes a cause for suspension of a license, dismissal of an officer, or others, the SAC takes appropriate measures.

A significant problem in this inspection power is the lack of well-qualified personnel who could effectively perform the duty. The SSB appears to have few lawyers and certified public accountants in its enforcement and inspection divisions. Like the SEC in the United States, the SSB needs to be equipped with experts in the area.

7. Discipline by the MOF and the SAC

The discipline of securities companies in Korea is threefold—discipline by the MOF, by the SAC, and by the KSDA. The MOF is empowered to revoke a license for securities business, whereas the SAC can only suspend all or a part of securities businesses or order a securities company to dismiss an officer. As a self-regulatory institute, the KSDA, though not as strong as the NSAD in the United States, may expel a member, suspend its membership, or issue a warning.

a. Statutory Causes for Disciplinary Sanctions

Under Article 55 of the SEA, the MOF may revoke the license for securities business if a securities company has:

(1) obtained its license through unjustifiable means; (2) not launched its business within one month from the date it could, or has ceased to do its business for more than one month; (3) taken or has transferred monies or securities from another person through unjustifiable means in relation to its business; (4) failed to meet within one month the terms and conditions imposed by the SAC's suspension order under Article 57 of the SEA; (5) violated or has been in default

---

305. *SEA*, Art. 53(2), (3).
306. *Id.*, Arts. 128, 129.
307. *Id.*, Art. 53(4).
308. *Id.*, Art. 53(5).

of a sales or purchase contract made on the exchange; (6) in contravention of the SEA effected a merger into or consolidation with another company, transfer of its business, or loan of its license to another person, or has, without having received required SAC approval, had its controlling shareholder effect a sale of control; (7) violated a SAC order issued under Article 54 of the SEA to prevent excessive speculation, or in the public interest or for the protection of investors; or (8) violated the SEA or any order or disposition issued or taken thereunder, and, as a result, appeared to meet difficulties to do business as a securities company.[309]

On the other hand, under Article 57(1) the SAC may suspend all or a part of a securities business, if a securities company has:

(1) violated any provision requiring minimum working capital, debt/asset ratio, or reserves for securities transactions; (2) violated any provision prohibiting its officers or employees from trading in securities or prohibiting it from acting both as a broker and as a dealer in the same transaction, or any provision limiting credit extension, securities savings, or category of business to do; (3) violated a provision of the book keeping rules or requirement of filing a business report with the SAC; or (4) violated a SAC order issued under Article 54 of the SEA to prevent excessive speculation, in the public interest, or for the protection of investors.[310]

In addition, under Article 57(3), the SAC may order a securities company to dismiss the officers involved, if the securities company has:

(1) failed to file a report with the SAC on the matters prescribed in Article 36 and the Presidential Decree thereunder; (2) violated the rule requiring it to state explicitly its function as a dealer or broker in every securities transaction or the rule prohibiting it from acting both as a broker and as a dealer in the same transaction; (3) violated Article 46 requiring it to report to its customer on the result of securities transactions immediately after the execution of an entrusted order; (4) violated Article 48 prohibiting its inside officers from engaging in business of other companies or their own business without SAC approval; or (5) violated Article 65 requiring the registration of its salesmen.[311]

b. Some Drawbacks

The foregoing disciplinary rules of securities companies included significant drawbacks and loopholes which prevented the MOF or the SAC from effectively enforcing the purposes of the SEA and

---

309. *Id.*, Art. 55.
310. *Id.*, Art. 57(1).
311. *Id.*, Art. 57(3).

Decrees or Rules thereunder. First, in enumerating violations of some specific provisions of the SEA as statutory causes for revocation by the MOF, Article 55 of the SEA included item 8, generally making it a category of the statutory cause that a securities company "has violated the SEA or any order or disposition issued or taken thereunder, and, as a result, appeared to meet difficulties in doing business as a securities company." No other guideline or indication exists, however, to determine what the phrase "appeared to meet difficulties in doing business as a securities company" actually means, and thus serious ambiguity remains as to its application. The legislature should have clarified the coverage of the phrase, such as financial difficulty, disqualification in light of ethical standard, or others.

On the other hand, the SEA adopted a limited enumeration in prescribing the statutory causes for the SAC's suspension order and included no general clause broadly covering any other violation of provisions of the SEA or Decrees and Rules thereunder, including those of the SAC, SSB, and KSE. Because of these limited enumerations and the vagueness of the phrase in Article 55, the authorities would have difficulty imposing a disciplinary sanction, and could not effectively exercise their disciplinary power when a securities company violated provisions of the SEA, Decrees and Rules thereunder, which do not expressly fall within the category of the statutory causes.

The authorities would meet such difficulties especially when a securities company violated the provision of the SEA prohibiting it from: (a) hypothecating or lending customers' securities in custody (Article 45); (b) effecting excessive trading in securities or unsound portfolio management as compared to its financial situation (Article 64); (c) making unsuitable recommendations, false statement of a fact, or false quotations of a price, or effecting any other acts or practices in contravention of investor protection or fair and equitable principles of trade, or detrimental to public confidence in the securities industry (Article 52) ; (d) disclosing or tipping any inside information or privacy of customers' accounts (Article 59) ; or (e) manipulating market prices of a security up and down or stabilizing in contravention of provisions of the Presidential Decree (Article 105). No violations of these provisions have explicitly been enumerated as a statutory cause for revocation or suspension. Therefore, the MOF could revoke the license of a securities company violating any of these prohibitions only when it determines that the securities company, as a result of such violation, "appears to meet difficulties in doing business as a securities company." Such determination, however, is left to the discretion of the MOF because of the vagueness and ambiguity of the phrase. In order to implement the purposes of disciplinary sanctions effectively, such loopholes or drawbacks should be cured by reappraising and amending the rules in an overall scheme.

Also, since the SEA adopted a limited enumeration in prescribing statutory causes for the SAC's dismissal order of an officer of a securities company, the coverage of such statutory causes is insufficient. In order for the SAC to perform its supervisory and disciplinary functions more effectively, the SEA should have included a provision authorizing the agency to issue a dismissal order. When any officers of securities companies have violated provisions of the SEA, Decrees and Rules thereunder other than qualifying a statutory cause, and when such violation appears to be inconsistent with investor protection or just and equitable principles of trade, the authority, at its proper discretion, should respond by selecting an appropriate sanction.

Finally, the SEA should require any authority, in making its final decision of a disciplinary sanction, to insure fairness. Such fairness can be attained by providing a person charged with a violation with an opportunity to defend himself against the charges. The SEA, however, failed to include such statutory proceeding for the accused person prior to making a final decision.[312]

C. The Korea Securities Dealers Association(KSDA)

1. Organization and Regulation

When securities companies have organized an association for the purpose of assuring fair trading in securities and protecting the interest of investors, a representative of the association must file a notification statement with the SAC.[313] Unlike the United States or Japan,

---

312. Under the pertinent laws, an aggrieved party can dispute its legality or fairness only in certain limited cases after the final decision has been made. For details, *see* the accompanying text of note 53 *supra*.

313. *SEA*, Art. 162. The notification statement must include the name and location of the association, names of officers and members, and articles of association.

the securities business association in Korea must be organized as one
central body; the organization is not required to be registered but
must notify the SAC of its association.[314] When the KSDA has
amended its Articles of Association or enacted, amended, or abro-
gated(hereinafter collectively referred to as "amend" or "amendment") its rules on business, the SEA only requires the KSDA to report such amendment to the SAC.[315]

But, the SAC may order the KSDA to effect amendments to its
Articles of Association or rules on business as the SAC deems necessary or appropriate to insure fair and equitable principles of trade or
protection of investors.[316] Also, the SAC was empowered to order the
SSB or the KSDA to inspect, investigate, and report such matters as
appeared to be necessary to insure the fair administration of the Association or the protection of investors.[317] Further, the SAC may order
the KSDA to dissolve it, suspend its business, dismiss its officers, or
take necessary measures, if any statutory cause therefore has occurred.[318]

2. Self-Regulation

The SEA granted the KSDA rule-making power for self-regulation
of its members to include in the Articles of Association provisions,

---

314. For the organization of the KSDA, *see* p. 118. in Ch. 5 *supra*. For those of the
United States and Japan, *see Securities Exchange Act of 1934*, Sec. 15A, 15
U.S.C.A. §780–3 and *Japanese SEA*, Arts. 67–69. In Japan, these had been
regional securities organizations until May, 1968, when 23 of these were
dissolved as an initial step toward a single national organization. In July,
1973, the 10 associations which formed the Japan Federation of Securities
Firm Associations were abolished again to establish a single national
organization, the Securities Dealers Association of Japan (SDAJ, or Japan
National Association of Securities Dealers). The Japanese Federation itself
was to be registered with the MCF. *See* Japan Securities Research Institute,
supra note 24, at 115–6; *see also Japanese SEA*, Art. 79.
        In the United States, the NASD is the only registered national association of
securities dealers, though brokers and dealers can organize their association
upon registration with the SEC.
315. *SEA*, Art. 164. But, from the viewpoint of the regulatory framework, it would
be better to have the KSDA's amendment to its rules be subject to the SAC's
review and approval.
316. *Id.*, Art. 167.
317. *Id.*, Arts. 169, 166, 53.
318. *Id.*, Arts. 168, 166.

inter alia, with respect to: membership and discipline, duties and rights of members, including dues, fees, and other charges among members; and rules of association designed to promote just and equitable principles of trade, and to prevent fraudulent and manipulative acts and practices, impositions of unfair commissions or charges, or other unjustifiable practices which are detrimental to public confidence in the securities industry.[319] In addition, the KSDA has been empowered by the 1976 Amendments to regulate the underwriting business and securities analysis and pricing, and the KSDA has taken over the Institute of Securities Training.

While membership to the KSDA is optional under the Articles of Association, all the securities companies and other institutions authorized to do securities business pursuant to relevant laws are affiliated with the KSDA.[320] Members are required to meet just and equitable principles of trade and protection of investors in purchasing, selling, underwriting, promoting, or effecting other transactions in a security. In its Articles of Association, however, the KSDA has only reiterated the phrases on basic principles as expressed in the SEA, and has failed to state such principles in more specific terms.[321] Although empowered to do so, the MOF or SAC never ordered the KSDA to specify and particularize the rule. The lack of specification and particularization of just and equitable principles of trade is a significant drawback in Korea, where the OTC market gains importance in terms of capital formation as well as efficient implementation of monetary and fiscal policies.[322] Exacerbating conditions include the KSDA's failure to be equipped with any lawyer, CPA, and other experts.

Discipline of the members by the KSDA includes expulsion from the association, suspension of membership, and a warning; the punishment is to be selected according to the degree of wrongdoing.[323] The causes for such discipline include any violations of the rules of fair practice which have not been particularized. Also, the causes

---

319. *Id.,* Art. 163 and *Presidential Decree thereunder,* Art. 78.
320. KSDA, *Articles of Association,* Art. 6 (Promulgated on November 25, 1953), as amended on May 13, 1975).
321. *Id.,* Arts. 7, 8, 9, and 48.
322. *See* pp.105–106 *supra.*
323. KSDA, *Articles of Association,* Art. 48.

include the imposition of suspension orders by the authorities, violation of administrative dispositions, rules of the association, or failure to stick to resolutions of the KSDA board or general meeting.[324] However, self-regulation by the KSDA in Korea has been far less active than the NASD of the United States. The KSDA has never taken the initiative in expelling or suspending its members.

As in the case of the KSE self-regulation, the SEA did not introduce a provision requiring the KSDA to notify authorities of the disciplinary sanction finally taken or under consideration. Nor did the SEA adopt a provision allowing an aggrieved member to bring an objection or appeal for review to the SAC or any court.[325] Also, no provision is included requiring the KSDA to provide an accused member with an opportunity to defend itself against the charges. Since all these devices are critically important to insure fair self-regulation, the legislature should deeply concern itself with solutions to these drawbacks.

Section IV. *Regulation of Securities Credit*

I. Types of Credit Extension

The SEA included two Articles on securities credit—Article 49 concerning credit extension by securities companies, and Article 147 concerning credit extension by the Korea Securities Finance Corporation(KSFC). Article 49(2) empowered the MOF Decree to prescribe the method of credit extension by securities companies, and Article 49(3) also empowered the SAC to designate the maximum limit, rate of collateral, collection method of loans, and other necessary measures on credit extension by securities companies. But the SAC has not yet exercised its rulemaking power, whereas the

---

324. *Id.*, These are any acts or practices which are:
   1) in contravention of just and equitable principles of trade or investor protection;
   2) fraudulent or manipulative;
   3) impositions of unjustifiable or unfair charges or commissions;
   4) in detriment to the promotion of public confidence in the securities industry; or
   5) in violation of the resolution adopted by a general meeting or the board of directors, or agreement among members.
325. *See SEA*, Art. 206.

MOF has prescribed in its Decree methods of credit extension within the mandate of Article 49(2).[326]

According to the foregoing provisions, securities credit in Korea may roughly be classified into four types: (1) credit extension by securities companies to investors in connection with margin trading; (2) credit extension by the KSFC to underwriting companies; (3) securities collateral loans by the KSFC to the KSE trading members and securities investment trust companies; and (4) securities collateral loans by the KSFC or securities companies to public investors.[327] Items (2) and (3) above, broadly speaking, involve regulation in the wholesale level for the purpose of facilitating distribution and trading in securities, whereas items (1) and (4) above involve direct regulation in the retail level for the purpose of facilitating trading in securities by public investors. The sources of funds, interest rates, terms, and conditions of such credit extensions vary with their respective types.

The regulatory framework of the foregoing credit extension on securities is similar to that of Japan.[328] The rules on securities credit

326. *SEA*, Art. 49; *MOF Decree thereunder*, Art. 12. Since the SAC has not yet exercised its rulemaking power, the writer hereinafter describes the limit, rate of collateral, including margin requirements, and other specific rules on credit extension, on the basis of the existing rules of the KSE and the KSFC.

327. *See id.* and Article 147 of the SEA.

328. *See Japanese SEA*, Arts. 49, 61 and 156–2 through 156–14; *MOF Order on Margin Transaction, Etc. under Article 49 of the SEA* (MOF order No. 75, promulgated on Aug. 27, 1953, as amended by MOF Order No. 31 in 1975) [Hereinafter referred to as "MOF Order on Margin Transaction"], Art. 1; Japan Securities Finance Company (JSFC), *Rules on Loan Transaction;* and Tokyo Securities Exchange, *Rules on Entrustment with Contract,* Arts. 12–16; *see also* Tatsuta 98–101; Japan Securities Research Institute, *supra* note 24, at 138–48. The Japanese SEA includes a provision concerning credit extension by securities companies to investors in connection with margin trading (Art. 49). Also, securities finance companies chartered by the MOF license under the Japanese SEA extend credit to securities companies for margin trading (called a "loan transaction"), "bond trading financing" (formerly called "underwriting finance" to facilitate the issuance of corporate bonds), and general securities collateral loans. In 1968, the maximum limit set for "bond trading financing" (¥5 billion to be loaned by the Bank of Japan) was abolished, and the coverage was extended to finance the issuance of government

covers only lending by securities companies and the KSFC. No provision governs this category of credit extension, although investors in both countries, especially in Korea, can borrow directly from a bank, non-bank financial institutions, or other lenders with securities as collateral.[329] Since an excessive credit extension on securities might result in destabilizing stock prices, excessive speculation, stock crashes, or even a monetary crisis, all categories of credit extension on

---

bonds and financial debentures. In addition, securities finance companies established a new system called "bond financing," which consists of temporary loans extended to securities companies to facilitate their underwriting or trading in bonds and to make loans to investors with bonds as collateral. The sources for "bond trading financing" consist of loans from the Bank of Japan and call money, whereas those for "bond financing" come from the comapny's own resources, deposits from the Capital Market Promotion Foundation and Japan Joint Securities Foundation, or bank loans.

The Japanese MOF is authorized to formulate rules on margin trading and margin requirements. The initial margin is required not to be less than 30% of the contract price. Deposit may be made in the form of collateral securities, the permissable loan value of which is fixed by the MOF order at 70% of the market price on the previous busines day. The details, including the maintenance margin requirements are prescribed in the rules of the securities exchange. Also, the Rules on Loan Transactions of the JSFC prescribes the coverage of loans, restrictions on credit extension, collateral rights, interest rates, and method of collecting loans, including the disposition of the collateral.

329. *See MOF Release for the Establishment of Capital Market Under the May 29 Presidential Special Measure* (June 8, 1974) MOF, *"Unpublished Documents on Major Policy and Its Content"* at 4; *also see* Japan Securities Research Institute, *supra* note 24, at 138, 148. In Korea, the MOF recommended that banks, insurance companies and other non-bank financial institutions give priority in extending credit to any loan secured by listed securities over those secured by real estate. This policy was intended to enhance the marketability of listed securities and to encourage more public participation in securities investment.

The banks of Japan did not accept stock as collateral for loans and the loan policy of the banks was oriented more toward emphasizing personal credit standing and not the form of material guarantee. However, since 1961, some city banks have begun to extend loans to individuals with securities as collateral as a form of consumer financing, and the aggregate amount of such loans is gradually increasing. Thus, it was pointed out that a careful study is necessary to design the sound development of such securities credit and the appropriate means of regulating it.

securities should be subject to adequate control and regulation as is done in the United States.[330]

II. Regulation of Credit Extension by Securities Companies

A. *Regulation of Margin Trading*

In the United States, the term "margin" has been judicially defined as collateral or security used in connection with the purchase of securities.[331] Ordinarily, margin is considered to be the amount deposited by a purchaser of stock with his broker, being a certain percentage of the purchase price of the stock involved, with the broker agreeing to advance the balance of the purchase price upon the condi-

---

330. *Securities Exchange Act of 1934,* Secs. 7, 8, 15 U.S.C.A. §78 g.h. *Federal Reserve Board Regs. T.U.G. and X.* 12 C.G.R. §220, 221, 207 and 224.

Section 7 of the Exchange Act mandated the FRB to "prescribe rules and regulations with respect to the amount of credit that may be initially extended and subsequently maintained on any security (other than an exempted security) registered on a national securities exchange" "[f] or the purpose of preventing the excessive use of credit for the purchase or carrying securities. . . . " Also, in order to reach the wholesale level where brokers finance their dealings through banks, Section 8 of the Exchange Act forbids both members of the exchanges and brokers and dealers to borrow on any exchange-registered securities except through a member bank or through a non-member bank which has filed an agreement with the FRB to abide by the provision of applicable margin regulations.

The FRB has, within the mandate, promulgated a series of regulations and amended them to close loopholes. Regulation T governs lending on securities by broker-dealers. Regulation U governs loans by banks secured directly or indirectly by any stock (including convertibles) "for the purpose of purchasing or carrying any margin stock." Regulation G, effective on March 11, 1968, governs lending by persons other than broker-dealers and banks, who engage in the business of making loans for the purpose of purchasing or carrying margin securities. Finally, Regulation X which was authorized by Act of October 26, 1970 (P.L. 91–508, 84 Stat. 1124, adding subsection (f) to Section 7 of the Exchange Act) governs borrowing by the United States residents from either domestic or foreign lenders in an attempt to stop the evasion of the margin requirements. For details of securities credit regulation, *see* F. Solomon & J. Hart, *Recent Developments in the Regulation of Securities Credit,* 20 J. PUB. L. 167 (1971); *see also* Lipton, *Some Recent Innovations to Avoid the Margin Regulations,* 46 N.Y.U.L. REV. 1 (1971); P.L. Kelly & J.M. Webb, *Credit and Securities; The Margin Requirements,* 24 BUS.LAW. 1153 (1969).

331. *See* Paul L. Kelly & John M. Webb. *supra,* at 1153, citing *Goldenberg v. Bache and Company,* 270 F. 2d 675 (5th Cir. 1959) and other concerned cases.

tion that he be entitled to hold the stock purchased as security for his advance. The use of margin is, therefore, a credit device which allows a purchaser to trade in securities while paying less than the full purchase price. Trading on margin is normally accomplished by investors by using one of two methods—either depositing the required with his broker in a mrgined account, whereby an investor is, with certain "maintenance margin" requirement, extended a loan equal to the remainder of the purchase price, or borrowing the balance of the purchase price directly from a bank, finance company, or other lender with no formal margin account being established.[332]

Margin trading in Korea, being substantially modeled after the Japanese rule, means either the purchase or sale of stock by a person who has been extended a credit by a securities company concerned in cash(in the case of a purchaser) or stock(in the case of a seller) equal to the remainder of the purchase price or of the stock sold.[333] Thus, a large portion of short-selling involves margin trading. When any investor intends to purchase or sell on margin, he must deposit a certain percentage of the purchase or sale price, the "initial margin," with his securities company in a margined account.[334] The

---

332. *Id.,* 1153–54. In case of the former method, the broker will often finance his lending activities by borrowing from a third party, usually a bank, and pledge the purchased securities as collateral for this secondary loan. Lending an investor the remainder of the purchased price, the broker retains the purchased stock as collateral and has the power to dispose of it if the investor fails to maintain an amount in his account equal to an established percentage of the current market value of such stock. The amount deposited by the investor at the time of purchase is the "initial margin," whereas the amount which must be maintained in accordance with a percentage of the market value is the "maintenance margin." "Initial" margins are percentages set by the Federal Reserve Board via Regulations T and U, whereas "maintenance" margins are set by the stock exchange themselves.

333. *MOF Decree,* Art. 12, item 2; *KSFC Rules on Entrustment with Order,* Arts. 6, 7, 12. Cf. *Japanese MOF Order on Margin Trading,* Art. 1 *Tokyo Securities Exchange Rules on Entrustment of Contract,* Arts. 12, 13–2.

334. In order for an investor to establish a margin account, he must deposit ₩ 100,000 with a securities company as guaranty money accompanied by an application. The amount of the "initial margin" varies with the respective stock and may from time to time be changed by the KSE. But it must not be less than 40% of the purchase or sale price. Also, unless the investor who opened the margin account specified the kind of transaction as either "spot"

deposit may be made either in cash or collateral securities, the permissible collateral value of which is dictated by the KSFC rules.[335] Thereafter, the securities company retains the purchased stock or other securities as collateral. The company has the power to dispose of the collateral if the investor fails to maintain an amount("maintenance margin") in his account equal to an established percentage of the current market value of the purchased stock or other securities held as collateral.

The KSE requires the maintenance of margins at the same level as that of the initial margin, and the securities company has a power to dispose of the securities held as collateral and may terminate an undermargined account, if the investor has failed to meet margin calls within three days.[336] It is also provided, however, that the securities company may dispose of the margined securities within the three day period, if the market price of the purchased stock or other securities held as collateral has dropped or risen so that the required maintenance level exceeds 30% of both the margined long and short positions. Unlike that of the United States or Japan, the Korean maintenance margin rule does not provide for sufficient leeway before market prices of collateral rise or fall to required maintenance levels to trigger margin calls.[337] Thus margin traders may become

---

or "margin" at the time of his entrustment, the order must be deemed to be intended for margin trading. In Japan, such an order must be deemed to be intended for spot transaction and the lowest amount of the initial margin must not be less than 30% of the contract price. In the United States, the Exchange Act initially required as a formula for the FRB that the margins be set at a flat percentage based on the lower of a current market price or lowest market price during the preceding three years. By the 1964 amendment, however, the FRB was empowered to set the percentage with more flexibility regardless of the old rule. See *KSE Rules on Entrustment with Order*, Arts. 12, 13, and 17–2. Cf. *Tokyo Securities Exchange Rules on Entrustment of Contract*, Arts. 12, 13, 13–2; *Securities Exchange Act of 1934*, Sec. 7(a) (b), 15 U.S.C.A. §78 g(a) (b).

335. *Id.*, Art. 17–2(3); *KSFC Rules on Designation of Collateral Securities and Standards of their Collateral Value*, Arts. 2 and 4 (promulgated on Dec. 19, 1973, as amended on July 1, 1974).

336. *KSE Rules on Entrustment with Order*, Art. 18.

337. Solomon & Hart, *supra* note 330, at 172–73, citing an example of the NYSE Rule 431 [NYSE Guide 2431(b)]; *also see* Tokyo Stock Exchange, *Rules on Entrustment of Contract*, Arts. 13–8 *et seq.*

frequently hardpressed to maintain margins. As a matter of public policy, the authorities should provide more leeway in order to give investors a measure of stability to the extent that credit makers' interest is not infringed.

As in the United States or Japan, the main purpose of regulation in securities credit is to prevent excessive market fluctuations.[338] To achieve this regulatory purpose, the authorities in Korea from time to time increase or decrease the margin requirements, including the categories and collateral value of securities that are held as collateral, as appears necessary and appropriate to confine market fluctuations. In addition, the authorities control securities credit in various other ways. Among other things, they control and adjust from time to time the aggregate amount of funds available for credit extension, and designate the categories of issues available for margin trading according to market conditions.

The sources of funds consist of the trading members' own funds and loans from the KSFC. The KSE, upon being granted approval by the MOF, may limit the aggregate amount of the members' own funds available for credit extension and may also limit the maximum

---

The NYSE in the United States requires maintenance of margins at 25% for long positions and 30% for short positions, and most brokerage firms have "house" maintenance requirements of their own, which are usually higher than the stock exchange margin, and which vary from account to account depending upon the kind of securities held as collateral and other factors. The net result is a built-in stability factor. Because the initial deposit required under the FRB's regulations is relatively high, market values of the collateral can decline a considerable amount before they breach the maintenance margin and trigger margin calls.

The Tokyo Stock Exchange in Japan currently requires 20% both for long and short positions.

338. *See* Loss, *supra*, note 91, at 1242–43; *also see* Tatsuta, 99; KSE, *Stock* (No. 103, Mar., 1977) at 70.

In the United States, three regulatory purposes were enumerated: (1) prevention of excessive use of credit for the purchase or carrying of securities; (2) protection of the margin purchaser by making it impossible for him to buy securities on too thin a margin; and (3) prevention of under market fluctuations in order to help stabilize the economy generally. Of these three, Professor Loss pointed out that the chief emphasis appears to have been placed on the third philosophy. The same philosophy seems to apply to Japan and Korea.

amount or percentage of such funds usable for a certain issue.[339] When any trading member is in danger of exceeding the limit or actually exceeds it, the KSE suspends further credit extension by the member. There also are quantity limitations on the loans extended by the KSFC to the trading members in connection with margin trading. The limitations are set in accordance with the respective issue and borrower by taking into account of the borrowers financial capability and business accomplishments.[341]

Unlike that of the United States, the Korean category of stock available for margin trading is relatively restricted to such issues as designated by the SAC.[340] Cash loans by securities companies to their customers can be given only with respect to the stocks listed on the KSE's Floor Section I. Moreover, the loaning of stock is limited only to specially designated issues.[342] However, investors can avoid any restrictions if they directly, or by the arrangement of a securities company, borrow money from banks, insurance companies, or other lenders using any listed securities as collateral.[343] This kind of regulatory loophole should be closed through an appropriate reform of relevant laws.

---

339. *Id.*, Art. 22–2. Effective on Oct. 21, 1976, the aggregate amount of credit extended by trading members (from their own funds) was allowed to increase up to twice their legal capital, due to depressed market trend, *see* KSE, *Stock* (No. 102, Feb. 1977) at 78.

340. *KSFC Rules on Margin Trading Finance* (promulgated on Mar. 2, 1974, as amended on Mar. 3, 1975) Arts. 3, 4, 5; *Guidelines for the limitation of Loans thereunder* (promulgated on Mar. 5, 1975). As of the end of 1976, the aggregate amount of KSFC funds was ₩ 20 billion (*see* KSE, *Stock supra*, at 79).

341. In the United States, by Act of July 29, 1968 (82 Stat. 452), Section 7 of the Exchange Act was amended to give the FRB the authority to regulate credit on OTC securities and to eliminate the prohibition against broker-dealers' lending on such securities. This authority has been exercised only with respect to a list of "OTC Margin Stocks" issued by the FRB. Thus, in regards to an OTC stock not on the list, broker-dealers still may not lend at all but banks may lend without restriction. *See* 12 C.F.R. §220. 3(a), 220.3 (c) (2), 221. 1(a).

342. *KSE Rules on Business*, Art. 48; KSE, *Stock* (No. 102, Feb. 1977) at 78–79. The number of issuers extended cash loan by the KSFC through the clearing house of the KSE was increased from 92 in 1975 to 149 in 1976, while that of lending stock increased from 11 in 1975 to 23 in 1976.

343. *See* note 329 *supra* and its accompanying text.

Other important devices designed to enforce the rules on credit extension in connection with margin trading are the bookkeeping rules, reporting requirements, inspection power, and the disciplinary rules discussed in the earlier section.[344] Securities companies must make and keep itemized ledgers on margin trading and specify the customers and the issuers. They must also specify the current extent of margin trading and credit extension and must file monthly and annual business reports with the SAC. Furthermore, the SAC and the SSB may inspect the books and records kept by securities companies and thereby may detect and prevent any violations of the rules on margin trading. The SAC may suspend the license of securities companies when they violate any of these rules.[345] However, the legislature has failed to empower the authorities to revoke the license or impose criminal penalties for violation of these rules. The first SAC suspension order which was imposed upon the Yoo Wha Securities Co. for the violation of the rules on securities credit, etc., appears too weak a precedent to either limit excessive credit extension or compel fair and equitable trading practices in Korea.[346]

---

344. *See* pp. 250–266 *supra*. Section 17(b) of the Exchange Act in the U.S. gave the FRB authority to require such reports "as necessary or appropriate to enable it to perform the functions conferred upon it" by the Exchange Act, and to make such inspections "as the Board may deem necessary to enable it to obtain the required information" of any person extending credit who is subject to margin regulations. Enforcement of the FRB's rules, however, is entrusted to the SEC, the Department of Justice, or private litigants.

345. *SEA*, Arts. 57, 47, 49; *also see* the accompanying text of note 310 *supra*.

346. Joongang Daily News, June 26, 1977, at p.2. The Yoowha Securities Co. violated the rules on credit extension by far exceeding the limit allocated to it. It also violated the rules prohibiting trading in securities by officers and employees and failed to liquidate and clear short-selling for a long period of time. Such violations were detected by the SSB's inspection conducted in May. The SAC suspended the Yoowha's business for five days in punishment for such violations. Although it was the first case detected and sanctioned by the SAC, such sanction appears to be overly mild in the light of the Korean situation where fair and equitable principles of trading have not been established. Considering the adverse impact of excessive credit extension on the securities market as a whole, the legislature should have empowered certain authorities to impose more strict sanctions for any violation of the rules of credit extension based on the degree of violation and market circumstances involved.

B. *Restriction of Credit Extension by Securities Companies on a Security Underwritten by Themselves*

Article 49(4) of the SEA prohibits a securities company from extending loans or other credit to investors, in connection with any security underwritten by itself, for a period of three months from the date on which the company became an underwriter of the respective security involved. Although there is no clear indication of legislative intent, the restriction was probably introduced to achieve the segregation of the functions of broker and dealer as exists in the United States and Japan.[347] However, the text of Article 49(4) included certain ambiguities which have not yet been clarified by the legislative process. These ambiguities of the restriction have been neglected in Korea because of the sustained oversubscription phenomena, but troublesome questions would be raised by its implementation.

First, a literal interpretation of the restriction is in conflict with the existing system of credit extension to public investors subscribing to

---

347. *See Securities Exchange Act of 1934*, 11(d) (1), 15 U.S.C.A. §78 k(d) (1); *also see* Loss, *supra* note 91 at 1269–76; *Japanese SEA*, Art. 61; Tatsuta, 98. Section 11(d) (1) of the Exchange Act and Article 61 of the Japanese SEA are the counterparts of Article 49(3) of the SEA, although there appear minor differences. By the 1954 amendments of the Exchange Act, the period of prohibition was reduced from six months to thirty days in the United States, while that in Japan is six months.

In the United States the prohibition of credit extension on an underwritten security is not part of a scheme of credit control by the FRB, but constitutes part of the segregation of the functions of brokers and dealers. The House committee described the section as following: it "strikes at one of the greatest potential evils inherent in the combination of the broker and dealer function in the same person, by assuring that he will not induce his customers to buy on credit securities which he has undertaken to distribute to the public." H.R. Rep. No. 1383, 73d Cong., 2d Sess. 22. (1934). Also, the House committee put it when the section was amended in 1964: "The apparent purpose was to provide that new issues would be initially placed with investors rather than with speculators," H.R. Rep. No. 1542, 83d Sess. 15 (1954). However laudable its purpose, the section has been one of the most troublesome provisions to construe in the United States.

Japanese Article 61 appears to have been modeled after the Section J 1(d) (1) of the Exchange Act for the same purpose. But this provision has seldom been discussed in Japan. This was because either the restriction was neglected or credit on securities was not over-extended as to necessitate the restriction. *See* Sujuki & Kawamoto, 63.

securities undergoing distribution.[348] A securities company which has become a manager of an underwriting syndicate can borrow additional money other than that for underwriting from the KSFC, and may in turn lend it to public investors who subscribe to the securities underwritten by the company. In order to reconcile the provision with the system of credit extension, it should be construed to prohibit a securities company from extending credit from its own resources to induce customers to buy the securities in distribution.

Second, intending to cover all members of the underwriting or selling group of a security, the provision fixes the period of prohibition for three months.[349] No other indication has been given as to whether the provision should apply to the members of a group which has already completed "full" distribution of an underwritten security and thus terminated the function within the three-month period. The provision should be construed to apply to the members of such groups which extend credit on such securities regardless of whether "full" distribution has been completed within three months. Insofar as the purpose of prohibition is to achieve the segregation of function, the legislature should have provided the restriction depending upon the completion of "full" distribution rather than upon the fixed three-month period.[350]

Finally, the provision includes another difficulty with respect to its enforcement in certain cases. From its text, Article 49(4) appears to include all the securities underwritten by securities companies whether or not they are exempted securities or new or outstanding issues, or whether or not the distribution is made under the registration or notification statement.[351] But, this provision appears to only

---

348. *See MOF Decree,* Art. 12 and *SEA,* Art. 147, item 4.
349. Because the text of Article 49(3) includes a phrase "in the case that a securities company sells the securities underwritten by itself" and the term "underwriting" is defined in Article 2(7) so as to cover the function as a selling group member, the prohibition is deemed to apply to a securities company which has become a member of the selling group.
350. *See* SEC Rule 11d 1–1(e), 17 C.F.R. §240, 11d 1–1(e).
351. This is because the legislature copied the provision after the Japanese model, which is different from the American one. In the United States, the requirement that the security must have been part of a "new issue" rules out the ordinary secondary distribution of outstanding securities, even when the distribution is made under the registration statement. This is because the

cover the securities which are underwritten and undergoing public distribution, and thus exclude other outstanding securities of the same class which were previously underwritten and distributed prior to three months. But, a difficulty arises as to how to distinguish the former from the latter. This identification problem should be given serious attention by the Korean authorities as is done by their counterpart in the United States.[352]

III. Regulation of the Korea Securities Finance Corporation (KSFC)
A. *Functions of the Securities Finance Corporation*

Since the call money market in Korea is not so well developed as that in the United States, the Korea Securities Finance Corporation (KSFC) was chartered to provide specialized finance in the area of securities credit.[353] The functions of the KSFC, as expanded by the 1976 Amendments,[354] mainly consist of several methods of credit extension on securities; (1) loans to KSE trading members to finance margin trading; (2) loans to underwriting companies in order to facilitate the underwriting and distribution of a security; and (3) loans to securities companies, securities investment trust companies, and public investors with securities as collateral. The KSFC's source of funds largely depends on borrowings from the Bank of Korea and other financial institutions.

---

seller is in a control relationship with the issuer. Also, the prohibition does not apply to exempted securities. *See* Loss, *supra* note 91, at 1271, 1275.

352. *Id.*, 1272, citing *Rule* 11d 1–1 (e) and *Sec. Ex. Act Rels.* 4038 (1947) (proposed), 4044 (adopted). In 1948, the SEC in the United States substantially alleviated the problem by creating an exemption for transactions entered into after the broker-dealer has ceased participating in the distribution of a new issue whenever the mixed issue is predominantly old—that is, when 11(d) (1) would otherwise apply with respect to 50% or less of all the securities of the same class which are either outstanding or currently being distributed. The exemption applies only during the thirty-day post-distribution period.

353. *SEA,* Arts. 145 through 161. The SEA requires that any person intending to engage in the securities finance business be a stock corporation chartered by the MOF. Thus, for only one corporation, the KSFC, has been authorized to do such business..

354. *SEA,* Arts. 147, 161. The 1976 Amendments permitted the KSFC to function as a limited repository for the KSE, securities companies, other securities institutions, and persons prescribed by the MOF Decree, and also permitted to function as a bond dealer.

Credit extension to the KSE trading members in connection with margin trading has become the predominant business of the KSFC. The KSFC makes loans, through the KSE's clearing house to the KSE trading members, in the form of either cash or stock. The members, in turn, extend credit to their customers. The mechanism is similar to the Japanese "loan transaction," which is effected between the member firms and a securities finance company in order to finance credit extension by the member firms to their customers who trade on margin.[355] The KSFC maintains a special account largely funded by the Bank of Korea. The aggregate amount of permissible credit extension is from time to time adjusted by the MOF in accordance with market movements and price behavior. In addition, a limit is set in accordance with both the borrower and the respective issue involved. As of the end of 1976, the aggregate amount of funds available for cash loans was at ₩ 2 billion.[356] Interest rates, collateral values, and terms of the loans are also subject to regulation.

Credit extension for the facilitation of underwriting and distribution of securities is offered in the form of cash loans from the KSFC's special fund. Loans which fall within this category include those used ;(1) for underwriting of a publicly distributed equity security or a bond; (2) for the "market formation" of a newly listed security; and (3) for subscription to such securities by the employee stock ownership union or public investors.[357] These extensions are offered where underwritten securities are not fully distributed and thus are placed in the accounts of underwriters. Unlike that for bonds, credit exten-

---

355. Japan Securities Research Institute, *supra* note 24, at 138–29.

356. *KSE, Stock* (No. 102, Feb., 1977) at 79–81. On the other hand, the limit on the lending of stocks was set in accordance with the respective trading members and was not to exceed 50% of its maximum amount of cash loans. The aggregate amount of the lending stocks available for all the trading members was set in accordance with the respective issue not to exceed 50% of the total stocks deposited with the KSFC as collateral on the previous business day. Such a respective limit on the borrower was not under the consideration of the size of assets and business, and the accomplishment of business operation, whereas the limit on issues was set in accordance with the size of legal capital of the respective issuer.

357. *SEA.* Art. 147 items 1, 4; *KSFC Articles of Incorporation,* Art. 2, items 1, 3. For the term "market formation," *see* the accompanying text of note 181 *supra.*

sion for the underwriting of equities has been rare because of the sustained oversubscription in offerings of equity securities.[358]

Securities collateral loans made by the KSFC to KSE trading members or securities investment trust companies are generally intended to facilitate trading in securities. The types of such loans include six kinds. The aggregate amount of funds available for these credit extensions increased from ₩ 6 billion in 1975 to ₩ 11 billion in 1976 because of increasing demand, especially in the area of general collateral loans, securities savings, and repurchases of certificates of securities investment trust.[359] The amount of another type of securities collateral loans made by the KSFC or by securities companies only to public investors, has been negligible because of the limited availability of funds and the relatively higher interest rates charged.[360]

B. Regulation of the Securities Finance Corporation

Since the securities finance company performs a critical role in the area of securities credit in Korea, the SEA gave the MOF and the SAC broad regulatory powers. The powers consist of entry restrictions and post-entry regulations. In order for any person to enter into a business, the person must be in the form of a stock corporation with a minimum legal capital of ₩ 2 billion and must also obtain a MOF license.[361] To facilitate the entry of foreign capital, the SEA permits

---

358. KSE, *Stock* (No. 102, Feb., 1977) at 83. The aggregate amount of credit extended for underwriting operations was ₩ 10 billion, of which ₩ 6 billion was allotted for equities and the remainder for bonds; provided, however, that ₩ 2 billion for equities was to be transferable to bond financing. As of the end of 1976, the balance of loans extended for equities was only ₩ 50 million, whereas that for bonds was ₩ 3 billion. Also, the balance of loans made for "market formation" was ₩ 13 million at the end of 1976, while it was ₩ 512 million at the end of 1975. No loan, however, was made to any employee stock ownership unions or public investors to finance their subscription to securities in distribution.

359. *Id.*, at 84–85.

360. *Id.*, The KSFC fund for securities collateral loans to public investors was established on Mar. 3, 1969, with ₩ 500 million under an agent agreement with the Korea Trust Bank (KTB). The purpose was to expand the participation in securities investment by public investors. The interest rate is 20% per year. As to the collateral loans by securities companies to investors, no material is available.

361. *SEA*, Arts. 145, 146. These requirements were modeled after the Japanese rule. Cf. *Japanese SEA*, Arts. 156–2 through 156–5.

any foreign national to serve as an outside officer of the company, subject to MOF's approval.[362] The SEA prohibits any inside officer or employee of a securities company from becoming an inside officer of the securities finance company for the purpose of avoiding possible conflicts of interest.

The post-entry regulation covers a broad area. First, any amendment to the articles of incorporation or business rules is subject to prior approval by the MOF or the SAC.[363] Also, the MOF may, to insure the fair administration of a business or to protect the interests of investors, order the company to amend the articles of incorporation or any business rules. On the other hand, the SAC may, if it deems it necessary or appropriate for the maintenance of fair and sound trading in the market, order a company to change means or terms of credit extension, but must give reasons for its actions beforehand.[364]

Second, the securities finance company is subject to a reporting requirement and possible inspection. It must file a report with the MOF every fiscal year on its budget, auditing procedures, and disposition of earnings.[365] This reporting requirement is not as stringent as that imposed on securities companies. The securities finance company, unlike securities companies, is required to follow the Presidential Decree on Accounting Principles and the MOF Decree on Terminology, Forms and Methods concerning Financial Statements which apply to listed corporations.[366] Article 53 of the SEA, which gives the SAC and the SSB a broad inspection power over securities companies, is made to apply *mutatis mutandis* to the securities finance company.[367]

Third, the MOF and the SAC are given broad disciplinary powers over a company which engages in illegal activities.[368] When the company has violated any provision of the SEA or any order thereunder, the MOF may suspend all or a part of its business within a six-month

---

362. *SEA*, Art. 149, But foreign nationals could not become inside officers.
363. *Id.*, Art. 151.
364. *Id.*, Art. 152.
365. *Id.*, Art. 156.
366. *Id.*, Arts. 195–196.
367. *Id.*, Arts. 157, 53.
368. *Id.*, Arts. 155, 153

period, after accounting reason therefor. If the company under such a suspension order fails to remedy its violation within a designated period, the MOF may revoke the license. When an officer of the company has violated either the SEA, or any order thereunder, or the article of incorporation of the company, or has been elected by an unfair means, the SAC may order the company to dismiss the officer.

Fourth, the general shareholders' meeting of a company, upon the MOF's prior approval, is required to be held upon its proposed date, at its proposed place, and must not deviate from the proposed agenda.[369] Also, Article 58 (re: civil liability of officers and controlling shareholders of securities companies) and 83 (re-prohibition of the KSE's officers and employees from misusing any inside information, trading in securities, or participating in the business of any securities institution) were required to apply *mutatis mutandis* to those of the securities finance company.[370]

From the foregoing description, it is clear from the start that the securities finance company in Korea is subject to relatively strong regulation by the MOF and the SAC in all areas of business. However, the rule appears to have some drawbacks. First of all, the relaxed reporting requirement does not give the authorities sufficient itemized and specific current data in the area of credit extension. The SEA requires only comprehensive annual report on budgeting, auditing, and the disposition of earnings. Furthermore, lack of specific bookkeeping rules similar to those imposed on securities companies would render any inspection by the authority ineffective. Since the nature and character of business of the securities finance company is totally different from those of business corporations, and is significant in regard to the public interest and protection of investors, the authority should have designed separate bookkeeping rules adequate enough to meet the regulatory purpose. Unless these reporting and bookkeeping requirements are appropriately amended, violations of the rules could not effectively be prevented and detected even through frequent inspections. Finally, in practice the enforcement of the civil liability provision would be almost impossible due to difficulties in establishing a case (*See* pp.255–58, *supra*, on the discussion of securities companies' liability.).

---

369. *Id.,* Art. 148.
370. *Id.,* Arts. 154, 58, 83, 42.

Chapter 8

Regulation of Trading in Securities (Two)

Section I. *Regulation of Takeover Bids*

I. Strong Implications to Discourage Potential Shift in Corporate Control

The basic purpose expressed in the 1976 Amendments to the SEA in Korea was to consolidate the securities markets into an institution which would effectively perform the function of capital formation designated by the Fourth Five-Year Economic Development Plan. To meet this purpose, the legislature concerned itself with inducing more blue chip corporations into going public and with further spreading equity ownership of publicly-held corporations. The fear of losing control was a formidable obstacle to both public offerings and wider distribution. Therefore, the legislature introduced in the 1976 Amendments several devices designed to discourage any potential shift in corporate control.

Such devices are: (1) ownership reporting requirements by a 10% shareholder ; (2) restrictions on any increase of existing shares held beyond a certain limit ; (3) tender offer rules ; and (4) proxy rules. These devices, with the exception of (2) above, were originally borrowed from the United States, but substantial modifications were made to harmonize with the Korean situation. The emphasis was placed on the protection of controlling shareholders' interest by discouraging any secret takeovers or challenges to existing control by would-be raiders.

However, the legislature in introducing such devices neglected the strong need to protect the interest of public investors. Since Korea at the time did not introduce modern anti-trust laws, which come into play in takeover, merger or consolidation process in the United

States or other developed countries, any legal implications arising under anti-trust laws are not covered in the discussion below.[1]

II. Restriction on Increase in Shareholding and the Ownership Reporting Requirement

A. Restriction on Ownership Increase

1. Statutory Rules

Article 200(1) of the SEA provides:

> "Any person, directly or indirectly, shall not hold the beneficial ownership of outstanding shares issued by a listed corporation beyond the following limit: (1) *the percentage initially held* in the case that a person has, at the time of listing, held more than 10% of the total shares issued and outstanding; or (2) 10% in the case of other than a 10% shareholder. In calculating the percentage of shareholding for the purpose of this Article, non-voting shares shall not be included in the total number of shares issued and outstanding." (Emphasis supplied.)

Any violation of this prohibition by purchase on the exchange market is subject to a fine of not more than ₩5 million, and any violation of the tender offer rules by purchase in the over-the-counter (OTC) market is subject to imprisonment of not more than two (2) years or a fine of not more than ₩2 million.[2]

Since the legislative purpose of this provision was to discourage challenges to existing control by raiders who increase their shareholding through secret accumulation of shares, this prohibition does not absolutely preclude increase in ownership. Article 200(2) enumerates four exceptions to this prohibition with the requirement that purchases be disclosed or do not result in a probable challenge to existing control. Ownership may be increased beyond statutory limits

---

1. Article 195–2 of the Japanese SEA provides that the anti-trust laws in Japan must preempt the securities laws. Federal securities laws in the United States include no explicit indication on the matter; however, takeover transactions must in advance comply with far-reaching anti-trust laws. *E.g.*, a pre-merger filing required under the Hart-Scott-Radino Antitrust Improvements Act of 1976. 15 U.S.C. §§7a(a)(2)(c) and 3(c).

2. For the purchase on the exchange market, *see SEA*, Arts. 211, item 2 and 215 (2); and for the purchase in the OTC market, *see SEA*, Arts. 209, 21 and 23. Both the 10% shareholder and the corporation concerned are subject to a criminal sanction for violation of the rules.

through (1) a tender offer solicitation, (2) a direct purchase from a 10% shareholder, (3) a purchase upon receiving approval of the SAC thereof, or (4) other purchases from such institutions as defined in Presidential Enforcement Decree promulgated under the SEA. The SAC enacted the Rules on Approval of Block Purchases, Etc., which enumerate specific standard required for approval.[3]

The restriction on ownership increases beyond a certain limit strongly assures continuing control by the incumbent management and thus may play a significant role in encouraging the decentralization of equity ownership. Any raider who intends to challenge the existing control or seeks to take over a publicly-held corporation cannot increase his percentage of shares by secret purchases. He is under the current law almost forced to resort to a tender solicitation,[4] against which existing management may employ various defensive tactics.[5]

On the other hand, the philosophy embodied in this restriction raises some significant questions. Among other things, the philosophy considerably restricts freedom of investment and economic activities in favor of the existing management. A substantial portion of acquisitions which are made only for investment purposes would be curtailed. Furthermore, it tends to protect control even by a possibly incompetent and unqualified incumbent management. The long run consequences of this particular philosophy should be reappraised in connection with the economic system as a whole.

2. Questions to Be Resolved

When the so-called "Daehan Flour Mills Case"[6] was publicly released, certain questions were raised with respect to the legal effect of the acquisition of shares in violation of the statutoty restriction on

---

3. *See* SAC Rule No. 3, as promulgated on March 23, 1977.
4. For detailed discussion of tender solicitation, *see* Section III of the discussion below.
5. The incumbent management of a target company may design and employ a variety of defensive tactics to defeat a take-over bid.
6. The Daehan Flour Mills case suddenly became a big news among the public through newspaper reports since February 28, 1980. For details, *see* Joong-Ang Daily Newspaper, February 28, 1980 at p. 9; Seoul Economic Newspaper, February 28, 1980 at p. 4; Joong-Ang Daily Newspaper, February 29, 1980 at p. 2; and March 7, 1980 at p. 7.

ownership increase. According to the newspaper reports, beginning on or about March 30, 1979, Mr. Yong K. Lee, the then controlling shareholder and President of Honam Flour Mills Co., Ltd. (*"Honam"*) which is a rivalry company of Daehan Flour Mills Co., Ltd., (*"Daehan"*) secretly accumulated the shares of *Daehan* through direct purchase from a ten-percent shareholder and continuing purchase on the exchange. On or about February 28, 1980, when *Daehan's* annual meeting of shareholders was scheduled to be held, Mr. Lee became the largest shareholder of *Daehan* by holding directly or indirectly about 1.2 million shares in *Daehan* representing more than 34% of the total shares issued and outstanding.[7] However, Mr. Lee never filed any ownership report or tender offer statement.[8] Being the largest shareholder, Mr. Lee demanded that the incumbent management of *Daehan* elect his nominees directors and auditors at the general shareholders meeting. The scheduled meeting was postponed due to the rival's sudden attempt to take over the control and after a long controversy among the government officials at the Ministry of Finance, the SAC and the SSB as to Mr. Lee's possible violation of any rule and measures taken by the authorities, Mr. Lee was criminally prosecuted. The Daehan Flour Mills Case raised a set of legal questions as to what would be the legal effect of the violation of the rule and what kind of civil remedies are or should be available to the persons injured or affected.

The SEC in the United States is broadly empowered to take enforcement action,[9] while the SAC is not. Except for the criminal sanctions, the SEA remains silent on the civil remedies available. Although the transaction is illegal, neither the transaction itself nor the shares acquired illegally would be held null and void. In order to enforce

---

7. *Id.* Of the 1.2 million shares purchased, 3,600,033 shares (9.8% of the total issued and outstanding shares) were held in the name of Mr. Lee and the remainder were held in the names of his nominees, including individuals with immediate relation and corporations controlled, directly or indirectly, by him.
8. A question is raised as to whether Mr. Lee's series of purchase on the market constitutes a tender offer for the purpose of the statutory provision. However, it is no doubt that Mr. Lee violated both the rule of ownership reporting and the rule of restriction on ownership increase.
9. *See Securities Exchange Act of 1934*, Sec. 21, 15 U.S.C.A. §78 w.

the rule effectively, however, the SAC should have been empowered to take enforcement action, including a power to compel the raider to sell all the shares which were illegally acquired through public auction or on the exchange within a specified period of time and to enjoin the voting of shares held by the raider until completion of the sale. In addition, the target, its controlling shareholders or certain other persons should have a standing to sue for damages or to seek an injunction under which such raiders are enjoined from exercising any voting rights of the shares illegally acquired.[10]

B. *Ownership Reports*

Article 201 of the SEA provides that "any person who owns more than 10% of the total number of shares issued and outstanding of a listed corporation shall file a report with the SAC whenever any change has occurred in his shareholding." Any violation of this provision is subject to a fine of not more than W500,000.[11] The text of Article 201 is vague and ambiguous in certain ways. Although the legislature appears to have borrowed this provision from the Williams Act of the United States,[12] it neither provided any detailed rules in the

---

10. In the United States, the voting of shares held by a dissident group was enjoined, the company having established the likelihood of its success on claims that bidders for corporate control had failed to make timely filing as required by Section 13(d)(1) of the Exchange Act. The obligation to file arose, with respect to a group which together owned more than 5% of the stock, when members of the group came together with the intention of acquiring control. See *Water* & *Wall Associates, Inc. v. American Consumer Industries Inc.,* (DCNJ April 19, 1973), 1973 CCH Fed. Sec. L. Rep. 93943.

11. *SEA,* Arts. 212, item 4 and 215(2). Both a 10% shareholder and the corporation concerned are subject to a fine for the violation of the reporting requirement.

12. See *Securities Exchange Act of 1934,* Sec. 13(d) 15 U.S.C.A. §78m(d), as amended by Pub. L. 90–439 (the Williams Act) effective July 29, 1968, and Pub. L. 91–567 effective Dec. 22, 1970; *Regulation 13D thereunder,* 17 C.F.R. §240. 13D; Sec. Ex. Act. Rels. No. 8370 (1968), No. 34–8392(1968), No. 34–8556 (1969), and No. 34–9060(1971).
In 1968, the Williams Act amended Sections 12, 13, 14 of the Exchange Act, and expanded the scope of that Act by bringing to bear regulatory, filing, and disclosure requirements with respect to certain securities transactions and certain actions pertaining to corporate takeovers. Specifically it deals with acquisitions of corporate equity securities by persons (including the issuer thereof), tender offers by persons other than the issuer, and changes in a majority

SEA, nor did it, with any specific guidelines, mandate a rule-making power to a regulatory agency for the enforcement of this provision. Recently the SAC, without any general or specific rule-making power granted by the SEA with respect to the ownership report, has included in the Rules on Approval of Block Purchases, Etc., a provision concerning the procedure of ownership reporting.[13] This provi-

---

of the board of directors of an issuer in connection with a takeover accomplished without a vote by stockholders at a stockholders' meeting.

Section 13(d) requires full disclosure of a certain shareholder who has, directly or indirectly, acquired more than 5% (prior to the 1970 amendment, 10%) of the beneficial ownership of equity security of a class which is registered under Section 12 of the Exchange Act, while Section 14(d) concerns tender offers. Such shareholder must within ten days after the acquisition send to the issuer and each exchange where such security is traded, and file with the SEC a statement containing such information as required in the same provision and as the SEC may by rules and regulations prescribe as necessary or appropriate in the public interest or for the protection of investors.

The SEC within the power mandated adopted Regulations 13D and 14D on July 30, 1968. Regulation 13D contains the rules applicable to Section 13 (d) and (e), while regulation 14D contains the rules applicable to Section 14(d) and (f) of the Exchange Act, which are operative provisions of the Williams Act. The Regulations provide that the statement pursuant to either Section 13(d)(1) or 14(d)(1) contain the information specified in Schedule 13D with respect to the identity, background and plans of the person or group making a tender offer of acquiring securities, the size of the holding of the person or group involved, the source of the funds used or to be used to acquire the shares, any contracts or arrangements relating to the securities of the issuer and, if the purpose of the acquisition is to acquire control of the issuer, any plans or proposals of the person or group to liquidate the company or make any other major changes in its business or corporate structure. Although Schedule 13D applies to the statement filed under both Sections 13(d)(1) and 14(d)(1), the basic distinction is that the person subject to Section 13(d) (1) is required to file a report after the acquisition, while persons subject to Section 14(d)(1) are required to make disclosure in advance. .

For detailed discussions of the Williams Act, *see* M.M. Brown, *The Scope of the Williams Act and its 1970 Amendments,* 26 BUS. LAW. 1637 (1971): P.J. Griffin, Jr. & J.R. Tucker, *The Williams Act, Public Law 90–439–Growing Pains?,* 16HOW. L.REV. 654 (1971).

13. SAC Rule No.3 *supra* note 3, Art. 4. The SEA included no counterpart to Section 23(a) of the Exchange Act, which gave the SAC, etc. a broad rule-making power to implement the provisions of the statute for which they are responsible or to execute the functions vested in them by the statute. Therefore,

sion requires that "any person who is subject to the reporting requirement under Article 201 of the SEA with respect to any change in his
shareholding file a report with the SAC in compliance with a specified
form within seven days following the occurrence of such cause."

However, it seems that the rules on ownership reporting include
such significant loopholes and drawbacks that the legislative purpose
could not be effectively implemented.

First, the rules require the disclosure of information only as to (1)
the identity of the person filing the report, and any relationship he
has with the issuer of the security concerned; (2) changes in the
number and percentage of shares held as compared to the total number of shares issued and outstanding; and (3) a short remark concerning the transaction effected.[14] Nowhere is there any requirement to
include further information, *i.e.,* as to the background, purpose, and
plan of the person acquiring the shares, source, and amount of funds
or other consideration used or to be used to acquire the shares, any
contract, arrangement, or understanding relating to the securities of
the issuer, and if the purpose of the acquisition is to acquire control
of the issuer, any plan or proposal of the person or groups to change
the business or corporate structure. Inclusion of such information
in the report, as is required in the United States, appears to be of
critical importance for both the public interest and the protection of
public investors.[15] The inclusion is also significantly important for
the protection of existing control as designed by the legislature.

•The legislature might have, because of the restriction on ownership increases by means of secret accumulation, intended that most
acquisitions subject to the reporting requirement would be effected
with considerable disclosure through the process of a tender offer,
or with the SAC's approval. However, this protects only the interests
of the controlling shareholders and does not fill the need for protec-

---

any rules and regulations promulgated by the SAC without any specific
power mandated by the SEA would raise a dispute as to the legality and en-
forceability. To avoid these questions, the legislature should have granted a
general mandate to the SAC by inserting a provision like Section 23(a) in the
United States.

14. *Id.,* Form 2 on "Report of Change in the Percentage of Shareholding."
15. *See supra* note 12.

tion of investors.[16] Therefore, the disclosure rule should appropriately be amended to require the person acquiring securities to report all the material information so that investors could fairly assess any potential changes in corporate control or business, and revaluate their investments. In addition, when any material change has occurred in the facts as stated in the report, an amendment reflecting such changes should be required to be promptly filed. Furthermore, to insure fair and full disclousre in the report, adequate remedies should be provided for fraud or misrepresentation of a material fact.

Second, ownership reporting rule includes another loophole by requiring the person increasing ownership to file only with the SAC. The SAC is not imposed any duty under the pertinent law to send copies of the report to the issuer or the exchange concerned, or to give public notice, or even to provide for public inspection.[17] The rule should, as it does in the United States, have required such person to send the report to both the issuer and each exchange where the securities are traded so that the management and public investors could be informed of any significant changes within a short time period.

Third, the ownership reporting rule, unlike the rule of ownership restriction, failed to specify in its coverage who is a 10% shareholder subject to the reporting requirement and how to determine a 10% ownership. Although the legislature seems to have intended to require

16. For the disclosure requirements of tender solicitation, *see* accompanying text of n. 61 *et. seq. infra.* In cases of authorized ownership increases or direct purchases from 10% shareholders, full disclosure is of critical importance. Any person who intends to purchase a block of shares upon the SAC's approval must make an application in compliance with Form 1, which requires them to state, in addition to such information as required in an ownership report, information as to the purpose of purchase and the period in which to such purchase. Public investors do not have access to learn of such information filed with the SAC (*See* SAC Rule No. 2, *supra*). In the case of ownership increases through a tender offer, inclusion of such information in the statement is necessary and appropriate, for public investors should be well informed of any potential changes in the business and management of the issuer.

17. Both registration statements and registration documents filed with the SAC are required to be available for public inspection under Articles 4 and 18 of the SEA. But no such provision is included in the SEA with respect to ownership report. Hence, the question as to whether ownership report filed with the SAC is available for public inspection remains to be answered.

those persons as defined in Article 200 (restrictions on ownership increase) to apply *mutatis mutandis* to the ownership reporting requirement for the purpose of Article 201, an express passage indicating such intention should have been inserted to avoid possible disputes. As provided in Article 200, any direct or indirect beneficial ownership should also be included in determining the 10% ownership limit in order to meet the legislative purpose of Article 201. Although the SEA requires in Articles 200 and 201 that 10% ownership be, regardless of any class, determined on the total number of outstanding shares, it would be more reasonable for the purpose of these Articles to define a certain percentage of ownership in classification of a respective class regardless of voting rights. It is because any person who owns an equity security of any class must approve at a shareholders' meeting of such class any changes in the articles of incorporation, or other matters pertaining to their interests.[18] Also, a shareholder who owns any non-voting shares of a class has a voting right in a shareholders' meeting of such a class. In determining a certain percentage of equity security of a class, the class of shares, as is required in the United States, should be deemed to consist of the amount of outstanding shares of the class, minus any shares of the class held by or for the account of the issuer or a subsidiary of the issuer, as voting rights of those shares must be suspended.[19] Also, the legislature should have required that any person be deemed to be the beneficial owner of securities of any class in which he has the right to acquire further shares through the exercise of presently exercisable rights, or through the conversion of presently convertible securities.

Fourth, the legislature, in designing the rules of ownership reporting, failed to allow for formations of a group and syndicate by two or more shareholders acting in concert for the purpose of controlling or influencing the business of the issuer. In order to meet the legislative purpose, the rule should be expanded to include in its coverage, as is the case in the United States, any persons acting as a group or syndicate for the purpose of acquiring, holding, or disposing of

18. *See Commercial Code* (Law No. 1000 of January 20, 1962, as amended), Arts. 435, 344 and 436.

19. *Securities Exchange Act of 1934*, Sec. 13(d)(4), 15 U.S.C.A. §78m(d)(4); also *Commercial Code*, Art. 369(2); 1 Hi-Chul Chung, *Commentary on Commercial Laws* 361 (rev. ed. 1972).

securities of the issuer.[20] In addition, the percentage of ownership subject to the reporting requirement should be lowered from the current 10% limit as the equity owership spreads further among the general public. On the other hand, the present rule imposed on a 10% shareholder may be too much of an impractical burden by requiring him to file a report whenever any change has occurred in his percentage of shareholding. Such a burden should be relaxed to a reasonable degree by providing some exemptions. At the same time, extending of the rule's coverage to registered corporations appears to be necessary and appropriate in the public interest and for the protection of investors.[21]

Finally, the ownership report rule, providing for a criminal sanction for any violation thereof, failed to include any specific rules relating to a filing period and determination of the time when any change in the shareholding of a person is deemed to have occurred for the purpose of ownership report.[22] Without having such loopholes inherent in the ownership report rule closed, enforcement of the rule would be almost impossible, and any criminal sanction cannot come into play.

III. Tender Offers

Together with the ownership reporting requirement and restrictions on ownership increases through secret purchases, a system of tender offers or takeover bids in Korea was, as noted earlier, recently introduced. The idea behind such introduction was, as noted earlier, to favor the incumbent management and discourages potential shifts

---

20. *Securities Exchange Act of 1934*, Sec. 13(d)(3), 15 U.S.C.A. §78 m(d)(3).
21. Under Article 4 of the SEA, corporations which are subject to the registration requirement are required to file registration documents with the SAC. The registration documents are to include shareholders registry of the corporation. However, since only "material changes" in the content of the documents are required to be reflected in an amended statement, it is not clear whether any change in shareholdings of a 10% shareholder constitutes a "material change" for the purpose of this Article. *See* note 11 *supra* at 102–103.
22. In the United States, a Schedule 13D is required to be filed within 10 days after the person becomes the beneficial owner of more than 5% of the security. For this purpose, a person will generally be deemed to have become the owner of the security when it has entered into a binding commitment to purchase the same.

in corporate control.[23] Although the management of a target company may employ various defensive tactics to defeat a takeover bid immediately after such a bid has been disclosed, the device can be used by raiders as an efficient and practical method of attempting to take over control. This is because any raider in Korea has the legal obstacles in increasing his shareholding of a target company through secret accumulation beyond his initial shareholding (if the initial shareholding exceeds more than 10%), 10% (if not a 10% shareholder), or 20% (upon a SAC's approval). An increase through a direct purchase from a 10% shareholder is practically impossible unless the target is friendly. The tender offer is also cheaper and simpler than the proxy contest in takeover attempts. But this area is unclear since no tender offer has been filed with the SAC to date. Therefore, the general rules of tender offer hereinafter will be discussed on the basis of statutory provisions in order to identify some legal problems prevalent.

A. Tender Offers Subject to Disclosure Requirements

1. Statutory Rules

The legislature copied the tender offer system after the Japanese model which had in turn been substantially copied after the Federal Securities Laws in the United States.[24] The legislature neglected to expressly define the term "tender offer" in the SEA or Decrees thereunder. Though the term "tender offer" has been expanded after the Williams Act of the United States to include stock exchange special bids, coordinated series of negotiated purchases, or even adoption proposals, it was conventionally understood to be a publicly made invitation addressed to all shareholders of corporation to tender their

---

23. *See* note 2 *supra* and its accompanying text.
24. *See SEA*, Arts. 21 through 27; *Presidential Enforcement Decree of the SEA*, Arts. 10 through 13; *MOF Enforcement Decree of the SEA*, Arts. 5 through 9. For the rules of tender offer in Japan and United States, *see Japanese SEA*, Arts. 27–2 through 27–8; *Cabinet Order of the SEA*, Arts. 6 through 15; *MOF Order on Filing Notification Statement, Etc. in Connection with Tender Offer* (MOF Order No. 38, promulgated on June 9, 1971, as amended by MOF Order No. 61 in 1971); *Securities Exchange Act of 1934*, Secs. 14(d)(e)(f), 13(e), 15 U.S.C.A. §78 (d)(e)(f), m(e), and SEC Regulation 14D, 13D (Rule 13e–1) and Schedule 13D thereunder. 17 C.F.R. §§240. 14 d–1 *et seq.* and 13 e–1. The term "tender offer" was not defined in the statutes of either the United States or Japan.

shares at a specified price.[25] The current state of the law is that open market purchases alone do not constitute a tender offer[26] and that pretender offer open market purchases, absent other factors, are not a tender offer and need not be integrated with a subsequent tender offer.[27] Probably the most important factors in determining whether purchases of securities, other than through a classic tender offer, constitute a tender offer for purposes of Section 14 (d) are the number of shareholders solicited, the extent of the publicity surrounding the purchases and, in the case of privately negotiated purchases, the extent to which the sellers have the opportunity to independently negotiate the terms of the purchases.[28] In 1979, the SEC released a proposed rule, which defines the term of tender offer, and if adopted, the proposed rule would effectively prohibit most stock purchase programs in excess of 5% of a target's outstanding shares.[29]

---

25. *See* Note, *The Developing Meaning of "Tender Offer" under the Securities Exchange Act of 1934*, 86 HARV. L. REV. 1250, 1251–2, 1260–70 (1973); *also see* M. Brown, *The Scope of the Williams Act and Its 1970 Amendments*, 26 BUS. LAW. 1637, 1644(1971). The special bid was made to be considered a tender offer within the meaning of Sections 14'(d) and 14(e) by a SEC release (Sec. Ex. Act of 1934 Rel. No. 8392, Aug. 30, 1968). The first judicial expansion of the meaning of the term tender offer came in May, 1972, in *Cattlemen's Investment Co. v. Fears*, 343 F. Suppl. 1248 (W.D. Okla. 1972), where a coordinated series of negotiated purchases from a large number of shareholders during a relatively short period of time was held to constitute a tender offer for the purposes of Sections 14(d) and 14(e). For another expansion re adoption proposal and limits to such expansion, *see* SEC Staff Advisory Ruling on *Yellow Freight System, Inc.*, and opinions of the courts in *A & P* and *Water & Wall* cases cited in the Note, *supra* 1266–70 (one limit was that the term does not encompass ordinary securities purchases made on an open market, even if done with the intention of gaining control of the issuer).

26. *See Wilfred P. Cohen Foundations Inc. v. Prevor*, (1974–1975 Transfer Binder) CCH Fed. Sec. L. Rep. 95,057 (S.D.N.Y. 1975); *D–Z Inv. Co. v. Holloway*, (1974–1975 Transfer Binder) CCH Fed. Sec. L. Rep. 94,771 (S.D. N.Y. 1974).

27. *See Indus. Inc. v. Great Atlantic & Pacific Tea Co.*, 356 F. Supp. 1066 (S.D.N.Y.) *aff'd on other grounds*, 476 F. 2d. 687 (2d. Cir. 1973).

28. *See Hoover v. Fugua Industries Inc.* CCH Fed. Sec. L. Rep. 97,107 (N.D. Ohio 1979); *also see Wellman v. Dickinson*, CCH Fed. Sec. L. Rep. 96,918 (S.D.N.Y. 1979).

29. The text of subparagraph (b)(1) as proposed to be added in Release No. 34–16385 (Report No. 835, Part II), November 29, 1979 is as follows:

Cash or other securities may be offered to shareholders as consideration, but in either case, the consideration specified usually represents a premium over the current market price of the securities sought. This opportunity to tender shares at a premium remains open for only a limited period of time, often about two weeks. A distinct aspect of the conventional tender offer is that offerors typically condition their obligation to purchase on the aggregate tender of stated number of shares. If greater than the stated number are tendered, the

---

(1) The term "tender offer" includes a "request or invitation for tenders" and means one or more offers to purchase or solicitations of offers to sell securities of a single class, whether or not all or any portion of the securities sought are purchased, which

    (i) during any 45–day period are directed to more than 10 persons and seek the acquisition of more than 5% of the class of securities, except that offers by a broker (and its customer) or by a dealer made on a national securities exchange at the then current market or made in the over-the-counter market at the then current market shall be excluded if in connection with such offers neither the person making the offers nor such broker or dealer solicits or arranges for the solicitation of any order to sell such securities and such broker or dealer and receives no more than the broker's usual and customary commission or the dealer's usual and customary mark-up; or

    (ii) are not otherwise a tender offer under paragraph (b)(1)(i) of this Section, but which (A) are disseminated in a widespread manner, (B) provide for a price which represents a premium in excess of the greater of 5% of or $2 above the current market price and (C) do not provide for a meaningful opportunity to negotiate the price and terms.

Under the proposed rule, an offer is a tender offer if it meets either of two tests. Under the first test, the following elements must be present for there to be a tender offer: (1) one or more offers to purchase or solicitations of offers to sell securities of a single class, (2) during any 45 calendar day period, (3) directed to more than 10 persons, and (4) seeking the acquisition of more than 5% of the class of securities (the offer must involve an attempt to acquire more than 5%; that is, securities already held by the purchaser would not be aggregated). The proposal would exempt, however, offers by a broker, its customers or a dealer at the current market price under certain conditions. Under the second test, there must be present all of the following three elements: (1) dissemination in a widespread manner; (2) provision for a price which represent a premium in excess of the greater of 5% of, or $2 above, market; and (3) no provisions for a meaningful opportunity to negotiate the price and terms.

offeror is not required to purchase the excess.[30] Meanwhile, during the period in which the overall response is being determined, the shareholder relinquishes control over his tendered shares. They are placed with depositary and the shareholder has only limited withdrawal rights.[31]

Modeled after the conventional tender offer in the United States, the tender offer in Japan or Korea is required by the statute to be effected only on the OTC market.[32] The SEA made it unlawful for any person to make a tender offer for, or request or invitation for tenders of a certain category of security toward many unspecified persons, and to acquire, either in cash or in exchange for other security, such security tendered unless a notification statement, filed with the SAC in compliance with the rules thereof, has become effective.[33] The category of security subject to acquisition through such tender offer is restricted to the securities of listed or registered corporations, *i.e.*, any equity securities, certificates representing a right to new shares, or bonds or debentures convertible to any equity securities (hereinafter collectively referred to as "securities"). In filing a notification statement with the SAC, a tender offeror is required to designate a securities company as his agent for the tender offer.

However, the SEA provides some exemptions from the requirements to file the statement in connection with a tender offer. The proviso of Article 21 (1) provides that a Presidential Decree may exempt a certain tender offer from the filing requirement under consideration of "the type and other circumstances" involving such tender offer. Although there is no indication of the meaning of the phrase "the type and other circumstances," a phrase borrowed from the Japanese rule,[34] the legislature appears to have intended to exempt

---

30. *See* Note, *supra* n. 25 at 1252 and note 12 therein. Although not obligated to do so, the offeror may reserve the option of purchasing the excess of tendered shares.

31. *Id.*, Such a position of a shareholder in a conventional tender offer is thus in sharp contrast with his position in ordinary market and negotiated transactions, where sellers retain control over their securities until sale is completed.

32. *SEA*, Art. 21(1); *Japanese SEA*, Art. 27–2(1).

33. *Id.*

34. Article 27–2(1), proviso of the Japanese SEA included the same phrase with some supplementary words, "appears to be unnecessary to require filing a notification statement."

such tender offers that appear not to influence the control of the issuer or do not otherwise violate the purpose of Article 21, especially in reference to full disclosure for the protection of investors. Under the Presidential Decree, a tender offer is exempted, if (1) the offeror, after the consummation thereof, directly or indirectly with "a person in special relationship" becomes the beneficial owner of less than 10% of the outstanding shares of such security; (2) the offer is a corporate repurchase for the purpose of redemption; or (3) the offer is defined by the MOF Decree as having the similar nature to that prescribed in items (1) or (2) above.[35] But no exemption has been added by the MOF Decree. The present two exemptions deserve some further comments as to their appropriateness.

2. Problems Raised

a. Corporate Repurchase and Redemption

Transactions involving the purchase by a corporation of its own shares arise in a variety of business contexts and include significant legal problems. Apart from a question of whether a corporation has the power to purchase its own shares, a corporation or its management frequently may meet a practical need to purchase its own shares to plow back the earnings and thus to realize capital gains rates on the increase of the stock's value, to keep the corporation closely held for the purpose of continuing control, or to support to manipulate the market price of the stock.[36] Shares purchased are treated as "treasury shares" unless formally retired by some form of statutory capital reduction or other method of redemption. While it is perhaps in some circumstances permissible to show treasury stock as an asset in the United States, if adequately disclosed, the dividends on such stock must not be treated as a credit to the income account of the company.[37] Furthermore, accounting experts who drew up and certified a false corporate financial statement was held criminally liable in

---

35. *See Presidential Decree,* Art. 12. The term "a person in special relationship" here refers to such a person capable of practically controlling the issuer by means of indirect stockholding or other means as specified in Article 39 of the Basic National Tax Act.
36. W.L. Cary, *Corporations* 1589–91 (4th ed. 1969).
37. Financial Accounting Standards Board (FASB), *Financial Accounting Standards* 9 (ARB No. 43, Sec. A) (1975).

United States v. Simon.[38] There accountants, knowing that an insider was looting corporate assets by means of borrowing money, certified as an asset a receivable whose collectibility was essential but collateralized by securities of the very company whose solvency was at issue and failed to reveal a known increase in such receivable. On the other hand, if the purchase of its own shares is not made out of reserved surplus, or if the amount paid for the shares exceeds the surplus, the purchase necessarily operates as a distribution to the selling shareholders of part of the capital, and to that extent impairs capital. The impairment may become permanent, where the corporation treats the purchased shares as retired without formally reducing capital, refrains from reselling the shares, or is unable to resell them except at a lower price. These consequences affect creditors and shareholders. The corporate repurchase also affects voting control by reducing the number of outstanding shares. Finally, it may frequently involve in manipulative or deceptive practices affecting public investors.

In response to the significant impact of corporate repurchases, including trading in its own shares, pertinent laws in the United States included several restrictions. Most state statutes restrict the corporate power to purchase its own shares by providing a surplus or capital impairment test with certain exceptions, which usually include repurchase of redeemable preferred shares.[39] They also concern the propriety of exercising such a power. On the other hand, Section 14(d) (8) exempted a tender offer made by the issuer of the security from Section 14(d), including the requirement to file a statement.[40] However, the Exchange Act provided a separate provision of

---

38. 425 F. 2d 796 (2d Cir. 1969), *cert. denied*, 397 U.S. 1006 (1970). The Second Circuit noted that, even in a criminal case, generally accepted accounting principles were not necessarily the measure of accountants' liability for allegedly misleading statements.

39. *Id.*, at 1593–94, citing as examples the provisions of state business corporation laws in Delaware, New York, Michigan, Ohio, California, Illinois, Minnesota, and Model Act.

40. *Securities Exchange Act of 1934*, Sec., 14(d)(8), 15 U.S.C.A. §78n(d)(8). It also exempted any offer not resulting in increase of more than 2% of the ownership together with all other shares of the same class acquired by the same person during the preceding twelve months, or other offers as the SEC by rules,

Section 13(e) concerning the regulation of corporate repurchases.[41] Recognizing that repurchases of securities may serve a number of legitimate purposes, the Congress was, in adopting the provision, concerned not only about the utilization of repurchases by management to preserve control or to counteract tender offers or other attempted takeovers, but also about the significant impact on market prices and the strong need for full disclosure of the company's activities and intentions.[42] Section 13(e) of the Exchange Act authorized the SEC to adopt rules and regulations regarding the purchase by a certain issuer of its own share in order to prevent any fraudulent, deceptive or manipulative acts and practices. It also specified certain material information which would be required to be disclosed. Furthermore, a purchase by or for a person in a control relationship with the issuer must be deemed to be a purchase by the issuer, with some exceptions as the SEC may prescribe. Since the SEC has adopted only Rule 13 e-1 thus far, repurchase by the issuer of the security under the Federal securities laws is prohibited during the period of a tender offer made by other parties and during the period of distribution of its own security.[43]

The Commercial Code in Korea, similar to the state business corporation law in the United States, includes some scattering provi-

---

regulations or orders exempts as not influencing the control of the issuer of otherwise not comprehended within the purpose of the Section 14(d).

41. *Id.,* §78m(e).

42. *2 U.S. Code Cong. & Adm. News* 12814–15 (90th Cong., 2d Sess. 1968).

43. 17 C.F.R. §240, 13 e-1. The rule provides that once such issuer receives notice that a tender offer is being made by another person pursuant to Rule 14 d–1, it must not thereafter during the period of the tender offer purchase any of its own equity securities unless it has filed with the SEC a statement containing the information required by the rule, and, within the past six months, has sent to its security holders substantially the same information as required in the statement. The information required closely tracks the statute but is more specified. Rule 13 e–1 is a balancing rule since it requires the issuer to provide disclosure before purchasing its own shares when the issuer is the subject of a tender offer by other persons. Therefore, the investors, with disclosures made by both sides in a contested tender offer, are able to make informed decisions as to whether or to whom they should sell or tender. For the restriction during the period of distribution, *see* 3 Loss, *Securities Regulation* 1595–1604 (2d ed. 1961). Also for the proposed Rule 13e–2 and an amendment to Rule 10b–6 under the Exchange Act, *see* SEC, *Sec. Ex. Act Rel. No.* 10539 (Dec. 6, 1973).

sions restricting the acquisition of shares by the issuer itself. It is illegal for any stock corporation to acquire its own shares unless the shares are acquired: (1) for the purpose of redemption; (2) in connection with a merger into or consolidation with another company, or an acquisition of the whole business of another company; or (3) in order to attain its purpose in the course of specific performance of its rights.[44] The major concern of such prohibition is, for the protection of the interest of general creditors, shareholders, and public investors, to maintain the financial soundness of the issuer and to prevent any possible speculation or manipulation by the issuer. Any acquisition in violation of such prohibition is construed to be null and void and subject to a fine.[45] Any shares lawfully acquired by the issuer are to rest dormant and hold no voting rights.[46] And the issuer must either retire them immediately following the acquisition (item 1 above), or sell or dispose of them, including those taken in pledge, within a certain period of time.[47]

Although acquisition of its own shares by issuer in Korea is more restricted than that in the United States, any issuer may purchase its own shares as far as such purchase is made for the redemption purpose. The Commercial Code again limits such acquisition for the redemption purpose to two categories only, *i.e.*, acquisitions effected in compliance with the statutory form of capital reduction and those

---

44. *Commercial Code, Art. 341.*
45. *See* Sup. Ct. Judgement, Minshang No. 229, April 7, 1955 (Da 156, May 30, 1963); *see also* 1 Chung, n. 28 *supra* I, 360–61; 1 Ton K. Suh, *Commentary on Commercial Laws* 321–22 (9th rev. ed. 1973); Won Sun Park, 1 *New Commercial Code* 286 (1962). Any acquisition or contract to acquire its own shares by the issuer itself is construed to be null and void by the supreme court and the majority of commentators on the ground that the purpose of prohibition is, in the public interest and for the protection of investors, to maintain the financial soundness of the company and to prevent any speculation and manipulation by the company. But a few commentators argue that such an acquisition should not be null and void in order to facilitate the marketability of securities and to protect the investors concerned. (*See* Park, *supra*). As to the criminal penalty for the violation of the provision, *see Commercial Code*, Art. 625, item 2.
46. *Commercial Code*, Art. 369(2).
47. *Id.*, Arts. 342, 635(1), item 17 (re criminal sanction for violation of Article 342).

paid for out of surplus usable for dividend payments.[48] Since reduction of capital must be made only by the methods prescribed by the Code, which requires amendment of the articles of incorporation by a shareholders' special resolution and an appropriate notice to general creditors, the redemption paid for out of earned surplus does not result in reduction of capital.[49] Redeemable or callable shares of a class such as preferred shares or all shares issued and outstanding may be redeemed under the Code. Redemption may also be effected through market purchases, by lottery or on a pro rata basis regardless of shareholders' intentions. Therefore, the statute requires a corporation to include in its articles of incorporation information on method, price, and other terms and conditions of redemption and to disclose such information in the subscription form and corporate registry. In addition, a public notice is to be given to each shareholder on the record whenever any redemption procedure is launched.[50] This regulatory framework concerning restrictions on corporate repurchase and redemption procedures is substantially modeled on the Japanese rules.[51]

From the foregoing analysis, one may conclude that public shareholders in Korea are ensured by the Commercial Code protection to a considerable degree by disclosures in the course of the corporate repurchase and redemption process. In this respect, the SEA seems to have exempted the tender offer which is effected for redemption purposes from the requirement of filing a statement. However, the

---

48. *Id.*, Art. 343.
49. *Id.*, Arts. 345, 438, 439(2), 232(2).
50. *Id.*, Arts. 343(2), 440, 441.
51. *See Japanese Commercial Code* (Law No. 48, March 9, 1899, as amended by Law No. 21, on April 2, 1974) Arts. 210–27 (restrictions on corporate power to acquire its own shares or to take them in pledge); Arts, 212, 377, 348, 375, *et seq.* (regulating the procedure of redemption with an earned surplus limit or requirement of reduction of capital). The regulatory framework is same between the two countries, except that Japan recently included a provision concerning appraisal rights of dissenting shareholders, which is substantially borrowed from state statutes in the United States. Thus, in Japan, a corporation may purchase its shares from a shareholder who opposes any proposal at a shareholders' meeting, concerning amalgamation, takeover, or other major changes in business or corporate structure. *See id.,* Arts. 210, item 4, 245–2, 349(1), 408–3.

present rule is insufficient in regard to the full protection of public investors.

First, the prohibition of acquisition of its own shares by the issuer, exclusive of the three exceptions, undermines the marketability of securities because any acquisition made in violation of the rule must be null and void. As far as capital is not impaired and legitimate purpose exists, certain repurchases may be allowed by introducing appropriate devices for investor protection. In addition, a public shareholder who dissents at a shareholders' meeing to a material change in corporate structure or business should be given freedom to retire his shares with fair payment through an independent appraisal proceeding.

Second, the present rule concerning redemption of shares which does not result in reduction of capital is also insufficient in protecting investors. Such retirement under the statute is required to be paid out of earned surplus as provided in the article of incorporation, by stating in the subscription form of shares and corporate registry information as to price, method, and other terms and conditions of retirement, and by giving a notice to shareholders on the record. However, many public shareholders who purchase such shares in the trading market may not be on record, and usually do not familiarize themselves with the corporate registry and articles of incorporation. Though they have access to all these materials in advance, they still are not guaranteed by the rule to be informed of any corporate purpose of retirement, source of funds used to retire the share, or other plans or proposals of the issuer involving the repurchase. Also needed is to establish accounting principles which require the shares held in the treasury to be fairly disclosed in a certain case where such shares may be shown as an asset.

Third, the SEA did not include a Section 13(e) type of prohibition (in connection with defense tactics) probably because the issuer is prohibited from repurchasing its own shares exclusive of the three exceptions. But the prohibition of corporate repurchases includes some loopholes that can be easily used by issuer who is the target of a tender offer. Above all, the rule encompasses within its coverage purchase by or for the issuer only. Any other purchase by or for a person other than the issuer is not deemed to be a purchase by or for the issuer, although such a person is controlled by, or under the common control of the issuer. As far as any fraudulent, manipulative, or deceptive practices and devices are concerned, the purchase by such a person should be deemed a purchase by or for the issuer. Such expansion of the rule gains further significance since the number of publicly-held corporations has increased rapidly since 1972, and the managements of such corporations appear to feel a strong need to support or manipulate the market prices through persons who are directly or indirectly controlled by the issuer.

b. The 10% Exemption

The present rule of the 10% exemption has some drawbacks, which includes methods that might be utilized by a raider in avoiding the requirement to file a statement. He may split the amount of shares intended to be purchased by the offer so as to keep his total shareholding after the acquisition below the 10% limit, and may thereafter effect another tender offer within some time interval, and thus avoid the rules of tender offers as far as the initial offer is concerned. Hence, the 10% limit as a standard for the exception is too generous as in the case of the ownership reporting requirement.

B. Disclosure in Connection with Tender Offers

1. Information to Be Included in the Statement

Article 21(2) of the SEA and Article 5 and Form 2 of the MOF Decree require tender offerors to include in the statement filed with and exhibits. Whereas the disclosure required in the ownership report was insufficient for the protection of investors as noted earlier, information included in the statement amounts to substantially a full disclosure as is required in the United States or Japan.[52] Tender offerors must include in the statement information, *inter alia,* as to:

(1) security and the issuer which is a target with specifications, operational status, and ownership distribution among controlling shareholders and officers; (2) identity and background of the offeror with detailed information concerning its business, capital structure, controlling shareholders and officers, and financial and operational status, if the offeror is a corporation; (3) source and amount of funds or other consideration used or to be used for the purchase; (4) purpose

---

52. *MOF Enforcement Decree under the SEA,* Art. 5 and Form 2 attached thereto. Cf: *SEC Regulations,* schedule 13D, 17 C.F.R. 240, 13D; *Japanese MOF Order on Filing Procedure, Etc. in Connection with Tender Offer,* Arts. 1, 2 and Form 1 attached thereto.

of transaction, with any plans or proposals concerning liquidation, sale of its assets or any material change in its business or corporate structure if the purpose of purchase is to acquire control; (5) terms, conditions, and number of shares to be purchased; (6) interest in securities of the issuer; and (7) any contracts, arrangements, or understandings with the issuer or its management, including persons to be employed, retained, or compensated.

A statement which has been filed with the SAC in compliance with the provisions of the SEA and Decrees thereunder becomes effective ten days after its filing. Since Article 11 of the SEA concerning the registration statement is required to apply *mutatis mutandis* to the tender offer statement, the offeror may, voluntarily or under the SAC's order, amend the statement when the original statement is incomplete in its form or includes any misstatement or omission of a material fact.[53] In this case the effect of the original filing is suspended, and the statement becomes effective ten days after the amended statement has been filed.

2. Public Notice and Prospectus

Any offeror who has filed the statement with the SAC is required to send a copy of the statement to the target company before the statement becomes effective.[54] The offeror must also give public notice in a daily newspaper more than two times, and if the security concerned is a listed security, must also send a copy of the statement to the KSE immediately after the statement has become effective. The required public notice is in effect an advertisement, and thus the tender offeror is required to submit to the SAC, at the time of filing the statement, a copy of the notice, which must also be made in compliance with a specified form.[55]

In addition, the tender offeror must draw up a prospectus concerning the offer. The prospectus must be made in compliance with the provision of the MOF Decree by stating all the information that is included in the statement.

However, the rule exempts information on financial matters from

---

53. *SEA,* Arts. 21(4), 11. The voluntary amendment may be filed until original statement has become effective.
54. *Id.,* Arts. 22, 21(3).
55. *Id.,* Art. 22(2); *MOF Decree,* Arts. 5(2), item 7,6 and 7.

the prospectus if the offeror is a corporation.[56] Although the legislative intent is not clear, such an exemption is not proper for the protection of investors even for cash tender offers. Like the delivery of a prospectus for public distribution of securities, a tender offeror is required to deliver the prospectus only when an offeree has asked for it.[57] To further the protection of investors, the prospectus should be delivered compulsorily to shareholders as it is in Japan.

Finally, the SAC is empowered to issue an order to tender offerors, the issuers which are targets, or other related persons, requiring them to file a report or to submit other relevant materials.[58] Also, the statement filed with the SAC must be kept for one year and must be available for public inspection.[59]

3. Some Drawbacks Included

In specifying the form of a public notice of a tender offer which is filed as a part of the statement, the SEA and Decrees thereunder failed to consider any other free-written materials or advertisements requesting or inviting tenders of the securities concerned. Neither are such materials or advertisements prohibited nor are they required to be filed as a part of the statement. In order to protect the interests of the investors concerned, the legislature should have inserted a provision which appropriately regulates requests, invitations, or advertisements. The SEA should have also included a provision treating two or more persons as a "person" for the purpose of the tender offer provisions if they act as a group or syndicate for the purpose of acquiring, holding, or disposing of the securities of the issuer.

In addition, the SEA and Decrees thereunder nowhere provide any indication, execpt in the voluntary amendment, as to whether the offeror is required to file promptly and material change that may have occurred in the facts as set forth in the statement. During the period of a tender offer, the offeror may extend the period of the offer, increase the consideration, or change his stated business pur-

---

56. *SEA*, Art. 24(1); *MOF Decree* Art. 8.

57. *SEA*, Arts. 24, 13; *MOF Decree*, Art. 9. In Japan, the prospectus must in advance be delivered (*Japanese SEA*, Arts. 2—5).

58. *SEA*, Art. 27.

59. *Id.*, Art. 261. Although all the reports, statements, documents, and materials submitted by persons in connection with a tender offer are to be kept and be available for public inspection, the text of Article failed to include these.

pose. Any such change, being material to the public interest and necessary for the protection of investors, should be promptly disclosed
as is required in the United States.[60]

C. *Restrictions on the Purchase*

The offeror may commence purchasing in accordance with the
tender offer if the statement has become effective, and if public
notice in a newspaper has been given at least twice in compliance
with the pertinent provisions. As in the United States or Japan,
however, the SEA requires that once a tender offer or exchange offer
has become effective, such an offeror must purchase the securities
of the target company pursuant only to the provisions of the tender
offer or exchange offer until such an offer by its terms expires.[61] The
purpose of this rule is to protect people who have deposited their
shares and who might otherwise obtain greater consideration for their
shares if the market rose above the tender prices and thus forced an
increase in the tender price. The rule also deprives the targets large
shareholders of potential for bargaining that the offeror give them a
greater consideration than that being paid to the public shareholders.[62]
To achieve these purposes, to wit, the protection of those who have
already deposited their shares, the rule should include within its
prohibition all direct or indirect purchases by persons who are controlled by, controlling, or under common control with the offeror.
However, the SEA, unlike the rules in the United States and Japan,
includes no phrases prohibiting such direct or indirect purchases by
persons other than the offeror.

Except for the rule prohibiting purchases outside the provisions
of the tender offer, the SEA and Decrees thereunder include no
other restrictions on purchases by the offeror. Rather Article 23(3)
of the SEA empowers the SAC to restrict by fiat, in the public interest or for the protection of investors, the method or terms and conditions of the purchases effected by the offeror. Thus, as partly im-

---

60. *See* SEC Rule 14 d-1(b), (d), 17 C.F.R. § 240. 14 d-1 (b), (d).
61. *See SEA*, Art. 23; SEC Rule 10 b-13, 17 C.F.R. 240, 10b-13; *Japanese SEA*,
   2—4(2).
62. *See* Griffin & Trucker, *supra* note 12, at 705; The Japanese Association of
   Practical Studies in Commercial Law, *Commentary on the Amended Securities
   Laws* 216 (1971).

plied in the note attached to Form 2, the matters concerning a right to withdraw or rescind, method of acceptance, such as pro rata or "first-come, first-served," and the price to be paid when the consideration has been increased before the expiration of the offer, are left to the full discretion of the offeror unless the SAC restricts them.[63] As a matter of legislative responsibility to the public, the legislature should have specified such matters in the SEA, rather than entrusting them to the discretion of a regulatory agency.

Indeed, the rules for tender offers should have been designed to reconcile the best interests of the persons involved. The rule should not have been made favoring either the target management or the persons making the takeover bid. It also should have been designed to insure full and fair disclosure for the benefit of investors, while at the same time providing the offeror and management with an equal opportunity to fairly present their case.[64] Although the investors have under the disclosure rules access to relevant information involved in a takeover battle, they are still far from being on an equal footing with the bidder. They should be provided with a fair opportunity in making their decisions whether to hold or to tender. They should have equal treatment if and when they tender their shares. In this regard, the rules in the United States and Japan allow persons who have tendered shares an opportunity to withdraw within a certain period of time.[65] The rules also require a tender offeror to accept

---

63. *See* Form 2 *supra,* attached Note items 9, 10.

64. *See 2 U.S. Code Cong. & Adm. News* (90th Cong., 2d Sess. 1968) 2813–14.

65. *Securities Exchange Act of 1934,* Sec. 14(d) (5) (6) (7), 15 U.S.C.A. §§78n(d) (5) (6) (7), and 1968 U.S. Code Cong. & Adm. News, *supra* at 2820; *Cabinet Order under the Japanese SEA,* Art. 13, and the Japanese Association of Practical Studies on Commercial Laws, *supra* note 62, at 129–31. In the United States, shareholders who have tendered are allowed to withdraw at any time within seven days after the tender offer is made or at any time after sixty days from the date of the original offer. In Japan, the withdrawal is allowed during the first ten days after the tender offer is made because the period of purchase is required to be between 20 and 30 days after the tender offer is made through a public notice.

Pro rata acceptance in the United States applies to the shares deposited within the first ten days after the offer is made public. If the offeror increases the consideration, a new ten days pro rata period is required in order to allow all shareholders a fair opportunity to participate in the offer. In Japan, pro rata

the shares deposited on a pro rata basis according to the number of shares deposited by each shareholder if a greater number of shares are tendered than tender offeror is bound or willing to take up. The rules further provide that where such offeror increases the amount of consideration offered prior to the expiration of the offer, he must pay the increased consideration to all the shareholders who have tendered.

The withdrawal right gives shareholders who tendered their shares immediately after the offer is made a period within which to reconsider. This right, particularly that in the United States which does not restrict the purchase period, also prevents tendered securities from being tied up indefinitely while awaiting a desision by the offeror as to whether he will purchase them or not. In addition, pro rata acceptances prevent a first-come first-served stampede, and meet the equal treatment test as the best-price requirement does in the case of increases in the consideration offered. In Korea, the rules on tender offers do not restrict the period of purchase nor do they give a withdrawal right to shareholders. Offerees are not permitted to change their minds and thus their shares tendered might be in a indefinite lockup. They also run the risk of rushing their decision and thus receiving unequal treatment solely because the method of acceptance and an increased payment are left to the discretion of the offeror.

D. *Communication to Shareholders and Fraud in Connection with Tender Offers*

The regulatory framework of a takeover bid should be designed to insure full and fair disclosure for the benefit of investors by requiring the bidder and the target company to fully present their case. At the same time, it should not be designed to materially aid any one party, either the bidder or the target company, in presenting its case or employing any offensive and defensive maneuvers. However, the

---

acceptance applies to all the shares deposited during the whole tender offer period. But, the MOF Order includes some adjustments in order to reduce the occurrence of odd-lot shares (*Japanese MOF Order, supra*, Art. 8).

The best-price requirement, in the case of an increase in the consideration offered, assures fair treatment of those who tender their shares at the beginning of the tender period and assured equality of treatment to all shareholders who tender their shares. *See id.*, Sec. 14(d) (7); Art. 13, item 4.

present statutory rules of tender offers in Korea are insufficient to meet such fundamental tests.

1. Regulation of Target Company Recommendations

a. Statutory Provisions

When a surprise takeover bid is publicly made, the management of the target company may employ various defensive maneuvers as the management's continued employment and company's independent control may rest on the outcome of a tender offer.[66] The most probable course of action for the target company is to communicate with the shareholders and urge them not to tender their shares. The SEA, being substantially copied after the Japanese rule which is in turn borrowed from that of the United States, includes a provision regulating communications by the target company with its shareholders.[67] The provision requires that "any expression of an opinion of the target company to its shareholders for or against the offer be made in compliance with the provision of the Presidential Decree, and a copy of the statement thereof be in advance filed with the SAC." Article 13 of the Presidential Decree thereunder in turn provides:

> "a target company who filed such statement under the SEA may, by means of an advertisement, letter, or other written document, express its opinion to its shareholders to accept or reject the offer; in communicating with its shareholders, the target company shall not include in the statement any material omission of a fact or misstatement which is misleading under the circumstances."

The foregoing provision dealing with target's communication with its shareholders does not require the company to respond to any type of tender offer by recommending to its shareholders either to

---

66. As in the United States, possible defensive tactics would include a recommendation to shareholders against the offer, direct or indirect repurchases of its own shares, dividend increases, stock-splits, litigations against offeror, or a defensive merger or competing tender offer. For defensive tactics employed in the United States, *see* W.M. Kennedy, *Defensive Takeover Procedures since the Williams Act,* 14 CATH. UNIV. L. REV. 158 (1969); D.S. Bardshow, *Defensive Tactics Employed by Incumbent Managements in Contesting Tender Offers,* 21 STAN. L. REV. 1104(1969).

67. *SEA,* Art. 25; *Securities Exchange Act of 1934,* Sec. 14(d), 15 U.S.C.A. §78n(d) and SEC Rules thereunder; *Japanese SEA,* Art. 27–6, Japanese SEA imposes on the target management the same requirement to file the documents with the MOF in compliance with the provisions of the Cabinet Order.

accept or reject the offer. Silence or neutrality is, therefore, permissible under the rule. In addition, the provision on communication "expressly" imposes the requirement to file a statement with the SAC on the target company alone and thus any person other than a target company may freely recommend to shareholders to reject or accept the offer. Furthermore, this provision, unlike that in Japan, does not require the target company to submit, at the time of filing, any documents or materials upon which the recommendation is based, nor does it require the company to include in the statement such specified information as required in Schedule 14D, which is required to be filed under similar circumstances in the United States.[68] Thus, such a broad freedom in making recommendations to its shareholders enjoyed by a target company in Korea, as compared to that given in the United States or Japan, would raise significant questions as to propriety and fairness.

    b. Some Drawbacks

    Although it is unlawful to include in the statement any material

---

68. *See Cabinet Order under the Japanese SEA*, Art. 27–6(2), and *MOF Order thereunder*, Art. 11. The target management is required to submit, at the time of the filing of the statement, to the MOF, the following information: (a) basis or grounds upon which the solicitation or recommendation is based; (b) a copy of the minutes of the board of directors reflecting the proceedings and the resolution concerned; (c) the number of each shares held by the officers; and (d) information as to any compensation or interest offered or to be paid by the tender offeror to any officer of the company, if any.

In the United States, the target management or any other person making the solicitation or recommendation is required to file a copy of statement in compliance with SEC rules and regulations at the time when the copies of the solicitation or recommendation are first published and sent to or given to holders of the security. Any material changes that occur in the facts as set forth in the statement must promptly be reported through amendment. Schedule 14D is a shortened form of Schedule 13D, which is filed by the bidder, and is patterned after Schedule 14B filed under the proxy rules. For the details of information included and materials filed as an exhibit, *see* SEC Rule 14 d–1, 4 and Schedule 14D, 17 C.F.R. § 240. 14d–1, 4, 101 (1969). Also Rule 14–d2(f) permits management of a target company to respond to a surprise tender offer before filing a Schedule 14D if the management statement does not more than state that management is studying the tender offer and request that security holders defer their decision until management makes its recommendation.

omission of a fact or misstatement which is misleading under the circumstances, the SEA and Decrees thereunder nowhere indicate what else the target company can or must disclose to their shareholders either in opposition to or in favor of a takeover bid made. Under the current corporate law, one may argue that if management of a target company is aware of any material, nonpublic information about the company, either favorable or unfavorable, it has a fiduciary duty to come forward and disclose this. In practice, however, it would be hard to determine whether the management would have such duty to disclose under a variety of circumstances. Because of the lack of any specific guidelines for disclosure and the failure to require the management to submit any relevant materials upon which a recommendation may be based, it would be almost impossible for public shareholders and the regulatory agencies to identify any fiduciary violation of such a management.

Thus, the broader freedom enjoyed by the target company due to the lack of such specified requirements creates a greater potential for abuse in that the company might deliberately misstate or omit nonpublic information to the detriment of the interests of public shareholders or to the detriment of the success of a desirable takeover bid. Hence, it would be appropriate to design a form in which a target company would be obligated to include specific information, either favorable or unfavorable, that might materially affect the judgement of shareholders in determining whether to accept or reject the offer, unless there exists some strong corporate reason to justify nondisclosure. It also would be advisable to require the management to submit relevant documents and materials, including a copy of the board's minutes, upon which the recommendation and the reasons therefor are based.

Second, the present rule contains a significant loophole in that it imposes the obligation to file a statement on the target company alone. Any other person who is controlling, controlled by, or under common control with a target company is exempted from the rule unless such a person represents the target company or is deemed to be the target company itself. Exemption of such a person from the rule is a significant loophole, which should be closed urgently.

Third, another drawback arises in that a target company must file a statement with the SAC before communicating with its shareholders. This requirement puts the target company at a disadvantage timewise, especially when a bid is secretly made by a hidden raider. Furthermore, if a bidder commences the tender offer at an attractive price under the condition that the desired number of shares will be accepted only for a short period of time on the first-come, first-served basis, and that no withdrawal right will be available for shareholders who tender their shares, many public shareholders might be induced to make a hasty decision to tender their shares without waiting for any recommendation from their management. Clearly, it is inconsistent with the basic purpose of the SEA to encourage public shareholders to make a decision without a reasonable opportunity to weigh alternatives. In order to mitigate such a disadvantage, the rules in the United States exempt from the requirement of filing a statement communication to the shareholders which does no more than identify the tender offeror and state that management is studying the matter, and will, on or before a specific date, make the recommendations to shareholders, and request them to defer making a decision until they receive management's recommendation.[69] There is a strong need for such exemption in Korea where the statutes do not cover pro rata acceptances, withdrawal rights, and best price guarantees.

Finally, a dispute may arise as to whether the target company must file an amended statement whenever any material change occurs in the facts as set forth in the statement that has already been sent to its shareholders. One may argue that the target company must file an amendment to reflect such a material change becuase the change constitutes a material omission or misstatement of a fact which is misleading. But, the text of the provision appears only to prohibit any material omission or misstatement of a fact made at the time of the filing of the statement. In order to avoid disputes and to insure full disclosure, the legislature should have inserted a separate provision requiring the target company to reflect the material changes that have occurred after the initial communication has been made.

2. Anti-Fraud Regulations

a. Lack of a General Anti-Fraud Provision

The last sentence of Article 13 of the Presidential Decree prohibits

---

69. *See* SEC Rule 14 d–2(f), 17 C.F.R. §240, 14d–2(f).

"a target company, in communicating with its shareholders, from making any material omission of a fact or misstatement which is misleading." The application of this provision is restricted to any material misrepresentation by a target company while communicating with its shareholders. Except for this one provision, the SEA and the Decrees thereunder nowhere provide any other anti-fraud provisions like Section 14(2) or 10(b) of the Exchange Act and Rule 10 b-5 thereunder in the United States, which broadly prohibit any fraudulent, manipulative, or deceptive acts and practices in connection with a tender offer or sale or purchase of a security.[70]

Therefore, the use of the various defensive or offensive maneuvers in Korea is subject to only the jurisdiction of civil and criminal laws, which is similar to regulation at the state level in the United States. This regulation includes mainly fraud doctrines in civil and criminal laws and fiduciary duty doctrines applicable to the management of companies under the Commercial Code.[71]

b. Regulatory Loopholes

The final sentence of Presidential Decree's Article 13 is, as noted above, the only provision dealing with fraud in connection with tender offers. However, the provision encompasses only a very limited area of fraud. It prohibits a target company, in making recommendation to the shareholders, from making "any material omission of a fact or misstatement which is misleading under the circumstances." The provision neglects any other fraudulent acts, practices, or devices used by a target company, and any misrepresentations or other fraudulent acts, practices or devices made by an offeror or other

---

70. *See Securities Exchange Act of 1934*, Secs. 10(b), 14(e), 15 U.S.C.A. §78j(b), n(e), and SEC Rule 10 b-5, 17 C.F.R. §240. 10b-5. Section 14(e) specifically prohibits in connection with any tender offer any misstatement or omission of a material fact, and any fraudulent, deceptive or manipulative acts or practices by any person in opposition to or in favor of such offer. Unlike Section 10(b), this subsection is automatically operative and does not depend upon rules adopted under it by the SEC to become effective. For Section 10(b) and Rule 10b-5, *see* pp. 380-86 *infra*.

71. For fraud doctrine in civil and criminal laws, *see* note 160, Ch.7 *supra* and its accompanying text. The directors and officers of a company in Korea, as in the United States, owe duties of care and loyalty to their company and shareholders, although the extent of the duties are not clearly defined or interpreted. *See Commercial Code*, Arts. 399, 415, 414, 382.

person in connection with the tender offer.[72] This failure to include a general anti-fraud provision appears to be a significant loophole, which should be closed as soon as possible. Inclusion of such a general anti-fraud provision in the SEA under special torts is of significance because establishing a case of fraud is usually beyond competence of a party under the civil and criminal laws.

Second, the SEA and the Decrees thereunder nowhere mention any civil and criminal remedies for any misrepresentation made by a target company in violation of Article 13 of the Presidential Decree. This raises the significant question of whether a bidder or shareholder of the target company has standing to sue under Article 13 for either an injunction against or compensation from the target company. In order to protect public investors and insure fairness in a contested offer, the legislature should have provided all the parties injured with a standing to sue for any misrepresentation or fraudulent, manipulative, or deceptive acts and practices. Also, it would be appropriate to insert a provision imposing a strict criminal sanctions which are at least equivalent to those for fraud in criminal law.

Third, another significant loophole in Article 13 is the failure to impose an affirmative duty on a target company and its insiders to disclose material, nonpublic information, regardless of whether the target company makes a recommendation to its shareholders after filing a copy of the statement. Hence, when the target company is silent on the offer, it need not disclose any material, nonpublic information in connection with the tender offer. Corporate insiders, officers and controlling shareholders of a target company do not owe such an affirmative duty of disclosure under Article 13, because they are not required to file a statement. Even when they tender the securities of a target company, they are not required to disclose this to public shareholders. Apart from the murky fiduciary duties owed under the Commercial Code, a target company and its insiders should be required under the SEA affirmatively to disclose any material

---

72. Although Article 209, item 4 of the SEA provides criminal sanctions for any violation of Article 21, the legislative intent appears to prohibit a bidder from effecting his tender offer in violation of statutory procedures, including filing statements, giving public notices, etc. *See SEA*, Arts. 209, item 4, 21; *KSE*, *Comment on Amended Securities Exchange Act in Stock* (No. 103, Mar., 1977) at 13, 19.

information to its shareholders. In order to enforce this duty effectively, it would be necessary and appropriate to define expressly the term "materiality" of information.[73] On the other hand, profit projections or generally optimistic statements about earnings should be prohibited as such statements tend to mislead investment decisions.

Section II. *Proxy Solicitations*

I. Introduction

Because stockholders of large publicly-held corporations do not get together physically to elect directors or vote on the matters of mutual concern, a surrogate mechanism was needed to allow all stockholders to be represented at corporations' annual meetings. The proxy vote process fills that need. Like state corporation laws in the United States, the Korean Commercial Code enables stockholders to designate other persons to act as their agents at such meetings.[74] However, because of a lack of any law governing the proxy solicitation process prior to 1976, shareholders as well as management were able to solicit proxies without any limitations. They could also use the proxies for a variety of questionable purposes.

The 1976 Amendments to the SEA[75] included provisions regulating proxy solicitations for the first time. It appears from the legislative history that the legislature adopted such provisions in order to attain two major purposes. First, such provisions were aimed at preventing possible abuses inherent in the proxy solicitation process by requiring any proxy solicitor adequately to disclose relevant information to public stockholders. Second, the provisions were intended to preserve existing control by granting management a mechanism of proxy so-

---

73. In the United States, the term "material," when used to qualify a requirement for the furnishing of information as to any subject, limits the information required to those matters in which an average prudent investor ought reasonably to be informed before buying or selling the security registered. *See* Rule 12b–2, 17 C.F.R. §240, 12b–2.

74. *Commercial Code,* Art. 368(3). A proxy-holder at a general shareholders meeting must file a written statement establishing his power of representation.

75. The legislature passed far-reaching Amendments to the SEA in 1976 (Law No. 2920 as amended on December 22, 1976), For the details of the 1976 Amendments, *see* pp. 102, *et. seq.*

licitation that would aid in discouraging takeover attempts.[76]

Article 199 of SEA provides that no person may solicit proxies from the stockholders unless he does so in compliance with the provisions of the Presidential Decree thereunder.[77] Article 85 of a Presidential Decree under the SEA in turn requires any solicitor of proxies to file copies of certain proxy statements with the SSB prior to or at the same time as the solicitation.[78] It also empowered the SAC to adopt rules as to the scope of information to be included in the proxy statement.[79] However, the present proxy regulation has some drawbacks and deficiencies as will be discussed below.

II. Statutory Proxy Rules
A. *The Coverage of Proxy Rules*

As do the Japanese rules, the proxy rules in Korea apply only to solicitations directed towards holders of listed stocks.[80] Solicitations directed towards holders of registered corporations' stocks are not covered by the rule. The term "solicitation" is not defined in the statute, but the text of Article 199 of the SEA limits the coverage of the rule to solicitation by any person who seeks execution of a proxy

---

76. *See*, in general, Dong-A Daily Newspaper, note 75, *supra;* for the second purpose, in particular, *see* Draft Committee for the 1976 Amendments of Securities Laws, *Basic Outline of Draft Amendments of Securities Laws,* Draft No. 60–200 (1976) at 10; *see also* Hyundae Economic Newspaper (*Hyundae Kyungje Ilbo*), July 31, 1976, at p. 1. It was reported that to further management control, the draft rule prohibited brokers and other securities institutions from soliciting proxies from beneficial owners of stock held in the street name. Shares held in the street name whose voting rights could, if directed by proxies, be exercised consist of those temporarily held by securities companies (brokerage houses), the clearing company, the Korean Securities Finance Corporation (*KSFC*), and financial institutions. *For details, see* Section II E *infra*.
77. Article 199 of the SEA reads:
   "It shall be unlawful for any person, in contravention of such provisions as a Presidential Decree may prescribe, to solicit for him or on behalf of any other person any proxy or authorization in respect of any security listed on the Exchange."
78. Presidential Decree No. 8436, as amended February 9, 1977. For the SSB. *see* note 79, *infra*.
79. Pursuant to the mandate, the SAC, on March 23, 1977, adopted its Rule on Proxy Solicitation (hereinafter *"SAC Rule on Proxy Solicitation"*)
80. *SEA*, Art. 199, *Cf. Japanese SEA*, Art. 194.

for himself or on behalf of other person. The legislature should have explicitly defined the term "solicitation" so that the rules would equally apply to any communication or request to revoke or withdraw a proxy, as the rules do in the United States.[81]

On the other hand, the proxy rules do not grant any exemptions. It is advisable to provide some exemptions for the cases in which enforcement of the proxy rules is neither in the public interest nor necessary for the protection of investors. Such exemptions, like those in the United States and Japan, could include: (a) solicitations made otherwise than on behalf of the management of the issuer where the total number of persons solicited is relatively small; (b) solicitations by a person in respect to securities of which he is the beneficial owner; (c) solicitations involved in a public offering or secondary distribution that is in compliance with the registration requirement; and (d) solicitations through the medium of a newspaper advertisement which informs security holders as to where they may obtain copies of a proxy statement, forms of proxy or any other soliciting material, and which does no more than name the issuer, state the reason for the advertisement and identify the proposals to be acted upon by security holders.[82] Though Article 4 of the SAC Rule on Proxy Solicitation exempts certain information which has been publicly released through newspapers from the requirements of a proxy statement un-

---

81. *See* United States Securities and Exchange Commission Rule under the Securities Exchange Act of 1934 (hereinafter "SEC Rule") 14a–1, 17 C.F.R. §240. 14a–1. The terms "solicit" and "solicitation" are defined by the SEC Rule to include:
   1) any request for a proxy whether or not accompanied by or included in a form of proxy;
   2) any request to execute or not to execute, or to revoke, a proxy; or
   3) the furnishing of a form of proxy or other communication to security holders under circumstances reasonably calculated to result in the procurement, withholding or revocation of a proxy.
   The terms do not apply, however, to the furnishing of a form of proxy to a security holder upon the unsolicited request of such security holder, the performance by the issuer of acts required by Rule 14a–7, or the performance by any person of ministerial acts on behalf of a person soliciting a proxy.
82. *See id.,* 14a–2; *also see Japanese Cabinet Order concerning the Proxy Solicitation of Listed Stock,* Art. 9. The Japanese Cabinet Order, unlike the U.S. counterpart, exempts only items a), b), and d) in the text.

der certain conditions, this does not waive the rules of the proxy statement but merely permits specific omissions from the statement.[83]

B. *The Form of Proxy*

Article 85 (2) of the Presidential Decree, like the Japanese rule,
requires that the form of proxy include a box-type ballot so as to
permit the security holder to choose between approving or disappro-
ving each matter that is to be acted upon.[84] Except for this one requirement, there is no other rule that designates the form of proxy, or
limits the amount of authority to be conferred.

Because of such simple requirements, significant disputes may arise
as to whether any unmarked proxies can be voted, or as to whether
authority can be conferred in absentia with respect to unanticipated
matters that may arise during the meeting. In the United States,
these problems are resolved by the SEC Rule. A proxy may confer
discretionary authority with respect to matters in which a security
holder does not specify a choice only if the form of proxy states in
boldface type how it intends to vote on each question.[85] Also, the rule
grants a proxy discretionary authority only with respect to some
specific matters, including unanticipated matters or matters incident
to the conduct of the meeting.[86] Though management can gain an
unfair advantage from stockholder inertia, adoption of such a rule
has its merits as noted by Professor Loss.[87] For instance, it is impossible to obtain the favorable vote of a majority or quorum of outstanding shares where speedy action is desired. Also, stockholders who in-
advertently fail to mark their ballots but evidence a pro-management
position by the very fact that they sign and return proxies to the

---

83. *See SAC Rule on Proxy Solicitation*, Art. 4.
84. *Cf. Japanese Cabinet Order, supra,* note 82, Art. 3. Article 2 of the SAC Rule on
Proxy Solicitation provides the same requirement as to the form of proxy.
In the United States, the rule gives special treatment as far as elections are
concerned, since there is no point in merely voting against a slate: if a security
holder does not like the nominees, he can either give his proxy to the opposition, if any, or simply not vote; but the authority must not be conferred to
vote any person into any office for which a *bona fide* nominee is not named in
the proxy statement. *See* SEC Rule 14a–4(b), (d), 17 C.F.R. §24;. 14a–4
(b), (d); 2 Louis Loss, *Securities Regulation,* 881 (2d ed. 1961).
85. SEC Rule 14a–4(b), 17 C.F.R. §240. 14a–4 (b).
86. *Id.,* 14a–4(c).
87. *See* Loss, *supra* note 91, Ch.7, at 882 *et. seq.*

management should not be disenfranchised. However, to avoid possible forgery or other abuses by management, it would be advisable to require that the form of proxy be impressed with the "registered seal"[88] of a stockholder and be effectively dated.

C. The Content of Proxy Statement

Article 3 of the SAC's Rule on Proxy Solicitation prescribes the content of the proxy statement required to be filed with the SSB when proxy solicitations are sent out. Information required in the proxy statement may be classified into two categories, *i.e.,* general information which is required regardless of the type of action to be taken, and specific information which is required in connection with a certain type of action.[89]

1. General Information

Information to be generally stated in the proxy statement consists of: (a) the names of the solicitor, persons solicited, and the person on whose behalf the solicitation is being made, and the kind and number of shares directly or indirectly held by "the person" who solicits or on whose behalf the solicitation is being made;[90] and (b) the relationship between the issuer and the solicitor or person on whose behalf the solicitation is being made. Identification of the person is not always possible under a rule which requires the disclosure of name only. Being modeled after the Japanese provision, the general information provision does not classify the solicitor in regards as to whether he is the issuer, its officer or some other person.[91]

---

88. The "registered seal" of a person is a device peculiar to Korea designed to prevent any forgery of a legal document and to lighten the burden of proving the effectiveness of a contract or agreement entered into. By requiring any person giving proxy to press the "registered seal" at the bottom of the signature with a copy of the certificate of such registered seal, the risk of abuses by management may largely be reduced.

89. *See SAC Rule on Proxy Solicitation,* Art. 3. Items 1 and 2 deal with general information, while item 3 specifies the information to be included in the proxy statement in accordance with the type of action to be taken at the meeting.

90. *Id.,* item 1. Though the text is not clear as to the coverage of the term "the person," the writer interprets it to cover a person who solicits or on whose behalf the solicitation is being made.

91. *See Japanese Cabinet Order on Proxy Solicitation,* Art. 2, items 1 and 2. In Japan, the rule requires full disclosure of the identity (name and address) and substantial interests, including beneficial ownership held, if the solicitation is not being made by or on behalf of the management.

The rule of general information has some drawbacks. First, the rule fails to require a solicitor to state the names of the persons who bear or will bear the cost of solicitation. Since the question as to who should bear the expenses for solicitation is frequently a legal issue, particularly in a contested solicitation for control, the legislature should have inserted an adequate provision as was done in the United States.[92]

Second, the rule requires a solicitor to disclose shareholdings held by him or other persons on whose behalf the solicitation is being made or any relationship between such persons and the issuer. However, the rule fails to require information on any possibly conflicting, or other substantial interests that a solicitor or certain related persons may have in the matters to be acted upon. The provision on specific information requires disclosure of any substantial interests only in the case of elections of officers or transfers of business. Since such information is material to the investor public in every shareholder action, the legislature should have generally required the disclosure of any substantial interests in the proxy statement.[93]

2. The Specific Information Required

Article 3, item 3, of the SAC Rule includes ten sub-items which specify the information that is required to be contained in the proxy statement in connection with certain types of action. Sub-item 1 deals with election of directors and auditors. The information required

---

92. *See* SEC Schedule 14A item 3 (a) (4) and (b) (5); *also see* note 97, *infra*. The SEC rules in the United States require the proxy statement filed to include specific information regarding the names of persons by whom the cost of solicitation has been or will be borne, directly or indirectly. An additional requirement is provided with respect to Rule 14a–11 solicitation involving election contests; if such cost is to be borne initially by any person other than the issuer, it must be stated whether reimbursement will be sought from the issuer, and, if so, whether the question of such reimbursement will be submitted to a vote of security holders. In addition, with respect to solicitations involving election contests, costs and expenditures within the meaning of the foregoing provisions include fees for attorneys, accountants, public relations or financing advisors, solicitors, advertising, printing, transportation, litigation and other costs incidental to the solicitation.

93. The SEC in the United States generally requires disclosure of such information. The coverage of related persons are separately specified in accordance with whether the solicitation is being made on behalf of the management, or whether the solicitation concerns election contests. For details, *see id.*, item 4.

includes the identity, business experience, and shareholdings of the nominee and any substantial interest he may have, other than shareholdings, in the issuer.[94]

Sub-items 2 through 10 relate to proposals of various other types. These include actions with respect to removal of officers, amendments of articles of incorporation, declarations of dividends, mergers or consolidations, transfers of business, increase or reduction of capital, and public offerings.[95] Financial statements are only required to be disclosed in the cases of certain actions, and this creates significant deficiencies in disclosure.

In order to insure that the public shareholders receive a fair payment during the issuance, modification or exchange of securities, the shareholders should have access to valuation data which accurately reflects the financial position and operations of both the issuer and any other company that is acquired by or merged with the issuer. However, the present rule does not meet such a purpose. Financial statements certified by qualified public accountants are required only if the action is with respect to the declaration of dividends. If action to be taken is in respect to a merger or consolidation, balance sheets and profit-loss statements of the companies for the latest fiscal year are required, but certification by an independent CPA firm is not required. In addition, no financial statement is required when the action to be taken is in respect to stock dividends paid from the coversion of reserved surplus,reduction of capital, or transfer of business. Furthermore, there is no disclosure requirement when the action to be taken is in respect to acquisition of all or a material part of the business of another company, through a fair disclosure under such circumstances is of critical importance to public shareholders.

D. *The Lack of Equalization*

As noted by Professor Loss,[96] a major problem in any system of proxy regulation is the practical equalization of the rights of both management and any dissident security holders. In this context the SEC rules in the United States approach this problem in three ways; (a) by assuring access to fellow security holders; (b) by imposing spe-

---

94. *SAC Rule on Proxy Solicitation,* Art. 3, item 3 (i).

95. *Id.,* Art. 3, item 3 (ii) through (x). *Cf., Japanese Cabinet Order on Proxy Solicitation,* Art. 2, items 4 through 10.

96. Loss, *supra* note 91, Ch.7, at 889.

cial requirements on all participants in contested elections; and (c) by opening the management's own proxy statement to legitimate proposals of security holders.[97]

Leaving the physical disclosure of security holder lists to state law, SEC Rule 14a-7 side-steps all the state-law problems of proper motive by giving management a choice. If management intends to make any solicitations subject to the proxy rules, it must either (1) furnish a reasonably current "shareholder list" upon the written request of any security holder entitled to vote on the matter, or (2) mail his proxy material for him, in either event at his expense.[98] In addition, Rule 14a-11, which applies only to solicitations involving contests for the election or removal of directors, requires every "participant" in such a solicitation to file with the SEC and stock exchanges a statement containing the information specified by Schedule 14B.[99] The SEC's attempt to be as neutral as possible, while at the same time assuring itself of the desired information at the earliest practical time, has produced a fairly complex provision on filing dates.[100] Either side in an election proxy fight may solicit prior to furnishing a proxy statement, but only under certain conditions.[101] Finally, 14a-8 offers

---

97. *Id.*, at 889–915: *also see* SEC Rules 14a–7, 8, 11 and Schedule 14B. 17 C.F.R. §§240. 14a–7 *et seq.* Rule 14a–8 dealing with shareholder proposals was extensively amended in November of 1976. For a detailed review of this amendment, especially its purposes and costs, *see* C.D. Schwartz & E.J. Weiss, *An Assessment of the SEC Shareholder Proposal Rule,* 65 GEO. L.J. 635 (1977).

98. The requirement is clearly in the "alternative." The security holder has no right to a list; and conversely, if the management elects to give him a list, he has no right to demand that the management do anything else for him under the rule. In most cases the mangement prefers the mailing alternative. *See* Loss, *supra* note 91, Ch.7, at 890–92.

99. SEC Rule 14a–11, 17 C.F.R. §240, 14a–11. Since this filing requirement makes the coverage of "participant" crucial, Rule 14a–11 (b) broadly defines that term. For the information required, *see* Schedule 14B.

100. Rule 14a–11 (c). A schedule for every non-management participant must be filed five business days before he solicits. For details of filing dates and amendments to statements, *see* the Rule; *also see* Loss, *supra* note 91, Ch.7, at 898–99.

101. SEC Rule 14a–11 (d) and (e). The conditions required, *inter alia,* are:
    1) schedule 14B must have been filed for each participant;
    2) no form of proxy may precede the proxy statement; and
    3) each communication must include at least the identity of each partici-

another procedure to security holders who are not willing or able to bear the expense of solicitation. It requires the management to include in its own proxy statement proposals by security holders entitled to vote at the meeting, if the action to be taken is not with respect to election.[102]

The proxy rule in Korea, being substantially modeled after the Japanese rule, does not include any of the foregoing devices designed to place opposing public shareholders on equal footing with management. Since the opposition shareholders' access to the shareholder list is left to the discretion of the management under the Commercial Code, any proxy solicitation in opposition to the management is in practice almost impossible to be carried out. In addition, because of the lack of a device imposing on the management the requirement of a mailing alternative or inclusion of shareholder proposals, public shareholders in Korea are excluded from forming any practical opposition through the proxy mechanism. Resultant advantages to incumbent management may be the result of legislative intent aimed at achieving further decentralization of equity ownership by diminishing fears of losing control and by rendering challenges to management impossible.

However, the present regulation of proxy solicitation leans towards the overprotection of management. Management enjoys every advantage. It possesses the current shareholder list. It has the overwhelming strategic advantage of access to the corporate treasury for the substantial costs of solicitation. It also gains from shareholder inertia. At such disadvantage, insurgent groups would be showing temerity to wage a proxy fight.

If the basic philosophy behind proxy rules is to further fair corporate suffrage and to promote public and shareholder interests, the present rule is improperly drawn. Under the present rule, even an incompetent management could perpetuate its control by using the proxy mechanism, so long as the company remains a going concern. As a matter of public policy, the operations of management should

---

pant, his principal occupation, and the amount of shareholdings, including beneficial ownership.

102. For details of the procedure and assessment of the rule, *see* Rule 14a-8; *also see* Schwartz & Weiss, *supra* note 97, at n. 17.

always be subject to surveillance by public shareholders, who should be able to remove an incompetent management. Efficient surveillance can be attained by the implementation of shareholder democracy through rules of fair participation in corporate governance by shareholders. Through implementation of rules furthering such shareholder democracy, the goal of capital formation can also be facilitated because the public in general will have more confidence in their investments. Therefore, the legislature should have moved more boldly in designing a program to implement shareholder democracy.

E. Securities Held in the Street Name

Although there are no available statistics, the amount of securities held in street names is substantial in Korea. Such securities may consist of those held in the margin accounts of broker-dealers, held as collateral in the accounts of the financial institutions, the KSFC or other persons, or in the names of nominees and various other kinds of fiduciaries. Such stock temporarily held by another creates significant questions revolving around the split of legal and beneficial ownership of shares. It also creates a substantial problem when proxies are solicited, because management knows only the holders of record.

In the United States, Section 14(b) of the Exchange Act gave the SEC a broad power to adopt rules regulating any activity by any member of an exchange or any broker or dealer to give a proxy in respect to securities carried for the account of a customer. The SEC has, however, left this problem to the exchanges to handle. The rules of the New York Stock Exchange (NYSE) require its members, with the proxy solicitor's reimbursement for out-of-pocket expenses, to transmit copies of proxy material they receive to all beneficial owners within the United States.[103] In addition, the members must be subject to additional requirements or restrictions in granting proxies as prescribed by their Exchange.[104]

The SEA and Decrees or Rules thereunder provide no phrase regulating the proxy solicitation process with respect to stock held in the street name. But,the Draft Committee for the 1976 Amendments

---

103. NYSE Rule 451 (a), CCH   2451.
104. *Id.*, 451 (b), 450, and 452. CCH   2450, 2452, The American Stock Exchange (AMEX) and other national exchanges adopted rules which are similar to those of the NYSE. *See* Loss, *supra* note 91, Ch.7, at 926–40.

included in its Basic Outline a clause that prohibits voting by proxy with respect to such a category of stock.[105] The purpose of such a prohibition was to discourage would-be take-overs through the use of proxies from such stock, and to prevent possible abuses through the influence of securities companies or other financial institutions. However, the enforcement of such prohibition is in practice questionable since the identification of the owners of the stock would be almost impossible at the meeting. In addition, the prohibition deprives shareholders of their right to vote by proxy as granted by the Commercial Code. Furthermore, shareholders should be given an access to the proxy statement in order to know the operation and financial position of their company. Therefore, it would be appropriate for the authority to allow voting by proxy to the beneficial holders of securities held in the street name, while confining itself to regulating possible abuses inherent in the process of soliciting and authorizing such proxies.

III. Enforcement of the Proxy Rules
A. Fair and Full Disclosure
Article 85(4) of the Presidential Decree prohibits:

> "any solicitor from effecting solicitation by means of any proxy statement, form of proxy, or other document which contains any (a) false statement of a fact, (b) misstatement which is false or misleading with respect to any material matter, or (c) omission to state any material matter necessary in order to make the statement therein not false or misleading."[106]

Any violation of this provision is subject to a criminal sanction of fine or imprisonment, or both.[107] Prohibiting such misstatements or omissions in connection with proxy solicitation, the legislature failed to consider how to effectively enforce fair and full disclosure and to provide civil remedies for any violation of the rule. No case has yet been brought to clarify the issue. Therefore, the author approaches the problem by analyzing the relevant provisions of the statutes to identify some possible enforcement techniques and regulatory drawbacks.

---

105. *See* note 76, *supra.*
106. *See Presidential Decree under the SEA,* Art. 85 (4).
107. *SEA,* Arts. 199, 209, item 9, 214 and 215.

Article 85(3) of the Presidential Decree requires any solicitor to file the proxy form and proxy statement with the SSB prior to or at the same time as his solicitation. Except for this requirement, the statute is silent on the administrative review, examination, and amendment requirements that are similar to those required in the case of registration for public distribution or tender solicitation in order to have any misstatement or omission of a material fact corrected.[108] Though there is no explicit phrase, the solicitor may voluntarily file an amendment to the proxy statement to correct any misstatement or omission or to reflect any material change in the facts set forth in the statement. However, in order to compel fair and full disclosure the legislature should have provided at least for an examination procedure, a reasonable waiting period and a correction requirement.

Second, the proxy rules offer no specific guidelines for fair and full disclosure. In practice, most solicitors would frequently disagree with the SSB as to what, depending upon particular facts and circumstances, may be misleading or material within the meaning of Article 85 (4). In this respect, the SEC Rule 14 a-9(b) in the United States enumerates some examples of misleading statements under a note. The examples include: (1) predictions as to specific future market values or dividends; and (2) material which directly or indirectly impugns character, integrity or personal reputation, or makes charges concerning improper, illegal or immoral conduct or associations, without factual foundation.[109] Because securities laws in Korea are in a developing stage and most participants in the securities markets are not familiar with disclosure standards, introduction of such specific guidelines would be an important step moving toward fair and full disclosure.

B. Remedies Available and Problems Raised

When a defective proxy statement is circulated, the corporation or individual shareholders may sustain a variety of injuries. They may be injured if a statement is employed to conceal waste of corporate assets or to mask self-dealing by the directors. The most ob-

---

108. *Cf. SEA*, Arts. 11 and 21(4). In the United States, there is no administrative proceeding comparable to the stop order proceeding under the Securities Act of 1933, though proxy statements filed are subject to examination and amendment to correct misstatements or omissions.

109. *See* SEC Rule 14a–9 (b), 17 C.F.R. §240, 14a–9 (b).

vious harm occurs when the terms of a given transaction, for example, the provisions relating to the exchange ratio in a merger contract, decrease the value of the shareholders holdings.[110] In order to implement the goals of the proxy rule, *i.e.*, insuring fair corporate suffrage and protecting investors, such injury should be effectively prevented or civil recovery should be allowed. Therefore, it is essential to identify some remedies available under the present law and the accompanying drawbacks, if any.

1. Non-Monetary Relief

Unlike the SEC in the United States, the SAC was not granted a power under the SEA to institute an action for injunctive relief for any violation of the SEA, Decrees and Rules thereunder.[111] A criminal sanction is the only remedy available for proxy violation under the SEA. But the SAC itself does not have a power to prosecute criminally nor does it have a legal obligation to recommend criminal prosecution when it discovers any violation through inspection. Such a lack of enforcement power and legal obligation to effect criminal prosecution is a severe drawback and must be remedied.

Under this regulatory framework, the seeking of non-monetary relief is left to actions by private parties. An important remedy may be found in the Commercial Code, though a question remains as to applicability. Article 376(1) of the Commercial Code provides that any shareholder or director may bring an action to rescind a passed resolution, if; (a) the meeting has been held in contravention of the "procedure" provided in the law, decree or articles of incorporation,

---

110. For a detailed discussion of types of injury, *see* Note, *Causation and Liability in Private Actions for Proxy Violations*, 80 YALE L.J. 107, 115 *et. seq.* (1970).

111. *See SEA*, Arts. 128 and 129. The SEC was given only a power to inspect violations of the securities laws. For the SEC's enforcement power, *see the Securities Exchange Act of 1934*, Sec. 21 (e), 15 U.S.C.A. §78 u, (e). The SEC has no express statutory authority to seek rescission, restitution or other forms of equitable monetary relief. However, it may institute an action for injunctive relief and, once the equity jurisdiction of the federal district court has been properly invoked, the court has power to grant all equitable relief necessary under the circumstances. And Section 27 of the Exchange Act confers exclusive jurisidiction on the federal courts to hear "all suits in equity. . . brought to enforce any liability or duty" created by the Act. For the discussion of the SEC enforcement actions, *see* Comment, *Equitable Remedies in SEC Enforcement Actions*, 123 U.PA. L. REV. 1188 (1975).

or held by a significantly unfair means; or the resolution has been adopted by a "means" which is in contravention of the law, decree, or articles of incorporation, or which is significantly unfair. The former category of causes relate to a procedural defect such as a failure to give the "call notice" (notice of a shareholders meeting), effective call notice in terms of content or statutory time limitations, or a meeting held at a distant place in volation of the articles of incorporation.[112] The latter category of causes on the other hand, relate to a substantial defect such as a vote by a person interested in the action, a failure to meet voting requirements, or an adoption of a resolution through blackmail or any extortionate means.

There is a question of whether the solicitation through a defective proxy statement may constitute a statutory basis for an action brought to set aside a resolution adopted at the meeting. This is because proxy solicitation is not a procedure that is statutorily required prior to convening every meeting, and thus is different from the call notice which is a prerequisite to convening every meeting under the Commercial Code. No decisional law can be found on the matter because the proxy rule has only recently been adopted. It seems, however, that a defective proxy statement may have even a greater impact than a defective call notice does. In addition, the Commercial Code includes as grounds for rescission of the resolution a meeting held by a significantly unfair means as well as that held in violation of statutory procedures. Therefore, it could be strongly argued that shareholders have standing to sue for any defective proxy statement as far as the defect in question is material under the circumstances.

Another important remedy would be to allow for an action to enjoin the meeting from being held or to enjoin the execution of the adopted resolution. However, the Commercial Code contains no general clause indicating whether or not shareholders may seek such injunctive relief, and leaves the question to the general rules on injunctions in the Code of Civil Procedure. Under this Code, injunctive relief is granted when it appears that otherwise the plaintiff would sustain irreparable injury or an injury for which recovery would be significantly difficult under the circumstances.[113]

---

112. *See* I Hi Chul Chung, *Commentary on Commercial Laws*, 375–78 (rev. ed. 1972).
113. *See Code of Civil Procedure*, Art. 714 (Law No. 547, promulgated on April 4, 1960, as amended by Law No. 1499 on December 14, 1963).

However, the Commercial Code makes two specific types of injunctive relief available for shareholders. One is that when a director commits any illegal act in contravention of the law, decree or articles of incorporation, and that act appears to cause irreparable damage to the company, a 5% shareholder may bring a derivative suit to enjoin the act.[114] But the 5% shareholder restriction on standing to sue is an impractical and difficult hurdle for individual shareholders. The 5% shareholder restriction on standing to sue, intended to deter a possible flood of lawsuits, means that an individual shareholder cannot attack any illegal or unfair conduct by the incumbent management unless he represents 5% of the total number of shares outstanding. This restriction being in practice so significant a hurdle, must be relaxed or eliminated for the protection of minority interests. The purpose in deterring a possible flood of lawsuits brought in bad faith could be met to a considerable degree by a provision which requires the plaintiffs in such actions to post a reasonable amount of bond as security if there appears to be any degree of bad faith.[115]

The other injunctive relief is a special type available only to plaintiffs in an action brought to remove a director who was illegally elected, or unjustifiably kept in office at the shareholders meeting.[116] The court, upon receipt of the allegation to that effect by the plaintiffs, may enjoin the discharging of duties by such director and appoint an acting director until the final disposition of the case. Since the applicability of these special reliefs is very limited, shareholders would in most cases have no alternative but resort to the general rules of injunction in the Code of Civil Procedure.

---

114. *Commercial Code*, Art. 402.
115. Article 403 (5) of the Commercial Code allows a court in a derivative suit for damages to order the plaintiffs to deposit a certain amount of security if defendants show bad faith on the part of plaintiffs. It is advisable to apply this security requirement to a suit for injunctive relief, in replacement of the 5% shareholder restriction.
116. *Id.*, Arts. 407, 408, 385, and 380. An individual shareholder may bring an action to remove any directors who have been illegally elected by asking a court of competent jurisdiction to declare null and void the resolution or to rescind the resolution. Also, a 5% shareholder may, within one month after the meeting which unjustifiably rejected a proposal to remove the directors charged with illegal conduct, bring an action against the company and the directors as joint defendants for removal.

2. Monetary Relief

Though Article 85(4) of the Presidential Decree prohibits material misstatements or omissions in connection with the proxy solicitations, it is silent on a private right of action for the recovery of damages incurred by such misrepresentations. It can be argued that any person who was injured may have standing to sue for recovery under this statute because the provision deals with frauds committed during the proxy solicitation process. But such an argument would encounter significant difficulties because of other provisions in the SEA which expressly create private rights of action for defective public distributions of securities, manipulations, and insiders' short-swing trading.[117]

In the United States, the private right of action for violation of Section 14 (a) of the Exchange Act and Rule 14a-9 thereunder was judicially recognized without any explicit reference to such a right in *J.I. Case Co. v. Borak*.[118] In this case, the court relied on the legislative intent expressed both in the history and in the language of Section 14(a).[119] In Korea, no documented legislative intent is available to clarify the matter, nor did the provisions include language similar to that of Section 14(a). Absent any indication, it may be reasonable to construe the statute to mean that civil remedies for violation of the proxy rule are left to the fraud doctrine in civil law and to provisions of a similar nature provided in the Commercial Code.[120] Even

---

117. *SEA*, Arts. 14–16, 106, 118, and 197.

118. 377 U.S. 426 (1964).

119. *Id.*, at 431–32, quoting H.R. Rep. No. 1383, 73d Cong., 2d. Sess. 14 (1934) and the language "as necessary or appropriate in the interest or for the protection of investors" expressed in Section 14 (a).

120. *See Civil Code* (Law No. 471, promulgated on February 22, 1958), Arts. 750, 760; *Criminal Code* (Law No. 239, promulgated on September 18, 1853), Arts. 347–48, 352. To constitute a fraud case under civil or criminal law, the following requirements must be established: (1) a misrepresentation of a material fact or failure to state it; or an employment of any fraudulent or deceptive acts, devices, or contrivances; (2) *scienter* or willfulness; (3) an intention to induce the plaintiff to act or to refrain from action in reliance upon the misrepresentation; (4) justifiable reliance upon the misrepresentation on the part of the plaintiff; and (5) damages resulting from such reliance (in civil cases only).

In addition to the remedy available under the statute above, shareholders may arguably have direct standing to sue directors under Article 401 of the Commercial Code in order to recover damages sustained. This Article pro-

though interpreted otherwise, this could make little difference unless
a new concept of fraud were created to allow for some flexibility in
effectuating a remedial purpose, as was created in the United States.

Indeed, should a civil law tort standard be applied to a case
brought against the makers of a defective proxy statement, the goals
of the proxy rule, *i.e.,* insuring fair corporate suffrage and protecting
investors, still could not be implemented. This is because the requirements of civil law fraud,[121] *inter alia,* plaintiff's proof of the presence of intent on the part of the solicitor to defraud, a causal relationship between the misstatement and the damage, and reliance by
shareholders of the misstatement, would present insuperable evidentiary bariers to recovery. Thus, the legislature should have included an explicit provision under which a court, with some flexibility, could expand the reach of the civil law fraud doctrine to
accomplish remedial purposes. However, a question arises as to what
extent the evidentiary obstacles implicit in civil law tort actions
should be relaxed to remedy violations of proxy solicitation legislation.

In adopting the United States securities laws, both the Japanese
and the Korean legislatures failed to include the far-reaching anti-
fraud provision of Section 10 (b) of the Securities Exchange Act of
1934 and SEC Rule 10b–5 thereunder.[122] Further, there has been

---

vides that "directors shall be jointly and severally liable for damages sustained by a *third person* due to their intentional or grossly negligent misconduct." (*Emphasis added*). Dealing with directors' liability to third persons, this
Article does not expressly designate a shareholder as a third person, and thus
raises some difficult questions as to the statute's coverage and the characteristics of liability in relation to the civil law concept of a tort. Though not unanimous in their opinions, commentators agree that directors should be held
liable under Article 401 for any damages sustained by a third person because
of the directors' intentional or "grossly" negligent missconduct: that a shareholder should be included in the coverage of the term "third person"; and
furthermore that directors should be held liable under the provisions of civil
law tort for any damages sustained by a third person because of directors'
"simple" negligence. For details, *see* I Chung, *supra* note 112, at 391–92;
also see I Ton K. Suh, *Commentary on Commercial Laws,* 364–66 (9th rev. ed.
1973).

121. *See* note 120 *supra.*

122. *See* 15 U.S.C.A. §78j (b); *also see* 17 C.F.R. §240. 10b–5. Both Japan and
Korea included as a sole insider trading rule the counterparts of American

no private action with respect to defective proxy statements in either Japan or Korea. Therefore, the United States history of private actions in the area would be an invaluable guideline for Korean courts and legislatures as well as administrative agencies in enforcing the rules.

In the United States, the concept of fraud under the securities laws has been judicially expanded far beyond the reach of the common law tort. The federal securities laws are not limited to standards of common law fraud and deceit;[123] and thus they are to be construed "not technically and restrictively, but flexibly to effectuate [their] remedial purposes."[124] The ambit of fraud under Section 14(a) and Rule 14a–9 has been judicially expanded even more broadly in some

---

short-swing profit rules of Section 16 (b) of the Securities Exchange Act, 15 U.S.C.A §78p(b), criticized by a commentator as being the "rule for dummy insiders only" because the reach of this section is very narrow and limited, and smart insiders may easily avoid it. *See SEA,* Art. 188(2); *also see Japanese SEA,* Art. 189; Bromberg, *Disclosure Programs for Publicly Held Companies—A Practical Guide,* 1970 Duke L.J. 1139 (1970). In the United States, Section 10 (b) and Rule 10b–5 have by virtue of their broad coverage of overreachings by insiders played a significant role in implementing the major purposes of securities legislation—adequate remedies as well as fair disclosure. However, it may not be too much emphasized that such failure to introduce a counterpart of American Rule 10b–5 has created a significant loophole both in Japan and Korea, and thus an injured party may not successfully bring a private suit to recover damages. For details of the insider trading rule in Korea, *see* Ch.8 section III *infra.*

123. The elements of common law fraud and deceit in the United States are the same as those in Korea. Under the rule 10b–5 of the federal securities laws, however, the plaintiff for recovery of damages is required to show: (1) misrepresentation or nondisclosure of a fact, or employment of any fraudulent, manipulative, or deceptive act, practice, device or contrivance in connection with purchase or sale of any security; (2) materiality; (3) *scienter or willfulness*; and (4) damages. Privity of contract is not required. With respect to causal relationship, loss causation is in general not required, but transaction causation (reliance by defrauded party on the misrepresentation or violation in question) is required to be shown, though the latter is easily inferred from the materiality of misrepresentation under the circumstances. *Scienter,* the showing of which was abandoned by many courts until recently, also is flexibly proved by circumstantial evidence to meet remedial purposes.

124. *Securities and Exchange Commission v. Capital Gains Research Bureau,* 375 U.S. 180 (1963).

contexts than the reach of Section 10 (b) and Rule 10b-5, which concern fraud in connection with purchase or sale of securities. The *Birnbaum* rule governing the latter is not applicable to the former.[125] More importantly, Section 14(a) does not require *scienter,* which is essential under Section 10 (b) and Rule 10b–5, and thus even negligence or reckless disregard of facts can bring Section 14 (a) into play.[126]

In connection with causal relationship between misstatements or omissions and the effected transactions, the Supreme Court of the United States considers "materiality" for purposes of Sections 10 (b) and 14 (a) to be identical. In *Mills v. Electric Acto-Lite Co.,* the court adopting a materiality test which still remains the guideline on this issue, stated:

> "Where the misstatement or omission in a proxy statement has been shown to be "material", as it was found to be here, *that determination itself indubitably embodies a conclusion that the defect was of such a character that it might have been considered important by a reasonable shareholder whose process of deciding how to vote."*[127] *(Emphasis supplied.)*

---

125. In *Birnbaum v. Newport Steel Corp.,* 193 F. 2d 461 (2d Cir. 1952), the court stated that a person who is neither a purchaser nor a seller of securities may not bring an action under Section 10 (b) and Rule 10b–5. The rule was cited with approval in *Blue Chip Stamps v. Manor Drug Stores,* 421 U.S. 723 (1975). On the other hand, in *Chris-Craft Industries, Inc. v. Bangor Punta Corp.,* 480 F. 2d 341 (2d Cir. 1973) *cert. denied,* 414 U.S. 910 (1973), CCI was granted standing to sue a person making a misleading tender offer or a responsible officer of a corporation making such an offer, and the court said it is a fair inference that a broader standing was intended under Section 14 (e). But, in *Piper v. Chris-Craft Industries, Inc.,* CCH Fed. Sec. L. Rep. 95,864 (Sup. Ct. Feb. 23, 1977), a tender offeror suing in its capacity as a takeover bidder was denied standing to sue for damages under Section 14 (e).

126. *See Gerstle v. Gamble-Skogmo Inc.,* 478 F. 2d 1281 (2d Cir. 1973). The alleged defect there was the failure to disclose the market value of unsold advertising plants at the time of the merger and the intent to realize large profits through the sales of such assets shortly after the merger.

127. 396 U.S. 375, 384 (1970). Plaintiffs in *Mills,* shareholders of Electric Auto-lite Co., sued to set aside a merger of Auto-lite and another company, and sought other appropriate relief for an alleged violation of Section 14 (a). The materiality test adopted by that court embodied three elements: a shareholder; an issue on which the shareholder's vote is solicited; and a proxy statement containing material omissions or misstatements which may be expected to influence the shareholder's vote. *See* Comments, *The Materiali-*

In *Affiliate Ute Citizens v. United States,* the court, citing *Mills* in the context of an alleged Section 10 (b) violation, stated that the test for materiality requires only that "a reasonable investor might have considered [the facts] important in the making of his decision.[128]

However, the materiality test under Section 14 (a) brings about another significant question as to whether a defect must "actually" be material in affecting the entire voting process, as well as important in affecting a single reasonable shareholder who is deciding how to vote, whereas the test of materiality under Section 10 (b) involves only the question of importance to an individual in deciding how to act under the circumstances. Justice Harlan, in the *Mills* case, posited that the defect have a "significant propensity" towards effecting the voting process as found within the express terms of Rule 14a-9, and this requirement adequately serves the purpose of ensuring that a cause of action cannot be established by proof of a defect so trivial, or so unrelated to the transaction for which approval is sought, that the correction of the defect or the imposition of liability would not further the interests protected by Section 14 (a).[129] Furthermore, he concluded that where there was a finding of materiality, causation was sufficiently proved upon showing that the proxy solicitation itself, rather than the particular defects in the solicitation materials, had been an essential link in the accomplishment of the transaction.

This objective test gains significant importance in that it could avoid the impracticalities of determining how many votes were affected. But, Justice Harlan explicitly left open the question of

---

ty *Text-Mills Revisited,* 14 DUKE. L. REV. 723, 727 (1976); Note, *Causation and Liability in Private Actions for Proxy Violations,* 80 YALE L.J. 107 (1970). This materiality test has recently been supported by the Supreme Court in *TSC Industries, Inc. v. Northway, Inc.,* CCH Fed. Sec. L. Rep. 95615 (June 14, 1976). There the court, citing *Mills,* held that an omitted fact is material if there is a substantial likelihood that a reasonable shareholder would consider it important in deciding how to vote. This standard does not require proof of a substantial likelihood that disclosure of the omitted fact would have caused the reasonable investor to change his vote, but contemplates a showing of a substantial likelihood that, under all the circumstances, the omitted fact would have assumed "actual significance" in the reasonable shareholders deliberations.

128. 406 U.S. 128, 153–4 (1972).
129. 396 U.S. 375. 384–5 (1970).

whether the existence of causal relationship and hence of liability could be shown where the management employed a defective proxy statement but controlled a sufficient number of shares to approve the transaction without any votes from the minority.[130]

The issue of materiality is a mixed question of law and fact, but the shareholders should be able to make an informed choice when they are consulted on corporate transactions. This should hold true even in a situation where management controls enough votes to approve transactions. Thus, shareholders should be allowed appropriate remedies, at least injunctive relief, even where the management employs a materially defective proxy statement to wield a controlling bloc of votes. In a situation where management does not have sufficient control and effects a transaction through a defective proxy statement, shareholders should be allowed recovery upon showing the materiality of the defect and the amount of damages sustained. Shareholders should be allowed to bring an action directly or in a derivative capacity for the corporation itself. The defendants in the action may avoid liability only when they meet the burden of proving that they could not have known about the defect even upon the exercise of due diligence.

IV. Related Areas: "Going Private" and the "Freeze Out"
A. *Introduction*

The term "going private" may be defined as any transaction or series of transactions engaged by an issuer or its affiliate, which would, if successful, permit the issuer to cease filing reports under the securities law and return to a privately held status.[131] Brought to public attention during the bear market of 1974 in the United States,

---

130. *See id.*, at 385 n. 7, citing some conflicting cases.

131. *See* SEC, *Sec. Act. Rel. No. 5567* (Feb. 6, 1975); *also see* Note, *Going Private*, 84 YALE L.J. 903, 904 (1975): A.M. Borden, *Going Private-Old Tort, New Tort or No Tort?* 49 N.Y.U.L. REV. 897, 987–9 (1974). In a wide sense, the term may be defined to include any transaction by an issuer or its affiliate which might directly or indirectly result in the issuer being able to cease filing reports under the Exchange Act or which might result in a significant impairment to the liquidity of the trading market in its equity securities. In any sense, going private shall be limited to refer only to transactions whose ultimate goal is the return of a corporation to a privately-held status.

going private has been a frequent technique which seeks to utilize market conditions to eliminate public shareholders at an advantageous price and thus enjoy the benefits as a privately held corporation. The benefits to a privately held corporation are varied, and include in the words of a dissenting Judge Moore in *Green v. Santa Fe Industries, Inc.*:

> "Freedom from worry about the impact of corporate decisions on stock prices; ability to take greater business risks than those sanctioned by federal securities agencies; a switch to more conservative accounting, resulting in lower taxes, the savings which results from no longer having to prepare, print and issue the myriad of documents required under federal and state disclosure laws; the removal of a pressure to pay dividends at the expense of long-term capital development or speculative capital investment—these are some of the advantages which may ensure to a corporation "going private."[132] (footnote omitted.)

Because of benefits of variety, going private may also frequently be attempted in Korea as has been in the United States. Going private could be a very attractive device, especially for controlling shareholders who fear losing control. It may be effected through a variety of techniques, including mergers, sales of assets and dissolutions, or bankruptcy reorganization proceedings.[133] These various techniques may fall into two basic categories: "one-step" acquisitions of publicly held shares, mostly through a merger; and "two-step" acquisitions, which involve a tender offer followed by a "mop-up" of any remaining publicly held shares.[134] In such circumstances minority shareholders may be "frozen-out" or "taken-out", in neutral terms, at the direction of the controlling insiders.

Under the Commercial Code, any contract involving a merger into or a consolidation with another company is required to be effected only upon a special resolution passed at a shareholders' general meeting.[135] Such a contract which is entered into between the representatives of two companies must be made in compliance with

---

132. CCH Fed. Sec. L. Rep. 95447 at 99244, 99265 (2d Cir. Feb. 18, 1976)
133. *See* V. Brudney, *A note on Going Private*, 61 VA. L. REV. 1019, 1021 (1975); Borden, *supra* note 131, at 990–1006.
134. *See* Note, *Going Private*, 84 YALE L.J. 903, 909 (1975). The same classification would apply to possible going private techniques in Korea. In the United States the more commonly prevailing technique is the latter, which begins with a tender offer followed by a mop-up device.
135. *Commercial Code*, Arts. 522, 436.

the form and content specified by the merger statutes.[136] It must, *inter alia*, include the total number of shares to be newly issued, their kinds and numbers, and exchange ratio between the old and new shares. However, the controlling persons of a corporation may initiate and effect a merger into a "shell" corporation also owned by them, requiring all security holders to accept cash or a newly created nonvoting senior equity or debt security which is unilaterally decided upon by the controlling persons. Dissenters at a shareholders' meeting under the Commercial Code are not even given rights to resort an appraisal proceeding to receive fair value determined by an independent appriaser. This creates a great danger to the interests of the minority shareholders who are to be taken out.

In the case of two-step acquisitions, minority shareholders are similarly faced with the fate of being frozen-out. This is because even an ostensibly voluntary offer is apt to have a compelling effect on the offerees. If the management or controlling person of a publicly held corporation makes a public solicitation for the tender of common stock in exchange for cash or redeemable securities, and announces that eventually the remaining shareholders will be merged out at a price which is not higher than that offered in the tender solicitation, this would be seen as a threat and thus shareholders would be induced to sell.[137] When such a person or management does not disclose that the tender solicitation will be followed by a forced merger, the same effect would be brought about by the destruction of public market for the company's shares. Indeed, in any situation where a company goes private, minority shareholders are faced with being unfairly frozen out at the whim and direction of the majority.

Therefore, going private raises numerous legal problems in relation to the protection of public shareholders who are frozen out. Hence, some restrictions on going private would be essential for the protection of their interests. From the point of view of the controlling insiders who wish to go private, such restrictions would be identified

---

136. *Id.*, Arts. 523, 524.
137. When the management proposes a repurchase program by means of public solicitation for the tender of common stock in exchange for either cash or redeemable securities, it must effect it in compliance with the provisions of the articles of incorporation. For details of corporate repurchase, *see* pp. 300–306 *supra*.

as justifications for going private. Thus, these restrictions should be considered in light of reconciling conflicts of interests between the controlling insiders and minority public. As a matter of public policy, it should first be resolved that to what extent the controlling insiders may enjoy freedom in reorganizing their enterprise by means of taking minority shareholders out; and that to what extent the interest of minority shareholders who are taken out should be protected.

Several approaches may be available for resolving this question. For example, full disclosure, fairness of payment, and existence of a legitimate business purpose are devices developed in the United States for the restrictions on, or the justifications for going private. Furthermore, appropriate remedies should be given to minority shareholders who are frozen out at the direction of the controlling majority.

All these questions are of significant importance in Korea, especially because the target of capital formation set in the long-term economic development plan could be aided by assuring public investors that they are guaranteed fair treatment by insiders and are free from the danger of any unfair freeze-out.

Neither the SEA nor does the Commercial Code include any special provision which directly regulates the methods of going private. Rather, some restrictions which apply to going private transactions can be identified by analyzing the provisions dealing with mergers, consolidations, transfers of business, tender offers, corporate repurchases, and the fiduciary duties of management, etc., which are scattered in the SEA and the Commercial Code.

On the basis of these scattered provisions, the following three basic questions will be discussed below. First, to what extent can management or controlling shareholders go private and take out minority shareholders? Second, how much are minority shareholders entitled to fair protection in terms of disclosure and payment? Finally, what are possible remedies for minority shareholders who are frozen out?

B. Restrictions on Going Private

1. The Propriety of the Transaction

As noted earlier, going private is typically effected through a merger, consolidation, or tender offer followed by a "mop-up" device. Unlike the United States, Korea does not have a "short-form merger" statute which enables a parent company owning a certain large percentage (80% or more) of the stock of a subsidiary to merge with

the subsidiary upon approval of the parent company's board of directors, and upon making cash payment to the minority shareholders.[138]
The Code, however, authorizes the majority shareholders who hold
or represent at least two-thirds of the total number of voting shares
present at a general shareholders' meeting (a quorum is met if more
than one-half of the total outstanding voting shares are present) to
approve by a "special resolution" any proposal for a merger, consolidation, transfer of business, or sale of material assets.[139] Since
corporate insiders can use corporate mechanism such as the proxy
solicitation, they can, without much difficulty, meet the requirements
of the special resolution and thus unilaterally slice the corporate pie
into portions which satisfy their appetite alone. The use of mop-up
techniques following a successful tender offer leads to the same results
because insiders can both dictate the terms of the take-out and assure
its acceptance by the necessary majority.

In the case of a merger or consolidation, the Commercial Code
requires additional statutory procedures which were included to
protect both shareholders and general creditors. It is, *inter alia,*
required that: (1) any agreement or contract of a merger or consolidation, which is entered into between representatives of the two companies, include certain terms and conditions prescribed by the Code;
(2) the company or companies to be dissolved make a public notice
to general creditors; or (3) the transaction, to become effective, be
approved by the court of competent jurisdiction if the remaining or
newly incorporated corporation is to be a stock corporation.[140] Item

---

138. Thirty-eight states adopted short-form merger statutes: *e.g., see Del. General
    Corporation Law,* Sec. 253. Though advance notice to or consent of the
    minority shareholders is not required, they must be notified within ten
    days of the merger's effective date, and any dissatisfied shareholder may
    petition the Delaware Court of Chancery for the payment of the fair value
    of his shares as determined by a court-appointed appraiser subject to court
    review.

    The percentage of the subsidiary's stock which must be owned by the
    parent varies with a state. Nebraska requires 80%, Illinois 99%, other
    twenty seven states including Delaware 90%, and the remaining nine states
    (including New York) 95%.

139. *Commercial Code,* Arts. 522, 436, 374.

140. For items (a) and (b) above, *see* notes 135 and 136 *supra*. For item (c), *see
    Commercial Code,* Art. 600.

(3) above, which requires a court's approval, was intended to protect general creditors and prevent any evasion by such corporation of the strict statutory procedures for incorporation and capital increase through a merger or consolidation.[141] Item (1) above concerns the interest of shareholders, and thus requires the terms and conditions of a merger or consolidation to be uniform because the fundamental principle of corporate law is that all the holders of the same class of stock are entitled to the equal treatment by the corporation in terms of dividends, liquidation distributions, and the like.[142]

As the foregoing discussion reveals, the present regulation allows majority shareholders to freeze out minority shareholders without much difficulty by changing the corporate structure. The only possible restriction applicable to going private would be the existence of a fiduciary duty. The Commercial Code, however, does not provide any indication as to whether controlling shareholders owe a fiduciary duty to the minority shareholders, nor has any case on that matter been brought to court since most corporations in Korea have been privately held. Furthermore, though directors and officers are expressly required to owe fiduciary duty to the corporation and shareholders, no precise standard has been either legislatively or judicially established as to the scope of such duty. Indeed, the lack of any clear standard against which to test the propriety of going private is a significant void in the laws in Korea.

In the United States, Section 1 0(b) and Rule 10b–5 thereunder came into play in this area. Recently, the supreme Court of the United States in *Santa Fe* has denied the reach of Rule 10b–5 to the instance of corporate mismanagement in a going-private transaction, reversed judgement of the lower court and remanded the case.[143] The Court held that a majority shareholder's alleged breach of fiduciary duty in effecting a short-form merger to eliminate minority interests without any justifiable business purpose did not violate Rule 10b–5 since the defendant's conduct was neither deceptive nor manipulative. Additionally, the Court held that:

---

141. *See* Chung, *Commentary* I, 456.
142. *Id.,* at 343–44.
143. *See Santa Fe Industries, Inc. v. Green,* CCH Fed. Sec. L. Rep. 95914 (Mar. 23, 1977).

". . . [T]he complaint in this case alleged fraud under Rule 10b–5 would
bring within the Rule a wide variety of corporate conduct traditionally left to
state regulation. *Absent a clear indication of Congressional intent, the Court should be
reluctant to federalize the substantial portion of the law of corporations that deals with
transactions in securities, particularly where established state policies of corporate regulation would be overridden.*" (Citations ommitted and Emphasis supplied.)[144]

---

144. *Id.* at 91, 448. The facts and lower courts' decisions are as follows. In 1974,.
Santa Fe Industries, Inc. ("Santa Fe") which held 95% of the stock of
Kirby Lumber Corporation ("Kirby"), a Delaware corporation, effected a
short-form merger under Section 253 of Delaware Corporation Law. The
statute does not require the consent of, or advance notice to, the minority
shareholders. However, notice of a merger must be given within ten days
after its effective date, and any shareholder who is dissatisfied with the terms.
of merger may resort to the appraisal procedure. Under the terms of the
merger, minority shareholders were offered $150 per share while Kirby's.
stock was alleged in the complaint to be worth at least $772 per share based
on the data, as revealed by the appraisal included in the Information Statement sent to minority shareholders. Minority shareholders objected to the
terms of the merger but did not pursue their appraisal remedy. Instead, they
brought a derivative suit under Rule 10b–5 seeking to set aside the merger
or to recover the fair value of their shares.
The District Court dismissed the complaint for failure to state a claim upon
which relief could be granted. 391 F. Supp. 849 (SDNY 1975). A divided
Court of appeals reversed. 533 F. 2d 1283 (1976). The court declined to rule
that a claim of gross undervaluation itself would suffice to make out a Rule
10b–5 case. However, the court held that although the Rule plainly reached
material misrepresentations and nondisclosure in connection with the purchase or sale of securities, neither misrepresentation nor nondisclosure was a
necessary element of a Rule 10b–5 action; the rule reached breaches of fiduciary duty by a majority against minority shareholders without any charge
of misrepresentation or lack of disclosure. It thus held that the majority has.
committed a breach of its fiduciary duty to deal fairly with minority shareholders by effecting the merger without any justifiable business purpose.
But the Supreme Court decided that the complaint failed to allege a material
misrepresentation or material failure to disclose. On the basis of the information provided, minority shareholders could accept the price offered or reject
it and seek an appraisal in the Delaware Court of Chancery, which is their
sole remedy under the Delaware state law for any alleged unfairness in terms
of the merger. Further, it found inapposite the cases relied upon by respon-
dents and court below, in which the breaches of fiduciary duty held violative
of Rule 10b–5 included some element of deception. *See Affiliated Ute Citizens
v. United States,* 406 U.S. 128 (1972) (misstatements of material fact used by
bank employees in position of market to acquire stock at less than fair

However, it can conversely inferred from the opinion of the Court that minority shareholders may successfully bring a suit under Rule 10b–5, if majority shareholders breach their fiduciary duty by effecting a merger to eliminate minority interests through any deceptive or manipulative act or practice, including misrepresentation or nondisclosure of a material fact.[145] Absent any deceptive or manipulative act or practice, corporate mismanagement or breach of fiduciary duty is left to state regulation. In addition, in *Popkin v. Bishop,* where a derivative suit, brought to enjoin a merger, was based on the grounds that the exchange ratios for the conversion of the common stock of the merged corporations into the stock of the surviving corporation was unfair to plaintiff, the second Circuit held that the complaint did not state a cause of action based on Section 10(b) and Rule 10b–5.[146]

In Korea, where no precise standard is available for determining the propriety of going private, it would be advisable to adopt a valid or justifiable business purpose test. However, the scope of a valid business purpose which justifies going private is difficult to visualize in practice. Even in the United States, this has not been clarified by either the court or the Congress.[147] Cases involving public corporations are too few to permit inferences of any clear standard between permissable and impermissable freeze-outs. However, some standards

---

value); *Super Intendent of Insurance v. Bankers Life & Cas. Co.,* 404 U.S. 6, 9 (1971) ("Seller of bonds was duped into believing that it, the seller, would receive the proceeds"); and other cases which involved an element of deception as part of fiduciary misconduct held to violate Rule 10b–5 are numerous as cited note 15 in the opinion at 91, 452.

145. *See id.,* holding at 91, 447–48, and opinion pt. III at 91, 452 *et seq.*
146. 464 F. 2d 714, 717 (2d Cir. 1972).
147. While the proposed Rule 13e–3B as contained in the SEC Release No. 5567 would require that the transaction have a "valid business purpose," the Release does in no way even purport to give examples of what might constitute such a valid business purpose. Also, while the Second Circuit adopted this test in *Marshel* and *Santa Fe,* there is no specific explanation on that meaning in both cases. *See* 533 F. 2d 1277 (2d Cir. 1976); 533 F. 2d 1283 (2d Cir. 1976).

Furthermore, state court decisions on the matter are sparse, and the bulk of it deals with closely held corporations. *See* Brudney, *supra* note 133, note 44 at 1031, citing as *e.g., Matteson v. Ziebarth,* 40 Wash. 2d 286, 242 p. 2d 1025 (1952); *Farmsworth v. Massey,* 365 S.W. 2d 1 (Tex. 1963) and so on.

for legitimate or permissible business purposes have been suggested by commentators. Borden suggested that this test be considered in connection with public policy.[148] However, apart from a consideration of all the social interests which revolve around the enterprise, its community of associated shareholders, creditors, employees, or the national economy as a whole, this test would be neither fair nor concerned with business reasons.

As to the savings argument for going private, Professor Brudney's criticism seems to be proper. He wrote:

> Whatever justification there may be for eliminating odd-lot holders in order to save the costs of servicing small stockholders, "going private" or reducing liquidity presents more serious questions. *As a matter of efficiency,* the corporate saving from the reduced costs of servicing public stockholders must be weighted against the expenses of going private and the cost of stockholder of losing a public market. *And as a matter of equity,* the distribution of benefits and costs between insiders and outsiders must be assessed. . . [T]he question would remain whether it is ever possible for business purposes to be legitimate if they produce only doubtful net savings of this type which are to be divided ultimately by one group of stockholders at the expense of other stockholders of the same class[149] (Emphasis supplied and footnotes omitted.).

Clearly, if savings could be an adequate justification for going private, every attempt to go private would be justified in and by itself.

A second justification suggested would be not only the elimination of the pressure from public stockholders for dividends and the elimination of blocking or delaying tactics by the minority but also the elimination of the threat of losing a challenge against control. However, this argument is based solely on a position favoring the freedom of controlling insiders. Considering the relevant social interests, the argument has its own limit in determining to what extent public policies should allow the freedom of corporate insiders in eliminating their minority shareholders. In Korea, where the top priority of economic policy has been placed on capital formation and the promotion of securities markets through inducing more privately held corporations to go public, the argument has little importance.

The most important justification for the standard of legitimate business purpose may be an economic justification. According to

---

148. *See* Borden, *supra* note 131, at 1022–23.
149. Brudney, *supra* note 133, at 1032–34.

Professor Brudney,[150] there must at least be a showing of an expected increase in the value of the enterprise such as from altered earning power, risk characteristics, or asset value available for all common stockholders, and not merely a claimed enhancement of the value of the shares of some common stock resulting from an alteration in the distribution of share or a shift in value among the stockholders. Furthermore, he noted, this standard is not met by the claim of savings in housekeeping costs, altered income division possibilities, or advantages in the use of privately held stock for acquisitions or employee stock option plans.

However, an expectation of corporate profit alone would not be sufficient since there would still remain an arms-length valuation process and sharing obligations. When the forced elimination of the public minority is a necessary condition for achieving any increase in value foreseen from going private, the minority taken out are entitled to a share of that increment.[151] But a difficult problem is how to identify and quantify those benefits and thus arrive at some basis for sharing. Professor Brudney, in this context, suggested the implementational, procedural safeguards that would require proponents of the contrived merger to disclose the purpose, amounts of expected benefits, and mode of sharing them, in terms which are specific enough to permit both assessment of the legitimacy of the proposal and the adequacy of the sharing, and to underpin liability if later events demonstrate culpable misstatement of the climed purpose, amounts, or division of benefits.[152] In addition, when the gains and purposes are not adequately identifiable, the insiders must carry a heavy burden of proof. Since the minority do not have an effective access to valuation data, the shift of burden of proof, which is strict, onto management appears to be appropriate.

Another suggestion relevant to economic justification is a test as to whether there exists any compelling corporate need.[153] When a corporation can demonstrate the existence of a compelling corporate need to revalue its shares, for example, in order to continue functioning as a viable economic entity, and an inability to achieve the

---

150. *Id.*, at 1036–38; *see also* Note, *Going Private,* 84 YALE L.J. 903, 923 (1975).
151. Brudney, *supra.*
152. *Id.*, at 1039.
153. *See* Note, *supra* note 150, at 923–24.

same result through a less drastic means, going private may be permitted. This test should be applied in Korea since this broader restriction on going private would meet the purposes expressed in both the economic development plan and the special statutes that were enacted to promote the securities market. In applying this standard to a specific case, a question arises as to the acceptable extent of a compelling need, but this question should be resolved on a case by case basis by measuring the necessity within a framework of the relevant social interest and public policy.

2. Full Disclosure and Fairness of Payment

A general supposition of securities law is that every investor should be allowed to exercise informed judgement in decisions to sell, purchase or hold securities. In order to exercise informed judgement, he must be supplied with all the material facts related to the transaction concerned. In a going private situation where insiders both dictate the terms of the take-out and assure its acceptance by the necessary majority, the full and fair disclosure of a material fact is essential in avoiding breaches of fiduciary duty or conflicts of interest. Among other important things that should be disclosed are: a justifiable business purpose; substantial valuation data to determine fairness of the consideration offered; and sources of funds to be used.

In order to approve the proposal of a merger, consolidation, or transfer of business, the management must under Article 363 of the Commercial Code send a written notice to every shareholder of record at least two weeks prior to the day set for a general shareholders' meeting. This written notice is, however, required to include information only as to the purpose of such meeting.[154]

The SAC Rule on Proxy Solicitation, substantially modeled on the Japanese rule, requires that a person soliciting proxies furnish, *inter alia*, the following information as to: 1) the identity of the person making the solicitation or the person who is to be given a power to exercise the proxy, the class and number of shares beneficially held by him, and his relationship with the issuer; 2) if the action to be taken is with respect to any plan for a merger or consolidation, a) the purpose of the transaction and a short summary of the events leading to the proposal, b) a short summary of the material contents of the pro-

---

154. *Commercial Code*, Art. 363.

posed agreement, and c) the balance sheets and profit-loss statements of the parties concerned for the latest fiscal year; or 3) if the action to be taken is with respect to transfer of whole or a material part of business, a) the identity of the proposed transferee, b) the material contents of the proposed agreement with a short summary of the events leading to the proposal, and c) any interest or relationship with the transferee, if any.[155] However, the proxy solicitation is not compulsory but is left at the discretion of the management. In addition, even in cases where proxies are solicited by the management, shareholders are not guaranteed by law to be given sufficient valuation data prepared by an independent appraiser on which to judge the fairness of the consideration offered.

Another disclosure rule in this area is included in the SEA. Two articles with respect to a merger, consolidation, or transfer of business were introduced by the 1976 Amendments to strengthen the disclosure rule.[156] One is Article 190 which provides:

> "Any shareholders' special resolution of a listed corporation under Article 522 of the Commercial Code which approves a proposed merger of a non-listed corporation into the listed corporation shall not become effective unless such a non-listed corporation has been registered with the SAC, in accordance with Article 3, six months prior to such resolution."

The other is Article 191 which also requires a listed corporation intending to transfer all or a material part of its business to another person, to make a report thereon six months prior to the date of a shareholders' meeting called to vote on the transaction. The SAC must, immediately after receiving such report, make a public notice thereon.

However, these two Articles have some significant loopholes and drawbacks. Article 190 does not requires the same disclosure when a listed corporation merges into a non-listed corporation. The legisla-

---

155. *SEA,* Art. 199, *Presidential Decree,* Art. 85, and *SAC Rule on Proxy Solicitation,* Art. 3. Cf. *Japanese SEA,* Art. 194 and *Rule on Proxy Solicitation of Listed Stock* (Japanese SEC Rule No. 13, promulgated on July 10, 1948, as amended by Cabinet Order No. 196 in 1955) Art. 2. In the Japanese Rule, there is no special indication requiring special disclosure as to the proposed transfer of business.

156. *SEA,* Arts. 190, 191.

ture clearly overlooked this matter, although Article 3, item 3, may possibly be deemed to include such a case within its registration requirement. Article 191 also gives rise to a significant loophole by failing to take within its coverage a case where a listed corporation takes over all or a material part of the business of a non-listed corporation. Furthermore, this Article provides no specific guidelines or standards as to the extent of information that is required to be filed in the report.

In the case of "two-step acquisition" involving a tender offer, the statute also does not guarantee public shareholders fair and full disclosure. The SEA exempted the repurchase of securites by the issuer from the tender offer filing requirement if such a tender offer is effected for redemption purposes. Though the Commercial Code contains several devices that insure a considerable degree of disclosure in the course of the corporate repurchase and redemption processes, public shareholders may not have access to information such as corporate purposes of retirement, sources of funds to be used, or other plans or proposals of the issuer involving the matter.[157] In addition, disclosure provisions concerning tender offers are insufficient to compel fair and full disclosure where the minority shareholders are taken out because of the lack of anti-fraud regulation.[158]

From the foregoing analysis, the present disclosure rule dealing with organic changes or going private is as a whole insufficient to enable public shareholders to make well informed judgements under the circumstances. If an increase in earning power is foreseen from the proposed organic change, public shareholders are entitled to a share of that increment. However, the present rule does not require the disclosure of valuation data necessary both to identify and quantify the benefits and thus to arrive at a basis for sharing. Indeed, if the existence of an economic justification for going private is required to be a necessary condition for the forced elimination of the minority shareholders, the management should by law be forced to disclose fairly all the relevant valuation data.

The SEC in the United States has recently proposed Rule 13e-3A, which is designed to protect investors, particularly in going pri-

---

157. *See* pp. 300–06 *supra*
158. *See* pp. 306 *et seq supra.*

vate transactions.[159] The proposed rule requires that the requisite information include, among other things, the sources of funds to be used for the transaction, intentions with respect to the future conduct of business, background information regarding affiliates, an opinion of counsel on the legality of the transaction, certain financial information, and a summary of an evaluation by two qualified independent persons of the consideration to be offered to the holders of the affected class of securities. It also requires that the consideration offered to such security holders be of a fair value as determined in good faith by the issuer or its affiliate, and not lower than the amount of consideration recommended jointly by two qualified independent persons. To guarantee the independence of the qualified persons, it is suggested that the relationship with the issuer or affiliate and other detailed information about them be included.

Unlike those in the United States or Japan,[160] minority shareholders in Korea who are dissatisfied with the terms of elimination are not entitled to resort to an appraisal proceeding to receive fair payment for their shares taken out. They thus can be forced out under the terms and conditions unilaterally determined by the controlling insiders. Under such circumstances, there is an urgent need for a device designed to insure fair payment for the minority taken out. It is advisable to adopt a rule which requires the management to disclose fully all pertinent information, including a summary of an evaluation by two qualified independent persons. Also, any dissenters should have access to an independent appraisal proceeding.

C. Remedies for the Minority Shareholders

Under state law in the United States, the remedy available for minority shareholders who are frozen out may usually be an appraisal proceeding or a suit claiming a breach of fiduciary duties. In addition, going private is under federal jurisdiction, and thus minority shareholders are protected by federal securities laws. Basic provisions applicable to going private transactions are Section 10(b) and Rule 10b–5, Sections 14(a) and (e), and Rule 14a–9. Section 10(b) and Rule 10b–5 broadly deal with fraud in connection with purchase or sale of security, whereas Section 14(a) or 14(e) governs fraud in con-

---

159. *See* SEC, *Sec. Ex. Act. Rel. No. 5567* (Feb. 6, 1975).
160. *See* notes 51 (Japan) and 138 (U.S.) *supra*.

nection with a tender offer or proxy solicitation. As for standing to sue, the coverage under Sections 14(a) and (e) is broader than that of Rule 10b–5 because the *Birnbaum* rule is not applicable to a former case. Also, culpability under Section 14(e) or Section 14(a) and Rule 14a–9 does not require *scienter*, an element which is essential under Rule 10b–5.[161] In addition, the prospectus requirement and remedy provisions of the Securities Act of 1933 govern exchange offers in which debt or redeemable securities are offered in exchange for outstanding equity securities, absent the exemption available pursuant to Section 3(a) (9).[162]

In *Popkin v. Bishop,* where an action was brought under Rule 10b–5 to enjoin a merger solely on the ground that the exchange ratios were unfair, the complaint was dismissed.[163] Recently the Supreme Court in *Marshel v. AFW Fabric Corp.,* as in *Santa Fe,* reversed the judgment below which granted an injunction against a proposed merger of Concord (a publicly held corporation) into AFW Fabric (a shell corporation incorporated as a vehicle for the controlling groups' stock interest in Concord).[164] The lower court had reasoned that notwithstanding the absence of any allegation of misrepresentation

---

161. *See Bangor Punta, supra* at note 52; *Gerstle v. Gamble Skogmo Inc.,* 478 F. 2d, 1281 (2d Cir. 1973). In *Bangor Punta,* the court held that the standard for determining liability under 14 (e) on the part of a tender offeror is whether the plaintiff has established that the defendant either (1) knew the material misstatements or omissions of a fact, or (2) "failed or refused to ascertain such facts when they were available to him or could have been discovered by his reasonable effort." In *Gamble-Skogmo,* where shareholders who were asked to approve a merger on the basis of a misleading proxy statement brought a suit for damages for violation of Rule 14a–9, it was held that they are not required to establish any evil motive or even reckless disregard of the facts. Under Rule 10b–5, however, knowledge of falsity, or at least reckless disregard which is tantamount to *scienter* is required; mere negligent conduct is not sufficient to permit plaintiffs to recover damages in a private action under Section 10(b) and Rule 10b–5 thereunder. *See Shemtob v. Shearson, Hammil & Co.,* 448 F. 2d 442, 445 (2d Cir. 1971); *Globus v. Law Research service, Inc.,* 418 F. 2d 1276, 1290–1 (2d Cir. 1969).

162. *Securities Act of 1933,* Secs. 10, 11, 3(a)(9), 15 U.S.C.A. §77 j.k.c(a)(9) Here, the offeror, directors, officers and controlling shareholders are subject to almost strict liability.

163. *See* note 146 *supra.*

164. *See* CCH Fed. Sec. L. Rep. 95919 (Mar. 17, 1977).

or nondisclosure, the controlling shareholders of Concord had devised a scheme to defraud their corporation and the minority shareholders to whom they owe a fiduciary obligation by causing Concord to finance the liquidation of the minority interest without any justifiable business purpose.[165] However, the Supreme Court has been reluctant to grant any remedy to minority shareholders under Rule 10b–5 if there is no allegation of nondisclosure or misrepresentation which is deceptive or manipulative, even though controlling persons or management lacked any justifiable business purpose in the elimination of the minority interest.

Modeled after the Japanese law, the SEA does not include general anti-fraud provisions like Section 10(b) and Rule 10b–5. Nor does it include any express indication as to a private right of action for any misrepresentation in connection with a tender offer or proxy solicitation.[166] Absent any clear indication, it is reasonable to assume, as noted earlier, that the legislature left civil remedies to the doctrines of civil and commercial laws which are tantamount to state laws in the United States.[167] Should it be construed otherwise, this would make little difference unless the concept of fraud was expanded at the same time. These are significant loopholes in implementing the purposes of the SEA, and should be closed as soon as possible in the public interest and for the protection of investors.

Some possible remedies may be found in the Commercial Code. First, the Commercial Code provides that a shareholder may bring an action against the remaining or newly incorporated company to nullify the merger or consolidation within six months after the transaction was completed.[168] However, the effect of the judgment nullifying the transaction, as that of nullifying the incorporation, need not be retroactive in order to protect the interests effected or created

---

165. *See* CCH Fed. Sec. L. Rep. 95448 (Feb. 13, 1976).
166. *See Presidential Decree under the SEA,* Arts. 13, 85 (4). While the proxy rule prohibits misrepresentation, the rules of tender offers prohibit misrepresentation only by a target company in connection with shareholder communication. But as to a private right of action, no indication is given either in the statutes or in the legislative history.
167. *See* the accompanying text of notes 72 and 120 *supra.*
168. *Commercial Code,* Arts. 529, 236–40, 186–91.

by the transaction.[169] However, the Code keeps silent as to what constitutes a cause for such an action, and precedents are too sparse to permit any inference. Commentators argue that the cause of such an action should be restricted to violations of the mandatory provisions or basic principles of corporate law since the provisions with respect to nullification of incorporation is required to apply to nullification of a merger in order to protect the new interests created by the transaction.

Another possible remedy available for minority shareholders under the Commercial Code may be an action attacking the effectiveness of a shareholders' resolution approving the merger or consolidation. Shareholders are given standing to bring an action to have any resolution either declared null and void or rescinded when the resolution contains certain defects. If the defect is procedural, such a defect constitutes statutory cause for the rescission; however, if the content of the resolution adopted is in contravention of any mandatory provisions of the statutes or articles of incorporation, or the basic principles of corporation law, the resolution is null and void.[170] While such a substantial defect makes the resolution null and void regardless of court's declaration thereof, a procedural defect nullifies the resolution only through a court decision, actions for which must be brought within two months after the resolution is passed.[171] Injunctive remedy may also be allowable under the Code of Civil Procedure if certain conditions are met.

However, a significant question arises as to the difference between an action for nullification of a merger and that for the nullification of a shareholders' resolution. The statutory causes for both actions are similarly restricted to material defects in the substance of the transaction concerned. But, an action for the nullification of a merger must be brought within six months after the completion of the

---

169. *Id.*, Arts. 529, 240, 189, 190, 417; Chung, *Commentary I*, 274; Suh, *Commentary I*, 505 and 296. Also, if any violation is remedied while an action is pending, the action must be dismissed.

170. *Commercial Code*, Arts. 376–81; Chung, *Commentary I*, 375–79; Suh, *Commentary I*, Suh, *Commentary I*, 341–48. For detailed causes of action for rescission, *see* the accompanying text of note 112 *supra*.

171. *Id.* But the effect of a court's judgement must not be retroactive in either case in order to protect the newly created social interests.

merger, otherwise the newly created interests may be unduly injured, whereas a shareholders' resolution could be pronounced null and void at any time if a statutory cause is proved either through an independent action or through allegation in other related actions. If any shareholder is allowed to resort to the latter course of action to nullify the resolution which approved the merger at any time, the six month restriction imposed on an action for nullification of a merger would be meaningless. No case has been brought on the matter neither have the commentators clarified it. Yet to reconcile the two remedies, it would be advisable to prohibit any shareholder from claiming nullity of a shareholders' resolution approving a merger six months after the merger was completed.

The most important weapon for minority shareholders who are unfairly treated by the management or the controlling shareholders would be an action for damages or injunctive relief. The Commercial Code contains several provisions dealing with such remedies. Directors and officers are required to fulfill duties of care and loyalty, and thus they may be held liable for damages sustained by their company and caused by a violation of the provisions of the statutes and articles of incorporation or by a failure to exercise due care and diligence in the discharge of their corporate duties.[172] Under such circumstances, if a company fails to bring an action within thirty days after a written request by shareholders, a 5% shareholder may bring a derivative suit on behalf of the company.[173] A 5% shareholder may also seek an action to enjoin any illegal activities of directors which otherwise appear to cause irreparable damage to the company.[174] But the statutory cause for this injunctive relief is restricted to the violation of the provisions of the statutes or articles of incorporation that appear to result in irreparable damage. In addition, a shareholder may have a direct standing to sue for damages against directors under Article 401 of the Commercial Code, which provides that "directors shall

---

172. *Id.*, Arts. 399, 414.
173. *Id.*, Arts. 403–406, Unlike in the United States or Japan, an individual shareholder was not given standing to sue in order to discourage possible abuses and a flood of lawsuits. Any shareholder may bring action even prior to the lapse of thirty-day period if the violation appears to cause irreparable damage to the company.
174. *Id.*, Art. 402.

jointly or severally be liable for damages sustained by a third person due to their intentional or grossly negligent misconduct.[175]

However, the statutory rules for actions that seek recovery and injunctive relief have some drawbacks. First, the 5% shareholder restriction on standing to sue, intended to deter a possible flood of lawsuits, means that an individual shareholder cannot attack any illegal or unfair conduct by management unless he represents 5% of the total number of shares outstanding. This restriction, being in practice so significant a hurdle, must be eliminated for the protection of minority interest. The purpose in deterring a possible flood of lawsuits brought in bad faith could be met to a considerable degree by a provision which requires the plaintiffs in such actions to post a reasonable amount of bond as security if there appears to be a certain degree of bad faith.[176]

Second, although Article 401 deals with directors' liability to a third person, not expressly designating a shareholder as a third person, raises some difficult questions as to the statute's coverage and the characteristics of liability in relation to the civil law concept of a tort. The statute exempts simple negligence from being a statutory cause for action, for the intended purpose of the exemption is to facilitate the directors' discharge of corporate duties, the nature of which is complicated and sophisticated and must be performed with flexibility according to circumstances. Though not unanimous in their opinions, commentators agree that directors should be held liable under Article 401 for any damages sustained by a third person because of the directors' intentional or "grossly" negligent misconduct: that a shareholder should be included in the coverage of the term "third person"; and furthermore that directors should also be held liable under the provisions of civil law tort for any damages sustained by a third person because of directors' "simple" negligence.[177]

---

175. *See id.,* Art. 401; *see also* Chung, *supra* note 169, at 391–92; Suh, *supra* note 169, at 364–66.

176. Article 403(5) of the Commercial Code allows a court in a derivative suit for damages to order the plaintiffs to deposit a certain amount of security if defendants show bad faith on the part of plaintiffs. It is advisable to expand this security requirement to a suit for injunctive relief, in replacement of the 5% shareholder restriction.

177. *See* Chung, *supra* note 169, at 391–92; *also see* Suh, *supra* note 169 at 364–66.

However, since directors owe no fiduciary duty to a third person who is not a shareholder, directors' liability to non-shareholders should be defined in a context different from that in liability to individual shareholders. Furthermore, directors' liabilities to a third person who is not a shareholder is reached by the provisions of civil law tort. In this context, Article 401 should be interpreted to govern directors' liability as an agent and a fiduciary for direct damages sustained by certain individual shareholders only, since shareholders' indirect damages sustained by the company can be recovered through a derivative suit under Article 399. Through such an interpretation, the legislative purpose can be met, and thus the phrase "third person" of Article 401 should be replaced by the word "shareholder."

Third, a question arises as to whether minority shareholders may have standing to sue for injunctive relief when corporate insiders effect or are going to effect a merger or consolidation, particularly for the purpose of going private. Under the Commercial Code, the statutory cause for injunctive relief is restricted to any illegal act of management that violates any provisions of the law, decree or articles of incorporation and appears to cause any irreparable damage to the company. Only a 5% shareholder may bring an action to enjoin such an act and only on behalf of the company. Because of these restrictions, it is difficult to believe that any individual shareholder may, by a *mutatis mutandis* application of the provisions of the Law on Civil Procedure, have standing to sue to enjoin any management misconduct that is not consistent with fiduciary obligation and appears to result in irrecoverable damage directly to minority shareholders only. Court decisions are not available on this matter, but for the protection of investors, minority shareholders should be given standing to sue to enjoin this category of management misconduct. In addition, since the legal powers of the management are for the most part vested in the board of directors, and majority shareholders most commonly exercise a dominating influence over the board by means of electing its majority, controlling shareholders should be required to owe a duty of good faith to the company and minority shareholders.

Though commentators call director's liability under Article 401 a special liability or special tort liability, they unanimously conclude that directors should be liable to a third party outside the company under a civil law tort, which includes even simple negligence.

Fourth, a critical question is to what extent corporate insiders should owe a fiduciary obligation to their shareholders and company in the case of a merger. Though the fiduciary concept has not been clarified in the area of corporations, the basic tests applicable to a breach of fiduciary obligation may be the absence of a valid business purpose, fair and full disclosure, and fair payment, as noted earlier. A subsequent questions arises as to whether an individual shareholder should be given standing to sue for recovery or for injunctive relief when a transaction lacks in only one of the foregoing three tests. This question should be resolved through the consideration of all the competing social interests involved. When top priority is placed on mobilizing resources from public investors and restricting going-private transactions, the minority public should also be protected whenever any of the three tests is met.

Section III. *Disclosure and Insider Trading*

I. Introduction: Equality of Bargaining

Directors, officers, and controlling shareholders("insiders") of a corporation usually have, by reason of their relationship to the corporation, access to material information which is not available to the general public. If such insiders or tippers trade in the shares of the corporation on the basis of non-public information, this results in gross inequality of bargaining power and injures outside investors either individually or as a group. Also, historical evidence, especially involving the series of stock crashes in Korea,[178] shows that insiders, if freed of legal restraints, tend to manipulate information and, possibly, corporate affairs to obtain trading advantages. Even if no injury to particular investors can be shown, public confidence in the market and the willingness of ordinary investors to provide financing for enterprises could be impaired or discouraged by a rule permitting insiders to trade freely on the basis of non-public information.

Until 1920 in the United States, serious controversies existed re-

---

178. For details of a series of stock crashes in the late 1950's and the 1960's, *see* Korea Stock Exchange(KSE), *The Ten-Year History of the Korea Stock Exchange* (*Cheongkwon gurueso Sipnyunsa*) 55–63 (1968).

garding the workability, and even the desirability, of the legal regulation of insider trading. After the leading Manne-Williamson controversy,[179] it is now well established that overreaching by insiders should be subject to strict legal constraints. As Professor Bromberg noted, "the market should not produce windfalls for some at the expense of others through control of information."[180] Indeed, the essential objective of securities legislation in the United States is to protect those who do not know market conditions from the overreaching of those who do.[181] In order to attain this goal, the Federal Securities Acts included two basic categories of provisions—provisions compelling the disclosure and dissemination of relevant information about securities and provisions prohibiting fraudulent, manipulative, or deceptive acts, practices and contrivances. The anti-fraud provisions are part of a statutory scheme which resulted from a congressional finding that securities are "intricate merchandise" and the determination that the public interest demanded legislation which would recognize the gross inequality of bargaining power existing between professional securities firms and the average investor.[182] These provisions, primarily Sections 12(2) and 17(a) of the Securities Act of 1933 and Section 10(b) of the Securities Exchange Act of 1934, which have greatly expanded the common law concept of fraud, also indirectly compel disclosure of information which might not otherwise have been disclosed.

Rule 10b–5, the broad anti-fraud provision promulgated under Section 10(b) of the Exchange Act, has become, through judicial interpretation, the most important weapon against insider trading.[183]

---

179. Brudney & Chirelstein, *Corporate Finance* 868–76 (1972), discussing the development of controversies among commentators, *inter alia*, H.G. Manne's *Insider Trading and the Stock Market* (1966) and *Insider Trading and the Law Professors*, 23 VAND. L. REV. 547 (1970) and O.E. Williamson's *Corporate Control and Business Behavior* 93–96 (1970).

180. 2 A.R. Bromberg, *Securities Law; Fraud-SEC Rule 10-5* §8.7(2) at 217–18, the accompanying text of note 78 (1977).

181. 3 Loss *Securities Regulation* 1435 (2d ed. 1961) and cases cited under note 18 therein.

182. H.R. Rep. No. 85, 73d Cong. 1st Secs. 8 (1933).

183. SEC Rule 10b–5 under the Securities Exchange Act of 1934 (19 C.F.R. §240, 10b–5) provides:

"It shall be unlawful for any person, directly or indirectly, by the use of

The Second Circuit in *Texas Gulf Sulphur* stated broadly the purpose of the securities laws: "to equalize investors' access to information so that no one in the market has an advantage over another by virtue of inside information."[184] For the purpose of Rule 10b–5, an insider was defined as anyone who has access to corporate information available for a corporate purpose.[185] Thus, a broad range of persons may be held to be liable, including (but not limited to) the company itself, outside professional advisers, persons in a business connection, communication media or regulatory agencies, and tippers.[186]

---

any means or instrumentality of interstate commerce, or of the mails, or of any facility of any national securities exchange,

(a) to employ any device, scheme, or artifice to defraud,

(b) to make any untrue statement of a material fact or to omit to state a material fact necessary in order to make the statements made in the light of the circumstances under which they were made, not misleading, or

(c) to engage in any act, practice, or course of business which operates or would operate as a fraud or deceit upon any person.

in connection with the purchase or sale of any security."

(Adopted in Release No. 34–3230. May 21, 1942, 13 F.R. 8177).

184. *SEC v. Texas Gulf Sulphur Co.*, 401 F. 2d 833, 848, 851–52 (2d Cir. 1968), *cert. denied*, 394 U.S. 976(1969). Although rule 10b–5 is not the only provision prohibiting insider trading on the basis of material information, it is the most generally applicable. The rule, like most other provisions which may govern insider trading, *e.g.*, Section 17(a) of the Securities Act, speaks in terms of fraud or deceit and does not specifically mention insiders. It was first recognized *In the Matter of Cady, Roberts & Co.*, 40 S.E.C. 907 (1961) that insider trading (face to face or in the impersonal market) on the basis of undisclosed or nonpublic material information violated Rule 10b–5.

185. *See* 401 F. 2d. at 848; 40 S.E.C. at 912.

186. Bromberg, *Disclosure Programs for Publicly Held Companies—A Practical Guide* 1970 DUKE L.J. 1139, 1142–43 (1970). Professor Bromberg enumerates possible insiders under the rule as (a) the company itself; (b) directors, officers, and major security holders; (c) outside professional advisers, including lawyers, accountants, financial advisers, management counsellors, public relations consultants, engineers, and testing laboratories; (d) business connections including lenders, underwriters, proposed merger partners, customers, and supplies; (e) personnel of the press, wire services, and other communication media; and (f) personnel of stock exchanges, self regulatory agencies, and government agencies. In addition, others who may be insiders, but are more likely to be considered tippees, include financial analysts, institutional investors, and firms and associates, families, brokers, or tippees of any of the above.

Section 16(b) of the Exchange Act prevents the unfair use of information which may have been obtained by insiders by reason of their relationship to the issuer.[187] It provides that the ('short-swing') profits realized by the insiders from the "purchase and sale" or "sale and purchase" of any equity security of the issuer, within a six-month period, inure to and are recoverable by the issuer. However, Section 16(b) produces a great potential for evasion because of the requirement of a purchase and sale within a six-month period, while Rule 10b–5 applies to any single purchase or sale. As Professor Bromberg noted, Section 16(b) is for stupid insiders and Rule 10b–5 is for smart ones.[188]

The Korean legislature in 1976 introduced for purposes of regulating insider trading Article 188 to the Securities and Exchange Act ("SEA"), which deals with short-swing profits.[189] However, the legislature failed to introduce a broad anti-fraud provision like Rule 10b–5. Therefore, a large portion of insider trading may be regulated only by the civil law fraud doctrine which, due to strict requirements of proof, cannot function effectively in terms of a broader remedial purpose and compelling disclosure of relevant information. The following sections discuss the statutory rules to identify: to what extent inside information is required to be disclosed under the SEA, mainly under the current report rule; and to what extent over-reaching by insiders can be prevented in Korea for the protection of investors. Discussion below also tries to compare regulations of disclosure and insider trading in Japan and the United States with those in Korea to identify some drawbacks included in the present Korean rule.[190] Final section discusses elements of a new far-reaching anti-fraud rule,

---

187. *Securities Exchange Act of 1934*, Sec. 16(b), 15 U.S.C.A. §78p(b).
188. *See* Bromberg, *supra* note 186, at 1142, note 7.
189. In 1976, the legislature passed a set of far-reaching amendments, the 1976 Amendments to the SEA (Law No. 972 of January 15, 1962) as Law No. 2920, which became effective December 22, 1976. For details of the 1976 amendments, *see* Dong-A Daily Newspaper (*Dong-A Ilbo*), July 29, 1976, at p. 3; and for details of Article 188, *see* Section III below.
190. Japanese regulation was largely modeled after federal securities regulation in the United States (the Securities Act of 1933 and the Securities Exchange Act of 1934), while Korean regulation has heavily depended on the Japanese regulation. Hence, a comparative analysis in the area would be meaningful.

introduction of which is urgent to improve the current regulation of disclosure and insider trading.

II. Disclosure of Information

A. *General Structure of Disclosure Rules*

In order to equalize bargaining power, the SEA includes a variety of provisions which compel the disclosure and dissemination of relevant information about securities being distributed or traded. At the primary market level, the SEA compels disclosure by requiring a certain issuer of securities to file registration documents or registration statements or to prepare and deliver a prospectus in compliance with the statutory requirements. At the secondary market level, the SEA requires certain persons to file periodic reports, proxy materials, and tender offer statements.

All the foregoing provisions of the SEA concern the disclosure of information in special instances. None of such provisions compels publicly-held corporations to disclose "current" material information which is critically important to public investors in the market. Prior to the 1976 Amendments, corporations listed on the exchange were required by the Korea Stock Exchange("KSE") Rules to make a current report whenever certain material information occurs.[191] Any violation of this disclosure rule was made grounds for delisting the issue. Until the 1976 Amendments, however, the KSE never exercised this power, because enforcement of the disclosure rule met with difficulties stemming from the rule's lack of precise standards and the issuer's lack of sufficient familiarity with the rule.

The amended SEA adopted Article 186 which requires listed corporations to make a current report whenever any statutory event occurs. Introduction of a current report system in the SEA is a significant development in terms of regulatory framework in Korea where the legislature failed to enact a broad anti-fraud rule. However, the rule has significant drawbacks because the statutory events listed are narrow in their coverage and lack a clear disclosure standard as will be discussed below.

---

191. *See KSE Rules on Listed Securities,* Arts. 2,3,7 and 22; *also see KSE Standards for the Administration of Listed Securities,* Art. 2 (Promulgated on July 1, 1974, as amended on January 20, 1976). The Article lists nine categories of material facts which fall under the current reporting rule.

B. *The Current Report Rule*

1. Coverage of Information Disclosed

Article 186 of the SEA enumerates certain statutory events, the occurrence of which imposes an obligation upon listed corporations to make an immediate report to the Securities Supervisory Board ("SSB") and the KSE.[192] No specific form like 8-k in the United States is required in filing the current report under the SEA.[193] Items 1 through 6 of Article 186 list specific events: (1) any default in the payment of commercial papers or checks, or "suspension"[194] from banking transactions; (2) suspension of a part or all of the business engaged in; (3) any action to begin legal proceedings for corporate reorganization or to undertake a *de facto* reorganization; (4) any change in the purposes of business; (5) significant damage sustained as a result of any disaster; and (6) any material legal proceeding. Item 7 of the Article, as a catch-all clause, generally requires a report of *"any other fact or event which appears to result in material influence on the operation of the corporation."*

Deciding whether certain information should be disclosed under the rule is a matter of judgment. In order to compel listed corporations to exercise fair judgment under the circumstance, it is essential to make the disclosure provisions specific in their terms and clear in their coverage. To enumerate as many specific instances as possible would be helpful in clarifying the coverage of information to be disclosed. The present disclosure rule, however, appears to be insufficient by these standards.

Article 186 enumerated six specific instances only, and left all other material events to be covered by the catch-all clause of item 7. The specific instances enumerated in items 1 through 6 are very narrow. Possible confusion could have been avoided if the legislature had listed a larger number of specific instances. For example, because item 1 refers only to defaults in the payment of commercial paper

---

192. *SEA*, Art. 186.
193. *Securities Exchange Act of 1934*, Secs. 13 and 15 (d), 15 U.S.C.A. §78m and o(d); SEC Rule 13a–11, 17 C.F.R. §240, 13a–11.
194. The term "suspension" in the text is author's. Item 1 of Article 186 includes the term "prevention" from banking transactions in lieu of the term "suspension," which more accurately reflects the legal and practical meaning of the term.

or checks, it is not clear whether information as to default in the payment of dividends, or default on contracts must be disclosed. Also, because item 5 provides only for significant damages sustained in a disaster, the question arises whether significant damage or loss caused by other means should be disclosed. The only test applicable to such information is the one set by the catch-all clause.

The catch-all clause includes a materiality test, which raises a significant question as to its propriety because of a statutory limitation. Any fact or event is required to have material influence "on the operation of the corporation." However, there would be information which is certain to have a substantial impact on the market or to affect the desire of investors to buy, sell or hold securities, even though such information is not certain to result in material influence on the operation of the corporation. Similarly, some defaults in the payment of debts, contracts, or dividends which are material for the investors might not materially influence the operation of the issuer, though there could be some overlap between the two tests. More significantly, information as to changes in accounting methods or principles,[194a] or the existence of a special relationship with an accounting firm or its members which is material for the public investors does not necessarily result in material influence on the operation of the issuer.

194a. In February, 1981, the new management (Sunkyong Ltd.) of Korea Oil Corporation(KOCO) attempted to replace KOCO's accounting method of FIFO (first-in, first-out) by LIFO (last-in first-out) with respect to appraisal of inventory. Such replacement was reported to create a deficit instead of net profits of more than about 30 billion won for the fiscal year of 1980; the two different accounting methods created a difference of about 100 billion won in the value of KOCO's assets. Although KOCO is a non-listed company, fifty percent of its shares are owned by Korea Oil Stock Holding Company (KOSHCO), which is publicly held. Hence a sudden newspaper release on the matter was a big shock to the public shareholders of KOSHCO. The incident reveals loopholes inherent in the current disclosure rule both in terms of its standard and its coverage of issuers. On the other hand, a question arises as to whether KOSHCO or its shareholders may bring a derivative action against Trans Ocean Gulf Oil Company (TGOC) in order to have such amount of excessive dividends, which has been declared, paid and remitted, returned to KOCO, since TGOC, the former management and controlling shareholder, looted corporate assets by the application of improper accounting methods and the illegal declaration and payment of excessive dividends.

Clearly, considering that the purpose of the disclosure rule is to protect the public investors, the materiality test should have been set to meet such purpose.

2. Other Drawbacks

a. Timing

Timely disclosure of material information is critically important for the protection of investors. Delayed disclosure may result in insider trading and "tipping" or leakage of information. The timing of disclosure is closely related to the determination of materiality. However, choosing the exact time is a dilemma in practice, especially when information concerned is tentative or incomplete. In this context, a question to be resolved is whether materiality is limited to "facts" which are fully established. In *Texas Gulf Sulphur,* the United States Court of Appeals for the Second Circuit stated that materiality is no longer limited to facts which are fully established; tentative or incomplete information can be material.[195] Further, if the information is still incomplete or tentative, another materiality test adopted is the probability of the expected outcome. The higher the probability, the greater the materiality.

Article 186 requires listed corporation to file current reports "without delay when any statutory event or fact has occurred." Failure to do so is made subject to imprisonment or a fine.[196] But the term "without delay" is vague and abstract, and this lack of a clear-cut time limit is a significant hurdle to the enforcement of the rule. A further difficulty arise due to vagueness of the clause "when any statutory event or fact has occurred." Many listed corporations have delayed disclosure of material information under the pretext that the information concerned was not completely established until a contract or agreement had been made, or an action finally approved by the board of directors.[197] However, no adequate measures have been taken by the authorities to compel fair and timely disclosure. Also, no criminal prosecutions have been made under the rule, probably because of its vagueness. Amendment of the rule is urgently needed

---

195. *SEC v. Texas Gulf Sulphur Co.,* 401 F. 2d 833, 840–50 (2d Cir. 1968), *cert. denied,* 394 U.S. 976 (1969).
196. *SEA,* Arts. 212, item 4, 186.
197. *See* Maeil Economic Newspaper, July 19, 1977, at P. 3.

so that disclosure of tentative or incomplete information can be compelled while it is still material.

b. Withholding from Disclosure

The requirement of disclosure of material information should not be an absolute rule, lest the result be a conflict among desired objectives. When there is a good business reason for withholding information from the public, non-disclosure or delayed disclosure is allowed in the United States.[198] But, such reasons should not excuse insider trading, tipping, or tippee trading.

The present rule is silent on justification for withholding information. To avoid possible conflicts among objectives, it is desirable to allow some exceptions as in the United States. However, as a prerequisite to such allowance of withholding, a broad anti-fraud provision like Rule 10b–5 should be adopted to prevent insider trading. In addition, in order to discourage possible abuses, justification for withholding should be specifically set forth. It may also be appropriate to require any non-disclosing issuer to get prior approval from the Securities Administrative Commission("SAC").

c. Coverage of Issuers

Article 186 imposes the obligation to make current reports only on listed corporations. The legislature clearly neglected to include registered corporations in the coverage. As the over-the-counter ("OTC") market grows, this exemption will raise a significant problem for the protection of investors.

d. Lack of Disclosure Pressure

As noted earlier, a broad anti-fraud provision plays an important role in the enforcement of the disclosure rule. In the United States, a great pressure for release stems from possible violations of Rule 10b-5 by insider trading with—or tipping of the information or by the tippee trading.[199] The longer the information remains non-public, the higher the risk of these occurrences.

---

198.   *see* 401 F. 2d 883 *supra* note 195 at 850; *Reynolds v. Texas Gulf Sulphur Co.*, 309 F. Supp. 548, 558 (D. Utah 1970); *American Stock Exchange Company Guide* 403 (1) at 104 (1970). In *Texas Gulf*, the need to acquire land surrounding the great mineral discovery furnished a good business reason for withholding. But such reasons do not excuse insider trading, tipping, or tippee trading (401 F. 2d at 848).

199.   Bromberg, *supra* note 186, at 1158.

Since there is no broad anti-fraud provision in the SEA, such an indirect enforcement of the disclosure rule cannot be expected. This is a critical loophole in the present regulatory framework. Enforcement of timely disclosure cannot be attained unless the legislature enacts a broad anti-fraud rule together with a strict criminal provision.

III. Insider Trading: Short-Swing Profits

In order to prevent short swing profits, Article 188(2) of the SEA provides:

> "In the case where any officer, employee, or major shareholder(a person who owns shares together with those held in the names of others, including ficticious persons, which total more than 10% of the total outstanding shares) of a listed corporations has realized profits from any purchase and sale or any sale and purchase of equity securities of the corporation within a six month period through the use of nonpublic information obtained in the performance of his duty or by reason of his relationship to the corporation may bring a suit to have such profits returned to it".

Although substantially modeled after the Japanese rule and Section 16(b) of the Exchange Act in the United States, Article 188(2) appears to include some modifications in its coverage and elements of liability.[200] No person has yet brought an action to get judicial interpretations of the provision, nor has the legislature clarified its coverage and elements of liability. Hence, the following discussion should largely depend on inferring the texts of the Article by comparing them with the American and Japanese rules after which Article 188(2) is substantially modeled.

A. *Coverage of Insiders*

Section 16(b) of the Securities Exchange Act in the United States was intended to correct abuses by insiders who used their positions of trust and access to confidential information in order to aid themselves in market activities.[201] The rationale of this section was explained by a statement made at congressional hearings that 16(b) "is simply an application of an old principle of law that if you are an agent and you profit by inside information concerning the affairs

---

200. Cf. *Securities and Exchange Act of Japan* (Law No. 25 of April 13, 1948, as amended; hereinafter "*Japanese SEA*"), Art. 189; *Securities Exchange Act of 1934*, Sec. 16 (b) 15 U.S.C.A. §78p(b).

201. *See* S. Rep. No. 792, 73d Cong., 2d Sess. 9 (1934); S. Rep. No. 1455.

of your principal, your profits go to your principal."[202] Thus, the insiders to whom the section is applicable are expressly defined to include directors, officers and 10% shareholders of registered corporations.[203] The Japanese version of 16 (b) also restricts its coverage to directors, officers and 10% shareholders.[204] Such a narrow designation of insiders may not be too serious in the United States because Rule 10b–5 is interpreted to cover a wide range of insiders and tippees. However, it would be serious in Japan and Korea because a broad anti-fraud provision has not been enacted without any clear reason.

Article 188(2) of the SEA applies to "employees" as well as officers and 10% shareholders, although it is restricted to listed corporations. The coverages of the term "employees" and "officers"[204a] are not expressly defined, and may be interpreted flexibly to deter the speculation which Article 188(2) was designed to control.

Trading by tippees is not reached by Article 188 (2). However, Article 188 (6) provides that "188 (2) and (3) shall *mutatis mutandis* apply to securities companies that have been an underwriter for a public offering or secondary distribution by a listed corporation."[205] Though the text of this provision is vague, the legislature probably intended to prohibit underwriters from profiting upon the confidential information which was obtained by reason of their performing underwriting services, by requiring that short-swing profits realized

---

202. *Stock Exchange Regulation*, Hearings on H.R. 7852 and 8720 before the House Committee on Interstate & Foreign Commerce, 73d Cong., 2d Sess. 133 (1934).

203. Early drafts of Section 16(b) made it unlawful for the insider to improperly disclose inside information and provided that the issuer could recover profits made by "tippees." *See* Hearings, *supra* note 202. These provisions were omitted in the final draft of the Section due to difficulties of proof. Also, the scope of Section 16(b) was enlarged by the 1964 amendments to be applicable to large OTC (registered) companies as well as listed ones. 48 Stat. 892 (1964).

204. *See Japanese SEA*, Art. 189.

204a. The term "officer" usually does not cover directors who are not officers at the same time. The term "directors" should have been expressly provided in Article 188(2) for the purpose of short-swing profit rules.

205. *SEA*, Art. 188(6). For Article 188(3) providing for derivative suit by individual shareholders, *see* the accompanying text of note 228 *et seq. infra*.

by officers, employees and 10% shareholders of underwirters inure to and are recoverable by the issuer.

Because of such *mutatis mutandis* application to employees and major shareholders of underwriting companies, the range of insiders covered by the Korean version of 16 (b) is expanded further. But, the legislature created a loophole by limiting the application of the rule to only securities companies, even though certain financial institutions also perform underwriting services and their access to confidential information creates the same potential for abuse.

An important question with regard to insiders arises concerning whether Article 188 (2) is applicable to a person who has been an insider within the meaning of the Article at only one end of the transaction. Article 188 (5), like Section 16 (b), provides that "Article 188 (2) shall not be applicable to a 10% shareholder at the time of purchase or sale." As to directors, officers and employees, the statute keeps silent. Thus, the question whether insiders other than 10% shareholders may be held liable under Article 188 (2) even when they have not been insiders both at the time of the purchase and sale or the sale and purchase remains unresolved.

B. Actual Misuse of Inside Information

Commonly termed "a crude rule of thumb,"[206] Section 16 (b) in the United States is not aimed solely at the actuality of evil, or the veritable employment of inside information for purely speculative purposes, but also at potentiality for evil inherent in all insider short-swing trading. To maximize its deterrent effect, the section is drafted

---

206. This often-quoted phrase is from a statement made by Mr. Thomas B. Corcoran, the chief spokesman for the draftsmen and proponents of the Act during the hearings on the proposed bill, in which he explained the purpose of the section by stating:

"That is to prevent directors from receiving benefits of short-term speculative swings on the securities of their own companies, because of inside information. The profit on such transaction under the bill would go to the corporation. You hold the director, irrespective of any intention or expectation to sell the security within six months after, because it will be absolutely impossible to prove the existence of such intention or expectation, and *you have to have this crude rule of thumbs, because you cannot undertake the burden of having to prove that the director intended, at the time he bought, to get out on a short swing.*" (Emphasis added.) Hearings before the Senate Committee on Banking & Currency, 73d Cong., 2d Sess. 6556–57 (1934).

in clear, straightforward terms, and it is no defense that the insider effected a transaction for legitimate reasons or did not actually make use of inside information.[207] Article 189 (1) of the Japanese SEA includes language similar to that of Section 16 (b) of the Exchange Act, but it has not been interpreted by the courts.[208]

Article 188(2) of the SEA, however, includes a clear indication ("through the use of non-public information") that proof of actual misuse of inside information is required. By this requirement, the criticism that an innocent insider may be held liable under Section 16 (b) can be avoided.[209] However, this requirement makes enforcement of the rule almost impossible, because it is practically impossible to prove that the insider intended, at the time he bought or sold, to get out on a short swing. This is a critical drawback which should be corrected by weighing the benefits of the rule against its costs.

C. A Purchase and Sale within Six Months

Article 188 (2), like its counterparts in the United States and

---

207. *See* the first part of Section 16(b) which reads in part: "For the purpose of preventing the unfair use of information *which may have been obtained by such* beneficial owner, director, or officer by reason of his relationship to the issuer, *any* profits realized . . . " (Emphasis supplied); *see also Newmark v. RKO General, Inc.,* 425 F. 2d 348 (2d Cir. 1970), *cert. denied,* 400 U.S. 854 (1970): Comment, *Stock Exchange Pursuant to Corporate Consolidation: A Section 16(b) "Purchase or Sale?",* 117 U. PA. L. REV, 1034, 1035 (1967): J.E. Munter, *Section 16(b) of the Securities Exchange Act of 1934: An Alternative to "Burning Down the Barn in Order to Kill the Rats,"* 52 CRN. L.Q. 69 (1966).

208. *See Japanese SEA,* Art. 189(1). It provides in part: "For the purpose of preventing the unfair use of information *which has been obtained* by a beneficial owner of more than 10% shares or officer in the performance of his duty or by reason of his relationship to the issuer, *any* profits realized . . . " (Emphasis supplied). The only difference from Section 16(b) is the clause, "which has been obtained" rather than the clause, "which may have been obtained."

209. Because Section 16(b) does not require proof of actual misuse of inside information and because it is no defense under the Section that the insider did not have or make use of inside information, there has been sharp criticism that "innocent" insiders can be held under the rule, even though innocent insider trading may serve some useful function for the company and the market as a whole. *See* Munter, *supra* note 207, at 71, 87 *et seq.* Also, for the benefits of insider trading, *see* the NYSE, *The Corporate Director and the Investing Public* (1965).

Japan, applies to only insiders who engage in a pair of transactions—a purchase and sale or vice versa—within a six-month period. Thus, it lets many "big fish" out of the net. If an insider holds his securities for exactly six months, for example, there can be no recovery despite proof of actual misuse of inside information. Nor does the rule reach the insider who only purchases or sells on the basis of inside information.

Another question raised is exact meaning of the terms "purchase" and "sale" for purposes of Article 188 (2). No definitions of the terms are included in the SEA or Decrees thereunder. In the United States, the definitions of these terms are found in the general definitional section of the Act. Unless the context otherwise requires, the term "purchase" includes "any contract to buy, purchase or otherwise acquire," and the term "sale" includes "any contract to sell or otherwise dispose of" a security.[210] However, the boom in corporate merger activity presents a difficult problem which cannot be resolved by mere reference to the words of the statute in ascertaining whether a "purchase" or "sale" was involved when insiders exercise conversion rights or participate in mergers, recapitalizations or exchanges of stock.

Previously, the so-called "objective" or "*per se*" test was applied without question to cases involving such "unorthodox" transactions.[211] This objective test was based mainly on the concept of Section 16 (b) as "a crude rule of thumb." It emphasized the automatic aspects of the statute and operated by applying it to every profit-making acquisition or disposition of securities, without regard to whether imposition of liability would further the purpose of the statute. An insider who found himself owning shares of stock after a conversion which he had not owned before was considered to have "acquired" those shares, and therefore to have "purchased" them within the meaning of Section 16 (b).

However, the "objective" test has been displaced by a "pragmatic"

---

210. *Securities Exchange Act of 1934*, Secs. 3(a) (13) and (14), 15 U.S.C.A. §78 c(a)(13) and (14).

211. *See, e.g., Smolowe v. Delendo Corp.*, 136 F. 2d 231 (2d Cir.), *cert. denied,* 320 U.S. 751 (1943); *Park & Tilford v. Schulte*, 160 F. 2d 984 (2d Cir.), *cert. denied,* 332 U.S. 761 (1947); *Heli-Coil Corp. v. Webster*, 352 F. 2d 156 (3rd Cir. 1965).

or "subjective" test because of its too harsh approach to application of Section 16 (b) to situations where an insider could not have taken advantage of his position.[212] The pragmatic approach emphasizes the Section's purpose of "preventing the unfair abuse of inside information," and requires initial consideration of whether the possibility of speculative abuse of inside information was present in a given transaction. In *Blau v. Lamb*,[213] where the insider defendants had purchased convertible preferred shares and converted them into common shares within a sixmonth period, the Court held that the conversion at issue was not a 16 (b) sale because of the insiders' lack of opportunity to realize a gain by speculative trading.

The same pragmatic approach has been applied to exchanges of shares pursuant to merger agreements by Courts in *Newmark*,[214] *Kern County*,[215] and *Crane*.[216] In *Kern County*, where the takeover bidder

---

212. *See, e.g., Roberts v. Eaton*, 212 F. 2d 82 (2d cir.), *cert. denied*, 348 U.S. 827 (1954); *Reliance Electric Co. v. Emerson Electric Co.*, 404 U.S. 418 (1972); *Kern County Land Co. v. Occidental Petroleum Corp.*, 422 U.S. 582 (1973); *American Standard, Inc. v. Crane Co.*, 511 F. 2d 1043 (2d Cir. 1974), *cert. denied*, 421 U.S. 1000 (1975). For critical analysis of the two approaches, *see* Comment and Munter *supra* note 207; Gadsby & Treasway, *Recent Developments under Section 16(b) of the Securities Exchange Act of 1934*, 17 N.Y.L.F. 687 (1971); Lowenfels, *Section 16(b): A New Trend in Regulating Insider Trading*, 54 CORN. L.Q. 45 (1968); Note *Reliance Electric and 16(b) Litigation: A Return to the Objective Approach?*, 58 VA. L. REV. 907 (1972).

213. 363 F. 2d 507 (2d Cir. 1966), *cert. denied*, 385 U.S. 1002 (1967). The pragmatic approach reasoned:
    "[I]n deciding whether a certain transaction is a Section 16(b) 'purchase' or 'sale' it is relevant to consider whether the transaction in any way makes possible the unfair insider trading that Section 16(b) was designed to prevent." *Id.*, at 522.
    For a detailed analysis of the courts' decisions which have developed the pragmatic approach, *see* Note, *Section 16(b) Liability for Profits Realized from a Cash Purchase and Sale Within Six Months of the Securities of Two Issuers Involved in an Intervening Reorganization* 75 COLUM. L. REV. 1323 (1975).

214. *See supra* note 207. The Second Circuit held that RKO's exchange of Central shares pursuant to the merger agreement constituted a "sale" for 16(b) purposes. The indispensible predicate to such holding was the court's finding that RKO's prior knowledge of the impending merger coupled with the ability to control it involved the possibility of speculative abuse which 16(b) was meant to deal.

215. *See supra* note 212. The court (the same court as *Newmark*) in *Occidental*

(Occidental) executed an option agreement and also exchanged Old Kern's shares for shares of a third company (Tenneco, into which Old Kern merged) incident to a defensive merger, the Court held that the transactions, which were not based on confidential information and were not susceptible to the speculative abuse that Section 16(b) was designed to prevent, did not constitute "sales" within the meaning of the section.[217] In so holding, the Court declared that the crucial question in deciding whether unorthodox transactions are within the reach of the statute is:

"[w]hether the transaction may serve as a vehicle for evil which Congress sought to prevent—the realization of short-swing profits based upon access to inside information—thereby endeavoring to implement congressional objectives without extending the reach of statute beyond its intended limits."[218]

---

pointed out the critical fact that placed RKO in a position which must be the dream of every speculator—"Heads I win, tails I do not lose." *See id.;* *also see Abrams v. Occidental Petroleum Corp.,* 450 F. 2d 157, 163 (2d Cir. 1971).

216. *See supra* note 212.

217. *See supra* note 212, at 584 *et seq.* There, Occidental on May 8, 1967, made a tender offer to Old Kern's public shareholders under which it acquired more than 10% within two days of the announcement. Having resisted Occidental's previous merger proposals, Old Kern moved to defeat the tender offer by engineering a defensive merger with Tenneco. Under the merger terms, Old Kern's assets were to be sold to a Tenneco subsidiary, with each Old Kern shareholder receiving one Tenneco preferred share for each share of Old Kern's common stock.

Occidental quickly negotiated an arrangement whereby it granted Tenneco an option to purchase all of the Tenneco preferred shares which Occidental would receive upon consummation of the merger. The option was exercisable by its terms no sooner than six months and one day after Occidental's tender offer expired.

Once the option agreement was executed, Occidental announced its non-opposition to the Old Kern-Tenneco merger, and on August 30, the merger transaction was closed. On December 11, Occidental exercised its exchange rights and immediately transferred newly acquired Tenneco shares to the optionee; in turn Occidental received about 84.2 million (making a total profit of $19.5 million).

Plaintiff sued under Section 16(b), contending that the transfer of Old Kern shares under the merger terms and the execution of the option agreement were both "sales" which could be matched against Occidental's purchase of Old Kern shares.

218. *Id.,* at 594–95. But Justice Douglas and two others dissented. For the dissenting opinion, *see id.,* at 605 *et seq.*

In *Crane,* where the post-merger successor to a target company brought a 16(b) action to recover profits from a defeated tender offeror (Crane) which was a competitor for control of the target, the Court applied the *Kern County* approach to the transactions at issue, despite the factual differences between the two cases.[219]

Some crucial facts noted to support the majority opinion were: (1) Occidental did not enjoy an insider's opportunity to acquire information about Old Kern's affairs at the time it made a tender offer as a non-ten-percent shareholder; (2) when Occidental extended its offer after having acquired more than 10% of Old Kern's shares, the possibility that Occidental had, or had the opportunity to acquire any confidential information about Old Kern was extremely remote because Old Kern's management vigorously and immediately opposed Occidental's efforts; refusing to discuss with Occidental, Old Kern's management negotiated and concluded a merger agreement with Tenneco; Occidental's requests for inspection of Old Kern records were frustrated by Old Kern's management which forced Occidental to litigate to secure the information; (3) critically, the exchange took place and was required pursuant to the defensive merger where Occidental did not participate in or control the negotiations or the agreement; (4) once the merger and exchange were approved, Occidental was left with no real choice with respect to the future of its shares of Old Kern because the merger left it with no appraisal right in California and because a disposal of shares prior to the merger would have left Occidental with a *prima facie* 16(b) liability; and (5) what Occidental granted was a "call" option in the agreement executed without having leverage in dealing with Tenneco, and the option did not appear to have been an instrument with potential for speculative abuse whether or not Occidental possessed any inside information about Old Kern's affairs *See id.,* at 596–604.

219. *See supra* note 212; for a detailed analysis of the two cases, *see* note *supra* 213 at 1339 *et seq.*

The factual similarities between the two cases are obvious. Both Occidental and Crane sought to gain control of target companies which responded by engineering a defensive merger with a third company. Being defeated, both attempted through litigation to halt the mergers. Failing, both exchanged their more-than-10% holdings in the target company for stock in the third company. Finally, both ultimately sold their holdings. However, some differences may be noted. Crane, unlike Occidental, did not give up the fight in the face of the defensive merger, and continued its purchase of the target's shares. In addition, Crane's cash sale of its standard preferred shares occurred less than six months after it had become an insider of Air Brake, while the option granted by Occidental was exercised after six months. although the "sale" at issue was not the exercise but the execution of the option agreement.

Such a judicial interpretation of Section 16(b)'s reach would be a helpful reference for the authorities in Korea in applying Article 188(2) to unorthodox transactions such as exercises of conversion rights or exchanges of stock incident to a merger or recapitalization. In order to prevent evasion of the Article, the scope of "purchase" or "sale" should be interpreted flexibly to reach such unorhthodox transactions. But the present rule, which requires proof of actual abuse of inside information, is stricter than the pragmatic approach in the United States. Only when an actual abuse is established, can the Article be applied to such unorthodox transactions.

Because of the difficulties of establishing an actual abuse of inside information, given the complexities of the commercial and financial world, such a strict test makes the statute almost unenforceable in practice. Moreover, Korea does not have a broad anti-fraud provision like Rule 10b–5 which might justify pragmatic application and limited coverage of Section 16(b) which result from various statutory limitations. The only solution is an appropriate amendment to relax the statutory requirements of Article 188(2) coupled with the adoption of a broad anti-fraud provision to counteract other shortcomings of the statute.

D. *Profits Realized*

The amount recoverable by the issuer under Article 188(2) is the "profits realized" by purchase and sale within a six-month period. In a single transaction, the amount of profit realized is simply the difference between the purchase price and sale price, disregarding all other transactions. But where there have been a series of purchases and sales at different prices within a six-month period, it is difficult to identify the amount of profits.

In the leading case of *Smolowe v. Delendo Corp.*, the Second Circuit in the United States established the law as to the method of computing profit.[220] The court rejected the following methods of computation: (1) the first-in-first-out rule; (2) averaging purchase and sale prices within a six-month period; and (3) identifying stock certificates. The test adopted by the Court requires that the lowest (lower) purchase price be matched against the highest (higher) sale price within

---

But the court declared that the similarities outweighted the differences. *See* 510 F. 2d 1043 (2d Cir. 1974).

220. 136 F. 2d 231 (2d Cir. 1943), *cert. denied,* 320 U.S. 751 (1943).

any six-month period.[221] No deduction is allowed even if some of the purchases are at a price higher than some of the sales during the same six-month period. This test therefore may result in the insider's paying a kind of punitive damages because judgement can be rendered against insiders who have actually lost.[222] In *Newmark*, the court included even control premiums in the damage award.[223]

The test adopted in the *Smolowe* case can be used in Korea in computing profits realized for purposes of Article 188(2). The awarding of punitive damages may be justified on grounds that Korean law requires proof of actual abuse of inside information. This test will also lighten the burden of proving the actual profits realized.

E. Enforcement

The SAC may, under its broad inspection power granted by the SEA, investigate any person who appears to have violated provisions of the SEA, Decrees and Rules thereunder.[224] The SSB may, under the SAC's control, investigate listed corporations and other persons to determine whether they have violated the rules relating to disclosure or insider trading.[225] Recently, for the first time, a short-swing trading case was detected by the authorities' inspection.[226] Sunchang Industrial Corp. (*"Sunchang Sanōp"*), a corporation listed on the KSE, was reported to have violated the disclosure rule on May 31, 1977, by falsely denying, in response to the KSE's official request, the fact that on May 27, 1977, it executed an agreement to take over the Choheung Construction Co. (*"Choheung Gōnsōl"*), a private company. As a result of the inspection, three employees of *Sunchang* were discovered to have engaged in short-swing trading on the basis of confidential information. The SAC on August 20, 1977, issued a warning to *Sunchang* for violation of the disclosure rule and directed the three short-swing traders to return their profits to *Sunchang*. However, no other legal actions, either criminal or civil, have followed to date.

---

221. *Id.*, at 239.
222. *See* Munter, *supra* note 207, at 82 *et seq.* and cases cited at p. 63.
223. *See supra* note 207.
224. *SEA*, Art. 128, However, the Statute failed to give the SAC a compulsory power of investigation; hence, efficient enforcement is doubtful.
225. *Id.*, Art. 135, items 4 and 5.
226. *See* Maeil Economic Newspaper, Aug. 20, 1977, at p. 3. Except for the facts described in the following text, no further details are available.

Under the SEA, anyone who has violated Article 188(2) is subject to the criminal penalty of imprisonment or fine, or both.[227] However criminal prosecution is left to the discretion of a prosecuting attorney, and the SAC and SSB have no legal obligation to ask for criminal prosecution when a violation is detected. In order to attain fair and impartial enforcement, it is advisable to require the SAC and the SSB, whenever they discern a violation of the provision, to refer the matters for criminal prosecution to the Prosecuting Attorney's Office of competent jurisdiction.

Civil lawsuits for the recovery of short-swing profits may be brought by the issuer or, if the issuer fails to bring suit within thirty days after request, by an individual shareholder in his derivative capacity.[228] Due to the statute of limitations, such suit must be brought within two years after such profits were realized.[229] Thus, early detection of violations is encouraged for enforcement.

However, the SEA does not contain a general provision like Section 16(a) of the Exchange Act, which requires insiders to report the extent of their ownership at the close of each calendar month.[230] Only ten percent shareholders are required to report their ownership changes under Article 201, and a director's ownership may be disclosed under the proxy rule. But, disclosure by the proxy rule is insufficient to serve the purpose of detection or deterrence. Introduction of a provision which requires, for the purpose of Article 188(2), a wide range of insiders to disclose the extent of their ownership appears to be essential.[231]

Another problem with the present mode of enforcement is the very low probability of instituting suit when violations are detected. The issuer's management usually is reluctant to take action against a fellow insider. In addition, the incentive for a shareholder to bring suit would be small because recovery runs to the corporation, and the individual shareholder's *pro rata* interest in recovery usually will be

---

227. *SEA,* Arts. 209, item 9, 214 and 215.
228. *Id.,* Art. 188(2) and (3). In the United States or Japan, a shareholder can bring a suit when the issuer fails to act within sixty days after the request.
229. *Id.,* Art. 188 (4).
230. *See Securities Exchange Act of 1934,* Sec. 16(a), 15 U.S.C.A. §78p(a).
231. In the United States, five-percent shareholders are required to report their ownership changes. *See id.,* Sec. 13(4), 15 U.S.C.A. 78m(d).

too small to induce him to act. In the United States, the major stimulus for instituting suit is the possibility of recovering attorney's fees which have amounted to one-quarter, one-third or even one-half of the company's recovery.[232] The American courts have also held that a person who was not a shareholder at the time of the transaction complained of can be a plaintiff under Section 16(b), regardless of the normal procedural requirements for a derivative suit.[233]

In Korea, sufficient recovery of attorney's fees for a derivative suit under Article 188(2) is doubtful. Also, it is not clear whether courts will allow a person who became a shareholder after the transaction complained of to bring suit in the name of the issuer. In order to implement the public policy in favor of vigorous enforcement of Article 188(2), both of these questions should be affirmatively resolved. Also, the legislature should clarify that the thirty-day waiting period can be waived if any demand that the corporation institute the suit would be futile.

One more question raised is whether the directors' failure to take appropriate action for recovery of short-swing profits may constitute a breach of fiduciary duty under the Commercial Code. This question should be considered in connection with the public policy of vigorously enforcing Article 188(2) and the issue of directors' liability under the Commercial Code. A possible reach of fiduciary duty exists if directors fail to settle the claim or institute suit in a case where violation of Article 188(2) was or could have been detected. Also, an argument can be made that the strong public policy in favor of enforcing the statute and the peculiar need of assistance

---

232. The recovery of attorneys' fees is one of several judicial developments relating to 16(b) suits which compounds the general negative reaction to such suits by a corporation which has decided not to prosecute the claim. The courts have recognized the public policy in favor of vigorous enforcement and have thus authorized substantial allowances. Further, courts have refused to consider charges of champerty, or any other allegations relating to the plaintiffs' motive for suing, as a defense to a claim for an award of attorneys' fees. For details of this area, *see* Munter, *supra* note 207, at 86; 2 Loss, *supra* note 91, Ch.7, at 1052 and cases cited therein; Note, *Insider Trading: The Issuer's Disposition of an Alleged 16(b) Violation,* 1968 DUCK L.J. 94, 102–104.

233. 2 Loss, *supra* note 91, Ch.7, at 1046 and cases cited therein. The courts have relied on the language and policy of the Section 16 (b).

from corporate officials to accomplish this policy impose a duty upon directors to take proper actions. Although the decisional law is sparse in the United States on the matter, a strong argument has been made that the established common law remedies governing director's fiduciary duty may be available in connection with Section 16(b).[234]

In Korea the statutory rule may be reenforced by attaching personal liability to directors in situations where the liability of the insider is relatively clear but the directors fail to take any action.

F. Prohibition of Short Selling

Article 188(I), modeled after the Japanese and American rules, absolutely prohibits officers, employees and 10% shareholders of a listed corporation from effecting short sales of any equity securities of the corporation.[235] Literally, the prohibition appears to be stricter than that of the United States because insiders in Korea are not given even the choice of delivering or depositing the securities within certain dates after the transaction. Such a strict prohibition of insiders' short sales was probably an expression of a strong legislative intent to prevent excessive speculation by insiders who have access to confidential information. However, effectiveness of the policy is quite doubtful because insiders can still sell long. Violators of this provision are subject to imprisonment and/or fine as is the case with insiders who violate the short-swing profit rules.

---

234. *See Note supra* note 232 at 108 *et seq. In Truncale v. Universal Pictures Co.,* 76 F. Supp. 465 (S.D.N.Y. 1948), the complaint alleged that the issuer's directors have violated their fiduciary obligations to the issuer by failing to act upon their knowledge that an officer had realized shortswing profits. More particularly, the directors were charged with conspiring to allow the two-year statute of limitations to run, thus permitting waste of a corporate asset. The court held that the "stockholder's claim under Section 16(b) is not, strictly speaking, derivative at all, but one possessing independent statutory origin." Since the stockholder had an independent claim against the profiting officer, the court reasoned, New York law required a showing that the directors had by means of fraud or negligent misrepresentation contributed "to the inaction of the stockholders in the enforcement of their statutory cause of action. . . . " *id.,* at 470.

235. *SEA* Art. 198(1). *Cf. Japanese SEA,* Art. 190; *Securities Exchange Act of 1934,* Sec. 16(c), 15 U.S.C.A. 78p(c).

IV. An Urgent Need for Enactment of a New Fraud Rule

A. Reappraisal of the Present Rule of Civil Liability

The foregoing analysis reveals that the present rule of insider trading governs very limited overreaching by certain statutory insiders.
The remedy available under Article 188(2) is the payment by the insiders of their short-swing profits to the issuer itself. No other provision in the SEA gives a party injured by insiders or tippees, in connection with securities transactions, standing to sue for direct recovery
of damages. Thus, in order to obtain recovery, public investors in
Korea must resort to the fraud rule in civil law under which it is
nearly impossible to prevail. Quite naturally under such circumstances, not a single private action has been brought, although there
were frequent reports of abuses[235a] against which a private fraud
action would prevail under the expanded fraud rule recommended
below.

The same loopholes or drawbacks are produced in the provisions
governing manipulations, proxy solicitations, tender offers, trading
or other activities of broker-dealers, and corporate mismanage
ment.[236] The SEA explicitly created private actions for manipula-

---

235a. Among other things, the recent newspaper report on the socalled "Lady
Jang Loan Scandal" or "Kong-young To-kun Case" created a big shock
among the public. According to the newspaper report, Kongyoung Construction co., Ltd. (*"Kongyung"*) which has been engaged in overseas
construction work for many years, became "de facto" bankrupt as of April
29, 1982 by virtue of the fact that its promissory notes with aggregate face
value of over 8 billion were dishonored by its prime trading bank on the
same date. Despite that fact, *Kongyoung*, on April 30, 1982, responded to the
KSE's formal inquiry that there had been no refusal to pay the promissory
notes issued by *Kongyoung*. Because of such report, *Kongyoung*'s securities,
trading in which was temporarily suspended by KSE due to widely disseminated rumors, were resumed. For three consecutive days thereafter, insiders
of *Kongyoung* institutional investors, and Donghae Life Insurance Co., Ltd.,
which is a subsidiary of *Kongyoung*, sold large numbers of *Kongyoung* shares
at the expenses of public investors. For details, *see* Dong-A daily Newspaper,
May 14, 1982 at P. 1; Maeil Economic Newspaper, May 15, 1982 at P.6.
However, the injured have never brought an action to recover the damages
incurred as a result of such insider Trading.

236. In the United States, Rule 10b–5 reaches mismanagement of corporate
affairs. *See Superintendent of Insurance of New York v. Bankers Life & Casualty
Co.,* 404 U.S. 6 (1971); also *see* A.S. Jacobs, *The Role of Securities Exchange*

tions, and implicitly, though not conclusively, created them for defective proxy statement and communication in connection with tender offers.[237] Whether private actions were created or not, however, could make little difference because neither the legislative history nor the language of the statute indicates any expansion of the existing fraud rule in civil and criminal laws.

Therefore, attainment of the major purposes of the securities legislation—implementing equality of bargaining power and adequate remedies—inevitably requires the legislature to design a new fraud rule, the scope of which is broad enough to fulfill these purposes effectively. Without introducing such a new fraud rule, public confidence in the market and the willingness of ordinary investors to provide financing for enterprises will be significantly impaired and discouraged. In the following section, two interrelated questions will be examined: what should be the elements of liability under the new fraud rule; and to what extent the new fraud rule should be implemented.

B. The Reach and Elements of the New Fraud Rule Designed

The effectiveness of the new fraud rule in attaining the two basic goals of equality of bargaining power and adequate remedy depends upon the creation of a new far-reaching concept of fraud. The history of private actions under Rule 10b–5 in the United States would be an invaluable guideline for designing the elements and coverage of the new fraud rule. But unique situations in Korea must be also taken into account.

1. Basic Elements

Recovery of damages under the new fraud rule may at least require a showing of: (1) misrepresentation or nondisclosure of a fact, or employment of any fraudulent, manipulative, or deceptive act, practice, device or contrivance in connection with the purchase or sale of any security; (2) materiality; and (3) damages. The term "in connection with the purchase or sale of any security" should be interpreted broadly and flexibly so that the rule will reach direct-

---

Act Rule 10b–5 in the Regulation of Corporate Management, 59 CORN. L. REV. 27 (1973).

237. *SEA,* Arts. 105, 106, 199 and 21–27. For details, *see* Young Moo Shin, *Securites Regulations in Korea: Problems and Recommendations for Feasible Reforms* (January, 1978, Yale Law School).

impersonal(*e.g.*, mergers, tender offers, or proxy solicitations) and indirect-impersonal transaction(*e.g.*, open market trades) as well as face-to-face or other direct-personal transactions. It should also reach trading in any security, whether registered or non-registered and whether traded on an exchange or on the OTC market. Privity should be unnecessary.

2. Scienter

A question arises as to whether the new rule should restrict liability to the presence of *scienter* or willfulness to defraud. In the United States, courts and commentators had long differed with regard to whether *scienter* is a necessary element for recovery under Rule 10b–5, or whether recklessness or even negligent conduct alone is sufficient to establish liability.[238] However, the Supreme Court in *Ernst & Ernst v. Hochfelder* held that "a private cause of action for damages will not lie under Section 10(b) and Rule 10b–5 in the absence of any allegation of *"scienter,"* *i.e.*, intent to deceive, manipulate, or defraud on the defendant's part.[239] The Court, reviewing the legislative history, emphasized that the language included in the statute—especially the word "manipulative"—"connotes intentional or willful conduct designed to deceive or defraud investors by controlling or artificially affecting the price of securities." The decision significantly curtailed the wide development of Rule 10b–5 private actions by restricting recovery to defendants who acted with *scienter*.

The *Hochfelder rule* limits the potential for vexatious litigation and for strike suits. On the other hand, as noted by the dissenters, it appears to be inconsistent with Congress' intent, repeatedly recognized by the Court, that the securities law be construed "not technically and restrictively, but flexibly to effectuate its remedial purposes."[240]

---

238. For details, *see* 2 A. Bromberg, *Securities Law Fraud: SEC Rule 10b-5*, §8.4 (500) at 204, 101 *et seq.* (1977).

239. *See* CCH Fed. Sec. L. Rep. ¶ 95479 (March 30, 1976) at 99413. Customers of a brokerage firm brought the action against the accountants, charging that they aided and abetted the broker's Rule 10b-5 violations by failing to conduct proper audits, and thereby failing to discover fraudulent internal practices of the broker. Two justices dissented, and the SEC in its *amicus curiae* brief contended that nothing in the term "manipulative or deceptive device or contrivance" limits its operation to knowing or intentional practices.

240. *Id.*, at 99425, citing *SEC v. Capital Gains Research Bureau*, 375 U.S. 180, 195

In Korea, where establishment of a fair and honest market is of cardinal importance to correct frequent abuses and practices of bad faith by insiders and professionals, there appears a strong justification for extending liability beyond the requirement of *scienter* to negligent conduct. Another justification for such expansion lies in the possible technical difficulties of proving an intent to defraud, which might exempt a large number of abuses from the reach of liability. Furthermore, historical evidence shows that no person injured by insider trading has ever brought a private action, despite frequent obvious violations. This suggests that the legislature should not concern itself with the possibility of vexatious litigation or strike suits, but rather should change the law to encourage victims of abuses to exercise their rights. Therefore, the new fraud rule should require a plaintiff to show only the three elements of misrepresentation, materiality, and damages to establish his case. The defendant may preclude liability by showing a lack of knowledge of the violation despite the exercise of due diligence.

3. Causation

Another question arises as to the need to show causal relationship, with regard to both loss causation (that the violations in question actually caused the economic harm) and transaction causation (reliance by defrauded party on the violations causing him to engage in the transaction in question). In the United States causation is required for recovery under Rule 10b–5 by judicial interpretations.[241] Loss causation, however, is rather easily demonstrated by showing some form of economic damage or sometimes absorbed into the element of reliance.[242] Transaction causation requires substantially more. In a representation case, a plaintiff must demonstrate that he relied on the misrepresentation in question when he entered into the transaction. In a nondisclosure case, a plaintiff need not show reliance but must show that the fact in question was material "in the sense that a reasonable investor might have considered it important" in

---

(1963); *Superintendent of Insurance v. Bankers Life & Casualty Co.*, 404 U.S. 6, 12 (1971); *Affiliated Ute Citizens v. United States*, 406 U.S. 128, 151 (1972).

241. See Bromberg, *supra* note 238, §§8.6 and 8.7 at 209–20; also *see Schlick v. Penn-Dixie Cement Corp.*, 507 F. 2d 374 (2d Cir. 1974), and other cases cited in Bromberg, *supra*.

242. *Id.*

making his investment decision.[243]

However, it would be more reasonable in Korea to require only a showing of the materiality of the violation in question in both the misrepresentation and nondisclosure cases, because, as noted by Professor Bromberg, reliance may be presumed from materiality.[244] Once the materiality of a fact is shown, the reasonably prudent investor can be presumed to rely on it. Professor Bromberg stated that this view is more straightforward than requiring an empty oral pleading and proof or playing word games with nondisclosure. The presumption would, of course, be rebuttable by appropriate evidence.

4. Standing to Sue

Due to the lack of explicit language, there has been much controversy over what class of persons were intended to be protected under Section 10(b) and Rule 10b–5 and over who should be granted standing to enforce the statute. Although the Court in *Birnbaum v. Newport Steel Corp.* held that only actual purchasers or sellers of securities had the right to bring a Rule 10b–5 action, many courts interpreted the *Birnbaum* rule liberally to allow recovery to injured persons who were not in fact purchasers or sellers.[245] In 1975, however, the Supreme Court reaffirmed the *Birnbaum* rule in *Blue Chip Stamps* on three primary grounds: (a) the longstanding acceptance of the rule by the courts, coupled with Congress' failure to reject the *Birnbaum* rule; (b) the inconsistency of allowing broader standing beyond the Congressional scheme evidenced, although not conclusively, by the statute's wording, which is directed at fraud "in connection with the purchase or sale" of securities and which stands in contrast with the parallel anti-fraud provisions of the 1933 Act; and (c) some countervailing advantages of limiting the danger of vexatious litigation and of speculative, perhaps limitless, damages which could result from a widely expanded class of plaintiffs.[246]

---

243. *Id.*, also *Affiliated Ute Citizens v. United States*, 406 U.S. 128, 153–154 (1972).

244. Bromberg, *supra* note 238 §8.6 (2) at 212. He also cites some judicial acceptance of his alternative approach.

245. 193 F. 2d 461 (2d Cir.), *cert. denied*, 343 U.S. 956 (1952). For the development of standing under Rule 10b–5 after *Birnbaum*, *see* note, *Standing Under Rule 10b-5 After Blue Chip Stamps*, 75 MICH. L.REV. 413, 414 (1976), and cases cited at notes 13 and 15.

246. *Blue Chip Stamps v. Manor Drug Stores*, 421 U.S. 723, 731–49 (1975). In a

In reaching its decision, however, the majority of the Court recognized a disadvantage of the *Birnbaum* rule by noting that three principal classes of potential plaintiffs were barred thereunder: (a) potential purchasers of shares, either in a new offering or on the post-distribution trading markets, who allege that they decided not to purchase because of an unduly gloomy representation or the omission of favorable material; (b) actual shareholders in the issuer who allege that they decided not to sell their shares because of an unduly rosy representation or a failure to disclose unfavorable material; and (c) shareholders, creditors, and others related to an issuer who suffered loss in value of their investment due to corporate or insider activities in connection with a purchase or sale which violate Rule 10b–5.[247] Although some shareholders of classes (b) and (c) above may in a limited class of cases be able to circumvent the purchaser-seller rule by bringing a derivative action on behalf of the issuer, implementation of this rule on standing to sue in Korea will prevent most of the above-mentioned deserving plaintiffs from recovering damages caused by violations of the new fraud rule. On the other hand, historical evidence in Korea shows that the danger of vexatious litigation would

---

civil anti-trust action brought by the United States against Blue Chip Stamp Co, which was engaged in the business of providing trading stamps to retailers, the court entered a consent decree which contemplated the merger of the Blue Chip into a newly formed corporation. The reorganization plan required the new corporation to offer a substantial number of its common shares to retailers who had used stamp services in the past but were not shareholders in the old corporation. The plaintiff retailer filed a class action on behalf of itself and other retailers who had failed to purchase, alleging that the defendant (new corporation) violated Rule 10b–5 by certain statements in the prospectus prepared and distributed by the defendant, which constituted an intentionally and overly pessimistic appraisal of the defendant's status and future prospects. Approximately 50% of the units offered to retailers were not purchased and apparently were sold to the public at a higher price one year later.

247. *Id.*, at 737–38. The Court further noted: Some shareholder members of classes (a) and (b) in the text may frequently be able to circumvent the *Birnbaum* rule through bringing a derivative action when the corporate issuer is itself a purchaser or seller of securities, while class (a) cannot claim the benefit of such a rule; *Schoenbaum v. Firstbrook*, 405 F. 2d 215, 219 (Ca 2 1968), *cert. denied, sub nom Maloney v. Schoenbaum*, 395 U.S. 906 (1969) are cited as an example for the circumvention.

be very low if standing is expanded to include the foregoing classes of potential plaintiffs. Thus, the strong need for implementing full disclosure and broad remedy in Korea outweighs the possible advantages of limiting the plaintiff class to actual sellers or purchasers.[248] The legislature should consider how to encourage the injured to exercise their right to recovery rather than how to discourage vexatious litigation.

Therefore, the term "in connection with the purchase or sale" should be interpreted liberally to cover "any attempt to purchase or sell" any security. If standing to sue is expanded to include all the foregoing classes of victims, it would be advisable to impose the additional burden on non-purchasers or non-sellers of proving causation between the violation in question and the victim's failure to sell or buy, as well as the amount of damages. This added burden of proof would significantly reduce the fear of vexatious ligigation and its resultant disadvantages. But still a question remains as to how much the plaintiff has to show to maintain his action. Considering possible difficulty in demonstrating causation in a non-purchaser or non-seller case, the burden of proof should be flexible and could be met, when plaintiff shows only materiality of information, depending on the circumstances.

5. Potential Defendants

The class of defendants liable under the rule should be large, in order to fulfill the proposed legislative purposes. They may include corporate persons as well as individuals such as insiders, tippees, outside conspirators, aiders or abettors, and participants in the violation.

---

248. In *Blue Chip Stamp,* the Court noted two separate grounds for the concern as to the danger of vexatious litigation by expanding the class of plaintiffs. The first was that a complaint with very little chance of success at trial may have settlement value to the plaintiff, and the very pendency of the suit may frustrate or delay normal business activity of the defendant which is totally unrelated to the lawsuit. The second ground was based on the concern that the abolition of the Birnbaum rule would throw open to the trier of fact, the proof of which would depend almost entirely on oral testimony.

SUMMARY

The vital functions of an efficient secondary securities market cannot be overestimated. Without a smoothly-functioning secondary securities market it would be almost impossible to achieve and maintain a well-functioning primary securities market. The preceding analysis of present laws relating to trading in securities points out various loopholes and drawbacks which have prevented the market from working efficiently. These loopholes and drawbacks may be classified into nine major categories.

First, the present disclosure rule, which concerns periodic and current reports, proxy solicitations, takeover bids, and stabilizations includes various loopholes and drawbacks in terms of its coverage, standards, timing, and withholding. Because of its incompleteness, the rule has failed to compel fair and timely disclosures of relevant information; as a consequence, the market has frequently been dominated by manipulative rumors, significantly impairing the public interest and fair trading order. There is an urgent need to improve the disclosure rule to ensure equal bargaining and to establish a fair investment climate.

Second, the lack of an effective antifraud rule is another critical loophole which hinders remedial actions and hinders disclosure of information. It is not clear to what extent civil actions are available under the several provisions preventing misrepresentations or omissions in proxy solicitations or tender offers. Explicit civil remedies provided in connection with manipulating market prices or short-swing trading are almost unenforceable because of the rigid requirements for recovery. Insiders, tippees, broker-dealers, conspirators, and aiders or abettors in Korea are almost exempt from legal restraints and can take advantage of regulatory loopholes at the expense of public investors. A similar danger of frequent manipulative or fraudulent acts and practices exists because of the lack of a provision preventing trading by persons interested in public distribution or rights offerings. Enactment of a rule preventing manipulative practices in this area is essential since the pricing system under the KSDA's rule can reflect the market prices of similar issues.

Third, the present rules governing KSE trading members and their activities are insufficient to ensure a fair and honest market. The disciplinary rules are extremely vague in their statutory causes, narrow in their coverage, and ineffective in their enforcement. Also, the rules lack measures ensuring fairness and impartiality in the exercise of disciplinary power. On the other hand, the SEA has failed to provide a provision designed to restrict frequent excessive speculations and left floor trading and short selling free from legal restraints.

Fourth, Korea has not yet organized the OTC market in spite of its vital economic functions, which cannot be attained by the exchange market, and in spite of the need for adequate protection of public investors. Also, various deficiencies are found in the rules regulating the securities companies in their entering, operating the portfolio, bookkeeping, reporting to and protecting customers, and regulating the areas of insiders' and salesmen's activities. More critical drawbacks exist in the disciplinary rules and enforcement measures both in governmental regulation of the OTC and in the OTC's self-regulation.

Fifth, the present rule governing the securities credit provides a great potential for excessive credit extension because it regulates only a limited area of securities credit. Financial institutions and other moneylenders are encouraged to extend credit on securities as collateral. Also, some drawbacks exist in the maintenance of margin requirements and in the supervision of margin trading, which is closely related to market fluctuations. In addition, the regulation of the KSFC should be strengthened, especially in the areas of reporting, bookkeeping, and insider trading.

Sixth, introducing measures to ensure continuing control of the existing management, the legislature failed to be seriously concerned about the interest of public investors. The regulatory framework of takeover bids is far from adequate to ensure the protection of public investors because it fails to require the bidder and the target company to present their case fully. It also fails to provide public shareholders with rights to pro rata acceptance, withdrawal, and the best prices. In addition, it lacks fairness and propriety in regulating employment of any offensive or defensive maneuvers by both parties. The proxy rule also fails to attain its basic purpose of adequate disclosure. More critically, the rule seems to disregard the equalization of the rights of management and of opposition security holders and overprotects the incumbent management, which already enjoys every advantage. The rule of ownership reporting also includes several shortcomings which require reforms.

Seventh, public shareholders in Korea are faced with the fate of being treated unfairly or even frozen out at the dictates of controlling insiders. The concept of fiduciary obligation imposed only on directors and officers is not well developed because actual public corporations were created only recently. Since controlling shareholders are excluded from fiduciary duty under pertinent laws, they can employ various techniques and dictate the terms of a reorganization to satisfy their interests alone. Dissenting shareholders are not given any right to an independent appraisal proceeding. In order to enhance the public participation in equity holding as well as to protect the existing public shareholders, such loopholes need to be eliminated.

Finally, the regulatory system, which was greatly reorganized by the 1976 Amendments, raises significant questions as to its effectiveness in administering and enforcing the securities laws. Although it may be too early to appraise the effectiveness of the new system after only a sixmonth experience, some fundamental drawbacks can easily be found as noted in several parts of the preceding legal analysis. Fundamentally, the legislature failed to give the SAC and SSB a variety of enforcement techniques. Even if the rules can be assumed to be complete, their enforcment is often ineffective because of the failure of the SAC and SSB to be equipped with well-qualified personnel such as lawyers, CPA's, or other experts. Without well-qualified personnel, any authorization of quasi-judiciary functions or even a present rulemaking function is very doubtful.

Part Three

Recommendations for Feasible Reforms

Chapter 9

Toward an Efficiently Functioning Securities Market

In the proceeding chapters, the writer reviewed the historical development of the Korean securities market together with the law reforms and resultant market activities. He also analyzed the present laws governing the securities market to identify some significant regulatory drawbacks and loopholes. To understand the laws and changes in the market activities, the importance of first understanding the policy goals placed on the securities markets in the national economy cannot be overestimated. Such an understanding is also a prerequisite to designing feasible reforms of regulatory drawbacks to form a proper and justifiable foundation on which recommendations for reform can be based.

Section I. *Formulation of Basic Policies*

I. Efficient Securities Market

The primary role of the securities market is allocation of ownership of the economy's capital stock. In general terms, the ideal is an "efficient" market, which is defined as a market where there are large numbers of rational, profit-maximizers actively competing, each trying to predict future market values of individual securities, and where important current information is almost freely available to all participants.[1] "Perfect competition"[2] among the many intelligent

---

1. The definition of the term, an "efficient market" is borrowed from Professor Eugene F. Fama's articles, *Random Walks in Stock Market Prices,* 21 FIN. AN-AL. J. 55, 56 (Sep–Oct., 1965) and *Efficient Capital Markets: A review of Theory and Empirical Work,* 25 J. FIN. 383 (1970). A market in which prices always "fully reflect" available information is called "efficient." Further, in the latter

participants in the market leads to the actual price at any point in time which signals for resource allocation. Firms can make production-investment decisions, and investors can choose among the securities that represent ownership of firms' activities under the assumption that securities prices at any time "fully reflect" all available information.

This notion of "efficiency" underlies the so-called "random walk" theory of market prices and a whole school of market analysis and investment behavior.[3] The efficient market theory has been stated in three different forms—"weak", "semi-strong," and "strong" forms—depending on the extent to which market prices are believed to reflect available information.[4] Both the "weak" and "semi-strong" forms have been supported by empirical evidence, though not conclusively, while the "strong" form of the efficient market theory has produced two deviations.[5] Corporate insiders and specialists are the

---

article, Professor Fama comprehensively reiewed, theoretical and empirical literature in the field.

2. *See* note 10 *infra* and its accompanying text.

3. The "random walk" theorists usually start from the premise that the major securities exchanges are good examples of "efficient" markets. They postulate that competition in an efficient market will cause the full effects of new information on intrinsic values to be reflected "instantaneously" in actual prices. They thus essentially assert that stock prices change in a random way so that past price movements provide no clue to future prices. *See* Fama, *Random Walk, supra; also see* R. Brealey, *An Introduction to Risk and Return from Common Stocks,* Ch. 1 (1969); B. Malkiel, *A Random Walk Down Wall Street* 121, 167–68 (1973).

4. *See* Fama, *Efficient Capital Markets supra* note 1; *also see* S.B. Cohen, *The Suitability Rule and Economic Theory,* 80 YALE L.J. 1604, 1614–17 (1971). Cohen, in his article summarized Fama's comprehensive review of theoretical and empirical literature on efficient securities markets for the integration of economic theory into the legal standard. The "weak" form postulates that it is impossible to identify and acquire undervalued securities on the basis of information concerning past price performance. The "semi-strong" form states that this is also true for all publicly available information. Finally, the "strong" form states that no investors have access to non-public information which they can use to identify and acquire undervalued securities.

5. Fama, *supra* at 415–16, citing Niederhoffer & Osborne, *Market Making and Reversal on the Stock Exchange,* 61 J. AM. STAT, ASS'N 897 (1966) and M. Scholes, *"A test of the Competitive Hypothesis: The Market for New Issues and Secondary Offerings,"* 1969 (unpublished Ph. D. thesis, Graduate School of

two groups whose monopolistic access to information has been do-cumented. If the ideal of efficient markets is implemented in the real world and there are no undervalued securities, or if those securities are impossible to identify, the theory of optimal investment choice is profoundly affected. Cohen has noted: "An investor seeking to maximize the return per unit of risk on his risky portfolio would have only one course of action-efficient diversification. Once efficiently diversified, a search for undervalued securities would be futile."[6]

Apart from the question of the adequacy of the empirical evidence in support of the theory of efficient markets, the notion of "efficiency" of "perfect competition" has been the basic goal and principle for structuring and regulating the securities markets in the United States. The two major sets of provisions relating to full disclosure and anti-fraud are good examples of the attempt to attain the basic goal of an efficient market under a competitive regime. The notion has been more strongly reflected in the 1975 Amendments of the Exchange Act that abolished the fixed minimum commission rates to eliminate restraints, and that introduced the central market system to prevent distortions or fragmentations of the markets.[7] The primary goal of the new market system is to attain "efficiency," or an "efficient mar-ket," as expressed in the SEC's Policy Study; the overall objective is

---

Business, University of Chicago). However, Fama argued that these devia-tions are unimportant for the overwhelming investment community by noting: there is no evidence that deviation from. . . the efficient market model permeates any further down the investment community.

6. Cohen, *supra* note 4, at 1615.
7. For a detailed analysis of the policy behind the 1975 Amendments of the Ex-change Act, *see* Warner, *Adventure in Social Control of Finance: The National Mar-ket System for Securities,* 75 COLUM. L. REV. 1233, 1269 *et seq.* (1975). The new law dealing with the market system begins with a declaration of congressional findings: the "securities markets are an important national asset which must be preserved and strengthened;" new technology creates the "op-portunity for more efficient and effective market operations;" investors and public will be served by markets achieving stated objectives and "the linking of all markets for qualified securities through communication and data proces-sing facilities will foster efficiency, enhance competition, increase the informa-tion available to brokers, dealers, and investors, facilitate the offsetting of investors' orders and contribute to best execution of such orders." *See id.* at 1269–70; *also see Securities Exchange Act of 1934,* Sec. 11A(a) (1), as added by the 1975 Amendments, 89 Stat. 97 §7.

"to encourage the development of capital markets with the ability to mobilize capital effectively and in so doing to allocate resources efficiently, establish realistic and fair valuation of investments, provide necessary liquidity for securities and produce satisfactory investment services and protection for those who commit their savings to the securities markets, in whatever form."[8]

In Korea since 1968, when the Capital Market Promotion Act (CMPA) was enacted, the securities market has been recognized as an important national asset to be promoted for the sound development of the national economy. In designing the national economic policy, the government has continuously placed a very high priority on promoting and developing the securities markets, especially as a strategy to mobilize capital resources needed for implementing long-term economic development plans. Because the success of the Fourth Five-Year Economic Development Plan for 1977–1981 largely depends on the performance of the securities markets, the government also amended the securities laws in a far-reaching reform from 1976 to early 1977. In the legislative history of the securities laws and their

---

8. SEC, *Statement on the Future Structure of the Securities Markets,* 37 FED. REG. 5286(1972). The immediate objective is to assure each investor "the best possible execution of his order," while maximizing market depth and liquidity so that securities can be traded "at reasonably continuous and stable prices." These anticipated benefits will flow from the new market system in which investors will be assured best execution by a composite tape, composite quotations system, and two trading rules giving priority to public orders through the system. *See* SEC, *Policy Statement on the Structure of a Central Market System* (March 29, 1973) SRLR No. 196, at D–3 to D–6 (1973).

The congressional subcommittees and the SEC never specifically endorsed the notion of "efficiency" or "efficient markets" which has been developed by the economists and financial theorists. However, they often referred to "efficiency" and "efficient markets" in a way broad enough to mean such a concept, as noted by Warner. *See* Warner, *supra* note 7, at 1274–75. He referred to the notion developed in the field of securities price theory as the "Treasury concept."

On the other hand, Warner noted that the specific goals of the ideal market are mutually inconsistent. Market liquidity and market stability are both important goals. But trading that provides liquidity often destablizes. Block positioning contributes to liquidity and is to be encouraged, but it undermines the agency auction market, also an objective of the new system of a central market. Clearly, such competing goals call for hard choices or delicate adjustments. *See id.* at 1273.

amendments, there has been no explicit indication that endorses the theory of "efficient" securities markets. However, the Securities and Exchange Act (SEA) has been substantially modeled after the federal securities laws in the United States. In addition, the 1976 Amendments of the SEA strengthened the disclosure system and anti-fraud rule together with the reorganization of the regulatory structure to attain an effective enforcement of the laws. The major objective for the enactment of the SEA and subsequent amendments was to structure and enhance the competitive regime as well as to prevent restraints or fraudulent practices.

On the other hand, the Korean securities laws included several devices which are inconsistent with the concept of an "efficient" market. Such devices include those through which the regulatory agencies strongly involve themselves in going public, securities analysis for the determination of offering prices, and the underwriting business in the primary securities market. The fixed minimum commission rates are a system restraining competition. Other devices such as restrictions on ownership increases are largely modified in favor of the incumbent management and also are inconsistent with a freely competitive market. However, the objective for strong government involvement in the primary market is mainly to create more supplies of commodities (securities) at a price favorable for investors because of unique situations in the Korean socity, and thus eventually to help, rather than to restrain, the competitive regime. The purposes of the present commission rate structure and the modifications employed in devices like restrictions on ownership increases are also to fit the systems into the present situations in Korea and thus are not so important in terms of characterizing the whole market structure. Indeed, the overall scheme of Korean securities laws is to develop securities markets capable of mobilizing capital effectively by establishing a competitive regime and a satisfactory investment climate. Therefore, the securities laws in Korea in principle are designed, or should be designed, to meet the ideal of the securities market, an "efficient" market, for the "optimal" allocation of resources in the "Pareto-efficient" sense.[9]

---

9. Any distribution, a change in which would have to hurt someone, is commonly called a "Pareto-efficient" distribution, after Vilfredo Pareto, the nineteenth-century Italian socialogist who first emphasized it in his studies. If any achie-

II. Actual Market Features and a Need for Government Intervention

A basic feature of the economist's definition of perfect competition ensuring optimal allocation is impersonality. More specifically, a market must satisfy the following four conditions to be perfectly competitive: (1) suppliers provide a homogeneous commodity or service; (2) participants (producers and consumers, i.e., issuers and public investors in the securities market) are so numerous in relation to the size of the market that, acting alone, they cannot affect the commodity's price; (3) all resources must be available to switch readily from one use to another, and participants must have complete knowledge of all relevant economic and technical data; and (4) barriers to entry are absent.[10]

No industry in the real world, now or in the past, has satisfied all these conditions completely although such a competitive market is the ideal toward which we should move. The actual features of the Korean securities markets are, however, far from meeting these conditions.

First, competition is seriously distorted because of the small number of suppliers and resultant scarcity in commodities, especially in equity securities. Due to continuously increasing consumers' demands, the scarcity results in a serious disequilibrium where only investors with larger subscription are able to be allotted odd-lot shares and investors with smaller subscription usually have no access to even a few shares; and where market prices fluctuate unusually in the trading market. As a consequence, the "penetration ratio" of stock ownership compared to the total population was below 1.6% in 1976, of which 62.7% hold 6.8% of the total stocks listed while 0.3% (1,700 persons) hold 61%. Clearly suppliers are so small in

---

vable redistribution of good makes someone better off without making anyone else worse off, the new allocation can be justified as a "Pareto-optimal-move."

10. For details of these conditions, *see* generally E. Mansfield, *Principles of Microeconomics* 204–05 (1974); J. Henderson & R. Quant, *Micro Economic Theory, A Mathematical Approach* 105–05 (2d ed. 1971). The fourth condition may be absorbed into the first three central conditions. Professor Samuelson noted another condition, that is, external effects imposed by parties on others without compensation are absent. For a description of the extenal effects, *see* P. Samuelson, *Economics* 474–76 (9th ed. 1974).

number that they can individually affect the market prices of securities. The corporate capital structure has been impaired due to the reluctance of a few monopolistic owners to allow the spread of equity securities to public investors.

Second, competition is seriously frustrated because timely disclosure of relevant information has never been attained. Rather, public investors are frequently misled by manipulated rumors and thus hurt by various dishonest practices of professionals and other persons having advantageous positions. When injured, the investors are usually unable to seek an adequate remedy.

Third, strict restrictions on entry into securities businesses maintain a smaller securities industry compared to the whole market; thus, a lack of competition discourages services of better quality for public investors.

Such deficiencies seriously restrain the securities markets in Korea from performing an efficient allocation of real resources. In fact, real resources are seriously misallocated. The capital structure of most business corporations, which has been highly leveraged, is worsened further due to insiders' (a few business elites) reluctance to spread equity ownership among the public who vigorously want to invest their savings into enterprises. When forced to go public, the insiders employ various dishonest practices, including disguising corporations as public and watering stock, to monopolize equity ownership. Despite a highly leveraged capital structure, the major means of corporate finance is still borrowings from the outside, such as financial institutions and other money lenders. The target of capital formation set in the Fourth Economic Development Plan and improvement of capital structure will be seriously frustrated unless the authorities institute another major reform to improve deficiencies in the market.

Clearly, the actual features and performance of the Korean securities markets require strengthening of the competitive regime so that the real national resources can be reallocated through the most socially desirable means. Such a reallocation requires that controlling shareholders transfer more shares to public investors. To attain such a reallocation cannot be left solely to the functions of the markets due to the insiders' unsound production and investment decisions and reluctance to spread equity ownership among the public; thus, the government is inevitably required to involve itself in the securities market, forcing the "haves" to transfer more securities to the "have-nots." Since this government intervention may conflict with the goal of our competitive regime, questions about the need for and the extent of such intervention arise.

Several approaches are available in Korea to justify this policy toward a wider spread of equity ownership. First, this policy is clearly the most efficient way of capital formation and a very "utilitarian" way of distribution which maximizes the "utility" in the society.[11] Second, it will also greatly contribute to the development of the securities markets by enhancing competition which has hitherto been distorted because of the shortage of suppliers and supplies of securities. Third, it will improve the highly leveraged corporate capital structure and thus contribute to sound development of the national economy. Fourth, the possible disadvantages or costs to the controlling shareholders can be reduced or eliminated by such measures as devices designed to protect the incumbent management or by rationalizing the pricing formula. Finally, although some costs or disadvantages may still remain, the controlling shareholders will be better off in the long run because of the benefits of the new policy. If not, the total benefits to be attained would be sufficient to outweigh any possible costs or disadvantages.

The foregoing justifications for strengthened government involvement imply certain limits. The initial government involvement in redistributing real resources should be restricted to the extent that utility achieved in the society can be maximized. It should also be restricted to minimize possible impairment to the competitive regime and mainly directed towards enhancing the conditions of perfect competition. More supplies will enhance the competition as does fairer disclosure. Therefore, a purely competitive market is basically still the ideal.

---

11. For the term "utility" and the "utilitarian" way of distribution, *see* N. Resher, *Distributive Justice* Ch. 2 (1966); B. Culbertson. *Distributional Equality and Aggregate Utility Comment,* 60 AM. ECON. REV. 435 (1970); Smart & Williams, *Utilitarianism: For and Against* (1973).

Section II. *Specific Recommendations for Reform*

I. Regulation of Distribution of Securities

A. Definition of Basic Legal Terms

To clarify the coverage of the SEA, some basic legal terms must be redefined. Also, the reach of the existing rules must be expanded for the purpose of the SEA by defining some basic legal terms which are not defined.

1. The Terms "Issuers" and "Underwriters" or "Underwriting"

The term "issuer" should be expanded to include, in addition to a corporate "issuer", any legal or natural person directly or indirectly controlling or controlled by the issuer, or any person under direct or indirect common control with the issuer. Through this expansion, the presently existing potential for evading the statutory requirements for registration, prospectus delivery, and even civil liability can be eliminated.

The term "offer to sell", "offer for sale", or "offer" should be defined as "every attempt or offer to dispose of, or solicitation of an offer to buy, a security for value." However, as in the United States, this term would not include preliminary negotiations or agreements between an issuer (in a broad sense) and any underwriter or among underwriters.

The term "prospectus" should be defined as "any notice, circular, advertisement, letter, or communication, written or broadcast on radio or television, which offers any security for sale or confirms the sale of any security". By such a broad definition, investors can have access to all information prior to making their investment decisions, and thus the goal of a purely competitive market may be realized. Only when the statutory prospectus prepared according to SEA requirements has preceded or has been delivered at the same time as such communication, may the communication be excluded from the foregoing definition.

2. The Term "Material" or "Materiality" as a Standard of Disclosure

The term "material" or "materiality", when used to qualify a requirement for furnishing information on any subject, should be defined to limit the information required to those matters which "an average prudent investor ought or might reasonably consider important in making his investment decisions as to sell, buy, or hold the security concerned." Such a definition may provide only a general guideline in determining the coverage of disclosure in a complex and delicate financial world; thus, more specific matters should be enumerated as examples in the respective disclosure provision.

B. Government Involvement in Going Public

The present policy which empowered the MOF to force selected corporations to go public is consistent with our basic goals. Actual designations, however, have been rare despite frequent failures to go public and increasing needs to create enough supplies for fair competition. Public investors cannot invest savings into enterprises which need their savings.

1. Impartial Exercise of Designation Power

When a corporation fails to go public within a notified period, the MOF should exercise its power to issue a designation order under the pertinent law. Further credit extension by financial institutions must be suspended or extremely restricted to those whose debt/equity ratio exceeds a certain level as well as to those who remain private in contravention of the designation order. In issuing designation orders and imposing restrictions on borrowings, the MOF or the SAC should be impartial and reasonably consistent. Restriction on borrowings as a punitive measure would be a strong inducement to corporations to resort to public equity financing because such loans have been the most prevalent sources for corporate finance. The policy would also stimulate corporations to improve their worsened capital structure.

2. Eliminating Unreasonable Restrictions on Going Public

The restriction on going public or public equity financing which requires the issuer's prospective dividend capability to exceed the level of the interest rate on one-year time deposits should be abolished. Many issuers whose earning capacity does not meet the requirement may qualify for public equity financing. Moreover, the restriction adversely affects corporate capital structure by encouraging listed corporations to declare dividends at an unreasonably high levels. When this restriction is abolished, the authorities should strengthen their supervision over securities analysis and pricing to provide offerings at reasonable prices. More corporations may be induced to seek public financing.

Medium industries should be also allowed access to public equity financing, if feasible. For the financing of such corporations, organization of the over-the-counter (OTC) market appears to be essential to enhance the marketability of such securities.

3. Preventing Abuses in Going Public

Such malpractices as disguising corporations as public or watering stocks employed in connection with going public should be strictly prevented. However, to effectively discourage and prevent such evils requires having the offering prices determined at a reasonable level. Also, enforcement techniques should be strengthened. For details, *see* pp. 164–69 *supra*.

C. *Regulation of Preliminary Activities*

1. Rationalizing Pricing Formula

Both underpricing and overpricing appear to be undesirable for moving toward the goal of an efficiently functioning securities markets.Pricing wholly based on the market prices is unavailable at this moment because the market has been too inefficient to yield a meaningful price. However, the present pricing formula which is largely based on the intrinsic value includes in its essential features unreason able factors which may lead to an underpricing or overpricing.

For the calculation of expected earnings for the next two years, the past record of performance during at least the past five years should formally be required to be taken into recount.

The automatic application of the interest rate on one-year time deposits for capitalization purposes should be abolished to reflect different degrees of risk involving the individual issuer. During the transition period, specific classifications of capitalization rate applied to several categories of issuers would be advisable. When a reasonable rate is to be applied for capitalization purposes, the automatic 25% reduction from expected earnings for risk adjustments should be abolished.

The pricing should eventually move toward the market pricing method. For such a move, listed corporations should be allowed to offer their securities at prices based on the market prices prior to the initial stabilization. To adopt this pricing method requires the enactment of a set of strict anti-manipulation rules preventing trading by person interested in a distribution and any other "manipulative or deceptive device or contrivance" as prescribed in SEC Rules 10b–6 through 10b–8. Allowing this category of market pricing would be a significant incentive for going public and public equity financing by corporations.

2. Strengthening Regulation and Supervision of Securities Analysis and Underwriting

Under an efficient securities market, securities analysis and underwriting will be accomplished solely by the self-regulation of the participants in the purely competitive regime. All the relevant information is available for them and is fully reflected in securities prices. No government restraints or involvements are necessary; the participants in the market, either through negotiations or competitive biddings, undertake underwriting business for public distribution of securities. Various sanctions or penalties for any malpractices indirectly compel the participants to act according to fair and equitable principles of trade. This is the ideal toward which we should eventually move.

However, actual features of the Korean securities market require regulatory agencies to involve themselves strongly in this area because of the ineffectiveness of self-regulation and frequent malpractices by underwriters. Also, deficiencies involving self-regulation should be eliminated.

a. Strengthening the KSDA's Role as a Self-Regulatory (in effect, Cooperative-Regulatory) Body

The Agreement on Underwriting Business should directly grant broad disciplinary powers to the KSDA rather than empowering the Association of Managing Underwriters (AMU). Also, the current Agreement on Underwriting Business should be amended as a KSDA rule to facilitate the rule's application as well as to avoid the vagueness and complexity inherent in the current Agreement.

The disciplinary sanctions available for malpractice should be diversified and strengthened. The KSDA should be empowered to issue a warning, to impose a fine (at least ₩ 500,000), to suspend membership (for at least six months), and to expel the member. The power should be expanded to discipline the securities analyists, CPA's and other persons who aided or abetted the malpractices. Disciplinary power should be exercised for any violation of rules on underwriting business.

Whenever one of the big-nine companies eligible for managing underwriters has been suspended or expelled from the underwriting community, it is advisable to authorize one or two additional companies to enter the business. The KSDA member whose business accomplishment and capabilities are the best among non-managing underwriters should be eligible for this new authorization. This additional authorization would supplement the contraction of the underwriting community and facilitate the KSDA enforcement.

The term "special relationship" between an issuer and a managing underwriter should be expressly defined to avoid conflicting interests. For this purpose, the term should be broadly defined as the equity holding, in a direct or indirect common control, exceeding 10% of the total outstanding shares. Such a broad definition is of significant importance in Korea where most securities companies or underwriters are controlled by the same person or group of persons controlling large industries.

Finally, the KSDA should be reorganized to ensure effective self-regulation and enforcement. The KSDA should have a strong enforcement division and a general council which are equipped with well-trained personnel, especially sufficient numbers of lawyers and CPA's. The personnel of these two divisions should be given strong inspection powers and considerably independent status to ensure impartial performance of their duties.

> b. Strengthening the Government Supervision

The SAC and the SSB should be given broad powers to supervise the KSDA's regulatory role. The KSDA should be required to make an immediate report to the SAC (or the SSB), in addition to the report on the result of inspection, as to any disciplinary measure under consideration or finally taken for malpractices by members. Upon review of this report, the SAC should be empowered to amend or revoke the sanction taken or independently impose a sanction on the KSDA member. Prior to a final action, the agency should give a violator an opportunity (a hearing proceeding) to defend himself against the charges.

D. Readjustment of the Disclosure System

> 1. Adjusting the Coverage of the Registration Requirement
>> a. Expanding the Coverage

In public sale or distribution of trust certificates, securities investment trust companies should be required to file a specified form of registration statement. When the securities trust investment com-

panies are required to register and meet the periodic reporting requirements, as they are in the United States, the registration for the
distribution of the trust certificates may be replaced in part by statements or documents already filed. The required registration statement should include all the relevant information about funds and
their management which appears to be necessary for public investors.

In the registration requirement, serious consideration should also
be given to including a security offered in an exchange for the security of another issuer. Though this category has been rare in Korea,
a great potential for such offers exists in the near future as the techniques of mergers, reorganizations, or tender offers are diversified
in a rapidly developing financial world.

b. Clarifying the Exempted Transactions

Exempted transactions should be explicitly provided in the SEA
to avoid possible disputes or evasions of the rules. One standard that
should be made specific is the standard for the "private placement"
exemptions. The general standard to determine the exemption's
applicability should be whether the particular classes of person affected need the protection of the registration requirement. As a
specific standard, it is advisable to limit the application by prescribing
the number of purchasers—for instance, twenty-five or less. However, because the number of offerees cannot be an absolute standard
for determining "private placements," other criteria should be met,
such as limitation on the manner of offerings, the nature of offerees,
and access to information, as prescribed in the SEC Rule 146 in the
United States.[12]

c. Relaxing the Full-Blown Registration Requirements

The present rule requiring listed corporations to file a full-blown
registration statement in the case of rights offerings and stock dividends should be relaxed to reduce the complexity, cost, and time-
consuming nature of the procedure. To accomplish this relaxation,
a specified form should be provided, requiring disclosure of information needed to meet regulatory purposes. When this relaxation is
proved successful in practice, it may be extended to the public offerings by listed corporations as in the Unites States.[13] However,

---

12. *See* SEC Rule 146 enacted under the Securities Act of 1933.
13. Form S–7 and Regulation C adopted by the United States SEC may be helpful in developing a form to fulfill such purposes in Korea.

specific items to be omitted or replaced in the registration statement should be seriously considered by weighing all the competing interests involved.

2. Clarifying the Restricted Transactions in Registration

Because of the conflicts between Article 8(1) (preventing any public distribution prior to the expiration of the additional seven-day cooling period) and Article 10 (preventing accepting offers to buy securities prior to the effective date), the category of restricted transactions in registration should be clarified. To meet the legislative purpose for adoption of the additional seven-day cooling period, which was intended to facilitate informed investements, the provisions should be clarified to be interpreted as follows: it is legal for any person to accept offers to buy only after the additional seven-day cooling period has passed; during the post-filing period, but prior to the expiration of the additional cooling period, it is legal for issuers, underwriters, or dealers to offer to sell or solicit for offers to buy securities; however, during the pre-filing period, all offers to sell are illegal.

3. Strengthening Regulation of Communication and Use of Sales Literature

The delivery of a statutory prospectus should be compulsory. Also, it is advisable to introduce devices such as a preliminary prospectus, a summary prospectus, and a "tombstone advertisement" which have been developed in the United States.[14] Use of other selling literature during the pre-effective period should be outlawed unless it has been preceded or is accompanied by a preliminary prospectus.

The filing of each form of the preliminary prospectus, summary prospectus, and "tombstone ad" should be required as a part of the registration statements. Such a preliminary prospectus prepared for use prior to the effective date should include substantially the same information as the forms required for the statutory prospectus in the SEA and Decrees thereunder. A special note should be printed on the front cover page to the effect that a registration statement has been

---

14. For the respective provisions relating to preliminary prospectus, summary prospectus and "tombstone ad", *see* SEC Rules 433, 434 and 434A and Section 2(10) of the Securities Act. Also, Rule 134 authorizes the use of an advertisement, an "identifying statement." This "identifying statement" contains additional information appearing to be appropriate.

filed with the SAC, but has not yet become effective; thus, the information contained is subject to completion or amendment.

To prepare the summary prospectus form (including the preliminary summary prospectus), a set of rules designed to protect investors should be enacted. This summary prospectus should contain the information specified in the form used for the registration statement. All information included may be expressed in a condensed or summarized form as may be appropriate for the circumstances under which the prospectus is to be used. A specific form should be developed to summarize the financial situation, earnings, and other information which are of cardinal importance for investors. A special statement should also be included on the front cover page: the information contained herein is based on a filed registration statement; copies of a more complete prospectus may be obtained from certain persons; these securities may not be sold nor may offers to buy be accepted prior to the expiration of seven days from the effective date.

The "tombstone ad" or "identifying statement" used in the United States is not intended to serve as a selling document but serves purely as a screening device to ascertain what persons are sufficiently interested to warrant delivery of the statutory prospectus. It does no more than state from whom a statutory prospectus may be obtained, identify the security, state the price thereof, and state by whom orders will be executed. Adoption of this device appears to be necessary to facilitate distribution. In addition, an expanded form of an "identifying statement" may be introduced. Any other form of advertisement should be outlawed unless the person has received prior approval from the SAC.

Such forms of preliminary or summary prospectus and "tombstone ad" may be subject to amendment, and the use thereof may be subject to suspension by the SAC. The use of the preliminary prospectus, as the name indicates, should be restricted to the time before the registration statement becomes effective. The summary prospectus, however, may be used even after the post-effective period. Any other selling literature may be sent to a prospective buyer after the effective date only when it has been preceded or is accompanied by a statutory prospectus. Finally, the term during which the prospectus (including the summary prospectus) may be validly used should be prescribed by the SEA.

4. Strengthening Regulation of Preparing the Registration Statement

a. Expanding the Coverage of Signers on the Registration Statement

A new rule should expand the coverage of signers on the registration statement so that persons who are subject to civil liability will perform their duty with full familiarity and responsibility. These expanded signers should include the majority of the board of directors and the senior staff members of the executive (or general affairs), the financial, and the accounting divisions who are actually in charge of preparing the registration statement or providing the material information for the preparation. In addition, the signers should include such engineers, appraisers, lawyers or other professionals who have prepared or certified any part of the registration statement, or any report valuation which is used in connection with the registration statement. The signatures of these professionals should appear in the relevant part of registration statement while those of corporate insiders should appear on the front page.

Considering the variety of legal questions and the complex technical problems involved in the registration statement, it is advisable to require the issuer to have the statement reviewed by a lawyer prior to filing. The reviewing lawyer or law firms should be required to state briefly their legal opinion of the registration statement. This compulsory requirement for lawyers' review will facilitate fair and full disclosure which in the past has been left entirely to the responsibility of corporate insiders who are laymen in the area.

b. Disclosing the Co-Managing Underwriters' Result of Securities Analysis

To facilitate fair and impartial securities analysis for pricing, the results of securities analysis performed by two co-managing underwriters along with the principal manager should be included in the registration statement as a special note. This short remark would also help public investors to make investment decisions. In addition, this statement is of cardinal importance for the co-managers' civil liability in determining whether they met a reasonable degree of investigation. This statement should be made in such specific and clear terms that public investors can understand any difference among the managing underwriters' securities analyses.

5. Enhancing the Functions of the Administrative Review and Regulation

To ensure an effective administrative review of the registration statement, the SSB should be equipped with qualified personnel, expecially sufficient numbers of lawyers, CPA's, and securities analysts. Also, to attain fairness and accuracy in issuing an amendment order or stop order, issuers should be given an opportunity in a hearing proceeding to defend themselves against any charges under consideration. When any clear, definite defect, detrimental to the interest of public purchasers, appears, however, the authority should be empowered to suspend the distribution of securities immediately even prior to a hearing.

E. *Regulation of Fraud in the Distribution of Securities*

1. Expanding the Coverage of Persons Liable

The coverage of persons liable should first to expanded to include at least such important inside figures as senior staff members of the executive (or general affairs), the financial, and the accounting divisions who are not directors but who are in charge of preparing the material information in a registration statement and thus are required to sign the statement. Inclusion of these inside figures, though not directors, is of critical importance to discourage aiding or abetting misrepresentation. The rule should also reach other participants in fraud and conspirators. Similarly, controlling persons of any person should jointly and severally be liable along with and to the same extent as such controlled persons.[15] Managing underwriters should be subject to liability regardless of the actual delivery of a prospectus.

The rule should include engineers, appraisers, lawyers, or any other persons whose profession gives authority to a statement made by them and who have consented to be named as having prepared or certified any part of the registration statement or any report or valuation which has been used in connection with the registration statement.

The rule must reach to such issuers, underwriters or dealers who effected distribution of securities, whether exempted or not, by

---

15. The term "controlling person or persons" should adequately be defined for the purpose of this provision.

menas of a false or misleading prospectus or oral communications as it does under Section 12(2) of the Securities Act in the United States. Furthermore, the rule must create absolute liability against such persons who effect distribution in violation of the registration requirement as Section 12(1) of the Securities Act does.

2. Relaxing the Elements of Liability

The elements of liability should be relaxed to meet broad remedial purposes. It would be advisable to require plaintiffs under the rule to show: (1) misstatement or omission of a fact; (2) its materiality; and (3) damages.

To require proof of the transaction causation (reliance on the defect in question) and the loss causation (the transaction causing the damages in question) would be almost meaningless when materiality of the defect in question has once been established and would create only insubstantial verbal argument.

To require privity of contract is also unnecessary for broad remedial purposes. However, under a new provision adopted after Section 12(2) of the Securities Act which, regardless of whether a registration statement was required to be filed, creates a broad civil liability for a false or misleading statement contained in a prospectus or any other written or oral communications, the presence of privity should be required to limit the danger of vexatious litigation and perhaps limitless damages which could result from a widely expanded class of plaintiffs.

Finally, when a distribution is effected in violation of the registration requirement, an absolute civil liability should be created. The fact that a prospectus prepared in good faith has been delivered to the plaintiff should not be available as a defense unless the prospectus was a part of an effective registration statement. Also included in this absolute liability is an offer of sale prior to filing the registration statement ("gun jumping"), during the time a refusal or stop order is in effect, or after a notice of stop order proceedings has been given prior to the effective date or expiration of the additional seven-day cooling period.

3. Classifying the Defenses Available

Generally, two categories of defense may be available for all the defendants. The first is the lack of the defendant's knowledge in the exercise of reasonable care. The second is the plaintiff's knowledge of the defect in question at the time of the purchase. However, these defense should not be equally available for all the defendants or applied to the same degree.

In order to meet broad remedial purposes and to prevent fraudulent or deceptive practices, the only defense available for the issuer should be to prove the plaintiff's knowledge. However, when a public distribution is effected in violation of the required registration, even the plaintiff's knowledge should not be available as a defense for the issuer, underwriters, dealers, or other participants or conspirators. For the defendants who distributed a security, whether exempted or not, by means of false prospectuses or oral communications, the only defense available should be restricted to proving the plaintiff's knowledge.

Both defenses may be available for all other defendants (directors, managing underwriters, CPA's, other important corporate insiders or professionals named) who are subject to civil liability because of false registration statements.

To meet the reasonable care defense successfully, the defendants have to show that "they had, after reasonable investigation, reasonable ground to believe, and did believe, at the time the registration statements became effective, that statements contained were true and that there was no omission of material fact required to be stated." In determining what constitutes reasonable investigation and reasonable grounds for belief, the standard of "reasonableness" should usually be "that required of a prudent man in the management of his own property." However, the degree of due care cannot be generalized for all the defendants but should be considered in connection with their respective duty, status, situation, and characteristics of the matter dealt with.

Corporate insiders should be held to a higher degree of investigation and due care than the outside directors. Whether a director is new or not may make little difference as long as he is an insider. The CPA's, engineers, lawyers and other professionals should be held to the same standard recognized in their respective professions. Another distinction on the degree of due care should be drawn between the expertised and non-expertised portions of the registration statement. As far as an expertised part is concerned, the degree of due care may be relaxed because it is reasonable to expect that a prudent man may usually rely on it. A statement made by an official person or a copy of or extract from a public official document should be treated like an expertised portion. However, the registration statement, having been reviewed by a lawyer, should not be considered an expertised one as a whole.

4. Rescission of Contract

To make rescission of the contract generally available as a remedy will significantly destabilize the social interests involved and the legal relationship already established. Also, it is difficult to determine if rescission would be available or should be limited when the plaintiff is not an initial purchaser. Therefore, it appears to be proper not to allow the rescission of contract for the purchaser of securities publicly distributed through registration.

However, in the case where the liability in question is based on a sale effected in violation of the registration requirement or by means of a false prospectus or oral communication, it would be advisable to allow the purchaser to sue for the rescission of contract as well as for damages as in the United States. Since privity should be required for standing to sue, the destabilization question would not be serious in this area.

F. Regulation of Financial Affairs

1. Enacting the SAC's Rule on Financial Affairs

The new rule to be enacted should include provisions requiring both listed and registered corporations to: (1) correct, for both dividend and disclosure purposes, financial statements in accordance with auditing by an independent CPA firm; (2) file copies in triplicate of the CPA firm's auditing report, corrected financial statements, and dividend proposal with the SAC and the exchange at least one week prior to the date set for a shareholders' meeting; and (3) set aside from net earnings a certain rate of special reserve, which should be used only for the purpose of improving capital structure. All the documents filed should be kept at least five years and available for public inspection.

2. Strengthening the Enforcement Techniques

In addition to the reporting requirement, any violation of the foregoing rule should be subject to criminal penalty of an imprisonment or a fine, or both. To enforce the rule effectively, the SAC should be obligated to ask for criminal prosecution whenever any violation occurs. When any corporation violates the net asset limit rule of the Commercial Code, the SAC should also immediately recommend criminal prosecution.

II. Regulation of Trading in Securities
A. Regulation of the Exchange Market
1. Strengthening Regulation of KSE Trading Members
a. Strengthening the KSE's Discipline

The statutory bases for disciplinary sanctions should be expanded by adding more specific cases (for example, excessive speculation or manipulation) to the current limited enumeration and by adopting a general, far-reaching provision to cover any violation of statutes, rules and orders, or fair and equitable principles of trade.

Sanctions available should be strengthened. The KSE should be given broader power to expel a member and suspend membership for longer than three months. KSE's exercise of this broad power should be appropriately limited and supervised by the MOF or the SAC.

b. Strengthening the Regulatory Agency's Supervision

The KSE should be required to report to the SAC as to a violation under consideration and the decision finally taken. Any failure to make an immediate report by the KSE should constitute a cause for disciplinary sanction against KSE officers. The SAC shoud also be empowered to revoke or amend the decision taken by the KSE, or impose directly any sanction on KSE members who violate law.

Any member charged with a violation should be given a hearing proceeding to defend itself. Also, an aggrieved person should be allowed to appeal for review of the sanction imposed (to the SAC for KSE's sanctions, and to the MOF for the SAC's or SSB's sanctions).

Officers or other senior staff members of the KSE or other regulatory agencies who have been removed or who have resigned by reason of misconduct should be barred from being employed by any securities institutions.

2. Strengthening the KSE's Supervision over Listed Corporations

Strong emphasis should be placed on compelling fair and timely disclosure. Effective sanctions should be provided for violation as well as a method of ensuring fair enforcement.

3. Restricting Floor Trading

Basically, it should be made unlawful for KSE trading members to effect transactions for their own account. A set of exceptions, however, should be provided if such exceptions do not tend to raise excessive speculation or allow unfair advantages to market insiders.

4. Restricting Short Selling

To restrict the destablizing effect of short selling, every order to sell must be marked to indicate whether it is "long" or "short." The price at which short sale may be made must be at or above the last regular way price at the opening and above the last regular way sale price thereafter. The KSE should enact detailed rules to define the coverage of short sales and other supplementary measures.

5. Allowing Off-Floor Block Transactions

The KSE should introduce measures designed to cope with large block orders. For this purpose, it is advisable to adopt a system of off-floor block transactions outside trading hours but under the exchange control. Other transactions impossible to execute on the floor because of the breakdown of communication facilities may also be allowed for off-floor transactions.

B. Manipulation and Stabilization

1. Expanding Coverage of the Rule of Manipulation

A new rule should be enacted to apply broadly to the use of fraudulent, manipulative, or deceptive acts, practice, and devices in connection with the purchase or sale of any security both on the exchange and in the over-the-counter market.

A new rule should also prohibit any persons interested in a distribution of a security from trading in such security prior to the completion of the distribution. Trading in similar issues whose market prices would be reflected in the offering price should also be prevented. It also should constitute a manipulative or deceptive act or practice for any person participating in a distribution of a security being offered through rights to sell the underlying security at a price exceeding a certain limit. However, a wide range of exceptions should be provided as they are under SEC Rules 10b–6 through 8 in the United States.

To enforce the rule effectively, elements of liability should be broadly expanded. This purpose can be met by creating a new fraud concept as is suggested in the section on insider trading.

2. Refining the Rule of Stabilization

Disclosure and reporting requirements should be strengthened. A stabilizer should be required to file a notification at least a few days prior to initiating the stabilizing operation. Also, unless the purchaser receives a prospectus, the stabilizer should give or send to the purchaser of a security in distribution a notice to the effect that stabilizing purchases may be or have been effected.

Stabilization before an offering price is set should be prohibited. The level of stabilizing should not exceed a price at which a security is being offered or distributed. The SEA also should explicitly require that if a security goes ex-dividend or ex-rights, the stabilizing price be reduced by an amount equal to the value of the dividend or right, computed to the nearest trading differential as is done in the United States.

C. *Regulation of the Over-The-Counter (OTC) Market and Securities Companies*

1. Enacting the SAC's Rule on OTC Trading

The new rule to be enacted should require all the brokers and dealers in the OTC market to register with the SAC and comply with certain rules of bookkeeping, periodic reports, inspection, qualifications, and discipline. The new rule should also require the OTC broker-dealers (market makers) to register with the KSDA and to comply with KSDA rules and regulations which are specified to enforce the SAC rule effectively. These KSDA rules should, among other things, include: qualifications for members or natural persons associated with members, and denial of membership or prohibiting association with a member; disciplining of members or persons associated with members; registration of securities traded in the over the counter; quotations; reporting and public release; detailed methods of trading and its settlement and clearance; supervision of issuers; and fair and equitable principles of trade.

The KSDA self-regulation, including its rulemaking power, should be subject to proper supervision by the SAC. KSDA disciplinary proceedings should be subject to SAC review, which may impose a sanction directly on members for any violation. Also, the KSDA rules should be enacted within the mandate of the SAC and be amended under the direction of the SAC.

Issuers eligible for OTC trading should include a wide range of securities. These OTC securities may comprise bonds, either governmental or corporate, equity securities of listed and registered corporations, and certain other securities issued by non-registered corporations. Also included should be issues delisted or suspended and odd-lot shares.

Disclosure rules and other protections for investors should be extended to certain registered corporations. These protections include rules on periodic reporting, ownership change reporting, proxy solicitation, prohibition of insider trading, and on manipulation or fraud.

2. Strengthening and Rationalizing Regulation of Securities Companies

Conflicts of interest created by business groups' domain in the securities industry should be eliminated by strengthened regulation of the activities of securities companies. Spreading the equity ownership of the securities companies should be seriously considered. Also, further takeover of securities companies by controlling persons of large industries should be prohibited. When any violation or dishonest practice by securities companies controlled by business groups is detected, the authority should order them to reduce their ownership below a certain level by means of public sale. On the other hand, the authority should allow more entries into the securities business to ensure services of better quality through enhanced competition. Existing entry restriction, in this respect, should be adjusted so that more qualified natural persons could be admitted.

The working capital requirement should be rationalized by controlling working capital on the basis of the business volume of each company. The SAC must enact specific rules on the coverage of debts and assets to enforce the maximum-debt asset rule. Also, the SEA should include a provision requiring securities companies to maintain liability reserves to be used for compensating investors.

The current bookkeeping rules should be strengthened by requiring additional ledgers reflecting separately for each security all "long" or "short" positions carried as of the clearance dates, reflecting dividends and interest received, securities not received or delivered. Also, securities companies should be required to record identification of the beneficial owner of each account.

Financial statements (or status) included in the annual and bi-annual reports of securities companies should be audited by an independent CPA firm.

Provisions (Article 41 and 58) on civil liability of securities companies and their officers and controlling shareholders should be clarified and rationalized. A general anti-fraud provision broadly expanding the concept of civil law should apply to securities companies and their employees. (See pp. 380–86 *supra*). Controlling shareholders may avoid liability only when they prove lack of knowledge.

To ensure suitable recommendations by securities companies and by their salesmen to customers, rules of fair trade should include specific standards of application. Among other things, securities companies recommending to their customers to buy or sell a security should be required to have reasonable grounds for believing that the recommendation is suitable for the customer based on his financial situation, needs, and other security holdings. In addition to a criminal penalty, any violator should be subject to civil liability and disciplinary sanctions. Accordingly, Article 52, item 2 should be reworded by eliminating subjective requirements.

Disciplinary rules should be amended to cover any violation of securities laws. In addition, a statutory proceeding should be provided for the accused person both prior to making a final decision and after the guilty decision. Finally, KSDA disciplinary proceedings should also be subject to proper supervision by the SAC.

D. Disclosure and Anti-Fraud Regulations

1. Eliminating the Shortcomings in the Current Report Rule

The materiality test set in Article 186, item 2 should be amended so that disclosure of information can be compelled in light of investor protection. Also, Article 186 should include more specific instances (such as any change in accounting principles or relationships with a CPA firm) to facilitate fair and timely disclosure. In addition, a specific form should be provided.

Certain specific guidelines should be adopted so that disclosure of tentative or incomplete information can be compelled while it is still material. Only when a clear-cut time-limit is established can the disclosure rule be enforced effectively.

Withholding or delaying disclosure may be allowed by showing a justifiable business reason or other legitimate cause.

2. Rationalizing the Short-Swing Trading Rule

Insiders and other persons liable under Article 188 should be required to report the extent of their ownership and changes therein every month to the SAC.

Actual misuse of inside information should not be required, but potential for speculative abuse should be present.

The term "purchase" or "sale" should include unorthodox transactions. The current six-month limit for short-swing trading should be extended to one year in order to prevent possible evasions.

Shareholders should be reimbursed for the actual costs (including attorney's fees) of a derivative suit. To facilitate enforcement, the directors' failure to take an appropriate action may also constitute a breach of fiduciary duty under certain circumstances.

3. Adopting a Far-Reaching, General Anti-Fraud Provision

In order to ensure equality of bargaining power and broader remedies in connection with securities transactions, the new provision should create a broader concept of fraud expanding the reach of the existing fraud concept. For the detailed elements and coverage of the rule, *see* pp. 379–88 *supra*.

Basic elements of the new fraud rule may require showing misrepresentation of a fact, or a fraudulent, manipulative, deceptive act or practice; its materiality; and damages. *Scienter* should not be necessary; proving the loss or transaction causation in general should not be required either.

The class of plaintiffs under the rule should not be restricted to actual purchasers and sellers. Also, to attain an efficient resolution of disputes, introduction of a class action system is advisable.

The class of defendants liable under the rule should be large to fulfill proposed legislative purposes. Defendants should include a wide range of legal and natural persons, such as insiders, tippees, aiders or abettors, conspirators, or other participants in the violation.

E. Regulation of Securities Credit

1. Broadening Regulation of Securities Credit

The current regulation is restricted to credit extension by securities companies, underwriters, and the Korea Securities Finance Corporation (KSFC). In order to control excessive credit extension and to prevent destabilizing stock prices, excessive speculations, or even a stock crash, the regulation should be broadened to control credit extended by financial institutions and other money lenders.

2. Adjusting the Maintenance Margin Requirements

The KSE rules, requring the maintenance of margins at the same level as the initial margin, made margin traders hardpressed because of the fear of frequent margin calls. Sufficient leeway should be provided to the extent that credit makers' interest is not impaired.

3. Strengthening Regulation of the KSFC

The KSFC should be subject to the same monthly reporting requirements imposed on the securities companies. The bookkeeping rules should require the KSFC to make and keep itemized ledgers, books, and records to fulfill the regulatory purpose. The civil liability provision applicable to securities companies should also apply to the KSFC.

F. Regulation of Takeover Bids

1. Strengthening Ownership Disclosure

Any person filing an ownership report should be required to disclose further information on his background; purpose or plan; source and amount of funds; and contract, arrangement or understanding relating to the securities of the issuer; and if the purpose of the acquisition is to acquire control of the issuer, any plan or proposal of the person or groups to change the business or corporate structure.

A copy of such a report should be required to be sent to each exchange and the issuer, and the exchange should give public notice and provide for public inspection.

The current 10% limit should be lowered to 5%. Specific guidelines should also be provided for the determination of a 5% ownership, including allowance for formations of a group or syndicate to control the issuer.

2. Rationalizing the Rules on Tender Offers

Adequate protection should be provided for public investors in connection with corporate repurchase and 10% exemptions from the filing requirement. The purposes of redemption, sources of funds, and other material information should be disclosed in connection with a corporate repurchase. A Section 13(e) type of wide prohibition should also be introduced to attain fairness in connection with the target's defensive tactics. To eliminate the potential for evasion, the 10% limit should be adequately lowered.

Deficiencies in disclosure rules should be eliminated. Unless filed as a part of the statement, any free-written materials or advertisements requesting or inviting tenders of securities should be outlawed. When any material change has occurred during the period of a tender offer, the offeror should be required to disclose it promptly.

All the shareholders should have fair and equal treatment when they tendered their shares by guaranteeing them pro-rata acceptances, best prices, and withdrawal rights.

Regulation of target company activities should be strengthened to ensure fairness in a takeover battle as well as to protect the investor benefits. In communicating with shareholders, the target management should be required to disclose relevant information and submit relevant materials and documents upon which the recommendation is based. The target management should also be subject to amendment requirements. Any person controlling or controlled by the target company should be treated like target management in this area. On the other hand, target companies should be allowed certain exemptions from the filing requirement as they are in the United States. It is also advisable to impose an affirmative duty (fiduciary duty) on the target to disclose its position and relevant information regardless of whether it makes recommendations or not.

Any fraud committed in connection with offensive and defensive maneuvers should be subject to both criminal sanctions and civil liability under a general anti-fraud rule.

3. Rationalizing the Rules on Proxy Solicitation

Certain categories of proxy solicitation in which the enforcement of the proxy rules is neither necessary nor appropriate should explicitly be exempted by the statute.

The proxy form should include specific information to clarify the extent of the authority conferred, and should require the impression of "a certified seal" to prevent forgery.

Information in the proxy statement should be expanded and made more specific. Especially needed is disclosure of relevant financial data certified by an independent CPA when actions to be taken relate to mergers, consolidations, transfers of business, changes in capital, or other material changes in business or corporate structure.

As in the United States, dissident shareholders should be given equal footing with the management. Either access to shareholder lists or mailing requirements and a system of legitimate shareholders' proposals should be seriously considered. Also, the authority should allow voting by proxy to those holding securities in the street name, while regulating possible abuses.

Remedies available for a defective proxy statement should be clarified. Under specific requirements, shareholders should be given standing to sue to enjoin a meeting or to revoke the resolution adopted. The private right of action should also be explicitly provided for recovery, both under the proxy rule and the general anti-fraud rule.

4. Strengthening Protection of Minority Shareholders Taken Out through Organic Changes

Controlling shareholders, as well as directors and officers, should owe fiduciary obligations to their corporations and minority public shareholders. In addition, the concept of fiduciary duty should be clarified and broadened in Korea to protect the minority interest in organic changes. Where either legitimate business purposes or fair disclosure, or fairness of payment is lacking in a given transaction, minority shareholders may be given standing to sue either for injunctive relief or recovery of damages on the grounds of breach of fiduciary duty. Also, they should have standing to sue under the general anti-fraud rule.

Dissenting shareholders should be freely allowed to retire their shares at a fair price determined by an independent appraiser.

The legislature should strongly concern itself with going-private transactions because of their possible adverse impact on the securities market and because of the strong need for the protection of the minority interests that are frozen out. Restrictions and remedies should apply more flexibly to going-private cases to fulfill such purposes (for details of the adequate restrictions and remedies proposed, *see* pp. 341 *et seq. supra*).

G. Role of the Regulatory Bodies

To enforce complex regulations of markets, both exchange and over-the-counter, and securities professionals is a crucial role of the regulatory agencies. The SAC and the SSB should be equipped with sufficient numbers of lawyers, CPA's, and securities analysts. Also, the commissioners and staff members should be guaranteed a substantial degree of independence to perform their duties impartially and to avoid pressures from the outside. In addition, to facilitate surveillance of market activities, an electronic market watching system should be installed in the regulatory agency.

Along with the strengthening of equipment, both personal and material, the legislature should seriously reappraise the effectiveness of the current functions given to the SAC and the SSB. Further, the legislature should consider strengthening the regulatory functions by granting some additional powers, such as a quasi-judicial power and the status to involve themselves in corporate reorganization proceedings.

SUMMATION

This study has explored methods of designing and enforcing the Korean securities laws in order to move toward the ideal, an "efficient" securities market, one which allocates the real national resources to maximize utility in the society. In analyzing the regulatory problems deterring movement toward that goal, this study has compared the Korean securities laws and their enforcement with those of the United States and Japan; the laws of the United States in particular offered very useful guidelines in identifying problems and designing feasible reforms. Since the best system for one society is not necessarily the best for another society, this study has closely examined the unique social situation in Korea and the role of the Korean securities markets. Therefore, many of the recommendations suggested here are for strengthening current regulations even though increased government intervention in the industry often conflicts with the concept of an "efficient" market and raises problems of increased administrative costs.

Since Korea is a country poorly endowed with natural and indigenous capital resources, the Korean securities market has a significant mission to function as a market-place mobilizing capital resources needed for long-term economic development plans, improving the highly leveraged corporate capital structure, and thus contributing to the sound development of the national economy. Thus, the market history during the past decade shows a strenuous struggle to attain an efficient allocation of the economy's real resources, beginning with the enactment of the CMPA of 1968 and culminating in the far-reaching 1976 law reform. Encountering various challenges, market crashes, and other failures, the movement has still been somewhat successful and has helped industries to sustain a high rate of investment in a rapidly growing economy.

In moving toward the goal—promotion of the securities market for an efficient allocation of the real national resources—securities regulation in Korea has been basically modeled on the federal securities laws in the United States to maintain a perfectly competitive market. However, unique situations such as the traditional reluctance to go public and the lack of the public's willingness to entrust their savings to the securities market has made the government make more drastic approaches: enacting a series of special laws, the government became strongly involved in going public, securities analysis and pricing, underwriting, and even in dividend policy; it has provided various incentives and privileges for going public and for decentralizing equity ownership further. Another special concern has been how to protect the interest and control of the existing shareholders after their corporations go public and spread their equity ownership. All the measures introduced in this concern matters such as restriction on ownership increases and regulation on takeover bids endangering the free ownership system and equalization of bargaining power among market participants.

Though such special legislation and measures are usually inconsistent with the concept of a perfectly competitive market, the legislative intent was to strengthen competition, especially by creating more suppliers and supplies of commodities; in fact, this special legislation played a large role in expanding the size and functions of the securities markets. However, the Korean securities laws and their enforcement have numerous legal problems seriously frustrating the move toward the ideal market. Indeed, because of deficiencies in laws and enforcement, actual market features in Korea reveal serious distortions of competition evidenced by such facts as significant shortages in supplies of equity securities and the lack of reasonable investment and production decisions; the lack of fair and timely disclosure; frequent dishonest practices and trading by insiders and market professionals hurting public investors; and services of low quality in the industry.

In sum, the development of the Korean securities market has been deterred by two major factors—the monopolistic control of the equity securities by a few business elites and the lack of a fair and reliable investment climate. Employing various evil practices, a few business elites try to monopolize the economy's real resources and do not spread their equity holdings. Such a reluctance to spread equity holdings actually leverages their capital structure further, resulting in serious disequilibrium in supply and demand and impairing market depth and liquidity; thus, securities have never been readily available at a reasonable price and on a continuing basis. Policies enacted by special legislation to resolve these problems have been seriously undermined and challenged by certain business elites.

Therefore, at the primary securities market level, this dissertation has recommended strengthening and rationalizing the current regulation of the market, which has been ineffective as well as unfair, inconsistent, and unreasonable. Special emphasis has been placed on enforcing the going public policy; reconciling conflicting interests; compelling fair and full disclosure; strenthening anti-fraud regulation; and strengthening and rationalizing the regulation of financial affairs, including declarations of dividends.

At the secondary market level, this study has also recommended strengthening and rationalizing current regulations to ensure a fair and honest investment climate, the common goal of capitalistic nations. Securities are intricate merchandise. A securities market can be developed only in an investment climate that compels timely and full disclosure to investors and directs the fair and equitable principles of trade as a standard to all those who participate in the market as professionals.

Investors will not entrust their savings to the securities market unless they have confidence in the mechanism which constitutes market and professional standards. In this concern, special emphasis has been placed on refining the disclosure rule; specifying the fair and equitable principles of trade; enacting a far-reaching anti-fraud rule, including insider trading; and protecting the interest of public shareholders, particularly in the area of mergers, consolidations, takeover bids, and other processes of organic changes.

All the recommendations for strengthening government regulation include the potential for impairing the ideal market. Thus, increased government involvement in the industry has its limits and can be justified only when it fulfills the purpose of the recommended policy.

Finally, no industry in the real world, now or in the past, has satisfied all the conditions of the ideal. The securities market in Korea will encounter numerous new problems in a rapidly changing, sophisticated financial world, problems which will challenge our goals. Even though Korea fails to reach its goals for the securities market, a strenuous effort by lawmakers and regulators to attain the ideal is clearly an important step and will thus contribute to attaining social objectives. This study, which begins to identify problems and to find solutions in an area which has been completely neglected by scholars in Korea, is to participate in that effort. If this study can affect the law-makers and regulators in Korea to reappraise the current rules and enforcement, its purpose will have been fulfilled.

Appendix

Recent Developments

Section I. *Steps Taken for Liberalization of the Capital Market*

The Government announced on January 14, 1982, that it intended to open the Korean securities markets to nonresidents through four steps to be taken during the period from 1981 through the early 1990s. The respective time periods and the policy targets set for the four-step liberalization of the Korean securities markets are as set forth in the Committee Report.

Committee Report (dated September 18, 1981) **on the Current Status of Promotion in the Internationalization of the Securities Market**

I. Basic Policy on the Promotion of Internationalization of Securities Market (as proclaimed by the Minister of Finance on January 14, 1982)

In compliance with the administrative policy of the President, in order to consolidate economic cooperation with the foreign countries of the world by maintaining an open economic system, and to actively meet the international trend of internationalizing various fields of the economy such as liberalization of trade and foreign exchanges, the government decided to internationalize our securities market on a gradual, step by step basis, as follows:

Steps of Promotion	Plan of Promotion
1st Step (1981–1984)	a) Limited allowance of international investment trust
	b) Allowance of inland operation of foreign securities companies (on official level)
	c) Training of personnel for securities institutions and preparation for accommodations
2nd Step (After 1985)	Limited allowance of foreigner's investment in domestic securities.

3rd Step (Latter half of the 1980s)	a) Full allowance of foreigner's investment in domestic securities
	b) Encouragement of offering and issuance by Korean companies of securities in the overseas capital markets.
4th Step (First part of of the 1990s)	Full liberalization of market and outflow of capital (Allowance of investment in foreign securities by domestic personnel)

1. *Current Status of Promotion in the 1st Stage* (1981~1984)
   a) Limited allowance of international investment trust
      (1) Basic plan:
> By the end of 1981, the two securities investment trust companies shall be allowed to establish Korea International Trusts for exclusive use by foreigners in accordance with the current regulations and their certificates shall be sold overseas.
>
> Around the first half of 1983, the operational scope of the Korea International Trusts shall be expanded to the establishment of investment trust companies (Korea Fund) in a foreign country and public subscription shall be invited for the Korea Fund which shall in turn be invested in domestic securities.

      (2) Current status of promotion:
          (i) Overseas sale of investment trust certificates for exclusive use by foreigners:
> Currently Korea Investment Trust Co., Ltd. and Daihan Investment Trust Co., Ltd. are continuing negotiations with certain foreign institutions in order to establish and sell their trust within this year. The promotion, however, is being carried out within the scope of the following regulations:
> 1) Limit of establishment: The promotion shall be regulated by the government taking into account the then conditions of the Korean securities market (factors of impact and possible supply limit of blue chip securities).
> 2) Types of trust and control of investment limit: The promotion shall comply with the current

regulations as contemplated in the Securities. Investment Trust Business Act.

3) Foreign exchange: Remittance of a certain amount of foreign exchange, which will be set by the government, shall be exempted from foreign exchange regulations.

4) The system: The promotion shall be in accordance with the current tax regulations.

(ii) Establishment and operation of Korea Fund:

With regard to Korea Fund, a preliminary consultation was made with International Finance Corporation (IFC) and other institutions during April of 1981, and continued negotiations with IFC are scheduled in the future. The following problems, however, must be solved;

1) Problems of economic conditions, overseas credit rating, economic level, balance of payment, functions of price and interest, and constitution of business management;

2) Conditions of securities market: Problems of supply of blue chip securities, function of prices, accommodating attitude by business circle, system of market (issuance at market price, system of transaction in real names, accounting system, etc.);

3) Problems of meeting legal and institutional requirements of the counterpart country; and

4) Problem of selecting convincing underwriters.

Also since the acceptance of Korea Fund means allowing the acquisition of stocks by foreigners, it is considered necessary to take measures on the following institutional regulations:

1) Regulation of investment limit (limitation on total amount);

2) Regulation of investment method and target enterprise;

3) Regulation of the kind of business invested in;

4) Regulation of foreign exchange; and

     5) System of taxation.

(iii) Current status of working level/operation:

In order to study supplementary problems in the working level in the wake of the policy to allow international investment trust, a working team was organized and operated twice, one in September, 1980 and the other in July, 1981.

    1) Organization: Composed of responsible persons in the related working levels of the Ministry of Finance, the Securities Supervisory Board, the Korea Stock Exchange, Korea Investment Trust Co., Ltd. and Daihan Investment Trust Co., Ltd.

    2) Items of study: Studied and examined operation plans on international investment trust and provided the government with the policy materials.

    3) The above team shall be absorbed into the newly formed working-level study team of the Consulting Committee for Internationalization of Securities Market and shall be operated as a special team for the working-level study of internationalization.

b) Allowance of inland operation by foreign securities firms:

(1) Basic plan:

At the present stage friendly exchanges are being made on the representative or liaison office level under the principle of reciprocity and, from the second stage, establishment of branch offices will be allowed and the internationalization of securities business and operation shall gradually be promoted.

(2) Current status of promotion:

The government approved in December, 1980 the establishment of the Seoul Representative Office of the Nomura Securities Co., Ltd. of Japan, and currently another application for establishment of a Seoul Representative Office has been submitted from Yamaichi Securities Co., Ltd. of Japan. Overseas operation of

domestic securities companies has not materialized.
c) Training of personnel for securities institutions and preparation for accommodations:

As for training of personnel for securities institutions a study
class for securities English was set up in the Securities Research Institute in November, 1980, and trained working-
level personnel from various securities institutions (first
training: 25 persons). In October, 1981, an audio-visual
training classroom is expected to be completed and it will be
used for teaching securities in English. Also, each institute
is sending its employees abroad for language and, practical
business education.

As for the preparation for accommodation of the securities
business circle: (1) Reinforcement of staff; (2) Innovation
of business operation and accumulation of capital for the
purpose of enhancing public confidence; (3) Solidification
of institutional footings, are some of the very extensive problems involved. First of all, translation of securities related
statutes into English and standardization of security terms
have been actively promoted since May, 1981 under the
sponsorship of the Korean Association of Securities Dealers
as follows:

(1) Organization of Promotion Committee: With president of the Association as Chairman, it is composed
of vice presidents from ten institutions.

(2) Target of Promotion: Translation into English of
sixty-five (65) items of statute under the four-year
plan, and the standardization of terms will lead to
publication of a dictionary by June, 1982.

2. *Future Problems for Internationalization of the Korean Securities
Market*

a) Supplementary measures for efficient operation of the international investment trust (in particular, Korea Fund):

(1) Regulation of investment such as the approval of investment and restriction on the kind of the enterprise;

(2) Regulation of foreign exchange;

(3) Problem of tax system;

(4) Problem of meeting legal requirements in the foreign

land;

(5) Problem of supplementing our security system and accounting system; and

(6) Selection of convincing underwriters.

b) Study of promotion plan for internationalization from the long range viewpoint:

(1) Examination of economical appropriateness of each policy measure:

(2) Judgment of conditions and timing of promotion for each policy measure; and

(3) Measure for supplementing regulations for each policy measure.

Outline of Procedures for Organization & Operation of Consulting Committee for Internationalization of Securities Market

Article 1 (Purpose)

This outline of procedures sets forth the matters required for the organization and operation of the Consulting Committee for Internationalization of the Securities Market (hereinafter called the "Consulting Committee") which will effectively promote the internalization of the securities market in accordance with Article 15 of the Regulations of the Securities Control Committee.

Article 2 (Composition)

1) The Consulting Committee shall be composed of one chairman who may be designated by the chairman of the Securities Control Committee and members corresponding to each item below:

a) Chief of Securities Section I, Bureau of Securities & Insurances, Ministry of Finance;

b) Chief of Foreign Exchange Policy Section, Bureau of Foreign Exchange, Ministry of Finance;

c) Two Assistant Vice Presidents of the Securities Supervisory Board who may be designated by the President of the Securities Supervisory Board;

d) One Director of the Korea Securities Exchange who may be designated by the President of the Korea Securities Exchange;

e) One Director of the Bank of Korea who may be designated

by the President of the Bank of Korea; and

f) Less than three men of learning and experience who may be entrusted by the Chairman of Securities Control Committee.

2) The tenure of members from Items a) through f) above shall be one year.

Article 3 (Tasks)

The Consulting Committee shall study and examine the following items and report their results to the Securities Control Committee thereby providing the Government with policy materials.

1) Promotion Plan for Internationalization of the Securities Market;

2) Regulations and institutions attendant upon promotion for Internationalization of the Securities Market;

3) Other consultative items regarding Internationalization of the Securities Market.

Article 4 (Meeting & Office Work)

1) A meeting of the Consulting Committee shall be called at any time when the theme of the discussion is decided and when deemed necessary by the Chairman of the Consulting Committee.

2) In case of an accident with the Chairman of the Consulting Committee one member who may be designated by the Chairman of the Securities Control Committee shall assume the office of the Chairman vicariously.

3) One of the Assistant Vice Presidents of the Securities Supervisory Board who are members and who may be designated by the Chairman of the Consulting Committee shall be appointed to the position of a manager to take charge of the office works.

Article 5 (Operation of Working-level Study Team)

1) The Consulting Committee shall organize and operate a working-level study team in order to supplement the business functions of the Consulting Committee.

2) The Working-level Study Team shall be composed of directors of pertinent institutions selected with the cooperation of presidents of the said institutions to the extent deemed necessary by the Chairman of the Consulting Committee.

3) The Team Master of the Working-level Study Team shall be assumed by the Manager of the Consulting Committee.

Article 6 (Operating Expenses)

1) For each attendance to the meeting each member of the Consulting Committee may be paid an amount not exceeding ₩20,000 as travel expenses.

2) All the expenses regarding the operation of the Consulting Committee shall be borne by the Securities Supervisory Board.

ADDENDUM

This outline of procedures shall be implemented from Angust, 1981.

II. Establishment of Korea International Trust Funds

With the strong encouragement of the Government, in November, 1981, the two investment trust companies successfully established Korea International Investment Trusts, the certificates of which were fully distributed to non-residents through private placements. The establishment of the trusts was a significant move toward the liberalization of the Korean securities market. Both trusts were established in the contractual type and differ in their structures from the mutual funds of the corporate type.

The following, up to page 458, are excerpted, from the Placing Memorandum dated November 12, 1981, which was prepared for the offering of beneficial certificates of Korea International Trust (the "Trust") managed by Korea Investment Trust Co., Ltd. ("KITC").

INTRODUCTION AND SUMMARY

The Trust was established under a trust deed dated as of 30th October, 1981 (the "Trust Deed") between Korea Investment Trust Co., Ltd. and Bank of Seoul and Trust Company (the "Trustee") and is the first vehicle for portfolio investment by non-residents to be authorised in the Republic. The principal objective of the Trust is capital appreciation through investment in listed equities of Korean corporations. The Trust Deed is governed by Korean law.

Investors in the Trust may require redemption of their Units at any time after 30th October, 1982. It is expected that subsequent issues of Units will be made in tranches, by the Manager, to international investors subject to the approval of the Minister of Finance (the "Minister") and the Investment Advisory Council of the Trust (the "Council"). Income distributions will be made annually, in or around June, beginning in 1982, and will be calculated with reference to current cash dividend and interest income. Net capital gains, realised and unrealised, will not be distributed as income.

The Trust's portfolio will be managed by KITC, the largest manager of funds invested in the Korean securities markets. Incorporated in 1974, KITC is owned by all of the city banks and the securities companies in the Republic. The Minister is empowered to regulate the activities of investment trust managers in the Republic and as a matter of policy exercises close supervision of these activities. Bank of Seoul and Trust Company will act as custodian of the Trust's assets, in addition to exercising certain limited trustee functions.

The Council will consist initially of five Korean and five non-Korean members and will review the Manager's activities in relation to the Trust, give advice and make recommendations to the Manager regarding policies and investments, organise the publication and dissemination of research on the Trust's investments and on Korean equities and the Korean economy and securities markets generally and exercise certain other functions on behalf of Holders.

The Trust's assets will be invested chiefly in equities listed on the Korea Stock Exchange. Up to 10 per cent. of the Trust may be invested in bonds of more than six months' maturity. The Manager is required under the Securities Investment Trust Act of 1969, as amended, and the Enforcement Decree, Regulations and Directives relating to it (together the "Law") to maintain not less than 10 per cent. of the Trust's assets in the form of cash and short-term monetary instruments. The Manager is also entitled to convert all the Trust's property into such a form. The Trust Deed and the Law contain several further restrictions on investments which may be made by the Trust.

Under current legislation, the Trust itself is not liable for Korean taxes in respect of income or capital gains. In accordance with the treatment of payments for Korean tax purposes which has been agreed by the Minister, Holders of Beneficial Certificates or IDRs will be liable to Korean taxes (which will be withheld from payments by the Manager), unless exempt under any applicable treaty or other arrangement, on income distributions and in respect of capital gains upon redemption. As detailed under "Taxation Aspects" below, the Republic has currently in force taxation treaties with 12 countries which involve some reduction in tax rates. Holders will be required to furnish certificates of residence and (in the case of a redemption of Units) evidence of terms of transfer in order to take advantage of any benefits available to them.

Fees totalling 1.4 per cent. per annum of the average net asset value of the Trust will be paid to the Manager, the Trustee and the Council for their services to the Trust. Further expenses arising from the operation of the Trust by the Manager, as detailed under "Valuation" below, will be reimbursable by the Trust.

Units in the Trust will be represented by Beneficial Certificates issued by the Manager which, except for those held by Japanese residents, will be deposited with Morgan Guaranty Trust Company of New York (the "Depositary"), who will issue IDRs in exchange. Thereafter, the Depositary will exchange IDRs for the underlying Beneficial Certificates at any time, upon request by Holders of IDRs. *The above Introduction and Summary is qualified by, and subject to, the remainder of this Placing Memorandum.*

THE TRUST

Establishment and Relevant Legislation

The Government of the Republic announced, on 14th January, 1981, that it intended to open the Korean securities markets to non-residents, initially through the domestic investment trust system. To this end, the Minister, by a letter dated 28th October, 1981, amended the Foreign Exchange Control Regulations of the Republic, giving general approvals for transactions by non-residents in Beneficial Certificates of Korean investment trusts. (See "Foreign Exchange Aspects" below.) Other forms of investment by non-residents in the Korean securities markets will continue to require case-by-case authorizations by the Minister. Such authorizations have not in the past been generally available (other than, from time to time, in relation to direct investments in Korean enterprises by foreign companies).

The Trust is the first to be established pursuant to these changes in official policy and regulation, for the purpose of channelling foreign portfolio investment into the Republic. While conforming in many respects to Korean investment trust practice, the Trust differs significantly from other domestic investment trusts, in that the Trust Deed contains more detailed provisions than is customary, particularly in regard to investment policy, valuation, redemption, remuneration and liability. In addition, the introduction of the Council and its advisory and supervisory functions and the provisions for meetings of Holders are without precedent in the Korean investment trust system.

The Trust Deed will be governed principally by the Securities Investment Trust Act of 1969, as amended, and the Enforcement Decree, Regulations and Directives relating to it (the "Law" as defined). The Law provides a framework for the establishment and operation of investment trusts in the Republic, vesting ultimate authority in the Minister (see "Government Supervision and Regulation" below). In addition to the Law, the activities of the Manager with respect to the Trust are affected by the Commercial Code and the Securities and Exchange Act of 1962, as amended.

Beneficial Certificates

The Units will be evidenced by Beneficial Certificates, which may be in either registered or bearer form, at the option of the Holder. Beneficial Certificates in bearer form will have coupons attached on issue, which will enable the Holder to obtain payment of income distributions, and title to them will pass by delivery. Beneficial Certificates in registered form may be transferred by endorsement in favour of a named individual or by a written instrument of transfer and the transferor shall be deemed to be the Holder until the transferee's name is entered in the register.

Investment Policy

Initially, the Trust's assets will consist of the Won equivalent of $15,000,000 to be invested primarily in equities listed on the Korea Stock Exchange (the "Stock Exchange"). The principal objective in the management of the portfolio will be capital appreciation of the Trust's assets, although cash dividends received or receivable in respect of the Trust's assets will not be reinvested but will be available for distribution. (See "Income Distributions" below.) The Manager intends to select a broad portfolio of equities, to be managed actively in terms of turnover. While investment policy will be the prime responsibility of the Manager, the Council will contribute regularly to the formulation of investment policy.

Apart from listed equities, the Manager may invest, on behalf of the Trust, in non-listed equities which are offered to the Manager on a perferential basis during the process of listing such equities and, subject as mentioned in (i) below, in national and local government bonds and bonds issued by statutory and private corporations. The Manager, under the Law, is required at all times to keep at least 10 per cent. of the Trust's assets in cash or short-term monetary instruments as a reserve to meet redemption requests by Holders and will further be permitted to convert the whole of the Trust into cash or monetary instruments (which includes bonds) authorised under the Trust Deed, subject to the restriction that the periods to final maturity of such monetary investments (apart from the amounts of investments allowed under (i) below) may not exceed six months.

The restrictions placed on investment of the Trust's assets either under the Law or the Trust Deed prevent the Manager from:

(i) investing more than 10 per cent. of the aggregate value of the Trust's assets in bonds of more than six months to final maturity;

(ii) investing in more than 10 per cent. of any one class of securities issued by any one issuer;

(iii) investing more than 10 per cent. of the aggregate value of the Trust's assets in securities of any one issuer;

(iv) dealing in commodities or commodities contracts;

(v) using the Trust's resources for underwriting activities;

(vi) investing in unlisted securities, except where such securities are acquired on a preferential basis during the process of their listing;

(vii) making loans, except to the extent that permitted investments in monetary instruments are in the nature of loans;

(viii) dealing short or on margin;

(ix) investing in real estate or real estate mortgages; and

(x) borrowing in the name of the Trust.

However, if the restrictions referred to in paragraphs (i), (ii) or (iii) are exceeded, except as a direct result of investment by the Manager, the Manager is not required to reduce the Trust's holding of the relevant asset until the end of 183 days.

The Law further requires that the Manager should purchase only those equity securities which either have been traded on the Stock Exchange for at least 10 of the 30 days preceding purchase (except equities in the process of being offered publicly); or have been issued by companies which have paid dividends during the latest fiscal year or which are reasonably expected to pay dividends in the following fiscal year; or which are reasonably expected to produce a yield (computed by reference to dividends and capital appreciation) or more than 15 per cent. per annum. Purchase of equity securities not falling into any of these categories requires specific authorisation from the Minister. Similarly, bonds eligible for purchase should yield more than 15 per cent. per annum.

With regard to the investment of the proceeds of the initial issue of Units in the Trust, the Manager will pay particular attention to the possible impact on Stock Exchange prices given the significance of the size of the issue in relation to the current total market capitalisation and average daily trading volume. The initial proceeds will be equivalent to approximately 0.34 per cent. of the total market capitalisation of companies listed on the Stock Exchange as at 31st August, 1981 and 1.3 times average daily market turnover in the year to that date.

As is customary in the Republic, there are provisions in the Trust Deed permitting the Manager to effect transactions between its own assets and those of the Trust at certain times, namely, during the period after any issue of Units, the period needed for realization of underlying assets in the case of a large-scale redemption of Units and the period before an accounting date, in order to provide liquidity and reduce pressure on stock market prices. In the first case, the Manager will be permitted to sell securities from its own portfolio into that of the Trust, and in the other cases, to buy securities from the Trust.

In transactions between the Manager's and the Trust's account, the applicable prices will be the relevant closing market prices on the Stock Exchange on the day preceding the day of the transactions, or where there is no closing price for the preceding day, then the latest closing market price (except where, in the opinion of the Manager, this would provide an unfair valuation, in which case the price will be determined on the basis of guidelines issued by the Minister).

In the case of securities transactions on the Stock Exchange, the Manager may apportion trading business to all of the securities companies.

Income Distributions

Distributions in respect of income will be made annually in or around June, beginning in June 1982. The amount of income available for distribution in respect of each accounting period will be calculated by deducting the operating fees and expenses of the Trust, any provision for taxation and any reserves made under the direction of the Minister, from the sum of cash dividends received, interest received or receivable and any reserves (the distribution of which has been approved by the Minister) in respect of income made in previous years. Certain expense items of a capital nature, notably brokerage fees, will be charged against capital instead of income. Net capital gains (whether realized or not) and stock dividends will not be distributed as income, nor will capital losses be charged against income. Although the Manager has the power to withhold a proportion of income available for distribution as a reserve for the purposes of equalizing income distributions or providing against capital losses, it is expected that such a withholding would occur only in extreme circumstances. Amounts available for distribution as income will be paid by the Manager into a separate, interest-bearing account and interest on that account will be credited to the Trust.

Reflecting the present timing of corporate accounting periods in the Republic, the Trust's accounting periods will run annually from 1st April to the following 31st March, except for the first accounting period, which will run from the Closing Date to 31st March, 1982. Most Korean companies have accounting periods which coincide with the calendar year and pay dividends by the end of March. It is possible that there will be changes in accounting dates of Korean corporations over the next few years, in which case income distributions from the Trust may, at the discretion of the Manager, become payable semi-annually.

Redemptions

Redemptions of Units may be made at the option of Holders of Beneficial Certificates at any time after 30th October, 1982 at a price calculated by reference to net asset value on the day following receipt of a Holder's request for redemption. Upon receiving a Holder's request for redemption, the Manager may either (a) purchase the Units for its own account at a price equal to net asset value per Unit less one per cent., or (b) cancel the appropriate number of Units upon receipt from the Trustee of the relevant amount from the Trust's cash reserves, or from the sale of securities from the Trust's portfolio, making payment to the Holder at the price of net asset value less one per cent., or if realization costs exceed one per cent., at a price of net asset value per Units less those costs. Under the Law, the Manager may, subject to the approval of the Minister, suspend redemptions during closure of the Stock Exchange or other *force majeure* events. The Manager is further entitled, under the Trust Deed, to suspend valuation in certain circumstances (See "Valuation" below).

Termination

The Trust will terminate in the year 2001 (unless it is extended), or in certain other circumstances, namely, if the Manager goes into compulsory liquidation, or has a receiver appointed over it, or ceases business; if the Trust becomes illegal or it becomes impracticable or inadvisable to continue the Trust as a result of a change in law; or if the Trustee retires and is not replaced within three months. The Trust may also be terminated by resolution of a meeting of Holders, subject to the approval of the Minister. In the event of termination of the Trust, Holders will be entitled to the portion of the net realization proceeds corresponding to the proportion of total outstanding Units represented by their holdings of Units.

Valuation

The net asset value of the Trust will be calculated by deducting actual and accrued (but not contingent) liabilities from the aggregate value of the Trust's assets (as determined in accordance with guidelines issued by the Minister) and net asset value per Unit will be calculated by dividing net asset value by the number of Units outstanding, including those held by the Manager. Expenses which may be paid from the Trust's assets by the Manager, in addition to the remuneration of the Manager, the Trustee and the Council as mentioned in the relevant sections below, include the fees and certain expenses of the Depositary (except those in relation to the initial issue) and stamp duties and certain taxation, brokerage, fiscal, auditing, communication, printing, legal and other operating expenses.

In calculating net asset value per Unit, securities held by the Trust will be valued at their most recent closing prices in the case of securities regularly traded on the Stock Exchange or otherwise in accordance with guidelines of the Minister regarding the valuation of securities by investment trusts, which contain detailed formulae for valuation in various special circumstances. The relevant guidelines are set out in the Trust Deed.

The Manager may, under the Trust Deed, suspend the calculation of net asset value per Unit for the purpose of any proposed cancellation of Units during any period when, *inter alia*, the Stock Exchange is closed or during which trading on that exchange is restricted, or when foreign exchange conversions for the purpose of remittance of distributions may not be made, or during any period when in the opinion of the Manager the determination of net asset value per Unit may not fairly be made.

All valuations expressed in Won will be translated at the then current spot selling rate for the Won against the Dollar as quoted by a leading foreign exchange bank in the Republic.

Payments

In order to obtain a distribution of income, a request for payment should be made to the Manager in Seoul and, in the case of a bearer Beneficial Certificate, the bearer of the relevant coupon appertaining to the Beneficial Certificate should present that coupon to the Manager in Seoul with such request for payment.

In the case of Beneficial Certificates represented by IDRs, the bearer of the relevant IDR coupon may present that coupon, and the Depositary will make the necessary request for payment of the distribution of income. Holders of IDRs will be notified of the gross amount of the distribution, the date on or after which the distribution may be requested and the number of the IDR coupon which should be presented with such requests.

Any request for redemption of a Unit (whether the Manager decides to repurchase or to have the Unit cancelled) must be accompanied by the relevant Beneficial Certificate evidencing that Unit. The Depositary, where it is the Holder of the relevant Beneficial Certificate, will make the request for redemption or payment on cancellation, on receipt of the IDR representing that Beneficial

Certificate, together with instructions to the Depositary to make the request.

In order to ensure that Korean tax is withheld from payments at the appropriate rate and, in the case of distributions otherwise than of income, that any capital gain arising is computed on the basis of the actual cost of acquisition by the person receiving payment, evidence of residential status and (in the case of distribution otherwise than of income) of the date, and cost of acquisition in the prescribed form should be presented together with the Beneficial Certificate or coupon or IDR or IDR coupon, as the case may be. (See "Taxation Aspects" below.)

Payments by the Manager will be made in Won at its office in Seoul, by bank cheque or transfer, except that payments made by the Manager to the Depositary will be converted into Dollars (subject to foreign exchange, fiscal and other regulations) and remitted to an account of the Depositary with a bank in New York City. The Depositary will pay the amounts so received by transfer to an account with a bank in New York City notified by the Holder of the IDR, or by a Dollar cheque drawn on a bank in New York City and sent to the address notified by the Holder, at the time of presentation of the IDR or IDR coupon by the Holder.

For further information, see "Description of Depositary Arrangements" below.

Prescription

No distributions of income or other amounts may be claimed after 5 years from the date on which they first became payable.

The Manager

The Manager will be responsible for the continuing administration of the Trust's affairs, including investing the assets of the Trust; executing redemptions and resale of Units; making distributions in respect of income and redemptions; calculating and publishing in the Republic the net asset value of the Trust daily and arranging for monthly publication overseas as described under "Information" below; instructing the Trustee to maintain, exchange and dispose of the Trust's assets as required; maintaining the books and records of the Trust; and making new issues of Units as approved by the Minister and the Council. The Manager will also arrange the calling to meetings of Holders of Beneficial Certificates (except where such meetings are called by the Trustee). The Manager will publish the semi-annual reports and annual accounts, to be provided to Holders, and is required to produce various reports to the Minister and the Council as described under "Government Supervision and Regulation" and "Investment Advisory Council" below. Further, any Holder of Beneficial Certificates may require the Manager to make available the books and records of the Trust for inspection.

In performing its functions, the Manager owes, under the Law and the Trust Deed, a duty of care to Holders of Beneficial Certificates but will be indemnified by the Trust in respect of claims not arising from actions or omissions involving gross, material or wilful breach of fiduciary duty. Such indemnity will be limited to $15,000 per claim where a reasonable person, in the position of the Manager and acting diligently and in good faith, would not have so acted or omitted to act. The Manager may be removed if it goes into liquidation (except for voluntary liquidation on terms approved by the Council), or if a receiver is appointed over its assets, or if Holders so decide by an extraordinary resolution (unless the Minister disapproves of such decision), or if the Manager's licence is cancelled.

The Manager will receive a fee of one per cent. per annum of the net asset value of the Trust, accrued daily and paid quarterly in arrears, as remuneration for its services, in addition to reimbursement for certain out-of-pocket expenses as described under "Valuation".

For other information about the Manager, see "Korea Investment Trust Co., Ltd." below.

The Trustee

Bank of Seoul and Trust Company is the only authorised trustee under the Law and is one of the five city banks of the Republic. As such, it is a shareholder of the Manager. At 31st December, 1980, it had total assets of Won 3,339 billion ($5.1 billion); 31.2 per cent. of the Manager that date was held by the Government.

As a result of the broad role played by the Manager under Korean law, the Trustee exercises only limited functions, and will act chiefly as custodian for the assets of the Trust, which are registered in the Trustee's name, but for which the Trustee will keep separate accounts. The Trustee also has the formal power under the Law to request rectification of any actions by the Manager with which it disagrees (although in the event of a dispute between the Manager and the Trustee in this context, the Minister acts as final arbiter) and is entitled to call meetings of Holders.

The Trustee will receive full indemnity from the Trust for any claims against it and a fee of 0.2 per cent. per annum of the net asset value of the Trust, accrued daily and paid quarterly in arrears.

Investment Advisory Council

Under the Trust Deed, the Council has the power to review the activities of the Manager and to advise and recommend to the Manager both the nature of securities and specific securities to be acquired by the Trust. The Council will have certain other rights designed to maintain the interests of investors, including the right to request the Trustee to exercise its rights or powers, to make reasonable requests for information from the Manager, to call, through the Manager, meetings of Holders and to approve any change in auditors and any new issues of Units by the Manager. The Council will have as one of its functions the preparation and dissemination of information about the Trust's performance and the Korean economy and securities markets generally, for the benefit of investors participating in the Trust.

The Council will consist of not less than six members, of whom the Chairman will always be non-Korean, with a casting vote where necessary. It is intended that membership will usually be institutional rather than individual. The Council will initially consist of five Korean members and five non-Korean members, who are expected to be as follows:

The Korean Development Bank
Korea Development Institute
Korea Securities Finance Corporation
Professor Y. D. Uh (a professor of international finance at Korea University)
Baring Brothers & Co., Limited
Credit Suisse First Boston Limited
Lazard Brothers & Co., Limited
Vickers da Costa Limited
Yamaichi Securities Company, Limited

Meetings will be held twice annually on a formal basis and more frequently as deemed appropriate; all meetings are expected to be held in Seoul. Members may appoint any person to participate in the affairs of the Council on their behalf. Members will generally be elected for terms of two years and elections are expected to be held annually. Members will retire by rotation. In the election process, the non-Korean members must approve the Korean members and *vice versa*.

Council members will receive a monthly report from the Manager containing a portfolio statement and record of transactions entered into on the Trust's behalf (in particular in relation to any transactions involving an exchange of assets between the Manager and the Trust as referred to under "Investment Policy" above) and such other information as may reasonably be required by the Council.

In addition, prior to each of the semi-annual meetings, the Manager will send a report to members of the Council on the activities and performance of the Trust and its investments, together with a schedule of all current investments and such further information as the Council may reasonably require which may include a review of developments in the economy and the securities markets.

Members of the Council will receive full indemnity from the Trust for any claims against them in their capacity as Council Members. A sum of 0.2 per cent. per annum of the net asset value of the Fund, accrued daily and payable semi-annually, will be paid to the Council, of which 20 per cent. will be paid to the Korean members for expenses of preparation and attendance and any research carried out and the remainder of which will be disbursed at the discretion of the non-Korean members for the preparation and dissemination of information on the Trust, Korean equities, the securities markets and the economy generally, for the benefit of Holders.

Auditors

The Auditors of the Trust will be Peat, Marwick, Mitchell & Co., who will audit accounts of the Trust on internationally accepted accounting principles for the purpose of the annual statement to be distributed to Holders.

Resales, New Issues and Marketability

The Manager may resell Units previously purchased and held by it at a price equal to net asset value per Unit plus one per cent. Any profit made as a result of resales will be retained by the Manager for its own account. Any new issues of Units will be made in tranches at a price equal to net asset value per Units plus an amount to cover fees and expenses for the issue and any costs arising from the purchase of investments with the proceeds of the new issue. Each new issue made by the Manager will require the prior approval of the Minister and the Council. It is expected that resales and new issues of Units will be made, to the extent permitted by the applicable laws and regulations, in the form of IDRs. Vickers da Costa Limited have indicated to the Manager that they will make arrangements for secondary market dealing in the IDRs on a "best efforts" basis.

Information

The net asset value per Unit in Won, the resulting Dollar equivalent and the exchange rate used will be communicated daily to Vickers da Costa Limited in London and to the Depositary in Brussels. The net asset value of a Unit in Won and the corresponding value in Dollars represented by an IDR will be published monthly in a major English-language daily newspaper which is expected to be the *Financial Times* in London.

Copies of an audited annual statement showing, *inter alia*, details of the calculation of the amount of income distributable for the period to which the statement relates, the composition of the investment portfolio and the net asset value per Unit on the date following the date to which the statement is made up, will be sent to Holders of registered Beneficial Certificates. In addition, an unaudited interim statement will be prepared and sent to registered Holders, containing similar information except in relation to details of income and expenses. All statements will be printed in English and will be further available on request from the Manager (and from the Depositary–see "Description of Depositary Arrangements–Reports and Notices" below).

Amendments to the Trust Deed

Amendments to the Trust Deed which, in the opinion of the Manager and the Trustee, would not prejudice the interests of Holders, may be made by the Manager and the Trustee, with the approval of the Council and upon receipt of a certificate from legal advisers to the Trust that any proposed change would not materially prejudice Holders' interests. In addition, meetings of Holders may also pass resolutions amending the Trust Deed. Any such amendments are subject to the approval of the Minister.

GOVERNMENT SUPERVISION AND REGULATION

Investment trust companies in the Republic are subject, principally, to the Securities Investment Trust Act of 1969 and the Enforcement Decree, Regulations and Directives made under that law (the "Law", as defined). Directives are issued by the Minister in relation to, *inter alia*, the general administration of trusts, the selection of investments and the method of valuation of assets.

Under the Law, the Minister has the power to license companies to carry on the business of managing a securities investment trust, and supervises and gives guidance to investment trust companies. In order to obtain a licence, the applicant, which must be a limited liability company having a share capital amounting to at least Won 500 million, must satisfy the Minister as to its constitution, management and method of operation. The Minister has wide discretion in deciding whether to grant a licence or not. In addition, the trust deed constituting each investment trust, any amendment made to a trust deed and any termination of a trust, require the approval of the Minister. As mentioned above, the Minister arbitrates in the event of a dispute between a manager and a trustee.

Certain matters affecting the status and business activities of a manuger also require the approval of the Minister; these include any amendments to a manager's articles of incorporation or to the portfolio management policy submitted by a manager at the time of its incorporation to the Minister, the establishment or reopening by a manager of a branch office, the voluntary liquidation of a manager, any merger, consolidation or transfer of the whole or any part of the business of a manager, and any acquisitions of the shares of a manager or any whole or any part of the business of a manager, and any acquisitions of the shares of a manager or any acquisitions by a manager of the whole or any part of the business of others. The Law requires that, if a manager is dissolved (whether as a result of a merger or consolidation or for any other reason) or has its licence revoked or terminates its business as an investment trust company, any deed of trust under which it is a manager must also be terminated, unless a successor company is appointed to the position of manager by the Minister, or unless the transfer of business as a result of the merger or consolidation has been approved by the Minister, or unless the company into which the manager has been merged or consolidated has been licensed to act as a manager.

The Minister also has the power to approve a postponement of any redemption of units by a manager where circumstances, such as natural disaster or suspension of trading in the stock market, render such postponement desirable and may direct a manager to make reserves (which may not be used without the Minister's approval) to provide for capital losses and to equalise distributions of income. The Law enables the Minister to order any manager to submit data or records concerning a trust or to appoint government officials to inspect a trust or the business activities or financial status of a manager and empowers the Minister, where a manager has violated any law or directive or the composition of the assets of a trust is unsatisfactory, or the method of operation of a trust is considered to be unreasonable and detrimental to the public interest or harmful to investors, to dismiss officers of a manager, to suspend the business or cancel a manager's licence, or to terminate or require an amendment to be made to a trust deed. A manager is required under the Law to furnish reports every five days to the Minister in relation to its administration of a trust, including statements of assets and portfolio transactions carried out, as well as more comprehensive monthly and annual statements. A manager must also report partial cancellations of a trust and the appointment or dismissal of any of the manager's officers to the Minister.

Full-time directors of a manager are prohibited by law from engaging on a full-time basis in the business of any other company or from operating any other business, and officers and employees of a manager may not, directly or indirectly, have an interest in the trust or purchase or sell, for their own account, trust assets.

TAXATION ASPECTS

Korean Tax

Under current legislation, the Trust is not liable to any form of Korean taxation on income or capital gains.

Payments from the Trust in respect of income and capital gains is non-residents are subject to Korean withholding tax, in the absence of any exemption under an applicable treaty or other arrangement, and subject to any reduction in the rate of tax available to the person entitled (for Korean tax purposes) to the payment.

The Minister has agreed that distributions of income and capital gains arising from the Trust will be treated for Korean tax purposes as follows:

(a) Liability

    (i) Distributions of income: Distributions in respect of income to non-resident individuals or foreign corporations having no permanent establishments in the Republic ("Non-Residents") are subject to Korean withholding tax. The liability for tax falls on the person whose name is entered in the register as holder of a registered Unit or who is the bearer of the relevant coupon relating to a Beneficial Certificate in bearer form or, where the Beneficial Certificates are held by the Depositary and represented by an IDR, the person is the bearer of the relevant coupon relating to the IDR.

    (ii) Capital gains: Capital gains realised by a Non-Resident of the Republic on the repurchase of Units by the Manager or a cancellation of Units are subject to Korean withholding tax. The liability for the tax falls on the person who presents the relevant Beneficial Certificate with a request to the Manager to repurchase or for payment on cancellation or (where such person is the Depositary) on the bearer of the IDR on whose instructions the Depositary is acting in making the request.

The Manager is obliged under Korean law to withhold tax from payment to all such persons ("Taxable Persons") and to account to the Office of National Tax Administration and to the Ward Office for all tax so withheld.

(b) Rates of Tax

If a Taxable Person presents to the Manager or (where his Units are represented by an IDR) to the Depositary a certificate as to residence in the form prescribed in the Trust Deed and in the Deposit Agreement, at the same time as requesting repurchase of or any payment in respect of the Beneficial Certificate or coupon (as the case may be), the Manager will withhold tax at the rate prescribed under any treaty or other arrangement between the Republic and the country within which the Taxable Person is resident, as evidenced by such certificates as to residence. In the case of withholding tax in respect of capital gains, the Manager will, where alternative rates are available, withhold tax at the rate which will result in the least tax being withheld. In the case of a Taxable Person who is the holder of an IDR (or a coupon relating thereto), the Manager will withhold tax on the basis set out above on receipt of a telexed notification from the Depositary specifying the residence of such holder (as so evidenced). In the absence of any such treaty or other arrangement, or if the Taxable Person fails to present a certificate as to residence in the form and by the time specified above, tax will be withheld by the Manager at the full rate prescribed by law, which is presently 26.875 per cent. in the case of distributions of income and either 43 per cent. of the capital gain or 26.875 per cent. of the gross proceeds of the realisation, whichever is the lower, in the case of capital gains.

Korean law does not entitle a person who has suffered a greater withholding from a distribution or payment to repayment of the excess of such withholding, even though he subsequently produces evidence that he should have been entitled to a withholding at a re-

	Rate of Taxation (per cent.)	
Country (1)	*Income*	*Capital Gains*
Belgium 15		0
Canada 16.125 (2)		0
Denmark 15		0
France 15		0
Japan 12		43 or 26.875 (2) (3)
Netherlands 15		0
Singapore 15		43 or 26.875 (2) (3)
Switzerland 15		0
Thailand .... 21.5 or 26.875 (2)		43 or 26.875 (2) (3)
West Germany 15		43 or 26.875 (2) (3)
United Kingdom 15		0
United States of America 16.125 (2)		0

(1) The Republic has also signed tax treaties with Finland, New Zealand and Sweden which presently await ratification. In addition, the Republic has signed memoranda which are expected to lead to tax treaties being signed with Australia, Malaysia, Morocco and Norway.

(2) These figures include a surcharge of 7.5 per cent. of the basic tax rate.

(3) Of net capital gains or gross sale proceeds, respectively.

duced rate. In addition, he may not be entitled to any tax credit in respect of such withholding to the extent that it exceeds the rate of withholding tax which should have been applied. However, Korean law, in general, provides that in the event of any overpayment of tax, an appeal may be made to the Office of National Tax Administration, with a subsequent right of appeal to a Korean court of competent jurisdiction.

The following table gives applicable tax rates for residents of countries with which the Republic has taxation treaties.

(c) Capital Gains Tax Computation

Where any tax is payable in respect of any capital gain arising on the cancellation or repurchase of a Unit, the amount of such tax, at the appropriate rate ascertained as set out above, shall be computed on the basis that the Units was acquired by the Taxable Person on the date and at the price notified by the Taxable Person to the Manager or (where the Taxable Person is an IDR Holder) to the Depositary at the time of the request by the Taxable Person for repurchase or payment. Such acquisition date and price must be evidence by a form of transfer and receipt (signed by the Taxable Person and by the person from whom he purchased the relevant Unit or IDR) substantially in the form set out in the Trust Deed and in the Deposit Agreement. In the absence of such notifications or evidence, the amount on which the withholding tax is calculated will be ascertained in accordance with the laws of the Republic.

(d) Inheritance and Gift Tax

Inheritance tax is imposed either (a) if the deceased is domiciled in the Republic or (b) the property transferred is situated in the Republic. The latter category includes interests in Units under the Trust. Gift tax is imposed in similar circumstances to the above and is payable by the donee. The taxes are imposed if the value of the property transferred is above a certain limit, which varies according to the identity of the deceased or donor. The rates of inheritance tax range from 7 per cent. to 67 per cent., subject to certain deductions in the case of inheritance tax.

(e) Stamp Duty

Any form of transfer referred to under "Capital Gains Tax Computation" above would, if executed in the Republic, be subject to stamp duty at a rate which varies up to 150,000 Won. Any other document, if executed in the Republic, would be subject to stamp duty at a rate of 50 Won per original document. In the case of the Beneficial Certificates, the Manager will be liable for the payment of stamp duty. No other stamp, issue, registration or similar taxes or duties will, under present Korean law, be payable in the Republic by Holders of Units or IDRs.

Belgian Tax

Under existing laws, no Belgian income, corporate, capital gains, withholding, stamp, transfer, issue, estate, gifts or wealth taxes will be imposed on the Holders of the IDRs or the Depositary in respect of holdings of Units or IDRs or in respect of distributions of capital or income relating thereto except in the case of persons who are subject to Belgian tax by reason of their residence or other connection with Belgium.

FOREIGN EXCHANGE ASPECTS

By virtue of a letter from the Minister dated 28th October, 1981, the following transactions, when carried out by or on behalf of a Manager who has been authorised to carry on business under the Law, are exempted from authorisations under the provisions of the Foreign Exchange Control Regulations of the Republic (the "FE-CR"):

(a) the issue and offer for subscription, underwriting, sale or re-purchase of Beneficial Certificates in a securities investment trust created exclusively for offering or distribution to non-residents (as defined by the Foreign Exchange Control Act); and

(b) the export, import or deposit of such Beneficial Cerificates.

Each remittance outside the Republic of payments of income and capital on such Beneficial Certificates will, under the FECR as so amended, require the approval of a "Class A" foreign exchange bank of the Republic. Such approval is designed largely to confirm that the amount being converted and remitted conforms with the amount payable under the Trust Deed or the Deposit Agreement.

Prior to the amendment of the FECR, all the above transactions required case-by-case approval by the Minister. The benefits of the amendment are applicable only to transactions in Beneficial Certificates as specified and all other types of transaction by non-residents relating to Korean securities will continue to require specific authorisations by the Minister.

DESCRIPTION OF DEPOSITARY ARRANGEMENTS

The IDRs will be issued pursuant to the provisions of the Deposit Agreement between the Manager, the Trustee and Morgan Guaranty Trust Company of New York in Brussels as depositary (the "Depositary"). The IDRs will be in bearer form, transferable by delivery and will represent Beneficial Certificates in respect of 1,000 Units, having endorsed thereon conditions setting out the relevant provisions of the Deposit Agreement. They will evidence the entitlement of the Holder to Beneficial Certificates which will be deposited at the specified office of the Depositary or any Agent appointed by the Depositary for that purpose (the "Agent") on behalf of the Depositary. Attached to each IDR will be a set of numbered coupons which will entitle the bearer to instruct the Depositary to request payment of distributions of income in respect of the Beneficial Certificates represented by the relevant IDR.

Copies of the Deposit Agreement will be available for inspection at the offices of the Depositary and each Agent as described in "General Information" below.

The Deposit Agreement and the conditions endorsed on the IDR contain provisions, *inter alia*, to the following effect:

Deposit of Beneficial Certificates and Issue of IDRs

Subject to the terms and conditions of the Deposit Agreement, including payment of the fees and expenses prescribed therein, the Depositary will accept for Deposit Beneficial Certificates representing 1,000 Units or integral multiples thereof, provided that they are accompanied by such other documents as are prescribed in the Deposit Agreement. Against such delivery the Depositary will issue and deliver to the depositor or upon his order, at the specified office of the Depositary or (at the request, risk and expense of the person entitled thereto) at the specified office of any Agent, IDRs evidencing the relevant Beneficial Certificates.

Withdrawal of Beneficial Certificates

Subject to the terms and conditions of the Deposit Agreement, including payment of the fees and expenses prescribed therein, the Holder of an IDR may, upon surrender, at the specified office of the Depositary or any Agent, of such IDR and all unmatured coupons appertaining thereto accompanied by such other documents (if any) as may be required under the Deposit Agreement, withdraw the Beneficial Certificates evidenced thereby. Against such surrender, the Depositary will, or will direct an Agent to, deliver to the former Holder of the IDR, or to his order, the relevant Beneficial Certificates and any other property held by it and attributable to the relevant IDR. Such delivery will be made at the specified office of the Depositary or (at the request, risk and expense of the former Holder of such IDR) at the specified office of any Agent.

Suspension of Deposit and Withdrawal

The Depositary may, after consultation with the Manager, suspend the issue of IDRs and the acceptance of Beneficial Certificates for deposit generally or in respect of particular Beneficial Certificates at any time. The withdrawal of Beneficial Certificates against the surrender of IDRs may be suspended by the Depositary during any period when the register is closed or, generally or in one or more localities, in order to comply with any applicable law or governmental regulation or, at the discretion of the Manager, to enable payment to be made under the Trust Deed in an orderly manner. The Depositary may also decline to act as agent of the IDR Holder to effect any realisation of the Beneficial Certificates while such realisation is not, for legal or other reasons, possible to carry out.

Charges of the Depositary

The Manager will pay the charges of the Depositary in connection with the initial deposit of the Beneficial Certificates now being issued and the issue of IDRs in respect thereof. The Manager will also pay the costs of notices required to be given by the Depositary to IDR Holders and insurance and other costs incurred by the Depositary in connection with the preparation and execution of the Deposit Ageement, an annual fee of $3,000, the charges of the Depositary on any withdrawal of Beneficial Certificates in the circumstances described below under the heading "Amendment of the Deposit Agreement and Conditions and Termination" and all other costs and expenses of the Depositary and any Agent not specifically referred to below. The Manager will be entitled to recover all amounts so paid by it from the assets of the Trust.

Except as mentione above any person depositing Beneficial Certificates in exchange for the issue of IDRs and any person surrendering IDRs in exchange for the delivery of Beneficial Certificates will be required to pay the Depositary $10 per IDR in each transaction. The Depositary will also charge $0.50 per coupon in respect of each income distribution against presentation of coupons and a reasonable charge for each IDR issued in exchange for an IDR when all coupons relating to that IDR have matured and for issuing replacement IDRs or coupons, or for exercising voting rights in respect of Units evidenced by IDRs.

The Depositary will not be liable for any taxes, duties, charges or expenses which may become payable in respect of the IDRs or the underlying Beneficial Certificates. Any such sum shall be payable by the Holders of the IDRs on request or may be deducted from any net amount due on the IDRs or the coupons appertaining to the IDRs in respect of any distribution. In default of payments, the Depositary may make payment out of the proceeds of sale of any appropriate number of the underlying Beneficial Certificates (representing not less than 1,000 Units) and the Holder of an IDR shall thereupon be bound upon request to surrender the IDRs in exchange for the balance of the net proceeds of sale of the relevant underlying Beneficial Certificates. Any such request shall be made by giving notice as specified below.

Distributions

Subject to the provisions of the Deposit Agreement and to all applicable laws and regulations, all distributions received by the Depositary in respect of the Beneficial Certificates will promptly be converted into Dollars and the proceeds of such conversion will be distributed by the Depositary to the Holder of the IDRs, after deduction of all fees, taxes, charges, duties and expenses which the Manager, the Depositary or any Agents is entitled or required to deduct in respect thereof.

Distributions and Payments

The Depositary may, with the approval of the Manager, appoint one or more Agents for the purpose of making payments and for such other purposes as are provided in the Deposit Agreement.

Notice will be given to IDR Holders of the date of any proposed distribution in respect of Beneficial Certificates, the amount of that distribution and the coupon which should be presented by the IDR Holder with the instructions to the Depositary to request payment in respect of the relevant Beneficial Certificates.

On receipt by the Depositary, either at its specified office or that of an Agent, of (in the case of a distribution of income) the relevant coupon appertaining to an IDR or (in any other case) an IDR, together in each case with a notice specifying an account with a bank in New York City or an address to which payment should be sent, the Depositary will request payment of the relevant distribution in respect of the Beneficial Certificate which is represented by the coupon or IDR presented. Under no other circumstances will the Depositary be obliged to make such a request.

Payments in Dollars will be made by Dollar cheque drawn on, or by transfer to a Dollar account maintained by the payee with, a bank in New York City. The Depositary or any Agent, as the case may be, is entitled to deduct from all moneys payable to the Holder of any IDRs all fees, taxes, charges, duties and expenses which are payable under the Deposit Agreement or under applicable law in respect of such coupon or the relevant underlying Beneficial Certificate.

At the same time as instructing the Depositary to request a distribution in respect of Beneficial Certificates, the Holder of an IDR or coupon should submit (in case of a distribution of income) a certificate of residence, or (in any other case) a certificate of residence, a form of transfer and a receipt, in each case in the form set out in the Deposit Agreement. Failure to sumit such certificate or form of transfer at such time and in such form may result in Korean tax being withheld at a higher rate, or (in the case of a capital gain) being computed on the basis of the gross proceeds of the realisation.

Voting Rights

The Holder of an IDR will have no right to attend or vote or speak at any meeting of Holders of Beneficial Certificates but will be entitled, upon depositing the IDR or (if required by the Depositary) the appropriate coupon at the specified office of the Depositary or any Agent, to instruct the Depositary as to the exercise of the voting rights attached to the Beneficial Certificates evidenced by such IDR. The Depositary will endeavour, insofar as is practicable and subject to any applicable provisions of law or of the Trust Deed, to exercise the voting rights attached to the Beneficial Certificates in accordance with such instructions. In the absence of such instructions the Depositary may, at its discretion, give a proxy to a person nominated by it in respect of such voting rights.

Limitation of Liability

The Deposit Agreement contains provisions for the limitation of the liability of the Depositary and any Agent and for the indemnification of the Depositary by the Manager. The Manager is entitled to recover amounts paid by it under such indemnity from the assets of the Trust.

Resignation and Termination of the Depositary

The Depositary may at any time resign as depositary and the Manager may at any time terminate the appointment of the Depositary if the Depositary shall have failed to a material extent to comply with its obligations to the Manager under the Deposit Agreement, in each case by giving at least 90 days' notice to the other party to the Deposit Agreement, provided always that such resignation or termination shall only take effect upon the appointment by the Manager of a successor depositary. Within 30 days after the giving of such notice, notice of such resignation or termination of appointment shall be given to Holders of IDRs.

Admendment of the Deposit Agreement and Conditions and Termination

Any provision of the Deposit Agreement and the conditions endorsed on the IDRs may be amended at any time by agreement between the Manager, the Trustee and the Depositary save that no amendment may impair the right of the Holder of an IDR upon surrender thereof to receive the Beneficial Certificates and any other property evidenced thereby. Any amendment which increases or imposes fees or charges payable by the Holders of IDRs or which is otherwise materially prejudicial to the interests of the Holders of IDRs shall not become effective as to outstanding IDRs until the expiration of the period of three months after notice of such amendment shall have been given to the Holders of such IDRs (which notice shall specify when such amendment shall become effective) during which period the Beneficial Certificates (and any other property) evidenced thereby may be withdrawn without payment of the charges of the Depositary mentioned in the relevant section above.

Either the Manager (if the Depositary has failed to a material extent to comply with its obligations to the Manager under the Deposit Agreement or if the Depositary refuses to agree to any amendment which the Manager is required by the laws of the Republic to request) or the Depositary may terminate the Deposit Agreement by giving at least 90 days' notice to the other. Within 30 days after the giving of such notice, notice of such termination shall be given to the Holders of IDRs. During the period from the giving of such notice to the Holders of IDRs until termination, each Holder of IDRs shall be entitled to withdraw the Beneficial Certificates (and any other property) evidenced thereby without payment of charges of the Depositary. If any IDRs shall remain outstanding after the date of termination, the Depositary thereafter shall suspend distributions to the Holders thereof and shall not give any further notices or perform any further acts under the Deposit Agreement, except that the Depositary shall continue to deliver Beneficial Certificates held by it and other property pertaining thereto in exchange of IDRs surrendered to the Depositary. At any time after the expiry of two years from the date of termination, the Depositary may sell the Beneficial Certificates held by it and other property then held under the Deposit Agreement, without liability for interest, for the *pro rata* benefit of the Holders of IDRs which have not been surrendered.

Reports and Notices

The Manager will (so long as any IDR is outstanding) furnish the Depositary with the semi-annual statements and the annual audited statements relating to the Trust. The Depositary will make such reports and financial statements available to the Holders of IDRs and will give the Holders of IDRs notice of such availability. The Depositary will give notice to the Holders of IDRs of the payment of all distributions to be paid or made in respect of Beneficial Certificates, together with other relevant details to enable the Holder of IDRs to procure payment or, as the case may be, delivery thereof.

Notices to Holders of IDRs will be given by publication in the *Financial Times* in London or such other newspaper or newspapers as may from time to time be agreed between the Manager and the Depositary.

Issue of Replacement IDRs

Upon receiving evidence satisfactory to the Depositary of the defacement, mutilation, destruction, loss or theft of any IDR or coupon and payment of its reasonable charges and, in the case of defacement or mutilation, upon surrender and cancellation of such IDR or coupon or, in the case of destruction, loss or theft, receipt of an indemnity satisfactory to the Depositary, the Depositary will issue at its specified office, or (at the request, risk and expense of the Holder of such IDRs or coupons) at the specified office of any Agent in replacement for such IDR or coupon, an IDR having attached thereto the same number of coupons as the defaced, mutilated, destroyed, lost or stolen IDR or (as the case may be) a replacement coupon.

Prescription

Holders of IDRs who have failed to claim distributions and/or rights within 5 years of their being made available to them will not thereafter be entitled to claim such distributions and/or rights, and the Depositary shall return the same to the Manager for the benefit of the Trust.

Governing Law

The Deposit Agreement and the IDRs will be governed and construed in accordance with English law.

III. Amendment of the Securities Laws

Following the release of the Plan for Liberalization of the Korean Securities Market, certain amendments were introduced in to the Securities and Exchange Act (the "SEA"). For the amendments relating to liberalization of the Korean securities market, *see* II. A of Section III below.

Section II.   *Market Activities*

I. Introduction

From late 1978 until the beginning of 1981, unfavourable market conditions prevailed on the Stock Exchange, reflecting the difficult economic and political circumstances of the time. The Composite Stock Price Index reached its lowest point in this period on the first trading day in January, 1981. Since then it has recovered substantially. The decline in stock prices was accompanied by falling turnover in value, although the number of shares traded increased in both 1979 and 1980. Total market capitalization fell from Won 2,893 billion at 31st December, 1978 to Won 2,527 billion at the end of 1980. New issue activity was brought almost to a standstill with only one company floatation in 1980. One cause of particular concern to investors was the effect of the 16.6 percent devaluation of the Won against the Dollar in January, 1980, which was accompanied by a sharp rise in interest rates. It was realized that high domestic interest rates would adversely affect the profitability of most listed companies, which tend to be highly geared by international standards. In addition, the decline in the value of the Won (which after the devaluation the decline in the value of the Won (which after the devaluation continued to float downwards, with a total fall in 1980 of 26.7 percent against the Dollar) while benefiting exporters resulted in exchange losses and weakened the balance sheets for the many companies which had outstanding Dollar borrowings.

During 1980, however, the bond market remained active. As part of the January, 1980 measures, the coupon rate on corporate bonds rose to 30.0 percent. After initial cancern as to whether interest rates would climb further, significant institutional and retail demand developed and coupons were cut successively to 28.0 percent in June, 26.0 percent in September and 23.5 percent in November. Record volumes of new corporate and public bond issues were absorbed during the year.

Towards the end of 1980, the stabilized political situation, coupled with a realization that the economic situation was improving, brought a renewal of investor interest in the equity market. The prevailing mood of cautious optimism was supported by the Government announcement on 14th January, 1981 that the securities markets would be gradually opened to foreign investors. An upswing in share prices resulted, based also on encouraging economic data-in particular, upward revisions in the Economic Planning Board's forecast for GNP growth in 1981, announcements of better-than-expected trade figures and the news of important overseas contracts secured by construction companies. The Composite Stock Price Index reached 226.1 on 7th July, 1981 while average daily turnover reached a high point of 37.9 million shares on 30th April, 1981. The authorities then acted to curb over-enthusiasm and the market declined. In August and September the market continued to fall slowly during quieter conditions, although the announcement early in October that the 1988 Olympics would be held in Seoul induced a rally, led by construction shares. Later in the month, the market resumed its slow decline.

As in 1980, the 1981 bond market has been absorbing record amounts of new issues. Coupons were reduced to 22.5 percent in April, 22.2 percent in June and 22.0 percent in July. However, investor resistance resulted in significant portions of the issues being left with the underwriters and secondary market yields increased. In early October coupons were raised to 22.5 percent and in the second half of the month they were increased again to 23.0 percent, although the bonds were offered in the primary market at 96 percent of their nominal value—the first time that bonds had been priced at a discount in the Korean market.

II. The Primary Markets

A. Equity Market

Securities companies, the Korea Merchant Banking Corporation and the Korea Investment Finance Corporation are permitted to underwrite new issues, and issue managers are required to endorse profit forecasts made in the prospectus; financial penalties are levied upon the managers if the company's profits are not within the permitted tolerance for the forecasts unless *force majeure* applies or a shareholders' meeting approves a dividend it deems to be satisfactory. All shares must have a par value, but the offering price of a new issue may exceed par value. Listed companies may issue new shares for consideration and this is normally done in the form of a rights issue to its existing shareholders at par. However, by law, up to 10 percent of the new shares may be allotted to employees irrespective of whether or not they are shareholders and most companies avail themselves of this opportunity to reward their staff. In addition, the Underwriters' Association Agreement permits the two securities investment trust companies, on behalf of the equity funds they manage, to subscribe preferentially for up to 10 percent, in the aggregate, of any new issue. Companies may also issue shares without consideration as bonus or scrip issues (figure for which are not included below). The following table indicates the growth of the primary equity

Year	Offerings by Listed Company Floatations		Total Equity Companies		Capital Raised	
	Number	In millions of Won	Number	In millions of Won	In millions of Won	In thousands of Dollars (2)
1971.. 2	2	850	7	2,090	2,940	7,876
1972.. 16	16	1,080	31	13,733	14,813	37,135
1973.. 40	40	21,475	52	29,623	51,098	128,548
1974.. 26	26	14,337	61	32,080	46,417	95,903
1975.. 62	62	39,876	68	82,929	122,805	253,729
1976.. 87	87	74,005	81	101,941	175,946	363,525
1977.. 49	49	44,113	97	141,859	185,973	384,242
1978.. 33	33	41,521	148	285,201	326,722	675,045
1979.. 5	5	4,875	98	211,927	216,802	447,938
1980.. 1	1	345	52	170,803	171,148	259,354
1981.. 2	2	3,045	81	302,996	306,041	436,889
1982(1).. .. —	—	—	29	81,054	81,054	109,340

(1) to 31st July

(2) Converted at The Bank of Korea Concentration Standard Rate at the end of the periods indicated.

Source: Korea Stock Exchange

markets over the past decade.

B. Bond Market

Most corporate bonds are issued through public offerings which are underwritten by securities companies, merchant banks and investment trust companies, while a very few private placements of unlisted corporate bonds also take place. The vast majority of corporate bonds are guaranteed by banking institutions. Since maturities are relatively short, currently three to five years, a significant number of new issues is required to meet maturing bonds. Levels of new issue activity in the corporate bond market are given in the following table:-

Bonds are also issued by the public sector in the name of or guaranteed by the Ministry of Finance, the Bank of Korea or institutions owned by the Government. Public bonds include Grain Bonds, Treasury Bills, Monetary Stabilization Bonds, Foreign Exchange Finance Debentures, Housing Bonds, Industrial Finance Debentures and Subway Bonds. Some of these are tax-exempt and not all of them

Year	Number of Issues	In millions of Won	In thousands of Dollars (2)
1971	—	—	—
1972	35	9,928	24,888
1973	12	3,450	8,679
1974	59	27,870	57,583
1975	·67	33,450	69,112
1976	112	86,280	178,264
1977	196	176,480	364,628
1978	306	326,340	674,256
1979	380	624,630	1,290,558
1980	465	963,700	1,460,373
1981	458	1,036,148	1,479,155
1982(1)	417	1,234,113	1,664,796

(1) to 31st July

(2) Coverted at The Bank of Korea Concentration Standard Rate at the end of
the periods indicated.

Source: Korea Stock Exchange

are listed on the Stock Exchange. Generally, public bonds yield less than corporate bonds and are held mainly by institutions.

It is difficult for small investors to participate directly in the bond market because bonds are only readily available in relatively large amounts. Instead, the small investor can buy units in securities investment trusts whose assets consist substantially of bonds and which offer higher yields than can be obtained on bank deposits. Consequently, the securities investment trusts are the largest underwriters of, and investors in, the bond market.

III. The Secondary Markets

A. Equity Market

Equities are traded on the Stock Exchange through securities companies, which act as brokers, but which may also buy and sell as principals. There are presently 27 member firms of the Stock Exchange. There is no significant over-the-counter market and no other stock exchange.

The stock market is divided into two sections. In order to be traded in the first section, a company must satisfy certain criteria. In respect of the previous accounting period, its profits after tax must have exceeded 10 percent of its paid-in capital; it must have declared a dividend; its auditors' opinion must not have been qualified in any material respect; and its net worth must be at least 90 percent of its paid-in capital. In addition, the company's shares must have been listed for more than six months, and at least 20 percent of its share capital must be freely traded and be held by 200 or more investors. Finally, the company must be classified as a publicly-held corporation within the definition of the Corporation Tax Act, the requirements for which are designed to ensure that the shares of such a company are widely held by small investors while at the same time providing tax benefits for the company. Companies which do not satisfy these criteria are traded in the second section. Of the 334 companies listed on the Stock Exchange as at 31st July, 1982, 220 were traded on the first section and 114 on the second section.

Brokerage is charged according to sales value as follows:

Sales Value	Rate
Less than Won 1 million	0.9 percent
Won 1 million to Won 5 million	0.8 percent plus Won 1,000
Over Won 5 million	0.7 percent plus Won 6,000

Brokerage of two percent is charged on that put of any order that is not a multiple of 100 shares. Securities transactions tax of 0.2 percent is levied on sales proceeds (except where the share price is below par, when tax is not charged). Sales by securities investment trusts are not subject to tax.

Purchases and sales of shares may be completed fully in cash or by means of a margin transaction. In the latter case a securities com pany will normally refiance itself with the Korea Securities Finance Corporation. Only shares in the first section of the Stock Exchange are eligible for margin transactions and the margin requirements are varied from time to time by the Securities and Exchange Commission. According to statistics prepared by the Securities Supervisory Board, margin transactions in 1981 amounted to 20.9 percent of the total trading volume by number of shares, and 29.7 percent of the trading volume of those shares eligible for margin transactions.

Movements in the Composite Stock Price Index (4th January, 1975 H 100) (the "Index"), currently incorporating the prices of 171 storks, are set out below, together with the associated dividend yield and price earnings ratios:

Year	Opening	High	Low	Closing	Closing Dividend Yield	Price Earnings Ratios
					(percent)	
1972	35.3	91.6	34.4	80.2	n.a.	n.a.
1973	76.3	139.4	76.3	110.2	7.5	n.a.
1974	101.9	121.1	95.1	105.0	13.7	4.8
1975	100.0	139.4	95.7	139.4	13.7	5.3
1976	134.1	154.6	134.1	146.8	12.7	6.6
1977	139.4	181.5	139.4	178.2	14.2	5.9
1978	166.0	228.8	166.0	207.2	12.9	5.9
1979	189.0	190.5	148.6	161.1	17.8	3.8
1980	135.2	162.2	134.6	139.6	20.9	2.6
1981	122.4	226.1	122.4	178.6	16.4	3.1
1982 January	164.6	173.2	162.8	167.2	16.6	3.3
February	167.2	180.7	165.4	180.7	16.2	3.3
March	180.7	187.6	173.9	176.1	13.4	3.4
April	174.3	174.7	165.0	166.3	13.1	3.2
May	164.2	164.2	146.8	160.1	13.7	3.1
June	161.4	175.5	158.8	174.8	13.2	3.3
July	171.6	175.2	164.0	174.1	13.0	3.4

Source: Korea Stock Exchange

Most shares are quoted 'ex-dividend' on the first trading day of the fiscal year, which accounts for the drop in the Index between its closing level at the end of one fiscal year and its opening level at the beginning of the following fiscal year.

Movements in share prices are confined to within fixed limits around the previous day's closing price as set forth below:

Previous Day's Closing Price	Fluctuation Limit
Less than Won 500	Won 30
Won 500 to Won 1,000	Won 50
Won 1,000 to Won 2,000	Won 70
Won 2,000 to Won 3,000	Won 100
More than Won 3,000	Won 130

This will, of course, limit the maximum movement in the Index on any day. By way of illustration, if every share in the Index had moved the maximum permissible amount in the same direction on 1st September, 1981, the Index, which stood at 186.1 on the previous day, would have risen or fallen by 12.2 points.

The number of companies listed and the corresponding total market capitalization at the end of periods indicated and the average daily trading volume for those periods are set out in the following table:

Year	No. of Listed Companies	Market Capitalization at 31st December		Average Daily Trading Volume		
		In millions of Won	In thousands of Dollars (2)	In thousands of shares	In millions of Won	In thousands of Dollars (2)
1971.. ..	50	108,706	291,203	169	115	308
1972..	66	245,981	616,648	289	242	607
1973..	104	426,247	1,075,319	439	543	1,366
1974..	128	532,825	1,100,878	528	602	1,244
1975..	189	916,054	1,892,673	1,056	1,136	2,347
1976..	274	1,436,074	2,067,095	1,986	2,110	4,360
1977..	323	2,350,835	4,857,097	4,310	4,662	9,632
1978..	356	2,892,512	5,976,264	4,671	5,944	12,281
1979..	355	2,609,414	5,391,351	5,382	4,579	9,461
1980..	352	2,526,553	3,828,691	5,654	3,897	5,905
1981..	343	2,959,057	4,224,207	10,565	8,708	12,431
1982(1).. ..	334	3,031,007	4,088,772	9,603	6,894	9,300

(1) to 31st July

(2) Converted at The Bank of Korea Concentration Standard Rate at the end of the periods indicated.

Source: Korea Stock Exchange

Details of the 40 most actively traded shares in 1981 are listed in the following two tables they account for 76.1 percent of the Stock Exchange's equity turnover by amount (67.0 percent by number of shares) during the period. All except six of these shares are included in the Composite Stock Price Index.

	End of 1981				
	Trading Volume			Price	
Company	In millions of Won	In thousands of Dollars(1)	In thousands of shares	High (Won)	Low (Won)
1. Korea Oil Holding Co., Ltd.	106,901	152,606	94,161	1,800	730
2. Jung Woo Development Co., Ltd.	105,900	151,178	111,227	2,005	450
3. Daelim Industrial Co., Ltd.	80,802	115,349	47,073	2,830	901
4. Dong-A Construction Co., Ltd.	76,287	108,904	48,445	2,600	790
5. Sunkyong Limited	75,957	108,433	79,868	1,428	621
6. Lucky Limited	75,824	108 243	82,639	1,170	640
7. Daewoo Development Co., Ltd. (2)	66,135	94,411	58,421	2,415	400
8. Daewoo Industrial Co., Ltd. (2)	64,372	91,894	91,951	1,011	381
9. Hanil Development Co., Ltd.	60,591	86,497	51,892	1,880	550
10. Hanil Bank	59,317	84,678	48,649	1,375	830
11. Han Yang Corporation	56,542	80,717	43,865	2,110	711
12. Kyung Nam Enterprise Co., Ltd.	55,865	79,750	51,701	2,300	502
13. Daewoo Heavy Industrial Co., Ltd.	54,425	77,695	86,630	940	330
14. Chinheung Enterprise Co., Ltd.	53,923	76,978	57,903	1,625	452
15. Samsung Electronic Co., Ltd.	53,691	76,647	60,365	1,208	645
16. Hanshin Construction Co., Ltd.	49,865	71,185	53,448	1,628	475
17. Daihan Electric Wire Co., Ltd.	49,417	70,545	74,881	880	445
18. Samwhan Enterprise Co., Ltd.	48,221	68,838	37,877	2,010	607
19. Samho Housing Co., Ltd.	47,692	68,083	54,080	1,520	365
20. Gold Star Co., Ltd.	46,587	66,505	54,039	1,180	610
21. Namkwang Construction Co., Ltd.	45,340	64,725	49,032	1,400	435
22. Pacific Construction Co., Ltd.	44,816	63,977	55,853	1,550	435
23. Bank of Seoul & Trust Company	44,554	63,603	40,836	1,331	780
24. Life Housing Development Co., Ltd.	38,984	55,652	42,674	1,620	474
25. Kongyung Construction Co., Ltd.	38,678	55,215	43,417	1,388	428
26. Keugdong Construction Co., Ltd.	38,201	54,534	31,917	1,980	600

27. Miryung Construction Co., Ltd.	36,765	52,484	30,609	1,910	511
28. Woochang Construction Co., Ltd.	35,690	50,949	63,059	945	143
29. The Cho-Heung Bank	34,963	49,911	31,261	1,350	800
30. Korea First Bank	33,522	47,854	30,542	1,340	820
31. Samsung Construction Co., Ltd.	33,126	47,289	47,284	1,260	211
32. Hankook Kunup Co., Ltd.	29,483	42,088	45,288	1,300	220
33. The Commercial Bank of Korea	28,754	41,048	23,454	1,455	860
34. Anam Industrial Co., Ltd.	27,166	38,781	29,974	1,139	700
35. Samick Housing Co., Ltd.	26,230	37,445	34,106	1,300	415
36. Samboo Construction Co., Ltd.	23,062	32,922	16,002	2,555	655
37. Hyundai Motor Company	22,911	32,707	53,882	575	280
38. Korean Air Lines Co., Ltd.	20,373	29,084	42,246	660	300
39. Samick Construction Co., Ltd.	19,523	27,870	25,063	1,100	421
40. Ssangyong Cement Industrial Co., Ltd.	18,542	26,470	35,687	662	370

(1) Converted at The Bank of Korea Concentration Standard Rate at 31st December, 1981.

(2) Shareholders of Daewoo Industrial Co., Ltd. and Daewoo Development Co., Ltd. had approved the merger of their companies. The merger became effective on 19th November, 1981 and the merged company is known as Daewoo Corporation.

Source: Korea Stock Exchange

	1981				
				Market Capitalization	
Company	Closing Price (Won)	Dividend Yield (per cent)	Price Earnings Ratio	In millions of Won	In thousands of Dollars (1)
1. Korea Oil Holding Co., Ltd.	841	14.3	9.1	88,018	125,650
2. Jung Woo Development Co., Ltd.	654	7.8	8.1	20,312	28,997
3. Daelim Industrial Co., Ltd.	1,605	9.4	2.0	63,269	90,320
4. Dong-A Construction Co., Ltd.	1,800	11.8	2.1	63,180	90,193
5. Sunkyong Limited	765	13.3	11.5	26,086	37,239
6. Lucky Limited	815	6.2	13.6	48,900	69,807
7. Daewoo Development Co.,					

Ltd. (2)	799	12.8	4.8	51,581	73,635
8. Daewoo Industrial Co., Ltd. (2)	660	14.5	3.3	53,856	76,882
9. Hanil Development Co., Ltd.	1,285	12.0	2.5	25,700	36,688
10. Hanil Bank	1,266	16.3	5.9	111,600	159,315
11. Han Yang Corporation	1,150	23.4	3.8	28,750	41,042
12. Kyung Nam Enterprise Co., Ltd.	835	8.9	10.0	16,340	23,326
13. Daewoo Heavy Industrial Co., Ltd.	645	10.0	12.2	41,925	59,850
14. Chinheung Enterprise Co., Ltd.	815	15.5	11.2	29,650	42,327
15. Samsung Electronic Co., Ltd.	862	—	—	60,340	86,138
16. Hanshin Construction Co., Ltd.	888	17.2	6.0	23,984	34,238
17. Daihan Electric Wire Co., Ltd.	500	—	84.3	33,130	47,295
18. Samwhan Enterprise Co., Ltd.	1,359	18.1	3.1	29,898	42,681
19. Samho Housing Co., Ltd.	750	7.6	17.6	18,900	26,981
20. Gold Star Co., Ltd.	868	—	—	60,760	86,738
21. Namkwang Construction Co.,	836	9.5	6.3	16,799	23,981
22. Pacific Construction Co., Ltd.	665	9.9	9.3	17,868	25,507
23. Bank of Seoul & Trust Company	1,083	13.3	9.9	97,953	139,833
24. Life Housing Development Co., Ltd.	700	14.3	9.3	20,330	29,022
25. Kongyung Construction Co., Ltd.	790	9.4	11.4	15,428	22,024
26. Keugdong Construction Co., Ltd.	1,195	8.6	3.0	23,422	33,436
27. Miryng Construction Co., Ltd.	1,382	6.2	4.3	27,640	39,458
28. Woochang Construction Co., Ltd.	540	2.4	4.4	10,450	14,918
29. The Cho-Heung Bank	1,141	12.2	10.2	100,008	142,869
30. Korea First Bank	1,111	13.0	9.4	97,680	139,443
31. Samsung Construction Co., Ltd.	608	—	—	18,830	26,881
32. Hankook Kunup Co., Ltd.	624	—	85.4	7,488	10,690
33. The Commercial Bank of Korea	1,290	17.7	3.7	113,250	161,670
34. Anam Industrial Co., Ltd.	830	6.4	8.3	9,462	13,507
35. Samick Housing Co., Ltd.	641	12.9	7.3	14,312	20,431
36. Samboo Construction Co., Ltd.	1,600	9.5	2.1	30,550	43,612

37. Hyundai Motor Company	353	—	—	29,835	43,523
38. Korean Air Lines Co., Ltd.	400	—	—	22,681	32,378
39. Samick Construction Co., Ltd.	745	11.5	4.9	8,700	12,420
40. Ssangyong Cement Industrial o., Ltd.	393	20.0	4.9	22,401	31,979

(1) Convert at The Bank of Korea Concentration Standard Rate at 31st August, 1981.

(2) Shareholders of Daewoo Industrial Co., Ltd. and Daewoo Development Co., Ltd. had approved the merger of their companies. The merger became effective on 18th November, 1981 and the merged company in known as Daewoo Corporation.

Source: Korea Stock Exchange

Sales and profits after tax for the year ended 31st December, 1981 and shareholders' equity and total assets as at the year-end for the 40 companies are set out below:

In millions of Won

Company/Business	In thousands of Dollars(1)				Total Assets
	Sales	Profit after tax	Listed Capital	Share-holders' Equity	
1. Korea Oil Holding					
Co., Ltd. (3)/	7,000	195	53,000	53,065	71,119
Holding Company	9,745	271	73,785	73,876	99,110
2. Jung Woo Development					
Co., Ltd./	104,934	3,225	16,000	23,417	97,561
Construction	149,800	4,604	22,841	33,429	139,273
3. Daelim Industrial Co.,					
Ltd./	757,548	23,897	19,710	131,011	609,125
Construction	1,081,439	34,114	28,137	187,025	869,557
4. Dong-A Construction					
Co., Ltd./	471,558	25,074	17,550	132,588	382,583
Construction	673,173	35,794	25,054	198,276	546,157
5. Sunkyung Limited/	1,017,950	3,563	15,000	28,725	435,903
General Trading	1,453,176	5,086	21,413	41,006	622,274
6. Lucky Limited/	249,102	3,961	30,000	44,616	203,194
Chemicals	355,606	5,655	42,827	63,692	290,070
7. Daewoo Development					
Co., Ltd./	—	—	—	—	—
Construction (2)	—	—	—	—	—
8. Daewoo Industrial Co.,					
Ltd./	1,898,018	62,290	68,300	191,437	1,179,201
General Trading (2)	2,709,519	88,922	97,502	273,286	1,683,370

9. Hanil Development Co., Ltd./	208,537	10,487	10,000	35,040	118,724
Construction	297,697	14,971	14,276	50,021	169,485
10. Hanil Bank/	486, 653	20,789	90,000	146,139	5,990,782
Banking	694,722	29,677	128,480	208,621	8,552,151
11. Han Yang Corporation/	490,693	13,373	22,500	53,305	384,427
Construction	700,490	19,091	32,120	76,096	548,789
12. Kyung Nam Enterprise Co., Ltd./	217,573	3,090	20,000	27,037	227,691
Construction	310,597	4,441	28,551	38,597	325,041
13. Daewoo Heavy Industrial Co., Ltd./	187,654	354	32,500	46,036	307,146
Machinery & Equipment	267,886	505	46,395	65,719	438,467
14. Chinheung Enterprise Co., Ltd./	198,433	4,909	20,000	31,161	194,301
Construction	283,273	7,008	28,551	44,484	277,375
15. Samsung Electronic Co., Ltd./	370,040	6,969	35,000	54,852	290,914
Electronics	528,251	9,949	49,964	78,304	451,295
16. Hanshin Construction Co., Ltd./	230,988	4,905	14,000	25,772	165,007
Construction	329,747	7,002	19,986	36,791	235,556
17. Daihan Electric Wire Co., Ltd./	265,819	510	33,990	48,757	306,892
Electronics Y Electric Wire Products	379,470	728	48,522	69,603	438,104
18. Samwhan Enterprise Co., Ltd./	242,841	12,335	11,000	47,116	200,901
Construction	346,668	17,609	15,703	67,261	286,797
19. Samho Housing Co., Ltd./	305,254	2,982	18,000	28,201	253,996
Construction	435,766	4,257	25,696	40,258	362,592
20. Gold Star Co., Ltd./	413,521	10,341	35,000	71,423	319,878
Electronics	590,323	14,762	49,964	101,960	456,642
21. Namkwang Construction Co., Ltd./	191,893	5,375	15,000	30,160	171,529
Construction	273,937	7,673	21,413	43,055	244,867
22. Pacific Construction Co., Ltd./	136,215	1,746	14,000	17,842	145,041
Construction	194,454	2,493	19,986	25,470	207,054
23. Bank of Seoul and Trust Company/	343,156	13,670	92,150	127,828	4,420,537
Banking	489,873	19,515	131,549	182,481	6,310,545
24. Life Housing Co., Ltd./	102,047	3,066	20,000	38,298	161,338
Construction	145,677	4,377	28,551	54,672	230,318

25. Kongyung Construction					
Co., Ltd./	224,391	5,490	16,000	24,060	247,253
Construction	320,330	7,837	22,841	34,347	352,966
26. Keugdong Construction					
Co., Ltd./	156,277	5,525	9,800	42,774	145,044
Construction	223,094	7,887	13,990	61,062	207,058
27. Miryung Construction					
Co., Ltd./	171,574	5,086	10,000	32,189	150,844
Construction	244,931	7,259	14,276	45,951	215,338
28. Woochang Construction					
Co., Ltd./	50,839	761	10,000	10,942	49,315
Construction	72,575	1,086	14,276	15,620	70,400
29. The Cho-Heung Bank/	412,694	10,884	90,000	121,543	5,417,531
Banking	589,142	15,537	128,480	173,509	7,733,806
30. Korea First Bank/	439,544	10,190	90,000	125,387	5,891,051
Banking	627,472	14,547	128,480	178,996	8,409,780
31. Samsung Construction					
Co., Ltd./	149,559	1,192	16,000	18,690	187,714
Construction	213,503	1,702	22,841	26,681	267,971
32. Hankook Kunup Co.,					
Ltd./	92,305	1,489	6,000	9,246	49,447
Construction	131,770	2,126	8,565	13,199	70,588
33. The Commercial Bank of					
Korea/	520,829	29,506	90,001	169,300	6,689,833
Banking	743,510	42,121	128,480	241,685	9,550,083
34. Anam Industrial Co.,					
Ltd./	19,037	625	5,700	8,035	19,820
Electronics	27,176	892	8,137	11,470	28,294
35. Samick Housing Co.,					
Ltd./	83,601	1,956	12,000	20,301	163,553
Construction	119,345	2,792	17,131	28,981	233,480
36. Samboo Construction					
Co., Ltd./	147,395	4,215	9,750	46,426	113,766
Construction	210,414	6,017	13,919	66,276	162,407
37. Hyundai Motor					
Company/	296,758	(16,447)	48,250	78,946	349,187
Motor Vehicles	423,637	(23,479)	68,879	112,700	498,482
38. Korean Air Lines, Ltd./	699,493	(7,117)	28,351	14,401	833,830
Transportation	998,562	(10,160)	40,473	20,558	1,190,335
39. Samick Construction Co.,					
Ltd./	73,638	2,539	6,000	9,642	70,651
Construction	105,122	3,625	8,565	13,764	100,858
40. Ssangyong Cement					
Industrial Co.,	362,999	(7,932)	28,500	100,265	644,676

Ltd./ Manufacture of
Cement   461,098   (11,323)   40,685   143,133   920,308

(1) Converted at The Bank of Korea Concentration Standard Rate at 31st December, 1981.
(2) Shareholders of Daewoo Industrial Co., Ltd. and Daewoo Development Co., Ltd. had approved the merger of their companies. The merger became effective on 18th November, 1981 and the merged company is known as Daewoo Corporation.
(3) Fiscal year end: 31st March, 1981 (Thousands of dollars were converted at The Bank of Korea Concentration Standard Rate on 31st March, 1982).

Source: Company Annual Reports

A breakdown of share ownership between certain categories of investors is set forth in the following table:

At 31st December	Government and Public Bodies	Banking Institutions	Other Corporations	Individuals
				(percent)
1971..	35.8	14.0	12.1	38.1
1972..	32.5	9.5	14.7	43.3
1973..	19.8	7.9	16.6	55.7
1974..	15.4	5.8	20.3	58.5
1975..	13.9	8.1	24.0	54.0
1976..	16.3	7.8	25.8	50.1
1977..	17.2	5.7	31.4	45.7
1978..	14.3	5.8	17.4	62.5
1979..	14.3	5.6	20.0	60.1
1980..	14.5	5.9	21.6	58.0
1981..	2.0	5.7	25.8	66.5
1982..	2.0	5.7	25.6	66.7

(1) at 31st March
Source: Korea Stock Exchange

The decline in the proportion of listed shares owned by the Government and public bodies as at 31st December, 1981 compared with 31st December, 1980 was principally due to the Government acquiring the remaining shares it did not already own in Korea Electric Company. As a result, Korea Electric Company was delisted on 5th June, 1981.

At 31st December	Unlisted Public Bonds		Listed Public Bonds		Listed Corporate Bonds		Total Listed	
	In millions of Won	In thousands of Dollars(2)	In millions of Won	In thousands of Dollars(2)	In millions of Won	In thousands of Dollars(2)	In millions of Won	In thousands of Dollars(2)
1971	17,811	47,712	44,060	118,028	—	—	44,060	118,028
1972	16,102	40,366	64,067	160,609	4,650	11,657	68,717	172,266
1973	18,380	46,239	120,369	302,815	5,250	13,208	125,619	316,023
1974	82,672	170,810	169,450	350,103	22,400	46,281	191,850	396,384
1975	149,894	309,698	167,883	346,866	52,150	107,748	220,033	454,614
1976	253,732	524,240	280,098	578,715	118,430	244,690	398,528	823,405
1977	498,978	1,030,946	339,692	701,843	232,290	479,938	571,982	1,181,781
1978	679,315	1,403,543	429,571	887,543	538,920	1,113,471	968,491	2,001,014
1979	1,037,662	2,143,930	540,081	1,115,870	1,001,430	2,069,070	1,541,511	3,184,940
1980	1,333,491	2,020,747	895,389	1,356,855	1,649,280	2,499,288	2,544,669	3,856,143
1981	1,745,008	2,491,089	1,534,586	2,190,701	2,365,800	3,377,302	3,900,386	5,568,003
1982(1)	2,114,105	2,851,889	2,455,069	3,311,842	2,579,070	3,479,118	5,034,139	6,790,960

(1) at 31st July.
(2) Coverted at The Bank of Korea Concentration Standard Rate at the end of the periods indicated.
Source: Korea Stock Exchange and The Bank of Korea.

B. Bond Market

In line with the sharp annual increases in the number of corporate bonds issued, the volume of issues outstanding has also shown large rises. In addition, the Government and other public bodies have had increasing recourse to the bond market with both listed and unlisted bond volumes showing substantial growth. The volume of listed corporate bonds outstanding exceeded that of listed public bonds for the first time in 1978. Volumes of outstanding bond issues since 1971 are given in the following table.

Trading volume of all listed debt securities has risen rapidly as illustrated below, increasing at a compound rate of 111 percent per annum between 1975 and 1981. No transactions tax is levied on bond sales. Bonds may not be purchased on margin or sold short. Details of trading volume are given in the table below:

Year	Public Sector Bonds		Corporate Sector Bonds		Total Bonds	
	In millions of Won	In thousands of Dollars(2)	In millions of Won	In thousands of Dollars(2)	In millions of Won	In thousands of Dollars(2)
1971	7,283	19,510	—	—	7,283	19,510
1972	8,550	21,434	128	321	8,678	21,755
1973	7,721	19,424	218	548	7,939	19,972
1974	3,232	6,678	199	441	3,431	7,089
1975	12,897	26,647	621	1,283	13,518	27,930
1976	30,030	62,045	6,667	13,775	36,697	75,820
1977	114,368	236,298	16,164	33,397	130,532	269,695
1978	195,141	403,184	43,541	89,961	238,682	493,145
1979	195,470	403,864	327,800	677,273	523,270	1,081,137
1980	246,013	372,803	643,863	975,698	889,876	1,348,501
1981	475,739	679,142	934,784	1,334,453	1,410,523	2,013,595
1982(1)	1,854,212	2,501,298	1,269,677	1,712,771	3,123,889	4,214,069

(1) to 31st July. (2) Converted at The Bank of Korea Concentration Standard Rate at the end of the periods indicated.

Source: Korea Stock Exchange

IV. Other Key Statistics

The following tables show certain key statistics of the activities of the Korean Securities Markets during the period from 1976 to September, 1982 and are updated versions of the respective tables included in chapter three of Part One at pp. 27–91 *supra*.

Table 3.9 Activities of Primary Market   (Amount: in Billion won)

Year	1976	1977	1978	1979	1980	1981	1982[a]
A. Public Offerings[b]							
a. Number	56	34	23	5	1	2	—
b. Amount	40.6	31.1	23.8	4.9	0.3	3.0	—
B. Secondary Distributions[c]							
a. Number	31	15	10	—	—	—	—
b. Amount	33.4	13.0	17.7	—	—	—	—
C. Capital Increases[d]							
a. Number	81	97	148	98	52	81	46
b. Amount	101.9	141.9	285.2	211.9	170.8	303.0	121.2
D. Corporate Bonds							
a. Number	111	196	306	380	465	458	610
b. Amount	86.3	176.5	326.3	624.6	963.7	1,036.1	1,810.5
Total (A + B + C + D)							
a. Number	278	342	487	483	518	541	656
b. Amount	262.2	362.5	653.1	841.4	1,134.8	1,342.2	1.931.7

Sources: 1) KSE, Yearbook (1981) at 268 for 1976–1981
         2) SSB, Monthly Review (October, 1982) at 87 for 1982
Notes: a; to 30th September
         b; Indicates public offerings of new shares by closely-held corporations
         c; Indicates secondary distributions of shares already issued and out-
            standing by closely-held corporations.
         d; Indicates offerings of new shares by listed corporations excluding
            stock dividends.

Table 3.10 Capital Increases by Listed Companies   (Amount: in Billion won)

	By Offering[a]		In Dividends[b]		Total	
Year	No.	Amount	No.	Amount	No.	Amount
1976	90	198.5	44	118.8	134	315.2
		△2.1				
1977	104	227.2	30	18.7	134	245.3
		△0.6				
1978	152	315.4	47	45.2	145	359.7
		△0.8				
1979	105	270.4	40	48.0	145	318.4
1980	60	221.1	41	79.0	100	300.1
1981	89	478.8	47	16.3	136	614.7
		△0.4				
1982[c]	46	121.2	39	57.7	85	178.9

Sources: 1) KSE, Yearbook (1981) at 194 for 1976–1981
         2) SSB, Monthly Review (October, 1982) at 92 for 1982

Notes: a; Indicates capital increases actually paid in.

   b; Indicates capital increases in the form of stock dividends by converting either reserved surpluses or asset revaluation surpluses into capital stock.

   c; to 30th September.

Table 3.11 Listed Companies by Size of Capital Stock

End of	No. of Listed Co.	1 Bil Won Less	1 Bil Won More	3 Bil Won More	5 Bil Won More	10 Bil Won More	20 Bil Won More	50 Bil Won More
1976	274	47	137	52	22	9	6	1
1977	323	46	158	61	39	11	7	1
1978	356	34	162	63	64	21	11	1
1979	355	26	150	72	67	24	10	6
1980	352	23	141	70	68	31	12	7
1981	343	18	132	64	65	40	17	7
1982a	334	14	127	57	64	37	27	8

Source: SSB, Monthly Review (October, 1982) at 91
Note: a; at 30th September.

Table 3.14 Distribution of Equity Ownership by Owners   (in million shares)

End of	1976	1977	1978	1979	1980	1981	1982a
A. Government & Public Bodies	263.1 (16.3)	371.8 (17.2)	438.3 (14.3)	518.4 (14.3)	585.2 (14.5)	86.7 (1.8)	86.8 (2.0)
B. Banking Institutions	125.6 (7.8)	124.3 (5.7)	178.2 (5.8)	203.9 (5.6)	239.7 (5.7)	239.9 (5.9)	249.8 (5.7)
C. Securities Cos.	176.9 (11.0)	331.1 (15.3)	54.9 (1.8)	59.8 (1.7)	90.8 (2.2)	95.6 (2.3)	113.0 (2.6)
D. Insurance Cos. & Other Legal Persons	239.9 (14.9)	350.0 (16.2)	477.0 (15.6)	666.3 (18.4)	785.3 (19.4)	1001.6 (23.8)	1048.2 (23.9)
E. Individuals	785.5 (48.7)	957.8 (44.2)	1871.1 (61.2)	2113.9 (58.3)	2268.7 (56.0)	2737.9 (64.5)	2804.2 (63.9)
F. Foreigners	22.1 (1.4)	32.3 (1.5)	38.9 (1.3)	65.9 (1.8)	80.6 (2.0)	83.2 (2.0)	89.8 (2.0)
TOTAL	1613.6 (100)	2167.2 (100)	3058.4 (100)	3628.4 (100)	4050.3 (100)	4244.8 (100)	4391.7 (100)

Sources: 1) KSE, Yearbook (1981) at 258–259 for 1976–1981
    2) SSB, Monthly Review (October, 1982) at 116–117 for 1982
Note: * Figures in parentheses indicate percentage compared to the total number of shares, which includes non-listed shares.
   a; at 30th June

Table **3.12** Key Statistics for Listed Stock

End of Year	1976	1977	1978	1979	1980	1981	1982[a]
A. No. of Listed Cos.	274	323	356	355	352	343	334
B. No. of Sec. Cos.	28	27	27	27	27	27	27
C. No. of SH's (thousand persons)	568.1	395.3	963.0	872.1	753.3	696.3	680.7
D. No. of Listed Shares (million Shs.)	1,583	2,117	2,959	3,507	3,876	4,048	4,467
E. Capital Stock Listed (W billion)	1,153	1,492	1,914	2,202	2,421	2,410	2,632
F. Market Value of							
a. Total Listed Stock (W billion)	1,436	2,351	2,893	2,609	2,527	2,959	2,927
b. Par Value of W500	635	780	738	610	522	617	556
G. Sales							
a. Volume (million Shs.)	591	1,272	1,368	1,561	1,645	3,075	2,086
b. Value (W billion)	628	1,375	1,742	1,328	1,134	2,534	1,487
H. Turnover of Market Value	53.7	78.0	66.4	52.5	44.4	85.7	50.4
Average of Year							
I. Stock Price Index							
a. Adjusted (W)	3,144	3,313	4,350	3,692	3,109	3,754	3,611
b. Composite Index	146.3	154.5	202.8	172.2	145.0	171.4	168.3

| J. Average Annual Yield(%) | 12.7 | 14.2 | 12.9 | 17.8 | 20.9 | 16.4 | 13.9 |
| K. PER (times) | 6.6 | 5.9 | 5.9 | 3.8 | 2.6 | 3.1 | 3.3 |

Sources: 1) KSE, Yearbook (1981) at 10, 18, 78 and 92 for 1976–1981
2) SSB, Monthly Review (October, 1982) at 104, 112; KSE, Stock (September, 1982) at 9, 14, 15 and 22 for 1982

Notes: a; at 30th September for the items A through F, to 30th September for the items G and H and average of nine months from January to September for the items I through K

* Stock Price Index = $\dfrac{\text{Current adjusted stock price average}}{\text{Base adjusted stock price average}} \times 100$

Adjusted stock price average = $\dfrac{\text{Aggregate of stock prices}}{\text{Constant divisor}}$

1) Basic date: January 4, 1972
2) Shift of Basic date: from Jan. 4, 1972 to Jan. 4, 1975
3) Adopted Issues (142 Issues)
4) The constant divisor is adjusted by the same method as that of Dow-Jones averages in case of the ex-right or replacement, etc. of any issue.

* Average Annual Yield = (average annual dividend per share/ average stock price) $\times$ 100
* Price Earning Ratio (PER) = stock price/earning per share after corporate income tax.

Table 3.13 Distribution of Equity Ownership by Shareholding

persons: in thousand
shares: in million

End of	1976	1977	1978	1979	1980	1981	1982[a]
A. Below 100 shares							
a. persons	355.4(62.6)	157.9(40.0)	244.2(25.4)	233.7(26.8)	197.7(26.3)	169.8(24.3)	156.7 (23.0)
b. shares	13.5(0.8)	5.2(0.2)	11.1(0.4)	9.2(0.3)	7.6(0.2)	6.5(0.2)	6.0(0.1)
B. 100–1,000 shares							
a. persons	136.0(23.9)	146.5(37.1)	500.9(52.0)	411.1(47.1)	331.4(44.0)	277.5(39.9)	276.4(40.6)
b. shares	44.1(2.7)	46.3(2.1)	190.7(6.2)	153.3(4.2)	132.8(3.3)	114.4(3.0)	113.7(2.6)
C. 1,000–10,000 shares							
a. persons	58.9(10.4)	68.1(17.2)	185.6(19.3)	188.0(21.6)	179.8(23.8)	196.2(28.2)	193.3(28.4)
b. shares	166.3(10.3)	199.9(9.2)	507.3(16.6)	532.3(14.7)	538.5(13.8)	635.8(15.0)	599.9(13.7)
D. 10,000–10,000 shares							
a. persons	16.1(2.8)	20.4(5.2)	29.8(3.1)	36.0(4.1)	40.2(5.3)	48.2(6.9)	49.3(7.2)
b. shares	408.4(25.3)	545.9(25.2)	766.2(25.1)	946.0(26.1)	1085.9(26.8)	1306.7(30.5)	1352.0(30.8)
E. Over 100,000 shares							
a. persons	1.7(0.3)	2.4(0.6)	2.4(0.3)	3.3(0.4)	4.8(0.6)	4.6(0.7)	5.0(0.7)
b. shares	980.7(60.8)	1369.9(63.2)	1583.1(51.8)	1987.4(54.8)	2285.5(56.4)	2181.4(51.4)	2320.1(52.8)
F. Total							
a. persons	568.1(100)	395.3(100)	963.0(100)	871.1(100)	753.3(100)	692.3(100)	680.6(100)
b. shares	1613.2(100)	2167.2(100)	3058.4(100)	3628.2(100)	4050.3(100)	4244.8(100)	4391.7(100)

Source: 1) KSE, Yearbook (1981) at 260–261 for 1976–1981
2) KSE (Listing Department) for 1982.

Notes: * Figures in parentheses indicate percentages compared to the total shareholders and shares outstanding.

* The total number of shares includes non-listed shares.

a; at 30th September

Table 3.15 Key Statistics for Listed Bonds

sales value and amount outstanding: in billion won

	1976	1977	1978	1979	1980	1981	1982[a]
A. Govt. & Public Bonds							
1. No. of Issues	254	253	240	217	230	274	367
2. Amount Outstanding	280	340	430	540	895	1,535	2,513
3. Sales Value	30.0	114.4	195.1	195.5	246.0	475.7	2,397.6
4. Average Yields (%)	21.6	20.7	21.6	25.2	28.8	23.6	17.5
B. Corporate Bonds							
1. No. of Cos.	105	165	278	356	434	457	465
2. No. of Issues	180	293	553	792	1,004	1,157	1,183
3. Amount Outstanding	118	232	539	1,001	1,649	2,366	3,023
4. Sales Value	6.6	16.1	43.5	327.8	643.9	934.8	1,850.2
5. Average Yields (%)	20.4	20.1	21.1	26.7	30.1	24.4	19.9
TOTAL							
1. No. of Issues	434	546	793	1,006	1,234	1,431	1,550
2. Amount Outstanding	398	572	968	1,542	2,545	3,900	5,537
3. Sales Value	36.6	130.5	238.7	523.3	889.9	1,410.5	4,247,8
4. Percentage in total Securities Trading (%)	5.5	8.7	12.1	28.2	44.0	35.8	74.1

Sources: 1) KSE, Yearbook (1981) at 12, 13, 105 and 115; KSE, Stock (January, 1982) at 37 for 1976–1981
2) SSB, Monthly Review (October, 1982) at 24, 25, 106 and 107 for 1982

Note: a; to 30th September

Table 3.16 Credit Balance in Margin Trading

in million won

End of	Money Loans			Stock Loans		
	Broker's Loans	KSFC's Loans	Total	Broker's Loans	KSFC's Loans	Total
1976	4,570 (19.4)	18,954 (80.6)	23,524	188 (35.5)	342 (64.5)	530
1977	19,940 (80.6)	4,802 (19.4)	24,742	93 (87.7)	13 (12.3)	106
1978	—	43,467 (100)	43,467	4 (1.0)	474 (99.0)	478
1979	3,750 (8.1)	42,804 (91.9)	46,554	39 (9.9)	356 (90.1)	395
1980	3,288 (9.2)	32,597 (90.8)	35,885	330 (66.5)	166 (33.5)	496
1981	9,011 (17.8)	41,516 (82.2)	50,517	195 (19.2)	818 (80.8)	1,012
1982[a]	14,519 (28.4)	36,547 (71.6)	51,066	3,390 (100)	— (0)	3,390

Sources: 1) KSE, Yearbook (1981) at 308 for 1976–1981
         2) SSB, Monthly Review (October, 1982) at 110–111 for 1982

Note: * Figures in parentheses indicate percentages compared to the total amount of money loans or stock loans.
      a; at 30th September.

Table 3.17 Growth of Securities Investment Trust Funds

in billion won

End of	KITC		DITC		CITC[a]		Merchant Banking Cos[b].	TOTAL		
	Stock Type	Bond Type	Stock Type	Bond Type	Stock Type	Bond Type	Bond Type	Stock Type	Bond Type	Total
1976	16.8	23.1	6.5	1.5			1.0	23.3	25.6	48.9
1977	30.0	48.5	17.0	27.0			9.5	47.0	85.0	132.0
1978	63.7	81.7	35.5	64.5			37.3	99.2	183.5	282.7
1979	39.2	146.2	20.1	131.9			65.9	59.3	343.9	403.2
1980	30.4	267.7	13.0	241.8			113.0	43.4	622.5	655.9
1981	29.7	583.6	27.7	559.6			210.1	57.4	1,353.3	1,410.7
1982[c]	89.3	1,090.3	57.3	955.7	3.0	41.0	350.9	149.6	2,437.9	2,587.5

Sources: 1) KSE, Yearbook (1981) at 314 for 1976–1981

2) DITC, Investment Trust (October, 1982) at 74–79 for 1982

Notes: a; CITC (Citizen's Investment Trust Company) was chartered by the Ministry of Finance and started its business on July 15, 1982.

b; There are currently six (6) Merchant Banking Corporations which are allowed to act as a manager of investment trust for bond type only.

c; at 30th September

Section III. *Recent Changes in the Securities Laws: The 1982 Amendments to the Securities and Exchange Act*

On November 24, 1981, the Government submitted to the National Assembly (the "Congress") a draft bill for the amendments (the "1982 Amendments") to the Securities and Exchange Act (the "SEA"). The bill for the 1982 Amendments to the SEA passed Congress on March 29, 1982, as Law Number 3541, and became effective on April 1, 1982. Together with the SEA, the Presidential Decree under the SEA and the Ministry of Finance (MOF) Decree under the SEA were also substantially amended in 1982. Major changes included in the 1982 Amendments are set forth below.

I. Regulation of the Distribution of Securities

A. Exemption from Registration Requirements

Article 8 of the SEA was amended to expand the coverage of transactions exempted from the existing registration requirements in two respects. First, an issuer whose public offering or secondary distribution is less than ₩50 Million was required to file a notification statement, which was simpler in form than the registration statement. The 1982 Amendments made such small issues exempted from the filing requirement of a notification statement. Second, prior to the 1982 Amendments even an issuance of new shares by listed corporations to the existing shareholders in the form of stock dividend was subject to the registration requirement. Article 8 of the SEA, as amended in 1982, exempts from the registration requirement the issuances of new shares by means of converting the reserves into capital stock.

B. Processing of the Registration Statements

First, the 1982 Amendments empowered the Securities Administrative Commission (the "SAC") to adopt rules on the coverage of information requred to be included in the registration statements, prospectus, and the documents attached thereto (Arts. 9, 12, SEA). Prior to the 1982 Amendments, the MOF was given such rule-making power. The purpose of the amendment seems to strengthen SAC's power in enforcing disclosure rules. Second, prior to the 1982 Amendments the registration statements were effective on the date as separately designated by the SAC, although notification statements required for small issues were to become effective immediately upon receipt. The 1982 Amendments made the registration statement take effect on the date when the prescribed period designated by the MOF Decree shall have expired (Art. 9, SEA). Within the mandate, the MOF Decree provides for the period as follows:

a) thirty (30) days for public offering or secondary distribution of equity securities;

b) ten (10) days for issuance of new shares (by listed corporation) by means of rights-offerings; and

c) twenty (20) days for public offering or secondary distribution of debt securities; provided; seven (7) days for debt securities guaranteed by financial institutions with respect to both principal and interest (Art. 3, the MOF Decree).

Third, Paragraphs 2 and 3, Article 9 of the SEA were deleted by the 1982 Amendments (for details, see Draft Bill for the Amendment of SEA, submitted by the government on Nov. 24, 1981. pp. 6, 35, 36). Fourth, the 1982 Amendments allowed registrants to amend the registration statements even after the effective date until they publicly offer or distribute the securities (Art. 11(3), SEA). Fifth, the 1982 Amendments required the issuers whose registration statements became effective to prepare a prospectus in accordance with SAC Rules and have the same kept for public inspection at the following places (Art. 12, SEA; Art. 4, MOF Decree):

a) the head office and the branch offices of the issuer;

b) the SAC;

c) the KSE; and

d) the places where any subscription for the securities is taken care of.

II. Regulation of Trading in Securities

A. *Regulation of Securities Companies*

1. Restriction of Sale of Control

Prior to the 1982 Amendments, Article 28(6) of the SEA required any oligopolic shareholder of a securities company to obtain prior approval of the SAC for any sale or transfer of his shares in the securities company. The term, "oligopolic shareholder" was not clear. Article 28(6) as amended in 1982 replaced the term "oligopolic shareholder" with "the largest shareholder," which was defined to mean "the shareholder with the largest shareholding among the shareholders." For the purpose of determination of the largest shareholder of a securities company, the statute required that all of the shares owned by certain close relatives and persons with special affiliation as defined in the Basic National Tax Act with certain modifications, expanding the coverage of special affiliates (*See* SEA Presidential Decree, Art. 15), be aggregated, or if held by one person. Further, amended Article 28(6) also required any purchase by a person of shares in the securities company to obtain SAC's prior approval, should such person, following such purchase, become the largest shareholder of the securities company.

2. Regulation of Entry into Foreign Capital Market

Prior to the 1982 Amendments, the SEA was silent as to whether Korean securities dealers may engage in securities business in foreign countries. Article 28(7) introduced in 1982 allowed Korean securities companies to enter into securities markets in foreign countries subject to an MOF's license and any other licenses required in the countries concerned.

3. Regulation of Foreign Securities Dealers

In order to open the Korean capital market to foreigners, the 1982 Amendments introduced for the first time provisions on foreign securities dealers (Article 28-2 of the SEA; Articles 17-2 and 18-3 of the SEA Presidential Decree). The new statute required any foreign securities dealer (as difined to mean a person who engages in securities business in a foreign country in accordance with the law in such foreign country) to obtain the license of the MOF prior to opening a branch or other business offices in Korea to engage in the securities business in Korea. As is the case with Korean securities dealers, the MOF license varies with the categories of the securities business, including dealership, brokerage and/or underwriting businesses. Any Korean branch or business offices opened by foreign securities dealers are treated as Korean securities companies for the purpose of the SEA unless there is a provision to the contrary. In granting a license to foreign securities dealers, the SEA adopted the principle of "reciprocity." For the details of the application procedure and regulation, *see* Articles 17-2 and 18-3 of the SEA Presidential Decree.

4. Regulation on Collaborative or Joint Trade Practices

The 1982 Amendments adopted a new Article in the SEA which prohibits securities companies, if they do not love the approval of the SAC, from engaging in certain collaborative or joint trade practices as provided in an MOF Decree by contractual arrangement, resolution or any other means in connection with issuance, sale and purchase of or trading in securities (Article 52–2). The idea of such restriction was to protect the interest of public investors and to maintain fair trade order in the securities markets. The SAC is empowered to suspend any collaborative or joint practices or actions as already approved, whenever it deems the suspension of the same necessary for the maintenance of a fair trading order in the market. Further, any violation by the securities company of provisions of Article 52–2 constitutes a cause for suspension of business (Article 57).

5. Salesman Regulation

Under the SEA as amended in 1982, the "Salesman" who solicits for and on behalf of his securities company an offer to buy or sell securities toward customers is known as an "investment consultant," in order to improve his image among the public (Articles 65 through 69). In addition, investment consultants are now required to be registered in the ledger kept at the SSB instead of the SAC. Further, unlike the salesmen under the old SEA, the investment consultants are no longer deemed to have the power to do and perform, on behalf of the securities company which they represent, any and all acts in the course of performing their duties, other than representation in legal actions (Article 67 of the Old SEA which empowered the salesmen the right to represent was deleted in the entirety by the 1982 Amendments).

B. *Regulation of Takeover Bids*

1. Restriction on Ownership Increase

Article 200(1) of the SEA prohibited any increase of shareholding beyond statutory limits in order to discourage secret challenge to existing control by raiders. Article 200(2) of the SEA enumerated four exceptions to the prohibition. However, the SEA was silent on any enforcement action by the SAC and civil remedies available, and the lack of enforcement devices proved to be a critical loophole at the time the so-called "Daehan Flour Mills Case" was publicly released. The 1982 Amendments introduced Article 200(3), which was intended to close such loophole. Under Article 200(3) of the SEA, any person who acquired shares in violation of the statutory restriction on ownership increase may not exercise voting rights with respect to such shares illegally purchased. Further, the SAC is empowered to issue, against such shareholder, an order to remedy the violation of the statutory restriction on ownership increases. Although there has not been issued any corrective order, it is clear that the SEA may compel any raider to sell all the shares illegally acquired through public auction or on the exchange within a specified period of time.

2. Request for Repurchase

Prior to the 1982 Amendments, the minority shareholders who are dissatisfied with the terms of a merger or elimination were not entitled to resort to an appraisal proceeding. The 1982 Amendments introduced Article 191 which gave the dissenting shareholders the right to request the company concerned to repurchase all the shares owned by them at the price agreed upon between the parties or equal to the arithmatic mean of the prices quoted on the exchange for the sixty (60) day period prior to the date when the Board of Directors approved the resolution of a merger. The method of calculating the arithmatic mean was provided in the Presidential Decree under the SEA, and the SAC has the power to adjust the price in the event that either the company or 30% of the minority shareholders concerned object thereto. The company is obliged to resell such shares repurchased within one year after the purchase (for details, *see* Article 84–2, the SEA Presidential Decree). Although the statute empowering the dissenting minority an option to force the company to repurchase their own shares was introduced, the statutory scheme for determining a purchase price does not give such minority shareholder an opportunity to ask for a fair appraisal proceeding.

C. Disclosure and Insider Trading

1. Recent Changes in the Current Report Rule

The 1982 Amendments include certain changes in the current report rule. First, Article 186 was amended to require listed corporations to make a current report to the Securities Administrative Commission ("SAC") and the KSE. Second, it was amended to require listed corporations to report the content of any resolution adopted by the board of directors with respect to a statutory event. Finally, Article 186 was amended to add to the existing statutory events a new item 7

"Any events prescribed in Articles 374 and 522 of the Commercial Code."

As a result, the statutory events were expanded to include:

i) any transfer or sale of all or a material part of corporate assets or businesses;

ii) execution, modification or termination of any contract or arrangement, under which all the business of the company are leased to another, under which the management of the company is entrusted to or undertaken by another, or under which all the profits and losses of the business of the company are to be shared with another or execution, modification or termination of any other contracts or arrangements similar to the foregoing;

iii) take-over or acquisition of all the businesses of another company; and

iv) merger or consolidation with another company.

Despite the foregoing amendments to Article 186, the drawbacks included in the current report rule are not cured at all, as discussed below.

2. Short-Swing Profits

The 1982 Amendments introduced into Article 188 of the SEA a set of new devices for better enforcement of the short-swing profit rules. First, prior to the 1982 Amendments, the term "a major shareholder" was defined in Article 188(1) to mean "a person who owns shares together with those held in the name of others, including ficticious persons, which total more than 10% of the total outstanding shares." The Article 188(1) as amended in 1982 redefined the term "a major shareholder" to mean "a person who is directly or indirectly the beneficial owner of more than 10% of the total outstanding shares." Second, SAC is, in addition to the corporation itself and shareholders, empowered to institute an action against insiders to have short-swing profits returned to the corporation. Third, Paragraph 4 newly inserted into Article 188 provided that the plaintiffs (shareholders or SAC), upon a favorable judgment being rendered may bring claims against the corporation for recovery of the legal expenses and reimbursement of other out-of-pocket expenses actually incurred in connection with the law-suit. Fourth, Article 188(6) and (7) improved the rule requiring disclosure of 10% ownership and any change therein. However, the combined effect of such 1982 Amendments on short-swing profits remains to be seen.

3. Other Changes in the Insider Trading Rule

The 1982 Amendments also introduced into Article 105 (Prohibition of Manipulative Practices) Subsection 4 which prohibits unfair trading practices. Subsection 4, Article 105 provides:

> "No person shall, in connection with the sale, purchase, of other trading of any securitiy make, employ or engage in any of the following:
>
> i) to make or employ intentionally, in order to make unreasonable profits, the dissemination of false information as to the rise or fall of security prices, untrue facts or rumors or scheme or device to defraud; or
>
> ii) to make monetary or economic profits by the use of any written document which has included a false statement of a material fact or omitted to state a necessary fact, and which has caused another person to misunderstand."

Any person who has violated Article 105(4) is subject to an imprisonment not exceeding three (3) years or a fine of not more than Won 20,000,000 (Article 200 of the SEA). In addition, any person who has violated Article 105(4) is liable to the injured for the loss and damages incurred in connection with sale or purchase of securities (Article 106 of the SEA). Although the introduction of Article 105(4) was clearly intended to prohibit fraudulent or manipulative practices employed by insiders in the interest of public investors, it is not clear whether the injured would successfully bring an action for recovery of the loss since the statute is not specific enough as to the elements of the causes of action. The combined effect of such amendments remains to be seen until courts set forth a set of detailed rules thereunder.

Table of Cases

Abrams v. Occidental Petroleum Corp. 373

Affiliated Ute Citizens v. United States 337, 344, 372, 383, 384

Birnbaum v. Newport Steel Corp. 336, 384

Blau v. Lamb 372

Blue Chip Stamps v. Manor Drug Stores 336, 384

Cattlemen's Investment Co. v. Fears 297

Chris-Craft Industries, Inc. v. Bangor Punta Corp. 336, 352

Daehan Flour Mills Case 288, 289

D-Z Inv. Co. v. Halloway 297

Ernst & Ernst v. Hochfelder 382

Farmsworth v. Massey 345

F.I. Case Co. v. Borak 333

Gerstle v. Gamble Skogmo Inc. 336, 352

Globus v. Law Research Service, Inc. 352

Gordon v. NYSE 199

Green v. Santa Fe Industries, Inc. 339

Hoover v. Fugua Industries Inc. 297

Indus. Inc. v. Great Atlantic & Pacific Tea Co. 297

Kaplan v. Lehman Brothers 179, 199

Kern County Co. v. Occidental Petroleum Corp. 372

Kong-young To-kun Case 380

Korea Wonyang Case 82, 162

Marshel v. AFW Fabric Corp. 352

Matteson v. Ziebarth 345

McGlynn v. Seymour 213

Mills v. Electric Acto-Lite Co. 336

Piper v. Chris-Craft Industries, Inc. 336

Popkin v. Bishop 345, 352

Reliance Electric Co. v. Emerson Electric Co. 372

Reynolds v. Texas Gulf Sulphur Co. 366

Roberts v. Eaton 372

Santa Fe Industries, Inc. v. Green 343

Schlick v. Penn-Dixie Cement Corp. 383

Scott v. Brown 213

Securities and Exchange Commission v. Capital Gains Research Bureau 335, 382

SEC v. Ralston Purina Co. 133

SEC v. Texas Gulf Sulphur Co. 360, 365

Shemtob v. Shearson, Hammil & Co. 352

Silver v. New York Stock Exchange 179, 198

Smolowe v. Delendo Corp. 375

Sunchang Industrial Corp. Case 376

Superintendent of Insurance v. Bankers Life & Casualty Co. 345, 383

Thill Securities Corp. v. New York Stock Exchange 179, 199

Truncale v. Universal Pictures Co. 379

TSC Industries, Inc. v. Northway, Inc. 337

United States v. Morgan 225

United States v. Simon 301

Water & Wall Associates, Inc. v. American Consumer Industries, Inc. 290

Wellman v. Dickinson 297

Wilfred P. Cohen Foundations Inc. v. Prevor 297

Wonpoong Idustrial Corp. Case 222

Yoo Wha Securities Co. Case 278

Index

A

accounting method 364
accounting principle 72, 416
accounting procedure 98
accounting reliability 143
accumulation of shares 287
Agreement on Underwriting Business
226, 230, 402
1976 Amendments of the SEA 242
amendment to the registration statement 149, 150
annual meeting of shareholders 289
anti-fraud provisions (or regulations)
120, 316, 317, 334, 359, 380, 416
appraisal proceeding 351
asset revaluation surplus 17, 79, 110
asset revaluation system 16
asset value 136
auction 189
auction market 235
auditing report 166, 167, 411
auditing standard 69
auditor 172, 173, 256
August 3 Emergency Decree 55, 61
authorized capital stock 17, 123
authorized capital system 123
automatic quotation 194

B

balance sheet 72, 164, 254, 324

bear market 338
big-seven securities companies 128
block trading (or transaction) 190,
193, 201
blue-chip corporations 122, 286
blue sky laws 116, 247
board of directors 123, 178, 357
bonding requirements 247
bonds 24, 247, 415
Bookkeeping Rules of Securities
Companies 252, 254
broker 178
broker and dealer 128
brokerage commissions 198
broker-dealer 171, 201, 237, 327, 414
broker's broker 175
bull market 226
burden of proof 158

C

Cabinet Order 238
callable share 304
call money market 281
capital formation 27, 269, 286, 341
capitalization rate 141
capital market 33
capital reduction 300, 303
capital stock 76, 123, 248, 249
certificate holders' meeting 172
certificate of contribution 71, 98, **173**
certificate of stock 115

charter 118

civil liability 134, 157, 260, 407

clearance 414

clearance transaction 11

clearing house 189, 282

closely-held corporation 47, 102

collateral 23, 273, 275

collateral right 108

co-managing underwriter 142, 407

commission 140

common shares 372

comparative market value 136

competitive commission rate 198, 202

compulsory redemption 173

consolidation 23, 254, 341, 419

construction interest 47

controlling person 346, 351, 408

controlling shareholder 68, 100, 163, 222, 255, 256, 416

conversion 144, 372

conversion right 375

convertible bond 84

convertible preferred share 372

convertible security 294

cooling period 145

corporate bond 55, 115

corporate insider 166, 346, 351, 359, 361, 410

corporate registry 304, 305

corporate repurchase 301, 302, 304, 350, 418

correction requirement 329

CPA auditing 104, 165

CPA audit of listed companies 72

CPA's auditing report 166, 167

credit extension 194, 265, 270, 276, 400, 417

current and bi-annual report 104, 362, 366

current shareholding 144

customer; customer protection 206, 255

customer registration system 77

customers' order 152

D

dealer 127, 178

debenture 24

debt/asset ratio 249, 265

debt/equity ratio 167, 168

debt securities 26, 55, 77, 190, 340

decentralizing equity ownership 95, 109, 169, 326

deferred clearance transaction 12, 51

Deliberation Committee 63

delisting 72, 163, 188, 242, 362

delisting standard 186

deposit of listed securities 247

deposit of security money 197

deposit requirement 196

depreciation 160

derivative suit 232, 355

designation order 64, 65, 73, 121

destabilization 411

disciplinary power 139

disciplinary rule 118, 177

disciplinary sanction 260, 264, 266, 402, 412

disclosure of information 98, 228, 292, 362

disclosure rule 228, 349, 362, 416

disclosure standard 148, 364

discretionary account 196

discretionary order 195

disguised-as-public corporation 162, 163, 397

distribution of securities 121, 154, 155, 224

distribution of trust certificate 403, 404

dividend 161, 300, 346

double-entry book-keeping 3

E

earned surplus 250, 304, 305

earned surplus reserve 111, 144, 164

efficient market 392

employee stock option plan 282, 347

employee stock ownership union 282

enforcement technique 221

entry restriction 247

equality of bargaining power 105, 381, 417

equity ownership 67

equity securities 17, 238, 282, 294, 352, 396

exchange market 175

ex-dividend 210, 230, 414

exempted securities 131, 280

exempted transaction 132, 404

expulsion 143, 178, 269

ex-right 210, 230, 414

F

fiduciary duty 68, 314, 345, 420

final prospectus 102

financial institutions 418

financial statements 72, 122, 167, 243, 254, 300, 411

financing for temporary clearance 20

firm commitment contract 226

fiscal year 80, 250

"first-come, first-served" 310, 311

five-finger rule 215

fixed commission rate 198, 202, 395

floor Section I 190, 277

floor Section II 190

floor trading 176, 203, 204

foreign capital 283

foreign controlled securities company 177

forgery 186, 322, 419

fraud rule 358, 367, 380, 381

free riders 225

free transferability of securities 242

free written material 152, 153

freeze-out 341, 343, 345

G

general shareholders meeting 285

going private 338, 339, 340, 420

going public 54, 65, 73, 121, 161, 395, 400

government bond 4, 12, 55, 115

government involvement 161

government-owned business 3

guaranteed bond 84

H

hearing proceeding 403, 408

I

incorporator 95, 179
indenture trustee 84
initial margin 274, 275
injunctive relief 355, 356, 420
inside auditor 156, 166
insider trading 20, 105, 261, 359, 361, 380, 414
inspection 414
inspection power 98, 149, 263, 376
institutional investor 71, 197, 202
institutional trading 198
interim certificate 116
intermediate dividend 80
internationalization of the securities market 244
interstate sales of securities 120
intrinsic value 135, 226, 401
investment company 38
Investment Deliberation Committee 49
investor protection 118, 259, 266
investment trust certificates 131
issuance of new shares 143
issued securities 154
issuer 125, 144, 228, 324, 375, 399
issuer meeting 237

J

January Government Bonds Crash 12
Japanese SEA 108, 115, 152, 171, 238, 367
joint managing underwriter 73

joint tort-feasers 161
June 3 Measure or Decree 52, 59

K

KSDA's Agreement on Underwriting Business 128, 139
KSDA's Rule on Securities Analysis 136
KSE Rules on Trading Members 179
KSFC stock crash 56

L

legal capital 109, 123, 204
legal entity 125
liability 215
liability reserve 250, 415
license 245, 246
license for the securities business 244
listed corporation 48, 76, 103, 143, 187, 349, 365
listed stock 151, 185, 186
listing of securities; standards 185, 186, 226
listing requirement 185
liquidity 185, 204
loan 281
loan transaction 282

M

maintenance margin 274, 275
managing underwriter 74, 129, 402
manipulation 15, 43, 56, 141, 142, 204, 211, 214, 380
margin requirement 13, 21, 52, 59, 89, 276

margin trading 43, 89, 186, 254, 274, 276, 278

marketability 238, 305, 401

market analysis 392

market formation (*Seejang Chosung*) 129, 224, 226

marekt price 216, 225, 392, 397

market watching system 223

matched order 211, 217

materiality 158, 363, 381

material misrepresentation 316, 381

May Crash 18

May 29 Special Instruction 70

membership regulation 177

merger 286, 303, 348, 419

method of settlement 194

minority shareholders 110, 188

MOF Decree 147, 153

municipal bond 71, 107, 115

mutual fund 90, 193

N

negotiated market 235

net assets 250

net asset limit rule 412

new shares 143

non-government shareholder 164

non-listed corporation 103, 349

non-participating preferred share 46, 164

non-trading-member securities company 175

non-voting share 287, 294

notification statement 133, 134, 150, 230, 267, 280, 299

O

odd-lot share 78, 86, 168, 190, 241, 396, 415

offering price 20, 118, 134, 138, 401

off-floor transaction 193, 413

option agreement 373

outside director 159

outstanding shares 78, 294

over-the-counter (OTC) market 70, 106, 119, 231, 236, 287, 366

ownership reporting rule 293, 306

P

paper-dividend 47, 111

partnership 249

periodic report 104, 188, 362, 414

pool manipulation 212, 218

portfolio 249

preallotment 226

preemptive right 46, 124, 144

preferential allotment 78

preferred right to dividend 164

preferred share 304

preliminary prospectus 102, 405

premium 298, 376

presumptive dividend 47, 111

price control technique 23

primary market 74, 95, 117

principal corporation 73

principal managing underwriter 73

principal office 172

private money market 33, 60

private offering 132

private placement 126, 131, 132, 133

241, 404

privity of contract 158

profitability value 136

profit and loss statements 254, 324

prohibition of insider trading 243

proportional allotment system 77

prospective issuer 103, 106

prospectus 83, 146, 149, 228, 307, 399

prospectus delivery 152, 399

prospectus requirement 151

proxy form 419

proxy regulation 319, 320

proxy solicitation 98, 101, 123, 318 326, 342, 415, 419

proxy statement 102, 319, 320, 322, 326, 331, 381, 420

public bond 241

public inspection 154, 166, 228, 293, 308, 418

public investment 64

publicly-held corporation 46, 161

public notice 293, 307, 342, 418

public offering 54, 74, 121, 125, 133, 152, 286, 320, 368, 404

public subscription 79, 168

punitive measures 66

Q

quotation 194, 235, 414

quoting systems 194

R

receipt for securities 116

reciprocal arrangement 162

reciprocal equity-holding 106

recommendation to shareholders 313, 314, 317, 416

redeemable preferred share 301

redeemable securities 340

redemption 99, 303

registered corporation 110, 167, 237, 415

registered securities 154

registrant 147, 148

registration requirement 69, 122, 131, 143

registration statement 103, 126, 144, 230, 307, 407

regular-way transaction 20, 189

release 117, 366

reorganization 111

reporting requirement 228, 362

representative's registered seal-impression 194

rescission of contract 411

reserved surplus 301

restriction on ownership increases 288, 292

retailer 127

revenue 250

revocation of registration 182

right offering 69, 233, 404

Rule on Proxy Solicitation 320, 322, 348

Rule on Salesman Registration 262

Rule on Approval of Block Purchases 288, 291

S

"saitori" member 176

salesman registration 262

salesman regulation 261

secondary distribution 75, 80, 121, 152, 320, 368

secondary market 86, 95, 117, 210

secret takeover 100, 101

Securities Act of 1933 125, 127, 154, 214, 257, 359

securities analysis 71, 74, 135, 142, 269, 395, 400, 407

securities business 129, 183, 269

securities collateral loan 271, 283

securities company 108, 173, 279, 415

securities credit 270, 271, 276

Securities Exchange Act of 1934 123, 177, 198, 257, 334, 359

securities exchange 171

securities finance company 282, 283, 284

securities held in street name 327, 328

securities industry 203

securities institution 174

securities investment trust 50, 90, 241, 281, 283

securities market 286, 391

securities savings 265, 283

securities transaction 108, 189

segregation 130, 245, 279

self-regulation 136, 240, 243, 268, 270, 402

self-regulatory agency 183

semi-annual report 187

settlement 414

shareholders general meeting 48, 339

shareholder registry 86, 243

short-sale or short selling 20, 206, 208, 209, 379, 413

short-swing profits 123, 361, 367, 379

short-swing trading 105, 210, 333, 376, 417

short-term profits 210, 241

short-term speculation 168

small issue 133

solicitation 258, 319

Soundness Rule 220

special guarantee fund 63

specialist 175, 204

special offer 193

special reserve 411

special resolution 123

specified-date transaction 189

Specific Rules on Disciplinary Standards 181

speculation 216

speculator 225

spot transaction 189

stabilization 151, 205, 224, 266, 414

stabilizing price 414

standard of diligence 159

statutory ledger 252, 253, 254

stock corporation 164, 176, 244

stock crash 272, 358, 418

stock dividend 110, 143, 324, 404

stock (securities) exchange 10, 171

stock re-registration 70

stock's price-earning ratio 141

stop-loss order 194, 195

stop order 149, 150, 221, 222, 408, 409

street name 102

sub-broker 176

subscription form 151

subscription rate 54

subscription right 115, 124

summary prospectus 405, 406

supervision of issuer 414

supervisory function 122

surplus reserve 255

surveillance of market activities 421

suspension 178, 183, 264, 363, 406

suspension of a license 108, 264

suspension of membership 140, 183, 269

suspension of transaction 181

swallowing 181, 190

syndicate 308, 418

syndicate manager 224, 225

syndicate of managing underwriter 138

T

takeover bid 163, 295, 310

target company 312, 315, 419

tax deduction 47

tender offer 101, 286, 295, 299, 309, 350

tender offer solicitation 288, 329

tender offer statement 289, 307, 362

total assets 250

trading member 175, 179, 183

trading report 243

trading unit 190

transfer 348

transfer of business 245, 324, 419

treasury share 300

U

underwriter 127, 149, 178, 368, 399

underwriting 121, 126, 402

underwriting business 128

underwriting syndicate 124, 128, 225, 226, 280

unguaranteed bond 84

unsuitable recommendation 259, 266

V

voting share 49, 68

W

waiting period 145, 329, 378

warrant 256

wash sale 211, 217

watering stock 111, 135, 397

when-issued transaction 52, 189

wholesaler 127

withdrawal right 311, 315, 419

Williams Act of the United States 290, 296

working capital 22, 249, 265, 415